W9-BHO-281

Computer Security Handbook

Computer Security Handbook

Second Edition

Edited by

Arthur E. Hutt
Seymour Bosworth
Douglas B. Hoyt

MACMILLAN PUBLISHING COMPANY
New York

Collier Macmillan Publishers
London

Copyright © 1988 by Macmillan Publishing Company
A Division of Macmillan, Inc.
Copyright © 1973 by Macmillan Publishing Co., Inc.

All rights reserved. No part of this book may be reproduced or
transmitted in any form or by any means, electronic or mechanical,
including photocopying, recording, or by any information storage
and retrieval system, without permission in writing from the
Publisher.

Macmillan Publishing Company
866 Third Avenue, New York, N.Y. 10022

Collier Macmillan Canada, Inc.

Library of Congress Catalog Card Number: 87-1735

Printed in the United States of America

printing number
1   2   3   4   5   6   7   8   9   10

Library of Congress Cataloging-in-Publication Data

Computer security handbook.

   Includes index.
   1. Electronic data processing departments—Security
measures.   I. Hutt, Arthur E.   II. Bosworth, Seymour.
III. Hoyt, Douglas B.
HF5548.37.C64   1987   658.4'78   87-1735
ISBN 0-02-915300-X

Contents

Data Output • Disposal Methods • Backup •
Microcomputers • Summary • Checklists

Software and Programming Services • Service
Bureaus • Facilities Management •
Documentation Service • Maintenance and
Repairs • Backup Facilities • Housekeeping,
Guard Service, and Deliveries • Legal
Considerations • Microcomputers • Summary •
Checklist Outside Contracted Services

List of Contributors

Lindsay L. Baird, Jr. is an independent management consultant specializing in computer crime, white collar crime, and systems security. He served in the U.S. Army Military Police Corps for twenty years and retired in the grade of lieutenant colonel. He developed a number of data processing systems in both law enforcement and intelligence areas and authored the first comprehensive Army Regulation establishing security criteria for automatic data processing systems; it was later adopted by the Department of Defense.

Mr. Baird has testified as an expert witness before both U.S. Senate and state legislative hearings.

His educational and professional certificates include: B.S. degree from the University of Maryland; an M.B.A. in management from Hofstra University; arbitrator, Commercial Panel, American Arbitration Association; Certified Information Systems Auditor, EDP Auditors Association; Certified Protection Professional, American Society for Industrial Security; and Fellow, Institute of Professional Investigators.

Mr. Baird's professional affiliations include: past chairman and vice-chairman of the American Society for Industrial Security's Computer Security Committee, and member of both the Privacy & Information Management and the White Collar Crime Committees; consultant to the Coupon Fraud Committee, and member of both the Expert Witness Group and Legislation Committee, of the Data Processing Management Association.

Robert Bigelow concentrates on the legal problems of the computer industry and is counsel to the Boston general practice firm of Warner & Stackpole. Bigelow received his A.B. and J.D. degrees from Harvard University. He served as law clerk to a justice of the Supreme Judicial Court of Massachusetts and as house counsel for a large insurance company. He has been in the private practice of law since 1966. He has written and lectured extensively on issues involving law and computers.

Mr. Bigelow is a founder and past president of the Computer Law Association. He was chairman of the ABA Science and Technology Section's Committee on Law Relating to Computers. He was also a founder and first chairman of the Route 128 Corporate Lawyers Forum, and a founder of the New England Computer Law Forum. Mr. Bigelow is a member of the Association for Computing Machinery, where he served as the first chairman of the Special Interest Group on Computers and Society. He has been an adjunct professor at Dartmouth College's graduate program in Computer and Information Science.

Mr. Bigelow is editor of the *Computer Law Newsletter* and author of *Contracting for Computer Hardware, Software and Service* (Matthew Bender, 1985) and *Computer Contracts* (3 volumes, Matthew Bender, 1987). With Susan Nycum he is co-author of *Your Computer and the Law* (Prentice-Hall, 1975). His articles on law and computers have been published in the *American Bar Association Journal, Harvard Business Review, Datamation, Computer Decisions,* and *Computerworld.* He has been a columnist for *Infosystems* and *ComputerData* (Toronto). He has also edited a number of books and journals relating to computers and the law.

G. J. (Jack) Bologna holds degrees in accounting (B.B.A.) and law (J.D.) and has done graduate study in business administration. His career spans a period of over thirty years and includes employment in banking, public accounting, federal law enforcement, industrial security, postsecondary education, management training, and consulting. His past consulting clients include a number of Fortune 500 companies as well as small and medium-sized banks and industrial firms, several government agencies, and many professional and trade associations. Currently, he is assistant professor of management at Siena Heights College in Adrian, Michigan.

Mr. Bologna has authored over forty technical articles on a variety of business and management topics. His books include: *Computer Crime: Wave of the Future, Strategic Planning for Corporate Directors of Security and Risk Management, Corporate Fraud: The Basics of Detection and Prevention, Guidelines on Forensic Accounting,* and *The Fine Art of Fraud Auditing.*

Mr. Bologna serves on the editorial board of the *Computer Law Reporter* and *Data Processing and Communications Security* magazine. He is listed in *Who's Who in Finance and Industry* and *Who's Who in the Midwest.*

Through his consulting firm, Computer Protection Systems, Inc., of Plymouth, Michigan, he publishes two monthly newsletters: *The Forensic Accounting Review* and *The Computer Security Digest.*

Seymour Bosworth is president of S. Bosworth & Associates, Plainview, New York, a management consulting firm active in computer applications for banking, commerce, and industry. He has been responsible for design and manufacture, systems analysis, programming, and operations of analog and digital computers for over twenty-five years. For his technical contributions, including an error-computing calibrator, a programming aid, and an analog-to-digital converter, he has been granted a number of patents and has others pending.

Mr. Bosworth was formerly president of Computer Corporation of America, manufacturers of computers for scientific and engineering applications; of Abbey Electronics Corporation, manufacturers of electronic test equipment and digital devices; and of Alpha Data Processing Corporation, a general-purpose computer service bureau. He holds a master's degree from the Graduate School of Business of Columbia University, and a Certificate in Data Processing of the Data Processing Management Association.

Mr. Bosworth is adjunct associate professor of management at the Information Technologies Institute of New York University. He is listed in *Who's Who in Computers and Data Processing,* published by the *New York Times,* and is the author of various technical articles.

Dick H. Brandon was the original author of the chapter on Employees in the first edition of the *Computer Security Handbook.* Until his death in 1981, Mr. Brandon was president of the Brandon Consulting Group, Inc., a diversified management and technical consulting firm in New York City.

Mr. Brandon was a recognized authority on the management of data processing, a well-known lecturer, and the author of several best-selling textbooks.

Carol W. Brown is vice-president of Winthrop, Brown & Co., Inc., in New York City. The firm provides custom software and computer consulting services for minicomputer users. Its clients include corporations in manufacturing, publishing, architecture, and other fields.

Prior to founding Winthrop, Brown & Co., Ms. Brown was manager of systems and programming for McKinsey & Co., Inc., an international management consulting firm. In 1980 she authored The *Minicomputer Simplified: An Executive's Guide to the Basics,* published by The Free Press. Ms. Brown has been active in the Special Interest Group for Business Data Processing of the Association for Computing Machinery, and has lectured for the National Computer Conference, the Data Processing Management Association, and other industry trade associations.

Ms. Brown holds a B.A., in economics from Wellesley College and a certificate in Systems and Programming from New York University. She was a contributing author to *Computer Handbook for Senior Management* published by Macmillan in 1978.

Peter S. Browne, president of Profile Analysis Corporation in Ridgefield, Connecticut, is an internationally recognized authority in computer security. His experience in information systems includes systems planning, quality assurance, data communications, information security, and audit. He has many years of experience as a computer systems analyst, security system designer, data processing staff member, and technical manager.

Since 1976, he has been a leading consultant in the areas of computer and network security. In this capacity, he has directed numerous management studies for over 100 commercial and government clients. He has conducted projects and design efforts in system software, disaster recovery planning, and information security implementation. He pioneered the area of security risk assessment.

Mr. Browne co-authored "Guidelines for Computer Security and Risk Management," published by the National Bureau of Standards, and is the author of the 1980 AFIPS System Review Manual on computer security. He has taught at the University of Nebraska and at the American University.

Mr. Browne has a B.A. from Syracuse University and an M.B.A. from the University of Nebraska. He was nominated as an industry representative to the Small Business Computer Security Advisory Council, chartered by Congress in 1984, and was elected its first chairman. He has also held other professional and industry offices, and is an active participant in security standardization efforts.

Theodore W. Christiansen has over twenty years of experience in data processing systems, including private management consulting and positions of staff systems analyst for IBM, project manager for TWA, and data processing manager for General Dynamics and Beneficial National Life Insurance Companies.

His consulting activities have included audits of computer installations; installation of data processing production standards and controls; and developing, programming, and implementing systems plus conversions to new computers.

He holds a B.A. in statistics from Lehigh University with graduate work at Syracuse and Rochester Universities in accounting and finance.

Mr. Christiansen has served as director for both the National Association of Accountants and the Association for Systems Management. He has published articles in *Business Automation,* the *Journal of Systems Management,* and the *Computer Handbook for Senior Management.*

Robert A. Daley, now retired, was supervisor of general services at the Savings Bank Trust Company, New York, where he was responsible for office services, purchasing, forms control, inventory control, and records management.

Mr. Daley's experience includes programming, systems, short interval scheduling, work simplification, and work measurement. Earlier he was operating supervisor at the U.S. Postal Service, New York, with responsibilities for training and scheduling personnel, planning, and supervision of clerical, delivery, distribution, and transportation operations.

Mr. Daley is a member of the Association for Systems Management. He has contributed to the *Computer Handbook for Senior Management.*

Cipher A. Deavours is a professor of mathematics at Kean College, where he teaches computer science and cryptography courses. Mr. Deavours was a founding editor of *Cryptologia* and is co-author of *Machine Cryptography and Modern Cryptanalysis* (1985).

Mr. Deavours has been involved in the design and testing of crytographic systems for over ten years and has served as a consultant to government and industry, both foreign and domestic. He is the author of several commercial cryptographic products and has been instrumental in the design of several large proprietary cryptographic networks outside the United States.

Dean P. Felton is a vice-president of Alexander & Alexander, Financial Products Group, headquartered in New York. The group is the national resource facility to A&A offices and their clients for specialty insurance, including computer related coverages such as computer crime and data processing errors and omissions.

Prior to A&A, Mr. Felton worked for another large national insurance broker, where he specialized in the design and placement of bonding, professional liability, and computer crime coverages for financial organizations.

The early part of Mr. Felton's career centered on both insurance claims and underwriting for large national insurance companies.

Mr. Felton is a graduate of Ohio State University. He has published articles and commentary on the subjects of bonding and computer crime.

Douglas B. Hoyt is president of Douglas B. Hoyt Co. in Hartsdale, New York, which provides management consulting services in systems and office management, financial controls, and organization and policy development.

Mr. Hoyt also has been associated with Johnson & Higgins, international insurance brokers, where he served as an internal financial systems consultant. Previously, Mr. Hoyt was research manager for the Financial Executives Institute, and headed systems operations for major manufacturers.

He is past president of the Society of Professional Management Consultants and founding member of the Institute of Management Consultants. He received the Distinguished Service Award from the Association for Systems Management. He received his education at Williams College and the Harvard Business School.

Mr. Hoyt was editor and chairman of the author groups that wrote the first edition of *Computer Security Handbook* (1973) and *Computer Handbook for Senior Management* (1978).

Arthur E. Hutt is an information systems consultant with extensive experience in the uses of data processing in banking, government, and a variety of industries. His innovative developments for on-line banking systems have received international recognition.

Mr. Hutt served as senior information systems executive for two major banks. As senior vice-president for Bank Leumi Trust Company, Mr. Hutt managed a multiple data center environment that provided on-line service for domestic and international banking. As vice-president for Bowery Savings Bank, he was responsible for the design and development of its on-line real-time banking systems. Mr. Hutt also served as a consultant to a number of financial institutions, specializing in strategic planning and the organization of information systems activities. He has served on many EFT planning groups for banking industry associations. He has been active in the development of technical standards, including plastic cards and magnetic stripe standards for national and international use.

Mr. Hutt was on the faculty of City University of New York and served as consultant to CUNY on data processing management. He was also a member of the Mayor's Technical Advisory Panel on Information Systems for the City of New York.

Mr. Hutt has been an editorial adviser to John Wiley & Sons, Inc., for a book series, *Business Data Processing*. He was co-editor and contributing author of *Computer Security Handbook* and *Computer Handbook for Senior Management*. He was a contributing author to *Real-Time Systems,* published by Infotech. He has also contributed numerous articles to professional journals.

Mr. Hutt holds a Certificate in Data Processing. He was a founding officer of the New York Chapter of the Association for Computing Machinery, and a founding officer of the New York chapter of the Information Systems Security Association. Mr. Hutt was educated at Brown University, the American Institute of Banking, and City University of New York.

Ralph E. Jones was manager of Cash Management Systems at ITT Corporation's executive offices in New York City, until his retirement in 1986. He now serves as cash management consultant.

He was recently awarded the ITT Harold S. Geneen Creative Management Award for designing and implementing a state-of-the-art computerized cash management system called ACTS, which creates a yearly savings to ITT of about $8 million.

Mr. Jones was closely associated with the new electronic payment systems using the National Automated Clearing House Association's processing network and bank computers. He has published articles for national cash management trade magazines and newspapers.

Mr. Jones also designed and implemented ITT's on-line interactive stock transfer system called STARS, which maintains the ITT shareholder records. He has designed and implemented many other on-line and batch data processing systems for ITT.

Mr. Jones earned his B.B.A. degree at Babson College. He is a founding member and past president of the New York City Cash Manager's Association. He was also a contributing author to the first edition of *Computer Security Handbook* and the *Computer Handbook for Senior Management*.

Javier F. Kuong is a management consultant and president of Management Advisory Services and Publications, an organization devoted to the EDP audit, security, and controls fields. Mr. Kuong is the editor of two journals: *COM-SAC Computer Security, Audit and Controls* and *COM-AND, Computer Audit News and Developments.*

Mr. Kuong has authored a series of books and audit practice manuals on computer security and has co-authored many others.

He has conducted numerous consulting engagements ranging from EDP operational audits to organization for EDP security, audit and quality assurance, and development of standards and guidelines for EDP internal controls. He is also director of the Contingency Planning Recovery Institute (CPR-I) and editor of the *Contingency Planning Report.*

Mr. Kuong holds a master's degree in chemical engineering from the University of Pennsylvania and a master's in business administration from Babson College. He has held positions in industrial chemical operations, corporate planning and computing at Atlas Chemical (now ICA America), as director of management information systems for Cabot Corporation, and as managing associate for Arthur Young & Company.

Robert W. London, prepared the revised version of Dick Brandon's chapter in the first edition of *Computer Security Handbook.* Mr. London is a vice-president of Brandon Consulting Group Division. His EDP consulting background includes resource and systems planning studies, hardware/software evaluations, and performance assessment of data processing organizations.

Mr. London started his business career at Sperry Univac and then moved to Westinghouse Electric Corporation. He was manager of systems and programming at Republic Aviation. He became vice-president of Brandon Applied Systems, and subsequently was head of management consulting and turnkey systems at Applied Computer Techniques.

Mr. London has a B.B.A. from City College of New York, where he specialized in production management. He has published a number of articles on various data processing subjects, is a member of the Association for Systems Management and the Data Processing Management Association, and was an officer of DPMA in England.

Belden Menkus is a management consultant based in Middleville, New Jersey. Since 1953 he has been helping management improve information handling techniques and operational security practices. He is accredited by the Society of Professional Management Consultants. He has also been certified as an Information Systems Auditor, a Systems Professional, an Office Automation Professional, and a Records Manager.

Mr. Menkus is editor of *Data Processing Auditing Report* and executive editor of *Journal of Systems Management.* He is a member of the editorial boards of *Computers and Security* and *Corporate Crime and Security.*

He is a Fellow of the British Institute of Administrative Management and the American Association of Criminology. He is a member of the Board of the EDP Quality Assurance Institute, the Panel of Arbitrators of the American Arbitration Association, the Association for Systems Management, the EDP Auditors Association, the American Society for Quality Control, the Information Systems Security Association, and the New York Crime Prevention Council.

Mr. Menkus was a contributing author to the first edition of *Computer Security Handbook* and to *Computer Handbook for Senior Management.*

Guy R. Migliaccio is managing director of *Commercial & Personal Client Services* of Marsh & McLennan, Inc., the world's leading and largest insurance brokerage firm.

Mr. Migliaccio began his career in 1961 as an underwriter with INA and subsequently joined the insurance brokerage firm of Flynn, Harrison & Conroy. Marsh

& McLennan acquired Flynn, Harrison & Conroy in 1967. In 1968, Mr. Migliaccio became manager of a department serving large corporate clients.

Mr. Migliaccio later managed the Plainview, Long Island, corporate office of Marsh & McLennan and then returned to New York City as manager of the Metropolitan Division. He was elected managing director in 1982.

He is a member of Marsh & McLennan's Management Committee, Automation Committee, and Professional Development Committee.

A graduate of the City University of New York with a B.B.A. degree in marketing, Mr. Migliaccio has also completed the Program for Management Development at the Graduate School of Business Administration of Harvard University. He was also a contributing author to the first edition of the *Computer Security Handbook.*

Eugene V. Redmond is president of EVR Associates, Inc., Riverdale, New York, an education and management consulting organization. Earlier, he developed and conducted courses and installed office and factory systems as senior consultant at Brandon Applied Systems, Inc. He was also director, management training, the Diebold Group; manager, Hazeltine Data Systems; director, Systems & Planning, Sterling Drug, Inc.; and manager of systems, Lily Tulip Cup Corporation.

During twenty-five years of management and data processing activities, Mr. Redmond applied his industrial engineering background to a wide range of marketing operations, training, and information systems tasks.

Mr. Redmond is professor of management at New York University. He is on the editorial review board of the *Journal of Systems Management,* a member of the Advisory Council at the Data Processing & Systems Analysis Institute of New York University, and a contributor to the Joint Accreditation Committee for Data Processing Standards. He was selected by the Vice-President of the United States to participate in the Invitational Workshop on Career Education.

Mr. Redmond has served as deputy general chairman of the International Systems Meeting. He was chairman of the Metropolitan New York Systems Council, and is a founding member of the Knickerbocker Chapter of the Association for Systems Management.

He was also a contributing author to the first edition of *Computer Security Handbook* and the *Computer Handbook for Senior Management.*

Richard S. Thompson has developed financial accounting skills both as an EDP auditor and as a systems analyst. He is now a senior systems analyst in the financial area of Corporate Systems Division at Combustion Engineering, Inc. He is concerned primarily with implementing accounting software and supporting its accounting users.

Previously, as a systems analyst on the information management staff of the Hartford Insurance Group, he developed new information-gathering and reporting systems in cooperation with its Comptrollers Operations.

Mr. Thompson had been an EDP audit consultant for Computer Audit Systems, Inc., a wholly owned subsidiary of Cullinane Corp., and later became an EDP auditor for a major public accounting firm. His accounting degree is from the University of Hartford.

Mr. Thompson has audited and tested a variety of business applications for major corporations in several industries. He has performed consulting services in areas of EDP security standards, EDP audit techniques, and inspections of EDP sites throughout the United States.

Mr. Thompson was a contributing author to the *Computer Handbook for Senior Management.*

Myles E. (Mike) Walsh is director of information systems for CBS Records, a division of CBS, Inc. He is also a teacher, a consultant, and an author.

He received a B.B.A. in economics from St. John's University and an M.B.A. in computer methodology from the Baruch School of Business. His books include *Understanding Computers: What Managers and Users Need to Know (1981), Database & Data Communications Systems: A Guide for Managers* (1983), and *Realizing the Potential of Computer-Based Information Systems* (1984). Mr. Walsh has contributed chapters to several other books and has written over forty articles.

Preface

The first edition of the *Computer Security Handbook,* published in 1973, began as a project of the Joint Research Committee of the Atlantic and New Jersey Divisions of the Association for Systems Management, which comprises nine chapters in the New York City and New Jersey areas. This committee undertook a study of computer security because, at the time, its members anticipated an emerging need to protect the vulnerabilities of computer operations.

As the project grew in scope, the need to expand the breadth of authorship became apparent. As a result, the committee was restructured into a Computer Security Research Group, and became independent of the initial sponsoring organization.

After the *Computer Security Handbook* was published in 1973, many of the authors collaborated with others to write the *Computer Handbook for Senior Management,* published by Macmillan in 1978. Subsequently, Macmillan requested us to revise the original *Computer Security Handbook.* A new Computer Security Handbook Group, formed for this purpose, has written and edited this revised edition. The handbook has been expanded from twelve to nineteen chapters and has been completely rewritten to cover current needs and technology. Three editors collaborated to make this work as complete, clear, consistent, and cohesive as was practicable. This review committee consisted of Arthur E. Hutt, Seymour Bosworth, and Douglas B. Hoyt. The handbook group's affairs were administered by Douglas Hoyt, chairman, Ralph Jones, secretary, and Arthur Hutt, treasurer. Carol Brown compiled and edited the glossary. She and Arthur Hutt prepared the index. David Chan was retained to provide additional editorial services on certain portions of the manuscript.

We wish to express our appreciation to the Negotiation Institute and to its president, Gerald I. Nierenberg, for furnishing meeting facilities for the review committee's many meetings. We also thank the following for allowing us to quote from or make reference to material of interest to our readers: IBM Corporation; Computer Law & Practice; Business Laws, Inc., publisher of *The Lawyer's Brief;* National Computer Security Center; and National Bureau of Standards.

While the publication was a joint endeavor, the authors are individually responsible for the contents of their chapters.

DOUGLAS B. HOYT, Chairman
New Computer Security Handbook Group

New Computer Security Handbook Group

Douglas B. Hoyt, Chairman	Douglas B. Hoyt Co.
Ralph E. Jones, Secretary	Consultant
Arthur E. Hutt, Treasurer	Management Consultant
Lindsay L. Baird, Jr.	Info-Systems Safeguards, Inc.
Robert P. Bigelow	Warner & Stackpole
G. J. (Jack) Bologna	Computer Protection Systems, Inc.
Seymour Bosworth	S. Bosworth & Associates
Carol W. Brown	Winthrop, Brown & Co., Inc.
Peter S. Browne	Profile Analysis Corp.
Theodore W. Christiansen	The Children's Village
Robert A. Daley	Savings Banks Trust Co.
Cipher A. Deavours	Kean College
Dean P. Felton	Alexander & Alexander
Javier F. Kuong	Management Advisory Services & Publications
Robert W. London	Brandon Consulting Group, Inc.
Belden Menkus	Management Consultant
Guy R. Migliaccio	Marsh & McLennan, Inc.
Eugene V. Redmond	EVR Associates
Richard S. Thompson	Combustion Engineering, Inc.
Myles E. Walsh	CBS Records

Introduction

Since 1973, when the first edition of the *Computer Security Handbook* was published, the proliferation of computers, and especially microcomputers, has increased both the opportunities for abuse and the number of people whose technical capabilities are adequate to that unwelcome task. As a result, the vulnerabilities associated with data processing have expanded markedly.

Now as then, fraudulent misuse receives the greatest media attention, although losses arising from inadvertent error continue to be of far greater magnitude. This second edition of the *Computer Security Handbook* addresses both intentional and accidental threats to the integrity of computer systems and to the assets of organizations that rely on them.

The nineteen chapters of the book fall logically into five categories: management's responsibilities, basic safeguards, physical protection, technical protection, and special protection issues. The authors' intention throughout has been to provide the breadth of coverage required by business managers with minimum technical knowledge, but also to provide sufficient depth to meet the needs of data processing practitioners.

Security problems and solutions relating to microcomputers are also emphasized in this handbook because of the increasing reliance of most organizations on microcomputers. Many of the chapters contain a section on microcomputers, and the last chapter in the book summarizes microcomputer issues.

In place of the sensationalism that often pervades works on computer security, the focus in the book is on practical realities. Each chapter concludes with a checklist summarizing the author's recommendations. These can be particularly helpful in evaluating and improving an organization's security status, but only if they are filled out to reflect the actual situation—not what the preparer thinks the answers should be, or would like them to be. Only then can they provide the guide to positive actions that will assist the prudent manager in achieving the necessary degree of computer security.

It is unrealistic to expect that this book or any other will eliminate the possibility of losses due to computer fraud or human error, The authors believe, however, that the sound procedures and practices described here will minimize these possibilities and reduce the risks to acceptable levels.

SEYMOUR BOSWORTH

Computer Security Handbook

PART I
Management's Responsibility

CHAPTER 1

Management's Role in Computer Security

By Arthur E. Hutt

Introduction

Computer security may be defined as the protection of computing assets from loss or damage. As a natural extension, the avoidance of loss or damage to other assets through abuse or misuse of computer facilities is also within the scope of this topic.

Protection encompasses prevention, detection, recovery, and insurance. Computing assets may be defined to include hardware, physical facilities, application programs, software programs, information or data files, and personnel. Loss or damage must be considered from any source, whether accidental or intentional, and for varying degrees of consequence.

The emergence of computer security as a major problem has been caused by the relative success of the computer and its proliferation. There is widespread use of data processing by all large organizations, by most medium-sized, and by many small ones. Quite significantly, data processing usually involves a concentration of vital facilities and assets. The rapid growth and acceptance of computer technology has not been accompanied by a parallel growth in the management of this technology. The management lag, coupled with the fact of concentration, gives rise to an exposure that can be detrimental to the very existence of even a large organization.

All organizations, of course, are not equally affected by this exposure to loss. In certain government computer installations, matters of national security are at stake, and the measures required to protect such facilities are elaborate and costly. At the other end of the spectrum are computers used exclusively for word processing of unclassified materials, requiring little or no security precautions. This book is not addressed to either of these extremes but rather to the bulk of user organizations, in business, government, and universities, where concentration of information and assets, and dependence upon the computer, create an exposure to loss. It is not addressed to the achievement of airtight security, but to situations requiring a balance of adequate security with cost effectiveness and common sense.

The Cause of the Problem

The use of computers has grown to the point where it has become almost indispensable to the continuing operations of many organizations. The techniques of information processing, with the computer as a focal point, have been well integrated into the daily fabric of user organizations. The computer has evolved from a laboratory curiosity, to a luxury, to a prestige symbol, and finally to a workhorse and a necessity. In most cases the value of the data and the physical value of the system are significant assets that require protection and attention.

Larger organizations, particularly, are dependent upon data processing because this resource has been used to extend, and often substitute for, scarce and expensive human resources in performing a variety of essential functions. In many instances loss of the data processing resource, even for short time intervals, may result in serious consequences to the user organization. On-line, real-time systems are particularly sensitive to disruptions.

Many commercial computer systems provide the same basic functions that were provided by noncomputerized systems in the past. If a bank or an airline could service its customers without a computer in the past, it would seem that the loss of computer service would not be seriously disruptive. If an on-line system was installed to improve the level of service, it is reasonable to assume that loss of access would result only in degrading the service function to its precomputer level.

Unfortunately, relatively few computer users can expect to achieve anything resembling precomputer service levels during system interruption. The reasons are that the organization of the end use service is often completely different, and recent changes and additions to end use service may have no parallel in terms of manual procedures. In a real-time system the minimum level of acceptable service may have increased, so that the customer expects service response and features available *only* through the computer. Finally, transaction volumes may have increased so greatly after computerization that it would be difficult or impossible to assemble, train, and administer an adequate staff to process manually.

After computerization, it is not uncommon to discover that continuity of essential activities is dependent upon continuity of data processing services. The computer system becomes a utility, and dependence upon this utility has evolved because the mechanics of the organization have been designed to function on the power it supplies. Just as a continuous source of electricity is essential for an electric motor, the operating elements of a business may be dependent upon information flow from a computer.

Dependence upon the computer is the basic phenomenon that gives rise to the need for protection of this utility. Concentration of data processing facilities serves both to aggravate and to mitigate the protection problem. The exposure becomes more acute because more value is focused in fewer physical locations. However, this concentration also affords greater opportunity to exercise control and to supply uniform protection to the computing assets.

Decentralization of information and computing power, an inherent characteristic of minicomputers and microcomputers, presents additional issues that must be addressed for the adequate protection of computer assets.

Management Responsibility

Management must concern itself with safeguarding the resources under its jurisdiction. Just as an investor seeks both a high rate of return and reasonable safety for his investment, so must the manager seek a high rate of return through the effective use of the resources under his command and must take adequate steps to protect the value of the resources.

The manager's function is essentially the management of resources: *human resources* and *capital resources*. In a computer operations environment, capital resources are represented by the investment in equipment and operating programs. Human resources are represented by skills needed to operate and control both hardware and software facilities. Human and capital resources are also represented by the completed operating programs. Information is another form of resource, one that is often created as a product of data processing, or concentrated at the computer facility in order to better utilize equipment resources.

Part of the data processing management task is to protect the information resources in its trust and to safeguard the human and capital resources that are essential to the services provided. Top management must concern itself with adequate recognition of the risks, and must be assured that adequate protective measures relative to these risks are in effect.

Kinds of Risks

The risks to data processing security may be categorized as follows:

Physical Hazards. The likelihood of threats, whether accidental or intentional, that can result in physical damage. Fire, water, power loss, explosions, vandalism, and civil disorders are all within this category.

Equipment Malfunction. The possibility of failures for computers and supporting equipment, such as printers, disk drives, and air conditioners.

Software Malfunction. The likelihood of loss and failures caused by computer programs, including operating system software and application programs.

Human Error. The threat of disruption or loss due to accidental or intentional action or inaction by employees. Computer operators, programmers, maintenance engineers, and service personnel can all precipitate loss.

Misuse of Data. The capacity for intentional misuse of information or facilities to perpetrate a crime, such as fraud, espionage, or theft of data or of some other asset controlled by the data.

Loss of Data. The intentional or unintentional loss of information through destruction of the physical media upon which the data reside, or the corruption or erasure of the data.

Magnitude of Risks

In addition to classifying risks by category of threat, it is useful to analyze risks by the magnitude of potential loss, the probability of loss, and the frequency and permanence of occurrence. Although magnitude of loss can be expressed in terms of time or dollars, it is more practical to use dollar cost as a common basis for measurement. Quantifications should be based upon reasonable and supportable estimates of the costs associated with the actual occurrences of adverse events.

Threats must be evaluated in terms of probability of occurrence. True risk is difficult to measure, but a reasonable priority of risks may be established by evaluating the likelihood of occurrence in conjunction with the magnitude of potential loss for each threat. An aggregation of consequential costs for each threat, over a common time period, and based upon the likelihood of occurrence for each threat, can serve to prioritize seemingly diverse risks.

Three convenient groupings for permanancy of damage are: Disaster, Solid Failures, and Transient Failures. *Disasters* are serious and lengthy disruptions usually involving costly reconstruction of data, alternative off-premises processing, loss of business, and high cost. *Solid Failures* are those that require cessation of use of part or all of a system in order to take corrective action. Cost of solid failures may range from simple inconvenience to substantial loss of business. *Transient Failures* are defined as temporary disruptions that do not recur regularly and therefore may be difficult to trace or correct. Like solid failures, their costs can vary widely.

Quantification of risk is imprecise at best and varies greatly from one organization to another and even between computer installations in the same organization. Nevertheless, quantification affords a means of ordering the relative importance of various threats and of substantiating the need for expenditure to counteract threats. Further discussion of the subject may be found in the chapter on Risk Analysis.

Determining Probability of Risk

A sample risk analysis table is shown for a typical medium-scale computer installation. It is assumed that the sample XYZ company has expended $1 million on equipment and site preparation. Its computer is used for a variety of applications of which two applications are critical to the normal continuation of business. One of the key applications involves the use of remote terminals. A disaster that disrupts the use of the computer facility for some extended period of time may result in loss of business due to curtailed service to customers. Vital financial records (e.g., accounts receivable) are also centralized at the computer facility. Records are backed up in the form of source documents. In the event of a major disaster, it is estimated that the loss could amount to $2 million including equipment, business impairment, and the cost of recreating essential records.

The XYZ company's computer is housed in a fire-resistant building in a medium-sized city. The fire underwriters rating indicates that the annual probability of a fire occurring is 0.5% or once in 200 years. The first column entry under *Fire* in the Risk Analysis Table (Table 1.1) is the probability of occurrence for that event in a one-year period. The adjacent column shows the range of loss in thousands of dollars. It is estimated that should a fire occur the loss may range from minor damage of about $5,000 to total destruction, or $2 million. The final column, labeled *Weighted Risk Values*, represents a simple multiplication of probability times the high and low estimated losses.

Similar estimates of probability of occurrence and ranges of loss have been made for additional physical hazards and for other categories of threats. In many instances, particularly equipment and software malfunctions and human error, precise data based upon actual experience may be used.

In the hypothetical case of XYZ company, it

Table 1.1 Sample Risk Analysis

Threat	% Probability	(000) $ Loss Range	Weighted Risk Values Low	High
Physical hazards				
-Fire	0.5	5–2,000	25	10,000
-Water damage	0.1	1– 100	1	100
-Power loss	1.0	1– 100	10	1,000
-Hurricane, windstorm, etc.	1.0	1– 200	10	2,000
-Explosions	0.1	10–2,000	10	2,000
-Vandalism	0.7	1– 100	7	700
-Civil disorder	0.1	1–2,000	1	2,000
Equipment malfunctions				
-Central processor				
Transient failures	20.0	.5– 20	100	4,000
Solid failures	10.0	1– 50	100	5,000
-Peripheral units				
Transient failures	50.0	.1– 2	50	1,000
Solid failures	50.0	.1– 10	50	5,000
-Communication equipment	15.0	.1– 20	15	3,000
-Air conditioning	25.0	1– 50	250	12,500
-Other supporting equipment	25.0	1– 25	250	6,250
Software malfunctions				
-Operating system executive	25.0	.1– 20	25	5,000
-Supporting software	75.0	.1– 10	75	7,500
-Application programs	90.0	.1– 20	90	18,000
-Data integrity software	50.0	.1– 20	50	10,000
Human errors & omissions				
-Computer operators	75.0	.1– 10	75	7,500
-Programmers	75.0	.1– 10	75	7,500
-Maintenance engineers	50.0	.1– 10	50	5,000
-Service personnel	50.0	.1– .5	50	250
-Terminal users	75.0	.1– .5	75	375
Misuse of data				
-Theft	1.0	.1– 100	1	1,000
-Fraud	1.0	1– 100	10	2,000
-Espionage	0.1	1– 200	1	2,000
Loss of data				
-Media damage	90.0	.1– 10	90	9,000
-Accidental erasure	90.0	.1– 10	90	9,000
-Malicious intent	2.0	.1– 100	2	2,000
Aggregate Low Value			1,633	
Aggregate High Value				139,675

is interesting to note that the threats that yield the highest weighted risk values are not necessarily the same as those that yield the highest maximum risks.

Since threat occurrences are expressed in terms of annual probabilities, the resulting weighted risk values can be equated to annual expected losses. Tables 1.2 and 1.3 present this comparison. Table 1.2, showing maximum exposures, includes all of the physical hazards as well as other externally initiated threats (theft, fraud, malicious intent). Table 1.3 lists only one threat (fire) that was included in the ranking of maximum exposures.

This example is useful in pointing out that different methods of viewing risks can yield dramatically different results. Substantial maximum exposures tend to be given much attention, and these threats certainly deserve concern. Unfortunately, these concerns often tend to overshadow

Table 1.2 Eleven Highest Maximum Risks

Threat	Maximum Loss
Fire	$2,000,000
Explosions	2,000,000
Civil disorder	2,000,000
Hurricane, etc.	200,000
Espionage	200,000
Water damage	100,000
Power loss	100,000
Vandalism	100,000
Theft	100,000
Fraud	100,000
Malicious intent	100,000

exposures that may not be as costly on a maximum risk basis, but that represent a far more probable actual loss.

In any specific situation it is management's judgment that will determine how much will be spent for insurance or other measures that will reduce or eliminate each risk. Risk analysis can serve as a basis for budgeting annual security expenditures. Aggregating all of the weighted risk values in Table 1.1 results in a total of $1,633 for the low values and $139,675 for the high values, or an average expected loss of about $70,000 per year. The individual risk values for each threat can serve to allocate expenditures, efforts, and emphasis.

The Dangers of Overreaction

No threat, however improbable, is completely impossible, for human ingenuity knows no bounds. However, it is essential to differentiate between probable and improbable threats, since the danger of overreacting to remote possibilities

Table 1.3 Eleven Highest Weighted Risks

Threat	Weighted annual high loss
Application program malfunctions	$18,000
Air conditioning malfunctions	12,500
Fire	10,000
Data integrity malfunctions	10,000
Central processor malfunctions	9,000
Media damage	9,000
Accidental data erasure	9,000
Supporting software malfunctions	7,500
Computer operator errors	7,500
Programmer errors	7,500
Other equipment malfunctions	6,250

is that it will divert energy and resources from the more likely threats. Avoid tilting at windmills.

An article in the *New York Times* on "Computer Scare Talk" berated the self-styled experts, with vested interests in selling security services and devices, who promote paranoia. Examples cited were *radical conspiracies to sabotage computers,* and the use of *special receiving equipment to sense radio waves* emitted by computers and line printers. Magnets in the hands of disgruntled employees were deemed ominous. All of these threats are possible, but hardly imminent and marginally probable.

Computer-related fraud has received increasing publicity recently, perhaps more publicity than it deserves relative to other risks. It cannot be denied that computer crime makes for interesting headlines and captures the public imagination. The use of a computer to instigate or expand a crime evokes secret admiration from those who fear or resent the supposed usurpations of technology.

Embezzlement, theft, fraud, espionage, and other crimes involving the dishonest acquisition of assets generates human interest because these acts appear bold. The larger the value of the assets the bolder the act appears. But large or small, if the act involves a computer, even in the remotest way, it is sure to create headlines. How much more interesting is the headline "BANK RIPPED OFF IN COMPUTER SCAM" than the more mundane "BANK EMPLOYEE EMBEZZLES $MILLION." Dishonesty is certainly no more of a threat under a computer-based accounting system, but it is apparently more newsworthy. There may be newer opportunities for criminals to utilize computer information for fraud, but there is also increased opportunity to apply controls in a consistent manner to protect assets. An undesirable side effect of computer fraud that cannot be ignored is the exposure to bad publicity. Many organizations are reluctant to reveal incidences of computer fraud lest it damage their public image.

An effective computer security program requires a balance of rationality and prudence. It also requires a continuing management commitment. Absolute security is an impossible dream unless one has unlimited resources. Surprisingly, even on a modest budget it is usually possible to achieve reasonable security. Many basic safeguards can be implemented for modest expenditures of time and effort.

Summary of Protective Measures

Location and Site Preparation

Computer security ideally starts with site selection and site preparation. The location of a computer facility should be chosen so as to avoid, or at least to minimize, the physical hazards.

- Avoid proximity to obvious explosion hazards, such as fuel storage tanks.
- Avoid buildings exposed to windstorm damage, either directly or from adjacent structures.
- Eliminate exterior windows in computer room.
- If possible, avoid lower floors of a building as there is higher exposure to break-in.
- Maintain a low profile. Avoid obvious identifying signs to minimize random exposure to sabotage or vandalism.
- Good drainage is important to prevent water damage. Avoid basements. Avoid locating near water mains. Protect the computer room against water by using watertight seals or by rerouting pipes and conduits.
- Proximity to flammable or explosive material should be avoided. Locations within a building near boilers, compressors, water or gas tanks should be avoided.
- The building housing the computer site should be protected against external fire damage. Blank parapetted fire walls, fresh-air intakes for air conditioning, and the use of noncombustible structural components are preferable.
- Computer rooms should be designed to prevent or minimize damage from fire. Large facilities should be subdivided, with fire walls or fire-resistant barriers to protect against fire intrusion. Fire doors at all openings should normally be kept closed.
- Storage facilities for paper and magnetic records should be separated from equipment rooms. If a vault or storage room opens into the computer room, a secondary access door should be provided in the storage facility as a personnel emergency exit and for fire-fighting access. Since paper and magnetic records can burn or melt, it is desirable to provide fire walls and fire doors both to protect the contents and to deter the spread of combustion to adjacent areas.
- Raised floors should be of noncombustible material. Under-floor drainage is essential. Carpeting in computer areas should be avoided unless fireproof and nonstatic. Floor tile pullers must be readily available for raising floor panels.
- Lowered ceilings should require metal supports. Fire walls must extend above dropped ceilings. Acoustic material should not fuel or contribute to the spread of fire or smoke or produce corrosive fumes.

Fire Protection

Protection from the physical hazard of fire is not unique to computer installations. An excellent body of knowledge is available about fire protection from its application to other facilities, where a high concentration of asset values exists.

- Warning devices should include alarms for smoke, heat, and fire detection.
- Hand extinguishers for controlling small fires should be conveniently located. Water extinguishers should be clearly marked "Not for use on live electrical equipment."
- Automatic carbon dioxide extinguishing systems may be used for under-floor areas, magnetic records storage vaults, and vital equipment. Usually activated by rate-of-rise thermostats, carbon dioxide can be dangerous to personnel in enclosed areas.
- Halon gas is a substitute for carbon dioxide that is regarded as considerably safer. Since a lower gas concentration is effective for extinguishing flames, the use of Halon still allows enough oxygen to sustain life in enclosed areas. In larger areas, a deep-seated major fire may cause the deterioration of Halon into corrosive gases that endanger life.
- For all automatic extinguishing systems it is important to enforce design safeguards. Computer power should be interlocked for automatic interruption. Air conditioning should be continued for gas extinguishing systems, with manual cutoff available. Smoke venting should be provided to ex-

haust corrosive fumes. A grid system is advisable for detection devices to prevent the triggering of an automatic extinguishing system by a single malfunctioning detector.

- Combustible material should be isolated wherever possible. Fireproof metal furniture should be used in computer rooms and tape libraries. Paper supplies should be stored separately, with only the minimum working requirement in the computer room.
- Personnel procedures must be established and rigorously followed. Smoking or the use of open-flame devices should be strictly forbidden at all times in value-sensitive areas. Emergency procedures should be posted and periodically tested. Fire drills are essential.

Water Damage

Good drainage is essential to minimize water hazards. While locations above ground level are preferable, it is also best to avoid top floors and the possibility of roof leaks. Water detection devices are especially useful for under-floor areas.

Other measures employed for water damage protection include a pumping system, plastic protective covers for equipment, and sandbags for dire emergencies.

Power Loss

Full protection from loss of power for a large computer installation can be quite costly; however, lesser degrees of protection can be realized for even modest costs.

As a minimum measure, a computer system, large or small, needs an orderly shutdown in the event of a power failure. Work in process must be preserved, and the equipment must be shut down in a normal manner so as to avoid damage to any components. A battery-powered uninterruptible power supply (UPS) can serve to bridge the gap between power loss and shutdown. The cost of this type of UPS depends upon the power load requirement; however, it is far less expensive than UPS for longer term use.

In large computer systems a variety of strategies can be used to protect against power loss. It is useful to employ a separate feeder line for the computer and supporting equipment with a different line for other electrical requirements. Another alternative is to install dual separately routed feeder lines from the power system (or even from different power systems) for computer

equipment. These measures offer some protection against minor disruptions but not against a general power failure.

Full-scale standby power facilities, where cost-justified, can allow the continued operation of a computer system for longer term power outages. Such standby systems require regular maintenance and periodic testing to ensure availability when needed.

Vandalism, Civil Disorders

In addition to the maintenance of a low profile (avoiding overt pointers or signs that disclose the high-value nature of the facility), physical access security is important. The extent of the measures utilized are a function of cost versus value. Locked doors are an obvious measure. Intrusion detection, door alarm systems, guards and watchmen, heavy-duty doors, taped doorways, sealed windows, desk alarms, and photoelectric and sonic alarm systems are commonly used protective measures. Contingency procedures for riots and intrusions should be worked out in advance and regularly reviewed.

Equipment Malfunctions

- Critical computer equipment should be duplicated where the cost of a lengthy breakdown is high; however, the user must avoid being lulled into a false sense of security by duplication of equipment alone. Complete duplication may entail the duplication of processing, such as updating of files, to afford more comprehensive protection. Too often computer duplication is regarded as a panacea when in fact the computer is usually the most reliable component of a system, and more attention should be paid to nonelectronic components.
- Air conditioning equipment is prone to malfunctions. Backup or redundant sources of air conditioning are advisable for medium to large-scale computer systems.
- Peripheral equipment, especially where mechanical components are present, are more prone to breakdown than are computers. Vital peripherals should be duplicated. Systems flexibility should allow continued operation without the requirement for specific peripherals.
- Alternative processing arrangements with

service bureaus or other users can ameliorate the effects of downtime. Backup arrangements of this sort must be tested regularly to assure their effectiveness when needed.

- Preventive maintenance on all equipment is essential and should be scheduled and monitored regularly by installation management.
- On-site maintenance service for critical and valuable systems should be considered.

Software Malfunctions

- Comprehensive testing procedures and stringent quality control can reduce the incidence of errors during development and subsequent production.
- Standards for development, documentation, modification, and operational turnover of programs can help to reduce software errors and facilitate correction.
- Structured programming and modularization of logic is beneficial in testing and maintaining software, as well as in reducing costs.
- Hardware memory protection can serve to limit damage from certain program failures, by preventing alteration of memory locations outside of the assigned program boundaries.
- It is important to treat the object program code as data, with the application of data integrity techniques. Externally stored object programs should contain check-sums, parity bits, and block sequence checks. These measures can prevent or detect loss of data or transfer errors that could cause faulty program executions. Ideally, the operating system environment will offer these features.
- Software failures may occur when "faulty" data crop up unexpectedly. Data integrity checks should be employed throughout a well-designed system. Application system consistency tests may range from simple tests of field length to elaborate checking for permissible values and relationships between data fields.
- Data parity checks should be provided by either hardware or software to prevent data corruption and the consequences of faulty programs.
- Utility software to aid in the rapid diagnosis

of faulty application programs is an essential tool. Software should be readily available to secure memory dumps, register contents, and other diagnostic data.

- Hardware bootstrap, or the ability to reload an operating system automatically and rapidly, can alleviate the effects of lost time due to software failures. In a multiprogramming environment it is also desirable for the operating system to permit restoration and resumption of all programs that had been operating when the failure occurred.
- Backup versions of programs are necessary in emergencies. Prior generations of application programs and other software should be maintained as well as duplicate copies of current operating versions. It is useful to record the essential differences between program versions to facilitate fallback to earlier versions.

Human Errors

Operating procedures should be designed to minimize the risk of deliberate or inadvertent alteration, manipulation, or destruction of programs, data files, or hardware by operators, programmers, engineers, or others.

- Personnel selection methods should stress stability, personal integrity, and conscientiousness. It is unwise to use unsupervised transient employees in sensitive areas.
- Separation of duties is essential to adequate control. Programmers should be prevented from operating the computer, even during testing. Operators and other personnel should not be permitted to program or make alterations to programs. Management authorization of program modifications should be enforced.
- It is important to review operating system information and exception reports to detect abnormalities in operations and to confirm compliance to authorization procedures.
- Audit trails can serve as useful tools to detect file manipulation or alteration.
- A control function that is separated from computer operations should be responsible for the independent verification of system safeguards, such as batch controls, file ex-

piration date controls, and program library controls.

- Backup copies of files and programs should be stored away from the operations area to assure availability when needed.

Misuse of Data

Dishonesty is a continuous threat to computer operations, as it is in all other activities. It is, of course, possible to use the computer to manipulate large masses of records to accomplish fraud, but the computer itself may also be used to detect dishonesty (or error) involving computerized records. The computer, when misused, can improve the economics of fraud, because it facilitates the mass manipulation of detailed records. These dangers are closely intertwined with programming since perpetration presumes that the system logic must first be altered.

The countermeasures required to protect against dishonesty and fraud remain the same whether or not a computer is involved: separation of responsibility and adequate independent control. "How much separation?" and "What constitutes adequate control?" are the questions that each organization must answer for itself. Some of the precautions to be considered include:

- The presence of audit trails throughout various levels of application systems
- Independent audit and testing of application controls
- Authorization requirements for program changes
- Separation of programming and computer operations; closed shop testing
- Separation of clerical control and data control from computer operations
- Rotation of assignments; programmers switch applications, operators change shifts, etc.
- Dual control of computer operations, with two operators always on duty so that collusion would be necessary to perpetrate a fraud
- Separation of program development and program testing
- Controlled access to program documentation and source decks for operational programs

- Restricted access to data files or file copies
- Insurance coverage and bonding of personnel

Loss of Data

Information loss or corruption represents the most probable and most common threat that every data processing installation faces. Data files, computer programs, and associated supporting material, such as source documents, output records, program documentation, and procedure descriptions are all part of the information resource that is the life blood and raison d'etre of data processing. Some common measures of protection include:

- Saving of files, using the minimum three-generation (grandfather, father, son) principle whereby the oldest file is not destroyed until after the current file has been backed up and validated
- Duplication of information, on a similar or different physical medium
- Off-site storage of backup file copies with limited access to the off-site facility
- Up-to-date record retention schedules covering all protected data files and documents
- Off-premises storage of vital reports on microfilm or other medium for emergency reconstruction
- An up-to-date emergency reconstruction plan for major disasters
- Development and periodic testing of backup computer programs to reconstruct data files

Management of Computer Security

The job of the manager is to provide leadership, and it must be provided in an organized and creative manner. Management is dynamic, not static, and the manager must deal with change—change in the organizational environment, change in people, and change in the methods of management. The laws of inertia apply, particularly in that change will be resisted. The challenge to the manager is to manage change.

Even a successful security program will usually result in higher costs as well as in changes in the organizational structure and in the working environment. To compound the problems, the benefits of a security program are not highly visible. Security is essentially preventive and often regarded as capital expenses and overhead of questionable value.

The tools of the manager include planning, organizing, integrating, and controlling. These are not independent activities that can be completely separated; rather they represent a matrix. Taken as an interrelated process, they achieve balance and direction.

Planning for Computer Security

The planning function of management includes the determination of objectives, policies, priorities, schedules, standards, and strategy.

It is important to define the scope and purpose of a computer security program in terms of objectives. There should be a clear statement of results to be achieved within a given period of time. Security objectives must be balanced with other organizational objectives, because conflicts may arise. As an example, the need for controlled access will naturally conflict with desires for user flexibility and convenience. Objectives should be imaginative and responsive to change and conflict.

Planning for computer security requires the participation of top management so that security objectives can be resolved with general organizational objectives, as well as for the establishment of financial priorities. It is also necessary to coordinate security activities between data processing and other areas of the organization. Auditing, insurance, legal, financial, and other groups are affected by, and should contribute to, a computer security program.

The objectives, policies, schedules, and standards that result from the planning process need to be communicated throughout the organization. While this is generally true for all planning, it is especially crucial to the success of a security program. Finally, feedback is essential to permit recognition of failures and departures from plans. Only by monitoring results is it possible to take corrective action or to readjust the objectives, policies, plans, schedules, and standards to the practicalities of the real world.

Organizing

Organization is the process of marshaling resources, grouping activities and responsibilities, and establishing relationships that will enable people to work together most effectively in determining and accomplishing the objectives of an enterprise.

The important elements of organization for computer security include:

- Obtaining resources of personnel, money, and facilities adequate to accomplish the assigned mission
- Fitting responsibility into the organization pattern
- Assigning responsibility and authority to individuals
- Formulating supporting methods and procedures
- Measuring organizational effectiveness

Traditionally, the organizing function is concerned with grouping activities into manageable components and grouping human resources into logical relationships to accomplish the desired results. It would be unusual to find an enterprise that was designed with an optimum structure to achieve security at the expense of other goals. Security is not an independent activity, nor does it represent the primary goal of a data processing organizational element. Data processing departments are usually organized into units that reflect the nature of the work performed, or user relationships, or some other structure designed to achieve an adequate service level for the end-user. Security measures quite often conflict with the service objective. That is all the more reason why security must be managed in order to be effective. It is also motivation for creating a separate functional activity, particularly in large organizations, so that information security can be administered independently of competing activities.

Computer security is frequently an afterthought to the organization of a data processing function. Security is also perceived as a passive activity. As a result, responsibility for security is often assigned haphazardly. Security should not merely be superimposed but, instead, should be carefully fitted into the organizational structure. Some important considerations are:

- Accountability for specific security tasks

should be included in formal job definitions at every job level.

- Training programs should include a complete review of security objectives and policies, as well as details relating to assigned security tasks.

- Supervisory and management personnel should be assigned responsibility for both performance and attitude of staff with respect to security.

- Certain line or staff positions could include responsibility for overall security, or a grouping of security tasks, or measurement and monitoring of security. It may be convenient to combine security and control of data processing into a single function. Monitoring of security effectiveness is sometimes assigned to the data processing auditor.

- EDP security should be coordinated and reviewed with security specialists in other areas of the organization. In a manufacturing concern the plant security personnel, or in a bank the bank security officer, should be consulted. It may be desirable to assign monitoring responsibility for security housekeeping tasks to these specialists.

- Wherever possible, policies should be translated into written methods and procedures to provide the detailed requirements for each task. Standards for performance of each activity must be formulated and applied.

In large organizations an independent security administration function is often the most effective method for accomplishing the overall objective of improved information security. The development of this specialized activity, along with typical responsibilities are discussed in the subsequent section.

The Need for Security Administration

The importance of information security has given rise to a new management specialty consisting of professionals involved in the planning and administration of protection for the integrity and security of automated information assets. Titles such as Information Security Administrator, Computer Security Manager, and Data Security Officer have been used to describe this activity.

Coordination of the information security function requires a combination of managerial and technical talents. The successful administrator must be a superior communicator capable of selling the concepts of security and maintaining security awareness at all levels of the organization. Sufficient technical knowledge is important so that the Information Security Administrator can evaluate and initiate appropriate technological solutions to meet corporate information security policies and to counteract threats. While technical skill, in the form of a data processing background, is important, a broader range of capabilities is really needed for maximum effectiveness. The ideal security administrator should possess the ability to communicate with all levels of management, and should have good knowledge of related functions such as auditing, internal control, and general security. It is also important to have some knowledge of the industry within which the organization operates.

The administration of information security can be centralized or decentralized depending upon the needs of the organization. Where multiple data center locations are involved, the decentralized approach may be more appropriate to accomplish the details of administration. However, it is important to have one focal point for overall coordination of information security policy. It is also essential to understand that responsibility for information security rests with all members of the organization and not just the security personnel. Security is a shared responsibility, and this concept must be widely promoted by the security administrator and strongly backed by senior management.

The responsibilities of the Information Security Administrator (ISA) should include the following:

Establishment of Policy Statements and Guidelines for Information Protection

While policy is the primary responsibility of senior management it is appropriate for the ISA to participate in the delineation of a formal policy statement covering this important organizational goal and to prepare appropriate guidelines. A sample policy statement is shown in Exhibit 1.1.

Exhibit 1.1
Sample Information Security Policy

General
This policy statement is intended to establish guidelines and responsibilities to protect the information assets of the company. The goals of this policy are to:

1. Protect against the loss or misuse of information
2. Define employee responsibility and accountability to maintain protection of information
3. Preserve the integrity and security of information through appropriate controls
4. Establish a basis for measuring security effectiveness
5. Preserve and support audit and legal compliance

Policy Statement
All information used by the company is to be considered an asset and shall be protected from damage, loss, misuse, or inappropriate disclosure. Protection of information is the responsibility of all managers and employees, and they are accountable to maintain appropriate protection. Management shall be further responsible to administer adequate controls to ensure the security and integrity of information.

Defintion of Information Assets
Infomation assets include all data and software, whether internally developed or acquird from outside the company. Information may be represented in a variety of formats, including hard copy, magnetic media, terminal display, or other mode.

Guidelines for Information Security

Infomation Ownership
Except for licensed software and data provided under confidentiality agreements, the company shall retain exclusive right of ownership of all information assets. Management representatives shall be designated as guardians of information assets in order to insure integrity and accuracy. Individual managers and employees may be designated as custodians responsible for information asset control. Specific individuals or groups will further be assigned owenership, guardian, or custodial responsibilities for major systems in order to insure accuracy, in-tegrity, security, and adequate control of information assets. Where proprietary software has been provided to the company under confidentiality agreements, it is the manager's responsibility to assure awareness of and compliance with the terms of such agreements.

Data Classification
A common system for data classification will be employed to provide defintitions for data sensitivity and information criticality.

Information Security Policies
Formal standards for information security shall be developed and applied, including a data classification system, a security self-assessment program, business resumption planning, and other information security categories. Specific guidelines will be developed for each area.

Information Security Self-Assessment
Management wil conduct an annual review to assure close adherence to formal information security controls and procedures. Management will also monitor information security awareness and the adequacy of education.

Business Resumption Planning
In order to ensure the continued functioning of essential information systems services, formal plans will be developed and implemented. The process of business resumption planning will include:

- Identification of critical applications
- Establishment of cost-effective alternatives in event of disruption of service
- Regular testing of alternatives to insure currency
- Coordination of planning between company groups and with other organizations to realize economies of scale

Identification of Vulnerabilities and Risks
The ISA serves as a consultant and coordinator in the process of risk analysis. The sensitivity of data resources must be decided by senior management but with full consensus and agreement by all affected sections of the organization. The ISA has special responsibility to identify specific risks that affect the automated data resources. The ISA should then coordinate the process of quantifying or otherwise prioritizing the value of the threatened data in order to establish a basis for selection and economic justification of protective measures.

Identify and Recommend Protective Measures

Major responsibility for identification of economic solutions to information security vulnerabilities is usually assigned to the ISA. Requiring a combination of technical knowledge and management analysis, this process entails the evaluation of protective solutions for technological, operational, and economic effectiveness. Appropriate recommendations must be coordinated with other affected sections of the organization, including audit, data processing operations, legal counsel, general security, and others. Implementation plans must also be developed, and there must be a management commitment for the implementation.

Control the Implementation of Protective Measures

Whether the final administration of the day-to-day security procedures is centralized or decentralized the coordination and control of implementation for major protective measures should be centralized. A prerequisite for implementation is the development of standards for information security to assure consistency in the application of protection. Important areas for standardization are security design for application systems, programming development, data sensitivity criteria, data base access, and program maintenance. In general, security standards should cover the entire system's life cycle.

Provide Measurement of Effectiveness

Feedback is essential to assess how effectively policies are being followed. Since the nature of information security is defensive, the measures adopted can easily fall into disuse unless there is ongoing confirmation of effectiveness. The ISA should have primary responsibility to conduct security audits for operational systems as well as for systems under development. Backup protection and disaster recovery procedures are especially sensitive plans that must be tested periodically. Monitoring of variances in security procedures is also important and is best controlled through the ISA function. In many organizations these activities would be coordinated with the auditor. Finally, the ISA should provide senior management with reports on the effectiveness of security policy, with identification of weaknesses and recommendations for improvement.

Exhibit 1.2
Sample Control Policy for Microsystems

General

This policy statement establishes the guidelines and responsibilities for the acquisition and utilization of microcomputer systems and for the protection of information assets controlled or affected by these systems.

Policy Statement

It is the policy of the company to encourage the acquisition and use of microcomputers and related technology if such use may improve personal productivity. It is a management responsibility to adhere to controls and guidelines relating to microsystems in order to:

- Protect against the loss or misuse of equipment, information, or other company assets
- Preserve the integrity and security of information
- Maintain operational efficiency and minimize duplication of effort in the development and administration of systems
- Ensure and maintain optimum return on investment

Definition of Microsystems

Microcomputer systems or microsystems, for the purpose of this policy, will include any standalone or connected terminal used in the workplace. While microsystems are traditionally defined as microprocessor-based computers, the purposes of this policy extend to any device that permits access to information in the workplace. Personal computers, intelligent terminals, word processing stations, executive workstations, and remote display stations are examples of devices that are intended to be covered by this policy.

Minimum Guidelines

Acquisition of Hardware and Software

All acquisitions will require appropriate cost justification and approval. For improved prospects of compatibility, for ease of training, and to simplify maintenance, all acquisitions will be made from an approved list of standard products. Whenever possible, volume purchases will be made to reduce costs.

Software Purchases

Whenever possible, software will l be acquired rather than developed internally. It is the responsibility of the staff to abide by licenses for use of the software, and to adhere to copyright protection requirements. Vendor registration of software is the responsibility of local management. Any employee misconduct with respect to software license or copyright abuse will result in disciplinary action and, where warranted, in dismissal.

User-Developed Software

If suitable packaged software is not available, then it is permissible to develop software. Cost justification and advance approval is required. All controls governing specification, development, testing, and maintenance of software must be followed.

Ownership of Information and Work Products

All information and other work products, including programs, documentation, procedures, data files, and reports, shall remain the property of the company unless otherwise agreed to in writing.

Personal Use of Microsystems

The acquired hardware and software shall be restricted to business use for the company. Personal use by an employee is not allowed unless permission is granted in writing by the employee's manager.

Physical Security

Company policies and procedures that govern the physical protection and movement of assets will also apply to microsystems. Protection against theft is important because these systems are of high value and are often easily transportable. Particular care must be given to provide adequate environmental protection, including safe electrical power, static elimination, magnetic media protection, and good housekeeping practices.

Information Security

Protection of information is necessary to assure integrity, availability, and confidentiality. Adequate controls must be employed to confirm and maintain the accuracy of data. Sensitive and critical information requires special protection. Access to data files and programs should be restricted to authorized individuals. Changes to information or software must be controlled and authorized. Information, whether on magnetic storage media or hard copy, should be managed, maintained, and disposed of in a manner consistent with its sensitivity and importance. Information that is difficult or costly to recreate should be duplicated and stored in a secure off-site location.

Business Resumption Planning

Whenever microsystems are used for information record-keeping or processing, the local management will be responsible to develop plans for recovery from an event that renders the system unusable. Plans should include:

*   Emergency procedures to be followed during the event

*   Continuation of business operations during and after the event
*   How to recover and restore the microsystem operations

Promote Security Awareness and Security Education

Another important area of responsibility for the ISA is security education and awareness. The concepts of security must be actively communicated to all members of the staff so as to maintain awareness of its importance. An effective program should achieve a workable balance between security and the utility of computer resources.

Standards

With the increasing awareness of the importance of computer security there has been a steady growth of products and services that profess to address security requirements. Large and small users are frequently exposed to promotions for hardware and software products intended to improve security. Many of these products and services can be quite useful. Unfortunately, there is little in the way of published standards or other measurement criteria that can serve to assess the adequacy of specific products. There is, nevertheless, a growing body of knowledge in the form of guidelines and standards that is being developed for this need from several quarters. Managers concerned with computer security will find it in their best interest to follow such developments on a regular basis.

Two useful sources for standards, such as they are or will evolve, are professional societies and the United States government. Professional societies and other groups that are currently engaged in defining standards or guidelines for EDP security topics are listed in Exhibit 1.3. All of these groups, except for Computer Security Institute, are nonprofit organizations.

Exhibit 1.3
Organizations Concerned About Computer Security

1. Association for Computing Machinery (ACM)
    11 West 42nd Street, New York, NY 10036

Ref: ACM Special Interest Groups on (1) Security, Audit & Control and (2) Software Engineering

2. IEEE Computer Society
   445 Hoes Lane, Piscataway, NJ 08854

3. Information Systems Security Association (ISSA)
   P.O. Box 71926, Los Angeles, CA 90071

4. EDP Auditors Association
   3735 Schmale Rd., Carol Stream, IL 60187

5. American Federation of Information Processing Societies (AFIPS)
   1899 Preston White Drive, Reston, VA 22091

6. Computer Security Institute
   360 Church Street, Northborough, MA 01532

7. American National Standards Institute (ANSI)
   1430 Broadway, New York, NY 10018
   Ref: Committees ANSC X 3, ANSC X 9

8. Institute of Internal Auditors
   249 Maitland Ave., Altamonte Springs, FL 32701

9. National Bureau of Standards (NBS)
   (see Appendix 13 for NBS FIPS Publications)
   National Technical Information Service
   Springfield, VA 22161

10. General Accounting Office
    441 G Street NW, Room 5077, Washington, DC 20408

11. National Computer Security Center (NCSC) - C13
    9800 Savage Road, Fort George G. Meade
    Maryland, VA 20755-6000

The standards development efforts can be useful to both vendors and users of security products. For the vendor it provides an overview of user requirements; it is a way for users to band together to tell the vendors what they need and want and how much they are willing to pay. For the user it provides a view of collective requirements for a group of users in similar straits. The minimum measures and guidelines that are collectively developed can serve as a useful tool for an organization to ensure that its own program is adequate. Such standards also serve as a basis for measuring the adequacy of vendor offerings.

Many topics of special interest need to be addressed from the viewpoint of developing a set of standards, or at least useful guidelines. The following is a representative list of security topics where standards or guidelines can be extremely beneficial:

- Contingency Planning / Disaster Recovery
- Computer and Data Security Organization
- Computer and Data Security Personnel Training
- EDP Facility Physical Security
- Personnel Management
- Systems Programmer Controls
- Database Management Security
- Hardware Security
- Systems Software Security
- Applications Security
- Operations Security
- Distributed Processing Security
- Microcomputer Security
- Telecommunications Security

Efforts at standardization have been more fruitful and have been more consistently funded by the federal government rather than by the private sector. Private efforts have been promoted primarily through professional societies, and are dependent upon voluntary participation by industry and government members. An example of the private sector standards efforts being promoted is evidenced by the efforts of the Information Systems Security Association (ISSA), which has organized standards projects for Disaster Recovery, Database Management Security, Systems Software Security, and Microcomputer Security.

Significant federal government standards efforts have been in progress for some time, notably by the National Computer Security Center (NCSC) and the National Bureau of Standards (NBS).

A number of government-sponsored standards that are useful for both government and commercial users have been promoted by the National Bureau of Standards, particularly *Guidelines for Automatic Data Processing Risk Analysis* (FIPS PUB 65), *Guidelines for ADP Contingency Planning* (FIPS PUB 87), and the *Data Encryption Standard* (FIPS PUBs 46, 74, 81). Other NBS standards are referenced in Chapter 4 (Legal Issues in Computer Security). Appendix 13 of the book furnishes abstracts of selected NBS Federal Information Processing Standards publications. Further discussion of the *Data Encryption Standard*, now widely used for communication security, may be found in Chapter 13 (Encryption).

The National Computer Security Center is part of the National Security Agency and the Department of Defense. Under presidential directive NSDD145, the NCSC is responsible for establishing policy and procedures for securing information deemed of value to the United States government.

NCSC has developed and published several important standards or guidelines, including the following:

- *Trusted Computer System Evaluation Criteria* (CSC-STD-001-83)
- *Guidelines on Password Systems*
- *Model Password Systems*
- *Audit Guidelines*
- *Discretionary Access Control*
- *Network Criteria*
- *Personal Computer Security Considerations* (NCSC-WA-002-85)
- *Guidelines on Security in Office Automation*

The *Trusted Computer Security Evaluation Criteria*, while primarily intended for government use, serves as an illustration of how such a standard can be useful in the commercial area as well. This standard establishes a basis for evaluating operating system security. The NCSC applies rigorous tests to various software and hardware configurations submitted by vendors, and rates each system in accordance with its criteria. The major access security software packages that are used on large-scale IBM processors (in conjunction with the IBM operating system software versions) have all undergone testing. Operating systems for Honeywell and DEC computers, with access security features incorporated, have also been evaluated. The existence and application of these procedures serves to assure both the government and the commercial buyer that the products meet designated levels of performance and expectation.

Exhibit 1.4A and Figure 1.1 show the Trusted Computer System Evaluation Criteria used by NCSC. There are four broad groupings or divisions, ranging from minimal to verified protection as follows:

Division D - Minimal Protection

Division C - Discretionary Protection
    Class C1 and C2

Division B - Mandatory Protection
    Class B1, B2, and B3

Division A - Verified Protection

Exhibit 1.4A
Trusted Computer System Evaluation Criteria
(U.S. Department of Defense - Computer Service Center)

Division D - Minimal Protection
- Relies upon procedural and physical control rather than hardware or software control.
- Systems evaluated have failed to meet requirements for a higher evaluation class.

Division C - Discretionary Protection
- Provides protection on basis of need to know.
- Provides accountability of subjects and actions via audit trails.
- Further subdivided into two classes: C1 and C2
- Class C1 Systems
    - Separates users and data by enforcing identification and authentication of users.
    - Allows for levels of data sensitivity.
- Class C2 Systems
    - All C1 features plus more stringent control.
    - Users can be individually accountable for actions through login procedures.
    - Resources, especially data, can be isolated with operational assurance and greater flexibility than for C1 systems.
    - Security-related events are recorded in an audit trail that is protected from modification or unauthorized access.

Division B - Mandatory Protection
- Provides and maintains sensitivity labels, representing security levels for the associated subjects and objects (e.g., users and data structures).
- The integrity of the sensitivity labels is strictly preserved and exported with the data. For example, when sensitive information is printed, each printed page would contain the readable representation of the level of sensitivity.
- Sensitivity labels are also used to enforce mandatory access control rules.
- The reference monitor concept, mediating access of subjects to objects, must be implemented.
- Further subdivided into 3 classes: B1, B2, B3
- Class B1 Systems
    - Provides at least an informal statement of the security policy model, data labeling, and mandatory access control.
    - Accurately labels information that is exported.
- Class B2 Systems
    - Provides formal security policy model that can control all subjects and objects in the data processing system.

-Resistant to penetration.

-Structured into critical and noncritical elements vis a vis protection requirements.

-Well-defined software and hardware interfaces.

-Proven authentication mechanisms. Secure configuration controls.

-Provides accurate and comprehensive documentation.

• Class B3 Systems

-Extends reference monitor control to all subjects and objects that are indirectly referenced.

-Must be tamperproof.

-Must be highly resistant to penetration.

-Can be subjected to thorough analysis and testing of all functions and features in a formal manner.

-Provides security administrator support features.

-Provides expanded audit mechanisms to signal security-related events.

-Offers system recovery procedures.

Division A - Verified Protection

• Contains all level B3 features and requirements.

• Provides high degree of assurance that implementation is correct through formal design specifications and formal verification procedures.

-A formal security policy model must be documented, with mathematical proof of consistency.

-A formal top-level specification must be provided, including definitions of the functions performed by hardware and software and firmware.

-Formal techniques should be used, where possible, to prove the consistency of the specification with the model.

-Consistency of the operational protection mechanism (hardware, firmware, and software) with the formal specification and formal model must be demonstrated and subject to reasonable proof.

-Covert channels, if present, must be identified and their presence justified.

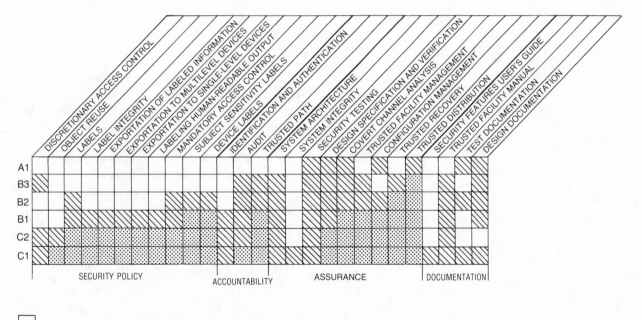

NO ADDITIONAL REQUIREMENTS FOR THIS CLASS

NEW OR ENHANCED REQUIREMENTS FOR THIS CLASS

NO REQUIREMENTS FOR THIS CLASS

Figure 1.1 Trusted Computer System Evaluation Criteria Summary Chart

The NCSC criteria for each division and class is intended to serve as a filter to identify the degree of protection that is provided by the product. Products are measured against the criteria rather than each other, and must meet all of the criteria for a given division and class to acquire that rating. Exhibit 1.4B summarizes the evaluation results for some specific host access system products, including the four major host access software packages that are used on large-scale IBM systems.

Exhibit 1.4B
Host Access Security Systems

The mission of the Department of Defense Computer Service Center (DOD-CSC) is to ensure that military and intelligence computers are secured against penetration by unauthorized entities. The *Trusted Computer System Evaluation Criteria* were developed for that purpose and have been used to evaluate commercially available products that provide host access control. The existence of these criteria, and their application by DOD, serves as a useful yardstick for assessing the protection afforded by various systems.

Some representative host access systems, and their DOD-CSC ratings under the *Trusted Computer System Evaluation Criteria* are:

1. RACF—Resource Access Control Facility (IBM Corp.) For use in large scale IBM systems: 30XX, 43XX. Rating: C1, but meets C2 criteria except for "Object Reuse."

RACF is IBM's facility under the OS/MVS operating system environment providing controlled access to system resources. Through the employment of user identification codes and passwords, RACF identifies, verifies, and limits the user to the authorized resources. User resource interactions are recorded and reported. RACF permits both protected and nonprotected resources to coexist.

A VM operating system version is also available; however, complete file protection features under VM are not implemented. Users of IBM's CICS application interface, which is widely used for on-line terminal access, have encountered other weaknesses in RACF, which fails to control CICS activities on system resources.

2. ACF2—Access Control Facility (Cambridge Systems Group, Inc.) For use in large IBM systems. Rating: C2

Designed to provide data security for computers using IBM OS/MVS or OS/VS1 operating systems. A VM version is also available. Resources are protected by default; all access to data or resources is denied unless specifically permitted for a given user or user group.

Cambridge Systems Group markets ACF2, but support is provided by the developer of the package, SKK, Inc. This division of responsibility is somewhat awkward; however, the users of the package have been satisfied with the support. ACF2 has been installed in over 1,500 sites.

3. TOP SECRET (Computer Associates, Inc.) For use in large IBM systems. Rating: C2

TOP SECRET provides logical protection of resources and facilities under control of IBM's OS/MVS by validating resource access. The IBM standard MVS Security Interface is utilized by TOP SECRET. Default philosophy and procedures are employed to strengthen protection. Over 600 installations of TOP SECRET have been completed.

4. OMNIGUARD and OMNIGUARD/CICS (On-Line Software, Intnl., Inc.) 1. For use in large IBM systems, and 2. for use in IBM CICS subsystems. Rating: N/A (not yet evaluated)

OMNIGUARD is a complete host access system that is offered for different versions of IBM Operating Systems. It provides comprehensive host access security for most combinations of VSE, VM, and CICS environments. Control of access to resources is handled by default.

OMNIGUARD/CICS is a special version of the software package designed to protect only the IBM CICS environment. CICS by itself lacks adequate security, good audit facilities, and limitations on user access to transactions and programs. OMNIGUARD/CICS (formerly known as GUARDIAN) can function as an independent CICS security system, or it can run under global packages such as ACF2 or TOP SECRET. With over 500 installations it is the most widely used CICS security package.

5. MULTICS—Multiplexed Information and Computing Service (Honeywell Information Systems, Inc.) For use on Honeywell model DPS 8/M computers Rating: B2

MULTICS is an operating system designed for the Honeywell DPS 8/M Series processors. An integrated security policy is enforced by software and hardware. MUL-

TICS protects against unauthorized use by three mechanisms:

  a. Access Control List for discretionary access
  b. Access Isolation Mechanism for nondiscretionary access, activated for highly sensitive information
  c. Ring Protection Mechanism to control intraprocess access

MULTICS is a total system with high-level security incorporated into the design of hardware and software. There are over 100 installations, usually with two or three processors per site.

Summary

Computer security is necessary in today's environment, because data processing represents a concentration of valuable assets in the form of information, equipment, and personnel. Dependence upon data processing services creates a unique vulnerability for many organizations. Centralized facilities increase the need for protection but also afford the opportunity for better control and uniform protection. The movement toward decentralization and the rising popularity of personal computers create new exposures and present special needs for security awareness.

Management must recognize the risks and identify the consequences of cost versus exposure for each type of threat. Probability of occurrence and magnitude of exposure to loss are both important in allocating protective resources.

It is important to avoid undue emphasis on improbable threats. Dramatic and widely publicized "dangers" are not necessarily serious exposures and may divert resources from more tangible, but less exotic, threats. Absolute security is unobtainable; reasonable security is achievable at a modest cost.

Management involvement is essential to a computer security program. Capital expenditures alone cannot accomplish security. Management concern and effort are needed to plan, guide, motivate, and control an effective computer security program. A balanced program, with proper concern for practicality and human values, will enhance the overall effectiveness of the information processing function.

Management Checklist for Computer Security

Yes No

Have the consequences of computer security threats been assessed thoroughly in order to determine the degrees and magnitudes of risk to the organization? ☐ ☐

Are protective measures in place to minimize risks and prevent threat occurrence with respect to:
- Facility Location? ☐ ☐
- Site Preparation? ☐ ☐
- Fire Protection? ☐ ☐
- Power Supply? ☐ ☐
- Physical Access to the Facility? ☐ ☐
- Equipment Malfunctions? ☐ ☐
- Software Malfunctions? ☐ ☐
- Human Errors and Omissions? ☐ ☐
- Intentional Damage, Theft, Fraud? ☐ ☐
- Protection of Data? ☐ ☐

Is there a formal definition of objectives and a formal policy statement on computer and information security? Are these policies and objectives communicated throughout the organization? ☐ ☐

Is accountability for security included in management and employee job descriptions? ☐ ☐

Do training programs include a review of security objectives and policies? ☐ ☐

Are management personnel given responsibility for security awareness on the part of the staff? ☐ ☐

Is there a security administrator? ☐ ☐

Is management involved in measuring the effectiveness of security? ☐ ☐

Are there adequate policies and procedures in place to secure microcomputer systems? ☐ ☐

Is computer and information security regarded as an ongoing management concern with review by senior management on a periodic basis? Is there sufficient management involvement to ensure the efficacy and importance of the program?

CHAPTER 2

Information Security Risk Management

By Peter S. Browne

Background

Information risk assessment is a vital business management task. It is a process that focuses on the need for implementing controls and security measures. It provides guidance for allocation of scarce resources that might otherwise be seen as being diverted from the primary business or mission objectives of the organization.

Perspective

The fundamental issues of data security are rooted in the conflict between efficiency and control. On the one hand, the computer industry has provided the mechanism for increased efficiency and expansion of business operations. On the other hand, traditional systems of checks and balances are many times overlooked by this expanded technology. Faster does not mean better controlled. Being able to do more work in less time does not mean that the principles of accountability should be missing. What happens all too often is that the computer has allowed corporate survival or has facilitated growth, but at the expense of internal controls.

The second issue of information security relates to the fact that demand for information processing invariably outstrips supply. Computing resources, be they hardware, software, or people, are scarce in relation to need. They are also costly. Thus, the first priority is throughput. The last priority typically relates to implementation of controls.

These problems are compounded by two additional factors. First, contrary to the need for a long-term view held by proponents of the Japanese style of management, most U.S. managers are still held accountable for short-term results. In such situations, the tendency is to readily ac-cept long-term risk. So threats of cataclysmic fires, tornados, large-scale uprisings, and even revolution tend to be thrust aside as minor irritants. The "can't happen to me" syndrome is prevalent. Thoughtful attention to risk management is sometimes viewed as counterproductive and contrary to organizational efficiency goals. In such a context, data security is a difficult marketing activity.

The second factor compounds the dilemma. Computer risk assessment has been postulated as a panacea—a tool that can cut through the fog of ignorance and lack of interest. In fact, risk assessment can only rationalize the need for control and for security.

Management problems addressed in data security are usually more economic and politically based than technical. They are subjective rather than objective. On the other hand, risk assessment traditionally has focused on objective or deterministic issues. There is, then, a gap between the management scientist and the manager. Yet thoughtful managers recognize the difference, and do use risk assessment techniques in their proper role—as a management tool, not as a substitute for good judgment.[1]

In a data processing environment, the treatment of risk *should* be an integral part of the analysis, design, development, production, and system maintenance tasks. It should apply to users as well as suppliers of EDP or telecommunications services. It is equally relevant to a standalone microcomputer and a large data center.

Problems Addressed

There are many risks faced by those who use and supply computing services. These risks include the following:

- Developing systems that do not meet user needs (the system is incorrectly designed or it is taking too much time to develop)
- Developing systems that are too costly
- Developing systems in which controls are insufficient or missing
- Implementing systems in an unstable environment in which operational errors, software errors, poor hardware stability, rapid organizational change, and external disruptions can cause costly delays or system unavailability
- Implementing systems in an uncontrolled environment in which costly computer resources can be misused or other organizational assets can be compromised
- Implementing systems in a vulnerable configuration in which power outages or disasters have traumatic effects

The first two types of risk listed above are beyond the scope of this discussion. They are covered quite thoroughly in other books, papers, training courses, and methodologies dealing with the system development process.[2]

Information Risk Management

Information risk management is concerned with the identification, measurement, control, and minimization of the impact of unexpected events on information systems and on the organization's functions supported by them. It is generally accepted that the state-of-the-art in computer security does not provide the capability to completely protect sensitive information and operations. Therefore, the implementation of compensating controls is essential. In any such implementation process, there will be competing alternatives. Certainly, there will be other projects competing for financial resources. The risk management approach is also useful in handling these issues.

Objectives
The overall goal of an information system risk management process is to ensure that the impacts of threats to the viability of computer and communications systems are known, and that cost-effective controls are applied (see Exhibit 2.1).

Exhibit 2.1
Information System Risk Management Objectives

Identify high-risk threats and protective measures
Identify threats affecting
 -Availability
 -Reliability
 -Confidentiality
 -Integrity of assets
Assess protection
Evaluate potential controls
Rank resources available
 -Time
 -People
 -Materials
 -Money
Define issues and develop planning objectives
Enhance awareness

The objectives are:

- To ensure that specific high-risk threats are identified, and that measures for reducing them are in place
- To identify specific threats that affect Computer system availability Computer system reliability Data confidentiality Integrity of organizational assets controlled by a given computer or communications system
- To assess current security and protection mechanisms
- To evaluate potential controls so that prudent implementation decisions can be made
- To rank in order the limited resources (time, materials, people, money) available for security and control
- To provide a viable tool for defining the issues and developing objectives for both long-range and short-range organizational planning
- To enhance system personnel and user awareness of system risks and potential losses

These objectives can be met by a wide variety of methodologies. The most common approaches are reviewed later. First, however, it is useful to describe some general principles that apply to all methodologies.

Nature

Information system risk management is:

- An approach to planning, controlling, and operating information systems
- A set of procedures
- A management process

Risk management attempts to define and quantify the tradeoffs inherent in any system of control by attempting to balance the cost of protection against the reduction in risk once a given set of protection measures (controls) is installed.

Risk management consists of two parts:

- The assessment of risks through a systematic evaluation process that attempts to describe the impact of given losses and the probability of loss occurrence
- The selection and implementation of controls that either reduce the threat of occurrence or minimize the impact of loss[3]

Uses of Risk Assessment

There are a number of reasons that an organization would want to identify or measure risk in a computer or communications environment. (Exhibit 2.2) They include:

- The need to convince management that a given control or set of controls is beneficial to the organization. In many cases this takes a specific direction to evaluate a specific measure, such as a data security package or encryption. In other situations, it may be a more general requirement to look at the overall set of risks, with the need to consider an entire security program.
- A requirement for assurance that there are no large or hidden problems that would lead to an unacceptable risk of disastrous consequences. It may be well to search for exposure before a serious outage or security breach occurs.
- A need to assess for compliance with regulation, laws, or corporate policy.
- A concern within the organization that there is either a proper mix and balance of controls, or that the controls in place are not proportional to risk. In the former case the concern is whether there is enough protection, and in the latter, there might be a feeling that there is too much security.

Exhibit 2.2
Benefits of Risk Assessment

1. Justify implementation of controls
2. Provide assurance against unacceptable risk
3. Assess compliance
4. Balance controls to risk

In any case, the risk review could be triggered by a specific event such as a publicized security breach in some other organization, by a perceived problem within the organization, or by an outside body such as the external auditor or an oversight agency.

Of greatest significance is the acceptance of an ongoing risk review process within the organization, so that users, software developers, and computer/communications providers all employ risk management as a normal business practice. As long as the assessment process is simple to do, and the results provide concrete guidance as to the kinds and levels of controls that are appropriate, then the benefits will invariably outweigh the costs.

Methodologies

The choice of method must, of necessity, depend on the purpose of the analysis, and the needs of the organization. It is useful to review how system security evaluation has evolved, since this provides a perspective on the use and intended purposes of risk management methods.

Evolution of Information Risk Assessment

Since computers were first used to manage an organization's financial transactions or books of account, the audit profession has identified the need to assess controls in application systems, data centers, and the business functions that are supported by computers. Initially these evaluations took the form of checklist audit or compliance reviews. In the 1970s a number of large accounting firms systematized their evaluation process and extended information security reviews to their management consulting practices. System vulnerability reviews and threat assessments became a common practice in both commercial and government EDP environments, especially as examples of disaster, fraud, and sabotage began to be publicized.

At the same time, concepts of risk management as defined by the insurance industry began to be applied gradually to data processing.[4,5] IBM and a number of consultants published articles and encouraged organizations to quantify risks, in order to convince sometimes reluctant management to spend money on controls and security.[6] Other efforts to apply the concept of risk assessment included work sponsored by the National Bureau of Standards, which led initially to the FIPS PUB 31 guidelines.[7] These efforts fostered the wider application of security techniques in both government and business circles.

These initial approaches to risk assessment almost invariably used quantitative techniques, which required the estimate of probability or occurrence rate of given threats, and dollar amount of loss per occurrence. The process of analysis considered a fundamental equation:

$$R = F \times L$$

where risk (R) is the product of a given threat frequency (F) times the single-time loss that occurs as a result (L). The output was usually expressed as an annualized loss exposure (ALE) for purposes of comparison (see Table 2.1).

Because of limitations on the ability to collect accurate statistical data, and the high cost of accomplishing risk evaluations, the trend in recent years has been to move away from quantitative techniques to those that describe or rate risk in more qualitative terms. Other trends relate to a renewed focus on applications or data, rather than on the computers and data centers alone, and the use of automated tools to provide a systematic and consistent analysis.

Elements

There are numerous methods and approaches to information risk assessment. All have as their purpose the greater understanding of the organization's susceptibility to information or information system viability. Given that the first step required in any kind of an analysis is to scope the problem, there are four succeeding analytical tasks (see Exhibit 2.3).

Exhibit 2.3
Determining the Scope of Computer Security Risk

1. Resource analysis
   - Identify potential losses and threats
   - Classify risks by criticality and sensitivity
   - Quantify cost of risk (potential loss)
2. Threats and vulnerabilities
   - Event-vulnerability combinations
   - Identify and classify threats
   - Identify weaknesses
3. Risk measurement
   - Risk scenarios
   - Risk ratings
   - Common measurement
4. Safeguards
   - Cost benefit analysis for proposed protective measures

Resources. An analysis of resources includes identification and estimates of potential loss for the facilities, applications, systems software, hardware, and people that are important to the data processing mission of the organization. A criticality and sensitivity analysis of resources is an essential task of a risk assessment. All identified resources should be quantified using a

Table 2.1 Sample Annualized Loss Exposures

Threat	Expected annual frequency	Expected loss (000)	A L E Annual loss exposure (000)
Fire	1/20	4,000	200
Water damage	1/10	100	10
Theft of data	1/2	100	50
Theft of equipment	1/3	150	50
Loss of data	4	25	100

standard measure of numeric value, such as dollars, that can adequately portray the replacement cost of the resource and the level of loss due to data processing disruption, data or software manipulation, and data or software disclosure.

Threats and Vulnerabilities. An analysis of threats identifies events that can, if they occur, compound a vulnerability in the security of a computer system or application. A threat assessment identifies and classifies threats and may determine their probable or actual occurrence rate. An analysis of vulnerabilities typically looks for flaws or weaknesses in design or implementation of controls.

Risk Measurement. The focal point of risk assessment is a measurement of risk (potential loss). Risk describes the potential loss or damage to an organization and is expressed in many ways. The simplest is a description: a scenario. Risk may also be expressed in linguistic terms (high, medium, or low) or in terms of a rating (1 to 5). A fully quantified assessment would tend to express risk in terms of both frequency over a given unit of time and the amount of potential loss to the identified assets. Annual Loss Exposure (ALE) is a common measurement of risk, determined by multiplying single-time loss by the frequency of occurrence of a threat.

Safeguards. An analysis of safeguards identifies the effectiveness of existing or proposed security controls relative to the identified threats and vulnerabilities. The evaluation of proposed safeguards may use cost-benefit analysis to select the risk management response that is most appropriate or cost-effective.

Each of the above are essential elements in terms of completeness. However, many studies include only a portion of the complete process and yet are called risk analyses. For example, it is common to look only at threats or vulnerabilities. Many times the risk study will stop short of determining the net benefit of proposed controls. And finally, it is sensible to consider working on a narrower scope than a complete data center or information system operation. A risk assessment on a single application, a remote terminal environment or a single set of threats is often all that is needed.

Types of Approaches

There are hundreds of differing approaches toward measuring and evaluating risk in a DP environment. Many organizations have developed their own, and the number of academic or proprietary methodologies grows each week. This may be due to the relative immaturity of the field as well as the difficulty in deriving credible data.[8]

All methodologies, however, can be grouped into the following two categories:

Qualitative Methods. The expression of risks in terms of descriptive variables such as high, medium, or low. Qualitative risks are based on the assumption that certain kinds of threat or loss data cannot be expressed in terms of dollars or discrete events, and that, in many cases, precise information is impossible to obtain. Examples include:

- *Delphi* methods in which a structured discussion of "experts" attempts to lead to a consensus of risks, usually expressed in descriptive terms. The concept was pioneered by M. Blake Greenlee, of Citibank, and was extended by Manufacturers Hanover Trust.[9]
- *Threat Scenario* techniques, which also use delphi techniques. Here a given scenario of potentially damaging events is mapped from initiation to completion and then documented. Some indication of frequency and effects is usually provided.[10]
- *Fuzzy Metrics*[11] techniques employ linguistic values to describe objects (assets), threats, and security mechanisms. The approach is statistically valid in terms of its mathematical relationships. It requires, however, an absolutely consistent definition and understanding of the linguistic variables, otherwise, one person's "medium" would be another's "high."
- *Scalar Techniques* often use a scale or range of values to portray losses or threats. Index values (1 to 5) or symbols can then be substituted for a description n of the range or scale. For example, an "A" can stand for a loss between $100 and $1,000, a "B" for $1,000 to $10,000, etc. The index values can then be manipulated or combined in some fashion.

Quantitative Methods. The use of statistically valid techniques to discern both loss exposures and threat occurrence rates. Formulas, ranges of values, and table lookup methods help provide the algorithmic base for deriving risk values. A single-time loss, expressed in dollar terms, is multiplied with a threat occurrence rate, expressed as a probability or an expected number of occurrences per year. Examples include:

- The *Fixed Effect* model used by many government agencies[12] and a few commercial organizations. This approach uses point estimates of loss and frequency and generally focuses on data center risk. It was developed in 1977 and has been used by a number of consulting organizations. It is the most widely used methodology in the federal government.

- The *IBM method*,[13] which uses a delphic approach to determine both expected loss and frequency. Each concept is expressed in terms of a range of values, usually an order of magnitude apart. Agreement is reached, and the resultant risk is calculated via a table lookup of formula.

- The *statistical evaluation*, in which the distributional nature of both threats and losses is recognized. The navy and Social Security Administration have used this approach.

- *Bayesian* decision models, in which varying distributional patterns are employed, and in which the fact that much risk data are not empirically based is recognized.[14]

In turn, each approach increases in complexity. Without automation, any statistical approach is dependent on intensive data collection and computation, a fact that limits its application and use.

Often methods are combined or integrated. Also, one approach may be used at one level, and another approach at another level. An example would be a qualitative assessment of overall risk, and an in-depth quantitative assessment of a particular system or risk area. In most cases, qualitative techniques are derived from Decision Analysis theory.[15]

Evaluation Criteria for a Methodology

Given a large number of differing approaches and methodologies for accomplishing risk management tasks, any organization contemplating the subject should consider a number of factors, not the least of which is the cost of performing a given methodology.

- What is the *depth of coverage?* Does the methodology provide a qualitative or descriptive assessment, very suitable for a broad overview of controls, or does it go into intense detail regarding the cost of loss or probability of threat?

- How *adaptable* is it to varying needs within the organization? Can it be used to evaluate a data center, a telecommunications facility, a single application system, a microcomputer, or a business function? Can it be integrated as an essential element of a security awareness program? Is it compatible with the view of controls held by management and the EDP auditors?

- What is the *functionality* of the methodology? Does it quantify risk in terms of dollar costs and benefits? Does it facilitate decision making in terms of control implementation? Does it support system design efforts? Or is it only useful for after-the-fact evaluation of existing systems or operations?

These questions should be asked of the risk assessment and management process. There is nothing wrong with employing more than one approach or method within an organization.

Automated Tools

There are a number of specific software products that can be used in carrying out all or part of a given risk management technique or method. In many cases they have made the difference between a usable methodology and one that was too complex or costly.

Uses and Benefits of Software Tools

Typically a software tool will *automate the tedious calculation* of a risk assessment, whether the underlying method is quantitative or qualitative in nature. To the extent that calculation is an administrative burden, the automated tool will save time and money. It may be possible to accomplish complex assessments at relatively low costs.

Software will also tend to provoke *consistency* and results that are *replicable*, thus removing one of the primary problems with any risk assessment process. This is especially important in distributed environments or in multiple locations.

To the extent that software is designed for use by nonspecialists, it will involve users and system managers. This involvement automatically increases security and control awareness, which is a major benefit to the organization.

From an analytical point of view, software allows "what if" modeling and thus facilitates the decision-making process. It may not be viewed as an "expert system," but at a minimum will allow the leveraging of one's own expertise.[16]

Types of Automated Systems
There are three general types of automated system that support the security evaluation of risk management tasks:

- *Spreadsheet models,* are usually run on microcomputers and employ standard software such as Lotus 1-2-3. In most cases, these models are developed by the organizations themselves. In other situations, they may be used by consultants or CPA firms as tools during an evaluation. They may also be sold separately as "templates" that can be used within an organization.
- *Qualitative assessment packages* are mostly microcomputer based. These generally present an easy to use front-end questionnaire to the user, who is led through a session focusing on his own environment or system. The answer will be weighted and scored, and the results portrayed on a scale or described. In some cases, the recommended controls or standards based on risk will be printed.
- *Quantitative packages* are either on microcomputers or mainframes. These may be as simple as automated calculators or as complex as a full risk analysis system, with a data base of actuarial statistics and complex statistical routines that take confidence factors into account.

Any one system may include both quantitative and qualitative elements.

Risk Analysis Software

Risk assessment encompasses an evaluation process that can range from simple procedures to time consuming, complex analysis. Full scale risk assessment requires comprehensive data collection and analysis for a variety of important risk factors. The resources needed for thorough risk assessment is often lacking even in large organizations. Automated risk assessment systems provide the means to organize and apply the risk assessment process. Several computer based risk assessment software systems are commercially available.

The evaluation functions provided by a typical system might include:

1. Delay loss - expected loss due to interruptions in data processing work flow.
2. Physical Damage - expected loss from damage threats.
3. EDP Fraud - expected application fraud loss.
4. Unauthorized Disclosure of Data
5. Physical Theft - expected loss from theft of data processing assets.
6. Master File Back Up - expected cost of alternative back up strategies.
7. Master File Privacy Sensitivity - expected cost of preserving file sensitivity based upon content privacy needs, file size and processing frequency.

Such an automated system might guide the user through a set of activities that include:

1. Project scope definition (objectives relating to security functions)
2. Define data collection (structure forms and files)
3. Evaluation of results (review of initial loss exposure estimates)
4. Classify the threats (groupings of losses)
5. Initial security measures data (recommendations for protection against loss)
6. Evaluation of results (quantitative evaluation)
7. Refine the data (reflecting cost implications)
8. Prepare an Action Plan - with summary of findings and recommendations

Appendix 1 contains a list of some of the software packages available for risk assessment.

Selection Criteria

The most important element in deciding on a given risk analytic tool is its suitability. What does it do, and how does it support the organizational objectives? Therefore, first determine the purpose and approach to risk assessment and then evaluate each software tool as to how well it meets the need.

Other factors must also be considered, such as:

- *Ability to run* in the systems and work environment of the organization. If microcomputers are routinely used throughout the organization and the purpose is to allow many diverse functions to accomplish their own analyses, then a micro-based product is absolutely necessary. If, on the other hand, only specialists within a large-scale data center perform the analyses, then a mainframe system is perfectly suitable.

- *User interface.* Does the system require security or systems expertise? Does it require specialized knowledge of the system under evaluation? Is research necessary before input is possible?

- *Software quality.* This includes the degree of difficulty of use, reliability, ability to withstand errors in data input, efficiency, and human engineering.

- *Vendor quality.* Product support, documentation, user training, and maintenance policies all have a bearing on the ability of the vendor to support present and future needs. An additional factor is the stability of the vendor.

- *Adaptability.* Can the package be adapted for diverse needs within the organization? Can it be adapted to fit the organization's own terminology, culture, and needs. Does the vendor provide customizing, or are there "hooks" or utility tools provided with the software?

- *Degree of expertise required.* Certain systems presume no expertise in the subject area or in risk analysis. Others may require extensive training and indoctrination.

These and other criteria must be considered whenever considering a given methodology and its associated implementation tools.

Approach

Regardless of size or function, most organizations can benefit from a corporate commitment to information risk management.

Scope of Review

A complete risk review should consist of three levels: First a broadly based, qualitative assessment that covers an entire processing environment or business function is needed. The result is descriptive, identifying areas of risk to be explored further.

The second level of analysis focuses deeper, taking an application, a physical system, a location, or an exposure as the object of evaluation. Here, the approach may extend to use of some quantitative techniques, but the main difference is that more data are collected.

Finally, there is an in-depth look at a given risk area, such as an application system, a threat, or a high-visibility computer installation. Here, it would be appropriate to collect empirical data for a quantitative analysis.

Because the multi-level approach of information risk management should never be confronted with a predisposition toward only one methodology, an organizational viewpoint is needed, often one that would require a number of differing risk management projects.

Approach to Assessment

The following actions should be considered prior to embarking on a potentially costly risk assessment or security audit project.

- *Determine needs and objectives.* The purpose of the analysis and its goals should be very explicit. In turn this will determine its scope. (It is inappropriate to schedule risk assessments based on routine or periodic time intervals.)

- *Review approaches and techniques of assessment.* Once the purpose is clear, then the decision can be made to commission a cursory review, an information system audit, a vulnerability study, a qualitative risk review, or a full quantitative risk assessment, as appropriate.

- *Survey vendors and other organizations.* Given the rapidly changing technology, vendor proposals should be solicited immediately before each study. In addition, other organizations in the same industry should be surveyed. Professional societies are also good sources of information. The organization's in-house and outside auditors may also be of assistance.

- *Consider the software packages available* to help make informed decisions and provide guidance. Most allow the modeling of different environments. Some allow tailoring to a given organization. Some provide explicit guidance in the form of recommended controls or security measures. All should reduce the need for direct consulting help.

- *Perform a make versus buy decision.* Given the wide variety of vendor approaches, including software tools, a decision to develop an in-house methodology or employ outside help is often resolved in favor of the outsider on purely economic reasons. However, many organizations feel that only inside personnel can shape their own approach to risk management.

- *Approach via a pilot project.* If a risk assessment process could become a major organizational management tool, or if a given project could be very costly (over $50,000), then the best way to approach it is via a pilot project of some limited scope. Here there will be a chance for evaluation without committing the organization heavily.

Risk assessment is a viable and useful management tool. It itself needs to be managed.

Implementation

Risk assessment is useless without action. Any plan for implementing controls must consider:

- *Balance of control strategies,* to include prevention, detection and recovery measures.

- A wide variety of *threat and loss scenarios.* It does little good to safeguard an on-line system yet allow the data base to be accessed freely with a batch job.

- A *changing technology.* Yesterday's physical security showcase is today's nightmare. The "hacker" wasn't considered much of a problem in the mid-1970s, but today the need for increased computer security is apparent.

- The *requirement for security and control awareness* as an essential prerequisite. There is no way an effective program of protection

or contingency planning can be put in place without awareness and concern at every level of an organization.

- The possibility of *accepting risk.* It may be entirely appropriate to withhold effort, and avoid costs necessary to prevent or recover from a given risk.

Once the mechanisms for cost-effective control have been identified, and the organization is convinced that benefits outweigh costs, it is a relatively easy task to implement a given control strategy.

Benefits

An aware organization can achieve significant benefits through the use of risk management techniques.

Some of the benefits include:

- The *alerting of management* to near-term problems with unacceptable consequences as well as what should be corrected over the long term. It can be argued that a good EDP or security audit will do the same thing. However, a risk assessment includes all the elements of a security audit.

- The determination of appropriate *control expenditures* for given risks. This is the bottom line of how limited security and control resources should be allocated.

- The critical side effect of overall *increased awareness* and support for control programs. This occurs particularly because a risk study encompasses the entire organization. Users who rarely get to voice their concern are heard. They tend to support the resultant recommendations. The security program is focused on the business functions of the organization.

- Evaluation criteria are developed for *further control efforts* in contingency planning, the systems development life cycle, and for logical access to application systems.

Computer risk management is an essential task of an information security program. The results of a risk assessment can provide the rationale for starting projects, training staff, and installing data security software and hardware with appropriate controls. A properly implemented plan can be expected to return more benefits than it costs.

Information Security Risk Management Checklist

Yes No

Is the treatment of risk an integral part of the analysis, design, development, production, and system maintenance tasks? ☐ ☐

Does the treatment of risk apply to users as well as suppliers of EDP and telecommunications services? Is it equally relevant to a standalone microcomputer and a large data center? ☐ ☐

Do risk management plans identify, measure, control, and minimize the impact of unexpected events in information systems? ☐ ☐

Are specific high-risk threats identified and are measures for controlling them in place? ☐ ☐

Are threats identified that affect computer system availability and reliability, data confidentiality, and the integrity of organizational assets? ☐ ☐

Have current security and protection mechanisms and potential controls been evaluated? ☐ ☐

Have the limited resources available for security and control (time, materials, people, money) been identified and ranked in order? ☐ ☐

Have system and user personnel been made aware of the system risks and potential losses? ☐ ☐

Has there been a systematic evaluation of the effect of potential losses and the probability of loss occurrence? ☐ ☐

Have controls been selected and implemented that either reduce the threat of occurrence or minimize the effect of loss? ☐ ☐

Is risk review a continuing process in which users, software developers, and computer/communications providers all participate? ☐ ☐

Have estimates been made of potential losses of resources including facilities, applications, systems software, hardware, and people that are important ☐ ☐

Yes No

to the data processing mission? Do these estimates identify replacement costs?

Do resource analyses classify risks by criticality and sensitivity? ☐ ☐

Are risks expressed in terms of both frequency over a given time and the amount of potential loss to identified assets? ☐ ☐

Has a cost benefit analysis been used to evaluate proposed safeguards to select the most appropriate management response? ☐ ☐

Is the risk management methodology adaptable to varying needs? Can it be used to evaluate a data center, a single application, or a microcomputer? Is it compatible with management's or the auditors' view of control? ☐ ☐

Does the risk management methodology facilitate decision making about control implementation and support system design efforts? ☐ ☐

Does risk assessment software save time and money and produce consistent results? ☐ ☐

Does the selection of a risk analytic tool take into consideration its ability to operate in the work environment, its reliability, and its adaptability to fit the organization's needs? ☐ ☐

Is there a corporate commitment to information risk management? ☐ ☐

Is the purpose of risk assessment explicit? ☐ ☐

Has a vulnerability study or a qualitative or quantitative risk review been made? ☐ ☐

Have auditors been asked to assist in planning security measures? ☐ ☐

If risk assessment may become a major project, has a pilot project of limited scope been planned? ☐ ☐

Does the implementation plan include prevention, detection, and recovery measures, and involve awareness and concern at every organizational level? ☐ ☐

Notes

1. Norman, Adrian, R. D., "Managing Computer Risks," in *Computer Insecurity*, pp. 311–329, Chapman & Hall Ltd., 1983.

2. Porter, W. Thomas and William E. Perry, *EDP Controls and Auditing.* Boston: Kent Publishing Company, 1984.

3. Browne, Peter S., *Security: Checklist for Computer Center Self-Audits.* Arlington, VA: American Federation of Information Processing Societies, 1974; rev. ed. Arlington, VA: American Federation of Information Processing Societies, 1979.

4. Rowe, William D., *The Anatomy of Risk*, John Wiley & Sons, Inc., 1977.

5. Wong, K. K., *Computer Security: Risk Analysis and Control: A Guide For Managers.* Manchester, England and Rochelle Park, N.J.: NCC Publications and Hayden Book Company, 1977.

6. Courtney, Robert H., *Security Risk Assessment in EDP.* National Computer Conference, 1977.

7. U.S. Department of Commerce, National Bureau of Standards: FIPS PUB 31: *Guidelines of Automatic Data Processing, Physical Security and Risk Management*, Washington, D.C., June 1974.

8. Nugent, W.; J. Gilligan; and Z. Ruthberg. *Technology Assessment: Methods for Measuring the Level of Computer Security.* U.S. Dept. of Commerce, National Bureau of Standards (NBS Special Publication 500–133) October 1985.

9. Heaps III, S. Wilson, "Assessing Risks in a "Deconcentrated" Computing Environment." *Computer Security* (July/August 1982), pp. 3–4.

10. Parker, Donn B., "Computer Abuse Perpetrators and Vulnerabilities of Computer Systems," Proceedings 1976 National Computer Conference, pp. 65–73.

11. Hoffman, L. J., and L. A. Netizel, *Inexact Analysis of Risk.* Proceeding of the IEEE 1980 International Conference on Cybernetics and Society. Boston, Mass., October 1980. Reprinted in *Computer Security Journal*, vol. 1., no. 1 (Spring 1981) 61–72.

12. National Aeronautic and Space Administration, *Self-Analysis Guide and Document for ADP Risk Analysis.* Washington, D.C., March 1982.

13. U.S. Department of Commerce, National Bureau of Standards: FIPS PUB 65: *Guidelines for Automatic Data Processing Risk Analysis*, Washington, D.C., August 1979.

14. Mosleh, Ali, *A Bayesian Approach to the Assessment of Risk for Computer and Communication Systems.* Paper presented at the Seventh Annual DoD-NBS Computer Security Conference, Washington, D.C., September 24–26, 1985.

15. Brown, Rex V., *Managing Diffuse Risks from Adversarial Sources (DR/AS) with Special Reference to Computer Security.* (DSC Working Paper 86-1). Falls Church, VA: Decision Science Consortium, Inc., January, 1985.

16. Carroll, John M., *Managing Risks: A Computer-Aided Strategy.* Butterworth Publishers, 1984.

CHAPTER 3

Employees

By Robert W. London and Dick H. Brandon

Introduction and Objectives

General Security Considerations of Personnel

It can be safely stated that employees are the key ingredient in the success of a data processing installation. By the same token, a chain is as strong as its weakest link, and in the data processing installation in many instances the employee often represents the weakest link in the security chain. Most of the emergencies for which security systems are built are in fact caused by people; and in most cases those people are either employees, or ex-employees of the organizations in which the emergency occurs. Thus, considerable care should be taken in recruiting and deploying personnel to insure maximum coverage in the event of emergencies.

It is generally agreed that there is no totally airtight security system; it is not possible to guard against all security breaches that may be caused by employees. However, it is possible to minimize the risks either by instituting preventive measures or by early detection and correction when they do occur.

This chapter will review four principal methods in which employee security can be controlled and maintained. If these methods are generally employed, and if care is taken in the operation of the organization to observe the conditions outlined, a great deal of potential difficulty can be avoided. The four components of a good employee security program are:

The Framework—By framework is meant the establishment of the appropriate organization structure, the requisite job descriptions, and lines of authority that provide for clear definitions of responsibilities and authority. This framework prevents unauthorized access to information and presumably prevents personnel from tampering with information in which they should have no interest or to which they should not have access.

Hiring Practices—The methods used in hiring personnel are the foundation upon which to build a sound security program. In-depth screening prior to employment can provide a practical means for assessing both the caliber and character of the individual, thus lessening the security risks within an organization.

Education and Employee Relationships—Morale in an organization can deteriorate through ineffective relationships with management, or through improper education of the employee. Thus, the establishment of reasonable policies with regard to employees can reduce dissatisfaction, which in turn will reduce the temptation for the employee to act in an irresponsible manner.

Effective Operation—By operating an organization that is continually security conscious, and that continues to follow a basic set of secure operating practices, both the temptation, the motive, and the opportunity for anything other than normal operation will be sharply reduced.

These four key areas are discussed in this chapter.

Classification of Security Breaches Caused by Employees

There are many breaches of security caused by employees. In examining security practices, and establishing the proper controls, it is highly desirable to recognize the different forms in which employees may cause a security problem. In effect, there are about seven ways in which an em-

33

ployee can participate in a situation that will ultimately be costly to the organization. These are as follows:

Theft—Theft is defined as the outright removal of an asset of the company by an employee. The asset in this case can be subtle; it could be the removal of an entire system or a program used by the organization, which might have value to another organization. In a recent case, some ex-employees of a major international airline reproduced copies of every single program of that airline's reservation system, and offered these for sale to competing airlines. The airline whose programs had been stolen in this manner went to court, obtained an injunction, and ultimately proceeded to prevent the actions by these employees. The fact that this was detected, however, was due solely to the fact that the airline industry is a relatively small one, in which information travels quickly and was rapidly reported back by the organizations to whom the programs were offered. Theft may also mean the theft of items of value such as tapes, disks, or other machine components. These are perhaps less important. Finally, theft may mean the removal of data vital to the operation of the company. Thus, the theft of a customer list, the theft of a payroll file, or the theft of a list of employee records could be of considerable value to competition, to employee recruiters, or to organizations interested in establishing a comparable business.

Fraud—Fraud for this purpose is defined as the obtaining by an employee of assets of the organization through intentional misrepresentation or misapplication of information. Fraud in this case may be the modification of a system by an employee to increase payments made on his paycheck or by several employees working in collusion who make use of a system for their own purposes, such as setting up phony accounts payable records for payments to bogus companies. Finally, fraud may also be the falsification of company records by an employee for his own benefit through the insertion or deletion of personal data maintained on computer files.

Another, perhaps more far-reaching aspect, is the potential for "inadvertent fraud," the unplanned misapplication of information due to lack of care, incompetence, or poor controls—such as the incorrect posting of transactions by clerical or data entry personnel. Although un-

intended, these processing errors can have severe implications for an organization, financial and otherwise. In today's environment it should be recognized that the proliferation and use of microcomputers throughout an organization can only exacerbate this problem.

Misuse of Information—An employee may make misuse of corporate information which is either proprietary to the organization or is embargoed through temporary confidentiality. Thus, it is possible, for example, for an employee to obtain advance information on the company's earnings which would enable the employee to purchase or sell securities of the company in advance of the general public. This, of course, is in violation of laws against "insider" trading, but this violation is not normally detected for anyone except corporate officers, who must disclose the amount of trading that they do in their company's shares.

Sabotage—An employee who is unhappy with his employer, for whatever reason, may intentionally perform acts to damage the organization as a means of revenge. Sabotage can be subtle, and may not be detected readily. A case in point is that of an employee who continually tampered with the computer equipment, causing it to malfunction on an irregular basis, which resulted in costing the organization millions of dollars in losses because the engineers were unable to identify the cause and correct the situation for a long period of time. Other forms of sabotage, of course, can include the modification or erasure of data maintained on computer media, as well as the physical destruction of files.

Rule Disobedience—Employees occasionally violate specific rules laid down to protect the organization or to protect the safety of other employees. In this case disobedience of a rule may cause accidents, may cause accidental destruction of data, or may cause other difficulty for the organization. For example, an employee who by accident destroyed a file on the night shift attempted, in violation of all normal library procedures, to reproduce the file in order to correct the situation so that it would not be noticed by his immediate supervisors. In this case, since he was not familiar with the exact contents of the file, the file he recreated was grossly inaccurate. However, the file was sufficiently accurate to escape detection until the monthly processing cycle some weeks later. At this point, however, a number of customer records had been permanently damaged.

Physical Accidents—A computer is a dangerous instrument. Many volts of electricity transformed to varying levels can represent significant danger of electrocution, and a number of design engineers, maintenance engineers, and even computer operators have been given significant electric shocks, and have even died through electrocution. In addition, the rapidly moving parts of the card reader, the printer, tape, and disk drives can be dangerous, if they were to catch a tie, an employee's beard, long hair, or any other part of the employee's dress. Thus, there are safety considerations to be emphasized in the use of essentially dangerous equipment, such as a computer or associated peripheral gear.

Emergencies—A number of different types of emergencies can take place in which the employee must act in a reasonable manner in order to insure that the company can in fact recover from whatever disaster has taken place. Disasters such as fires, floods, power failure, or air conditioning failure must be coped with in an orderly manner, if data files are to be properly protected, and if programs and program documentation are to be taken care of prior to evacuation of the premises. Again, operating rules should be established to cope with emergencies of all types and descriptions, and employee training programs should be provided for this instance.

The remainder of this chapter deals with the precautions and cautions which must be taken in the four areas outlined earlier.

Framework for Effective Security

The first precaution that an organization must take in order to insure that security consciousness permeates throughout is to establish the proper framework for security purposes. In part this means the establishment of the proper lines of authority and the proper employee relationships. In addition, however, it means that an appropriate organization structure must be established to insure that the opportunities for security breaches are minimized.

Organization Structure

There are many organizational precepts that must be considered in structuring a data processing organization. Of these, those concerned with security are certainly not the most important. However, the rules that must be considered in structuring an organization and the rules that should be considered from the viewpoint of security are not significantly different, and a careful assessment of organizational objectives will indicate that the organization structure that results from both considerations tends to look the same.

An organization structure can assist only in the prevention of deliberate breaches of security, such as theft, fraud, sabotage, and misuse of information. Clearly no organization structure can prevent natural disasters, nor can it effectively prevent accidents that occur under normal operating conditions. However, a carefully planned organization can, in fact, reduce the risk of theft, fraud, and sabotage when the following precepts are considered:

1. In general, the only way in which fraud should be capable of being perpetrated is by requiring the collusion of more than one individual. Thus, by structuring the organization in such a way as to require collusion among individuals, for fraudulent purposes, a significant protective device is created. If collusion is required, it will discourage employees. Collusion also makes fraud more difficult since it requires more than one person with comparable inclinations and comparable disaffections. And finally, of course, where collusion does exist, it is more readily detected, since it is possible that one or more partners will not in fact be available to participate when surprise audits take place, or when other unexpected situations arise.

2. By specializing the organization along functional lines, it is more readily possible to prevent employees from entering areas in which they do not belong. Functional specialization provides each employee a specific set of tasks within a specific area of operation. He should, therefore, never be in any other area of operation, unless it falls within his specific job description. This permits ready detection if an employee should be in an unauthorized area. Functional specialization has the secondary benefit of providing a chain of people involved in the development of a system or in the production of a set of reports. This means that the organization will never be wholly dependent on a single individual who has all of the necessary knowledge capable of altering a system. In functional specialization if three or more people are required to make a change to a system then obviously it is difficult for a single individual to make an unauthorized change to a system or to a report.

The basic organizational precepts which come from this type of consideration are:

- Where feasible, segregate systems analysis and programming functions. These two functions essentially represent conflicts of interest in that one is supposed to optimize user interest and the other to optimize machine or data processing interests. By segregating these two functions, controls can be built into the system and only collusion between the two can effectively create a systems control breach.

- Segregate the systems development function from the systems maintenance function. This will not allow changes to be made in a system once it is out of development, unless such changes are made and authorized by the maintenance organization.

- Segregate the software maintenance organization from the operations function. This will prevent direct relationships between maintenance and operations, and will also eliminate from the operations organization any type of programming capability.

- Segregate project control functions from development activities. By segregating the quality control functions from the actual operating functions it will necessitate collusion between people in data control and people in operations. Similarly changes in a system can only take place by authorization of project control, and, therefore, require both project control personnel and systems development personnel. A simplified organization chart which embodies these basic principles is shown as Figure 3.1

- Rotate software maintenance and computer operations personnel within their own areas. Since both are ongoing, production activities, they are more susceptible to fraudulent acts. Maintenance programmers can be ro-

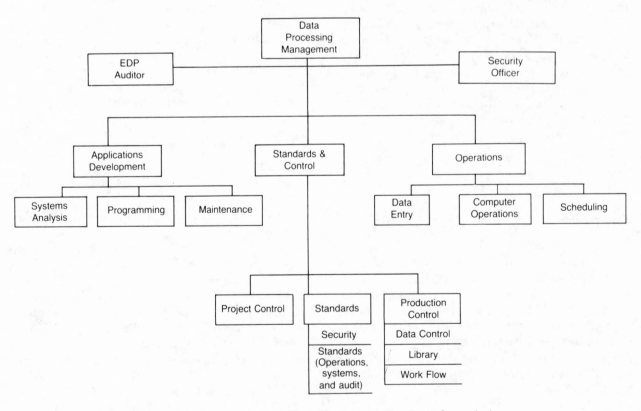

Figure 3.1 Organization Chart (Illustrating Desirable Functional Separation)

tated by application area; operators by work shift. Such organizational procedures would not only tend to deter frauds and collusion but can be used effectively for the cross-training of personnel in a job enhancement program.

- Ensure, wherever possible, that family relationships do not exist between employees in sensitive components of the organization. A man and wife in programming and operations could jointly access both programs and data files and thus could breach a basic security principle. Similarly, close friends should be discouraged from working together in sensitive situations.

3. In large organizations the establishment of a security function within data processing can be instrumental in ensuring that its assets—people, information, and equipment—are adequately protected. The optimum corporate structure to achieve maximum security levels would involve three independent groups:

- Corporate Security Chief—to establish corporatewide security objectives and plans, and to oversee their implementation.
- Internal Auditor—to review the appropriateness of the security procedures, and to conduct periodic (random) audits to assess the level of adherence.
- EDP Security Officer—to establish, direct, and coordinate all security activities within the department in conjunction with corporate policy and predefined standards, procedures, and measures.

Job Descriptions
Another principal component of an effective security framework is to have clear and detailed current job descriptions for all the activities in the data processing organization. These job descriptions will then provide clear statements of authority and responsibility. Each job description should disclose to whom the employee reports and whom the employee supervises.

In addition, a job description should provide for a clear delineation of the duties of the employee, and the areas within the organization where such duties are to be performed. Thus, the physical access that the employee is allowed under normal circumstances should be specifically detailed in the job description.

Finally, a job description should stipulate specifically the duties of the employee in the event of a disaster. If the employee is responsible for protecting specific data files, or specific documents or documentation components, this should be clearly spelled out in a job description. Copies of the job description must, of course, be made available to the employee and to all of the necessary supervisory personnel.

Performance Evaluation
Observance of security should be incorporated as one criterion in the periodic assessment of employee performance. This will serve to stress its criticality to the organization and to provide a means for constant review and reinforcement. In addition, incentives and penalties could be assigned to further ensure compliance with corporate policies. As part of this program, the organization should make its employees aware of any legal liability for misconduct in this area.

The Standards Manual
A final component of the framework prerequisite to effective security management is, of course, a standards manual. One component of the standards manual will specify all of the security practices. However, these are not the only standards that are of importance to security. Other types of standards insure that the organization can survive even if employees leave, and ensure that the policies, procedures, and practices of the organization are clearly understood and spelled out for all employees. A sample table of contents for security standards is presented in Appendix 2.

Hiring Practices

An examination of the background of instances of theft, fraud, misuse of information, and sabotage by employees or ex-employees, would probably show that some of these might have been prevented if the hiring practices had been more carefully thought out and applied.

An important time to determine whether or not an employee is going to be an honest, hardworking member of the organization is when he is being hired. At that point much information about him is readily accessible, both from the in-

38

dividual and from his previous employers or other references.

There are, however, serious limitations in the screening of applicants for security purposes, in particular the legal restrictions in revealing and using derogatory information. Most companies are understandably hesitant to give adverse comments about former employees, a condition widely known. Therefore, applicants can often hide or misrepresent information without detection.

Since the screening of applicants can not assure honesty and reliability, it is essential to observe and monitor behavior and performance after employment, especially during a probationary period.

Nevertheless, it is important that members of the personnel organization responsible for hiring be made aware of the overall security practices of the organization and of the specific emphasis that should be taken with highly sensitive positions in the data processing activity. If a security manual does not exist for the organization as a whole, then component sections of the data processing standards manual that deal with employee security should be provided to the personnel department to acquaint them with the objectives of the data processing security standards.

Initial Security Checks

By the time that an individual becomes a prospective employee of an organization he has already established for himself a considerable trail that can be checked quite extensively. He has for example an educational record, potentially a military record, previous employment, and other activities, such as marriage, divorce, personal bankruptcy, litigation, court action, or other events, which will be available as a matter of public record. It is highly important to obtain all possible information about prospective data processing employees, especially if they are going to be in highly sensitive positions. These are primarily positions in systems analysis, programming, and operations with direct access to information and information flow.

The types of checks that should be performed for sensitive employees include the following:

Reference Checks—At a minimum for all employees at least three business and three personal references should be checked. In checking both

of these types of references, it should be recognized that persons given by the employee as personal references are not likely to be terribly negative about that employee. By the same token, though, they will be relatively honest in the event there have been severe problems in the employee's background. Consideration should be given to the source of the reference, so that employees on their application blanks should be requested to give references who have fairly long-standing relationships with the employee, other than a family relationship. Professional personnel such as lawyers, doctors, dentists, clergymen, or other professionals who may have known the employee personally in some form are preferred over other forms of acquaintances. Employment references should be checked in any event. When an employee is an applicant it may not be feasible to check his present employer. In any event, after he has given notice to that employer he must extend permission to have his present employment reference checked, and his employment must be contingent on such a check. Thus, in any case as many as six references should be checked, and the information taken from the reference recorded as part of the employee's personnel file if hired.

Specific information that should be reviewed with the references other than work competence is information as to the employee's medical history, his habits, his honesty, and his educational record. Any discrepancy between information given by a reference and information given by the employee should be carefully checked with the employee. If it is determined that the employee deliberately misstated any facts on the application blank, regardless how trivial, then the employee should not be considered further for employment. Any minor misstatement on an employment application is an indication of the employee's potential dishonesty and can lead therefore to future discrepancies far more significant. In fact it should probably be considered good practice to note on the application blank that if any facts thereon are found to be inaccurate after employment then that will be automatic cause for dismissal as well.

Special Checks—For employees in supersensitive management positions it may be desirable to run a special check. Special checks were made famous when General Motors commissioned one on Ralph Nader, who in turn managed to sue General Motors and win a considerable settlement for invasion of privacy. However, there are a number of services who perform special checks on employees or prospective employees for a fee, without the ultimate invasion of privacy. In this case the service simply checks all available public records to determine whether the employee has any negative elements on his or her record. Litigation, court records, marital records, and all other types of public documents are checked to insure that the employer is given all of the necessary information about the prospective employee. Services such as Proudfout and Bishop are considered private reporting services who for a nominal fee will provide the basic public facts about prospective employees. Similarly, credit bureaus can provide a more limited check on the prospect.

Military Record—The fact that a prospective employee has been in the military is usually noted on the employment form. Depending on the sensitivity of the position, a brief request for any information on the military record that might be deemed to be detrimental can be forwarded by the appropriate authorities.

Law Enforcement Record—It may be possible to check with the proper law enforcement authorities to determine if a prospective employee has any type of criminal or law enforcement record. It is currently required for employees in the financial community, in Wall Street, to have their finger prints taken prior to employment. These finger prints are checked to insure that no one is employed in sensitive positions dealing with securities who has in the past had any type of criminal conviction.

Educational Record—The educational record of a prospective employee often provides insight into his character and capability. Comments by professors, possible instances of cheating, or possible activities in school that may have influenced the employee in some way might all be considered factors that would have a bearing in combination with other information on the employee's ability to handle sensitive information.

Probation

After an employee has been checked and has been hired, it is desirable to place the employee on probationary status. There is always a reluctance on the part of the employer to terminate an employee. This reluctance can be assuaged in the event some negative aspects of the employee are discovered, by virtue of the fact that the employee is still on probation. It is far easier to terminate an employee on probation, both psychologically and economically, than a permanent employee. A permanent badge should not be issued to employees on probation. During the probationary period an opportunity can be taken to observe the employee in action and to complete the final checking of his background and qualifications that may not have been obtained during the hiring process.

Insurance and Bonding

It is possible to obtain a surety bond on employees at an approximate average cost of about $300–$400 per year. These bonds reimburse organizations primarily for the theft of specific assets, defalcations, and fraud. They do not typically guard against damages caused by sabotage, and they certainly do not guard against accidents or emergency procedures. A more detailed discussion of insurance provisions will be found in the chapter on that subject. If an employee is to be bonded, it is desirable to initiate the procedure at the time the employee is hired. This will also prompt additional checks by the bonding company.

Nondisclosure Agreements

To guard against the possibility of misuse of information, or to attempt to insure that the employee will not obtain corporate information and use it for his own benefit, it is possible to execute a nondisclosure agreement (see Appendix 3) with each employee. It is difficult to enforce such an agreement, except in the case of outright sale by the employee of company trade secrets or specific information which can be traced back to the company. Nondisclosure agreements typically provide that they survive beyond the employment of the employee regardless of method of termination, and that the employee will recognize the irreparable damage that could occur if he were to disclose information confidential to the organization. This recognition may be of some use in a court of law; however, it is extremely difficult to prove and even more difficult to enforce.

Conflict of Interest

One subtle means of defalcation, perhaps more insidious than other forms, is "conflict of interest." In this instance, an employee participates in the selection of a vendor and, without disclosing it to the corporation, may receive a commission or fee from the vendor for having made the necessary arrangement. This form of kickback is just as illegal and just as fraudulent as any other form of defalcation. Essentially the company loses the amount of money or the goods or favors that are returned by the vendor to the employee. This practice is widespread in the purchase of things like supplies and accessory equipment. It is especially prevalent in the printing industry or in any industry in which the selection of a vendor is not dependent on proprietary techniques or products.

In other forms of conflicts of interest the employee may be a shareholder of a vendor organization, or he may be entitled, on some basis, to a percentage of the profits of the organization. This practice has been used on occasion by software companies wishing to advance themselves with potential client companies. Again the practice is illegal and indefensible. To guard against it, vendor selection of all types should be based on competitive bids and should be supervised by at least two levels of management, thus minimally requiring some collusion. Contracts should be periodically reviewed, and prices obtained from vendors checked against other independent vendors, perhaps by the auditing organization or by data processing management.

Temporary Personnel Security Practices

On occasion it becomes necessary for organizations to hire temporary employees. In this case it is common practice to ignore the basic security checking since the employees may not be employed for a significantly long period of time. In general this is an acceptable procedure, but it should be exercised with caution. If a temporary employee is going to be employed for so short a period as to prevent him from becoming totally familiar with the company's operating practices and, therefore, to prevent his access to vital and sensitive information on some basis, then it is probably acceptable to rely on the bonding provided by most reputable temporary personnel agencies. If, however, the employee is going to be on board for a considerable period of time, say in excess of two weeks, and the employee is going to be in a relatively sensitive area where he will have access to information, as, for ex-

ample, a contract programmer employed for more than three months at a given site, then it becomes necessary for the organization itself to perform the necessary reference checking much in the same way as references are checked for regular employees. Thus a temporary employee should no longer be considered temporary or special or exempt from security practices if his tenure with the organization is going to exceed a month or two. In any event, it is necessary to check the references of the supplying organization and to insist on bonded or insured personnel.

Employees of Vendors, Contractors, Building or Outside Users

It is clear that there will be contractors and vendors whose employees will require access to the premises, such as maintenance engineers repairing the equipment, air conditioning personnel, building personnel, or occasional outside organizations using the computer of the organization on a spare time basis. All of these are potentially hazardous, unless the organizations they represent have posted the requisite bonds and have indeed been checked. Almost all major computer vendors have bonded engineering personnel to ensure against liability. It should be noted that in the case of employees of other organizations a certain amount of risk can be taken by the host organization, when the liability will in fact be assumed by the organization that acts as the employer of these individuals. Notwithstanding this, if this liability is not effectively assumed, or if the organization itself is not financially responsible, then the risk taken may be significant. In any event, it is likely that bonding and assumption of liability alone may not be sufficient to offset the inconvenience and damage, which could be significantly more than that which is compensible in dollar terms.

Education and Employee Relationships

The third precaution that should be taken by a prudent organization is to make sure that its relationship with its employees is maintained at a reasonable level, so that except for isolated incidents of potential disaffection, the entire work force is generally loyal to the employing organization. This implies that the organization will be relatively careful in treating the entire work force with the necessary respect, and with consideration for any individual problems that may arise. It is clear that regardless of the amount of care taken by the employer organization there may still be isolated instances of employee dissatisfaction, occasionally caused by totally spurious situations.

Morale as a Factor in Security

There can be no question but that employee morale is a significant factor in the data processing installation's security. Employees who believe that in some way they have been disenfranchised may feel that it is their right to correct this situation. If they believe that their employer has cheated them, or has taken from them what is theirs, or has failed to compensate them properly for work they have done, then they have no hesitancy about correcting the situation, much to the detriment of the employer. Thus, employee morale, in specific instances, must be protected whenever possible. In the general case, if the morale of the entire organization is poor, then the employees will not work together as a team, and they will not attempt to prevent individual employees from committing acts such as rule disobedience, which might, in fact, endanger or damage the employer.

One method of overcoming this problem is to maintain a continuing relationship with each employee in the organization. This can be done through the establishment of an effective personnel management program, with a principal emphasis on the continued professional development of employees in the data processing organization. This approach is especially applicable to the data processing organization, where the technical skills are so diverse and so rapidly changing that almost every employee can benefit from continued professional development programs. As a result, the conduct of professional development programs will not only have the benefit of increasing employee morale but will also increase the effectiveness and efficiency of employees as well.

In addition, management should be aware that there are certain problems that are more acute in data processing than in most other areas, such as meeting frequent and unrealistic deadlines. Compensatory time, bonuses, and recognition of accomplishments are some of the means available to management for lessening the effect of such conditions.

Training Needs

One method of maintaining or improving morale in the organization is to provide professional development and continued education. Another method is to demonstrate the cost of poor security. This can be considered a form of training, exposing employees to the risks, damages, and costs that can be caused by situations resulting from breaches in security. In effect this type of training can appeal to the employees' solidarity and to their sense of belonging to the organization. It can be shown that if the organization is damaged significantly, so will they be. Thus, continued training and education are necessary factors in employee relationships.

Employee Communication

In addition to the normal methods of employee communication through training and through staff meetings. other communication with the data processing employee are available. These may take the form of suggestions, although these have fallen into disrepute since most organizations do not really consider suggestions as a significant form of communication. A more positive form of communication is to have group meetings with all of the personnel of the data processing organization so that employees may air their gripes without punitive results. This also gives management an opportunity to explain new policies, new developments, and their attitude toward the issues that have been raised.

Another effective technique for increasing communication between employees and management and among employees is to have an employee-produced newsletter. This type of communication device can be significant not only in improving the morale of employees by giving them a voice, but also in maintaining a high level of interest and concern in matters relating to computer security.

Operation

A final safeguard or precaution that must be taken in the organization is to have a security conscious continuing operation of the data processing organization. This takes many forms.

Continuing observation

The first and most logical form is to have a watchful management, which continually observes the operation of the organization, which determines whether or not employee morale is maintained, and whether or not security practices are being followed. Thus, the organization must continually be observed either by management, by special audit groups, or by personnel assigned within data processing.

Part of this can be accomplished through effective supervisory training. It is desirable to teach supervisors within the data processing organization to look out for specific symptoms of possible problems that might exist in the organization. Included among these problems are deteriorating morale and the symptoms associated with that, such as increased employee grievances, complaints about the working environment, increases in turnover, exit interviews with employees who have resigned that indicate potential danger signs, and the like.

There are, however, a number of other problems that are more individual in nature and that a trained supervisor should be capable of detecting. Alcohol and drug use have increased dramatically in the last few years in modern organizations. Unfortunately, these are merely symptoms of the problem, rather than being the problem itself. These two influences tend to rapidly deteriorate an employee's effectiveness and create substantial additional problems. A habitual drug user, for example, who is required to pay up to several hundred dollars a day to support his habit, is very likely to be contemplating any fraudulent method of obtaining such sums of money. Many companies provide counseling services to employees with addiction or emotional problems, which are often interrelated. Such supportive programs generally are considered a sound investment; the benefits obtained by the employer more than justify the rather large costs associated with such programs.

Another potential problem area, which is not often publicly reviewed, is on-the-job sex. Although this subject is more often the butt of washroom jokes, it requires serious consideration. This type of situation can lead to concurrent problems as a result of potential blackmail, employee frustration, and lowered morale. When circumstances of this type are discovered, they must be handled in accordance with clearly defined company policies.

Job Rotation

As part of a continuing operation it is desirable to ensure that no one person continually stays at the same job. It is beneficial to institute job rotation to prevent an employeee from being in total control of one segment of the entire job. Such total control might readily result in data modification, theft, fraud, or misuse of information. If such rotation is not possible, employees in sensitive areas should be given extended vacations and should be forced to take their vacations on contiguous days. This would mean that the entire cycle of their operation would be under the control of other persons, so that inadvertent or fraudulent errors would be detected. It is common practice, and in certain instances state law, that banking employees must take at least two weeks of their vacation on a contiguous basis, to ensure that problems arising from their work will be detected by others.

Rotation, either horizontally or through promotions, is seldom difficult within a data processing organization, where growth and turnover open up significant career opportunities for most employees. It is unlikely to find anyone in a data processing organization who has been in the same position for more than five years. If someone were to be in a sensitive position for a longer period of time, it might be desirable to consider that person for promotion or transfer.

Access Control

The chapter on monitoring devices covers the details of access control. Elements of the organization that contain sensitive information, or which contain assets of the organization that can be misused by employees, should be subject to significant controls for access. It is desirable for each employee in the data processing organization to have an identification card. This identification card, complete with picture, will enable guards stationed in sensitive areas to identify each individual and to insure that these individuals are in fact authorized to enter sensitive areas. It is not at all uncommon to color code or letter code the identification cards to indicate which areas the employee has access to within the data processing complex.

The increasing use of guards in data processing is a clear indication that people are interested in physical protection of their site. Guards or some forms of card-operated automatic entry systems are desirable for areas such as the computer room and the data file library, both of which could be sabotaged, and both of which could be significant to the survival of the organization. It is a reasonable investment to provide an entry system to control access to these specific areas. In that event, employees would be checked prior to their entry into these areas, and any packages that they are carrying would either be left behind or would be subject to inspection.

In large installations, programmers are usually not permitted free access to the computer area or library, partially to prevent the opportunity for them to manipulate the data or programs improperly. However, programmers are usually encouraged to bring up failed systems as quickly as possible, even if they must enter the computer room to do so. Also, access through remote terminals is as potentially dangerous as physical access to the machine room. In small installations, programmers and operators are frequently the same persons. Thus, even though programmers' presence in machine rooms and libraries should be discouraged where possible, other means must be used to prevent their improper use of or modifications to data and programs.

Standards and Compliance

Finally, of course, any data processing organization needs a comprehensive set of standards, not only for purposes of security but also for purposes of ensuring that the quality of the product is uniform, understandable to all concerned, and capable of being measured qualitatively and quantitatively. Standards can help enforce security practices. Emergency procedures, for example, should be detailed in a standards manual. Turnover procedures by which a program is given over to maintenance and maintenance turns over a program to operations, all should be part of a standards manual, and the procedures should be designed to recognize the potential collusion that might exist between personnel of the two organizations. As a result, procedures should be designed so that additional personnel are part of the turnover cycle, thereby making collusion more difficult.

It is obviously not possible in even the best and most comprehensive standards manual to prevent collusion among employees. But it can be made more difficult and more subject to rigorous rules and regulations, thus making it more difficult to perform and easier to detect, acting

as a psychological deterrent. In point of fact, the primary purpose of a good security program is to act as a psychological deterrent to the would-be thief or the would-be saboteur. Clearly there may be cases in which no psychological deterrent is sufficient to stop someone who is determined to do damage to the employer. However, the careful design and enforcement of standards and procedures could prevent collusion or other fraudulent acts and will provide the necessary environment for effective security.

Standards should be enforced. A breach of regulation, which can be damaging but may not always be, should be punished whether or not damage has, in fact, been done. If rules are not complied with, then general disobedience will follow, with the result that personnel will find themselves in a gradually loosening environment, so that ultimately they will find it very easy to commit acts that could be damaging. Standards must be complied with, and their compliance is the responsibility of the supervisory staff. Data processing supervisors have the responsibility for reviewing the work of their subordinates, for ensuring that it meets the qualitative standards of the organization, but also for ensuring that it meets the standards established for methodology, for controls, and for security practices. In the event noncompliance is discovered for any reason, it should be treated in exactly the same way as any other rule disobedience is treated. The offending employee should be warned, disciplined if the situation is serious, and, if it recurs, the offending employee should be dismissed.

The general laxity of data processing practices in the past is now being replaced by an increasing concern for security. Management is now much more aware of the need for effective security practices. Good data processing security is a matter of common sense, but it also requires the application of knowledge and a management commitment for enforcement. Few situations justify a relatively foolproof, but costly, system such as might be used at a major intelligence agency. What needs to be done is to institute careful practices in consideration of the fact that the data processing organization is more sensitive than almost any other element of the organization.

Since employees are the most sensitive component of the data processing organization, employee security practices must clearly be a focal point. If employee security practices have been established and employees are security conscious, the remaining controls built into the hardware, the software, and the other activities of the organization will follow suit.

Appendix 2 provides a sample set of contents for a manual of security standards.

Termination

Termination of an employee occurs through transfer, promotion, resignation, death, retirement, or firing. In any case, it is desirable to be security-conscious, and it is especially important if the termination occurs under a cloud of negative feelings. In such circumstances, it is of preeminent importance that the terminated employee be requested to leave immediately, accompanied by a manager or security guard.

Much as most companies have a hiring checklist, which prescribes the forms to be filled out, orientation to be supplied, and the like, a similar checklist should be established for termination. It should include, depending on type of termination:

- Surrender of keys
- Surrender of identification cards
- Exit interview
- Return of other company materials
- Changes in passwords
- Changes in locks
- Changes in access or authority codes

Microcomputers

Micro or personal computers (PCs) used in business are of particular concern from a security standpoint. Unlike most on-line video terminals, they are not only programmable, but they can have ready access to the data bases maintained on the mainframe computer, either directly or by downloading for local storage. Alternatively, the micros themselves are accessible to remote personnel, through dial-up telephone lines or local area networks (LAN).

The human relations issues relating to security for microcomputers are similar in many ways to the related issues for minicomputers and mainframes. However, certain security needs for microcomputers are significantly different from

the security requirements for larger computers. How they are different, and how to provide adequate security, are indicated in Exhibit 3.1.

Exhibit 3.1

How Microcomputer Needs Are Different	Security Measures to Provide
It is easy to remove floppy disks containing sensitive data from the premises.	Keep disks for sensitive data locked up when not in use. Prevent the making of unnecessary copies. Make efforts to assure reliability and loyalty of persons using sensitive data or in its vicinity.
Most PC users are not computer specialists.	Provide training in PC use and controls.
Microcomputer data are accessible to more people.	Institute password systems where data are sensitive.
It is easy to copy software illegally.	Publish rules stating that copying illegally is against policy, and remind all concerned of the rules frequently, both orally and in writing; apply appropriate penalties for noncompliance.
Microcomputers are not usually centrally located nor centrally controlled.	Establish standards and guidelines centrally. Spot check for compliance with standards. Offer training in sound control practices.
Microcomputers connected to mainframes make information vulnerable to unauthorized access or, possibly, modification.	The organization responsible for the main computer must establish password and other control procedures, by category of sensitive information, to prevent its misuse.

The security measures presented in this chapter for the data processing staff must be extended to all personnel throughout the organization who are involved with microcomputers. Only through such an investment, which may be costly, will management be able to protect the corporate assets and minimize any liabilities related to the loss of such assets.

The establishment of a microcomputer information center is advisable in organizations with widespread use of microcomputers, especially where some of those microcomputers handle sensitive data. Such centers do not exercise direct control over computer users; rather they provide training and assistance in the use of PCs and disseminate bulletins with helpful information, standards, and procedural guidelines. These training and guideline roles should help to make microcomputer users aware of the security risks they are involved with, and suggest measures to provide protection from security dangers.

Summary

A chain is as strong as its weakest link, and often, when breaches of security are uncovered, the weak link turns out to be an employee.

Good security practices must therefore concern themselves with the employee, by:

- Establishing the proper framework for effective security
- Realistic and careful hiring practices
- Continuing attention to employee relationships
- Attention to rotation, promotions, and, where necessary, terminations
- An effective and aware operation

Employee Security Checklist

	Yes	No
Is there an individual or department responsible for computer-related security?	☐	☐
Are employee references and background fully checked prior to employment?	☐	☐
Are employees in security-sensitive positions bonded?	☐	☐
Is there a standard employee confidentiality agreement? (See Appendix 3 and Appendix 7)	☐	☐
Do all employees sign this agreement?	☐	☐
Are all new personnel advised on internal security practices?	☐	☐
Is there a formal manual defining the organization's security standards and procedures? (See Appendix 2)	☐	☐
Is this manual mandatory reading for new personnel?	☐	☐
Are changes in security practices incorporated in the manual and disseminated to the staff? (See Appendix 2)	☐	☐

	Yes	No
Is there an ongoing program of computer security education for data processing and user personnel?	☐	☐
Is the program kept current?	☐	☐
Is there an individual or department responsible for monitoring compliance with security standards and procedures?	☐	☐
Is a security check carried out for contract and temporary personnel?	☐	☐
Are the security arrangements for temporary personnel the same as those of full-time employees?	☐	☐
Are badges used to identify personnel?	☐	☐
Do the badges indicate the level of employee security (i.e., access or restriction to various work areas)?	☐	☐
Are all personnel engaged in confidential or other sensitive work requested to leave immediately on resignation or dismissal?	☐	☐
Is all work-sensitive material, including badges or passes, collected upon termination of employment?	☐	☐
Are security responsibilities included in personnel performance evaluations?	☐	☐
Are personnel appropriately penalized for security violations?	☐	☐
Is there a log maintained for personnel working "after hours"?	☐	☐
Is there a planned program of work rotation for computer operations personnel?	☐	☐
Are nondata processing personnel having access to computer systems apprised of internal security measures and responsibilities?	☐	☐
Are passwords used for terminal access to computer systems?	☐	☐
Are the password procedures (level of access, changes, recording of violations, etc.) adequate in terms of organizational security?	☐	☐
Are guards used to monitor access to restricted or sensitive areas?	☐	☐

CHAPTER 4

Legal Issues in Computer Security

by Robert P. Bigelow

Introduction

Legal issues are particularly important in considering computer security. The company's liability for violation of its legal commitments in the security area can be substantial; indeed, in certain situations, management could be personally liable. This chapter will discuss these questions, but it should not be considered as a substitute for consultation with the corporation's law department. The particular facts in any situation determine the legal ramifications.

These legal questions will be discussed under several topics: management problems, proprietary legal rights, privacy, computer abuse and crime, data communications, legal liability, and specific governmental controls.

Management Problems

While all the matters considered in this chapter (as, indeed, all the matters discussed in this book) are management problems, there are some legal issues with which the data security officer should be familiar that are particularly appropriate concerns for management.

Corporate Recordkeeping

Business lives on the records it maintains, particularly as to accounts receivable and accounts payable. These records are generally admitted into court proceedings as business records kept in the ordinary course of business, provided the business relies on them. However, with computerized records in which the material is updated

periodically without hard copy, there may be difficulty in proving the accuracy of the records, particularly if considerable amounts of money are involved and the opposing part in a lawsuit questions the validity of the records.

To prove the records' authenticity, it may be necessary for the company's lawyer to show how the programming was performed, that all patches were fully documented, that input controls were in place, and that the hardware functioned properly. (Appendix 4 is an Australian statute outlining what must be shown to a court in South Australia in order to prove that the computerized records are reliable. While American courts are not as particular in their proof requirements, such kinds of proof could be required if the validity of the computer system is questioned.)

The Internal Revenue Service has also established rules for corporate recordkeeping, and failure to observe the requirements of Revenue Procedure 86-19 (Appendix 5) and Revenue Ruling 71-20 (Appendix 6) may prevent the corporation from relying upon its computerized records when audited by the IRS. Revenue Procedure 64-12 requires (1) that the system must have the ability to produce a detailed audit trial at a later date, and (2) that the company completely document the system. These are specific rules for database management systems. Revenue Ruling 71-20 requires that punched cards, magnetic tapes, disks, and other machine-sensible data media used for recording, consolidating, and summarizing accounting transactions be kept by the company so long as the contents may become material in the administration of the internal revenue laws. The IRS will make agreements with companies as to what tapes must be preserved and for how long, and the company's tax

©Copyright 1984 Robert P. Bigelow

or accounting department will lay down these rules for the particular organization. However, the security of this information and its availability could well fall within the responsibilities of the data security officer.

Labor and Management Relations

In some companies, unions represent data processing employees, particularly input personnel. It is particularly important when dealing with unionized personnel that the requirements of the collective bargaining agreement as to disciplinary action and consultation on work rules be followed; the advice of the company's labor attorney is essential.

In any situation where employees (union or nonunion) are in conflict with management, it is possible that attempts may be made to compromise or damage the company's computer system; the company should have in place mechanisms to prevent damage in such situations.

Personnel who service computer systems may also be unionized; there have been reported instances of injury to a customer's computer system when the employees of a computer company were engaged in a dispute with their employer. Again, contingency plans to protect against such situations should be designed and implemented when appropriate.

Many companies have agreements with employees protecting the company's trade secrets and inventions (see Appendix 7 for one example). As will be discussed later, the protection of trade secrets requires considerable vigilance so that these valuable proprietary rights are not lost, including procedures for making sure that valuable papers are locked up at night and that access to them is limited at all times to those with a need to know. Methods of ensuring that such papers are not removed, particularly when employees are terminated, should be instituted.

Proprietary Rights and Obligations

Probably the most important part of the security officer's duties from a legal point of view are those concerned with guarding the company's proprietary rights in its software and complying g with the company's contractual commitments in the protection of software belonging to others.

Forms of Protection

Two major ways are used to protect proprietary rights in software: trade secrets and copyrights. (In certain unique situations, a patent for software may be available.)

Trade secret law, a state developed and enforced doctrine, is based on the concept of confidentiality: when a business discloses its secrets to another in confidence, the person to whom it is disclosed must keep that information confidential. Copyright, on the other hand, is established under a federal statute and proceeds from the concept that in order to get information available to the public, some method of remunerating its author must be established. Copyright, therefore, protects the "method of expression" used by the author but not the ideas that are disclosed.

Copyright and trade secret complement each other: trade secret protects the idea disclosed in confidence, and copyright protects the way that idea is expressed. However, in certain situations, if proper procedures are not used, the copyright law may preempt the trade secret, and trade secret protection may be unavailable.[1]

The standard legal definition of trade secret is:

A trade secret may consist of any formula, device, or compilation of information which is used in one's business, and which gives him an opportunity to obtain an advantage over competitors who do not know or use it. It may be a formula for a chemical compound, a process of manufacturing, treating or preserving materials, a pattern for a machine or other device, or a list of competitors.[2]

Trade secrets are often also protected by statute, and theft of a trade secret may well be a criminal act. For example, in Massachusetts the larceny statute specifically defines a trade secret as follows:

The term "trade secret" . . . means and includes anything tangible or electronically kept or stored, which constitutes, represents, evidences or records a secret scientific, technical, merchandising, production, or management information, design, process, procedure, formula, invention or improvement.[3]

A recent federal court decision involving the copying of a computer program gave the following definition:

Trade secret protection may be afforded to any idea, process, or compilation of information valuable and useful in one's business which is not generally known. A trade secret is any special knowledge developed through skill and ingenuity and the expenditure of money and effort which, by being secret, gives the owner an advantage over his competitors.[4]

The judge in this case also pointed out that in deciding whether a particular program was entitled to protection, the court must consider not only the information, but:

The degree of secrecy imposed by the developer

The amount of effort the developer expends in developing the secret and preserving secrecy

Its value to the developer

How difficult it would be for others to duplicate the trade secret

The Company's Needs

When the company develops its own software, precautions must be taken to protect trade secrets. This rule applies when applications programs are used in the company's computer systems in its daily operations; even more so, when the company itself is involved in the software business.

To protect trade secrets, eternal vigilance is necessary, because the accidental disclosure of a trade secret can lead to its loss. The only practical way to protect a trade secret disclosed outside the company is by contractual agreement. While there is an implied duty of employees not to disclose trade secrets, most companies concerned with protecting these rights require employees to sign an explicit agreement under which they are obligated to respect the confidentiality of the company's information (see Appendix 7).

Courts have held that the company has a duty to advise employees of what it considers a trade secret. Not every bit of information will qualify, and selection of what is to be protected is a matter for decision by management. An attempt to classify *everything* as a trade secret will undoubtedly make it very difficult to prove that *anything* actually qualifies. On the other hand, failure to make clear what are trade secrets, and, particularly, failure to take appropriate security precautions with respect to these secrets will lead the court to declare that the company did not make sufficient efforts to protect its rights, and that the information is no longer secret. Therefore their disclosure—even accidental—can lead to the loss of the secrets.

Computer programs and manuals are also protected under the Federal Copyright Act, which protects the way the words (and code) are expressed, but not the ideas themselves, which are the subject of trade secret protection. The copyright begins at the moment the source code or the manual is written and belongs to the employer. (When programs or manuals are prepared by outside consultants, particular care is required to make sure the company retains the copyright in these products by way of contract.)

When a copyrighted work is published (i.e., offered for sale or voluntarily disclosed to a wide audience), a copyright notice must be included or the company may lose its copyright protection and find that the program or manual is in the public domain, to be copied freely by anyone.

However, until the copyrighted work is published (with or without a copyright notice), the author's or other copyright owner's rights are protected under the federal law in almost the same way as if the document disclosed a trade secret. While copyright protects the expression and not the ideas, the effect may be very similar, and the procedures that the company should use in protecting these "unpublished" documents are much the same.

Among the procedures that a data security officer should consider are:

Numbering each copy of the trade secret or unpublished copyrighted document

Keeping a log of to whom the document is issued

Checking the files and workstation of each recipient to be sure that the document is being treated as confidential

Making sure that all unissued documents are locked up and their distribution controlled

Instituting appropriate safeguards to prevent employees to whom such documents are issued making copies for any reason

Since a failure to take appropriate security precautions can lead to the loss of a trade secret, the security officer should give more attention to documents disclosing trade secrets than to unpublished works that do not contain trade secrets but are protected by copyright (such as systems manuals). The major problem in distributing unpublished copyrighted documents is the possibility that the document will be so widely distributed that the company's copyright will be lost at that time. However, if someone steals the document and makes it public, the law does provide the company with a remedy against all who copy the document. The same relief is not available when a trade secret is widely distributed against the wishes of its owner.

Appropriate security precautions for copyrighted products that are not being distributed to the public is a logical responsibility of the security officer.

Contractual Commitments to Protect Proprietary Rights

When computer programs are supplied by a software developer or other computer company, the programs are usually licensed and not sold outright. The license agreement often contains a number of provisions relating to the security of the programs and manuals. Failure to observe these requirements can lead to termination of the license and can expose the company to substantial monetary liability if, through its failure to observe security requirements, the proprietor of the software loses its trade secrets and profits that would otherwise have been earned.

Excerpts from the January 1983 version of IBM's standard program license are reprinted in Appendix 8. Among the points that the reader will want to notice are:

A customer's use is limited to the United States and Puerto Rico

The term "use" means only copying the licensed materials into a machine for processing

IBM can terminate the license immediately if the customer fails to comply with its requirements

Programs in machine-readable form can be used only on designated machines

Materials in non-machine-readable form may not be copied

If a data base is licensed, it is for the use of the customer only

The customer shall not reverse assemble or reverse compile the programs

The customer may change the designated machine on notice to IBM

No copies of the program materials may be distributed by the customer to anyone else without IBM's consent

The customer must maintain records of the number and location of all copies of the program materials

The customer will not make the program materials available without IBM's consent except to the employees of the customer or of IBM or to other persons on the customer's premises for work related to the program

When the license has ended, the customer must return or destroy the materials

It is important that the data security officer be aware of all the contractual commitments on security required by software licensors. He should find out what these are and institute appropriate precautions to see that they are followed. Sometimes, for example, the license will require that employees who have access to the program sign a nondisclosure agreement (Appendix 9). If these precautions are not taken, the company may find itself being sued for failure to protect highly proprietary programs and data bases. With software license fees running in the tens of thousands of dollars, the liability for loss of trade secret protection could be in the millions.

Particularly important are license requirements limiting the use of programs to specific machines, specific locations, or specific kinds of problems (for example, the IBM requirements that the programs be used only in the United States and Puerto Rico and only on designated machines). The licensor's requirements should be examined and strictly adhered to (for example, IBM's requirement that the customer maintain records of the number and location of all copies). These may include requirements for reprinting copyright notices (the IBM license does), and this must be followed.

Even if the software confidentiality is not compromised, failure to follow these rules may result in the licensor revoking the license and demanding the return of all the software. If these programs are integral to the customer's data processing operations, the result could be disastrous.

Privacy

Security has sometimes been defined as protecting the computer against people, and privacy as protecting people against the computer. The law of privacy originally developed as a protection against individuals' private affairs being reported in the press and against the exploitation of their names and pictures for advertising purposes. The concept of information privacy in the computer age developed from a mid-1960s proposal that the Bureau of the Budget establish a Federal Data Center in which would be placed machine-readable data in the possession of many branches of the federal government—approximately 30,000 computer tapes and 100 million punched cards.

Congressional reaction to this proposal was vociferous, and there were a series of hearings on whether such a data center could properly protect individual privacy, since information from the Internal Revenue Service, the Census, the Bureau of Labor Statistics, and Social Security might all be included. In commenting on the problems of the computer in privacy, Thomas J. Watson, Jr., then chairman of the board of IBM, stated:

> Today the Internal Revenue Service has our tax returns.
>
> The Social Security Administration keeps a running record on our jobs and our families.
>
> The Veterans Administration has medical records on many of us, and the Pentagon our records of military service. So in this scatteration lies our protection.
>
> But put everything in one place, computerize it, and add to it without limit, and a thieving electronic blackmailer would have just one electronic safe to crack to get a victim's complete dossier, tough as that job may be.
>
> And a malevolent Big Brother would not even have to do that: he could sit in his office, punch a few keys, and arm himself with all he needed to know to crush any citizen who threatened his power.
>
> Therefore, along with the bugged olive in the martini, the psychological tests, and the spiked microphone, the critics have seen 'data surveillance' as an ultimate destroyer of the individual American citizen's right to privacy—his right to call his soul his own.

Opposition to the federal data bank, particularly from the computer industry itself, was responsible in large measure for the fact that we do not have one today. Also helpful were a report by the Department of Health, Education and Welfare under Secretaries Elliot L. Richardson and Caspar W. Weinberger, and studies of the Presidential Domestic Council Committee on the Right to Privacy. These led eventually to the Privacy Act of 1974, sponsored by Senator Ervin of Watergate fame, and signed by President Ford on January 1, 1975.

Federal Privacy Act

This act applies only to records maintained by certain branches of the federal government, specifically executive departments, independent regulatory agencies, government corporations, and government-controlled corporations such as the Federal Reserve Banks. It is not applicable to Congress, the judiciary, or to territorial subdivisions of the United States such as the District of Columbia. It is important for the security officer to note that when a covered federal agency contracts with a private business or a state or local government to run the agency's federally controlled record system, the contractor's employees are liable to the same criminal penalties for failure to comply with the act as are the agency's employees.[5]

The act defines a "record" that is subject to the act in very broad terms:

> Any item, collection, or grouping of information about an individual that is maintained by an agency, including, but not limited to, his education, financial transactions, medical history, and criminal or employment history and that contains his name, or the identifying number, symbol, or other identifying particular assigned to the individual, such as a finger or a voice print or a photograph.

Agencies can maintain information about individuals only when it's relevant and necessary to accomplish the agency's purpose. The act generally prohibits the disclosure of any records except within the agency maintaining it unless the individual makes a written request for the data; there are, however, a number of exceptions to this general rule. The agency must also give public notice of the existence of the record system, keep track of certain disclosures, establish rules of conduct for those who design and operate the systems, and:

> establish appropriate administrative, technical, and physical safeguards to ensure the security and con-

fidentiality of records and to protect against any anticipated threats or hazards to their security or integrity which could result in substantial harm, embarrassment, inconvenience, or unfairness to any individual on whom information is maintained.[6]

In addition to exceptions to its disclosure provisions, a number of records and record systems are completely exempted from its operation. These include investigative records maintained by the CIA or a law enforcement agency, and national defense secrets.

If an individual proves that an agency intentionally or willfully violated the Privacy Act, he can recover at least $1,000 in damages and his attorneys' fees. There is also a provision for criminal penalties against agency employees (which include, as noted above, employees of contractors with the federal government) who willfully make a prohibited disclosure—a fine as high as $5,000 can be levied.

The act also established specific rules prohibiting any federal, state, or local government agency from denying an individual benefits or privileges because he refused to disclose his social security number. There are several exceptions to this provision, particularly one authorizing the use of social security numbers for drivers' licenses.

The Privacy Protection Study Commission

The Privacy Act of 1974 also established a seven-member Privacy Protection Study Commission to make a study of data banks and computer programs, and recommend to Congress which requirements and principles of the Privacy Act should be applied to private industry and other organizations. This commission delivered its report to President Carter and Congress in July 1977 and made a number of recommendations affecting primarily the federal government, although there were specific proposals for the credit-granting, investigative reporting, banking, insurance, and medical care industries. Some of these recommendations have been introduced in Congress, but as of this writing none has been passed.

State Acts and Regulations

Even before the federal government acts, several states enacted Fair Information Practices Acts regulating the information that state agencies could maintain about individuals. As of this writing, there are such statutes in Arkansas, California, Connecticut, Indiana, Massachusetts, Minnesota, New Hampshire, New York, Ohio, Utah, and Virginia (see Appendix 10 for citations). Some municipalities, such as Berkeley (California), Wichita Falls (Kansas), Charlotte (North Carolina), and Dayton (Ohio) have enacted citywide ordinances on privacy.

In some instances, there also are statutes regulating the information that may be kept by private organizations; these are often based on recommendations of the Privacy Protection Study Commission. For example, Rhode Island has enacted a statute on the confidentiality of health care information, and Virginia has included privacy in its statute on unfair insurance trade practices.

International

A number of European countries also have privacy acts covering both governmental and private corporate records. Usually these laws apply only to computerized data banks, which must be licensed by a governmental authority. The rules on disclosure are quite strict, and there are particular prohibitions against the transfer of information in these data banks across national boundaries.

If the company has computerized records in such a foreign country, the development and enforcement of security precautions to enable the company to comply with that act are particularly important.

What to Do

The data security officer employed by an organization subject to a privacy act should regularly review with the legal department exactly what is required by the act, prepare appropriate procedures to comply with the act, and make sure that these procedures are enforced and the enforcement documented. Otherwise, the organization may be liable for penalties arising from invasions of an individual's privacy.

Computer Abuse and Crime

This subject is covered in considerable detail in the chapter on crime and only a few comments are offered here. (See Appendix 11 for a paper prepared by Mr. Bigelow on this subject.)

While there is a new federal computer crime statute, individuals have been convicted under other statutes for computer-related offenses. For example, in *U.S. v. Seidlitz*, 589 F.2d 152, an individual was convicted of wire fraud under 18 U.S.C. Section 1343 for transferring a program from a computer in Maryland to his terminal in Virginia. In *U.S. v. Girard*, 601 F.2d 69, an individual was convicted of larceny under 18 U.S.C. Section 641 for theft of information from a computerized data base.

Most of the action has been at the state level. In 1972, a programmer was convicted in California of theft of a trade secret; the case is reprinted in Appendix 12. However, California has recently amended its law against stealing trade secrets, Penal Code Section 499c, to cover programs specifically.

Approximately half the states now have computer crime laws of one type or another; the quality of these statutes is variable and may not be as effective as some might wish. For example, the definition of a computer in the Florida statute (Section 815.03(3)) is: "an internally-programmed, automatic device that performs data processing"—a definition that covers a digital watch or a microwave oven.

"Computer program" is defined in Section 16-9 of the Illinois laws as "a series of coded instructions or statements in a form acceptable to a computer, which causes the computer to process data in order to achieve a *certain* result." The difficulty with this definition is the word "certain." While the legislature probably used the word in the sense of "prescribed" or "specified," it can also mean "inevitable." It is unlikely that any computer program of any value that might be the subject of theft would be absolutely bug free. Since this is a criminal statute, any ambiguity is resolved in favor of the accused. Will the prosecutor be able to prove that the program alleged to have been stolen achieved "a *certain* result"?

It is hoped that these criminal laws will deter theft of machine-readable information, but their operation is uncertain, and the difficulty that many prosecutors still have in understanding data processing makes it problematic whether the state will prosecute.

This doubt makes it all the more imperative that a data security officer establish and enforce controls that will prevent as much as possible computer abuse and crime. This is particularly true in protecting against the computer hacker, because so often these are juvenile offenders. Even if a computer crime law is applicable, the defendant in such a case may not be subject to the penalties spelled out in the law, but only remanded to the custody of the juvenile authorities. Many criminal laws cannot be applied to youthful hackers. Even when these penalties do apply, district attorneys do not like to prosecute youngsters, and convictions can often be difficult to come by. Prevention is always preferable to detection and prosecution.

Data Communications

In a computer system of any size, there will be telecommunications links between terminals and the CPU or between CPUs. These communication links are usually provided either by the local telephone company or by an interstate carrier—AT&T, MCI, Telenet, etc. The contracts between the communications company (usually called a common carrier) and the customer organization are known as tariffs, because they are filed with state public service commissions (for telecommunications within a state) or with the Federal Communications Commission (for interstate communications).[7]

In practically all tariffs and in many communications contracts, the carrier limits its liability to the customer for any defects in transmission to a very small amount. This, in turn, means that the responsibility for security of the communication rests, as a practical matter, entirely on the customer and not on the common carrier. The protection of these communications is discussed in the chapter on cryptology and the chapter on communications and networking, but the legal liability for poor security may be a substantial risk on the corporation.

Sometimes contracts for remote computer services (for example, in banking) may include a requirement for encryption of data during transmission. The data security officer should be aware of such requirements and see that they are obeyed. Failure to meet such contractual obligations could create a major liability for the company.

Legal Liability

Any organization with a computer system may be liable to individuals and other entities who are injured by any one of a variety of problems in the computer system. These range from programming errors through libel to violation of criminal law. There could even be personal liability for the data security officer, the management information systems manager, other officers, and the board of directors, as the discussion below indicates.

While the company may be liable for violation of its contractual commitments on security to providers of software, as previously discussed, this section concerns the liability imposed by statute and by the courts particularly for injuries to third parties who do not have a contractual relation with the company. Such lawsuits are based on the law of "torts" or civil wrongs, and are usually founded upon negligence or wrongful misdeed. As such, there are no contractual limitations on the amount that the company (and possibly the data security officer) may be compelled to pay. The actual damages will be determined by a judge or jury, and punitive damages may, in appropriate cases, be added.

Programming Errors

The data security officer, while not responsible for the accuracy of computer programs, is responsible for taking reasonable precautions to prevent the loss of a program, or its unauthorized revision. Such precautions would include ensuring the availability of backup versions, limiting access to the program library to authorized personnel, and enforcement of password security and other techniques to limit terminal access. The same considerations apply when dealing with data bases.

An example of liability in such a situation might be where the company provided programs to control air traffic operations. Such programs must, obviously, because of the danger involved to thousands of people, be constructed and tested with extreme care. Assume the program is properly designed, but it is later determined, because of lack of security, an interloper was able to place a logic bomb in the program requiring it to crash at a specified date and time. Because the bomb works, the program becomes inoperable, and two commercial aircraft collide. The damages in such a case could be astronomic.

Product Liability

Similar considerations could apply in errors in data bases arising out of breaches of security. For example, the company is maintaining a data base in which are recorded the strengths of concrete; this data base is accessed by engineers designing bridges. A computer hacker gains access to the data base and changes certain figures by an order of magnitude (for example, say that in a certain situation, concrete that has a strength factor of 1 is modified to show a strength factor of 10). An engineer relying on this data base designs a bridge that collapses, and several automobiles drop into the river. While the data base company has probably limited the amount it will pay in damages to the engineering company for inaccuracies in the data base, it has no protection against the next of kin of the individuals who drowned when the bridge collapsed. The executors of their estates will sue not only the company that built the bridge but the engineering company and, when they find out about the data base error, the company providing the information. If it is shown that the data base company did not take reasonable precautions to ensure the security of the information, it could well be held liable for substantial amounts of money.

Libel

Particularly with data bases that include personal information, the company maintaining the data base may be liable for inaccurate information or inaccurate output. In one instance, a computerized credit reporting service misidentified a specific individual because the system lacked the necessary auditing procedures to ensure that when reports were rendered the individual was properly identified. A credit-worthy individual was misidentified and sued the credit bureau, recovering $10,000 for humiliation and mental distress and $4,485 in attorneys' fees (*Thompson* v. *San Antonio Retail Merchants Association*, 682 F.2d 509). While this lawsuit was brought under the federal Fair Credit Reporting Act authorizing the award of damages and attorneys' fees for improper handling of credit references, the disclosure to merchants of inaccurate information about credit applicants could well be considered by a court to be libelous, an invasion of privacy, or both.

If a computer hacker were able to access the system and change the records of another individual to his detriment, the company could be held responsible in tort. Or a disgruntled employee might access the data base and release sensitive information to the press—leading to a lawsuit by individuals injured by the publication of the information.

Foreign Corrupt Practices Act

Among the disclosures of the Watergate era were a number of questionable and even illegal acts where foreign officials had been bribed to grant benefits to American businesses. To stop these practices, the Securities and Exchange Commission undertook a campaign to require corporate disclosure and, in 1977, Congress passed the Foreign Corrupt Practices Act.[8] While the act was aimed primarily at improper foreign operations, it also applies to all companies whose securities are registered under the Securities Exchange Act of 1934 or that file reports under that act—whether or not the company does business abroad.

Section 102(b)(2) requires that affected companies must keep books, records, and accounts in reasonable detail that accurately and fairly reflect the transactions of the company, and they must maintain an internal accounting control system that ensures, among other things, that access to assets will be allowed only in accordance with management's general or specific authorization. This act, therefore, mandates for companies whose securities are traded on a stock exchange the institution of a security program, including a data security program for its accounting records.

Willful violation of the statute is a criminal act, and the SEC may also ask for injunctive relief, i.e., ordering the company to clean up its act. While most commentators on this act have felt that the protection of assets is subject to a cost-benefit analysis, the failure to make such an analysis, or failure to institute the controls and security techniques required thereby, could make the corporation liable for fines in litigation with the SEC; and if these failures were willful, the individuals involved (and possibly the data se-

curity officer) could be subject to criminal prosecution.

Failure to Observe Standards

The National Bureau of Standards has published a number of national standards in the computer security area. Known generally as FIPS PUBS (standing for Federal Information Processing Standards Publications), they are distributed, for a small fee, by the National Technical Information Service, Springfield, VA 22161. EDP security standards include the following:

> 31: *Guidelines for ADP Physical Security and Risk Management*
>
> 39: *Glossary for Computer System Security*
>
> 41: *Computer Security Guidelines for Implementing the Privacy Act of 1974*
>
> 46: *Data Encryption Standard*
>
> 48: *Guidelines on Evaluation of Techniques for Automated Personal Identification*
>
> 65: *Guideline for Automatic Data Processing Risk Analysis*
>
> 73: *Guidelines for Security of Computer Applications*
>
> 74: *Guidelines for Implementing and Using the NBS Data Encryption Standard*
>
> 81: *DES Modes of Operation*
>
> 83: *Guideline on User Authentication Techniques for Computer Network Access Control*
>
> 87: *Guidelines for ADP Contingency Planning*
>
> 102: *Guidelines for Computer Security Certification and Accreditation*

Abstracts of these standards are included in Appendix 13.

Failure to follow recognized standards may frequently be used by plaintiffs in tort cases to indicate negligence, even when compliance is mandatory only for government agencies. In any lawsuit in which a breach of security is claimed, the existence of these standards and the failure of the company to implement NBS guidelines and similar standards could well be the most telling piece of evidence in the case.

Personal Liability

The law of torts operates on the principle that anyone whose action or inaction was a proximate cause of the injury to the plaintiff is responsible financially to pay money to the plaintiff who was injured. This liability is usually joint and several, which means that each defendant is fully liable for the entire amount until it is all paid.

The liability extends not only to the employer, but also to the employee, although, as a practical matter, the employer, unless bankrupt, will be the source of funds for payment of any judgments. However, there are some situations in which the employer may have a defense that is unavailable to the employee. For example, the employer may be bankrupt and have no assets. Or it may be a governmental or charitable organization and immune from suit except as specifically authorized by law. (The federal government and many states now waive their sovereign immunity in certain cases, and in some situations charitable immunity is limited to a certain amount.)

How this works in a specific situation was illustrated in a 1983 Massachusetts case, *Mullins* v. *Pine Manor College*, 449 N.E.2d 331. In this situation, because of poor security, a trespasser was able to invade a college dormitory and rape a student. She sued the college and its vice-president in charge of security, who had designed and was responsible for the enforcement of the security system. There was evidence that if the system had been properly designed and operated, the rape would have been unlikely. The court held that the jury could find both the college and its vice-president negligent because of the way the security system operated, and that negligence was the proximate cause of the injury. Both were held financially liable.

The jury awarded $175,000 jointly and severally against the college and the individual. But because the college was a charitable organization and the injury arose out of an activity (on the college's part) that was carried on to accomplish directly its charitable purposes, the maximum amount for which the college was liable was $20,000. The security officer argued that his liability should be limited too. But the court held that, as an employee, he was not entitled to the benefit of his employer's immunity, even if he was acting on his employer's behalf. Therefore, the individual was financially responsible for $155,000.

While the injury in this case was rather foreseeable and was a violent attack, the same rea-

soning could apply to any kind of security breach where the information is sensitive or its misuse dangerous.

Specific Governmental Controls

Security of hardware and software may be affected also by legal requirements imposed by statute or regulation. The security requirements of the Privacy Act have been discussed previously. Similar requirements may be imposed if the corporation is doing work under a government contract. For example, when the design, development, or operation of a system of records on individuals is required to accomplish an agency function, government contracting officers are required to insert in the contract two clauses relating to the Privacy Act, including an agreement to comply with the act and the agency's rules and regulations thereunder.[9]

Regulations of specific departments, particularly those dealing with national security, may have additional requirements that must be included in the contract. Even if there is no required contract language, such clauses may be included in the contract and be binding upon the company. In any such government contracts, the security officer should discuss with the company's contract administrator any specific security requirements that may be involved.

Another example are the requirements of the export control regulations, which require governmental licenses before some kinds of computer hardware and software can be exported from the United States. The purpose of these rules is to prevent militarily valuable materials from falling into the hands of unfriendly nations, and failure to obtain the appropriate licenses can expose the company to heavy fines.

If the company is operating overseas, the law may impose data security requirements that will fall within the responsibility of the data security officer.

There can also be specific requirements applicable to particular industries. For example, banks are audited by state and federal agencies; among the items usually checked in such an examination are the security precautions not only against bank robbery but also against data diddling and other ways of breaching security or avoiding controls. One example is the directive from the Chief National Bank Examiner requiring that the board of directors of each national bank review annually what would happen if the bank lost its EDP support and whether the contingency procedures for reducing or eliminating this risk are adequate.[10]

Personal Computers

The legal considerations with personal computers in the business organization are much the same as with mainframes. However, a particular problem is likely to be the unauthorized copying of software, and there have been lawsuits by software suppliers against corporations for making and distributing within their organization unauthorized copies of spreadsheet programs and other software.

Every company should establish a policy on acquisition and use of programs, making sure that this policy is widely circulated within the company. Appendix 14 is an excerpt from a periodical discussing such a policy and suggesting a memorandum to PC users.

Summary

This chapter has outlined some of the legal considerations with which data security officers and other management personnel should be familiar; a checklist at the end of the chapter covers some of the points discussed. Particularly important from the company's point of view is the need to examine legal obligations and contractual commitments undertaken by the company as to security of data processing systems programs and data bases.

There are many situations that management must analyze from a security viewpoint. For example:

- When acquiring software from a new vendor, review the license agreement for clauses requiring specific requirements about security.
- When license agreements with previous software vendors are amended, review the amendments to see if there are any changes in the security requirements.
- When the company licenses others to use its software, review to see whether there are any

security requirements imposed on the licensee that the company as licensor should supervise.

- Consult with the company's tax accountants to be sure that security precautions required by the Internal Revenue Service are being followed.
- Review security procedures to protect the company in situations where there is labor unrest.
- If the company has undertaken government contracts that involve records on people, review security procedures to be sure that they comply with privacy acts.
- Consult with the personnel department to be sure that data processing security of personnel records is appropriate.
- Compare security techniques used by the company with those promulgated by the National Bureau of Standards; if there are differences, document the reason for not following the federal standard.
- Review contracts between the company and governmental agencies to determine whether they include any specific data security requirements.

While following the foregoing outline will not guarantee that the company—or management—will escape from legal liability, compliance with the various suggestions will make such liability much less likely.

A Legal Checklist

	Yes	No
Are records needed for tax purposes kept in accordance with Revenue Procedure 86-19?	☐	☐
Has the company agreed with the IRS on which records must be kept (Revenue Ruling 71-20)?	☐	☐
Are records agreed to with the IRS kept securely?	☐	☐
Are contingency plans in place against damage to the EDP system during a strike by employees of the company?	☐	☐
Are contingency plans in place against damage to the EDP system by employees of striking suppliers?	☐	☐

	Yes	No
Have these strike contingency plans been tested?	☐	☐
Has each software license under which the company acquires software been reviewed for security requirements?	☐	☐
Have the security requirements of each software license under which the company acquired software been implemented?	☐	☐
Has each employee with access to secure programs and data signed the appropriate confidentiality agreements?	☐	☐
Is a log being kept of who has access to each piece of software belonging to others?	☐	☐
Are proprietary manuals serially numbered and their distribution logged?	☐	☐
Are all employees with access to trade secrets and confidential information as they leave the company informed of their obligations to return all company property?	☐	☐
Has the Legal Department advised data security of what steps should be taken to protect the company's trade secrets and copyrights?	☐	☐
Has the Personnel Department advised data security of what files contain sensitive information?	☐	☐
Has Data Security developed written procedures for protecting trade secrets, confidential and sensitive information?	☐	☐

	Yes	No
Are these procedures being followed?	☐	☐
Have all contracts with government agencies been reviewed for specific privacy and security requirements?	☐	☐

Notes

1. Under Section 301 of the Copyright Act, copyright protection preempts any state law protections that are equivalent to copyright. In one case, *Avco Corp.* v. *Precision Air Parts, Inc.*, 210 U.S.P.Q. 894 (M.D.Alab. 1980), aff'd 676 F.2d 494 (11th Cir. 1982), cert. den. 103 S.Ct. 450 (1982), it was held that since a trade secret disclosed on drawings could be protected by copyright, trade secret protection was unavailable.

   However, there have been cases holding that a claim of copyright in computer manuals is not inconsistent with trade secret protection, the copyright protecting the words used and the trade secret protecting the concepts disclosed. *Technicon Medical Information Systems, Inc.* v. *Green Bay Packaging, Inc.*, 211 U.S. P.Q. 343 (E.D.Wisc. 1980), aff'd 687 F.2d 1032 (7th Cir. 1982), cert. den. 103 U.S. 732 (1983); *Warrington Associates* v. *Real Time Engineering Systems*, 522 F.Supp. 367 (N.D.Ill. 1981).

2. Restatement of Torts, Section 757, Comment b(1939).

3. Chapter 266, Section 30(4).

4. *Dickerman Associates, Inc.* v. *Tiverton Bottled Gas Co.*, 594 F. Supp. 30, 222 U.S.P.Q. 529 (D.Mass. 1984).

5. 5 U.S.C. Section 552(a)–(m).

6. Subsection (e)(10).

7. As a result of a series of FCC inquiries, certain services provided by common carriers are now a matter for individual contract between the carrier and the customer.

8. 15 U.S.C. Section 78.

9. Federal Acquisition Regulation, Subpart 24.1 and Sections 52.224-1 and 52.224-2, 48 Federal Register 42277 and 42539 (September 19, 1983).

10. Banking Circular 177, June 29, 1983.

CHAPTER 5

Computer Crime and Computer Criminals

By Jack Bologna

Introduction

A computer-related crime may be defined as one in which a computer is used to commit a crime, or as a crime in which a computer itself is the target. The usual crimes committed using computers include embezzlement, larceny (theft of property and proprietary information), fraud, forgery, and counterfeiting. Crimes committed *against* computers include sabotage, vandalism, electronic burglary, wire-tapping, and gaining illegal access, either by impersonating an authorized user, or by exceeding one's authority.

Computer crime is generally considered to be a white-collar crime when it involves an internal theft, fraud, or embezzlement by an employee or official of an organization.

Computer-related crime can be viewed as a phenomenon brought about by advances in information processing technologies. Before computers, there was no computer crime. But before computers there was crime—of both the white- and blue-collar variety. There were also crimes of violence against people and crimes against property. The computer did not usher in a new wave of crime; it merely changed the form of older crimes. Embezzlers could now steal by making electronic entries in magnetic books of account, rather than by pen and ink or in paper ledgers.

Computer-related crime today is mainly an occupational crime committed by people with requisite skills and knowledge. But, in addition to skills and knowledge, a computer criminal must also have access to a computing system. Access can be gained more easily by organizational insiders (employees) than by outsiders (in-

truders, hackers). Therefore, insiders represent a greater potential computer crime threat than do outsiders, despite the opinions of mass media commentators, who often suggest the opposite.

One might therefore conclude that computer-related crime is a phenomenon that involves knowledgeable people with criminal predispositions. But the idea that certain people are born crime-prone is the subject of much controversy. Behavioral scientists suggest that cultural and environmental conditioning are equally significant factors in understanding crime.

The phenomenon of computer-related crime may be viewed from a number of perspectives:

- The individual criminal, and his motivations
- The environmental factors that exacerbate motivations
- The organizational cultures that minimize the probability of such crimes
- The incidence rate of computer-related crime and its longer term trend
- Security countermeasures to computer-related crime

History and Evolution of Computer-Related Crime

Electronic computers were first introduced for commercial use in the United States in the mid-1950s. Prior to that time, the few computers that existed were used for governmental purposes, i.e., for the tabulation of the national census, for military applications, and for scientific research.

Until 1958, no systematic tracking nor tabulation of computer-related crime existed. In 1958, Stanford Research International (SRI) began tracking publicly reported incidents of computer "abuses," some of which were criminal and others which involved the breach of civil laws such as the copyright and patent acts. SRI grouped these incidents into four categories:

- Vandalism against computers
- Information or property theft
- Financial fraud or theft
- Unauthorized use or sale of computer services

The first year in which 10 or more of the above incident types were reported was 1968. There was a total of 13 that year. Such reported incidents increased annually thereafter:

Year	Total Number
1969	20
1970	38
1971	59
1972	72
1973	76
1974	74
1975	81
1976	57
1977	85
1978	31

SRI discontinued tabulating such abuses after 1978 for several reasons. First, the publicly reported incidents bore no demonstrable relationship to the total number of incidents. Many, perhaps most, incidents of computer abuse were not publicly reported. So tabulating reported incidents by year could create the impression that computer abuse was growing or declining when in fact the reported incidents might not be fairly representative of all actual incidents. Also, with more and more computers being used, one *should* expect an increase in the *number* of incidents of abuse. Secondly, tabulating reported incidents of abuse would shed no light on the phenomenon itself or its causative factors. So SRI elected to look at each case individually for whatever insights it could give on causations and on other variables, such as the mental dispositions of the computer abusers, the employment conditions that made abuse more likely, and the demographic characteristics of abusers.

The Computer Criminal

White-collar criminologists like Cressy and Sutherland suggest that white-collar criminals tend to be trusted employees of long tenure with unresolvable personal problems, usually of a financial nature, such as indebtedness for sickness in the family, or because of gambling, alcoholism, expensive tastes, or sexual pursuits. In police vernacular, these precedent conditions of dishonesty are usually referred to as the three B's, "booze, babes and bets." However, it is yet to be demonstrated that computer criminals meet the above criteria; egocentricity seems to be a more distinguishing characteristic. Perpetrators often commit their crimes to prove how smart they are and how easily controls can be compromised by a dedicated and knowledgeable intruder.

The typical computer thief, as often described in the literature of computer crime in the United States, is:

- Male; white; young, 19–30 years old
- Has no previous criminal record
- Identifies with his own technology far more than with his employer's business
- Is employed in the data processing or accounting field
- Is bright, creative, and energetic; outwardly self-confident and willing to accept challenge; adventurous; and highly motivated
- Feels desperate because of economic problems resulting from high living, expensive tastes, family sickness, gambling, or drug or alcohol abuse
- Feels exploited by his employer and wants to get even
- Does not intend to hurt *people*, just a cold, indifferent, impersonal, and exploitative employer
- Sees self as a "borrower," not a thief

Other motives ascribed to modern day embezzlers, as reported in the media and in law enforcement and security journals, include:

- Resentment—brought on by being passed over for promotion; pay inequities, such as unequal pay for equal work, no distinction in pay for longevity, and bonuses paid on the basis of unfair performance criteria

• Financial pressures—brought about by girlfriends, boyfriends with expensive tastes, or by gambling debts

• Deceiving the "establishment" is fair game because the establishment is deceiving everyone else

• The challenge. Beating the system is fun. The motive need not be economic

In addition, there are symptoms that may indicate crimes in progress. These include:

• High living—beware of the programmer who shows up at the plant gate with a new Rolls Royce

• Super dedication—beware of the bookkeeper or teller who has not had a vacation for 10 years

• The aging process—beware of those employees, male and female, going through divorce or sporting young girlfriends or boyfriends

• Chronic lateness—beware of the employee who is always late with reports. They may be taking longer because they have to fabricate, cover up, or counterfeit the information.

The motives and symptoms are generalizations and cannot be applied with certainty to any specific instance. In fact, there is a lot more not known about computer crime and computer criminals than is known. The best tools available are a number of generalizations, and common sense. But that realization should not embarrass us, because there still is no single generally accepted theory of crime causality even among the experts in criminology, after 100 years of research.

Dispelling Myths

A false notion that should be dispelled is that fraud by or through a computer requires some special talent, particularly in the realm of programming skills. While certain programming frauds, such as "salami slicing," "trap doors," "trojan horses," "time bombs," may require such skills, the typical reported computer-related fraud does not fall within that category. The typical computer fraud is not a *throughput* (programming) fraud but an *input* fraud, whereby false, fraudulent, or fabricated data are entered into a computer. This technique is generally referred to as "data diddling" and can be accomplished by people with little or no knowledge of computer programming, e.g., data entry clerks and computer or terminal operators. Most computer crimes involve the creation of a false or fake debit, such as a fabricated or raised vendor invoice, a false benefit or insurance claim, an improper payroll claim, spurious expense vouchers, etc. Falsification was an underlying problem in the manual era of accounting as it is today. In that sense, not much has changed over the years. The *form* of the journal entry or input is the main distinction—machine-made versus handwritten.

It is useful to examine what we *do* know about computer-related fraud versus what the public has assumed to be true. First, the computer crime phenomenon is not significantly different from what businesses experienced 30 years ago. Its form has merely changed. There is also no conclusive evidence that the current incidence rate of insider computer-related business crimes, like employee theft, fraud, and embezzlement, is greater than it was in the past. But computing systems (accounting and information) may be more vulnerable to *outsider* attack by way of electronic eavesdropping and other improper or illegal access attempts by computer "hackers," "phone phreaks," computer "time thieves," and "information pirates," or predatory competitors.

The why, when, where, and how of computer-related crime can be summed up in a concept called MOMM's:

1. Motivations (Who and why?)

Motivations for crime can be classified by a variety of conditions, caused by either internal or external conditions.

2. Opportunities (What, when, and where?)

Opportunities to commit crime can exist wherever there are inadequacies that create an environment permissive of crime. Weaknesses in either system controls or management controls are the chief types.

3. Means (How?)

The means for commission of computer-related crime usually involve the compromise of safeguards or ethics in some fashion. Where controls are improperly utilized, where personnel are disloyal, or where technology can be diverted to dishonest use, are representative categories.

4. Methods (How much, how often?)

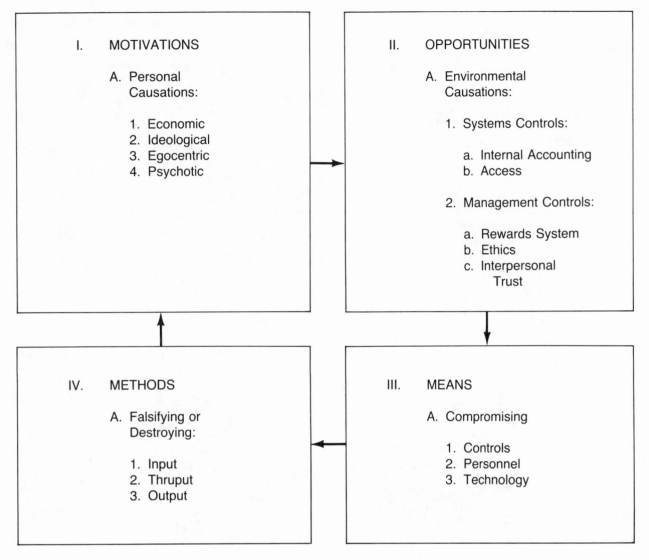

Figure 5.1 The Computer Theft Iteration

The methods of committing computer-related crime are scams that entail the falsification or destruction or fabrication of information. The most convenient classifications are by input, by throughput, and by output.

Figure 5.1 depicts computer-related theft as an iterative process.

Nature of Computer-Related Crime

Crimes such as embezzlement and employee thefts of funds were not unheard of before computers. Accountants attempted to discourage such crimes by requiring a separation of duties between persons handling cash or other assets and those making entries in the books of account. Accessibility to assets and accountability for the recording of transactions concerning such assets were thereby divided on the theory that forcing persons to conspire to commit a theft of assets would reduce the likelihood of theft.

An additional control measure relied upon by accountants was called the paper trail, or audit trail. In essence, that control measure required that all business transactions be entered into journals and be supported by source documents, such as vendor invoices, purchase orders, receiving reports, canceled checks, disbursement vouchers, sales receipts, and customer invoices.

Despite these control measures, employee theft, fraud, and embezzlement were still possible. Accounting systems were not designed to be foolproof or fraud proof. A determined defrauder could still find ways to circumvent or override controls.

Computers have not changed the human disposition. Fraud, theft, and embezzlement are still possible in the computer era. It has been argued that such crimes are even more likely now because the classic accounting controls have been diluted. Paper audit trails have often been replaced by electronic audit trails, which are not as easily verified by traditional audit methods. Speed of processing has taken precedence over effective controls, or so it is claimed. Some traditionalists, therefore, recommend more intensive internal auditing for firms with computerized accounting systems, as an added measure of protection.

Despite auditors' concerns over the adequacy of internal controls in the computer era of accounting, there is little reliable data to support the claim that crime by computer (mainly employee theft, fraud, and embezzlement) is more prevalent than before computers. Individual losses from such crimes do appear much higher now, but the incident rate may not be higher than before. However, the risk or threat of loss is greater, particularly if the frequency and severity are considered as well as the new opportunities for misbehavior.

New opportunities for employee fraud, theft, and embezzlement have been created by computer technology itself. A whole cadre of new employees can now access accounting systems. Not only are such systems accessible by the so-called user community, i.e., employee and management personnel who have a need for accounting information, but are also accessible to computer analysts, programmers, operators, and data entry clerks. In essence, computers have made financial information more easily accessible to more people for more purposes. With proper skills and criminal inclination, even outsiders can access the information and thereby manipulate or compromise the assets that lie behind the information.

Computer-Related Crime Typology

Computer-related crimes and more specifically those crimes in which a computer has been used as a means or instrument to commit or abet a crime, can be grouped into three categories, which parallel the three stages of data processing: input tampering, throughput tampering, and output tampering. An input type crime involves the entry of false or fraudulent data into a computer. Examples include data that have been altered, forged, or counterfeited—raised, lowered, destroyed, intentionally omitted, or fabricated. So input tampering is euphemistically called "data diddling."

While there are many reasons for entering spurious information into a computer, the main reasons are to overstate revenue and assets and to understate expenses and liabilities. These forms of manipulation of data input are sometimes directed by managers to deceive superiors, shareholders, and creditors. At lower levels, spurious data may be entered to commit a special fraud against the company as, for example, when an accounts payable clerk adds a phony vendor's name to the vendor master file, then submits invoices from that vendor to embezzle funds.

Input scams are probably the most common computer-related crime and yet the easiest to prevent with effective supervision and controls, such as separation of duties, audit trails, control totals, and access controls (authorization limits, terminal access controls.)

Throughput scams, accomplished by altering computer instructions, require a knowledge of programming. Such colorful expressions as salami slicing, trojan horses, trap doors, time bombs, and logic bombs have been used to describe this type of computer abuse. A typical example would be modifying a computer program so as to credit all fractional pennies arising from interest calculations to the perpetrator's account. Based upon publicly reported cases, there are far fewer incidents of throughput scams than of input scams.

Output scams, such as theft of computer-generated reports and information files (customer mailing lists, R&D results, long-range plans, employee lists, secret formulas, etc.) seem to be increasing in this era of intense competition, particularly among high technology manufacturers.

Among the publicly reported cases of computer crime, most have been of the input and output type and have involved lower level data processing personnel—entry clerks and computer operators. However, since throughput crimes are more difficult to detect, it cannot be said that their number is exceeded by the other two types. It is simply not known. Furthermore, throughput crimes may not be reported for other reasons. Proof is often quite complex, and admitting the occurrence may be an embarrassment to top management. These types of crimes have a greater probability of going undetected and, even if detected, are rarely brought to the attention of police or prosecutorial authorities. When reported, such crimes may be mismanaged by the authorities. Few police detectives know how to investigate computer crimes and few prosecuting attorneys know much about presenting such cases. They often recommend a case be handled by the civil courts rather than the criminal courts.

The Most Common Computer-Related Crimes

While computer hacking (electronic break-ins of computers by teenage pranksters) has received most of the recent media attention, the more serious and most prevalent computer crime has been the fraudulent disbursement of funds, which is generally preceded by the submission of a spurious claim:

- Phony vendor, supplier, or contractor invoice
- Phony governmental benefit claim
- Phony fringe benefit claim
- Phony refund or credit claim
- Phony payroll claim
- Phony expense claim

This crime usually involves a data entry clerk in accounts payable, payroll, or the benefits sections, either acting alone or in collusion with an insider or outsider—depending on how tight the internal controls are. From an accountant's perspective, the claim is a fake debit to an expense, so that a corresponding credit can be posted to the cash account for the issuance of a check. Auditors assert such disbursement frauds represent more than half of all frauds by lower level employees.

At higher levels of management the typical fraud involves the overstatement of profits by the fabrication of such data as sales, which are increased arbitrarily or by artifice (sales are booked before the sales transaction is completed), and the understatement of expenses which are improperly reduced or disguised as deferrals to the next accounting period. There are numerous variations on these two main themes—overstatement of sales and understatement of expenses. One of the more common ploys to overstate profits is to increase the ending inventory of manufactured goods or merchandise held for sale. That ploy results in understating the cost of goods sold and thereby increases the net profit.

The incentive to overstate profits is often brought about by the executive compensation system. If bonus awards depend on profits, executives have an economic incentive to "fudge the numbers." They may also be tempted to do so, if they own a great deal of company stock, whose value depends on investor perceptions of profitability. If profits are down, investors are not happy and may rush to sell; thus causing a lowering of the stock's price and depressing the value of the executive's own stock.

Manipulations of the above type often require the joining of both line executives and personnel in accounting and data processing capacities. The Equity Funding case is an example. Such conspiracies are becoming a recurring theme in business. The pressure on executives for high performance grows with each passing year. It is, therefore, likely that there will be more of such frauds in the future.

Computer Criminal Motivations

Motivations for computer-related crime can be distinguished by those that are personal to the crime perpetrator and those that are environmental.

The *personal motives* that can lead to the commission of a computer crime are:

- Economic
- Egocentric

- Ideological
- Psychotic

The economic motive influences the perpetrator whose main purpose is the need or desire to secure financial gain from the crime—money or things that can be disposed of for money.

The egocentric motive provokes the need or desire to show off the perpetrator's talent in committing what others may tend to see as a complex crime. Stealing money may be included in the criminal act but it is not the primary purpose of the act. The stolen funds are a secondary consideration—the more funds the better, but only to demonstrate the prowess and ingenuity of the perpetrator. The youthful "hackers" of recent fame fall into this category. Their intentions are not generally to steal money, but information, so that they can demonstrate how bright and gifted they are.

The ideological motive incites the perpetrator who feels compelled to seek revenge against someone or something that he believes is oppressing or exploiting him or others. Terrorist bombings of computer centers is an example of that mindset. Sabotage against computers by disgruntled employees is another example. Such criminals may feel computer technology threatens their economic and political survival or well being.

Psychotic motives include a distorted sense of reality, delusions of grandeur or persecution, and sometimes exaggerated fears or hatred of computers or their representative institutions to a point where bizarre behavior is directed against them to relieve anxieties. There have been few reported incidents of computer abuse where psychotic motives were attributed to perpetrators.

Environmental conditions that have provided motivation for computer-related crime and abuse include both the internal environment of the firm that operates a computer and the external environment, i.e., the world or marketplace in general. Internal influences that can aggravate the motives for computer-related crime and abuse include such things as:

- The work environment
- The reward system
- The level of interpersonal trust
- The level of ethics

- The level of stress (pressure for performance)
- The level of internal controls

Much thought and consideration continue to be given to the development of better internal and accounting controls to ward off or defend against computer crime and abuse. Other defensive measures include enhancement of the physical security of computer centers and protection of information and telecommunication systems from climatic disasters and outside intruders. Considerably less thought has been given to the enhancement of the work environment, the reward system, and the levels of trust, ethics, and stress. These factors are more difficult to assess as influences on risks, so they are often overlooked as defensive measures.

Externally, motives for computer-related crime and abuse may be provided by the current mores and social values of society, competitive conditions in the industry, and economic conditions in the country or the world.

Computer-Related Crime in the Future

With more and more businesses, governmental agencies, and consumers acquiring computers and with more and more people trained to use and program them, society should expect more computer-related crimes in the future. Furthermore, making computers more secure against tampering has not been a paramount consideration in designing new computers. Security tends to be an afterthought, because it slows down the speed of processing, requires more memory capacity, and makes operations more complicated and expensive.

Computer-related crime is primarily an occupational offense; it is a type of crime that requires access to and some knowledge of the operation and programming of computers in order to be carried out successfully. In that sense, computer crime is part of the phenomenon we call white-collar crime. White-collar crimes are generically referred to as occupational crimes and include such offenses as fraud, embezzlement, commercial bribery, price fixing, issuing false and fraudulent financial statements, padding contracts, etc.

In a survey conducted by the author of 40 personnel directors, 67 percent of the survey respondents believed computer crime would rise in the future.* The sample group of personnel directors can hardly be called representative of the mass public, but they do tend to be more knowledgeable about such matters in industry.

The respondents ranked computer crime as number six for its present frequency and seriousness, but they ranked computer crime as number one in terms of its future frequency. Their assessment no doubt takes into consideration the fact that many more computers will be used in the future and that many more people will understand the technology and thus be able to compromise computer systems.

The following is a ranking by current prevalence of white-collar crime as perceived by the survey respondents:

Perceptions of White-Collar Crime Prevalence

Current Rank	Crime Type
1.	Bribing political leaders
2.	Padding the bill on government contracts
3.	Employee theft, fraud, and embezzlement
4.	Polluting the environment
5.	Pilfering small tools and supplies
6.	Computer-related crimes
7.	Bribing union leaders
8.	Expense account padding
9.	Corporate income tax evasion
10.	Stock frauds and manipulations
11.	Falsifying time and attendance reports

In terms of the perception of future white-collar crimes that will occur with greater frequency, the rank ordering is as follows:

Expected Future Rank	Crime Type	Current Rank
1.	Computer-related crimes	6
2.	Bribing political leaders	1
3.	Expense account padding	8
4.	Bribing union leaders	7
5.	Employee theft, fraud, and embezzlement	3
6.	Falsifying productivity reports	25

*Jack Bologna, ''Computer Crime: Wave of the Future,'' *Assets Protection Journal,* 1981.

Expected Future Rank	Crime Type	Current Rank
7.	Padding the bill on government contracts	2
8.	Corporate income tax evasion	9
9.	Bribing foreign officials (tie)	21
10.	Stock frauds and manipulations	10
11.	Polluting the environment (tie)	4

The Control "Environment": Key to Computer Crime Prevention

If it could be assumed that all people are honest, there would be less need for internal controls. Some employees seem to steal under the best of employment circumstances; others would not consider stealing if they worked for Ebenezer Scrooge. The design of internal controls often reflects past experience; it has, for example, been said that a conservative is a former liberal who has been mugged. Rational individuals and societies tend to build or legislate constraints on human behavior by creating laws, norms of acceptable behavior, minimum standards of behavior, and even absolute prohibitions against certain forms of conduct.

But because not all people are prone to steal or are tempted to steal, it is counterproductive to build so many constraints on behavior that people begin to feel oppressed, untrusted, or under constant surveillance.

As a society, the United States boasts of personal freedoms—freedom of speech, religion, assembly, etc. As a society, these freedoms are kept in a state of creative tension by a set of countervailing rights. For example, while I have a right to speak my mind freely, I have no right to slander or libel another individual. And, while I have a right to select my own religious faith, I have no right to foist that faith on others or compel them to join my sect.

Ideally, internal controls should take into account a similar set of checks and balances. On one hand, consideration must be given to the risks, threats, and vulnerabilities that are faced in the marketplace, and how critical they are to survival and profitability. On the other hand, one must consider responsibilities toward employees, the value of their contribution to the success of the firm, and how their satisfaction with employment and working conditions may affect their performance and efficiency and the company's profitability.

A competent systems analyst or accounting systems designer can build controls upon controls in any firm. But controls must be balanced against the nature and extent of the risk. Controls must be cost effective and should not place undue burdens on the people who monitor them or work under them. So the "internal control environment" does not mean a "siege" mentality nor a fortress environment. Internal control mindedness should be a matter of balance and equilibrium not of paranoid fear.

Figure 5.2 below depicts the author's proposed plan to prevent internal theft.

The implications of this view of employee theft and the theft prevention process are as follows:

• Most prevention efforts concentrate or focus on building more accounting and access controls or physical security controls.

• It is necessary to recognize that there are limits to technological and procedural controls. It is difficult and costly to match the rate of growth of EDP technology with the rate of improvements in protection and detection mechanisms.

• An alternative for securing company assets in an EDP environment is to shift the concentration of effort and cost to *decreasing the probability of commission*. The technique for executing that strategy lies in strengthening *management* controls, improving the motivational and ethical climate and interpersonal trust in the firm.

The author's theory, then, is that an organization's internal controls are optimal when two sets of interacting environmental conditions are counterbalanced. The environmental factors that encourage and discourage crime are itemized under I and II, respectively, below.

I. Factors that enhance the probability of the commission of internal theft, fraud, embezzlement, and corruption.

   A. Motivational environment
      1. Inadequate rewards
         a. Pay, fringe benefits, bonuses, incentives, perquisites, job security, meaningful work, promotional opportunities
      2. Inadequate management controls
         a. Failure to articulate and/or communicate expected mini-

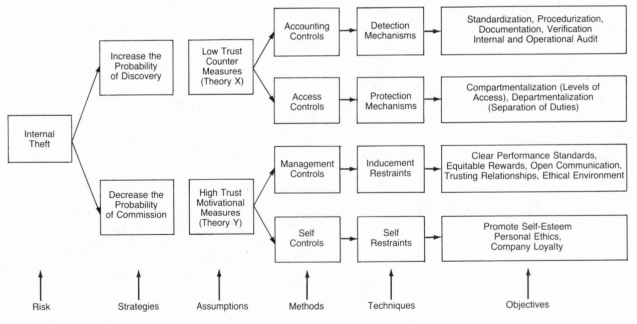

Figure 5.2 An Internal Theft Prevention System

mum standards or job-related performance and on-the-job personal behaviors

  b. Ambiguity or lack of clarity in job roles, relationships, responsibilities, and areas of accountability

3. Inadequate reinforcement and performance feedback mechanisms

  a. Lack of recognition for good work, loyalty, longevity, and effort

  b. Lack of recognition for truly outstanding performances

  c. Delayed feedback or no feedback at all on (1) performance inadequacies or (2) unacceptable on-the-job behaviors

  d. Failure to counsel when performance levels or personal behaviors fall below acceptable levels

  e. Lack of challenging job-related goals and objectives—acceptance of mediocre performance as the standard

4. Inadequate support

  a. Lack of adequate resources to meet mandated standards, e.g., to complete tasks within quantity, quality, and cost parameters and within time frames for completion

5. Inadequate operational reviews

  a. Lack of timely or periodic audits, inspections, and follow-through to assure compliance with company goals, priorities, policies, procedures, and governmental regulations

6. Condoning influences

  a. Unspecific or ambiguous corporate social values and ethical norms

  b. Tolerance or indifference toward antisocial behavior

7. Fostering hostility

  a. Promoting or permitting destructive interpersonal or interdepartmental competitiveness

  b. Promotion of a low interpersonal trust philosophy

  c. Bias or unfairness in selection, promotion, compensation, or appraisal

B. Personal and Personnel Inducements

  1. Inadequate standards of recruitment and selection

  2. Inadequate orientation and training on security matters and company policies with respect to sanctions for security breaches

  3. Unresolved personal financial problems

  4. Unfulfilled status needs

  5. Failure to screen applicants for sensitive positions before appointment

    a. Employment verification

    b. Educational verification

    c. Financial reliability

    d. Character

  6. General job-related stress or anxiety

II. Factors that discourage acts of, and enhance the probability of *discovery* of, internal theft, fraud, embezzlement, and corruption

A. Prevention measures

  1. Internal accounting controls

    a. Separation of duties

    b. Rotation of duties

    c. Periodic internal audits and surprise inspections

    d. Development and documentation of policies, procedures, systems, programs, and program modifications

    e. Establishment of dual signature authorities, dollar authorization limits per signatory, expiration dates for signature authorizations, and check amount limits

    f. Off-line entry controls and limits

    g. Batch totals, hash totals

  2. Computer access controls

    a. Identification defenses

      (1) Key or card inserts

      (2) Passwords and code names

(3) Exclusion—repeated error lockout

(4) Time activator/deactivator

(5) Periodic code and password changes

b. Authentication defenses

(1) Random personal data

(2) Voice, fingerprint, or palm geometry recognition

(3) Call backs

c. Establishment of authorizations by levels of authority or levels of security (compartmentalization and "need to know")

B. Detection measures

1. Exceptions logging systems

a. Out of sequence, out of priority, and aborted runs and entries

b. Out of pattern transactions: too high, too low, too many, too often, too few, unusual file access (odd times and odd places)

c. Attempted access beyond authorization level

d. Repeated attempts to gain access improperly—wrong password, entry code, etc.

e. Parity and redundancy checks

2. Management information system

a. Monitoring operational performance levels for

(1) variations from plans and standards

(2) deviations from accepted or mandated policies, procedures, and practices

(3) deviations from past quantitative relationships, based upon ratios, proportions, percentages, trends, past performance levels, indices, etc.

3. Intelligence gathering

a. Monitoring employee attitudes, values, and job satisfaction level

b. Soliciting random feedback from or surveying customers, vendors, and suppliers for evidence of dissatisfaction, inefficiency, inconsistency with policies, corruption, or dishonesty by employees

High Fraud/Low Fraud Environments

Employee fraud, theft, and embezzlement are more likely to occur in some organizations than in others. Organizations that are most vulnerable are usually hampered by management and inadequate accounting and security controls. Solutions often proposed are:

- Tight accounting and audit controls
- Thorough screening of applicants for employment
- Close supervision and monitoring of employee performance and behavior
- Explicit rules against theft, fraud, embezzlement, sabotage, and information piracy and strict sanctions for their breach

While those solutions are obvious, other considerations also affect the likelihood of employee crime. Organizations that are most vulnerable to employee misbehavior can also be distinguished from those that are less vulnerable by the following environmental and cultural contrasts:

High Fraud Potential	Low Fraud Potential
1. Management style	1. Management style
a. Autocratic	a. Participative
2. Management orientation	2. Management orientation
a. Low trust	a. High trust
b. X theory	b. Y theory
c. Power driven	c. Achievement driven
3. Distribution of authority	3. Distribution of authority
a. Centralized, reserved by top management	a. Decentralized, dispersed to all levels, delegated

High Fraud Potential	**Low Fraud Potential**
4. Planning	4. Planning
a. Centralized	a. Decentralized
b. Short range	b. Long range
5. Performance	5. Performance
a. Measured quantitatively and on a short-term basis	a. Measured both quantitatively and qualitatively and on a long-term basis
6. Profit focused	6. Customer focused
7. Managed by crisis	7. Managed by objectives
8. Reporting by routine	8. Reporting by exception
9. Rigid and inflexible rules, strongly policed	9. Reasonable rules fairly enforced
10. Primary management concern	10. Primary management concern
a. Capital assets	a. Human, then capital and technological assets
11. Reward system	11. Reward system
a. Punitive	a. Generous
b. Penurious	b. Reinforcing
c. Politically administered	c. Fairly administered
12. Feedback on performance	12. Feedback on performance
a. Critical	a. Positive
b. Negative	b. Stroking
13. Interaction mode	13. Interaction mode
a. Issues and personal differences are skirted or repressed	a. Issues and personal differences are confronted and addressed openly
14. Payoffs for good behavior	14. Payoffs for good behavior
a. Mainly monetary	a. Recognition, promotion, added responsibility, choice assignments; plus money
15. Business ethics	15. Business ethics
a. Ambivalent; rides the tides	a. Clearly defined and regularly followed
16. Internal relationships	16. Internal relationships
a. Highly competitive, hostile	a. Friendly, competitive, supportive
17. Values and beliefs	17. Values and beliefs
a. Economic, political, self-centered	a. Social, spiritual, group centered
18. Success formula	18. Success formula
a. Works harder	a. Works smarter
19. Biggest human resource problems	19. Biggest human resource problems
a. Burnout	a. Not enough promotional opportunities for all the talent
b. High turnover	
c. Grievances	
d. Absenteeism	
20. Company loyalty	20. Company loyalty
a. Low	a. High
21. Major financial concern	21. Major financial concern
a. Cash flow shortage	a. Opportunities for new investments
22. Growth pattern	22. Growth pattern
a. Sporadic	a. Consistent
23. Relationship with competitors	23. Relationship with competitors
a. Hostile	a. Professional
24. Innovativeness	24. Innovativeness
a. Copy cat, reactive	a. Leader, proactive
25. CEO characteristics	25. CEO characteristics
a. Swinger, braggart, self-interested driver, insensitive to people, feared, insecure, gambler, impulsive, tight fisted, numbers and things oriented,	a. Professional, decisive, fast paced, friendly, respected by peers, secure, risk taker, thoughtful, generous with

High Fraud Potential

profit seeker, vain, bombastic, highly emotional, partial, pretends to be more than he is

26. Management structure, systems and controls
    a. Bureaucratic
    b. Regimented
    c. Inflexible
    d. Imposed controls
    e. Many tiered structure, vertical
    f. Everything documented; a rule for everything

27. Internal communication
    a. Formal, written, stiff, pompous, ambiguous, CYA
28. Peer relationships
    a. Hostile, aggressive, rivalrous

Low Fraud Potential

personal time and money; people, products, and markets oriented, builder, helper, self-confident, composed, calm, deliberate, even disposition, fair, knows who he is, what he is and where he is going

26. Management structure, systems and controls
    a. Collegial
    b. Systematic
    c. Open to change
    d. Self-controlled
    e. Flat structure, horizontal
    f. Documentation is adequate but not burdensome; some discretion is afforded

27. Internal communication
    a. Informal, oral, clear, friendly, open, candid
28. Peer relationships
    a. Cooperative, friendly, trusting

Security Countermeasures to Computer Crime

A variety of methods has emerged as potential countermeasures to computer crime. The following is a partial list of specific measures:

1. Computer and Terminal Access Controls
   a. Passwords (alpha and numeric).
   b. Compartmentalization—Restricts users to only those files and programs that they are authorized to use.
   c. Error lock-out—Shuts down the terminal's power after successive incorrect attempts to log on.
   d. Voice print recognition.
   e. Finger print recognition.
   f. Palm geometry.
   g. Magnetic card access.
   h. Automatic shut-off—After transmission is completed, if operator fails to sign off.
   i. Time lock—No messages can be received or transmitted at the terminal after normal working hours.
   j. Call back—Before user gains complete access, a phone call is made to the terminal site, to verify the user's identity.
   k. Random personal information––Before the computer fully accepts an access request, it poses random personal history questions, stored in its memory, such as "What is your mother-in-law's maiden name or date of birth?" "In what hospital was your oldest child born?" "When will you celebrate your 25th wedding anniversary?" (Usually personal information which is not carried in a wallet. If the wallet were stolen, the thief could not use the information therein to impersonate its owner to gain access to a computer.)
   l. Personal identification number (PINS)—Used in conjunction with a magnetic card that has a coded authorization. One must present or insert both the card *and* his "PIN" number (a 4-digit or 5-digit number committed to memory) as proof of identity.
   m. Personal signature recognition—After logging on, the terminal operator writes his name with a light pen and the computer matches that signature with an authentic sample in its memory.

2. Data Communications Controls
   a. Cryptographic transmission and storage of data to avoid interception and casual perusal of sensitive information.
   b. Scramblers—To garble the computer message being transmitted.
   c. Dial back devices—The computer will not grant access unless terminal identification, user identification, password, and authority have been verified. Logs are kept and monitored of all access attempts. Those that were aborted for impropriety are further investigated. An alarm may be sounded when an improper access is being attempted.
3. Needed Improvements: Internal and Other Controls, Policies, Laws, Etc.
   a. Clear and explicit policies with respect to the proper and authorized uses of computers, and sanctions for abuses thereof.
   b. Better accounting controls.
   c. Better defensive countermeasures to ward off attacks and intrusions by outsiders.
   d. Better internal controls.
   e. Better supervision of employees with computer responsibilities.
   f. Better laws against criminal acts committed *by* computer and *against* computers.
   g. Better education of computer users with respect to the security and privacy of information.
   h. Better computer auditing methods.
   i. Better hardware protection.
   j. Better software protection.
   k. Better telecommunication systems protection.
   l. Better physical security of computer centers.
   m. Better proprietary information protection methods.
   n. Better personnel policies.
      - Reward systems
      - Standards of performance
      - Recruitment standards
      - Confidentiality agreements
      - More trust and less pressure
      - Clearer job-related goals and objectives
      - More involvement in decision making
      - More recognition for jobs that are well done

SOME SELECTED RECENT COMPUTER CRIMES

Computer Protection Systems, Inc., 150 North Main St., Plymouth, Michigan, 48170 has for the past several years, published a monthly newsletter called the *Computer Security Digest*, edited by Dr. Timothy A. Schabeck. A review of that newsletter provided information on the computer crimes which follow:

Issue Date: June 1982
Computer Crime Victim: 1. A state university's hospital
Details: A computer operator at the hospital was charged with embezzling $40,000 by submitting false invoices that were processed through the hospital's computer. Another case involved a charge against the hospital's former assistant data processing manager, that he accepted a $41,000 bribe from a data processing consultant and conspired with another data processing consultant to steal $126,000 from the hospital by submitting false invoices for software services. *Both* the operator and the assistant data processing manager had previous convictions for computer-related crime. The hospital did not as a matter of course conduct background investigations on data processing employment applicants.
Conclusion: Conduct thorough background checks on all employees in sensitive data processing and related operations.

Issue Date: June 1982
Computer Crime Victim: 2. A manufacturer of magnetic peripherals
Details: A subsidiary of a major computer manufacturer was another victim of computer crime. An accounts payable terminal operator and her boyfriend conspired to defraud the company by fabricating invoices from a fictitious

vendor firm, which they had earlier formed. Five checks totaling $155,000 were then issued to the phony vendor after which the terminal operator and her boyfriend left for sunnier climes. The operator finally turned herself in and disclosed the fraud to police when her boyfriend tried to effectuate a reconciliation with his estranged wife and began to physically abuse the terminal operator. The investigating police officer alleged that the company was too busy with all its business to build in any safeguards for its computer.

Conclusion: Verify the authenticity of large invoices and payments and spot check smaller transactions of this nature. Management must fulfill its legal responsibility to provide proper safeguards.

Issue Date: October 1982

Computer Crime Victim: 3. A top oil company

Details: A former EDP employee and his wife were indicted for stealing $18,000 from the company in an accounts payable-type scam. The employee instructed the company computer to pay his wife rent for land she allegedly leased to the company by assigning her an alpha-numeric code as a lessor and then ordering that payment be made.

Conclusions: Never let a data entry clerk in accounts payable who processes payment claims also have access to the approved vendor master file for additions or deletions. Doing otherwise violates the separation of duties principle of internal controls.

Issue Date: April 1983

Computer Crime Victim: 4. A Netherlands bank

Details: The head of the bank's foreign transfer department and his assistant were arrested on suspicion of forgery and embezzlement for a scheme that involved the taking of at least $65 million over a two-year period. Police believe the money was embezzled by breaking the bank's computer code, allowing funds to be funneled into outside accounts. The alleged fraud was discovered through audit. The bank's management is also under investigation for tax evasion.

Conclusion: More trained EDP auditors, doing routine EDP audits, can detect this type of crime sooner.

Issue Date: June 1983

Computer Crime Victim: 5. Insurance company

Details: A guilty plea by an insurance company employee marks the second conviction under Florida's computer crime law. The employee, a benefits analyst with the insurance company, used her remote terminal in a Dade County field claims office to defraud the company out of $206,000 between April 1981 and January 1983. Case highlights: (1) The employee used her position of trust and knowledge of claims systems to execute the fraud; (2) she used false names to submit fictitious claims but used the addresses of herself, her father, and her boyfriend. The repetition of the same addresses eventually tipped off the insurance company's security department; (3) under Florida's computer law HB.1305, she faces restitution of the $206,000, a fine, and a possible prison term of one to five years.

Conclusion: Blank claims forms should be kept under lock and key, preserialized, and under the strict control of an employee other than a data entry clerk.

Issue Date: July 1983

Computer Crime Victim: 6. A university in Michigan

Details: On December 19, 1982, the university's computer system was accessed by one or more people who damaged nearly 43,000 student records stored on the system. Many students' first names were changed to "Susan," student telephone numbers were replaced with the phone number of the university's president, grade point averages were modified, and some files were deleted completely. The university's outside auditors reported that the computer's security system was penetrated either by someone who had extensive knowledge of the system or by misuse of the password used by the Admissions Office. The admission files were recreated by hiring a lot of temporary help.

Conclusion: Change passwords periodically, use individual (vs. departmental) passwords, make passwords more complex, i.e., alpha and numeric, and monitor system users' security practices.

Issue Date: July 1983

Computer Crime Victim: 7. A transportation authority

Details: A 31-year-old bus scheduler has been acquitted of criminal charges involving extortion and violation of the state's 1980 computer crime law. The scheduler, who developed seven report generation programs for the transportation authority, attempted to collect $19,500 in payment for the programs after he was fired. The programs were developed with built-in security access blocks, which made accessing the source code difficult. The scheduler was said to have demanded the $19,500 before he would turn over the access codes needed to alter the source code. The programs were developed over a two-year period in his free time. The scheduler's attorney contended that the programs saved approximately $150,000 over the past two years.

Conclusion: Make it clear to new hires (orally and in writing) that software applications designed by employees during their employment are the property of the employer. Establish programming standards, and monitor compliance via regular reviews of work in process as well as completed projects.

Issue Date: August 1983

Computer Crime Victim: 8. A diversified corporation

Details: Criminal charges have been filed against two former employees of a food corporation. The two allegedly programmed "logic bombs" that would erase inventory and payroll information processed by the company for 400 retail franchise operations. The programmed commands, one of which was set to activate on June 7, would also have shut down the computer system and erased all traces of the destructive commands. The motive is still unknown.

Conclusion: Use careful hiring practices and promote a positive working environment as basic preventive measures. Employ operating procedures that present and detect internal sabatoge; for example:

- authorized turnover of operational programs
- independent testing of new and revised programs
- audits of program changes.

Issue Date: January 1984

Computer Crime Victim: 9. California Welfare Department

Details: Although the exact amount of loss sustained by the Alameda County, California, Welfare Department is unknown, it is quite evident that over $300,000 has been lost owing to fraud committed by a supervisor and clerk. Again, this is a case of an input falsification fraud. A welfare department compliance unit supervisor and one of her former clerks falsified dozens of claims over at least a period of a year and collected unauthorized payments for the claims. The two were caught when one of the welfare department's data entry clerks discovered incomplete information on an input document authorizing a claims payment. The clerk then checked with the eligibility worker whose name had been forged on the document. When the eligibility worker denied authorizing the claim or signing the document, an investigation was started.

Conclusion: Rotate employees in sensitive positions. Do more intensive auditing of cash and disbursement functions.

Issue Date: February 1984

Computer Crime Victim: 10. Australia case

Details: A *Computerworld* article reports that an operator at a state-run horse betting agency was changing the time clock in the computer system by three minutes. After a race was run, the operator would quickly telephone his girlfriend, an input clerk, and give her the winning horses and the amounts to bet. Loss: unknown. Detected: when his girlfriend got mad at him because he left her for another woman.

Conclusion: Any change in input parameters, even a change of time, should be logged by the system, preferably in an automatic manner, so as to create an audit trail of operational activities. Sensitive on-line operations may require the use of more than one operator at all times.

Summary

One of the peculiar things about the field of computer-related crime is that one can say almost anything about it and not be challenged. One opinion tends to be as acceptable as any other. Since the field is new and generally unresearched, practitioners are free to make personal predictions, assessments, categorical statements, and generalizations. Rarely are they asked to support their judgments or conclusions with reliable facts.

One statement that is repeated so often that it seems to have moved up from mythology to universal acceptance is that computer crimes are committed mostly by people with highly developed knowledge and skills, i.e., mainly programmers and analysts. A logical extension of that plausible but questionable rationale might naturally cause an uninformed person to wonder what it is about computer professionals that makes them so crime prone. In the absence of hard data, the mass media gives us the following answers:

- EDP technicians are more dedicated to their profession than to their employers.
- EDP technicians tend to be highly ambitious, energetic, naturally curious, creative, and challenge seeking.
- They tend to be young, psychologically immature and easily frustrated when facing obstacles like unreasonable deadlines, programs that cannot be de-bugged quickly or simply, large backlogs of work, and demanding users who do not understand their technology, their jargon, or their value to the organization.

The speciousness of the rationale is not that the above circumstances do not exist in the EDP environment. Indeed they do. But the same thing could be said for other professions as well. Engineers, accountants, lawyers, and doctors suffer similar frustrations. They also tend to be more loyal to their profession than to their employers, clients, or patients. (If they were not, they might be sued more often or disciplined by their professional ethics board.) They likewise tend to be young, ambitious, energetic, curious, creative, etc. They are professional problem solvers, too. But the mass media does not paint *them* as people who might use their positions of trust to violate their clients', patients', or employers' interests and what makes the EDP profession different or special.

It may be that EDP technology is more suspect because it is new. Since the public does not understand it, they may be fearful about it and may believe negative allegations about computer technology and the people who work in the field.

The fact is that while most reported cases of computer-related crime involved at least one person with sufficient knowledge to gain access and manipulate data for personal economic gain, the inspiration for the scheme was, as often as not, an outsider or non-EDP employee. Most computer crimes involving the theft of company assets have been conspiracies. Internal controls, which require separation of duties, make conspiracies more likely than individual acts of computer-related theft. (But acts of sabotage against computers do tend to be individual acts, most usually by disgruntled EDP employees or terrorists.)

It is a simplistic and erroneous notion that EDP professionals, by virtue of their extreme youth and alleged lack of company loyalty, are more crime prone than other professionals. That myth is just too convenient to be true. Worse yet, it has discouraged research in computer crime motivations and has branded and labeled a large group of mostly innocent people.

Another cherished myth is that most computer-related thefts, frauds, or embezzlements are discovered by accident, not by audit or exceptions controls. If that were factual, it would be logical to conclude that criminals are more intelligent, more clever, or more cunning than noncriminals, particularly noncriminals who design systems, programs, and controls.

Frankly, very little is known about computer crime in an empirical sense. It is understood to involve substantial sums of money, to occur with some frequency, and is likely to increase in both frequency and amounts lost. These are conjectures based on two of the few realities in the field:

1. The proliferating use of computers will increase the probability of computer-related crime.
2. Our ability or willingness to design control mechanisms in computer systems has not kept pace with our ability to build more sophisticated hardware and software, and that also increases the probability of computer crime.

Therefore, the prudent businessman will give appropriate attention to the maintenance of sound controls and will foster an environment that discourages criminal activity.

Security in the Microcomputer and Office Automation Era

Office information today is much more than correspondence between the headquarter's sales staff and distant customers and field representatives. The automation of American offices permits access to sensitive information by way of local data base, word-processing equipment, on-line computer terminals, and networking services, i.e., financial, research, technological, economic, and competitive data bases.

The sensitivity of information flowing through modern office machines can be evidenced by a number of recent cases. At one Wall Street law firm, an office manager accessed information about proposed mergers and acquisitions by way of "browsing" on his word processing unit. He, in turn, sold such "inside" information to a few friends and relatives who made several million dollars trading in the securities of the about-to-be-acquired firms.

In another New York City law firm, a proofreader and a word processing operator jointly deciphered the internal office encryption code contained in the word processing system and thereby gained access to data about the firm's clients who were about to make tender offers. They passed the information to several outsiders in exchange for a share of the profits—$60,000 on one series of transactions alone.

A Michigan labor union was shocked to receive a monthly phone bill showing a balance due of $320,000, as its average phone bill was $600. "Hackers" had gotten the union's telephone credit card number from an injudicious remark and had posted the number on electronic bulletin boards all over the country.

In another incident, a word processing system in the corporate offices of Ford Motor Co. was used for gambling on sports events and horse races—to the tune of $25,000 in wagers per week.

Office employees have been apprehended while leaving the premises with all manner of confidential and proprietary data in disk, diskette, and tape form, i.e., listings of customers, clients, vendors, and employees; research and development studies; software applications packages for micros, etc.

There was a time when a clean-desk policy offered some immunity to after-hours browsing by the cleaning crew or by nosy colleagues who worked late. Today, information security takes far more time than placing the contents of your "in/out" box in a locked file cabinet at night.

Now, program and file disks and backup media must be secured, that is, stored in tamperproof, fireproof, and climatically controlled cabinets or vaults. Microcomputers, electronic typewriters, and word processors may need to be secured by time locks after working hours to protect them from unauthorized persons. Even paper waste and carbons of confidential and sensitive documents may need to be destroyed (burned or shredded) to insure against late-night viewing by outsiders and daytime viewing by unauthorized insiders. And terminals and word processors need to be anchored in place, or they may not be available in the morning. So securing the office workplace is no longer a matter of locking doors and placing documents in file cabinets at night. Clean terminal policies are far more important than clean desk policies today. Employees must be educated and trained in security principles, policies, plans, and procedures.

The fundamental purpose of security is to *minimize the risk* of loss from (1) physical damage or destruction, (2) human errors and omissions, and (3) theft or unauthorized disclosure. That purpose is best fulfilled by effective loss-prevention efforts. Loss-prevention efforts involve the identification and assessment of risks to capital, human, informational, and technological assets, and the development of suitable and cost-feasible countermeasures.

Employee Security Survey Questionnaire

	Yes	No	Not Applicable/ Don't Know
1. Does your company have *written* policies which restrict or prohibit the following: a. Outside employment (moonlighting)?			
b. Conflicts of interest?			
c. Accepting gratuities, expensive gifts or lavish entertainments from vendors, contractors, and suppliers?			
d. Compromising or bribing customers?			
e. Disclosing company trade secrets to unauthorized persons?			
f. Fixing prices with competitors?			
g. Gambling on-the-job?			
h. Drug and alcohol abuse?			
i. Fighting on-the-job?			
j. Stealing company property?			
k. Destroying company property?			
l. Falsifying time and attendance reports?			
m. Falsifying production reports?			
n. Falsifying personal data on job applications?			
o. Falsifying or forging accounting records?			
p. Destroying accounting records?			
q. Falsifying expense accounts?			
r. Allowing non-authorized persons to gain access to confidential records, i.e., payroll and personnel records, customer and vendor's lists, research results, product and marketing plans, etc?			
s. Allowing non-authorized persons to gain access to company buildings or critical work areas?			
t. Loaning company building access identification cards, badges, or door keys to non-authorized persons?			
u. Disclosing computer log-on codes to non-authorized persons?			
v. Allowing non-authorized persons to use computer terminals?			

	Yes	No	Not Applicable/ Don't Know
2. Does your company conduct background inquiries to confirm: a. Identity of applicants?			
b. Educational achievements?			
c. Credit standing?			
d. Satisfactory past employments?			
e. Freedom from criminal convictions? (Name and/or fingerprint checks)			
f. Reputation?			
g. Character?			
3. Does your company administer any of the following to new hires or applicants: a. Polygraph?			
b. Paper and pencil honesty tests?			
c. Voice stress analysis?			
d. Handwriting analysis?			
e. Intelligence tests?			
f. Psychological diagnostic tests like the MMPI, PF 16, etc?			
4. Does your company conduct and/or provide: a. Security orientation training for new hires?			
b. On-going security awareness training programs for all employees?			
c. Written rules of employee conduct?			
d. Hearings for employees charged with punishable offenses?			
e. Employee representation at such hearings?			

	Yes	No	Not Applicable/ Don't Know
5. Does your company utilize or provide:			
a. Job descriptions?			
b. Organizational charts?			
c. Standards of performance?			
d. Performance appraisals?			
e. Coaching and counseling of employees whose work is unsatisfactory?			
f. Counseling of employees with substance abuse problems?			
g. Technical training programs?			
h. Human resource development programs?			
i. Quality of work life programs?			
j. Quality circles programs?			
k. Tuition reimbursement?			
l. Time off for study?			
m. Time off for family emergencies?			
n. Employee involvement programs?			
o. Job enlargement/enrichment/rotation programs?			
p. Exit interviews of departing employees?			

	Higher	Lower	Same
6. How does your company compare with other firms in your industry and/or areas of operation with respect to: a. Salaries?			
b. Fringe benefits?			
c. Blue collar turnover?			
d. White collar turnover?			
e. Absenteeism?			
f. Employee firings?			
g. Promotions from within the company?			
h. Ability to recruit new employees?			
i. Skills of its employees?			
j. Educational level of employees?			
k. Employee attitudes toward their work?			
l. Employee loyalty?			

7. Does your company, as a matter of written policy, refer incidents of employee crimes on-the-job to police or prosecutorial authorities? _____

8. Does your company have:
   a. Internal auditors? _____
   b. EDP Auditors? _____
   c. At least one Data Security Officer or Administrator? _____
   d. A Corporate Security or Loss Prevention Unit? _____
   e. An investigative staff? _____

9. During the past five years, has your company experienced:
   a. A substantial inventory shortage corporate-wide? _____
   b. A substantial inventory shortage in a major operating division? _____
   c. A major embezzlement, involving a loss of more than $10,000? _____
   d. A successful penetration of your main office computers by outsiders? _____
   e. An accounts payable, accounts receivable, payroll or benefit claim fraud of any amount? _____
   f. Commercial bribery of purchasing or other personnel? _____

PART II
Basic Safeguards

CHAPTER 6
Contingency Planning

by Arthur E. Hutt

Requirements for Contingency Plans

Contingency planning is an essential underpinning for an adequate computer security program. It provides the necessary framework for achieving security by establishing the goals and strategies to be adopted and setting forth the basic plans needed to achieve those goals.

A contingent event is a chance event, an uncertainty, something that has a possibility of occurrence but may or may not actually come about. Contingency planning for computer security is concerned with providing alternatives for those chance events that could be detrimental to the functions normally performed. The question addressed is how to protect against the potential of loss due to these adverse occurrences.

Major interruptions in the availability of information services can result in severe impairment for organizations that depend upon such services. One of the most important aspects of contingency planning is disaster recovery planning, which deals with the management of recovery following a disaster. The consequences of vital service disruption can be greatly eased by carefully detailing, in advance, the responses necessary to react quickly and effectively to such emergencies. Every issue that is resolved in advance contributes to the primary objective of restoring service promptly and efficiently.

While it is incumbent upon management to plan for chance events, particularly where the events might seriously endanger the well-being of the enterprise, it must also be recognized that it is impossible to protect against all contingencies. At best, contingency planning should provide reasonable security within the economic constraints mandated by the nature of the processes performed. Comprehensive risk analysis is needed to provide a basis for economic justification. However, it is important to recognize that the economics of contingency measures will vary widely based upon strategy, and that many contingency plans cost little more than continuing management vigilance to ensure effectiveness.

This chapter reviews the basic requirements and elements of contingency planning, including the establishment of backup strategies for all aspects of the data processing environment:

- Emergency response requirements
- Personnel resources
- Hardware backup
- Software and datafile backup
- Documentation backup
- Backup for related and special activities

Various options are described for backup solutions, along with the pros and cons of the different alternatives. Backup of computer hardware and data communication systems is treated in depth, and also the need for regular testing and monitoring of contingency measures. While much emphasis is given to disaster protection, other aspects of backup are also addressed. This chapter explains how to appraise the costs and benefits of the selected backup options, and how to determine the economic impact of potential interruptions in computer services.

The issues of contingency planning are addressed from the management viewpoint, assuming that the reader has either direct or indirect responsibility to ensure the adequacy of contingency plans for securing computing resources. The value of the information resources or services, rather than computer size, is assumed to be the major factor determining the economic feasibility of backup alternatives.

The discussion of contingency planning presented here addresses the need for reaction to potentially detrimental events. It does not cover other related computer security issues that are discussed elsewhere in this book, such as prevention and detection of threats, insurance against undue risk, audit controls, and other important topics. Contingency planning for fortuitous events is not included in the discussion. Prudent management requires saving for the rainy day.

Basic Elements of Contingency Plans

Defining Contingency Planning Goals

The initial phase of contingency planning must be to define and establish the goals that are expected for the activity. Just as a requirements definition is the logical starting point for a new system, so too should a statement of requirements be utilized to guide the planning processes for "contingencies." The purpose of goals definition is to direct the proper allocation of resources in order to counter threats, to devise effective strategies for backup, to assist economic justification and to ensure the effectiveness of the program. Goals guide strategies, and strategies guide actions. A statement of goals for a contingency plan is necessary to serve as a basic guide for the development of the contingency plan details in a manner that is effective in carrying out management's intentions.

In order to provide adequate direction for the planning process the goals should contain the following:

- A statement of importance as to the need for business resumption following disruption or loss of the computer facility. The ultimate objective of every plan is to restore service promptly and efficiently; however, not every enterprise is affected in the same way by the loss of a facility for short or long periods of time. By indicating the value of computer services it is then easier to shape strategies that are cost effective.

- A statement of priorities as to the relative importance of the functions or applications

performed. Not every application is of equal importance, except in unusual circumstances.

- A statement of organizational responsibility. This is important in order to establish authority and responsibility for implementing the plan and to foster cooperation across all organizational elements. While a data processing department might be given primary responsibility for contingency plans, it is essential to have user involvement.

- A statement of urgency and timing. Management should establish at the outset firm target dates for the implementation of the plan and also indicate the need for maintaining operational effectiveness through regular updating and testing.

Because the underlying purpose of contingency planning is the resumption of business, it is essential to consider the entire organization, and not just data processing services, when developing plans. Ideally, there should be an overall business interruption and resumption plan covering all organizational elements, identifying essential services, providing alternatives for emergency operations, and identifying responsibility for coordination. If there is an overall plan, the data processing plan should then be a major subset and should be integrated with the separate action plans for the other units of the organization. Where a unified business resumption plan does not exist, the plans for data processing should be extended to cover planning for all units that are dependent upon the data processing services to'sustain its vital functions. In any event, the data processing plans must extend to the user areas to cover the sources of information, transmittal of data to the data processing department, and delivery and deployment of processed results to the user units.

The end purpose of a data processing facility is to accomplish useful results in the form of information products. The application system utilized to process information into its final form is equally important for realistic recovery as the hardware environment and the supporting software. Application recovery is often relegated to a lesser role in contingency planning. It is important not to lose sight of the need to recover application functions and data as well as to restore the basic capabilities to process data.

Contingency planning should properly embrace normal backup requirements as well as disaster backup and recovery. Most disruptions are far short of disasters, but many elements of planning are applicable to both. The integration of strategies for disaster recovery and normal backup can be beneficial in terms of economy and efficiency.

Contingency planning strategy must not preclude flexibility of action. Preconceived attitudes and procedural rigidity may backfire. While it is important to develop detailed plans to cope with emergencies in a systematic way, it is also essential to place the preconceived plans in the proper perspective. One of the most important objectives of contingency planning is to take care of the routine procedures and thereby free up personnel to function more effectively during a crisis. Advance planning for emergencies covers those details that can be foreseen; it serves as a checklist of actions to take following a crisis, actions that have been thought through in advance in order to be helpful in the management of recovery. While the purpose of advance planning is to take care of many situations that might occur, provision for the unforeseen must also be made. It is necessary to maintain flexibility of decision in applying the appropriate procedures effectively, possibly curtailing unnecessary actions, or devising spontaneous actions to handle special situations. The Recovery Management Team bears the responsibility for applying flexibility and common sense to the execution of contingency plans.

As important as it is to recognize the necessity to back up and recover vital information functions it is also important to recognize that there are limits to recovery. There is a need for advance consensus on the extent and timing of recovery. Every capability has an associated cost. There are very few free rides. Total backup and immediate recovery can be very expensive, sometimes far more expensive than the value of the functions being protected. The economics of backup and, in particular, disaster recovery should be carefully considered when developing strategies. Management must also recognize the differences between disasters and short-term or "normal" disruptions. Disaster recovery measures are usually not meant to be activated for short-term problems, such as a temporary power outage. Unfortunately, this distinction is often not fully understood by senior management, with the result being a gap in expectations and sometimes unwarranted interference with recovery procedures.

Development of a comprehensive contingency plan can be accomplished in several different ways. Plans can be formulated by an in-house staff, presumably within the responsibility of data processing, or by outside consultants. A combination of the two is often effective because it will offer the opportunity to capitalize on outside expertise while ensuring that those responsible for carrying out the action plans are involved with its development. Regardless of the approach, in-house or consultant or combination, it is imperative that firm target dates be established for the development and implementation of the plans. Management must choose how to develop the plan, commit the resources to ensure that it is accomplished, assign responsibility for both plan development and plan implementation, and set target dates for these accomplishments.

Finally, management must insist on adequate feedback to assure itself that the contingency plans are indeed workable and that procedures are kept current. Recovery testing, like fire drills, can be either cursory or extensive. Inadequate testing and mere lip service can result in vulnerability to damage when real emergencies occur. Management cannot afford to delude itself about the effectiveness of contingency plans. It is simply too important to leave it to chance. Recoverability must be verified on a regular basis, and it should extend to the recovery of applications not just the data processing facility. The key ingredient needed to provide this assurance is a continuing management commitment.

Emergency Response Procedures

An important element of contingency planning is the basic reaction to an emergency situation. When an emergency arises it must be addressed with dispatch and efficiency. Often, the initial response, or knee-jerk reaction, to an emergency can be the critical factor affecting its ultimate outcome. Emergency response procedures represent that set of prepared actions that are meant to cope initially with disruption. It is the first line of defense in dealing with crisis.

When an emergency occurs it is essential that the choice of action be made swiftly and effectively. Those responsible for managing any portion of the crisis situation must be armed with the wherewithal to respond. Procedures to facilitate emergency response must, of course, be prepared in advance. Clarity is important in the formatting and presentation of procedures in order to assure ease of use. Of equal import is familiarity and current knowledge; key personnel must be adequately trained and kept up to date in order to assure effectiveness.

Some emergencies are unpredictable, as are the nature and scope of the associated threats. Protection of life is of paramount importance, followed by protection of property and limitation of damage. Emergency response procedures should be prioritized to reflect these basic protective purposes. For example, general emergency response guidelines for use by supervisory personnel might start out in the following manner:

Emergency Response Guidelines

1. In event of any life-threatening emergency (such as fire, earthquake, harmful chemicals, or explosives) the supervisor-in-charge is responsible FIRST to commence EVACUATION of personnel in an ORDERLY fashion. Designated emergency wardens will assist the supervisor-in-charge, as required. Established evacuation routes and procedures will be used.

2. Whenever evacuation is required, ALL individuals known to be on the premises must be accounted for. This includes vendor personnel and visitors as well as regular staff.

3. The supervisor is responsible for prompt NOTIFICATION of the emergency to appropriate authorities, such as:
   - Fire Department
   - Police Department
   - Emergency Rescue groups
   - Medical Emergency groups
   - Internal Security
   - Management, vendor support staff, etc.

4. If feasible (that is, if it can be done WITHOUT ENDANGERING LIFE), remove crucial data files during evacuation. Also, if feasible, shut down equipment and utilities in prescribed sequence.

5. If the emergency is NOT life threatening, the supervisor should arrange for an orderly termination of jobs in progress prior to equipment and utility shutdown.

6. Establish damage control coordination to guide recovery and repair activities and to facilitate notification.

7. Activate Emergency Control Center procedures if the scope of the emergency or the expected duration is sufficiently serious.

8. Recall personnel for special assignments, if required. Initiate recovery and repair procedures. Notify users and customers of conditions, if necessary.

Actual instructions for emergency response use must be concise and clear. Checklists are probably the most convenient format to use. Ideally, separate checklists should be prepared for different emergency scenarios. It is also desirable to differentiate between short-term and long-term disruption of business.

The importance of advanced training and preassigned responsibility for emergency response procedures cannot be overemphasized. Especially since lives may be at risk, it is important that all management and supervisory personnel be aware of their roles during an emergency. The assigned roles may very well be different from the normal chain of command. For example, a computer operator could be designated floor warden during evacuation procedures and thereby overrule the activities of a shift supervisor for the duration of the immediate emergency. The entire staff should know who is responsible and what action is expected in an emergency. General assignments of responsibility are not adequate. Specific assignments should be made, in writing, and regularly kept up to date. Periodic drills may be necessary to ensure compliance and effectiveness.

Emergency response procedures are, of course, applicable to any environment where groups of people gather for a common purpose, whether it is work, school, play, etc. Most large organizations already have procedures for emergencies. The general emergency response guidelines or procedures that apply to the total organization should be used as the starting point for data processing emergency response, and modified to reflect additional requirements.

Hardware Backup

Hardware backup is often regarded as synonymous with contingency planning. It is only one of the elements needed for adequate protection; in fact hardware backup alone will usually be inadequate to assure continuity of activities. Nevertheless, backup for physical equipment is an important element of the contingency plans. It is also highly visible and represents a focal point for the other ingredients of protection.

Procedures to back up computer hardware should embrace both on-site and off-site protective strategies. Both are important. Experience dictates that the most frequently encountered disruptions will involve localized emergencies, usually nondisasters, and often affecting a single component of equipment. Lengthier and more costly outages, particularly disasters that impair the primary physical facility, require off-site backup alternatives.

Because of the importance of off-site backup to contingency planning, it is accorded separate treatment in a subsequent section. A number of alternatives are examined and reviewed for applicability to different needs for protection.

On-site backup represents the first line of defense for contingency planning. It should be regarded as a natural precursor to off-site measures. Several important goals can be satisfied by adequate on-site backup. Disaster prevention and disaster containment are both furthered by on-site backup. Nondisastrous disruptions provide the primary motivation for on-site backup; however, the distinction between disasters and non-disasters is meaningful only in terms of time and cost.

It is useful to classify disruptions in order to aid in developing hardware backup strategies. Three categories are readily identified:

1. *Nondisasters.* Disruptions in service stemming from system malfunction or other failure. Requires action to recover to operational status in order to resume service. May necessitate restoration of hardware, software, or data files.

2. *Disasters.* Disruptions causing the entire facility to be inoperative for a lengthy period of time, usually more than one day. Requires action to recover operational status, usually the use of an alternate processing facility. Restoration of software and data files from off-site copies may be required. It is necessary that the alternate facility be available until the original data processing facility is restored.

3. *Catastrophes.* Major disruptions entailing the destruction of the data processing facility. Short-term and long-term fallback is required. An alternate processing facility is needed to satisfy immediate operational needs, as in the case of a disaster. In addition, a new, permanent facility must be identified and equipped to provide for continuation of data processing service on a regular basis.

The relationships between the categories of disruption are fairly obvious. Many of the same procedures will be required, particularly in the earlier phases of the emergency. As the expected time interval increases, the nature of the response changes from short-term fixes to longer-term solutions, but both may be needed.

Situations that are less than disasters account for the major portion of data processing disruptions. It is more timely and more convenient to respond to such downtime situations with on-site backup. The purpose of on-site backup measures is to minimize disruption by providing either redundancy or substitute processing within the same facility. Usually, critical hardware components, such as computer processing units and disk drives, are duplicated. As a rule, systems should be designed to minimize dependency on unique hardware components in order to encourage flexibility in processing, and thereby facilitate backup. Sometimes a degraded mode of operations, entailing slower or partial processing, may be acceptable for emergency use. Larger data processing facilities that normally require multiple computer systems often have an advantage in that on-site backup can be more economically justified for multiple computers and backup can be more easily accommodated by sharing computers when required.

Development of specific on-site backup measures requires a thorough technical and economic analysis to identify the appropriate strategies and costs. A sound technical assessment is needed to assure that all necessary critical equipment units are either backed up by alternate units or may be bypassed. It is important to include environmental equipment, such as air conditioning units, in this assessment. Generally, the technical assessment process will involve evaluating the effect upon the overall system of failure for each of the separate equipment units, identifying which units can be replaced by other units or temporarily bypassed, and identifying those units that are essential. Statistics for *mean time to failure* and *mean time to repair* may be used to support economic analysis in order to select equipment units that need to be duplicated.

On-site backup and off-site backup, no matter how intricate or detailed, no matter how expensive or redundant, would be wasted if data are not retrievable and recoverable. A crucial element of any contingency plans for on-site and off-site recovery is adequate data. Duplication of important data is a prerequisite for any type of recovery, and off-site storage of such backup data is essential.

Hardware backup sites for alternate processing may be categorized into three basic types of sites:

1. *Hot sites.* These are sites that are fully configured and ready to operate within several hours. The equipment, and systems software, must be compatible with the primary installation being backed up. Usually, the only additional needs are staff, programs, and data files.

2. *Warm sites.* These are sites that are partially configured, usually with selected peripheral equipment, such as disk drives and tape drives and controllers, but without the main computer. Sometimes a warm site is equipped with a smaller CPU. The assumption behind the warm site concept is that the computer can usually be obtained quickly for emergency installation (provided it is a widely used model), and since the computer is the most expensive unit, such an arrangement is less costly than a hot site. After the installation of the needed components the site can be ready for service within hours; however, the location and installation of the CPU and other missing units could take several days or weeks.

3. *Cold sites.* These are sites that have the basic environment (electrical wiring, air conditioning, flooring, etc.). The cold site is ready to receive equipment but does not offer any components at the site in advance of the need. Activation of the site may take at least several weeks.

The major distinctions between the three types of sites are activation time and cost. The hot site affords a reasonably fast response to a disaster situation. Even nondisaster disruptions could be alleviated by the ready availability of alternative processing. The cost of hot site backup is usually high. The warm site is a less expensive alternative, but obviously less satisfactory in terms of activation time. The cold site is the least expensive approach, but it is only meant to accommodate longer term needs. In event of a long-term disaster or a catastrophe it may be useful to have either a warm site or a cold site to turn to as a secondary facility, after initially utilizing a hot site for a short term, in order to reduce operating costs.

Software and Information Backup

Without software the computer hardware is of little value. Software in the form of an operating system, programming languages, utilities, and application programs provides the necessary processing logic needed to support the information functions of the organization. Information in the form of records, data files, data bases, and input/output documents, provides the raw materials and the finished products for the data processing cycle. Contingency planning must provide for protection of software and information in an adequate and thorough manner in order to achieve meaningful security.

The nature of information and software is such that it is less tangible and more dynamic than hardware. The usual representation of information and software in a data processing system is in machine-readable format that permits rapid sensing and rapid alteration. In order to preserve these nonhardware elements it is necessary to consider both the physical storage environment and the fluidity, or frequency, of change. Backup for information and software must allow for the continuing occurrence of change.

There are several approaches to backup for information and software. All entail copying files onto machine-readable media. The straightforward copying of an information file or a software file is easy to apply if the file is of manageable size. Since data processing updating often involves the creation of a "new" master file, as in the case of batch updating and program modifications, it is usually desirable to retain the prior file for two or more file generations, along with the applied changes, and thereby backup the latest file without extra copies of the most recent file. On-line files may require creation of backup on a record by record transaction log basis, together with copies of individual records prior to alteration. Regardless of the technique, the principles are the same. A copy of the file or record as of some point in time is retained for backup purposes. All changes or transactions that occur during the interval between that copy and the current time are also retained. In the event of the need to reconstruct the current file, all subsequent changes are applied to the backup copy. Obviously, if there are few or no changes to be applied, then the backup file has greater value for immediate emergency use.

As in the case of hardware, there is a definite need for both on-site and off-site backup of information and software. As a rule, security is improved and accessibility is decreased as the backup storage facility becomes more remote. On-site backup copies are readily accessible and afford protection against most nondisaster downtime, but may be inadequate for disaster situations. Off-site storage locations may be chosen to optimize either convenience or protection. A nearby off-site location would be convenient for access but might be vulnerable to the same environmental hazards as the computer facility. A very remote storage location frustrates the need for access but it will improve protection against a common environmental disaster. It is not unusual for larger organizations to establish a tiered strategy, employing several levels of backup to achieve a balance of safety and convenience.

The following is a hypothetical arrangement of storage facilities to achieve tiered backup:

1. *On-site local backup*. A fire-resistent safe located in a tape library adjacent to the computer room. Used to house the most recently created backup files until replaced by newer generation.

2. *Off-site local backup*. A fire-resistant vault located in the basement of another building within a half-mile radius of the computer site. Used to store backup files for up to one week in duration. Accessed daily for rotation.

3. *Off-site remote backup*. A fire-resistant vault located at least five miles from the computer site. Used to retain remaining backup files in active use for more than one week. Accessed weekly.

4. *Archival storage*. An underground, fire-resistant and earthquake-resistant storage facility located at least 50 miles away from the computer site. Used to house permanent records to be retained for several years, including microfilm, printed reports, and selected backup files such as year-end data.

When several levels of backup are employed using different facilities, it is obvious that the required logistics become complex. Backup files must be moved on a regular basis from accessible to more remote storage based upon the updating cycles of the files. The constant juggling of files between facilities requires well thought out procedures in order to minimize confusion. Good procedures and good practices are needed for file

rotation to foster accuracy and prevent misfilings. Written, up-to-date file library records must be maintained indicating the status and location of each backup file. (The status records should also be periodically backed up at the remote off-site storage area.) There is also a continuous need to ensure security, both information security and physical security for backup files across any and all of the storage facilities.

When actual reconstruction of files is required, it is advisable to employ a special set of procedures in order to enforce protection of data and prevent operational oversight. As a rule, original backup files should be recopied to create extra backup copies prior to using the originals in any updating processes. During special reconstruction it is also advisable to suspend the release of other, older backup file generations that may be scheduled for recycling until the reconstruction has been successfully completed and checked out. Management must be alert to the need for close supervision to assure that system controls are not bypassed, inadvertently or otherwise.

Reconstruction of files needs to be accomplished in an atmosphere of calm, efficiency, and thoroughness. Management should recognize the need for order, despite the difficulties of the particular situation, and assist in insulating the recovery team from unnecessary interruptions and undue pressure.

Advanced technical planning, based upon systematic reviews of each computer application, can provide the basis for more effective reconstruction techniques. If special computer programs are needed to accomplish reconstruction, such programs must be thoroughly tested, and often retested, to assure currency. Even so-called automatic restart and recovery routines that are provided as operating system utilities must be tested under realistic conditions. If necessary, testing should include cycling through successive generations of files to ensure compatibility with "normally" updated files. Sometimes, specialized computer programs for contingency support may be useful to handle various problems; however, all such programs must be created and tested well in advance of the actual need. Examples of such specialized programs include:

- Detection of file and record inconsistencies
- Full and partial file reorganization

- Resequencing of records
- Reestablishment of indexes
- Correcting record elements (field values)
- Elimination of "garbage" records

The establishment of well thought out schedules for backup files is an important part of any effective backup strategy. Some of the considerations relating to backup schedules include the following:

- Frequency of backup cycle and depth of retention generations must be determined for each data file.
- Backup strategy must anticipate failure at any step of the processing cycle.
- Master files should be retained at convenient intervals, such as the end of an updating.
- Transaction files should be preserved to coincide with master files, so that a prior generation of a master file can be brought completely up to date to recreate a current master file.
- Real-time files require special backup techniques, such as duplicate logging of transactions, use of before images and/or after images of master records, time stamping of transactions, communication simulation, etc.
- Data Base Management Systems (DBMS) require specialized backup, usually provided as an integral feature of the DBMS.
- File descriptions need to be maintained over time to coincide with each version of a file that is retained; for DBMS systems this may entail keeping separate versions of data dictionaries.

Backup for system software requires much of the same attention that applies to data files; however, some important distinctions should be noted. Since software "files" are seldom updated regularly or with great frequency, the most convenient form of primary backup is a copy of the current software file rather than the previous generation of a software file. Software backup versions should be maintained at both the main computing facility and at a secure off-site storage location, because they must be accessible for short-term disruptions and for disasters. There may be a need to configure and test special ver-

sions of software for use at an alternate site. It may be necessary to secure the license to use certain vendor software at an alternate site, and this should be arranged in advance of the need. Backup for software must include both object code and source code software libraries, and must include provision for maintaining program patches on a current basis at all backup locations.

Procedures and Documentation

Written instructions are essential for many business activities and, most certainly, for information processing. All too often the written instruction is taken for granted or ignored, until something unusual occurs. The prevailing rule appears to be "When all else fails, read the instructions."

Procedures and documentation are an important extension of hardware and software and are equally vital to ensure the continuity of business activities. Operating procedures may consist of application run books, job stream control instructions, operating system manuals, and special procedures. Operating procedures should be treated as crucial data files. Copies should be maintained at off-site locations for emergency use in the event of disaster or any destruction of the original copy. As in the case of data files, it is important that the off-site copies be kept up to date to ensure their usefulness when needed.

Systems and program documentation also require attention, and must be protected through the use of off-site backup. Such documentation may be in the form of both machine-readable data files and hard copy. Systems and program flow charts, program source code listings, program logic descriptions, error conditions, and other descriptions are important elements of documentation that need to be preserved. Without such documentation the maintenance and revision of software would be difficult, and often impossible. It is, of course, essential that copies of such information be kept up to date on a regular basis. Backup documentation can serve a dual purpose. In addition to serving as backup for a disaster it can be a useful archive to protect against the inadvertent loss of original documentation, a quite likely occurrence in the life of many systems.

Special procedures must also be accorded adequate attention and protection. Special procedures refer to any procedures or instructions that are out of the ordinary. Several variations of special procedures should be considered:

1. *Exception processing.* Procedures to accommodate unusual conditions, such as rejects and inconsistencies identified by the application software. In the life cycle of many systems such exception processing is developed on an ad hoc basis as the need arises. All too often these procedures are documented poorly or not at all, when in fact they may be of serious consequence.

2. *Variations in processing.* System variations, run sequence changes, and special shortcuts in processing also represent a body of knowledge built over time to handle practical situations that arise in the operational life of a system. As in the case of exception processing, variations in processing are usually not well documented.

3. *Emergency processing.* Special procedures for the recovery of files, restart of processing after failures, and other procedural responses to emergencies are critical to successful contingency planning.

All of these special procedures should be documented and kept up to date as a normal activity of the data processing function. Contingency planning should provide for both regular documentation and "special documentation" to be treated as valuable records, to be kept current, and to be preserved in the form of off-site copies. It is important to audit the adequacy of all documentation regularly, and to audit compliance with off-site backup policies.

The documentation of disaster plans also warrants particular attention, for this, too, represents a "special procedure." It must be regarded as a key set of plans that needs to be kept up to date and to be readily accessible in an emergency. Off-site copies are essential. In large organizations, where numerous copies may exist, it is important to control the location of the various copies and to ensure that all are kept current. Comprehensive, detailed disaster plans may require special resources or automation to assist in their maintenance. The use of word processing systems and data base management systems can simplify the requirements of keeping a disaster plan up to date. Most importantly, a recovery team under the direction of a senior manager

must be ready and equipped to deal with any contingency.

Backup for Related Activities

Concern about backing up the data processing function must extend beyond the central data processing activities to the sources and recipients of information. Evaluations of risk and contingency plans should embrace the full information spectrum, and not merely the processing of machine-readable information by a central processing system. The information cycle begins with an external source or stimulus that is transformed at some point to computer input. An important end product of most information systems is humanly readable output, or hard copy, that is distributed in order to assist in furthering the business activities of the organization.

Protective procedures are often required for the source documents themselves as well as for the mechanisms used to deliver and transform source information into machine-readable input. As a rule, if source documents are critical and there is exposure to loss or destruction, then provision should be made to copy the source documents so that the basic information may be reconstructed in an emergency. Backup of source documents may be in the form of duplicate copies, photocopies, microfilm, microfiche, or other media.

Key entry equipment, particularly when centralized, can be critical to the capability to transform source information into machine-readable format. A central data entry facility can be wiped out by fire or some other disaster, and the effect upon the organization's ability to continue to do business can be as serious as a disaster affecting the central computer facility. In order to protect against this threat, contingency plans should provide for the use of alternative facilities for key entry. It is generally easier to back up standardized batch type key entry operations than specialized or on-line key entry operations. It is essential, especially where unique equipment or specialized procedures are employed, to consider the consequences of losing the data entry capability.

Delivery of information from the source to the data entry preparation unit, from the data entry facility to the data processing facility, and from data processing to the end user also warrants attention in contingency planning. It is important to recognize in advance that the use of an alternative data processing facility may disrupt normal delivery activities and thereby necessitate alternative procedures for the receipt and delivery of information.

Alternatives for Backup Planning

The following is a review of various alternatives that may be employed for disaster backup of computer hardware and physical facilities.

Vendor or Third Party Resupply of Hardware

In an emergency the hardware vendor is usually the best source for replacement of equipment; however, this will often involve a waiting period that is not acceptable for critical operations. Most vendors will exert themselves to meet an emergency, but it is unlikely that any vendor will guarantee specific reaction to a crisis. At best, this particular source of hardware replacement may be activated for longer term restoration needs following a disaster but should not be depended upon for short-term operational needs.

Another source of equipment replacement is the used hardware market. Dealers and brokers in used hardware can often supply critical components or entire systems on relatively short notice, often at a savings in cost. Effective utilization of this source suggests the cultivation of dealer relationships well in advance of actual emergencies.

On-the-shelf Hardware

The ideal situation, in which replacement of equipment can occur quickly, is one where components are readily available from inventory. Obviously, if the equipment needed to resupply an installation is available from suppliers on short notice and with minimum need for special arrangements, then vulnerability is reduced. This requires an underlying system strategy that:

- Avoids the use of unusual and hard-to-get equipment
- Regularly updates equipment in order to keep current
- Maintains software compatibility to permit operation on newer equipment

Mutual Aid Agreements

Reciprocal agreements between two or more organizations with similar equipment or applications, represents another method for backup protection. Under the typical agreement, participants promise to provide time to each other when an emergency arises.

Mutual aid agreements are, at best, a secondary option for backup and disaster protection. The agreements are usually not enforceable. Differences in equipment configurations often necessitate program changes in order to operate effectively. Changes in workloads or equipment configurations can undermine the usefulness of such agreements.

Despite the inherent shortcomings, many organizations rely upon mutual aid agreements because of their low cost and, in some cases, because it is the only option available. Non-IBM users often employ mutual aid agreements because they have fewer commercially available hot site options.

In order to be effective the mutual aid agreement should satisfy several critical questions:

- How much time will be available at the host computer site?
- What facilities and equipment will be available?
- Will staff assistance be provided?
- How quickly can access be gained to the host recovery facility?
- How long can the emergency operation continue?
- How frequently can the system be tested for compatibility?
- Are the participants willing to maintain a high degree of compatibility?

In-House Dual Sites

Hot site alternatives, and variations thereof, represent the most reliable form of backup but also entail the highest cost. A dedicated, self-developed hot site can back up critical applications that cannot afford even one day of downtime.

Self-developed in-house sites can range from standby hot sites to the mutual aid variety. It is usually assumed that there are fewer problems in coordinating compatibility and availability in the case of in-house backup sites; however, this fact should not be taken for granted. Larger organizations, in particular, especially where departmental or divisional data centers are separately managed, may encounter problems similar to those of mutual aid agreements between unrelated companies. Several essential principles are necessary to ensure the effectiveness of in-house sites to serve as backup in time of need:

1. Coordination of hardware/software strategy. A reasonable degree of compatibility must exist to serve as a basis for backup.

2. Resource availability must be assured. The workloads of the sites must not be allowed to grow to the point where availability for emergency backup use would be impaired.

3. Regular testing is necessary. Even though in-house sites are under common ownership, and even if the sites are under the same management, testing of the backup operations is necessary.

Third Party Hot Sites

Fully operational, dedicated to disaster recovery or emergency operational needs, with a guaranteed configuration of equipment and software, third party hot sites are usually available to subscribers with notice of 24 hours or less. Hardware typically includes a central processor, front end processors, disk drives, tape drives, printers, and communication equipment.

Costs for the use of a commercial hot site may be high but are often justifiable for critical applications. Costs include a basic subscription cost, usually a monthly fee, plus activation costs that may apply when the site is used for an actual emergency, plus hourly or daily use charges. Pricing structures vary between vendors. Some hot site suppliers impose a high activation fee in order to discourage the frivolous use of the facility. Other vendors have no activation fee and encourage the use of the facility for nondisaster purposes such as overload processing.

Apart from subscription fees, the additional costs incurred in the actual use of a hot site following a disaster may be offset by proper insurance coverage.

The hot site is usually intended for emergency operations for a limited time period, but not for long-term extended use, because such utilization would impair the protection of other subscribers. The hot site should be viewed as a means of accomplishing the continuation of es-

sential operations for a period of up to several weeks following a disaster or major emergency. Further plans are still necessary to provide for subsequent operation.

Third Party Cold Sites and Warm Sites

Longer term operational needs for backup can be addressed by subscribing to a cold site service. The cold site provides all of the environmental support needed for a computer facility: power, climate control, raised flooring, telephone wiring, access security, etc. This shell facility lacks only the computer and peripheral equipment.

The cold site does not serve immediate back-up needs. It is intended to provide for longer term backup requirements, after computer equipment is physically installed.

A variation on the cold site is the partially configured site described earlier. The warm site is a basic facility equipped with some peripheral equipment, and sometimes with a small central processing unit. With installation of additional components the warm site can be made ready for operation within a matter of days. If the warm site contains a small CPU, some more immediate emergency processing is also feasible.

Alternative Ownership for Hot and Cold Sites

Self-ownership and cooperative ownership are the other alternatives for either hot sites or cold sites. If it can be economically justified, the self-developed and self-owned hot site provides the best assurance for backup protection. Cooperatively owned backup sites exist in several areas of the country and are useful in providing backup protection at reasonable costs, usually lower than third party vendors.

Mobile Backup Sites

At least two vendors of backup processing facilities offer computer-ready trailers that can be set up in a subscriber's parking lot or other site following a disaster. Supplementary trailers can serve as emergency office space.

This arrangement provides certain advantages:

• It can serve to back up multiple sites from a single source, which has a special appeal for decentralized organizations.

- It can avoid or minimize travel to recover a computer operation. This is particularly desirable following a natural disaster when employees may be reluctant to travel and leave injured relatives or damaged property.

Management Responsibility

Management has the final responsibility for ensuring that essential functions of the enterprise can continue even after a disaster or catastrophe. Contingency plans must be endorsed by management and must be regulated and monitored by management.

Strategies

Two important strategies that are needed as a basis for contingency plans are a system strategy and a backup strategy. The system strategy motivates policies for the MIS function and can greatly affect contingency planning. An ideal strategy would:

1. Avoid the use of unique hardware or software
2. Utilize mainstream technology when possible
3. Maintain currency and compatibility for equipment and software

Backup strategy must be predicated upon three essential points:

1. Identification of critical functions
2. Identification of short-term contingency needs
3. Identification of long-term requirements

Once requirements have been properly identified, a strategy can be formulated based upon the tradeoffs of cost versus protection. There is no single strategy that is suitable for every organization. Each organization must select a strategy that is appropriate for its own needs. Costs and protection should be carefully balanced.

Sharing of backup facilities, either through a cooperative plan or a commercial service, is a primary means of containing the cost of a backup facility. Some special concerns relating to shared backup sites are:

- Is access strictly on a first-come first-served basis or is there provision for sharing the facility in event of concurrent disasters?

- It is important to keep informed about the subscriber base for a shared facility. Too many subscribers reduces the chance of protection for all. Some sites use a cutoff of 20 to 30 subscribers for a single site, whereas others may allow several hundred. Larger services sometimes offer multiple site coverage to a large body of subscribers, which statistically reduces vulnerability.

- Too few subscribers for a commercial shared facility may be a sign of a failing business. If the economics of the venture are undermined so is the protection.

- A geographic concentration of subscribers is unhealthy because the risk of concurrent need for disaster backup is increased.

Monitoring and Testing Results

Testing of backup facilities should be scheduled from one to four times per year. In addition to scheduled tests it is useful to have surprise tests conducted by an objective third party. Some organizations allow auditors or consultants to stage surprise tests without the prior knowledge of data processing management. Testing should permit key members of the recovery team to go through operational procedures to be employed in the emergency. This provides an important basis of familiarity with the backup site as well as training in the emergency operation.

Two types of tests should be considered. The regularly scheduled tests should cover the basic use of the backup facility and procedures to be employed. Periodically, and less frequently, a full-scale disaster simulation may be staged in order to test thoroughly all aspects of the disaster plan under close to actual emergency conditions.

Reviewing and Updating Plans

Plans and strategies for disaster backup should be reviewed and updated on a scheduled basis to reflect continuing recognition of changing requirements. Backup is a form of insurance, and for crucial data processing functions it is important protection that can only be effective if it is available when needed. A strategy that is appropriate at one point in time may not be adequate as the needs of the organization change. New applications may materialize. Changes in business strategy may alter the significance of critical applications; a previously noncritical function may suddenly be very important to the health of the enterprise.

Periodically management should address the critical issues relating to backup:

1. What are the current and future needs of the organization for backup and disaster protection?
2. Are these needs likely to be served by the selected strategies?
3. Is there reasonable assurance of backup effectiveness if needed?
4. How can effectiveness be improved?

In the final analysis, contingency planning is a management responsibility. It cannot be ignored or transferred to others. Many details may be delegated, and it is important to involve all members of management and staff in the process; however, overall effectiveness depends upon the concern and involvement of senior management.

Checklist for Contingency Planning

Contingency Planning Goals

	Yes	No
Have the overall goals of contingency planning been defined in terms of		
• a business concern as well as a data processing need?	☐	☐
• the consequences of outages even more than the possibility of occurrence?	☐	☐
Is contingency planning supported by a formal risk management program?	☐	☐
Is there an ongoing preventive action plan for reducing threats and vulnerabilities?	☐	☐
Is there an up-to-date action plan for dealing with events during a disaster?	☐	☐
Is there a statement of priorities for data processing applications and functions?	☐	☐
Has responsibility been established for implementing and maintaining contingency plans?	☐	☐

Considerations of Risks and Responsibilities

	Yes	No
Have all primary consequences of loss of service been considered?	☐	☐

- Total business collapse
- Partial business collapse
- Loss of personnel
- Loss of capital assets
- Loss of revenue
- Loss of customers
- Loss of shareholders
- Loss of information
- Risk of prosecution

	Yes	No
Is there an up-to-date awareness by management of legal and regulatory requirements?	☐	☐

- IRS 64-12 makes senior management *personally* responsible for record retention
- Foreign Corrupt Practices Act permits civil and criminal prosecution for violations
- Comptroller of the Currency requires financial institutions to adopt policy to reduce impact of data processing related losses
- Potential for lawsuits by shareholders and employees for gross negligence in the absence of a plan
- Insurance company requirements in order to maintain coverage.

	Yes	No
Has adequate consideration been given to equipment failures?	☐	☐

- Central Processing Unit failures
- Data storage device failures
- Communication device failures
- Other peripheral device failures
- Power supply failures
- Environmental device failures

	Yes	No
Has adequate consideration been given to software failures?	☐	☐

- Is software adequately and currently maintained?
- Is software constructed with built-in survivability?

	Yes	No
Have risks from accidental and man-made threats been adequately considered?	☐	☐

- Fire
- Power outage
- Nuclear disaster
- Environmental disaster
- Human errors and omissions

Yes No

- Disgruntled employees
- Strikes
- Sabotage
- Terrorism

Have risks from natural events been ☐ ☐
adequately considered?
- Earthquake
- Flood
- Storm, hurricane, blizzard
- Tornado
- Volcanic erruption
- Drought

Implementation of a Contingency Plan

Have preventive controls been in- ☐ ☐
stalled?
- Fire detection
- Smoke and water detection
- Environmental controls
- Access controls
- Media storage separation
- Redundandant components
- Audit controls

Have critical applications been iden- ☐ ☐
tified and classified using appropriate
criteria?
- Effect upon organization's survival
- Effect upon organization's cash flow
- User's ability to carry out functions
- Legal requirements
- Competitive requirements
- Control over other assets

Is there a vital records management ☐ ☐
program in place?
- Data files
- Documentation
- Application software
- Systems software
- Rotation of backup files

Have appropriate alternative com- ☐ ☐
puting strategies been adopted? Has

Yes No

consideration been given to the var-
ious options for alternative process-
ing?
- Service bureaus
- Time brokers
- Hot-site contingency facility
- Cold-site contingency facility
- Warm site contingency facility
- Communications alternatives
- Short-term contingency operations
- Long-term contingency operations

Is a phased disaster plan in place? ☐ ☐
- Emergency phase
      Protection of personnel
      Minimization of damage to equipment
      and media
- Backup phase
      Activation of alternative processing
      Crisis management
- Restoration phase to resume permanent
  processing at new or rebuilt facility

Is there adequate testing of the plan? ☐ ☐
- Can all critical applications be recovered and
  resumed?
- Do all personnel understand their roles and
  responsibilities?
- Has the plan been shaken down and revised
  to ensure effectiveness when needed?
- Is there a realistic estimate of recovery time?
- Is the plan complete and comprehensive?

Is the plan adequately maintained? ☐ ☐
- Does the contingency plan meet current pro-
  cedural requirements?
- Are the latest business changes and process-
  ing changes reflected in the contingency
  plan?
- Are personnel adequately trained and kept
  informed on plan changes?
- Is the plan documentation kept up-to-date?
  Is the plan documentation automated?

CHAPTER 7

Computer Risks and Insurance

by Guy R. Migliaccio & Dean P. Felton

Introduction

Complete assessment of the risks to any data processing operation must be an integral part of data processing management. Only then can guidelines for adequate protection be formulated. The most effective means of protection is a plan for preventing or at least minimizing potential threats. However, a carefully considered computer insurance program can help reduce the financial impact on the organization if data processing service is disrupted. The right computer insurance program can also mitigate the financial consequences of crime, fraud, inadvertent error, malpractice, and other damages. This chapter addresses the role of data processing insurance in managing computer risks.

Problems Addressed

Choosing a computer system best suited to an organization's needs is recognized as requiring a large investment of time and money; but often little thought is given to the risks inherent in critical data processing operations. These risks make an organization vulnerable to serious losses that could jeopardize its viability.

Data processing risks are especially significant for several reasons:

- Data processing equipment is expensive and can take time to replace.
- High values are often concentrated in one room or area. Therefore, even relatively minor incidents affecting a small area can be serious.
- Information can also be concentrated. In some organizations all accounting records, inventory records, and production schedules may be on magnetic media stored in a single area.
- Vulnerability is high. Computer equipment, magnetic media, and the processing itself are highly sensitive to heat, smoke, flood, and a host of environmental dangers.
- Dependency on data processing is high. It is very difficult for an organization to survive an extended interruption in processing once it has come to depend on its automated capabilities. Rebuilding automated capability involves tremendous effort.
- A growing and potentially major errors and omissions exposure is computer programming and data processing malpractice.
- The impact of crime and fraud can run into millions of dollars.

The potential losses make computer insurance a subject of major importance for data processing managers.

Insurance Protection

Insurance, though not a substitute for loss prevention and disaster recovery planning, should be an integral part of risk planning. However detailed or comprehensive the planning, there are always risks and eventualities that cannot sensibly or economically be borne by an organization with its own resources. In such cases insurance provides a valuable alternative. This chapter describes the types of protection available to data processing users and discusses how to design a program that is tailored to the organization's needs.

Too strong a fear of the risks and eventualities arising from obscure circumstances could

97

lead to overinsuring the organization against loss. Though preferable to being underinsured, over-insurance is costly and unnecessary. The data processing manager should assess the organization's risks, protect itself where feasible, and insure externally those risks that the organization cannot afford to carry itself.

The 1965 and 1977 New York City blackouts exemplify the potential risks facing a data processing facility. In 1977, loss of power, looting, vandalism, and bomb scares triggered the evacuation of many buildings creating havoc in the world's heaviest data processing concentration.

The headquarters of one large supermarket chain and 16 of its stores were wrecked by looters. An office computer was destroyed as well as disks containing company sales, inventory, and other financial data for the May to July quarter; disk packs scattered on the floor were later ruined by fire and water; and computer printouts were rendered useless. The computer was not difficult to replace, but it took months to reconstruct the records. The situation could have been worse—fortunately, the printouts and disks of previous records were stored away from headquarters. Although uncommon, such events do occur.

Some new risks have also materialized. For example, minicomputers and microcomputers present the risk of theft. Many manufacturers now offer computer portability, a feature that unfortunately makes theft easier and increasingly more common. "Computernapping"—holding computer records and programs for ransom—is another new threat. An employee of a company that performed data processing for medical labs demanded a ransom of $100,000, after stealing all the records and programs, and hid in the San Bernardino Mountains in California. He was captured, but the computer material was impounded by the sheriff for evidence. This delay threatened to close down the firm.

Many risk factors can disrupt data processing operations, with varying consequences. If the disruption is accompanied by destruction of vital information or records, repercussions may continue for months. Lengthy downtime and subsequent erosion of goodwill among clients and customers can be expected. In some cases, disruption can result in loss of business or business failure.

Insurance has but one function in protecting an extremely vulnerable, yet critical, operation against these dangers: it provides funds to reduce the financial impact of the interruption. It does not prevent disasters and other losses from occurring; nor does it provide ready-made solutions. To be effective, insurance must work in conjunction with data processing standards and prevention procedures (which attempt to avoid losses and interruptions) and recovery measures (which attempt to minimize the effect of interruptions).

Data processing standards and procedures cover effective design and engineering of the computer center, fire protection, maintenance, training, security, and safety. All these can affect operational efficiency and the frequency and severity of loss.

Recovery measures, on the other hand, minimize the impact following a loss. These include emergency procedures, evacuation plans, procedures for resumption of operations, alternate power sources, alternate processing arrangements, salvage operations, and disposal—all factors in the quick and efficient resumption of data processing operations.

If an organization's loss record is good and in-house prevention procedures and a recovery plan have been implemented, insurance will be more readily available and less costly.

Cost is only one factor when purchasing data processing insurance; the terms of the insurance contracts are perhaps more important. A low-priced insurance policy with numerous exclusions, such as flood and earthquake, is of little value. Cost must be balanced against the policy conditions. Wording of the policy is all-important.

Equipment

Computers can be purchased, rented, or leased. There may be an intervening third party such as a computer broker, and other parties may be responsible for transportation, delivery, or installation. A computer may even be on the premises of one user but owned and operated by another organization. In each situation, the data processing manager must be aware of the extent of responsibilities of each party and of the exact moment when these responsibilities take effect.

If equipment is purchased, risk usually passes in contract when the equipment is placed on the user's premises. The key date in this transaction is customarily the installation date, because the manufacturer's insurance usually terminates then and responsibility is wholly transferred.

Two points should be clarified with the manufacturer before the contract is signed:

- The purchaser's responsibility during the delivery and installation of the machine. The manufacturer usually employs a third party for delivery and installation, and the purchaser is asked to provide staff and equipment to assist during the installation. The extent of everyone's liability should be carefully checked.
- The purchaser's liability during acceptance testing. The machine could be damaged (e.g., by negligence) while undergoing acceptance tests. The purchaser should check to see if any claims could possibly be made against the organization during this period.

A clear understanding must be established with the manufacturer to ensure that insurance coverage is continuous.

Once a machine is in the user's possession, that user has certain responsibilities over and above any contract liability; neglect of those responsibilities might result in common law liability. A machine lacking complete indemnity from the manufacturer should be fully insured by the purchaser as soon as it enters his premises. The possibility of an insurance overlap during a limited period is a small price to pay for complete safety.

Leasing

Liability must be clear in leasing agreements. Organizations sometimes incorrectly assume that the manufacturer or leasing firm is responsible for loss or damage. This may be true, but the insurance of the manufacturer or lessor does not automatically free the user from liability. The manufacturer or lessor could file a subrogation claim—the rights of a company to recover damages from a negligent third party. A waiver of subrogation is free if inserted into the contract. This insertion must be made in writing prior to the loss. The lease will show that equipment responsibility falls into one of the following categories:

- The user is relieved of all (or almost all) responsibility for the equipment.
- The user is relieved of responsibility for the equipment if damage is *not* due to user negligence.
- The user is relieved of responsibility for the equipment if damage is caused by any of several named perils. The user is responsible for damage *from any other* cause.
- The user is totally responsible for the equipment.

Tailor-Made Coverage

The owner's coverage may only address itself to certain perils. Equipment is only one part of a data processing operation. Be aware that negligence on the user's part may cause certain losses. Negligence has a very broad application in some jurisdictions.

What Risks Should Be Covered

Users should take advantage of the opportunity to design tailor-made coverage. Standard forms of insurance for data processing really do not exist. For example, the standard fire insurance policy will not suffice, because limitations and exclusions are virtually endless. Several insurance companies offer data processing policies that insure against all risks of direct physical loss or damage to data processing equipment.

These all-risk policies, however, exclude losses resulting from:

- Errors in machine programming
- Latent defects and wear and tear
- Gradual deterioration
- War and nuclear destruction
- Dishonest and criminal acts by employees

The means to protect against some of these exclusions is through data processing standards and procedures: better training resulting in fewer errors, effective maintenance anticipating breakdowns, and careful employee selection.

Valuations

After basic coverage is established, the amount of insurance to carry must be considered. Valuations must then enter into the picture. Data processing policies offer a choice; *replacement cost new*—the cost to replace new at current prices without a deduction for depreciation—or *actual cash value*—which is the new replacement cost at current prices less a deduction for physical depreciation.

If obsolescence is a problem, the policy should cover losses on a current replacement basis. This requires frequent upgrading of the amount of insurance. If the equipment used is no longer manufactured or available, the policy should state that the amount of insurance recovery will equal the equipment value specified in the policy. This will establish the amount of claim, because new retail replacement prices are not available.

All remote locations should be covered, as well as equipment in transit. Policies requiring listings of serial numbers should be avoided. Otherwise, a claim could be denied if a piece of equipment has since been replaced and the new serial numbers do not match those in the policy.

Media

The most important protection measures for magnetic media is keeping duplicate media in a secure, separate location. Only those tapes needed for current operations should be kept in the processing room.

Data processing management should set standards for media backup and ensure that they are followed. Even if operators appreciate the need for stringent security measures, the pressures of daily operations can lead to neglect of backup procedures. Operations must therefore be audited frequently.

In general, policies covering data processing equipment do not insure media unless specified. Contents of insurance policies cover only the blank value of the media and simple transcription expenses.

The media insurance required is a function of *duplication, storage,* and *update frequency.* If media are duplicated and stored in separate locations, the possible destruction of the original media no longer threatens the organization. In fact, this is a possible area for self-insurance, either in the form of outright assumption of risk or a hefty deductible.

Determining media value is the most difficult aspect of any data processing insurance survey. A realistic value will avoid both over- and underinsurance. In a nutshell, the coverage should pay for the blank value of the media and the costs of reconstruction.

Media loss presents potentially catastrophic expense, particularly if it involves accounts receivable data. Accounts receivable insurance premiums, however, are relatively low and policy conditions fairly liberal. These policies are of the all-risk type and will reimburse the user for losses resulting from:

- Inability to collect
- Extra costs of collection
- Expenses to reestablish records
- Interest charges on any loan to offset impaired collections

Again, duplication plays a key role in minimizing losses. The value of a comprehensive disaster recovery plan cannot be overemphasized.

Business Interruption and Extra-Expense Insurance

Nowhere is the need for disaster recovery capability more evident than in the area of business interruption and extra-expense insurance. One source estimates that only one in ten small firms can survive a major data processing loss. This is true even if the firm is covered by business interruption insurance. It is further estimated that the average company can survive 10 to 11 days without its computer; after that, it loses 91 percent of its business activities.* The loss of data processing facilities can also harm large corporations; it is often difficult to predict whether a downtime of hours, days, or weeks would be critical to the corporations' financial well-being.

Business Interruption Insurance

Business interruption insurance covers the loss of net profits caused by computer or media damage. Income lost after damage to the premises should also be included in the coverage. For example, if data processing facilities are on the

---

* Simon, E. "Computer Failure Could Pull the Plug on Many Firms," *Business Insurance*, Vol. 14 (August 11, 1980).

sixth floor and the first five floors are burned out, operations will be interrupted even though the data processing facility is unaffected. The amount of business interruption insurance needed depends largely on the organization's recovery measures. The faster normal operations can be resumed after a disaster, the less insurance is required.

Extra-Expense Insurance

Extra-expense insurance covers the costs of continuing operations while normal processing is being restored. Like business interruption insurance, it is directly related to the organization's recovery measures. Replacement of the simplest equipment can take as long as 12 weeks. If outside data processing services are purchased in the interim, the cost can be twice that of normal processing. If normal costs are, for example, $600 per hour, and temporary costs are $1,200 per hour, extra expense for the 12 weeks needed to replace the equipment and (assuming 40 hours processing time per week) will total $288,000.

Extra-expense insurance should be part of the policy that covers equipment, media, and business interruption. The amount of extra-expense insurance needed is based on the availability and cost of backup facilities and operations. Some insurance companies offer such policies for organizations with data processing installations valued at less than $500,000. Data/media coverage of up to $5,000 is provided without a separate premium charge.

Errors and Omissions Insurance

Data processing professionals' errors and omissions policies provide legal liability protection in the event that the professional commits an act, error, or omission that results in financial loss to a client. For many years this type of coverage had been available only for service bureaus, but several insurance companies now offer similar protection for systems analysts, software designers, programmers, and consultants.

Most claims alleging errors or omissions are the result of poor communication between the software vendor and the customer. The biggest problem is a misunderstanding of what the other person will provide. Usually there is not a clear-cut error, but rather the program does not do what the customer expected. Communications between the vendor and the buyer must be specific, with as many details as possible about what the buyer wants and what he will get. The contract should be very specific and to the extent possible, everything written down.

Historically, insurers have been reluctant to cover computer consultants, claiming they preferred not to insure a nonregulated professional group. Even those companies that insured service bureaus for years were unwilling to insure professionals involved in program design, program development, or consulting. Companies now providing independent consultant insurance include Shand Morahan & Co., Lloyd's of London, St. Paul Fire and Marine, American International Group, and Fireman's Fund.

Deductibles for errors and omissions coverage generally range from $1,000 to $10,000 but can climb to hundreds of thousands of dollars. Protection limits vary from $100,000 to $25 million. Underwriters generally want to know the type of data being processed, the type of software being manufactured, the kinds of services being performed, the level of staff experience, the type of equipment used, the age of the company, and the rate of employee attrition.

Although all software professionals should probably buy errors and omissions insurance, contract provisions that limit liability to clients can reduce losses and help keep insurance costs down.

Crime and Fraud

In this section we describe the impact of computer crime and fraud on individuals and on business. We discuss the nature of an insurable risk as it relates to automation and comment on available crime insurance. Lastly, we outline procedures that can reduce or eliminate computer crime and fraud both at home and in the workplace.

Impact of Crime and Fraud on Users of Computers

There has been much written about the human and worldly elements surrounding the individuals who commit crimes and their motivation.

Regardless of the reasons for thefts, crimes, or fraud, one common fact remains: crimes and frauds are committed by people, against people, for the benefit of the criminal. This benefit can be for financial gain or for ego boosting only. Either way, such behavior has a detrimental effect on the private and public community alike. It is useful to examine ways in which individuals and businesses use computers and see how computer crime and fraud affect them.

Individual Consumer   Today, we are computer dependent. There is an integration between the home and business in this institutional environment in which we live that we cannot escape. Computer systems support our banks, hospitals, stores, utilities, investments, schools, military, churches, and transportation. Accordingly, the individual must be satisfied that the integrity of the computer-based systems is unfaltering, dependable, and accurate.

A second concern of the individual is that information in the systems be used only for legitimate purposes and that such personal information as one's income, debt, investments, donations, etc., not be accessible to others than those with a "need to know."

Small Business   Today's entrepreneur can start with a small operation personally counting the widgets, paying the bills, ringing up the cash register, and keeping the books, always aware of whether or not income is sufficient to cover expenses. As the business grows, the computer can extend the range and effectiveness of its user.

Unfortunately, as the business becomes increasingly dependent on the computer, the opportunity for computer crime and fraud increases as well. A business owner has a greater likelihood of "getting out of touch" with the intimate details of day-to-day operations when computers are utilized. Inventories may be manipulated, sales overstated, and payrolls inflated, until the small business is financially undermined.

Large Commercial Business   Large businesses use computers for the same functions as small businesses, but the technology is generally more advanced. With network-based on-line computers and with multiple interfaces using remote access techniques while controlling large monetary and property values, with complex programming, there exists a high potential for fraud and inadvertent error.

If a large firm has sizable resources, a major fraud loss may not mean its demise. However, earnings can be substantially reduced whenever the company's assets are compromised through computer fraud or error.

Financial Organizations   Traditionally, financial organizations are defined as banks, savings and loans, stockbrokers, insurance companies, mutual funds, and pension plans—organizations that maintain inventories of money and securities mainly as impulses in computer memories. Criminals will attempt to penetrate those systems that are most accessible and in which the possibility of detection is minimal. With values that exist in today's financial organizations' computer systems, the temptation to "attack" them is enormous. Control and security become extremely important.

Exposure to Crime and Fraud

For both financial organizations and commercial businesses, losses from computer fraud have high potential. Some exposures are:

*   The change of critical information on a primary source or input document
*   The alteration of firmware or hardware allowing a bypass of security or control systems
*   Fraudulent entry into or fraudulent manipulation or modification of applications or systems programs
*   The theft of disks or tapes containing critical data
*   The holding of stolen tapes and disks for ransom
*   The interception of data communications be it land line, microwave, via satellite, etc.
*   The use of computer programs to fraudulently void or bypass built-in electronic controls or reconciling systems
*   The use of "tag on" computer instructions on legitimate programs that allow unauthorized modification to instructions of data within an application
*   The complete destruction of a data base by a "logic bomb"
*   Fraudulent use of utility programs to avoid detection of access under normal control systems

- Stealing of microcomputer processor and related disks or diskettes
- Utilization of programming to access CPU data, which circumvents data security and/or data audit
- Wire tappings, the interception of information from data transmissions
- The theft of asset sensitive output data whether hard copy or in machine-readable form

Traditional Insurance

One risk management alternative against computer crime is insurance.

Insurance is a risk transfer method to reduce the effects of an event, called a loss, on the insured. There are eight basic characteristics of an insurable event.

1. The loss must be sufficiently large so as to require that it be averaged over either a large group or over an extended period of time.
2. The circumstances of loss should not affect a significant portion of the total insured population. The event that causes the loss, at any point in time, should apply to only a small population within the large group.
3. The event causing loss must have a relatively small chance of occurrence.
4. The event of loss should have the likelihood of equally occurring on any member of the group or class making up the population.
5. The event causing the loss should be unexpected and unpredictable in time.
6. The event of loss should be undesirable as an end result and generally not controllable.
7. The event of loss should be clearly definable.
8. The event of loss should be statistically identifiable in terms of mathematical relationships between claim expense, premium income, and profit margins.

Several of the ways traditional insurances apply to the computer-related risk are reviewed above. Without exception these characteristics of an insurable event are satisfied. However, when computer crime is considered, all is not black and white. Consider: Is an event of loss clearly definable? Is it likely that a loss will occur equally on any one member of a group? Is it likely the event causing the loss has a relatively small chance of occurrence?

As of this writing, 22 states have legislatively addressed events of computer crime. However, legislators do not agree on what constitutes a criminal act under the statutes. Furthermore, the federal government still has the issue of computer crime under wraps, with congressional committees studying the problem. Lack of a clear definition affords legal loopholes to the computer crime felon.

Underwriters, too, do not agree on the definitions of a computer system. Are switches included? Does the definition of computer include distributed CPU's? Answer: Not always. This lack of uniformity requires careful scrutiny on the part of the insurance buyer to assure the definitions within the policy do not preclude valuable needed coverage.

To provide your business with a more comprehensive coverage we suggest the following points:

1. Coverage to the systems utilized should be specifically addressed by definition or by designating all electronic funds transfers systems, communication systems, clearing house systems, computer networks in which you participate, and list or schedule of the mainframe, mini- or microcomputers along with a summary of applications processed in that hardware.
2. Make sure that not only your own employees are bonded but also that your computer fraud policy covers acts of employees working within systems utilized such as Federal Reserve systems, switch operators, and communication networks.
3. If transferring funds over the telephone by voice instruction, make sure your insurance addresses the exposure.
4. Independent software contractors performing services for you either on location or remote using a modem connection should be covered.
5. Service bureaus under contract should be addressed in your policy wording.
6. Acts of former employees who have critical knowledge about your systems and controls have high exposure potential. Make sure you understand how your insurance coverage will attach to protect your business against this risk.

It is true the vulnerable computer systems tend to be those that are unsecured. Depending on the motivation and desire of the would-be computer criminal: banks, stockbrokers, retailers, with their inventories of money, securities, and widgets, respectively, all have worth attractive to the criminal. Accordingly, some groups of business are more susceptible to computer crime than others.

Vendor-purchased software designed by the developer "with fraud in mind" opens the way for multiple frauds within a whole industry that uses the software. So, the computer criminal could attack a whole class of insureds on an unequal basis.

Lastly, predicting criminal intent is not scientifically or statistically based, like many types of insurable risks. The chances for occurrence of computer crime are unknown. As a result of the use of computers in the home, at work, and at play, the opportunity for foul play is increasing. The technology generation of today will handle the records in computer systems with the ease and familiarity of yesterday's bookkeepers, and more than one bookkeeper has had his fingers in the till.

Available Crime Insurance

For commercial businesses, crime insurance has been traditionally extended through three basic insurance vehicles, (1) the Commercial Blanket Bond or Blanket Position Bond, (2) the 3-D Policy, and (3) the Blanket Crime Policy. The Commercial Blanket Bond and Blanket Position Bond provide for employee fidelity coverages only. Both the 3-D and Blanket Crime policies provided for several named perils including fidelity, burglary, robbery, wrongful abstraction (theft), mysterious and unexplainable disappearance, destruction, and forgery coverages as it relates to the insured's property. The agreements are drawn along the lines of traditional property insurance to protect tangible assets against loss by specified perils.

Insurance for financial organizations follows basically the same perils listed above but expands the definition of property to include those financial instruments commonly dealt with by financial organizations. The policies include Bankers Blanket Bond, Stockbrokers Blanket Bond, Insurance Company Blanket Bond, etc.

Difficulties arise when insurers take tradi-tional crime policies designed to address tangible property and extend those policies in an attempt to cover losses connected with electronic or magnetic representation of such property as may exist within a computer system. The focus of this problem is the lack of a uniform definition as to what constitutes computer crime.

Although several states have attempted to give definition to this peril, there is a lack of consistency in approach to the criminal issue. One recent incident involved what was known as the 414 Gang—a group of computer hackers in the Milwaukee, Wisconsin (414) area code who accessed governmental, financial, and commercial institutions alike. Because there were no specific criminal statutes in place, charges could only be made for telephone harassment.

How Underwriters Are Now Addressing the Computer Crime Exposure

Underwriters are generally taking the step to redefine the current perils in the Premise clause of the commercial bond to include "computer theft" as it relates to electronic representations of money and securities on the insured's premises or the insured's bank's premises. The "Loss Inside the Premises Coverage" extends to "loss of Money and Securities by the actual destruction, disappearance or wrongful abstraction thereof within the Premises or within any Banking Premises or similar recognized places of safe deposit."

The most common method of converting a commercial bond to pick up "computer theft" is to redefine "wrongful abstraction" to include losses sustained by computer theft.

Definitions vary but generally fall within similar points of coverage and underwriting intent.

1. "Computer Theft" means the fraudulent removal and unlawful taking of Money or Securities
   a. from within the premises or banking premises or similar recognized places of safe deposit, or
   b. while being conveyed by a messenger or any armored motor vehicle company by electronic access of any other method of access from inside or outside the premises through the use of any computer located anywhere.

2. "Computer Theft" means the fraudulent removal and unlawful taking of money or securities from within the premises or banking premises or by electronic access or other method of access from outside the premises through the use of any computer located anywhere.

3. "Computer Theft" means the fraudulent removal and unlawful taking from within the premises or banking premises or by electronic access or any other method of access from outside the premises of money or securities through use of any computer located anywhere.

The premium of the insurance varies but generally adds only nominal cost to the overall price of the bond for commercial businesses unless the computer usages are great. Nominal costs range between nil to 15 percent of the commercial businesses' bond program. The deductible for the bond is also applicable to computer theft. Small business owners will find deductibles as low as $100, while large commercial businesses reach self-insurance levels well in excess of $10,000.

Not many commercial firms have large money and securities exposures directly subject to computer crime, as financial organizations do. Accordingly, insurers deal with financial institutions' computer crime exposures in a much more cautious and calculated fashion. Specific underwriting conditions of coverage may vary from carrier to carrier, but the general approach is to cover stated or defined perils related to loss of assets or liabilities from the fraudulent entry into or modification of information within a mainframe, electronic cash dispensing or automated teller machines, communication and funds transfer systems, or by software independent contractors and service bureaus. Commercial bonds are generally rated by underwriters guided by the following factors:

1. Number of employees
2. Number of branches/facilities or ratable locations
3. Size—in assets or deposits (financial institutions only)
4. Limits of liability
5. Deductibles or self-insurance applicable to the limits of liability
6. Type of institution or business
7. Number and type of EDP systems
8. Perception of internal controls and operations
9. Competitive forces in the marketplace

While there are some other less significant variables that can come into play when determining premium, these are the most important. Only two of these factors are outside of the control of the insured—the underwriter's perception of the risk and the state of the marketplace. All others are directly determinable by the actions of the insured.

While it is not practical to assume an insured would change the overall nature of its business, a refocus of the primary market addressed by a business can cause a reclassification of that business and create a change in the insurance rate.

The use of deductibles or SIRs (self-insurance retentions) can have a dramatic effect on premiums. Most company rating plans are filed with regulators on the basis of a graduated scale. Limits of liability assumed by the insurer closest to the first dollar of coverage are loaded with a higher rate than for liabilities assumed at a greater distance away from possible loss. Accordingly, "self-insuring" the high frequency area of potential liability can greatly reduce premium.

However, we would caution that some underwriters perceive the computer crime exposure as independent of the exposures relating to the bond. Therefore, they price their product independently of the rates relating to the bond. This is because computer crime and fraud is not considered a "frequency" coverage but catastrophe coverage only, and deductibles have little effect on rates necessary to support catastrophic loss.

To the extent that the underwriter does relate the computer crime exposure to the bond, the premiums can vary between 10 percent and 20 percent of the bond premium for commercial business and 15 percent to 25 percent of the bond premium for financial organizations.

The number and type of EDP systems and the limits of liability also help determine the premium. The more systems that are utilized by an organization create a larger exposure. The values of the information and data base contained within those systems will alter the premium. Obviously, the more insurance that is purchased to protect those values, the higher the premium. Again, because premiums are rated on a sliding scale, coverage limits purchased further away from the frequency loss area are less of an expense.

The last three areas of rate determinants are number of employees, number of ratable locations, and size of business. Of these, the employee count generally has the most influence on premium (on average 50 percent to 60 percent). Insureds having a large number of locations (thus increasing the exposure) will likewise have a surcharge to their premiums of some significance.

This is a transitional time for computer crime and fraud insurance. Some of the reasons are:

1. There is a need for uniform laws and regulations to define computer crime and the liabilities associated with such activities.

2. Insurers need to be better educated on the exposures represented by today's high technology society. With such specific knowledge the insurance industry can better address the insurable events of the computer age.

3. With an enlightened insurer come new insurance products, which are not "stopgap" but which specifically relate to the electronic era where the computer is now the vault containing valuable, although intangible, property.

Market Capacity

Computer crime coverage is relatively new. It has been generally tied to fidelity bond coverages. Individual policies can cover losses as little as $2,500 or as great as $50 million. When structured as a cosurety contract (underwriters share liability at a set percentage under a single contract) or in a layered policy approach (underwriters accept liability excess of underlying insurance), policies to levels of maximizing insurance market capacity can be achieved. There is no widely applicable rule of thumb as to how much coverage is enough when it comes to computer crime. Each manager must weigh the costs against the risks in periodic reappraisals. However, computer crime coverage is generally taken at levels equal to the Fidelity Bond limits of liability.

Like fidelity losses the computer crime is hidden. Unlike fidelity it usually takes place over a short period of time but can involve sizable sums. Funds or securities are moved globally in milliseconds and can be withdrawn or disbursed before reconciling procedures could detect a discrepancy. In an uncontrolled situation, the exposure could equal the total financial resources of an organization.

Dilemma of Underwriters—Handling the Risk of Computer Crime and Fraud

With the word "underwriting" comes a presumption of professionalism in the insurance industry. This presumption contemplates that the individual assessing risk and exposure has comprehensive knowledge of the subject at hand. In fact, the insurance products in the marketplace today for computer crime have been developed by a few knowledgeable individuals. This leaves the majority of underwriters in a "me too" position. That is, they agree that there is a need for the products offered, and they offer them sometimes without knowledge of the associated risks. This is not a condemnation of the industry, but rather demonstrates that in areas of rapidly changing technology insurers may have difficulty fulfilling the role of traditional crime insurance underwriters while creating new computer crime policies. Following the lead of those who develop a new product may be dangerous. The underwriting standards may not generate revenues sufficient to cover future losses. Underwriting standards on management, internal controls, and audits will constantly have to be updated as computer technology and computer operating controls change.

Insurers must cultivate an attitude of creativity and flexibility when working with insurance relating to computer crime and fraud.

Several companies and markets have taken innovative steps in the computer crime area. They include Aetna C&S, Chubb, Lloyd's of London, St. Paul, and Shand Morahan. The Surety Association of America has also introduced products for its members.

As purchasers of insurance, consumers have a right to request that insurance companies continue to reevaluate existing products, particularly as new technology creates new exposures. Insurers need help in both identifying and understanding these exposures. Insurers and consumers must be partners in this era of rapid technological change.

Preventing Computer Crime

To the extent that computer crime can be controlled, reduced, or eliminated the cost of insurance will be more affordable. Therefore, controls for data security need to be in place. The controls that should be enforced are:

1. Be sure that the information going into the computer system is correct. The user responsible for the information should verify its accuracy.

2. Reduce the ability to address critical programs or portions of applications by limiting user access with passwords, personal identification numbers. Make sure authority levels are defined and constantly updated. Availability of any information within a system should be on a "need to know" basis.

3. All tapes, disks, and hardware should be physically protected. The premises' controls can include access controls, badges, guards, alarms/detection systems. Use of fire suppressants, Halon, and CO_2 should also be considered. Library controls should include a system that masks tape and disk contents and monitors their use. Tapes should be duplicated and the backup tapes stored away from the data processing facility in the event the original is lost, stolen, or destroyed.

4. Test control systems regularly to assure they are in place and working properly.

5. Hire competent auditors to review program details to assure that unauthorized instructions are not tagged to existing programs.

6. Set up effective dual controls over use of utility programs. Management should be aware of each instance they are used, and audit and data security should review all changes in data.

7. Change data audit and data reconciling points routinely. EDP auditors should review and sign off on all program changes on asset-sensitive or information-sensitive data and test. This helps to assure continuity of good internal controls in a dynamic data processing environment.

8. To reduce wiretapping during data transmission consider segmenting the data so if captured, they would be meaningless. Also consider shielding the lines, use of encryption or electronic compression techniques.

9. Identify all printouts that contain asset-sensitive or critical data and set up a control facility for destruction of the printouts after use.

Two other general points need to be emphasized. All systems should be designed for a high degree of auditability; hire good, competent, highly qualified people. Remember, system privileges in the hands of incompetent or poorly managed people are no less a threat than a fire in your computer room. Both destroy data.

Recommended Courses of Action

The cost of data processing insurance and the still unpredictable offerings in this area make it critical for data processing management to plan and control operations to reduce risks. In general, it is wise to self-insure the smaller and more predictable risks and buy insurance to cover catastrophic losses. Regardless of the extent of coverage, the policy should be tailored to reflect the organization's environment.

Important considerations for determining data processing insurance needs include:

- Systematically examining the potential losses
- Awareness that insurance available is not standardized
- Careful comparison of costs and coverages
- Checking the terms of equipment leases to see if they correspond to the terms of the insurance policy
- Checking what risks are covered and what measures have been taken to deal with uninsured areas
- Determining if all locations are covered
- Obtaining errors and omissions liability insurance if the organization does data processing related work for outside clients.

Insurance for Personal Computers

Generally, personal computers are treated as personal property under your homeowner's policy. The owner must be aware of conditions in the contract that can require that such equipment be specifically scheduled and appropriate replacement costs should be shown.

Personal Computer Supplement   Here are some helpful hints in reducing risks associated with your personal computer:

- To deter theft anchor your PC to the desk
- If your PC is near a window or an area where there is possible water exposure, cover the PC with a waterproof cover.
- If you use your PC at home in conjunction with your business, ensure confidentiality of data by:
  1. storing sensitive data disks in locked files
  2. storing sensitive data printouts in locked files
  3. destroying obsolete media prior to disposal
  4. always masking PC passwords to on-line access
  5. rotating passwords often
  6. turning off PC when leaving machine unattended
- Avoid copying software provided by your employer. Software is proprietary and subject to copyright and trade secret laws. Your employer and the PC user may be subject to possible penalties for violations.

Checklist

	Yes	No
When purchasing equipment and during installation, are the responsibilities of each party clearly understood by all concerned?	☐	☐
Were equipment leases checked to determine the liability of each party?	☐	☐
Is this routinely done before each lease is signed?	☐	☐

	Yes	No
Were proper values established, and does the insurance respond on the basis of those valuations?	☐	☐
Are exposures covered at remote locations, and while equipment is in transit?	☐	☐
Were appropriate media insurable values determined?	☐	☐
Have operations and financial people agreed on business interruption and extra-expense loss potentials?	☐	☐
Are these losses covered?	☐	☐
Has professional liability been properly considered?	☐	☐
Have the computer systems been evaluated for fraud potential inherent in complex programming?	☐	☐
Does data security emphasize control over accessibility to a system and continuous monitoring?	☐	☐
Is computer crime clearly and uniformly defined in each insurance contract?	☐	☐
Have the data processing insurance requirements been reviewed regularly?	☐	☐
Does the fire insurance coverage adequately protect against the possible consequences of a fire or other cause of physical damage?	☐	☐
Does the liability coverage adequately protect against claims that may be brought against the organization?	☐	☐
Does the business interruption coverage adequately protect against losses resulting from the possible inability of the computer to perform?	☐	☐

CHAPTER 8

Auditing in the EDP Environment

By Richard S. Thompson

Introduction

Internal controls are the raw materials for auditing. Internal controls serve many purposes and are heavily relied upon by management for consistently accurate and complete information, as well as to assure continuity of operations. The auditor's purpose is to provide management with a competent, independent appraisal of information management control and of the accuracy and integrity of information presented by automated systems.

Internal control is defined by the AICPA Committee on Auditing Procedures as follows:

Internal Control comprises the plan of organization and all of the coordinate methods and measures adopted within a business to safeguard its assets, check the accuracy and reliability of its accounting data, promote operational efficiency and encourage adherence to prescribed managerial policies.

Under this definition there are four primary objectives of internal control.

1. *Safeguarding assets.* The safeguarding of important assets of a business is a significant responsibility of management. Assets requiring protection include not only the physical assets but also documents and records.

2. *Accurate and reliable information.* Without accurate and complete information about the activities of the organization, management may not be sufficiently prepared to make important business decisions. Control of a business depends very heavily on the adequacy and reliability of information. There are also legal obligations for management to maintain accurate and timely records.

3. *Promotion of operational efficiency.* Another important goal of management is to elim-

inate duplication and waste of resources and to promote economical and efficient operation within the organization. Although not directly related to computer security, internal control methodology offers an opportunity for management to encourage and measure efficiency, and thereby to promote the general health of the organization.

4. *Adherence to prescribed policies.* Management must delegate tasks and responsibilities to appropriate organizational levels in order to operate the business effectively. It is essential for management to institute procedures and guidelines to coordinate and regulate the activities of all personnel in meeting agreed-upon goals of the business. Internal control can serve as a feedback mechanism to provide assurance that prescribed policies are followed by personnel.

Internal control objectives do not change with the introduction of EDP systems, although the nature and emphasis of some control elements may. The basic elements required for internal control in any system, manual or automated, include:

1. Able and trustworthy personnel
2. Clearly defined lines of authority and responsibility
3. Adequate separation of responsibility
4. Proper authorization procedures
5. Adequate documentation and records
6. Good recordkeeping procedures
7. Sufficient physical control over assets and records
8. Independent verification of performance
9. Checks and balances to assure that reported statistics and data are correct

It is convenient to classify EDP system controls into two categories: *Overall EDP Controls* and *Individual Application Controls.* An overall control, such as data center access restrictions, relates to and serves as a foundation for all EDP applications. Application controls relate to the specific use and requirements of an individual system, such as payroll provisions, and may include such procedures as balancing input transaction totals. In audits of EDP systems, the overall controls are usually evaluated first. If the overall controls are adequate, the application controls are specifically examined for each system in order of criticality or magnitude of assets at risk. If the overall controls are not adequate, the application controls cannot be relied upon. If the internal controls are judged inadequate, then a complete audit including verification of transactions and balances may be required. The following is a brief list of EDP Control categories:

Overall EDP Controls

1. A plan of organization to define responsibilities and reporting relationships
2. Procedures for authorizing, testing, documenting, and reviewing changes to systems and programs
3. Hardware and system software controls to ensure system integrity
4. Controls over access to equipment, programs, and data files

Individual Application Controls

1. Input controls
2. Processing controls
3. Output controls

From the auditor's point of view, it is first useful to identify and document the presence or absence of specific controls for specific objectives. After that, the auditor can recommend controls where they are absent or found weak and can perform periodic tests on certain controls to assure they are functioning adequately and consistently. Audit tools can facilitate both the identification and the testing of internal controls. The goal of this chapter is to describe what EDP internal controls are, who is responsible for them, and how auditors address them.

What Is EDP Control

A company's management is responsible for the security of any computer-based programs and data files that are relied upon for the delivery of goods and services and the preparation of reports on production, profitability, taxation, and more. Such security is generally provided by developing several tiers of control expressed here in the form of a pyramid (Fig. 8.1).

Organizational and administrative controls are the foundation on which every security practice eventually rests. Accordingly, the functions of a business may be integrated in a way that provides for accountability of assets and enables continuity and effective review of operations.

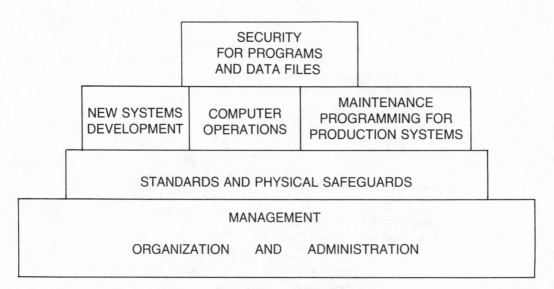

Figure 8.1 Pyramid of EDP internal control

Overall Controls

There is a level of control whose benefits are available to all application systems. Overall controls encompass a range of activities common to most computer applications. The sharing of EDP resources among users from all areas of a company makes them subject to the same control strengths and weaknesses. Important overall controls include:

1. Separation of responsibilities
2. System development controls
3. Computer operation controls
4. Production programming controls
5. Program library controls
6. Data library controls

Separation of Responsibilities A system of checks and balances eliminates opportunities for misappropriation of assets. For example, users of a payment disbursement system exert control over checks issued. Unauthorized requests for payment may be curtailed by giving approval authority to a separate person or department unit without the authority to originate payment requests.

A computer environment supports this effort by:

1. Providing a single transaction entry procedure available only to the area authorized to submit invoices
2. Providing distribution of output transaction detail and summary reports to both the unit that accounts for checks and a company official responsible for the unit on whose behalf the checks are drawn
3. Providing distribution of printed checks to a unit responsible for the inventory of checks and separate from the one that authorizes the payments

In a company whose accounting systems are computer based, misuse of or abuse to data files and programs may be prevented or detected by assigning departmental functions on a responsibility basis. For example, computer operators and programmers should not have authority nor opportunity to enter a transaction related to any application system. Conversely, those with authority to enter transactions to a particular system should not have occasion nor opportunity to change any of its programs or operate the system.

Further separation of responsibilities provides that:

1. Access to a computer room by people other than computer operations personnel should be supervised
2. People other than computer operations personnel should not be permitted to operate computer equipment
3. The separation of functions should be exercised consistently during each working shift throughout the year
4. If appropriate, require more than one operator to be on duty

System Development Controls The development of systems should be guided by an overall policy or strategy. Adhering to a sound policy should provide that:

1. Development resources be applied only toward company authorized projects on the basis of written approval
2. Systems specifications be rigorously prepared and controlled at levels suited to establish scope, business requirements, identification of data, definitions of processes, and correlation of data and processes at every summary and detail level
3. Systems specifications represent the complete body of knowledge and understanding about a particular application to be shared between user and system design personnel
4. Systems specifications be reviewed for approval by management parties responsible for both user and system design areas
5. A test plan be designed and employed to ensure the correct operation of all programmed routines
6. A plan for acceptance of a design, for its implementation and for any requisite conversion of data assures a smooth transition

Computer Operation Controls The objectives of computer operation controls are to ensure compliance to management policies such as separation of duties, efficient operation and protection of facilities, data, software, and other assets.

1. Approved standard operating instructions should be available and should be used for every scheduled job.

2. Computer usage should be logged to provide a complete history of each machine's workload in detail.

3. The computer usage log should be supervised to ensure that all scheduled jobs were done, only scheduled jobs and no unauthorized jobs were run, and all abnormal endings, malfunctions, and reruns are investigated.

4. Only tested and approved versions of computer programs should be available to run in production.

5. Backup and recovery procedures are tested and documented as part of standard operating instructions to help assure continuity of operations.

Production Programming Controls The responsibility of making changes to production programs differs from that of developing new programs. Programs are written based on the programmers' best informed understanding of the business requirements. Over time, both the requirements and the understanding may change. The maintenance programmer interprets the original and adds new lines of code in the context of the original. A recorded understanding of the maintenance activity can give some indication as to the orderliness of making changes and reasonable assurance against unauthorized changes.

1. Additions or changes to production programs should be authorized by user and programming management areas in writing at each stage of the procedure—to approve definition of requirements, to approve a design for program modification, to approve the results of testing, to signify approval for implementation, and to indicate acceptance.

2. Documentation authorizing program modifications should be kept in a way that allows retrospective reviews for ensuring the proper approval for programming activity, and for determining causes of delays in commencement or completion of projects.

3. Production programming specifications should include scope of activity, business objectives, details of proposed design and programming, layouts of data records or reports to be modified, testing procedures and acceptance criteria.

4. Controls over changes to production programs apply to both application systems and operating systems.

Program Library Controls As a condition for acceptance, each individual program and the entire system must demonstrate fitness for operational use. A program library may be vulnerable to tampering or to errors undetected by inadequate testing. Incomplete or incorrect understanding of user or system requirements can also introduce errors into a program library. One of the auditor's commitments is to ensure that standards are upheld on the basis of the following:

1. Written EDP and user management approval of testing methodology and results, system documentation, and user interface procedures and timing of implementation

2. Identified and testing controls providing that no unauthorized changes be entered and that authorized versions be entered in an approved manner

3. Congruity between "source" and "executable" versions of programs in the library

4. Immediate identification and review of emergency changes to production programs

5. Program management routines (either programmed or manual) to enable a thorough review of actual changes introduced, new program version numbers, and a date and time stamp indicating when programs were last modified

Data Library Controls Programmed security can reduce the risk of accidental destruction or misuse of data files. Where available, a data management system records file name, application name, creation date, library retention period, and possibly a generation number. In these instances, the system itself can detect a mismounted or unavailable data file to be reported and resolved.

Data files should be available for access by programs only as authorized by proper schedules. As tape files are moved in and out of storage, vault or library inventory records should be kept to ensure that only those files needed for scheduled production are issued and that issued files are returned on time.

Password protection is a further means of limiting "READ" and/or "WRITE" access to data. Currently valid passwords should be required in order for the system to allow a particular user to initiate activity concerning a particular file.

A data base administrator may supervise the operation of password assignment and periodic reassignment, may oversee programmed data library controls, and may ensure that proper standards are observed for systems being developed by reviewing specifications of new data representations.

Details of access to data files should be logged for reporting of deviations from acceptable patterns. Such details may consist of the date and time of access, duration of use, and identification and location of user.

Individual Application Controls

Specific control requirements may be geared to the sensitivities of a particular application with emphasis in areas vulnerable to misappropriation. Individual controls are further intended to prevent errors during input, update, and conversion processing, and to prevent unauthorized access to or manipulation of company data.

Without adequate assurance that the overall installation controls are functioning properly, the individual application controls, even if functioning properly, cannot necessarily be relied upon. Assurance that controls function properly is provided by testing, responsible supervision, and periodic audits or third party reviews.

Application controls should be designed to protect against anticipated errors and irregularities. A convenient and widely used classification of application controls is the following:

1. *Input controls.* Provide the first line of defense in an automated system. Includes the detection of lost or duplicated data and ensures the accuracy of the data. Also includes the identification of transaction sources and the authorization of transactions. A variety of techniques may be employed to satisfy specific input control requirements. Some common techniques are:

- Verification—Verification of key entry by a second key entry or by visual review. Use of check digits. Use of preprocessing edit checks.

- Batch Controls—Validation of quantitative data by accumulating field totals and balancing to source document totals.

- Master File Reference—Systems using on-line master files may be designed to extract some data on-line to complete the transaction input. Direct verification of critical input data is also possible and desirable.

- Edit Programs—Substantial verification of input may be accomplished by comparison of fields against tables of expected values and the testing of logical relationships with other fields.

2. *Processing controls.* Protect against accessing or updating the wrong file or record, incomplete processing, incorrect results, untimely or inappropriate transactions, and lost files or programs. The processing control category is often difficult for the auditor to assess without thorough technical knowledge because there may be little external visible evidence to rely upon. Nevertheless, it is the foundation of system integrity. Some specific techniques include:

- Test Decks—Verification of processing results may be accomplished by using prepared input data for which totals and processing results are known or have been established. Ideally, the test data should include a broad range of transactions and conditions that will be encountered under actual operations.

- Batch Controls or Total Controls—It is necessary to ensure the continuity of control, from source to input to processing. Batch controls established for input validation should be further verified as a by-product of processing. Once control totals are established the subsequent validation can be automated so that the system is essentially self-checking during the processing stage.

- Crossfooting Tests—Logical tests for data consistency, such as crossfooting of totals, may be incorporated into the processing function for additional verification.

- Application Reruns—Processing consistency can be validated by the simple expedient of a rerun with comparison of the results to the original run. In an on-line real-time environment this may be complex because it could require the trapping of transaction input data in a manner that permits the simulation of randomly received message segments. Alternatively, some on-line system transactions may be regenerated using a straight forward batch format and employing a completed transaction log as the source. However, this may not recreate the original conditions for on-line updating, and hence may fail to pinpoint certain processing inconsistencies.

3. *Output controls.* Output controls include the procedures necessary to ensure proper distribution of output results, to protect against lost reports or late reports, to detect erroneous information, and to provide for correction of errors.

4. *Other controls.* Necessary to properly monitor compliance with organizational policy, such as limitations of access to input, processing and output functions, and conformity to generally accepted accounting practices.

Examples of common application controls that can be identified, tested and evaluated include:

1. Item-by-item checking to verify accuracy of detail
2. Batch total and file count reconciliation to verify completeness of an input and update process
3. Sequence checking for reporting of missing items
4. Matching transactions with master file data to facilitate review of nonmatching items where a match is expected (e.g., payment voucher with no vendor data)
5. Reasonableness checks to bring attention to payments or pay rate increases over some established limit and shipments of goods in unusually high or low quantities

Individual system controls need not be excessive or burdensome but should provide protection that is both effective and consistent. Ideally, controls should be considered from the inception of the system and incorporated during the design stage. Important minimum considerations from an audit standpoint are:

• Cost Effectiveness—The cost of controls must be appropriate to the value of the information and the underlying assets that are protected.

• Trap Errors Early—The earlier that errors can be detected and corrected in the system the fewer the problems that will result later. Once updating of a file or a record has taken place it is costly and time consuming to have to back out a transaction.

• Correcting Errors—The correction of errors should provide for an audit trail, particularly after the updating of a master record. If a transaction has been applied in error and needs to be reversed, it should be completely documented, ideally as a special transaction that is maintained in transaction history. System utilities should not be used for this purpose except under strict supervision and with thorough documentation of each use.

In the EDP environment, there should be an awareness of things that can go wrong, such as:

1. Computer files or programs lost
2. Customer account details recorded incorrectly
3. Unauthorized disbursement of cash or data
4. Detected errors not corrected properly
5. Usage or replenishment of materials not recorded or recorded incorrectly
6. Facilities damaged by fire, smoke, flood, storm, or intrusion

When something does go wrong, a preventive control may be missing or may have been circumvented. Even where strong preventive controls are in place, they cannot be regarded as failsafe protection. Inevitably, problems will occur. If one cannot prevent an undesirable occurrence, then the next level of defense is detection.

Detection controls are critical to minimize the consequences of:

1. Prolonged business interruption
2. Inventory excess or shortfall
3. Incorrectly priced sales invoices or cost of goods sold details
4. Improper purchase orders or payments
5. Failure to bill for goods and services
6. Disclosure of proprietary customer, financial, or production data to competitor
7. Failure to collect accounts receivable or interest due
8. Theft

Cooperative participation in EDP controls at all levels of management and staff is in the interest of personnel safety, confidence and goodwill of customers and vendors, and safeguarding of company assets.

Who Is Responsible for Control of EDP?

Top Management

Management uses certain internal controls to validate the reliability of results of operations. The type and extent of internal controls vary as do the volume and scope of operations. Management is responsible for the approval and, in some cases, the initiation of controls.

Data Originators

A key operator may have responsibility for exercising basic control such as item-by-item checking, key verification, and balancing of totals. A further control at the input source is provided by adequate supervision of key operators.

System Developers

The design of adequate controls in automated systems is a systems development responsibility. This activity requires sensitivity to the goals and objectives of management, awareness of pitfalls, and knowledge of remedies.

Computer Operators

The basic control exercised by operations staff occurs in the execution of scheduled workloads. Supervisory operations personnel extend control by verifying the usage of programs and data files in accordance with established and documented procedures.

Data Users

The end user responsibility for control consists of numerous activities. Among these are the review of detailed transaction logs for accuracy, completeness, and proper authorization, the follow-up on error, omission, and unauthorized entry, reentry of corrections, review for reasonableness, and supervision of review, follow-up, and reentry.

Internal Auditors

The role of internal auditor is control advisor and consultant to management. To avoid conflict of interest (or the mere appearance of one) in a postimplementation audit, production auditors do not usually design controls. Design phase audit involvement is concerned with whether or not sound standards and policies are consistently applied and specific controls are properly planned. Production phase auditing stresses the identification and testing of controls. The auditor is responsible for notifying management of absent controls and recommending suitable controls over the specified exposure.

External Auditors

Unless an external auditor is specially engaged to perform some other consulting activity, he typically limits his scope to the fair presentation of published financial statements. Where those statements are produced by or dependent upon computer-based systems, the external auditor may need computer audit skills to be assured they are fairly presented. To obtain this assurance, there must be evidence that correct accounting procedures were used consistently throughout the period covered by the statements.

Auditing Modern Computer Applications

In an ordered approach to auditing in the EDP environment, it is useful, first, to identify the overall controls and, second, to test them to determine the current status as to the absence, presence, and adequacy of overall control. The quality of the overall control relates directly to the integrity of control available to each application system.

Where the overall controls are poor, a user must be satisfied that the fundamental objectives are met through the ability to calculate any result using detail shown in the output reports. With this ability, the user is not so dependent on "invisible" programmed routines nor is the auditor so reliant upon weak controls.

Where the overall controls are strong, there can be more economy of detail in printed output, and the user may devote fewer resources toward proving the integrity of data with more toward using it. Likewise, the auditor may be more comfortable with the individual system controls and the presentation of reports.

Certain objectives must be met by users of computer systems regardless of EDP department controls and audit findings. Through the phases of authorization, preparation, conversion, editing, correction, reentry, and updating of data, there must be demonstrable accuracy and completeness. The information provided must be useful and timely. These assurances are necessary whether or not the controls are present.

Since many systems have been designed to make the full consummation of a transaction possible within a few seconds, the systems must quickly identify the validity of input data using rigorous criteria. Batch systems may survive brief delays in error correction, but on-line systems without quick on-line validation may not meet objectives for accuracy, authorization, and completeness.

The most cost-effective and practical time to audit a system is during the design stage, before it is programmed. While *performance* cannot be evaluated as in audits of systems already in operation, the early disclosure of functional or control inadequacies can save the cost of redesign, redocumenting, reprogramming, and retesting. The analysis of auditability is an important part of preprogramming review. An auditable system is one that lends itself to an independent control appraisal.

Some users are choosing to decentralize operations to a greater extent by installing microcomputers in their offices. Also gaining acceptance rapidly are "fourth-generation" programming tools that permit speedy changes to programmed routines. In these instances, management is electing to negate some of the overall controls described earlier. It must compensate for this decision by installing alternative controls in order to provide the necessary assurances of integrity within a given decentralized application.

With many on-line systems, the interactive nature of "user friendly" programming tools can make the end user directly responsible for the development and integrity of programmed accounting routines, where formerly it may have been the responsibility of separate system development and production programming areas.

The decentralized use of microcomputers presents a similar shift of control responsibility. The secure storage of microcomputer media containing data and programs must be established within each user area. Otherwise, there can be no grounds for relying on reports produced by the microcomputer.

Audit Tools

Audit tools and techniques vary in cost, in complexity, and in applicability to specific situations. Audit workpapers are, traditionally, one of the auditor's most important tools. They are nearly always mandatory, linking detailed staff work to the final audit report.

Workpapers represent formal documentation of audit work. They contain a statement of the scope of activities, records of related meetings, exhibits, reports, documents, correspondence, checklists used, details of identified controls to be tested, proposed methods of testing, details of tests performed, results of tests, details surrounding a finding of missing controls or controls functioning unsatisfactorily, and, usually, a summary concluding statement about the overall adequacy of controls considered in the statement of scope.

In the survey for initial identification of internal controls, there is a need to establish and document the absence or presence of numerous specific controls within a limited period of time. Auditors often use checklists or questionnaires tailored to the types of controls for which they are looking. The checklist or questionnaire itself should be tested and revised frequently to improve the understanding obtained about specific controls.

Sample questionnaires can be found in the appendix, and a checklist appears at the end of this chapter. Appendix 15, *FDIC Examination Questionnaire*, and Appendix 16, *Work Program for Electronic Data Processing Examinations*, were provided by the Federal Deposit Insurance Corporation to illustrate their examination of bank data centers. The "Implementation and Integrity Control Checklist" contains a specimen list of questions used by a public accounting firm to build an understanding of a client's data processing controls.

Manual tracing, usually called an audit trail, is employed to assure the accurate flow of transactions through a system. Each detail of a given input source document or transaction must be traceable to an output report or file, and vice versa. The tracing technique may be applied on a single transaction basis for a quick test to provide some indication of the presence of control, but to provide assurance that the control functions consistently, the test must be extended to cover large volumes of data over differing periods of time. Audit trails should be built into each production system as a normal part of its internal controls.

Generalized EDP audit software is an essential tool for internal and external auditors to verify the validity of data and systems. This is especially true for large-scale computer systems where sizable data bases would otherwise be difficult to verify.

Audit software was developed to facilitate verifying the integrity of computer data bases. It also helps to improve the effectiveness of the auditor by improving the quality and scope of the audits, and by allowing the auditor to be more independent of the data processing staff. EDP audit software extends the auditor's technical skills and thereby provides better flexibility for using the computer to help evaluate automated information.

Two major types of programs used by auditors are *data audit* programs and *source compare* programs. The characteristics of these programs are as follows:

Data Audit Programs   These programs allow the auditor to sample the processing of transactions and to validate processing. The auditor can examine computer files, establish tests for data validity, and produce reports. The audit program functions usually include data extraction, file handling, calculation of formulas, and crossfooting of values. Some representative features may include:

- *Data Sampling*
  Interval sampling—selecting items based upon specific interval occurrences, such as nth item
  Random sampling—random selection
  Statistical sampling—based upon population characteristics and statistical rules
  Monetary value samples—based upon set monetary values, such as all balances over $10,000

- *Data Calculations*
  Reperforming critical calculations such as earned interest, payroll amounts, unearned

income, discounts, and expense distribution amounts.

- *Data Summarization*
  Allows independent aggregation of numeric values for proof of controls.

- *Data Resequencing*
  Helps to verify data values or to isolate abnormalities by listing in sequence by date, serial number, time, amount, account number, or any desired field.

- *Rule Violations*
  Checks for violations of rules that apply to changes and inputs, such as authorization for privileged transactions or overrides of special conditions.

- *Analysis and Reporting*
  Application-oriented analysis, such as aging of receivables, overdue payables, payroll or general ledger irregularities.

- *Creating Special Files for Audit Use*
  Allows the creation and maintenance of separate automated files for use by the auditor. For example, data records extracted from an accounting master file can be set up as an independent audit work file, and all further processing such as recalculations, resequencing, and recoding can take place without changing the original data.

- *Confirmation Preparation*
  Ability to prepare confirmations or other documents necessary for direct verification of financial records. Selective confirmation capabilities and the creation of independent follow-up files are desirable.

- *Reporting of Sampling Results*
  Diagrams, histograms, and other graphic formats are sometimes provided for the summarization and reporting of sampling results. These features can aid in reducing large masses of raw data to understandable form.

- *Data Base Support*
  Data dictionaries and the ability to accommodate a variety of data structures, file structures, and access methods are offered by some systems.

Source Code and Other File Comparison Programs   These programs allow the auditor to track changes made to a program. The source code for two different versions of a program can be compared and the differences identified. This serves as an investigative aid to verify that only authorized changes have been implemented. It is useful if the programs are capable of comparing different types of media and data files, as well as source code. Useful comparisons for audit purposes can be made between:

- Magnetic data files, whether on tape or disk
- Program source code files
- Program object code files
- Input transaction files
- Output transaction files
- Output reports (on magnetic media)

Flexibility for source program comparison is enhanced if the comparison program can ignore line numbering between source program versions or even allow comparison of restructured programs. Other useful features are those that permit comparison of entire program libraries to prior versions and identify differences between versions.

Following is a brief description of several EDP Audit Packages that are commercially available. No single product meets all desirable criteria, and the packages cover a wide range of costs and functionality. Neither the listing nor the exclusion of any package is the result of comparative judgments or evaluation.

EDP Audit Software Packages

1. ADR/THE LIBRARIAN
Applied Data Research, Inc.

This program tracks changes to source code at the statement level. It provides a history for each version tied to data record changes, and an audit trail on disk, tape, and printer. It performs file comparisons, data resequencing, and file creation. Audit trails, data summarization, and reports describing file modules or total files are generated. The Librarian is written in assembler, and although source code is not available, exit facilities are provided to permit modification by the auditor.

2. AUDIT ANALYZER
TSI International, Inc.

The Audit Analyzer offers data validation, audit planning, simulation, various analyses, sample selection, confirmation requests, and exception reports. Source code, in assembly language, is provided with the system. The auditor

can modify functions and add new functions to the system using assembler or a high-level language. An audit trail is available on disk, tape, and printer. The programs perform file comparisons, computations, data resequencing, statistical analysis, data summarization, file creation, and aging. It generates audit trails, sampling reports, histograms, and confirmation labels.

3. CQS–AUDITEC
Carleton Corp.

Designed as a replacement for earlier audit retrieval and report writer software, this system uses a data dictionary and can be run in an interactive environment. It verifies processing, including complex calculations, and provides audit trails of data changes and source code changes. Sophisticated sampling options are offered. The system is written in COBOL. Source language is not provided but high-level language links are offered.

4. EDP AUDITOR
Cullinet Software, Inc.

The EDP AUDITOR verifies correct processing and complex calculations, detects rule violations, and audits data and source code changes. It provides a wide range of sampling options and confirmation options. The programs analyze IBM's SMF (Systems Maintenance Facility) files for compliance with security and integrity rules. It can measure resource use efficiency. Source code is provided in assembler and the CULPRIT language.

5. MS/CS–Multifunction Security Control System
Legist Automation, Inc.

This low-cost, interactive program, protected by special passwords, allows supervisory monitoring of all screen images in an on-line system. It provides an audit trail on disk of terminal logins and logouts, hardware malfunctions, system starts and shutdowns, job starts and stops. Since source code is not provided, the system is not alterable except for reporting.

6. PANAUDIT PLUS
Pansophic Systems, Inc.

This is a comprehensive collection of preestablished audit routines. Together with the EASYTRIEVE PLUS language, it facilitates programming of new audit tests. Preset routines are categorized as general (integrity tests, date and time routines, test data generation, aging, and data conversion), statistical (distribution analysis, sampling, and statistical projections), and operating system job information (system utilization, performance and workload analyses, throughput analysis, abnormal program terminations, media allocation, and application trend analysis). Source code is provided in the EASYTRIEVE PLUS language.

7. RES-Q

Quality Systems Development Corp.

Designed to compare source code between program versions to detect program changes and to create audit trails of changes, RES-Q accommodates restructured programs and some data files. It can be used for COBOL, PL/I, JCL, and other languages. RES-Q is written in COBOL, but source code is not provided except for input/output file modifications.

8. SOURCE PROGRAM COMPARE

MacKinney Systems, Inc.

This package shows differences between two versions of the same program. It can print an entire program file or just differences: however, it will accommodate only sequential input and fixed length records. A statement-oriented audit trail is printed. Source code in COBOL is available.

9. TEXT COMPARATOR

Dataware, Inc.

This utility program compares source or object code files and reports differences based upon content. An audit trail is provided on disk, tape, or printer. The program handles fixed or variable length records, and can compare programs, libraries, or partial data sets. Written in assembler, the source code is not provided.

Microcomputers

Auditing of microcomputers, as with mainframe computers, must be concerned with the accuracy and integrity of input data, processing, and outputs. However, special audit approaches are needed for personal computers because of the diffused responsibility for their use, and the largely uncontrolled environments in which they operate. These special approaches should be applied to verify the integrity of important personal computer output, to assure that sensitive data are properly protected, and to check as to whether vital data are backed up to prevent their loss.

However, not all microcomputer work need be audited. Only microcomputer activity that produces data that are used for important decisions or are incorporated into major information systems requires auditing. Word processing work is an example of a microcomputer function that is usually not subjected to audits.

Any microcomputer output data that are used for management decisions or which are used as input in important information systems should be subject to audit to substantiate their correctness. This audit should verify three aspects: (1) the source data must be accurate and complete, (2) the computation procedures must be sound, and (3) the source data and output should be identified with their creation dates so that users are aware of how current the data are.

The auditor should make sure that adequate measures are taken to confirm that important sensitive data cannot get into the wrong hands. Personal computer data are particularly vulnerable since they can be quickly copied to a small floppy disk, which can easily be removed from the premises. Therefore, the auditor should check to see that sensitive data are identified and that the responsibility and methods for their protection are clearly defined. The protective methods can take a number of forms: locking up all copies when not in use, key controls, library custodial controls, and encryption.

The personal computer data backup methods should be audited to make sure that vital data are not vulnerable to accidental loss. A main value of proper backup procedures is also to prevent the necessity of arduous and costly reconstruction of records, which can be destroyed due to mechanical failure or erroneous operation. The auditor should verify that backup methods are defined for each important type of data used on microcomputers, covering how often and on what medium they are duplicated, whether the duplicated data are kept on site or off site, and whether data can, in fact, be reconstructed from the backup media.

Finally, the auditors should intend their audits to verify compliance with the organization's policies on microcomputers, especially if such policies are written. As examples, the auditors may check to determine whether acquisitions of microcomputers are preceded by required cost justifications, whether acquired software conforms to policies and standards, and whether copying of a software package does not breach the vendor's license agreements.

Summary

The physical controls an auditor looks for in the EDP environment are usually found in the fabric of well-organized companies and well-planned, well-designed systems. EDP auditors have a responsibility to identify both an organization's strengths and its weaknesses in the computer environment, and then to follow up and reevaluate periodically. The strengths should be tested for consistency while the weaknesses are examined to determine whether a material loss resulted or could result from them. Preventive or detective controls should be recommended as appropriate to prevent the potential losses inherent in weak systems. The auditor should monitor progress in implementing recommended controls. Most importantly, a cooperative approach between auditor, data processing functions, and user departments can benefit each of them individually and their organization collectively.

Checklist for EDP Auditing

Job Functions

1. Who may enter the computer room?
2. Under what circumstances may these rules be overridden and by whose authority?
3. How are these rules enforced?
4. Who may operate computer equipment?
5. Under what circumstances may these rules be overridden and by whose authority?
6. How are these rules enforced?
7. Where and how are registers and records, which are used to control data being processed, stored?
8. Who has access to these documents?
9. How does the company ensure that only these personnel have access?
10. Under whose authority and under what circumstances may these procedures be overridden?

11. List and describe transactions of an accounting nature that can be initiated within the operations or system development departments?
12. In each case, who authorizes these transactions and how is this authorization evidenced?
13. Who are responsible for the custody and issuance of
    a) data files?
    b) program and system files?
14. Describe the functions of these personnel; what other duties do they have?
15. Describe for the first six questions above the variations in procedures that occur:—
    a) during shifts outside the normal working day and at weekends
        1
        2
        3
        4
        5
        6
    b) during periods of nonproduction work (e.g., program testing).
        1
        2
        3
        4
        5
        6
16. In each case, who is responsible for reviewing and supervising the described procedures?
17. What evidence exists that this review and supervision are carried out?

Computer Operations

18. What are the installation standards with respect to the preparation and use of operating instructions for each application (attach copy of standard)?
19. Have such operating instructions, in accordance with these standards been prepared for all applications?
20. How are these documents filed?
21. Who approves operating instructions? How is this approval evidenced?

22. Is a manual log of computer operations prepared (attach specimen copy)? What information is included in the log? Does the log show details of how all computer time is spent? Does the log show all unusual situations (e.g., hardware malfunctions, reruns, abnormal endings)?

23. Is a log of computer operations prepared by the computer in hard copy form? Describe the software used to generate these logs?

24. Describe the information included on the systems console and/or in the system log?

25. Does the printed log and/or system log automatically record all system and operator interaction during the start of a job, file set up, processing and end-of-job routines?

26. If a system log is being recorded, describe the software used to examine and print the log.

27. What standard options have been included and/or what nonstandard amendments have been made to software used to generate and print logs?

28. How does the company ensure that the logs are complete and that all pages are accounted for and seen by the reviewer?

29. Who reviews the logs?

30. Describe the procedures carried out by the reviewer. How does the reviewer evidence his review?

31. How does the reviewer ensure that any corrective action necessary as a result of the reviews is carried out?

32. Is a processing schedule prepared? Are this schedule and all changes thereto authorized? How is this authorization evidenced?

33. When, how often, by whom, and to what extent are the logs compared to the processing schedule?

34. Are all reruns and the reasons for the reruns recorded? How does the company ensure that all reruns are recorded?

35. Who investigates and reviews the reasons for the reruns? How is this review evidenced?

36. How does the company ensure that the correct authorized programs are being called by each step in a job stream?

37. Provide a list and describe all standard and nonstandard utility programs which have the capability of making run-time amendments to data files and object programs?

38. Describe the procedures for the access to and usage of these special utilities and name the personnel entitled to use them.

39. Is each use of such a utility recorded?

40. How does the company ensure that this record is complete and that all usages are accounted for?

41. Who reviews and approves this record? How is this approval evidenced?

42. In each case, who is responsible for reviewing and supervising the procedures described?

43. What evidence exists that this supervision is carried out?

44. Who reviews the outstanding change forms to identify those that have been delayed? How is this review and the reason for the delay documented?

Software Testing

45. Describe the procedures for testing or reviewing output to ensure that all new facilities and capabilities are functioning properly.

46. How are these procedures documented?

47. Do the procedures apply equally to the selection of options and changes? If not, then list the differences.

48. Who reviews and approves the results of the testing? How is this approval documented?

49. How, and under what circumstances, are urgent modifications made (e.g., by the use of utility programs) bypassing the normal testing procedures described above?

50. Who authorizes the waiver of the normal procedures? How is this authorization documented?

51. Describe the procedures for subsequently checking such modifications.

52. How does the company ensure that all such modifications are subsequently checked?

Software Implementation

53. Who is responsible for the final review and approval of all new operating systems? How is this approval documented?

54. How does the company ensure that all new operating systems and software are implemented as authorized and that no unauthorized amendments are made between the time of approval and when they are put into use?

55. Do the procedures apply equally to all the selections of options and changes? If not list the differences.

56. How does the company ensure that operating systems and software remain correct and up to date and that no unauthorized changes are made?

Systems Development
New Systems

57. What are the installation standards with respect to the preparation and contents of outline systems descriptions (attach copy of standard)? Have such systems descriptions, in accordance with these standards, been prepared for all systems or applications (attach a sample copy)?

58. How are these documents filed?

59. Who in the user department has the authority to review and approve these outline systems descriptions? How is this approval evidenced?

60. Who in the data processing function has the authority? How is this approval evidenced?

61. What are the installation standards with respect to detailed system descriptions (attach a copy of the standards)? Have such detailed system descriptions been prepared for all systems or applications (attach a sample copy)?

62. How are these documents filed?

63. Who in the user department has the authority to review and approve these detailed systems descriptions? How is this approval evidenced?

64. Who in the system development function has the authority? How is this approval evidenced?

65. Who in the computer operations function has the authority? How is this approval evidenced?

Application Program Modifications

66. Describe the procedures for requesting changes to operational production systems or programs?

67. Are all changes documented on a standard change form (attach copy)? who reviews and approves the changes? How is this approval evidenced?

68. How are the change forms filed?

69. How does the company ensure that a change form is prepared in every case?

70. How does the company ensure that all changes are carried out?

71. How does the company ensure that all change forms are authorized?

72. Who reviews the outstanding change forms to identify those that have been delayed? How are this review and the reason for the delay documented?

Testing

73. For new systems, what are the installation standards (attach a copy of the standard) with respect to:
    a) program testing?
    b) systems testing?
    c) testing of clerical and administrative procedures?

74. How does the company ensure that all testing is carried out in accordance with these standards? Have all programs and systems been tested in accordance with these standards. Describe the procedures for retaining and filing test data, test results, and other evidence of successful testing.

75. Do the procedures apply equally for all application program modifications? It not, list the differences.

76. Do the standards require that systems testing be reperformed for every program change? If not, describe the extent of the testing.

77. Who in the systems development function has the authority to review and approve the

results of the testing? How is this approval evidenced?

78. Who in the computer operations function has this authority? How is this approval evidenced?

Immediate Modifications

79. How, and under what circumstances are urgent modifications made (e.g., by the use of utility programs) bypassing the normal testing procedures described above?

80. Who authorizes the waiver of the normal procedures? How is this authorization documented?

81. Describe the procedures for subsequently checking such modifications?

82. How does the company ensure that all such modifications are subsequently checked by both the data processing function and user departments?

Acceptance and Implementation

83. As part of the final acceptance procedures, prior to implementation of a new system, who is responsible for ensuring that the following are prepared in accordance with the installation standards in each case, and how is this approval evidenced for:
    a) program documentation?
    b) systems documentation?
    c) operating instructions?

84. In the case of modifications to systems do the procedures ensure that the documentation and instructions are amended so as to be up to date and in accordance with the company's standards?

85. Describe the procedures for using and controlling the program libraries, including where applicable source statement libraries, object code library, executable libraries, procedures libraries, system files, data base definitions and libraries. Name and describe any librarian packages used.

86. Who is authorized to read and execute programs in these libraries?

87. Who is authorized to change these libraries?

88. How does the company ensure that all unauthorized uses of the libraries are detected?

89. How does the company ensure that all programs are implemented as authorized and that no unauthorized amendments are made to approved systems between the time they are approved and when they are put into operation?

90. Who is responsible for ensuring that changes made to executable program libraries are also made to source statement libraries or vice versa?

91. Who is responsible for reviewing and approving this work? How is this approval evidenced?

92. How does the company ensure that all program libraries remain correct and up to date and that all errors are detected?

93. Who in the data processing function is responsible for giving the final review and approval on systems for operational use? Does this review include an assurance that all necessary reviews and approvals have been performed? How is this final review evidenced?

94. Are users notified in writing of the effective date when new systems, and modifications to systems, become operational? Where is this notification filed?

95. Does this function ensure that all documentation and instructions remain correct and up to date?

Bibliography

American Institute of Certified Public Accountants, *Auditing Standards and Procedures* (SAS #3), New York, NY, 1963.

Canadian Institute of Chartered Accountants, *Computer Control Guidelines*, Toronto, 1971.

Canadian Institute of Chartered Accountants, *Computer Audit Guidelines*, Toronto, 1975.

Coopers & Lybrand, *Implementation & Integrity Control Checklist*, New York, NY, 1976.

Federal Deposit Insurance Corporation, *Work Program for Electronic Data Processing Examinations and Serviced Bank Questionnaire*, New York, NY, 1978.

Institute of Internal Auditors, *System Auditability and Control Study*, (Researched by Stanford Research Institute under a grant from International Business Machines Corporation), Altamonte, FL, 1977.

Thompson, Richard S., "Computer Auditing: Organization and Techniques," *Computer Handbook for Senior Management*, Macmillan Information, New York, NY, 1978, Chapter 14.

Wasserman, Joseph J., "Plugging the Leaks in Computer Security," *Harvard Business Review*, September/October 1969.

Wasserman, Joseph J., "Computer Auditing," *Computer Security Handbook*, Macmillan Information, New York, NY, 1973.

Yourdon, Edward and Constantine, Larry, *Structured Design*, Yourdon Press, New York, NY, 1978 pp. 42–57, 81, 114, 155–169.

CHAPTER 9
System Application Controls

By Javier F. Kuong

Introduction

Application Controls and Relation to Other Controls

This chapter deals with the subject of internal controls for computerized application systems. In order to process business data, organizations require computer hardware, operating systems and software, adequate facilities, and knowledgeable personnel. All these elements require controls if they are to function properly. However, it is through the application systems with its key files or data bases, that computerized decisions are determined and processed.

If a data center is compromised, an intruder could damage or destroy the physical devices and media that store and process information. Appropriate access controls could minimize this possibility, just as contingency planning would minimize its effect in the event of an actual occurrence. On the other hand, if the application system itself lacks controls, the end result can range from minor disruptions to catastrophic situations, including misstatement or loss of assets, improper decision making, and programmed fraud. All of these can have substantial adverse consequences on an organization, ranging from lost profits to violations of legislative or regulatory mandates.

Figure 9.1 shows the role of application controls with respect to other control layers. The other controls are discussed elsewhere in this handbook. The illustration shows that application system controls are an integral part of the total protection grid for the organization's data and information.

The chapter deals with some of the methods that are available to design and evaluate appli-

cation controls. The chapter discusses several methods in order to provide the reader with a choice of methods from which he can arrive at the best approach to suit his needs. It may be shortsighted to consider only one single method since the selection of the proper method can vary depending upon the level of sophistication desired in relation to the complexity or nature of the application system that one is contemplating. In actual practice, the control and security professional can use a combination of the methods explained in this chapter, as the methods are not necessarily mutually exclusive and will tend to reinforce one another.

Approach Used

The method by which security and audit specialists go about handling application controls depends upon a number of factors, such as the type of system involved, the system complexity, and whether one is building or evaluating the application controls. The dynamic evolution in computer-based systems over the past two decades has also brought about a major need to examine the various ways by which the control and security specialist deals with application controls.

This chapter reviews the importance of internal controls for application systems and presents three main approaches to design and evaluation of controls. Next, it provides a description of each of the methods discussed in sufficient detail to permit the controls specialist to obtain a practical understanding of each method, enable him to make an informed decision on each method and permit him to apply it to his particular environment. It also discusses the advantages and disadvantages of each method and suggests when

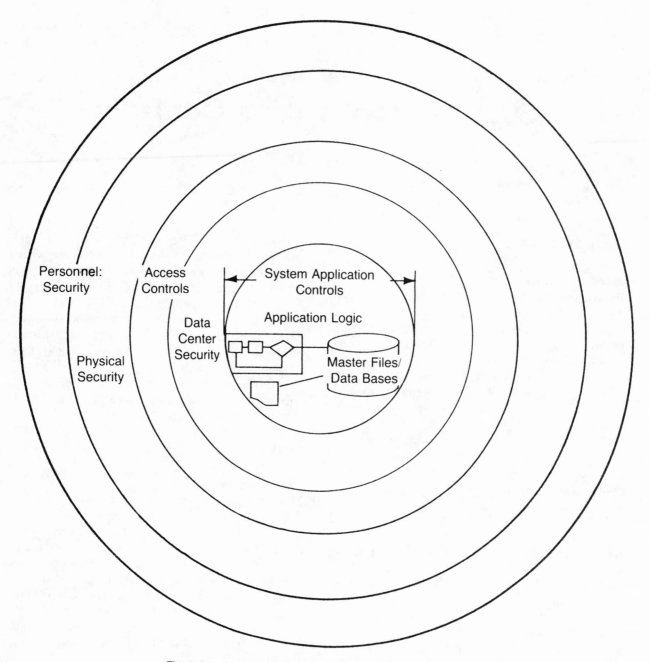

Figure 9.1 Application controls in relation to other control layers

or for what types of systems, each of the methods discussed would be most appropriate.

The material presented addresses controls with particular reference to computerized application systems. However, a great deal of the information applies to other aspects of data processing and business systems in general, including the control of special situations such as microcomputers or personal computers.

Methods for Designing and Building Application Controls

There are a number of methods to deal with application controls. The various methods and their suitability depend upon the purpose for which the given approach is used, (whether controls building or review), and to a good extent the type and level of complexity of the application system that one is dealing with. The methods that will be covered are:

1. Checklists and questionnaires
2. Input, output, and processing (I.O.P.)
3. Control zones/Control points risk analysis

The first two are the most conventionally used and the most popular. The checklists and questionnaires approach is often employed in connection with the "review" of internal controls in conventional or simple systems and for data centers. The second method, input-output and processing approach, has been traditionally used with regard to both building and reviewing internal controls with particular reference to application systems. The third method is the most comprehensive of all three. It is based on risk analysis methods and on a progressive breakdown of all areas of the application system exposure into specific control zones and points and their associated control objectives. This approach offers a structured methodology that is ideally suited to *designing and building* internal controls in general and in particular for application systems.

Checklists and Questionnaires Method

Although most systems and security professionals are familiar with the checklists and questionnaires method of dealing with internal controls, it will be explained here to clarify a few key points not normally discussed in the literature, and in the interest of providing a balanced coverage of each of the methods discussed in this chapter.

It is a well-known fact that auditors, and particularly external auditors, have used the checklists and questionnaires method in the process of "evaluating" internal control for years. Before one can understand the reason for their popularity, it is well to discuss why auditors use application system checklists and questionnaires.

When business applications are developed, it is seldom that a set of control practices and procedures are clearly defined, specified, and documented. One of the main reasons is that most organizations lack a formal and systematic methodology for designing and building internal controls. Another key reason is the absence of control standards and guidelines for the most common application systems.

Therefore, when evaluating application internal controls, the auditor or security specialist is quite handicapped in the conduct of the evaluation process, as there are no clear-cut "measures of performance" against which to gauge the adequacy of application controls. Contrast this situation to what is the case, for example, in engineering design. Equipment design usually requires a precise articulation of the specifications for the construction of a given piece of equipment with a minimum of ambiguities. If the designer or another individual wishes to evaluate either the adequacy of the design or the soundness of operation of the equipment, it is possible to take the set of specifications or the documented operating standards and turn them into a set of checklists and questionnaires for evaluation.

An example will illustrate this point:

Device XYZ

Specification or Standard Practice	Questionnaire	Yes	No
Design			
• There should be a safety latch provided to prevent the unit from starting when loaded.	• Has a safety latch been provided to prevent inadvertent start which can cause the unit to be damaged?		
Operation			
• The safety latch must be in the "ON" position at all times before equipment is started.	• Have you ensured that the safety latch is in the ON position before starting the unit?		

In the cited example, the specification or the standard practice is described on the left and the corresponding questionnaire item is shown on the right column. Usually, the questions are set up so that if the answer is "yes" the condition under review is satisfactory. A "no" answer would indicate a control deficiency.

Translating this general method from the design engineering field to the applications control field, the applicability of the method to controls is direct. In fact, the contents of the left column can make up the checklist portion, and the contents of the right column can constitute the questionnaire portion. Another way to look at this method is to think of the left column contents as being the *control specification or requirement* (the design portion) and the contents of the right column as being the basis for *controls evaluation or testing of the controls*.

This method shows that in engineering, design and operation standards are developed and prepared *in advance* of building the device. It is thus possible not only to construct a safe device but, also, to evaluate its soundness.

Because clear control specification and standards are often lacking in EDP applications systems, auditors and security specialist are forced to develop checklists and questionnaires "after the fact," which are intended to be a mirror-image view of the controls that should have been present in the first place, in order to have an adequately controlled system. In this sense, then, the controls checklist and questionnaires are a form of a "measure of controls adequacy" and, in many cases, a form of the "minimum acceptable control standards" that should exist in order for internal controls of the application system to be judged adequate.

Examples of checklists and questionnaires are shown at the end of this chapter with particular reference to checklists for input, processing, and output controls.

Application of the Method   The *checklists and questionnaires method* was developed at the time when computerized business systems were mostly manually operated, relatively simple, and supported by individual and separate files. By contrast, many of today's highly computerized systems are far from being manual, simple, or limited to using separate files, but rather are quite integrated. Thus, this raises questions as to whether this method, by itself, is adequate for dealing with application controls in today systems.

Listed below are the conditions under which this method for controls building and evaluation is best suited.

- When dealing with simple, manually operated systems, such as batch processing systems
- When there are no clear standards, specification, and documentation on the application controls on which to base the controls review
- When time limitations do not permit the use of other more comprehensive methods

The Input-Output-Processing Controls Approach

The input-output-processing method (I.O.P.) is the most commonly known and used. In this approach, the designer or auditor views the application system into three major control subdivisions. It then focuses on the controls that apply to each of the three subdivisions. An overly simplified way to view this approach is to think in terms of "what goes out must be reconcilable to what went in after considering how it was processed en route to becoming the output." The fundamentals of the I.O.P. approach are described in the following sections.

Types of Procedural Controls or Control Phases   Procedural input-to-output controls are concerned with controls over the flow of data. Most books and the literature consider three types of controls for applications:

1. Input controls
2. Processing or throughput controls
3. Output controls

Although this classification is useful, it is often more educational to think in terms of the three main equivalent phases, namely:

1. Input phase (Source document control, pre-processing)
2. Processing phase
3. Output phase (Output control-error control, distribution-user controls)

A schematic view of these phases and what they encompass is shown in Figure 9.2. The input

The objectives of input controls are:

1. To ascertain that all transactions have been properly recorded at the source level.
2. To insure that all transactions that are to be processed are accounted for at source level and at the pre-processing stages (e.g., Keypunch).
3. To insure proper authorization of transactions.
4. To insure that all transactions are transmitted from point of origin to point of processing.
5. To insure that error-re-entry procedures are followed.
6. To insure data batches are logged properly (signed in and out).

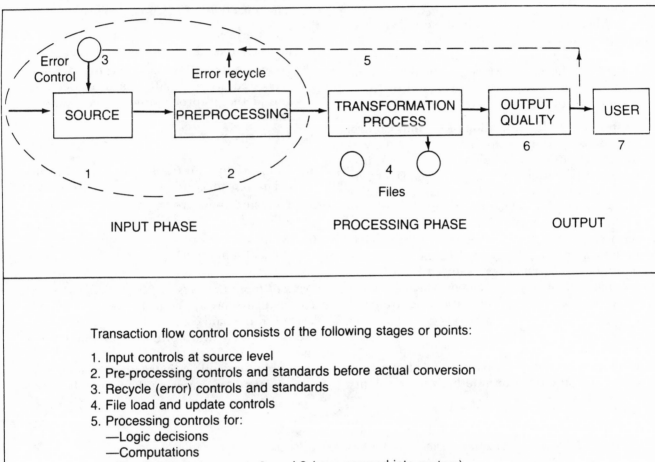

Transaction flow control consists of the following stages or points:

1. Input controls at source level
2. Pre-processing controls and standards before actual conversion
3. Recycle (error) controls and standards
4. File load and update controls
5. Processing controls for:
   —Logic decisions
   —Computations
   —Quality controls over 1, 2, and 3 (programmed into system)
6. Output quality controls
7. User end-use controls (quality, quantity, accuracy, timeliness, security, etc.).

Each of the above has a series of steps or sub-stages which must be considered on their own merits. For example, for the INPUT PHASE, we can distinguish the following important stages:
   I-1. Source data preparation (usually manual preparations, tickets)
   I-2. Data authorization
   I-3. Data conversion   } These may be subject
   I-4. Data transmission   } to both manual
   I-5. Input validation   } and computerized
   I-6. Error correction and re-entry procedures } procedures.

Figure 9.2 Transaction flow in a system application

phase generally encompasses both the source document and preprocessing stages. The processing phase deals with the actual transformation stages, and the output phase usually includes the data center output quality controls and distribution procedures and user-end control procedures.

When viewed in this light, we obtain a more complete understanding of the whole transaction flow process from transaction initiation to the time when the end user receives the required information. Both processing steps and the associated controls are considered in this manner.

Responsibility for Execution of Various Control Functions   It is useful to show which of the various functions or tasks belong to the input, processing, and output phases, and which Data Center units are responsible for execution of these steps. Table 9.1 tabulates functions pertaining to the main three stages of transaction flow along with responsibility for execution. These basic functions are directly related to the processing of applications. Figure 9.2 showed Data Center internal administrative functions which are more directly concerned with operations control.

Input Phase Controls

Definition and Objectives
Input phase controls constitute a set of procedures to ensure the proper authorization, validity or normality, and completeness of source documents and data to be processed. A large number of these procedures can be performed manually by the source and/or user department. Many can also be mechanized by programming them into the application system.

The objectives of input controls are:

1. To ascertain that all transactions have been properly recorded at the source level
2. To insure that all transactions that are to be processed are accounted for at source level and at the preprocessing stages (e.g., data entry)
3. To insure proper authorization of transactions
4. To insure that all transactions are transmitted from point of origin to point of processing
5. To insure that error-reentry procedures are followed
6. To insure data batches are logged properly (signed in and out)

Types of Input Controls
The controls may apply at the source document level or at the data contents level, which includes the data itself and control over master file changes.

Computers follow instructions exactly. This requires that data entering the system be trans-

Table 9.1   Application Control Phases in Relation to Functions Responsible for Execution

Function/Task	Application Control Phase			Performed by
	Input	Processing	Output	
Input control (Logging)	X			Users and control clerks
Microscheduling/Dispatching	X			Control
Data Preparation	X			Data preparation (preprocessing)
Job Assembly	X			Control
File Library	X		X	Control–librarian
Processing Functions		X		Machine operations
Job Disassembly			X	Control
Report Quality Control			X	Control
Report Finishing and Distribution			X	Control
Error Discrepancy and Management	X		X	Control and users

lated into machine-readable language and in correct form and content. If input is captured accurately and completely, the processing of data will be relatively simple once computer programs have been debugged. The development of formal procedures, written instructions, and the minimization of transactions requiring special treatment will increase input accuracy and strengthen internal control.

Control over Source Documents

The need to provide controls over source documents and computer input is important. Prenumbered documents and sequence checks could be used wherever possible, together with written approvals wherever appropriate. All transactions should originate outside of the data processing department and a register should be maintained, or multiple copies provided. Document counts, dollar control totals, and control totals for other fields should be developed for each batch of documents sent to Data Processing. Regular deliveries should be scheduled and transmittal forms should be used with each request.

Special emphasis should be placed on the need for control over master file changes. Changes to these files can influence dollar answers. For instance, a vendor added to a master file of approved vendors might be the basis for approval of an invoice upon a match in the computer. In this situation, there is an obvious need for this vendor to be genuine and to be approved by authorized personnel. A written authorization for changes to master files is a good operating practice.

It should be noted that many controls that contribute to improved validation of input data can be programmed into the computerized system to detect anomalies for subsequent corrections. These are dealt with in the next section. Exhibits 9.1 and 9.2 summarize the needs for transaction controls.

Exhibit 9.1
System Application Transaction (Data) Control Needs

Transaction controls are needed to insure that:

1. The transaction is complete.
2. The transaction is normal (not anomalous). For example:
   Alpha instead of numeric
   Quantity larger than normal, etc.

3. All transactions in a group are transmitted and/or processed. Control totals in the control log to reconcile input controls with controls (totals) generated upon processing. Example:
   A batch control total on:
   A. Number of transactions per batch ensures that all clock cards in a payroll application (documents, checks, cards) are received. However, this is not good enough for accuracy of the amount. Therefore we use:
   B. A field total (say, hours worked). This can be used to validate the computer processed output against input controls received.

For Items 1 and 2, input validation techniques are available. They are listed in Exhibit 9.2.

Exhibit 9.2
System Application Controls for Input Validation

For data completeness and normality checks, it is common practice to use input validation control techniques.

Input validation should be practiced as soon as possible. This is usually done through computerized (programmed) edit controls (or filters) for the following needs or conditions:

1. Validity (transactions, codes, fields.) Accept/reject type. Reject relative to:
   • Validity
   • Reasonableness
   • Limits
   Criteria can be against
   • Quantity
   • Amounts
   • Codes
   Relative to:
   • Values given
   • Tables of values
   • Actual master file accounts, items
   • Official values, rates, discounts, etc.
2. Completeness
3. Limits
4. Logical tests. Relationship to other things: Branch code, transaction code teller no., terminal no. and assigned password, etc.
5. Control totals
6. Sequence
7. Self-checking digits
8. Ratio tests
9. Pattern analysis
10. Conversational or dialogue controls

Processing Phase Controls

Definitions and Objectives

Processing controls encompass a set of manual and mechanized procedures and techniques designed to help meet basic quality, accuracy, and regulatory requirements of information during the computer processing phase at the data center.

The basic objectives of processing controls are to:

1. Detect loss or nonprocessing of data
2. Determine if arithmetic or mathematical calculations were performed correctly
3. Determine whether all relevant transactions were posted to the proper record or file
4. Spot possible program deficiencies or errors and aid in their resolution
5. Insure that proper files are loaded for a given job
6. Minimize operator errors or job assembly mistakes

Nature of Processing Controls

The accuracy of processing depends upon the checks designed and built into the equipment by vendors and the programmed controls included by users and data processing professionals in the programs. Naturally, the adequacy of the programmed controls also depends on the accuracy and correctness of the conception, testing, and execution of the programs during the system design and development phase of the application systems, as well as the proper documentation, review, and approval process.

All EDP equipment manufacturers have checks built into the equipment to ensure that data are correctly read, processed, transferred within the system and recorded on output media. These checks are sometimes referred to as "hardware" controls, and include parity checks, dual read-write heads, dual circuitry, and file protection rings.

In addition to the hardware checks, data processing accuracy in EDP systems is achieved by programmed controls or checks to detect loss or nonprocessing of data including record counts, control and hash totals, and sequence checks. Programmed checks of arithmetic calculations include limit checks, crossfooting, balance checks, proof figures, zero balancing, and reverse arithmetic.

Programmed Controls

The amount of control that can be built into a program is limited only by the ingenuity of the designer. It is much easier to build in controls at the beginning than later. It is sometimes contended that controls reduce the operating speed of the computer and, under certain circumstances, this may be true. Usually, the incorporation of a few additional controls would not add to the running time significantly.

One of the cardinal rules of data processing has always been never to proceed to another process until you are absolutely sure the previous process was completed. This has generally been accomplished by proving to predetermined totals or control totals, by crossfooting, by downfooting, and by proving the accuracy of computations. In addition there are limit or tolerance tests, sign checking, and duplicate or complement arithmetic. Linkage between programs or the fact that one program should precede or follow another, and that certain characteristics should be present in both, can be used to advantage. Sequence checks can be used in many situations. A good deal of this is accomplished by Job Control language instructions and run-to-run controls.

Programmed checks for proper postings are used to achieve accuracy in files and records. The problem of file integrity is a significant one in EDP systems because of the absence of "visible" records and because of the ease with which wrong information can be written on magnetic tapes and disks. In order to assure that proper tapes or disks are used, and that records are not lost, controls should be maintained for:

- Tape and disk labels
- Record counts which are checked from program to program as a file passes through the system
- Hash totals for the same purpose
- Redundant identifiers, such as an alpha code corresponding to the last name of an account
- Memory protection and file protection to prevent valuable information from being wiped out in error
- Suspense accounts for the accumulation of the amounts of error records which are discarded from the system

Suspense accounts help in balancing the data and point out the errors to be corrected.

Output Phase Controls

Objectives and Scope

The objectives of output phase controls are to:

1. Reconcile output data with input controls during processing
2. Determine reasonableness of the information produced
3. Check for normal format and quantity of information
4. Control rejected input data produced during processing and take the necessary steps to route it to the appropriate people for disposition
5. Review and control the distribution of output reports to authorized users according to established quality, quantity, timeliness and security acceptance criteria

During the output phase, the control unit has the last opportunity to ensure that data processing output is correct, free of obvious abnormalities, and that, in fact, it reaches only authorized personnel.

Another set of output controls are those practiced by the originating or user group through review of abnormal items or conditions. This process is greatly aided by a combination of the programmed controls mentioned above and the use of exception report capabilities built into any one system, to warn the user of any possible anomalous situations.

Control over Reports

Adequate control of reports and documents requires participation by departments outside of Data Processing. A sound system should include regular systematic review of output by these using departments to ascertain that established requirements are being met. Since most reports are used by someone, and in this use are subject to some scrutiny, it might be contended that this requirement is automatically fulfilled. The key to effectiveness of review, however, is the planned approach on a regular basis using such yardsticks as predetermined totals, appropriate budget amounts, standards of performance, results of prior periods, and other tests of reasonableness, along with exception reporting. It is also possible to relate present balances on a recent report to balances of previous reports for the previous period plus the net of new transactions for the new

period. In other words, by conducting a period-to-period balance.

Error Control and Resubmission of Corrections

One of the problem areas created by EDP is the computer-detected error. In most manual systems, and in some machine systems, many of these errors would go undetected or would be dismissed as immaterial. Unless told to do so, the computer cannot process even the slightest error. Many of these errors are due to carelessness in preparing the original source document or an anomalous condition. A good system should provide information that can be used in improving performance of the data originators. Reducing the number of source document errors is obviously one of the best ways to improve computer performance.

Procedures should provide assurance that all error data are investigated, corrected, and resubmitted. Generally, all errors from a given application should be controlled by one department outside of data processing, with that department contacting others as required. This department should be provided with an error register and the applicable source documents should be filed in such a way as to allow the particular document in which the error exists to be located. Written approvals should be used for error correction, wherever appropriate, and further control is necessary to ensure that the error is corrected and resubmitted. This is normally done through the control section within EDP.

Distribution of Reports

Control over distribution of output reports is needed to ensure that the final products of the system are disseminated in compliance with requirements for timeliness, security, and confidentiality. Exhibit 9.3 provides a useful report profile for distribution control.

Exhibit 9.3

Report Distribution Control List

Report Specification Data

- Report name
- What is the report intended for (brief description)
- Who is the report intended for and who will use it in the user group
- Size of report (no. of pages)
- No. of copies and authorized roster for distribution

- Retention cycle (file copies, microfilm)
- Sample copy of report or report format layout
- Schedules and due-out dates. Frequency of processing (daily, etc.)
- Specification of official programs used to generate report according to run book
- Table of data elements of items printed in the report, including where these originate from, regarding data source and how arrived at in processing
- Special instructions for security and confidentiality

Application of the Input-Output-Processing Method

This method can be applied to almost every type of application system, whether manual or computerized. The method is best suited to manual and batch computerized application systems where the breakdown of the application into the three main input, processing, and output control zones is quite adequate. For advanced/on-line and complex systems, the input-output-processing method may not provide the level of detail needed for a thorough analysis of application system controls.

The Control Zones/Control Points/ Risk Analysis Method

This approach represents one of the most comprehensive methods available for the design, selection, justification, and assessment of internal controls. Although the fundamental concepts have been available in other areas, such as corporate planning, decision theory, and economic analysis, the methodology has been further refined in connection with the development of EDP controls.

Under this method, the controls designer or reviewer focuses on control zones and points as the main points of application system processing activity. He then uses risk analysis and control objective concepts to select the appropriate controls.

The methods differ from the input-processing-output controls approach in that instead of limiting oneself to just three major control zones, as many control zones as may be required to permit a more thorough analysis of the situation can in fact be conceived. In this sense, the methods discussed in this chapter can be considered actually complementary and all three methods can be used to reinforce the other two.

Generalized Procedure for the Control Zones/ Controls Point Method   A detailed description of this method would require a complete treatise or manual on the subject itself. Figure 9.3 describes and illustrates the main phases of this controls design methodology in schematic form.[3,4,5]

The methodology comprises four submethodologies:

Sub-Methodology	What It Addresses
1. Risk Analysis	What is the exposure?
2. Management by Objectives	What must be done?
3. Controls Design and Selection	What controls meet the objectives?
4. Cost/effectiveness Analysis	What controls are economical to implement?

In brief summary, the first submethodology determines the extent of exposure derived from the threats that attack the control zones in the application system. The second submethodology produces a set of detailed control objectives to be met. The third component helps select the most desirable controls that would meet the control objectives specified in the second component. The last component determines which of the selected controls can meet the cost-effectiveness criteria for subsequent implementation.

In the process, this methodology produces a far more thorough documentation of the controls analysis and design process for subsequent controls evaluation. This documentation can be used for:

- Controls design documentation
- Control evaluation documentation
- Compliance to the Foreign Corrupt Practices Act
- Communications documentation to help all concerned with application controls

An Illustration

The essence of the method is explained below.

Consider the Data Entry area of an application system. This area can become the first control zone. To enter data in an application system, one could conceive at least the following "control points":

- The data entry *operator*
- The *terminal* through which transactions are entered

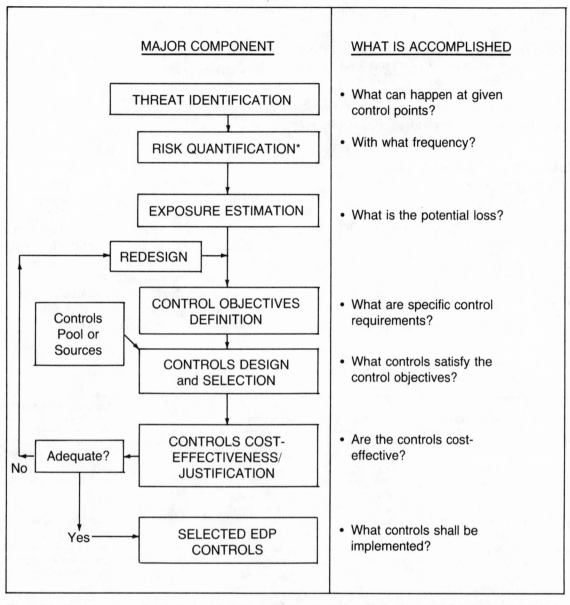

MAJOR COMPONENT

WHAT IS ACCOMPLISHED

THREAT IDENTIFICATION
- What can happen at given control points?
- With what frequency?

RISK QUANTIFICATION*

EXPOSURE ESTIMATION
- What is the potential loss?

REDESIGN

CONTROL OBJECTIVES DEFINITION
- What are specific control requirements?

Controls Pool or Sources

CONTROLS DESIGN and SELECTION
- What controls satisfy the control objectives?

CONTROLS COST-EFFECTIVENESS/ JUSTIFICATION
Adequate?
No
- Are the controls cost-effective?

Yes

SELECTED EDP CONTROLS
- What controls shall be implemented?

Figure 9.3 Overall process of designing and justifying controls by the Control Zones, Control Objectives and Risk Analysis Approach.

- The various types of *transactions* that the data entry operator enters into the application system

In considering the control point "terminal," one could postulate a number of "threats" that could beset the control point terminal. For example, common threats may be:

- Danger that unauthorized personnel may access the system via the terminal

- Possibility that the terminal may become disabled and thus cause a discontinuity in business operations

Now the risk could be estimated by one of the various methods of risk quantification covered in the literature. See reference (7) for example. Using one of these methods, the risk and the exposure incurred are as follows:

- Illegal accesses could occur at the rate of 30

per month with a potential loss of $300 each time it happens.

- The calculated exposure is the product of these two numbers or 30 × $300, or $9,000 per month, or $108,000 per year.

Knowing the threat and the extent of exposure, we can articulate a specific "control objective":

- Ensure that unauthorized access to the sensitive terminal does not occur.

Now that a specific control objective is known, the control techniques or solutions must be found, as follows:

- Ensure the terminal is enclosed in a locked room.
- Ensure that the terminal has physical locks.
- Ensure that the terminal requires personal

identification and authentication codes, such as passwords, etc.

- Provide authorization tables to discern the various level of access and authority pertaining to different users.

The next step in the methodology is to work out the economics of the proposed controls. If the savings or reduction in exposure are in excess of the cost of implementing the controls, the controls are adopted. Otherwise, either fewer controls are installed or intangible values are postulated for management decision. This completes the design and justification cycle. The next steps to include are the "documentation" of the selected controls and the preparation of "detailed" implementation instructions.

The procedure outline above is applied to every control point defined in the application system situation at hand.

Table 9.2   Advantages and Disadvantages of the Three Methods

Checklists and Questionnaires	Input/Output/Processing	Control Zones/Control Points/Risk Analysis
Advantages • Simple to understand • This method is well known by the controls and security community and widely used in reviewing internal controls • If the questionnaire for the situation under review is already available, the method provides the fastest way to review application controls • It can be used by relatively inexperienced personel **Disadvantages** • The method is not comprehensive and does not relate to the idea of threats and risks • The checklist-questionnaire may not be available for each particular application situation so that often general checklists are made to apply to a wide variety of situations • It does not relate findings to control objectives and it is difficult to apply to complex applications and to systems that are logically interrelated.	**Advantages** • Simplicity in understanding and application • Widespread use of the method all over the world, which leads to ease of communications on work papers among professionals • The method is not as laborious as other methods since it focuses on controls at only three main zones • It can provide an overall view of the controls and their interrelatedness **Disadvantages** • The method is relatively crude and fails to show the reason for building the control. That is to say, it does not give a measure of exposure, unless this is documented outside the description of the controls • The method controls at only three main zones. The possibility exists that other important areas can be missed	**Advantages** • The method is rational, structured, and thorough. It proposes controls only in proportion to risk/exposure • The method forces the user to formulate specific control objectives before selecting control solutions at key control points • The method is ideally suited for the controls building process and provides sound and detailed documentation for controls assessment purposes • The method forces detailed thinking that leads to the selection of specific controls to satisfy specific control objectives. • The method provides detailed information for the process of justifying internal controls **Disadvantages** • Additional effort is required to detail the control zones and control objectives. This is actually an advantage in terms of forcing the analyst to do a more thorough job • It requires reindoctrination of personnel in risk analysis concepts and on the details of this new methodology. (With new personnel, this is not an issue.)

Advantages and Disadvantages of the Three Application Control Methods

As can be expected no single method for dealing with application controls is ideal and perfect. Each of the methods presented has advantages and disadvantages. Table 9.2 presents a comparative summary of the pros and cons of each method.

Summary

This chapter highlights the vital importance of application controls, indicating that it is from the application systems, its programs, files, and logic, that many of the most serious exposures to a company may derive. The application controls present a major supplementary barrier to errors of omission and commission, to fraud, and to potential information and asset loss.

As application systems become increasingly computerized, and by increasingly complex methods of computerization, such as by advanced, on-line, data base and data communication networks, the method for dealing with application controls should be commensurate with the complexity of the new computerized environment. The checklists and questionnaires method and the traditional input-output-processing (I.O.P.) method for building and reviewing controls by themselves, are becoming increasingly limited to deal with controls design and evaluation needs of modern complex systems. The control zones, control points, control objectives approach, based on risk analysis, can be used to supplement and enhance the checklists-questionnaires method and the input-processing-output method of dealing with application controls. The third method is also quite useful in the process of "building" internal controls into application systems. It should also be pointed out that all three methods are applicable to controlling microcomputer applications, which represent just another special case of application systems.

Accordingly, auditors and security specialists should urge management to support their efforts to improve the methods by which application systems controls are conceived, designed, and cost-justified. This process requires a significant amount of effort and a reindoctrination program for users, data processing and audit and security professionals. Regardless of the control method used, the most important consideration is that security and control professionals use application system controls to safeguard their application systems. The question of which method to use becomes a matter of style and preference.

System Application Controls Checklist

	Yes	No
Are the persons responsible for computer operations different from those responsible for the writing and maintaining of programs?	☐	☐
Are they different from those personnel with accounting (control) responsibility?	☐	☐
Are EDP operations personnel the only ones to have unsupervised access to computer files?	☐	☐
Are there formal written operating procedures in the computer area? (Run Book)	☐	☐
Are there formal, written programming standards in effect?	☐	☐
Are there formal policies in effect for the request, tracking, and testing of new systems and programs?	☐	☐
Are such policies enforced as to changes to existing programs?	☐	☐
Is the operating system maintained to the most recent version?	☐	☐
Is access to the computer and its files controlled by password security, and are such passwords regularly changed?	☐	☐
Are violations to any of the above procedures recorded in a log subject to review by some non-EDP management?	☐	☐
Are proofs or totals of input developed independently by the user rather than the EDP department?	☐	☐
Are all internal requirements enforced on purchased systems (i.e., documentation, changes, access, etc.)?	☐	☐

	Yes	No
Is there a formal policy of retention of files?	☐	☐
Are copies of all programs, including the operating system, maintained either off site or in a safe location?	☐	☐
Are there up-to-date systems flow charts and/or narratives on all major applications?	☐	☐

Input Phase Controls Checklist

Control over Input Data

Although the review of controls over input data must be done for each application eventually, general questions regarding these controls may be used to ascertain whether use of control procedures is evident.

	Yes	No
Are source departments required to establish independent control over data submitted for processing (through the use of batch totals, document counts, record counts, hash totals, etc.)?	☐	☐
Is the number of basic types of input documents limited so as to facilitate control and processing efficiency?	☐	☐
Are all input documents prenumbered (preprinted)?	☐	☐
Are all numbered documents accounted for by the control unit?	☐	☐
Are data processed in serially numbered batches?	☐	☐
Are all source documents identified by batch number and canceled to prevent reprocessing?	☐	☐
Are data controlled by the number of documents processed and by hash totals as well as by dollar amount?	☐	☐
Does the control unit use a document register or other positive method of comparing machine run totals with control totals?	☐	☐
Is responsibility fixed, and are adequate procedures in effect, for tracing and correcting input errors?	☐	☐

	Yes	No
Are corrections identified and recorded in such a manner that duplicate correction will not occur and subsequent audit will be possible?	☐	☐
Are all instructions to data entry operators (or machine operators preparing data tapes) written in clear, concise form?	☐	☐
If the computer writes checks or other negotiable instruments, are the requisition and use of blank stock closely controlled?	☐	☐
Are both master files and transaction files handled properly insofar as controls and verification are concerned?	☐	☐
Do source/user departments maintain independent control over master files?	☐	☐
Are all data batches identified and perferably serially numbered?	☐	☐
Is each batch accompanied by a batch control document (ticket) created by the originating department? (A copy of the source document should be maintained by the control unit for verification purposes.) Does this ticket show: batch number, date, control totals by important field, transaction count, previous batch number?	☐	☐
Are sequence controls and quantity control totals used, such as hours, units, items?	☐	☐
For on-line systems, are adequate "dialog" or interactive controls provided to ensure the correctness and propriety of input data? (6)	☐	☐

Error Procedures

Controls should ensure that rejections are corrected and reentered into the system. Sometimes rejection reports, cards, etc., are lost and the corrected data are never reentered. Better systems keep open files of rejections and clear them only when they are reentered correctly. Also, it is usually best to have rejections printed on separate reports rather than on reports containing other information. This makes them easier to isolate and correct.

	Yes	No
Are batch contents listed for user review?	☐	☐

	Yes	No
Is erroneous data captured in an error listing that accompanies each batch input printout?	☐	☐
Are there procedures for rejecting erroneous data?	☐	☐
Are errors that cause out of balance conditions spotted and rejected to keep the system in balance?	☐	☐
Are source documents canceled to avoid reentry or reprocessing?	☐	☐
Are errors and rejected input managed by the control section, sent to originating departments and records kept for reentry later?	☐	☐
Are errors removed preferably before final processing? It is preferable to catch errors, correct them and then reenter them in a new batch.	☐	☐
Are corrections actually made by the source department rather than the control unit?	☐	☐
Are master files listed and purified at appropriate intervals to reduce error sources?	☐	☐
If error stems from master file contents, are there specific procedures to correct master files?	☐	☐
Does the control unit follow up reprocessing of rejected data?	☐	☐
Are all error corrections reviewed and approved by persons who are independent of the data processing department?	☐	☐
Are records maintained of errors occurring in the EDP system?	☐	☐
Are these error records periodically reviewed by someone independent of data processing?	☐	☐

Data Preparation/Conversion

	Yes	No
Are there up-to-date written procedures for all data preparation/conversion applications, including data formats, forms, and controls?	☐	☐
Are check digits used for account codes or item numbers, where appropriate?	☐	☐

	Yes	No
Is there a manual that describes all record applications formats and layouts, including special instructions?	☐	☐
Are there controls for data conversion to machine-readable form for all types of data conversion (keypunch, keyverify, optical scanning, key-to-tape, using document counts, batch totals)?	☐	☐
Is personnel properly trained on verification procedures and on handling of discrepancies?	☐	☐
Are there procedures to prevent reentry of canceled documents?	☐	☐
Are records kept of volume of transactions processed and number of errors made?	☐	☐
If data transmission is used, are there adequate transmission controls to determine correctness of transmission or message loss?	☐	☐
Are there sound retention procedures for documents for an appropriate time period to enable reprocessing in the event of magnetic file loss?	☐	☐

Processing Phase Controls Checklist

	Yes	No
Are operator's run manuals up to date giving run instructions and including:		
(a) Complete job description	☐	☐
(b) Source, form, and condition (sorted) of input	☐	☐
(c) I/O files and which peripheral unit	☐	☐
(d) Operating steps	☐	☐
(e) Console switch settings	☐	☐
(f) Halts and required operator action	☐	☐
(g) File labels	☐	☐
(h) Job Control Language (JCL) instructions	☐	☐
Are there rules on the use of utility programs to copy files or other media?	☐	☐
Are there procedures to print out program constants (rates, discounts, prices) and reviewed by authorized personnel?	☐	☐

	Yes	No
Are there adequate procedures over use of console by operators?	☐	☐
Are console listings reviewed by a group outside EDP?	☐	☐

Programmed Control over Processing

Programmed controls are usually evaluated in terms of each application. For further details on program processing review, refer to system application review questionnaires for system audits.

	Yes	No
Are control totals used to check for completeness of processing? These may include trailer file labels, run-to-run totals, etc.	☐	☐
Are programmed edit controls used to test processing of significant items?	☐	☐
(a) Limit and reasonableness test		
(b) Crossfooting test	☐	☐
Does the program check for improper switch settings (if sense switches are used)?	☐	☐
Do programs provide an adequate console printout of control information (switch settings, control violations, operator intervention, etc.)?	☐	☐
When a program is interrupted, are there adequate provisions for restart?	☐	☐
Are there adequate controls over the process of identifying, correcting, and reprocessing data rejected by the program?	☐	☐
Is the handling of unmatched transactions (no master record corresponding to transaction record) adequate?	☐	☐
(a) Reject and note on error log		
(b) Reject and write on suspense record	☐	☐
(c) Other	☐	☐
Does the system input data in such a manner as to minimize errors?	☐	☐
Has due consideration been given to the design of foolproof source documents?	☐	☐
Have checking procedures been set up, both manually and within the computer, to detect errors?	☐	☐

Output Phase Controls Checklist

Output controls are utilized to determine the accuracy of the processing system and to insure the output goes to the proper user.

Report Distribution

After a job has been processed, the output should be returned to the operations control area.

	Yes	No
Is the job logged out in the log book and the output or outputs routed to the authorized recipients?	☐	☐
Have open output bins been avoided?	☐	☐
Is all output maintained in a controlled environment until the courier can take them directly to the user?	☐	☐
It is useful to have a set of report distribution instructions. Is a checklist of control data maintained for each important report as shown in Exhibit 9.3?	☐	☐
Are batch controls checked by the control unit: predetermined controls vs. printout of input?	☐	☐
Does the control unit compare source media against the printouts on a 100 percent or test basis? (100 percent at the start of any new system.)	☐	☐
Is the source media and a copy of the printout returned to the originating data preparation unit, which should perform its own checks for accuracy?	☐	☐
Are output reports and documents reviewed before distribution to ascertain the reasonableness of the output?	☐	☐
Are there adequate procedures for control over the distribution of reports?	☐	☐
Is there a control of usage of sensitive forms such as checks and the use of check signing devices by other than EDP personnel?	☐	☐
Do processing programs report errors or exceptions?	☐	☐
Are output totals balanced to the original input control totals?	☐	☐

	Yes	No
Is there a record of errors from all sources maintained in report form and summarized periodically for review?	☐	☐
For on-line systems, are there appropriate authorization controls for the display of sensitive data according to authorization profiles?	☐	☐

Control Zones Checklist

	Yes	No
Have the various risks and control points of the system been identified?	☐	☐
Have the risks been evaluated in financial and nonfinancial terms?	☐	☐

	Yes	No
Have control objectives been formulated and agreed upon by management?	☐	☐
Are the controls selected and designed to meet the risks that have the most important consequences?	☐	☐
Have the controls that are selected been measured in terms of their cost?	☐	☐
Are the costs of the controls applied balanced in relation to the risks they are designed to monitor or prevent?	☐	☐

Bibliography

1. CICA, "Computer Control Guidelines" vols. 1 and 2, *Canadian Institute of Chartered Accountants*, 250 Bloor Street, Toronto, Ont. M4W 1G5, Canada.

2. Klee, O.A., "The EDP Control Environment as Seen by a Systems Executive," *The Interpreter*, June 1979, pp. 19–23.

3. Kuong, J.F., "Alleviating EDP Auditing's Work Load, Improving Internal Controls Quality and Fixing Responsibility for Controls Via a Controls Design Methodology," *COM-AND, Computer Audit News and Developments*, Management Advisory Publications, Vol 1, No 2., 1983.

4. Kuong, J.F., "How To Design and Build EDP Internal Controls," course notes for seminar by the same title, *Management Advisory Services & Publications*, Wellesley Hills, MA 02181.

5. Kuong, J.F., "Checklists and Guidelines for Reviewing Computer Security and Installations," Publication MAP-4, *Management Advisory Publications*, Wellesley Hills, MA 02181.

6. Kuong, J.F., "Controls for Advanced/On-Line/Data-Base Systems," Publication MAP-19, vol 1 and 2, *Management Advisory Publications*, Wellesley Hills, MA 02181.

7. Perry, W.E. and Kuong, J.F., "EDP Risk Analysis and Controls Justification," Publication MAP-16, *Management Advisory Publications*, Wellesley Hills, MA 02181.

8. Sharrat, J.R., "Data Control Guidelines," *NCC Publications*, National Computing Centre, Manchester, U.K.

PART III
Physical Protection

CHAPTER 10

Hardware Elements of Security

By Seymour Bosworth

Introduction

A comparison of today's automobiles with those of thirty-five years ago would reveal few, if any, improvements in speed, reliability, cost, or usefulness. In contrast, this same brief period of time has seen the computer progress through four major design changes. From vacuum tubes to transistors to integrated cirucuits, to very large-scale integrated circuits, each generation has produced faster, more reliable computers—each smaller, less costly, and far more useful than earlier models. For automobiles, a 5 or 10 percent improvement in any one of these areas would be noteworthy. With computers, the improvement in each has been by factors of hundreds or even thousands. The revolutionary technological advances that made these gains possible have had equally significant, although not always beneficial effects on every aspect of computer security and data integrity. To understand how, and in what measure, requires some knowledge of computer hardware.

The development of electronic computers has proceeded along two quite different paths. One has produced the analog computer, and the other the digital machine. In the analog computer, now principally used for real-time simulation of aircraft, missiles, and dynamic systems, electronic elements are interconnected so as to behave like the physical systems they represent. The voltages in the analog then vary in a manner analogous to such physical quantities as acceleration, velocity, and displacement. In one setup, for example, 100 volts might represent a velocity of 1,000 miles per hour; 50 volts would then be equivalent to 500 miles per hour, and so on. Theoretically, in this arrangement 87.55 volts would represent 875.5 miles per hour, but in practice,

due to the inherent accuracy limitations of this technology, the actual velocity might be anything from 874.6 to 876.4 mph. An error of ±0.1 percent is usually acceptable in engineering studies, but it would meet with something less than full approval from an auditor who could not be certain if an entry should be $874.60 or $876.40, or something in-between.

Although the first commercial production of analog computers preceded their digital counterparts by more than five years, there was never a contest as to which would be more suited to commercial use. From the beginning, the digital computer aimed at absolute accuracy and total reliability. Because it uses discrete pulses of electrical energy, rather than continuously variable voltages, the digital computer is capable of approaching this goal.

Binary Design

Although there are wide differences in computer architecture and in the hardware designs that follow, all digital computers have at least one thing in common: each utilizes a uniquely coded series of electrical impulses to represent any character within its range. Like the Morse code with its dots and dashes, computer pulse codes may be linked together to convey alphabetic or numeric information. Unlike the Morse code, however, computer pulse trains may also be combined in mathematical operations or data manipulation.

In 1946 Dr. John von Neumann, at the Institute for Advanced Study of Princeton University, first described in a formal report how the binary system of numbers could be used in var-

145

ious computer implementations. The binary system requires combinations of only two numbers, zero and one, to represent any digit, letter, or symbol, and by extension, any group of digits, letters, or symbols. In contrast, the conventional decimal system requires combinations of ten different numbers, from zero to nine, to convey the same information. Von Neumann recognized that electrical and electronic elements could be considered as having only two states, on and off, and that these two states could be made to correspond to the zero and one of the binary system. If the turning on and off of a computer element occurred at a rapid rate, the voltage or current outputs that resulted would best be described as pulses. It is the nature of these pulses and the methods of handling them that provide the ultimate measure of a computer's accuracy and reliability.

Pulse Characteristics

The ideal shape for a single pulse may be straight-sided, flat-topped, and of an exactly specified width, amplitude, and phase relationship. It is the special virtue of digital computers that they can be designed to function at their original accuracy despite appreciable degradation of the pulse characteristics. However, when certain limits are exceeded, errors will occur, and the integrity of the data will be compromised. Because these errors are difficult to detect, it is important that a schedule of preventive maintenance be established and rigidly adhered to. Only in this way can degraded performance be detected before it is severe enough to affect reliability.

Circuitry

To generate pulses of desirable characteristics, and to manipulate them correctly, requires components of uniform quality and dependability. To lower manufacturing costs, to make servicing and replacement easier, and generally to improve reliability, digital computer designers attempt to utilize as few different types of components as possible, and to incorporate large numbers of each type into any one machine.

First-generation computers used as many as 30,000 vacuum tubes, mainly in a half-dozen types of logic elements. The basic circuits were flip-flops or gates that produced an output pulse whenever a given set of input pulses was present.

However, vacuum tubes generated intense heat, even when in a stand-by condition. As a consequence, the useful operating time between failures was relatively short.

With the development of solid-state diodes and transistors, computers became smaller and cooler. With advances in logic design, a single type of gate, such as the NAND circuit, could replace all other logic elements. The resulting improvements in cost and reliability have been accelerated by the use of monolithic integrated circuits. Not least in importance is their vastly increased speed of operation. Since the mean time between failures of electronic computer circuitry is generally independent of the number of operations performed, it follows that throughput increases directly with speed; speed is defined as the rate at which a computer accesses, moves, and manipulates data. The ultimate limitation on computer speed is the time required for a signal to move from one physical element to another. At a velocity of 186,000 miles per second in air, an electrical signal travels 9.82 feet in 10 nanoseconds (0.000,000.01 seconds). If components were as large as they were originally, and consequently as far apart, today's nanosecond computer speeds would clearly be impossible, as would be the increased throughput and reliability now attainable.

Coding

In a typical application, data may automatically be translated and retranslated into a half-dozen different codes, thousands of times each second. It would be gratifying to report that each of these codes is necessary, or even desirable, but in fact many of them represent earlier technology that is retained for economic reasons only.

In any given code, each character appears as a specific group of pulses. Within each group, each pulse position is known as a bit, since it represents either of the two binary digits, zero or one. Table 10.1 illustrates some of the translations that may be continuously performed as data move about within a single computer.

Because translations are accomplished at little apparent cost, any real incentive to eliminate them is lacking. However, all data movements and translations increase the likelihood of internal error, and for this reason parity checks and validity tests have become indispensable.

Table 10.1 Common Codes for Numeral "5"

Code	Bits	Typical Use	Bit Pattern for "5"
Hollerith	12	Card Reader/Punch	000000010000
EBCDIC	8	Buffer	11110101
EBCDIC, zoned decimal	8	Main Memory	11000101
EBCDIC, packed decimal	8	Arithmetic Logic Unit	01011100
Binary, halfword	16	Arithmetic Logic Unit	0000000000000101
Binary-Coded-Decimal	6	Console Indicators	000101
Transcode	6	Data Transmission	110101
Baudot	5	Paper Tape	00001
Hexadecimal	4	Console Switches	0101
USASCII	7	Data Transmission	0110101
USASCII-8	8	Data Transmission	01010101

Parity

The concept of redundancy is central to error-free data processing. By including extra bits in predetermined locations, no additional information is conveyed, but certain types of errors can be immediately detected. In a typical application, data move back and forth many times, from tape to buffer to main storage to register, to storage to buffer to printer, and so on. During these moves the data may lose integrity by dropping one or more bits, or by having erroneous bits introduced. To detect these occurrences, parity bits are added before data are moved and checked afterwards.

Vertical Redundancy Checks, VRC

In this relatively simple and inexpensive scheme, a determination is initially made as to whether there should be an odd or an even number of "one" bits in each character. Using the binary-coded-decimal representation of the numeral "5," we find that the six-bit pulse group 000101 contains two "ones," an even number. Adding a seventh position to the code group, we may have either type of parity:

Even Parity	0000101	2 "ones"
Odd Parity	1000101	3 "ones"

If odd parity has been selected, a "one" would be added in the leftmost checkbit position. After any movement the number of "one" bits would be counted, and if not an odd number, an error would be assumed and processing halted. Of course, if two bits, or any even number had

been improperly transmitted, no error would be indicated since the number of "one" bits would still be odd.

To compound the problem of nonuniformity illustrated in Table 10.1, each of the 4, 5, 6, 7, 8, and 16-bit code groups may have an additional bit added for parity checking. Nor is there any standardization of odd or even parity amongst manufacturers, or even within the equipment of a single supplier.

Longitudinal Redundancy Checks, LRC

Errors may not be detected by a vertical redundancy check alone, for reasons discussed above. An additional safeguard, of particular use in data transmission and magnetic tape recording, is the longitudinal parity check. With this technique, an extra character is generated after some predetermined number of data characters. Each bit in the extra character provides parity for its corresponding row, just as the vertical parity bits do for their corresponding columns. Figure 10.1 represents both types as they would be recorded on 7-track magnetic tape. One bit has been circled to show that it is ambiguous. This bit appears at the intersection of the parity row and the parity column, and must be predetermined to be correct for one or the other, as it may not be correct for both. In the illustration, the ambiguous bit is correct for the odd parity requirement of the VRC character column; it is incorrect for the even parity of the LRC bit row.

In actual practice, the vertical checkbits would be attached to each character column as shown, but the longitudinal bits would follow a block of data that might contain 80 to several

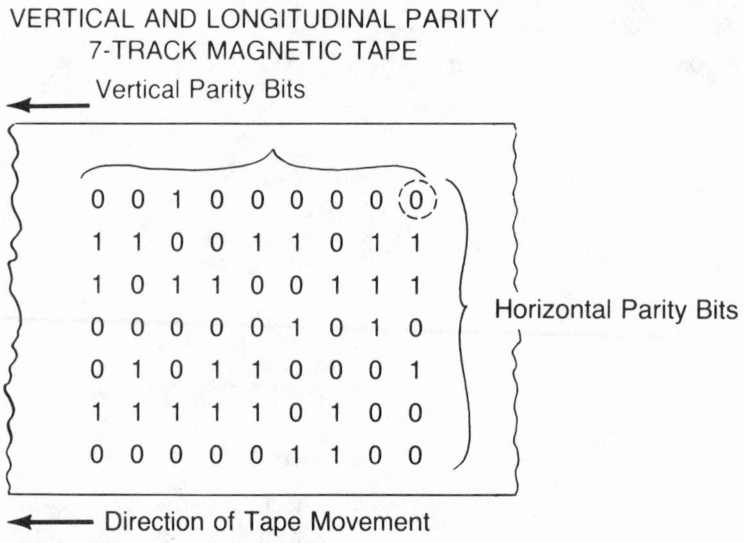

VERTICAL AND LONGITUDINAL PARITY
7-TRACK MAGNETIC TAPE

Vertical Parity Bits ←

```
0  0  1  0  0  0  0  0  (0)
1  1  0  0  1  1  0  1  1
1  0  1  1  0  0  1  1  1
0  0  0  0  0  1  0  1  0        } Horizontal Parity Bits
0  1  0  1  1  0  0  0  1
1  1  1  1  1  0  1  0  0
0  0  0  0  0  1  1  0  0
```

← Direction of Tape Movement

Figure 10.1 Vertical and longitudinal parity 7-track magnetic tape

hundred characters. Where it is possible to use both LRC and VRC, any single data error in a block will be located at the intersection of incorrect row and column parity bits. The indicated bit may then be automatically corrected. The limitations of this method are: (1) multiple errors cannot be corrected, (2) an error in the ambiguous position cannot be corrected, and (3) an error that does not produce both a VRC and LRC indication cannot be corrected.

Cyclical Redundancy Checks, CRC

Where the cost of a data error could be high, the added expense of cyclical redundancy checking is warranted. In this technique a relatively large number of redundant bits is used. For example, each 4-bit character requires three parity bits, while a 32-bit computer word would need 6 parity bits. Obviously, much extra storage space is required in main and secondary memory and much longer transmission time is used. The advantage, however, is that *any* single error would be detected, whether in a data bit or a parity bit, and its location would be positively identified. By a simple electronic process of complementation an incorrect zero would be converted to a one, and vice versa.

Self-checking Codes

Several types of codes are in use that inherently contain a checking ability similar to that of the

parity system. Typical of these is the 2-of-5 code, in which every decimal digit is represented by a bit configuration containing exactly 2 "ones" and 3 "zeroes." Where a parity test would consist of counting "ones" to see if their number was odd or even, a 2-of-5 test would indicate an error whenever the number of "ones" was more or less than 2.

Hardware Operations

Input, output, and processing are the three essential functions of any computer. To protect data integrity during these operations, several hardware features are available.

Read-after-Write

In card punches and magnetic tape drives it is common practice to read the data immediately after they have been punched or recorded, and to compare them with the original values. Any disagreement signals an error that requires rewriting.

Dual Read

To check the accuracy of punched-card readers, the read operation is performed twice and the results compared. Any disagreement should produce a machine check halt.

Echo

Data transmitted to a peripheral device, to a remote terminal, or to another computer can be made to generate a return signal. This echo is compared with the original signal to verify correct reception. One common example is impact printers in which each hammer generates an identifying code when it is actuated. Timing errors caused by uncontrolled signal delays, jammed keys, and other printer malfunctions produce echoes that do not agree with the original signals.

Overflow

The maximum range of numerical values that any computer can accommodate is fixed by its design. If a program is improperly scaled, or if an impossible operation such as dividing by zero is called for, the result of an arithmetic operation may exceed the allowable range, producing an overflow error. Earlier computers required programmed instructions to detect overflows, but this function is now generally performed by hardware elements.

Hardware Multiply

Multiplication of binary numbers is carried out by a series of additions and register shift operations. Although programmed instructions or a standard subroutine could be called when required, faster and more reliable results are attainable with hardware implemented multiplication.

Validity

In any one computer coding system, some bit patterns may be unassigned, and others may be illegal. In EBCDIC, for example, the number "9" is represented by 11111001, but 11111010 is unassigned. A parity check would not detect the second group as being in error, since both have the same number of "one" bits. A validity check, however, would reject the second bit configuration as invalid.

Similarly, certain bit patterns represent assigned instruction codes, while others do not. In one computer, the instruction to convert packed-decimal numbers to zoned-decimal is 11110011, or F3 in hexadecimal notation. 11110101, or F5, is unassigned and a validity check would cause a processing halt whenever that instruction was tested.

Replication

In highly sensitive applications, it is good practice to provide backup equipment on-site, for immediate changeover in the event of failure of the primary computer. For this reason it is sometimes prudent to retain two identical, smaller computers rather than to replace them with a single unit of equivalent or even greater power.

Fault-tolerant, or fail-safe computers use two or more processors that operate simultaneously, sharing the load. If one of the computers fails, the others pick up its share of the work without pause.

Many of these sensitive applications, such as airline reservation systems, have extensive data communications facilities. Where these are handled through a front-end processor, it is important that this equipment be duplicated as well as the central processing unit.

Replacements should also be immediately available for other peripheral devices. In some operating systems it is necessary to inform the system that a device is down and to reassign its functions to another unit. In the more sophisticated systems a malfunctioning device is automatically cut out and replaced.

Interrupts

The sequence of operations performed by a computer system is determined by a group of instructions—the program. However, many events that occur during an actual run require deviations from the programmed sequence. Interrupts are signals generated by hardware elements that detect exceptional conditions, and initiate appropriate action. The first step is immediately to store the status of various elements in preassigned memory locations. The particular stored bit patterns, commonly called program status words, contain the information necessary for the computer to identify the cause of the interrupt, to take action to process it, and then to return to the proper instruction in the program sequence after the interrupt is cleared.

Five types of interrupts are in general use. Each of them is of importance in establishing and maintaining data processing integrity. In order of probable frequency of occurrence they are:

Input/Output Interrupts

I/O interrupts are generated whenever a device or channel that had been busy becomes available. This capability is necessary to achieve error-free use of the increased throughput provided by buffering, overlapped processing, and multiprogramming.

After each I/O interrupt, a check is made to determine whether the data have been read or written without error. If so, the next I/O operation can be started, but if not, an error-recovery procedure is initiated. The number of times that errors occur should be recorded so that degraded performance can be detected and corrected.

An I/O interrupt is also generated when the "Request" key on the console keyboard is pressed. This is an important factor to consider in establishing security precautions, since operator intervention can precede the suppression of logging data, and the execution of unauthorized programs. To prevent this, separate machine utilization records should be continuously compiled, and these records closely compared to an authorized job list.

Supervisor Calls

The supervisor, or monitor, is a part of the operating system software that controls the interactions between all hardware and software elements.

Every request to read or write data is scheduled by the supervisor when called upon to do so. The I/O interrupts are also handled by supervisor calls that coordinate them with read/write requests. Loading, executing, and terminating programs are other important functions initiated by supervisor calls.

Program Check Interrupts

Improper use of instructions or data may cause an interrupt that terminates the program. Attempts to divide by zero and arithmetic overflow that would produce erroneous results are voided. Unassigned instruction codes, attempts to access protected storage, and invalid data addresses are other types of exceptions that would cause program check interrupts.

Machine Check Interrupts

Among the exception conditions that will cause machine check interrupts are parity errors, jammed card readers, and defective circuit modules. It is important that proper procedures be followed to clear machine checks without loss of data or processing error.

External Interrupts

External interrupts are generated by timer action, by pressing an "Interrupt" key, or by signals from another computer. When two central processing units are interconnected, signals that pass between them initiate external interrupts. In this way, control and synchronization are continuously maintained, while programs, data, and peripheral devices may be shared and coordinated.

An electronic clock is generally included in the central processor unit for time of day entries in job logs, and for elapsed-time measurements. As an interval timer the clock can be set to generate an interrupt after a given period. This feature should be used as a security measure, preventing sensitive jobs from remaining on the computer long enough to permit unauthorized manipulation of data or instructions.

Trapping

Trapping is a type of hardware response to an interrupt. Upon detecting the exception, an unconditional branch is taken to some predetermined location. An instruction there transfers control to a supervisor routine that initiates appropriate action.

Data Storage

The modern digital computer is known as a stored program calculator to distinguish it from earlier machines that required external initiation of program phases, and differently wired boards as well. It was the ability to "memorize" long lists of instructions, and to act upon them, that was originally responsible for characterizing these machines as "Giant Brains." However, just as the human mind is subject to aberrations, so is computer memory. In the interests of data security and integrity, various therapeutic measures have been developed.

Main Memory

Whether of magnetic cores, thin films, plated wires, or metal-oxide semiconductors, all primary storage elements share the necessary quality of being easily accessed for reading and writing of data. Unfortunately, this necessary characteristic is at the same time a potential source of difficulty in maintaining data integrity against unwanted read/write operations. The problems are greatly intensified in a multiprogrammed environment, especially with dynamic memory allocation, where the possibility exists that one program will write improperly over another's data in main storage. Protection against this must be provided by the operating system.

One form of protection requires that main memory be divided into blocks, or pages, typically of 2,048 eight-bit bytes each. Pages can be designated as read-only when they contain constants, tables, or programs to be shared by several users. Additionally, pages that are to be inaccessible except to designated users may be assigned a lock by appropriate program instructions. If a matching key is not included in the user's program, he will be denied access to that page. Protection may be afforded against writing only, or against reading and writing.

A significant characteristic of magnetic core memories is their nonvolatility; stored data remain unaltered even in the event of total power failure. Semiconductor memories, on the other hand, are usually volatile, and as they have replaced magnetic cores, precautions against loss of data have become even more important.

Read-only Memory, ROM

One distinguishing feature of main memory is the extremely high speed at which data can be entered or read out. The set of sequential procedures which accomplishes this and other functions is the program, and the programmer has complete freedom to combine any valid instructions in a meaningful way. However, where certain operations, such as multiplication, are frequently and routinely required, they may be performed automatically by a preprogrammed group of memory elements. It is then necessary that no change, intentional or inadvertent, occur in the preset program. For this purpose, a class of memory elements has been developed in which read-out is even faster than from main memory. Further-more, once programmed they cannot be changed at all, or at least they require a relatively long time and usually external equipment to do so. This class of memory is called read-only memory, or ROM. The process by which sequential instructions are set into the elements, or the function they perform, is known as microprogramming. The technique can be used to advantage where data integrity may be safeguarded by eliminating the possibility of programmer error.

Variations of the principle include programmable read-only memories, PROM, and erasable, programmable read-only memory EPROM, all of which combine microprogramming with a somewhat greater degree of flexibility than read-only memory itself.

Secondary Storage

As the cost of primary storage continues to decline, computers are built with ever larger main memories. At the same time, the size of programs, and the number run concurrently in a multiprogramming mode, continues to increase so that main memory remains an important constraint on throughput.

To increase the effective size of main memory, a variety of secondary storage devices has been developed. Unlike primary storage, secondary memories are not an integral part of the central processing unit, although they may appear to be, as in virtual memory systems.

Typical devices include magnetic disks, diskettes, tapes, and tape cartridges. Punched cards are also considered secondary storage, particularly when used to contain programs and data read from or to main memory as required.

Hardware safeguards described earlier, such as redundancy, validity, parity, and read-after-write, are of value in preserving the integrity of secondary storage. These safeguards are built into the equipment and are always operational unless disabled or malfunctioning. Other precautionary measures are optional and, as a consequence, are too often neglected. An example of this is found in the many installations that have not adopted standard internal labeling procedures for magnetic tapes and disks. These installations do not avail themselves of the error-preventing capabilities built into their equipment. Standard internal labels can include identification numbers, record counts, and dates of creation and expiration. Because software systems provide for operator intervention to ignore error messages that result when labeling is not properly used, there is no impetus to adopt proper procedures unless management forces it. Most installations do use pressure-sensitive external labels on tape reels and disk packs, but these are not an adequate substitute for computer-generated labels, magnetically inscribed on the medium itself, and automatically checked by programmed instructions.

Another security measure sometimes subverted is magnetic tape file protection. A hardware interlock prevents writing on tape in any reel that does not have an enable ring in its hub. The ring, properly installed on an output reel, should be removed immediately when the tape is unloaded. Failure to do so will cause the data to be destroyed if that same reel is improperly mounted in an output drive.

Magnetic disks and drums are classified as direct access storage devices. Unlike magnetic tapes with their exclusively sequential processing, DASD's may process data randomly as well as in sequence. This capability is essential to on-line operations, where it is not possible to sort transactions prior to processing. The disadvantage of direct access is that there may be far less control over entries, and far more opportunity to degrade the system than exists with sequential batch processing.

One possible source of DASD errors arises from the high rotational velocity of the recording medium, and except on head-per-track devices, the movement of heads as well. To minimize this possibility, areas on the recording surface have their addresses magnetically inscribed. When the computer directs that data be read from or into a particular location, the address in main memory is compared with that read from the DASD. Only if there is agreement will the operation be performed.

Through proper programming the integrity of data can be further assured. In addition to the address check, comparisons can be made on identification numbers, or on key fields within each record. Although the additional processing time is generally negligible, there can be a substantial improvement in properly posting transactions.

Several other security measures are often incorporated into DASDs. One is similar to the protection feature in main memory, and relies on determining "extents" for each data set. If these extents, which are simply the upper and lower limits of a data file's addresses, are exceeded, the job will terminate.

Another safety measure is necessitated by the fact that defective areas on a disk or drum surface may cause errors undetectable in normal operations. To minimize this possibility, tapes and disks should be tested and certified prior to use, and periodically thereafter. Further information is provided by operating systems that record the number of tape and disk errors encountered in each program run. Resurfacing or replacement must be ordered when errors exceed a predetermined level.

Lastly, unlike magnetic tape where the read/write heads must be in direct contact with the oxide surface of the tape, it is imperative that the heads of a DASD never touch a moving surface. These heads are designed to operate while separated from the magnetic surface by a thin cushion of air. This "air bearing" is created by the disk's rapid rotation, and disappears when the disk is slowed down or stopped, or when a mechanical malfunction occurs. To prevent the serious loss of data that could result from a "head-crash," sensors are built in to determine when the air cushion is in danger of dissipating. At that instant, the heads are retracted mechanically, and contact is prevented.

It is a sensible precaution to ensure that if restoration of files is required, the backup disks not be loaded into the same drive on which the errors occurred until it is determined that the drive itself is functioning properly. Otherwise, there is a considerable risk of destroying all of the backup disks before the operator realizes that the hardware itself is at fault.

Time

Within the computer room a wall-clock is usually a dominant feature. There is no doubt that this real-time indicator is of importance in scheduling and regulating the functions of people and machines, but the computer's internal timings are equally important.

Synchronous

There are many computer operations that are independent of the time of day but that must maintain accurate relationships with some common time and with each other. Examples of this synchronism include the operation of gates, flip-flops, and registers, the reading of punched cards, and the transmission of data at high speeds. Synchronism is obtained in various ways. In the card reader, mechanical gears and clutches are used. For gates and other circuit elements, electronic clocks provide accurately spaced pulses at a high-frequency rate, while tape and disk drives are maintained at rated speed by servomotor controls based on power-line frequency.

Of all computer errors, the ones most difficult to detect and correct are probably those caused by timing inconsistencies. Internal clocks may produce 10,000,000 pulses per second, every second that the computer is turned on. The loss of even a single pulse, or its random deformation or delay, can cause undetected errors. Even more troublesome is the fact that if the errors are detected, their cause may not be unless the random timing faults become frequent or consistent.

An example of the insidious nature of timing faults is the consequence of an electrical "brownout." During this type of emergency overloaded generators may reduce the frequency and voltage of their generated power. Since disk drives are synchronized to the power-line frequency, they will slow down proportionately, and if sectors are being recorded, their physical size will be correspondingly smaller. Then, when the brownout is ended, sector sizes will become larger again. The result could be erroneous data or data lost in overlapped sectors.

A further example of the need for precise timing arises from the fact that data and instructions are completely indistinguishable within a computer. Table 10.1 lists 11110101 as the valid EBCDIC code for the numeral "5," but as an instruction this same code is not assigned a recognized value and will cause a validity check halt. The difference is in the time when the code is tested. Computers alternate between an instruction cycle and an execution cycle, in accordance with the ticking of their internal clocks. Pulse patterns moving from main memory to a storage register during the instruction cycle are expected to be instructions; during the execution cycle they are expected to be data. A momentary lapse in synchronism will hopelessly garble all operations.

Asynchronous

Some operations do not occur at fixed time intervals, and are therefore termed asynchronous. In this mode, signals generated by the end of one action initiate the following one. As an example, slow-speed data transmissions are asynchronous. Coded signals produced by the random depression of teletypewriter keys are independent of any clock pulses.

Some computers are organized entirely around asynchronous timing. In the main, these are scientific computers—very fast in executing instructions, but usually more complex and more expensive than the synchronous types.

Natural Enemies

To preserve the accuracy and timeliness of computer output, there are environmental dangers that must be guarded against. Most obvious of these is the fire hazard, discussed fully in another chapter. Less well publicized, but equally important, are the following:

Power Failure

Probably the most frequent cause of computer downtime is power failure. Brownouts and blackouts are visible signs of trouble; undetected transients, or voltage spikes, are far more common, although hardly less damaging.

Lightning can produce voltage spikes on communications and power lines of sufficient amplitude to destroy equipment or, at the very least, to alter data randomly. Sudden storms and intense heat or cold place excessive loads on generators. The drop in line-voltage that results can cause computer or peripheral malfunction. Even if it does not, harmful voltage spikes may be created whenever additional generators are switched in to carry higher loads.

To detect power-line fluctuations, a recording indicator may be used. At any time that out-of-tolerance conditions are signalled, the computer output should be carefully checked to assure that data integrity has not been compromised. If such occurrences are frequent, or if the application is a sensitive one, auxiliary power sources should be considered. These range from simple voltage regulators and line conditioners to "uninterruptible" power supplies.

Heat

Sustained high temperatures can cause electronic components to malfunction or to fail completely. Air conditioning is therefore essential, and all units must be adequate, reliable, and properly installed. If backup electrical power is provided for the computer, it must also be available for the air conditioners.

A frequently unrecognized cause of overheating is obstruction of ventilating grilles. Printouts, tapes, books, and other objects must not be placed on cabinets where they can prevent free air circulation.

Humidity

Either extreme of humidity can be damaging. Low humidity, below about 20 percent, permits buildup of static electricity charges that may affect data pulses. Because this phenomenon is intensified by carpeting, computer-room floors should either be bare, or covered with antistatic carpeting.

High humidity, above about 80 percent, may lead to condensation that causes shorts in electrical circuits, or corrodes metal contacts. To ensure operation within acceptable limits, humidity controls should be installed and a continuous record kept of measured values.

Water

Water introduced by rain, floods, bursting pipes, and overhead sprinklers has been responsible for more actual computer damage than fire or any other single factor. Care taken in locating computer facilities, in routing water pipes, and in the selection of fire-extinguishing agents will minimize this significant danger.

Dirt and Dust

Particles of foreign matter can interfere with proper operation of magnetic tape and disk drives, and of printers, card readers, and other electromechanical devices. All air intakes must be filtered, and all filters must be kept clean. Rubber bands, pencils, and paper clips must not be permitted to fall into equipment that can be

jammed or shorted out. Cups of coffee seem to become especially unstable in a computer environment; together with any other food or drink, they should be banned entirely.

Throughout the installation, good housekeeping principles must be rigorously enforced.

Radiation

Much has been written about the destructive effect of magnetic fields on tape or disk files. However, because magnetic field strength diminishes rapidly with distance, it is unlikely that damage could actually be caused except by large magnets held very close to the recorded surfaces. Metal containers are a simple, foolproof precaution to prevent this type of sabotage or inadvertent destruction.

Strong signals from a nearby transmitter have been blamed for the introduction of erroneous pulses. If the computer room cannot be sited so as to prevent this, magnetic shielding is an expensive but effective solution. Radioactivity, on the other hand, is a great threat to personnel, but not to the computer or its recording media.

Downtime

It is essential to the proper functioning of a data center that preventive maintenance be regularly performed, and that accurate records be kept of the time and the reason that any element of the computer is inoperative. The more often the computer is down, the more rushed operators will be to catch up on their scheduled workloads. Under such conditions, controls are bypassed, shortcuts are taken, and human errors multiply.

Downtime records should be studied to detect unfavorable trends, and to pinpoint equipment that must be overhauled or replaced before outages became excessive. If unscheduled downtime increases, preventive maintenance should be expanded or improved until the trend is reversed.

Data Communications

One of the most dynamic factors in current computer usage is the proliferation of devices and systems for data transmission. Within the next few years, computers that do not function at least part time in a teleprocessing mode may well become rarities.

The necessity for speeding information over great distances increases in proportion to the size and geographic dispersion of economic entities; the necessity for maintaining data integrity and security, and the difficulty of doing so, increases even more rapidly. Major threats to be guarded against include human and machine errors, unauthorized accession, alteration, and sabotage. Accession defines an ability to read data stored or transmitted within a computer system; it may be accidental or purposeful. Alteration is the willful entering of unauthorized or incorrect data. Sabotage is the intentional act of destroying or damaging the system or the data within it. For each of these threats, the exposure and the countermeasures will depend on the equipment and the facilities involved.

Two types of wired facilities are in widespread use; leased lines and dial-up networks. Within each type several classes of service, or tariffs, are available from the common carriers. A third type of wired interconnection is one that can be made and maintained independently. Both common carriers and independent systems may employ various media for data transmission. The increasing need for higher speed and better quality in data transmission has prompted utilization of coaxial cables, fiber optics, microwave, and communication satellites. Where devices are not in the data center itself, but are fairly close, they may be "hardwired" directly to the computer, or into local area network.

Generally, decisions as to the choice of service are based on the volume of data to be handled, and on the associated costs.

Dial-up Lines

Computer input ports may be reached by any subscriber to the public telephone system. Some method of identification is therefore necessary to detect and deter unauthorized callers. Passwords are the most common means for accomplishing this, but their use must be well planned and systematically guarded. It is advisable to:

- Establish a hierarchy of programs and data files, and restrict users to specified levels.

- Maintain close supervision over passwords and change them often—at once, if it is suspected that security has been breached.

- Compile a log of unauthorized attempts at entry, and use it to discourage further efforts.

- Compile a log of all accesses to sensitive data, and verify their appropriateness.

- Equip all terminals with internal identification generators, or answer-back units, so that even a proper password would be rejected if sent from an unauthorized terminal. This technique may require the availability of an authorized backup terminal in the event of malfunction of the primary unit.

- Provide users with personal identification in addition to a password if the level of security requires it. The additional safeguard could be a magnetically striped, or computerized plastic card to be entered into a special reader. The value of such cards is limited since they can be used by anyone whether authorized or not. For high security requirements, other hardware-dependent identifiers such as handprints and voiceprints should be considered.

With proper password discipline, problems of accession, alteration, and data sabotage can be minimized. However, the quality of transmissions is highly variable. Built into the public telephone system is an automatic route-finding mechanism that directs signals through uncontrollable paths. The distance and the number of switching points traversed, and the chance presence of cross-talk, transients, and other noise products will have unpredictable effects on the incidence of errors. Parity systems, described earlier, are an effective means of reducing such errors.

Leased Lines

Lines leased from a common carrier for the exclusive use of one subscriber are known as dedicated lines. Because they are directly connected between predetermined points, they cannot normally be reached through the dial-up network.

Wiretapping is a technically feasible method of accessing leased lines, but it is more costly, more difficult, and less convenient than dialing through the switched network. Furthermore, no statutes exist to prohibit calling any telephone number at all, while wiretapping is clearly illegal. The result, of course, is that leased lines are generally more secure.

To this increased level of security for leased lines is added the assurance of higher quality reception. The problems of uncertain transmission paths and switching transients are eliminated, although other error sources are not. In consequence, parity checking remains a minimum requirement.

Wireless Communication

Data transfers between multi-national corporations have been growing rapidly. At the same time, transoceanic radio and telephone lines have proved too costly, too slow, too crowded, and too error-prone to provide adequate service. An important alternative is the communications satellite. Orbiting above the earth, the satellite reflects ultra-high-frequency radio signals that can convey a television program or a computer program with equal speed and facility.

For communications over shorter distances, the cost of common-carrier wired services has been so high as to encourage competitive technologies. One of these, the microwave radio link, is used in many networks. One characteristic of such transmissions is that they can be received only on a direct line-of-sight path from the transmitting antenna. With such point-to-point ground stations it is sometimes difficult to position the radio beams where they cannot be intercepted; with satellite communications it is impossible. The need for security is consequently greater, and scramblers or cryptographic encoders are essential for sensitive data transfers.

Because of the wide bandwidths at microwave frequencies, extremely fast rates of data transfer are possible. With vertical, longitudinal, and cyclical redundancy check characters, almost all errors can be detected, yet throughput remains high.

Terminals

Data communications are carried on between computers, between terminals, or between computers and terminals. The terminals themselves may include teletypewriters, magnetic tape drives, cathode-ray tube stations, "intelligent" terminals, and microcomputers.

In the simplest of terminals the only protection against transmission errors lies in the inability to record characters not included in the valid set. At small additional cost, almost any terminal can be equipped to detect a vertical parity error and print a question mark or other symbol when it occurs. More sophisticated terminals are capable of detecting additional errors

through longitudinal and cyclical redundancy characters, as well as by vertical parity and validity checks. Of course, error detection is only the first step in maintaining data integrity. Error correction is by far the more important part, and retransmission is the most widely used correction technique.

Slow-speed terminals generally receive characters asynchronously, one at a time, storing them in a buffer until tested. If accepted, the buffer is cleared and an appropriate signal returned. Otherwise, a signal is sent to the originating station requesting retransmission of the erroneous character. This process may be programmed to repeat itself any number of times, until some other action is taken. Faster operation is possible if the transmitter does not wait for an acceptance signal after each character, but instead transmits continuously until an error signal is returned.

High-speed terminals are similar in their action except that blocks of information containing hundreds of characters may be transmitted at once, stored in a buffer, checked for parity and validity, and retransmitted as a block upon receipt of an error signal.

Intelligent terminals and microcomputers are capable of high-speed transmission and reception. They can perform complicated tests on data before requesting retransmission, or they may even be programmed to correct errors internally. The techniques for self-correction require forward-acting codes such as the Hamming cyclical code. These are similar to the error-detecting cyclic redundancy codes, except that they require even more redundant bits. Although error correction is more expensive, and usually slower than detection with retransmission, it is useful under certain circumstances. Examples include simplex circuits where no return signal is possible, and half-duplex circuits where the time to turn the line around from transmission to reception is too long. Forward correction is also necessary where errors are so numerous that retransmissions would clog the circuits, with little or no useful information throughput.

A more effective use of intelligent terminals and microcomputers is to preserve data integrity by compression or compaction. Reducing the number of characters in a message reduces the probability of an error. Terminals, therefore, are programmed to replace long strings of spaces or zeros with a special character and a numerical count, reversing the process when receiving data.

Finally, the intelligent terminal or microprocessor may be used to encode or decipher data when the level of security warrants cryptography.

All terminals, of every type, have at least one thing in common—the need to be protected against sabotage or unauthorized use. Although the principles for determining proper physical location, and the procedures for restricting access are essentially the same as those that apply to the central computer facility, the problems of remote terminals are even more difficult. Isolated locations, inadequate supervision, and easier access by more people all increase the likelihood of compromised security.

Cryptography

Competitive pressures in business, politics, and international affairs continually create situations where morality, privacy, and the laws all appear to give way before a compelling desire for gain. Information, for its own sake or for the price it brings, is an eagerly sought after commodity. We are accustomed to the sight of armored cars and armed guards transporting currency, yet invaluable data are often moved with no precautions at all. When the number of computers and competent technicians was small, the risk in careless handling of data resources was perhaps not great. Now, however, a very large population of knowledgeable computer people exists, and within it are individuals willing and able to use their knowledge for illegal ends. Others find stimulation and satisfaction in meeting the intellectual challenge that they perceive in defeating computer security measures.

Acquiring information in an unauthorized manner is relatively easy when data are communicated between locations. One method of discouraging this practice, or rendering it ineffective, is cryptographic encoding of data prior to transmission. This technique is also useful in preserving the security of master files within the data center itself. If such files were stored on tape, disk, or drum in cryptographic cipher only, the incidence of theft and resale would unquestionably be less.

There are many types of ciphers that might be used, depending on their cost and the degree of security required. Theoretically, any code can be broken, given enough time and equipment. In practice, if a cipher cannot be broken fairly quickly the encoded data are likely to become valueless. However, since the key itself can be used to decipher later messages, it is necessary that codes or keys be changed frequently.

For further information refer to Chapter 15.

Backup

As with most problems, the principal focus in computer security ought to be on prevention rather than on cure. No matter how great the effort, however, complete success can never be guaranteed. There are four reasons for this being so:

1. Not every problem can be anticipated.

2. Where the cost of averting a particular loss exceeds that of recovery, preventive measures may not be justified.

3. Precautionary measures, carried to extremes, can place impossible constraints on the efficiency and productivity of an operation. It may be necessary, therefore, to avoid such measures aimed at events whose statistical probability of occurrence is small.

4. Even under optimum conditions, carefully laid plans may go astray. In the real world of uncertainty and human fallibility, where there is active or inadvertent interference, it is almost a certainty that at one time or another the best of precautionary measures will prove to be ineffective.

Recognizing the impossibility of preventing all undesired actions and events, it becomes necessary to plan appropriate means of recovering from them. Such plans must include backup for personnel, hardware, power, physical facilities, data, and software. These are discussed more fully elsewhere in this book.

Backup plans should be evaluated with respect to:

- The priorities established for each application, to ensure that they are properly assigned, and actually observed.

- The time required to restore high-priority applications to full functioning status.

- The degree of assurance that plans can actually be carried out when required. For important applications, alternative plans should be available in the event that the primary plan cannot be implemented.

- The degree of security and data integrity that will exist if backup plans are actually put into effect.
- The extent to which changing internal or external conditions are noted, and the speed with which plans are modified to reflect such changes.

Too much emphasis cannot be placed on the assignment of priorities in advance of an actual emergency. In most data centers, new applications proliferate, while old ones are rarely discarded. If backup plans attempt to encompass all jobs, they are likely to accomplish none. Proper utilization of priorities will permit realistic scheduling, with important jobs done on time and at acceptable costs.

Personnel

The problems of everyday computer operation require contingency plans for personnel on whose performance hardware functioning depends. Illnesses, vacations, dismissals, promotions, resignations, overtime and extra shifts are some of the reasons why prudent managers are continuously concerned with the problem of personnel backup. The same practices that work for everyday problems can provide guidelines for emergency backup plans. These practices include cross-training, advanced training, and overstaffing.

Cross-training provides for each person to be able to perform any of several functions. A practice that should not be allowed is the fairly common one of developing applications specialists. Some applications, for example, are always run on second shift because documentation is poor, and only the second shift operators are familiar with the job. Documentation must be improved, and jobs rotated so that no one person or group is indispensable.

One contingency plan that should be available is the replacement of automated procedures with manual operations. This apparent regression could be the most cost-effective way to overcome a temporary computer problem. Personnel should be periodically retrained in the manual operations necessary to provide continuity of important services.

Hardware

Hardware backup can take several forms:

- Multiple processors at the same site to protect against loss of service due to breakdown of one unit.
- Duplicate installations at nearby facilities of the same company.
- A reciprocal agreement with a similar installation at another company.
- Maintaining programs at a compatible service bureau, on a test or standby basis.
- A contract for backup at a facility dedicated to disaster recovery.

The probability of two on-site processors both down at the same time due to internal faults is extremely small. Consequently, most multiple installations rarely fall behind on high-priority job schedules. However, this type of backup offers no protection against power failure, fire, vandalism, or any disaster that could strike two or more processors at once. A possible further disadvantage arises from the fact that in some instances dual computers could be replaced by a single unit with more power at less cost, if an alternative method of backup were available.

With duplicate processors at different, but commonly owned sites, there is little chance of both being affected by the same forces. Although the safety factor increases with the distance separating them, the difficulty of transporting people and data becomes greater. An alternate site must represent a compromise between these conflicting objectives. Furthermore, complete compatibility of hardware and software will have to be preserved, even though it places an undue operational burden on one of the installations.

Backup by reciprocal agreement was for many years an accepted practice, although not often put to the test. Unfortunately, many managers still rely on this outmoded safeguard. One has only to survive a single major change of operating system software to realize that when it occurs, neither the time nor the inclination is available to modify and test another company's programs. Even the minor changes in hardware and software that continuously take place in most installations could render them incompatible. At the same time, in accordance with Parkinson's Law, workloads always expand to fill the available time and facilities. In consequence, many who believe that they have adequate backup will get little more than an unpleasant surprise, should they try to avail themselves of the privilege.

The backup provided by service bureaus can be extremely effective, particularly if the choice of facility is carefully made. Although progressive service bureaus frequently improve both hardware and software, they almost never do so in a way that would cause compatibility problems for their existing customers. Once programs have been tested, they can be stored off-line on tape or disk at little cost. Updated masters can be rotated in the service bureau library, providing off-site data backup, as well as the ability to become fully operational at once.

Effective hardware backup is also available at independent facilities created expressly for that purpose. In one type of facility there is adequate space, power, air conditioning, and communication lines to accommodate a very large system. Most manufacturers are able to provide almost any configuration on short notice when disaster strikes a valued customer. The costs for this type of bare standby facility are shared by a number of users, so that expenses are minimal until an actual need arises. However, if two or more sharers are geographically close, their facilities may be rendered inoperative by the same fire, flood, or power failure. Before contracting for such a facility, it is therefore necessary to analyze this potential problem; the alternative is likely to be a totally false sense of security.

Another type of backup facility is already equipped with computers, disk and tape drives, printers, terminals, and communications lines so that it can instantly substitute for an inoperative system. The standby costs for this service are appreciably more than for a base facility, but the assurance of recovery in the shortest possible time is far greater. Here, too, it would be prudent to study the likelihood of more than one customer requiring the facility at the same time, and to demand assurance that one's own needs will be met without fail.

Power

The one truly indispensable element of any data processing installation is electric power. Yet, because of its high cost, backup for a central utility is not often provided. This may have been acceptable when utility-supplied power was more dependable, and when data processing was less vital to corporate survival, but it can no longer be. Several types of power backup are available. The principal determinant in selection should be the total cost of anticipated downtime and reruns, versus the cost of backup to eliminate them. Downtime and rerun time may be extrapolated from records of past experience. The direct tangible cost per hour is obtained by dividing the annual expenditures by the annual standard hours of operation. To this figure should be added a factor for any intangible costs that can be quantified.

Problems due to electrical power may be classified by type and by the length of time that they persist. Power problems as they affect computers consist of variations in amplitude, frequency and wave-form—with durations ranging from fractions of a millisecond to minutes or hours. Long-duration outages are usually due to high winds, ice, lightning or vehicles that damage power lines, or to equipment malfunctions that render an entire substation inoperative. It is usually possible, although costly, to contract for power to be delivered from two different substations, with one acting as backup.

Another type of protection is afforded by gasoline or diesel motor generators. Controls are provided that sense a power failure and automatically start the motor. Full speed is attained in less than a minute, and the generator's output may power a computer for days if necessary. The few seconds delay in switching power sources is enough to abort programs running on the computer and to destroy data files. To avoid this, the "uninterruptible" power supply was designed. In one version, the AC power line feeds a rectifier that furnishes direct current to an inverter. The inverter in turn drives a synchronous motor coupled to an alternator whose AC output powers the computer. While the rectifier is providing DC to the inverter, it also charges a large bank of heavy-duty batteries. As soon as a fault is detected on the main power line, the batteries are instantaneously and automatically switched over to drive the synchronous motor. Because the huge drain on the batteries may deplete them in a few minutes, a diesel generator must also be provided. The advantages of this design are:

• Variations in line frequency, amplitude, and waveform do not get through to the computer.

- Switchover from power line to batteries is undetectable by the computer. Programs keep running, and no data are lost.
- Millisecond spikes and other transients that may be responsible for equipment damage and undetected data loss are completely suppressed.

Testing

The most important aspect of any backup plan is its effectiveness. Will it work? Certainly it would be a mistake to wait for an emergency to find out. The alternative is systematic testing.

One form of test is similar to a dress rehearsal, with the actual emergency closely simulated. In this way the equipment, the people, and the procedures can all be exercised, until practice assures proficiency. Periodically thereafter the tests should be repeated, so that changes in hardware, software, and personnel will not weaken the backup capability.

Recovery Procedures

The procedures required to recover from any system problem will depend on the nature of the problem, and on the backup measures that had been taken. Hardware recovery ranges from instantaneous and fully automatic, through manual repair or replacement of components, to construction, equipping, and staffing of an entirely new data center.

Contingency plans should include recovery procedures that will restore conditions to normal as soon as possible. Otherwise, it may be necessary to draw up a second level of backup plans.

Almost every data center is a collection of equipment, with options, modifications, additions, and special features. Should it become necessary to replace the equipment, a current configuration list must be on hand, and the procedures for reordering established in advance. An even better practice would be to keep a current list of *desired* equipment that could be used as the basis for replacement. Presumably, the replacements would be faster and more powerful, but additional time should be scheduled for training and conversion.

If manual operations had temporarily replaced automated systems, it could be of advantage to run new or repaired equipment in parallel for a time. Manual operations should be discontinued only after confidence has been fully restored in the automated system.

Just as with original backup scheduling, the recovery of individual applications should proceed in accordance with updated priority ratings and detailed cost analyses.

Microcomputer Considerations

Four factors operate to intensify the problems of hardware security as they relate to small computers:

- Accessibility
- Knowledge
- Motivation
- Opportunity

• Accessibility is a consequence of operating small computers in a wide-open office environment, rather than in a controlled data center. No security guards, special badges, man-traps, cameras, tape librarians, or shift supervisors limit access to equipment or data media in the office as they do in a typical data center.

• Knowledge, and its lack, are equally dangerous. On the one hand, as microcomputers pervade the office environment, technical knowledge becomes widely disseminated. Where once this knowledge was limited to relatively few computer experts who could be rather easily controlled, its growing universality now makes control extremely difficult, if not impossible. On the other hand, when computers are operated by people with minimal knowledge and skills, the probability of security breaches through error and inadvertence is greatly increased.

• Motivation exists wherever valuable assets can be diverted for personal gain, or where real or fancied injustice creates a desire for revenge. The profitable sale of corporate assets to others has always provided motivation for theft; now, with many employees owning computers at home, the value of stolen equipment, programs, and data can be realized without the involvement of third parties.

In the past, large computers have been singled out as targets for sabotage. As long as they are associated by radical elements with government, the military, and social or economic ills, such acts are likely to continue. While microcomputers are not presently involved with these major issues, in the minds of some employees they are a high-visibility link to any management policy or practice of which they disapprove. In consequence, the motivation for sabotaging microcomputers is more likely in the near term to increase than it is to disappear.

A third, relatively new motivation for breaching computer security must also be considered—the challenge and excitement of doing so. Whether trying to overcome technical hurdles, to break the law with impunity, or merely to trespass on forbidden ground, many "hackers" find these challenges irresistible. To view such acts with amused tolerance, or even mild disapproval, is totally inconsistent with the magnitude of the potential damage. The technology exists to lock out all but the most determined and technically proficient hacker; it is gross negligence not to use it to protect sensitive systems.

• Opportunity. With so many microcomputers in almost every office, with virtually no supervision during regular hours, and certainly none at other times, opportunities are plentiful for two types of security breaches: intentional by those with technical knowledge, and unintentional by those without.

Among the most significant threats are those pertaining to:

- Physical damage
- Theft
- Electrical power
- Static electricity
- Data communications
- Maintenance and repair

Physical Damage

Microcomputers and their peripheral devices are not as impervious to damage as telephones, typewriters, TV sets, and other common electronic equipment. Disk drives are extremely susceptible to failure through impact; keyboards cannot tolerate dirt or rough handling; and printers are easily damaged when changing ribbons, printwheels, or paper feed devices. It is essential that computers be recognized as delicate instruments and that they be treated accordingly.

Even within an access-controlled data center, where food and drinks are officially banned, it is not uncommon for a cup of coffee to be spilled when set on or near operating equipment. In an uncontrolled office environment, it is rare that one does *not* see personal computers in imminent danger of being doused with potentially damaging liquids. The problem is compounded by the common practice of leaving unprotected floppy disks lying about on the same surface where food and drink could easily reach them. Although it may not be possible to eliminate these practices entirely, it is necessary that greater discipline be enforced to protect data media and equipment from contamination.

Damage can also result from blocking vents necessary for adequate cooling. Such vents, located on the side or back of a housing, can be rendered ineffective by placing the equipment too close to a wall, especially one with an additional heat source. Vents on top of a cabinet are too often covered by papers or books that prevent a free flow of cooling air.

As a result, the internal temperature of the equipment increases, so that marginal components malfunction, intermittent contacts open, errors are introduced, and eventually the system is brought to a halt. When heavy objects are placed on top of computers and peripheral housings, or when people lean on them, as is common in offices, the effects are further worsened by short circuits resulting from distorted printed circuit boards, and even more catastrophically, by data corruption and head crashes due to excessive stress on disk drives.

Theft

The opportunities for theft of personal computers and their data media are far greater than for their larger counterparts. Floppy disks containing proprietary information or expensive programs are easily copied and removed from the premises without leaving a trace. External disk drives are small enough to be carried out in an attache case, and the widespread practice of taking portable computers home for evening or weekend work eventually renders even the most conscientious guards indifferent. In offices without guards, the problem is even more difficult. Short of instituting a police state of perpetual surveillance, what is to be done to discourage theft? Equipment can be chained or bolted to desks, or locked within cabinets built for the purpose. Greater diligence in recording and tracking serial numbers, more frequent inventories, less "solo" overtime, and a continuing program of education can help. Most of all, it is essential that the magnitude of the problem be recognized at a sufficiently high management level so that adequate resources are applied to its solution. Otherwise, there will be a continuing drain of increasing magnitude on corporate profitability.

Power

In a controlled data center, brownouts, blackouts, voltage spikes, sags and surges, and other electrical power disturbances frequently cause loss of data integrity. This occurs even though most data centers are constructed with full regard for the power sensitivity of computer equipment. The situation is much worse in a typical office, where microcomputers are plugged into existing outlets with little or no thought to the consequences.

Some of the rudimentary precautions that should be taken are:

- Eliminating, or at least controlling, the use of extension cords, cube taps, and multiple outlet strips. Each unit on the same power line may reduce the voltage available to all of the others, and each may introduce noise on the line.

- Providing line voltage regulators and line conditioners where necessary to maintain power within required limits.

- Banning the use of vacuum cleaners or other electrical devices plugged into the same power line as computers or peripheral devices. Such devices produce a high level of electrical noise, in addition to voltage sags and surges.

- Connecting all ground wires properly. This is especially important in older offices equipped with two-prong outlets that require adapter plugs. The third wire of the plug *must* be connected to a solid earth ground for personnel safety, as well as for reduction of electrical noise.

The services of a qualified electrician should be utilized wherever there is a possibility of electric power problems.

Static Electricity

After walking across a carpeted floor on a dry day, the spark that leaps from fingertip to doorknob may be mildly shocking to a person—to the computer it can cause serious loss of memory, degradation of data, and even component destruction.

To prevent this, several measures are available:

- Use a humidifier to keep the humidity above 20 percent R.H.

- Remove ordinary carpeting. Replace, if desired, with static-free types.

- Use an antistatic mat beneath chairs and desks.

- Use a grounding strip near each keyboard.

- Touching the strip before operating the computer will drain any static electricity charge through the attached ground wire. Spray the equipment periodically with an antistatic spray.

Some combination of these measures will protect personnel, equipment, and data from the sometimes obscure, but always real dangers of static electricity.

Data Communications

Although microcomputers perform significant functions in a stand-alone mode, their utility is greatly enhanced by communications to mainframes, to information utilities, and to other small computers—remotely or through local-area networks. All of the security issues that surround mainframe communications apply to microcomputers with added complications.

Until the advent of personal computers, almost all terminals communicating with mainframes were "dumb." That is, they functioned much like teletype machines, with the ability only to key in or print out characters, one at a time. In consequence, it was much more difficult to breach mainframe security, intentionally or accidentally, than it is with today's fully intelligent microcomputers.

The image of thousands of dedicated hackers dialing up readily available computer access numbers for illicit fun and games, or for illegal financial gain, is no less disturbing than it is real. Countermeasures are available, including:

- Two-way encryption
- Checksums and testkeys
- Frequent password changes
- Automatic call-back before logging on
- Investigation of unsuccessful logons

- Monitoring of hackers' bulletin boards
- Tighter controls in all areas

Despite the fact that several widely publicized thefts have been effected by data communications, there has been remarkably little activity in instituting countermeasures. The reasons most often cited are high cost, customer inconvenience, and low priority as compared to other system requirements. New legislation that makes directors and senior officers personally liable for any corporate losses that could have been prevented is certain to have a marked effect on overcoming the present inertia. Prudence dictates that preventive action be taken before, rather than corrective action after, such losses are incurred.

Maintenance and Repair

A regular program of preventive maintenance should be observed for every element of a microcomputer system. This should include scheduled cleaning of disk drives and their magnetic heads, monitor screens, printer platens, and paper chaff. A vital element of any preventive maintenance program is the frequent changing of air filters in every piece of equipment. If this is not done, the flow of clean, cool air will be impeded, and failure will almost surely result.

Maintenance options for microcomputers, in decreasing order of timeliness, include:

- On-site maintenance by regular employees
- On-site maintenance by third parties under an annual agreement
- On-call repair, with or without an agreement
- Carry-in service
- Mail-in service

Unlike mainframes and minicomputers, the majority of microcomputers are not covered by annual contracts calling for on-site repair within a specified number of hours. There appear to be three major reasons for this:

1. The cost of contracted on-site repair is not warranted by the value of a microcomputer's limited functions.
2. The cost of having a complete spare microcomputer available is low enough to justify this approach.
3. Because of limited demand, on-site maintenance is not widely available at a reasonable cost.

4. The inherent reliability of microcomputers is high enough so that many users underestimate the risk of failure.

As microcomputers are increasingly applied to functions that affect the very existence of a business, their maintenance and repair will demand more management attention. Redundant equipment and on-site backup will always be effective, but the extended time for off-site repairs will no longer be acceptable. For most business applications, "loaners" or "swappers" will be immediately available from service companies, so that downtime will be held to an absolute minimum.

Management must assess the importance of each functioning microcomputer and select an appropriate maintenance and repair policy.

Accessibility, knowledge, motivation, and opportunity are the special factors introduced by small computers that threaten every microcomputer installation. Until each of these factors has been addressed, no system can be considered secure.

Conclusion

This chapter has dealt principally with the means by which hardware elements of a data processing system affect the security and integrity of its operations. Many safeguards are integral parts of the equipment itself; others require conscious effort, determination, and commitment.

An effective security program, one that provides insurance against computer catastrophe, cannot be designed or implemented without considerable expenditures of time and money. As with other types of insurance, the premium should be evaluated against the risk. Once a decision has been made, however, the "policy" should not be permitted to lapse. Premiums must continue to be paid in the form of periodic testing, continuous updating, and constant vigilance.

Hardware Security Checklist

	Yes	No
Are security and integrity requirements considered when selecting new equipment?	☐	☐

	Yes	No
Is a schedule of preventive maintenance enforced?	☐	☐
Is a log kept of all computer malfunctions and unscheduled downtime?	☐	☐
Is there an individual with responsibility for reviewing the log and initiating action?	☐	☐
Are parity checks used wherever possible?	☐	☐
Is there an established procedure for recording parity errors and recovering from them?	☐	☐
Are forward-acting or error-correcting codes used when economically justified?	☐	☐
Do operators follow prescribed procedures after a read error or other machine check halt?	☐	☐
Has the hardware multiply option been incorporated to improve reliability?	☐	☐
Are all operator interventions logged and explained?	☐	☐
Is a job log maintained and is it compared regularly with an authorized run list?	☐	☐
Is the interval timer used to prevent excessively long runs?	☐	☐
Are storage protect features such as data locks and read-only paging used?	☐	☐
Are keys to software data locks adequately protected?	☐	☐
Are precautions taken to prevent loss of data from volatile memory during power interruptions?	☐	☐
Are standard internal and external tape and disk labeling procedures enforced?	☐	☐
Are file protection rings always removed from tape reels immediately after use?	☐	☐
Is there a rule that new tapes and disks must be tested or certified prior to use? At regular intervals thereafter?	☐	☐
Are tapes and disks refinished or replaced before performance is degraded?	☐	☐

	Yes	No
Are air conditioners adequate for peak thermal loads?	☐	☐
Are air conditioners backed up?	☐	☐
Is there a schedule for frequent filter changes?	☐	☐
Have all static electricity generators been disabled?	☐	☐
Have all sources of water damage been eliminated?	☐	☐
Is good housekeeping enforced throughout the facility?	☐	☐
Is access to data termals restricted?	☐	☐
Are terminals and surrounding areas examined frequently to detect passwords carelessly left about?	☐	☐
Is a log maintained of unsuccessful attempts to enter the computer from terminals? Is the log used to prevent further attempts?	☐	☐
Is a log maintained of all successful entries to sensitive data? Is the log used to verify authorizations?	☐	☐
Are terminals equipped with automatic identification generators?	☐	☐
Are test procedures adequate to assure high quality data transmission?	☐	☐
Is cryptography or scrambling used to protect sensitive data?	☐	☐
Has a complete backup plan been formulated? Is it updated frequently?	☐	☐
Does the backup plan include training, retraini..g, and cross-training of personnel?	☐	☐
Is on-site backup available for the CPU? For peripherals?	☐	☐
Are reciprocal agreements in force for backup at neighboring facilities?	☐	☐
Does your backup advise you of all changes to their hardware configuration and operating system?	☐	☐
Does your backup have enough free time available to accommodate your emergency needs?	☐	☐
Do you monitor power line voltage and frequency?	☐	☐

	Yes	No
Are the effects of brownouts, dimouts, and blackouts known?	☐	☐
Is advance warning available, and if so is there a checklist of actions to be taken?	☐	☐
Are power correctors in use? Voltage regulators? Line conditioners? Lightning spark gaps?	☐	☐
Is backup power available? Dual sub-station supply? Motor generators? Uninterruptible power supplies?	☐	☐
Does your equipment provide automatic restart and recovery after a power failure?	☐	☐
Are backup plans tested realistically? At frequent intervals?	☐	☐

Microcomputers

	Yes	No
Are floppy disks always kept in a closed container when not actually mounted in a disk drive?	☐	☐
Is it forbidden to put food or drink on or near computer equipment?	☐	☐
Are microcomputers securely fastened to prevent dropping or theft?	☐	☐
Are air vents kept free?	☐	☐
Are accurate inventories maintained?	☐	☐
Is electrical power properly wired?	☐	☐
Has static electricity been eliminated?	☐	☐
Are data communications secure?	☐	☐
Is there an effective maintenance plan?	☐	☐

CHAPTER 11
Computer Facility Physical Security

By Belden Menkus

Introduction

When the computer first appeared in most organizations it was exhibited freely to stockholders, employees, officials of other companies, and the general public. Installation of this equipment marked a major milestone in company progress and represented investment of a lot of organization funds. Management wanted as many as possible to have a good look at what was being done with that money. Data processing operations were turned into veritable fishbowls. Glass was used liberally in the walls to provide for viewing by visitors and to display the computer at work to casual passersby. Work area decorations were designed to be visually impressive to these observers.

Accessibility was emphasized in computer facility placement and physical layout. The computer room location was well marked on doorways and building direction signs. In some instances, automatic electric door opening equipment that would admit anyone was installed at data processing operations area entrances. Almost no one thought of assigning security guards to this area. In fact, very little thought was given to possible threats to the safety of the computer equipment, the people who worked with it, or the information that was processed by it. The design of computer facilities established at that time reflects the fact that few saw the computer as a menace and few were a menace to it.

More recent events, however, have demonstrated clearly that real threats to data processing activities do exist and that the computer must be protected against them. Improved approaches to computer room layout and design are called

for. It is not realistic to turn the computer operations area into some sort of fortress. This location must be made secure, yet it must retain its workplace environment. Thus, any plan for controlling access to this area and for safeguarding its physical contents should be designed to enhance the employee's sense of well-being on the job.

Where the computer has been installed and operational for some time, physical security deficiences may be somewhat difficult and costly to remedy. After the fact construction changes and improvements are always very expensive. The work can cost three to five times as much as new construction. In some organizations the simplest—and possibly the least expensive—solution to this dilemma may be relocation of the computer to a new and more secure site. Then, management can start fresh in dealing with physical computer security problems. Most of the basic requirements can best be met through careful advance planning *before* the computer is installed at a particular location. This is the time to deal with such things as:

- Locating the computer away from main building traffic areas
- Avoiding a location with outside walls and windows
- Providing secure door locks and related access control devices
- Installing power sources and air conditioning systems that can function independently of regular utilities during an emergency.

The most effective program for protecting the computer is one developed as an integral part of the selection and installation process.

166

Selecting and Preparing the Physical Location

Most computer equipment manufacturers offer site selection and preparation help. In many instances, organization policy may require that a particular architect or engineer prepare or review plans for computer facility layout. And, in some instances it may be wise to have these plans examined as well by a competent fire protection engineer. *Caution:* Be sure that the people selected to do this are thoroughly familiar with the physical and fire security requirements of a computer facility. Someone who is more than competent in other design areas in this instance may commit serious security errors. For example, air conditioning system vent closures installed in the tape library room may be designed to shut automatically when the temperature of the ambient air exceeds 150°F. In a fire, stored tape will have been damaged seriously well before that happens. As another example, computer area power and air conditioning sources may not be adequately isolated from those used in the rest of the building. Thus, service frequently may be cut off automatically because of power load fluctuations or a fire elsewhere in the building. This may happen even when there is no direct threat to computer operations. Serious processing interruptions and equipment damage may result.

A number of considerations are essential to selection and preparation of a secure site for the computer.

The Building

The building in which the computer is to be placed should meet basic requirements for a fire-secure location. It should be situated well away from the obvious hazards posed by gas stations, airports, garages, paint storage structures, chemical plants, fire walls, and electrical generation substations. Data processing operations should not be located adjacent to a factory area used for machining or other basic production activities. While airborne dust accumulations may not adversely affect humans in the area, they will create serious operating and maintenance problems in the computer area.

The building chosen also should be located in an area free of possible flash flood danger. While it need not be located on particularly high ground, the building should be situated away from creeks, springs, and other sources of ground water. Drainage in the area should be away from the building itself and should have sufficient runoff capacity to handle maximum anticipated rainfall accumulations.

The site chosen for the computer within the building should be located well away from main traffic areas and exterior building entrances and walls. Avoid the temptation to make the computer room so accessible to the users of the data, that it becomes even more accessible to every peril that threatens it.

Make the computer facility as inconspicuous as possible. Remove door and direction signs that identify the computer's location. (It may be desirable to leave computer facility entrances unmarked and to remove any location identifications from the company telephone book.) Instruct company telephone operators and security officers, as well as members of the data processing operations staff, not to give unseen telephone callers directions to the computer room. A single telephone call can compromise this aspect of computer security.

Determine that the walls and ceiling of the site chosen for the computer are sufficiently watertight to prevent possible damage to the equipment and contents in the event of rupture of steam, water, or plumbing lines that pass near the room or through its walls. Check the air conditioning system for possible leaks. (This test should be repeated periodically after the computer has been installed and is operational.) Be sure that drainage under the facility's raised floor is adequate to avoid water accumulation wherever flooding may occur or water might be used to extinguish a fire. Typically the base floor in an area like this will be poured concrete. Drainage will be virtually nonexistent. Accumulating water will be held by a sort of *bathtub effect* and must be bailed or pumped out of the underfloor area. Generally this problem can be remedied by installing a swimming pool type drain opening and cutting through the concrete floor to locate a drain pipe to connect with the nearest water or plumbing line.

Air Conditioning

Install an air conditioning system that functions—and can be maintained—independently of the equipment serving the rest of the building. When the computer room is located in a *controlled* environment, the air conditioning system associated with it should also be able, in an emergency, to cool adjacent service areas and offices. Otherwise these areas may prove to be uninhabitable during a summertime loss of the basic building air conditioning system.

The computer room air conditioning system, however, should be connected to the fire detection and extinguishing system that functions in that area of the building. Detection of a fire within the area immediately surrounding the computer site should automatically cut off the air conditioning supply to it. Supplemental smoke exhaust facilities may be required for emergency use. A simultaneous audible alarm to persons working in the computer area should allow sufficient time for a smooth system halt without unduly delaying their evacuation of the area.

Power Supply

Provide an independent power generation source that will compensate for random voltage surges or reductions and for failure of utility power. Supplement this with reserve battery packs placed in selected computer room fluorescent light fixtures. These batteries should provide sufficient power for at least 90 minutes of sustained illumination during emergency operations. Incidentally, this will meet U.S. Occupational Safety and Health Administration requirements. Install an uninterruptible power source (UPS) generation system. It will isolate the computer facility from fluctuations in the primary power supply load. In its simplest form, the UPS consists of a bank of storage batteries linked by a direct current to both a rectifier/battery charger and a direct current to alternating current inverter. While the utility power supply level remains within normal operating limits, the rectifier/charger smooths voltage transients to maintain power load consistency. It also retains the charge on the batteries. When the normal power supply fails, the batteries instantaneously begin to supply power to the computer through the inverter. Where extended power outages are possible, or when critical real-time data processing systems must be safeguarded without interruption, battery power will be maintained only as long as is necessary to start up a local conventional diesel-powered generator and shift

the power load to it. Typically, in an emergency an independent UPS system should have batteries capable of sustaining required load for a minimum of from 15 to 18 minutes. Even though longer operating periods are feasible under this system, this should allow sufficient time on noncritical data processing systems for reaching the nearest program restart point and for shutting down operations in an orderly fashion. A smaller and less expensive UPS is required when it is to be used during the emergency in conjunction with a conventional diesel generator. The UPS, in this environment, need be able to sustain the electrical load involved only while the generator is started and becomes fully operational. Typically, this will take from three to eight minutes after the basic power load is lost.

Whatever emergency electrical power supplies are installed should be able, especially when the computer room is located on an upper floor of a high-rise building, to support work area, hallway, and stairwell lights, at least one elevator, work area heating and air conditioning, and a pump of sufficient capability to supply water to strategically located lavatories and drinking fountains. An audible warning device to whatever emergency power source is used will assure that the shift console operator on duty and others in the immediate area are notified promptly of the shift to reserve power.*

Document Destruction

Place document destruction units near the computer operations area. Two basic types of equipment are available: (1) *shredders* that slit documents into strips as narrow as $\frac{1}{32}$ inches wide, and (2) *disintegrators* that grind and pulverize documents under water pressure or in the presence of chemicals. Spoiled impact printer output, continuous form carbon paper accumulation, used machine tabulation cards, and similar data processing generated waste products should be processed through one of these units before transfer from the data processing operations vicinity to the building's trash collection site. (Failure to provide for this extra processing before this type of material is consigned to the trash

---

* For more information on this subject see [U.S.] Federal Information Processing Standards 94, *Guidelines on Electrical Power for ADP Installations,* [U.S.] National Bureau of Standards, 1983. Available from National Technical Information Service, 5285 Port Royal Road, Springfield, VA 22161.

has resulted in compromise to industrial spies of budget plans, marketing and research plans and cost data, and similar sensitive information.) While special plumbing connections are not required for shredder installation, these units do tend to increase the overall bulk of the material that they process. And, in most organizations, use of shredder output for product shipment packing is difficult to justify economically and operationally. In some facilities it may be desirable to secure a single large-scale unit with sufficient capacity to serve the entire operation. But, in many other organizations it may be preferable for financial and administrative reasons to place smaller *office size* shredders at several strategic locations.

Leased Computer Site

A number of special problems may develop when a computer facility located in leased space must be safeguarded. Among other things:

- Lease terms may prohibit permanent structural alterations or changes in the nature and location of such things as electrical service and plumbing facilities, or they may discourage changes by requiring that the site be restored to its original condition upon occupancy termination.
- Building design may impose restrictions on floor loads and fire wall placement.
- The semipublic nature of leased space makes it difficult to fully control access to the area in which the computer is located. (For instance, building security, maintenance, and cleaning personnel—who are not under your direct control—may require almost unlimited access to the area.)

If the space leased for the computer is located in an urban high-rise, controlled-environment building, the possible fire effects of two basic construction features of this building type must be considered. Openings between the exterior and interior building walls have been made to facilitate floor to floor heat and air conditioning circulation. They breach conventional fire walls and may encourage fire spread to various parts of the building. The sealed windows commonly installed in a building of this type may intensify heat build-up by offering no openings through which it might dissipate naturally.

Fire Prevention and Detection

To be effective the fire protection plan for the computer facility must be developed and operate independently of that for the rest of the premises. The area in which data processing equipment is physically located—together with the physically separable tape and disk library—must be isolated as a unit from the rest of the building and protected as a single unit. Suitable perimeter fire walls and fire doors will accomplish this. (Doors normally should remain closed. However, they can be held open when necessary by electromechanical or electromagnetic catches linked to the smoke detection system for this area. This linkage will assure that the doors close automatically as soon as a fire is detected.) If proper controls are maintained over custody and handling of data files and program materials, office space used by computer facility management and staff may be excluded from the special protected area.

In general, the computer fire protection plan must conform to the requirements of the local government's fire protection code. National Fire Protection Association Standard 75[1] provides useful guidance on those aspects of computer facility fire protection with which the local fire code does not directly deal. Work closely with the local fire marshal or fire protection bureau staff in designing fire detection and prevention features into the computer facility. Arrange, at least annually, for the nearby fire department crew to review the layout and contents of your computer area. (This yearly visit could include a thorough check of fire detection and extinguishing system circuitry. However, this might be done by a contract inspection service, if one is available in your area. The annual visit is especially critical when the computer facility is located in a remote semirural area. Fire crews there are often composed largely of volunteers and they may not be familiar with fires involving sensitive electronic equipment.)

Fire is less likely to strike in a data processing operation in which certain housekeeping rules are strictly adhered to. Basically this means prohibiting smoking or eating within the computer facility and requiring prompt removal of accumulating waste.

---

[1] Available from NFPA, Batterymarch Park, Quincy, MA 02269.

Computer Room Specifications

Effective computer facility fire protection really begins when plans are made for equipment installation. Construction specifications should satisfy a number of safety requirements. These include use of:

- Flame-resistant floor and wall surface finishes
- Acoustical ceiling tiles and ductwork installation certified by Underwriters' Laboratories—or some other recognized fire rating laboratory—as having flame spread, fuel contribution, and smoke development ratings of not more than 25
- Glass diffusers on lighting fixtures[2]
- Fluorescent light fixture ballasts that do not melt when overloaded nor drip hot plastic when they fail

Construction specifications also should call for placement of clearly marked *master power control* switches at each of the computer facility main exits. Ideally these switches (preferably located adjacent to the fire extinguishers placed at these points) should be deactivated by the last person leaving the computer area in an emergency evacuation. These switches, covered with a plate to guard against accidental activation, should be positive pull types, rather than the commonly used toggle or push button switches.

Avoid placing, within the computer area, data processing equipment in which foamed rubber or plastic, not rated by fire test as fire resistant, has been used to deaden machine sound or vibration. In the presence of flame, unsafe insulation materials of this type can give off dangerously corrosive fumes.

Extinguishers and Detectors

Place portable fire extinguishers at main room entrances and exits and other unobstructed strategic locations. Pair 10-pound carbon dioxide[3] and 2.5-gallon pressurized plain water units at each location. (Prohibit use of foam, dry chemical, loaded stream, and soda-acid extinguishers in the data processing facility.) A set of the proper extinguishers should be within 50 feet of every

point in the protected area. Clearly mark the water extinguishers: *Do not use on live electrical equipment.* The other units may be used on any type of fire.

Install smoke and fire detection equipment approved by Underwriters' Laboratories or another recognized testing organization. Guided by a thorough engineering study of computer facility airflow patterns and structural obstructions place detectors (Figure 11.1) at critical locations throughout the computer operations area. (Supplemental detectors should be placed in underfloor space with thermostats activated by rate of heat rise.) Define monitor zones for each detector to assure prompt identification of the danger source. Panels over underfloor detectors should be especially marked or be of a distinctive color to facilitate access to the trouble spot. Place a prominently marked extra floor panel lifter near a centrally located extinguisher pair. There, it will be readily available for emergency use.

Make available breathing apparatus similar to that used by fire fighters. (Again, these units should be located near key extinguisher sets.) Assigned operators of key extinguishers should put on breathing devices as soon as the fire detection system is activated. (Correct use of this equipment should be reviewed routinely as an integral part of the regularly scheduled fire drills.) Activation of the smoke detection system should result in several things: (1) sounding an audible alarm in the computer area; (2) automatic notification of organization security officials and the nearest fire department location; (3) automatic switching of the area air conditioning system to a nonrecirculating operating mode; and (4) startup of required additional fans and blowers. Smoke and combustion products should be exhausted by an emergency outlet into the outside atmosphere with the least feasible contaminant deposit in the computer area. Removal is recommended by the Factory Mutual Association at the rate of three cubic feet per minute, per square foot of computer operations space, and four cubic feet per square foot of tape library and vault space. Be sure that adequate exhaust capacity has been provided in the underfloor space where dangerous quantities of hydrogen chloride gas produced by cable insulation breakdown during a fire, may accumulate.

Wherever local fire codes permit, remove water sprinkler fire extinguishing equipment

---

[2] Plastic diffusers, having a flame spread rating of 25 or less, may be used on individual light fixtures.

[3] Or Halon 1301, a freon agent. Its use is covered by NFPA Standard 12A and is subject to limitations noted elsewhere in this chapter.

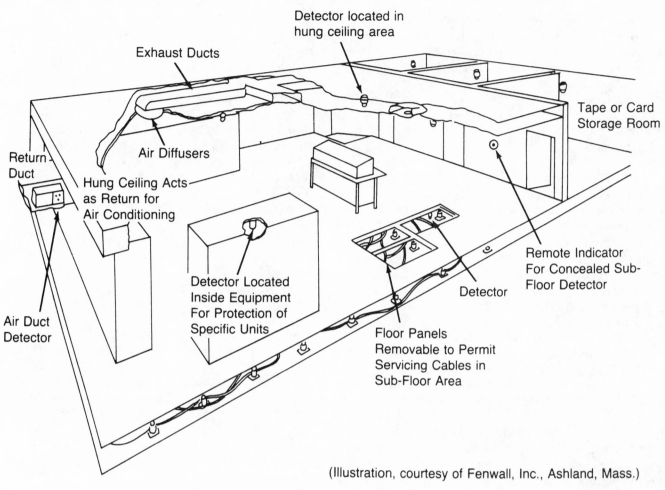

Exhaust Ducts

Detector located in
hung ceiling area

Return Duct

Air Diffusers

Hung Ceiling Acts
as Return for
Air Conditioning

Tape or Card
Storage Room

Air Duct
Detector

Detector Located
Inside Equipment
For Protection of
Specific Units

Remote Indicator
For Concealed Sub-
Floor Detector

Detector

Floor Panels
Removable to Permit
Servicing Cables in
Sub-Floor Area

(Illustration, courtesy of Fenwall, Inc., Ashland, Mass.)

Figure 11.1 Placement of Smoke Detectors in a Typical Computer Room

from the entire computer facility. (A sprinkler is activated mechanically by a heat fusible plug in its head. Once activated a single sprinkler head will discharge 20 gallons of water per minute in a closely defined area. Sprinklers at times may fail to operate during a fire or may discharge prematurely and cause serious local flooding. At such times water damage can be minimized by use of a *Sprinkler Stopper* to inactivate temporarily a single defective sprinkler head.[4]) Where sprinkler removal is not possible, plan use of *multiple-vehicle systems* (which apply several suppression mechanisms) to extinguish fires. Install *preaction sprinklers* (which are dry until activated by a fire) in the main computer room and

provide for automatic power cutoff and de-energizing of the equipment as soon as water movement is detected in the system. Use automatic carbon dioxide flooding equipment in the underfloor or overhead plenum space in the data processing facility.[5] Design system operation to provide instantaneous cutoff of the computer room main power supply and air conditioning system when carbon dioxide discharge begins. Since carbon dioxide is toxic to humans, discharge should be delayed until personnel can safely evacuate the area. Since Halon 1301 normally will not harm humans, consider substituting it for carbon dioxide use in enclosed areas in which people regularly work. Computer equipment need not be de-energized before Halon

[4] Details available from Corde, Inc., 9 Second Road, Great Neck, NY 11021.

[5] System design and performance are discussed in NFPA Standard 12.

1301 discharge; this can be important when fire strikes a critical real-time system. (Halon 1301 use in the computer room or underfloor space can prove undesirable in some circumstances. Its application to smoldering or deep-seated fires may cause it to decompose into corrosive hydrogen fluoride, hydrogen bromide, and bromine. This danger may limit use of Halon 1301 portable extinguishers.)

Other Considerations

Have flame-retardant waterproof plastic covers fitted for the major equipment units in the data processing area. Make particular employees responsible on each shift for covering these units in the event of a fire, sprinkler system discharge or air conditioning duct leakage. Store these covers, along with mops and other emergency cleanup gear, in special containers in the computer room alongside each unit.

Reduce exposure to arson attempts by moving air conditioning and ventilation air intake ducts that serve the computer operations area. They should be relocated from ground level to well up on the building side—when possible even up under the eaves. When computer room emergency power generation equipment must be located outside the building, reduce its vulnerability to arson or vandalism by placing it in a below ground vault.

Limit the storage of forms, paper, and supply stocks within the computer room. Maintain reserve quantities at an adjacent location and authorize an operator on each shift to withdraw from that storeroom only the material to be used on that shift.

Hold frequent emergency action drills; at least one should be scheduled each month for each shift. Review system shutdown and personnel evacuation procedures. Test smoke detection and fire extinguishing equipment operation periodically.

Access Controls

Access to the computer facility must be closely controlled on a continuing basis to reduce its vulnerability to arson and vandalism and to avoid possible compromise by industrial spies of the data it processes. Something more is required than simply stationing an armed security guard at the main computer facility entrance and asking visitors to sign a register. At one large installation where this seems to be the extent of the access control effort, a visitor who signed himself as *Adolf Hitler, Berchtesgaden, Germany* was admitted without question. Later this same visitor spent several hours wandering without challenge throughout the facility. Similar vulnerability can be demonstrated in countless other data processing operations. Effective access control is built upon consistent application of sound security procedures and employee awareness that no unusual action, thing, or person should be ignored.

A successful access control plan is based on this principle: Limit entry only to those company employees whose assigned duties require that they be in the area. The formal policy on the matter might be phrased in this fashion:

- Access to the computer center will be on a *need to enter* basis. Company employees not regularly assigned to the computer center will *not* be granted automatic admission to the facility. They will be required to justify their reason for entering the computer center and will be subject to the normal controls placed on visitors to the area. Where access must be monitored very closely, a *personal access control booth* (often improperly termed a *mantrap*) may be installed. It consists of two sets of doors separated by a short corridor. The corridor is outfitted with some combination of a closed circuit TV camera or one-way window to permit observation of individuals attempting to secure access—and a standard badge reader access control system. Normally, the outside door is unlocked when no one is in the corridor; and the inside door remains locked. When entrants are cleared visually, the access control system is activated: The outside door locks and then the inside door opens until those in the corridor enter the facility. The inner door then locks and the outer door reopens. A one-way revolving door or turnstile may be installed in place of the corridor and double doors.
- Vendor representatives, auditors, building cleaning and maintenance employees, and other visitors will be required to (1) provide positive identification before admittance; (2) record the date, time, and purpose of their

visit; (3) wear a distinctive visitor's badge while they are in the computer center; and (4) be escorted during their visit by an assigned member of the computer center staff. (When building employees require access to the center after hours, they will be escorted by one of the center management group.)

- Computer center employees will be expected to question *unescorted visitors* about their right to be in the facility, even when they are wearing the required visitor's badge.

- Messengers and vendor representatives will be instructed that deliveries are *not* to be made directly to the computer center. Form stocks and other supplies are to be delivered to the regular receiving area. Messengers are to deliver materials to the company mail room for routine rehandling.

Safeguarding the computer facility requires that it be kept secure against entry of unauthorized persons.

Determine the total area for which access is to be controlled. Generally this will include the office space used by data processing management and the systems and programming staff, as well as computer operations and the tape library. Establish a perimeter around the area that is to be safeguarded. The access control plan should be built upon existing controls on personnel entry into and circulation through the building. For instance, if employees are issued a personnel identification card by the company, a distinctive one should be issued to computer center personnel. Where a larger plan for maintaining building security exists, computer facility security plans should form an integral part of it. In most instances the computer area perimeter will function as a second—or even third—line of defense.[6]

Eliminate or block any doors in the perimeter not essential to safe emergency evacuation of the computer area. Remove outside door knob hardware on all doors in the perimeter that are not to be used as *entrance* points. Local fire codes normally will require that panic-bar door opening hardware be placed on the perimeter interior side of all of these doors. To assure that assigned computer room employees use designated access points, attach audible exit alarms to each of the other doors. The noise made by these alarms will alert security officers and others to surreptitious exits from the computer facility. These alarms should help deter thefts from the computer room and discourage unauthorized removal of files and records.

External Threats

Physical attacks against computer facilities have been relatively rare. (Unfortunately those that have been reported have been very well publicized.[*]) However, data processing activities do offer a tempting target for the rioter, bomber, or vandal. Plans for dealing with these threats should be integrated into the organization's overall plans for handling these contingencies. In particular, management must determine the circumstances under which computer operations will be shut down. And, it must decide how and when critical real-time systems are to be kept operating during an emergency. For instance, the formal policy for handling bomb threats might state that:

- Upon receipt of a written or telephoned bomb threat against the computer center or discovery of a suspicious object in or near the computer center, operations will be terminated immediately and all personnel evacuated from the area. Company security officers will be responsible for: (1) contacting the police department bomb squad, (2) preventing unauthorized access to the computer center until after the device has been safely removed, and (3) conducting a search of the premises to assure that they are safe before permitting center employees to return and resume operations.

The various formal contingency plans should be tested at least twice annually.

When a computer must be placed where it may be subjected to acts of vandalism or may be threatened during a possible civil disorder, a number of supplemental security measures may be taken to prevent unauthorized access. For example, perimeter doors and their frames and hardware must be specially reinforced.

---

[6] When the facility occupies its own building a number of access control problems exist whose solution lies beyond the scope of this chapter. For detailed information on means for resolving these problems see *Design for Security, Second Edition,* by Richard Healey. New York: John Wiley and Sons, Inc.; 1983.

[*] For a discussion of one aspect of this problem, see Belden Menkus, *Notes on Terrorism and Data Processing in Computers and Security,* p. 2. New York: Elsevier Scientific, 1983.

Establish several *access points* in the perimeter. During hours that the computer center is operational each of these entrances should be continually observed by a receptionist or security guard. In many organizations it will be desirable for the security guard to also act as the receptionist. (Normally data processing management will have almost no control over the conditions under which security guards will be used. General management policy on organization security will determine such things as use of a contract security guard service and arming of guards.[7]

The work station at this access control point should be placed where the normal traffic flow will force all visitors to pass that point when they approach the door to the computer facility. The work station should be equipped with electric controls for unlocking the adjacent door into the computer area, a telephone call director that will permit direct push button access to extensions in the computer center, and some means for unobtrusively summoning assistance in an emergency. Sufficient space should be available for opening and inspection of the contents of brief cases and parcels on both entry and departure. This routine inspection would discourage unauthorized removal of tapes and papers.

Place a visitor's register at each work station and provide a stock of numbered visitors' badges. The badge itself can be a distinctively colored plastic laminated printed card. An alligator clip affixed to the badge can be used to attach this identification to the visitor's clothing. Enter the assigned badge number opposite the register entry for each visitor. This practice will aid control of the badges themselves and will assure that all visitors are accounted for on departure.

Designate *after hours* entrance and exit points for use by assigned computer facility employees. Strictly limit issuance of keys for these locks and assure that they are recovered from terminating employees prior to delivery of the final paycheck. Use of removable core locks will facilitate rapid change of locks when an employee leaves under questionable circumstances. (Use of Sargent *Keso* brand or comparable lock hardware would offer greater security against surreptitious entry. However these lock cylinders can not be

readily changed on short notice.) Where data processing operations are sensitive, it is desirable to install additional access controls. These could include (1) locks that are opened by a special identification card issued to computer center employees, (2) keyboard-activated combination lock hardware, or (3) equipment that will recognize the unique geometric outline of the hands of authorized employees and admit them.

Periodic security officer checks of the computer facility premises will provide some measure of after hours security. This should be supplemented by installation of intrusion detection devices[8] at strategic points in the computer facility. Placed in operation when normal computer center activities are shut down, these units will react automatically to intruders or emergency conditions and alert security officers, as well as the local police or fire departments, to them.

The procedures for controlling access to the computer facility are relatively simple. They must be routinely followed if they are to be successful. Yet this same routine compliance can undermine their effectiveness. There is a constant danger that a well-meaning employee may circumvent these controls "just this once" and compromise all of the efforts made to safeguard the computer. To avoid this problem, access controls should be reinforced by a continuing employee education effort. Posters and other materials can be used to stress the value and significance of computer security in assuring uninterrupted continuance of business operations and in avoiding industrial espionage.

Safeguarding Data Processing Records

Efforts to protect the computer against a variety of perils will become close to pointless if the information that it processes is not also kept secure. While data processing equipment can be replaced or repaired, lost or distorted information may be impossible to replace at any price. Many of the general precautions suggested in this chapter will aid in safeguarding the tapes and disks that contain this information. In addition, these media must be protected against assaults by magnets and from fire and water damage.

---

[7] For additional information see *Design for Security and Locks, Safes and Security: A Handbook for Law Enforcement Personnel* by Marc Weber Tobias. Springfield: Charles C. Thomas, Publisher; 1972.

[8] Discussed in detail in Chapter 12 of this book.

Stories have circulated in the data processing field for several years about use of small magnets to damage or destroy the content of computer records. These stories have revolved around the activities of vandals, disgruntled employees, and unthinking visitors to the computer center. Studies of computer record vulnerability to assault by magnets indicate that (1) it is difficult and extremely time consuming to erase completely the contents of a tape or disk with a common relatively small magnet, but (2) application of these magnets can cause random data loss on tapes or disks.[9] The strength of a magnetic field decreases in proportion to the cube of its increasing distance from the surface of the object being affected by it. Thus, a magnet strong enough to alter or erase data when in direct physical contact with a tape or disk surface will fail to cause these changes when it is moved a small distance from that surface.

The real problem with magnetic assaults on data processing records is the randomness of those assaults. In a large tape library it may be necessary to printout its entire contents to locate and correct damage done by magnets. Consistent use of tape rings and disk pack locks will offer some protection by making it more difficult for an intruder armed with a magnet to get direct access to the recording surface. Critical tape files can be housed in antimagnetic shielded containers. But, magnetic shielding can be cumbersome and extremely expensive to apply to the entire contents of a tape library. However, portable or stationary magnetometers, similar to those used in airline luggage inspections, can be installed at computer facility access points to screen visitors and employees. (Informal tests at airline inspection stations indicate that there is little likelihood that magnetometers will adversely affect the contents of data processing records.) Unfortunately, these instruments are not infallible and may fail to detect every magnetic threat. Thus, computer facility employees should be encouraged to examine the tape library and their work areas periodically for such potential dangers as pocketsized magnets and magnetized screw drivers and flashlights. Employees should also be alert for damaged electrical connections,

unlatched doors on operating disk drives, and other evidences of possible sabotage.

Data processing tapes and disks consist of a plastic substrate coated with a fine oxide powder suspended in a binding substance. Excessive heat will distort both the substrate and the coating. In addition, a sharp temperature rise may force the binder to break down and give up some of its constituent moisture. Temperatures above 135°F. can cause distortion. Those above 170°F. will accelerate surface decomposition. Conventional insulated record storage containers are designed to protect paper records from fire damage by keeping the temperature of their contents below 350°F., just below the flash point of paper. These containers do this by releasing stored moisture into their interiors. Excessive moisture in this temperature range will accelerate the deterioration of stored tape, disk, and microfilm records. Clearly the conventional records fire protection equipment is not suitable for safeguarding tapes or disks from fire damage. Bank vaults (which are designed for burglary rather than fire protection) and the typical tape library area offer little additional security.

Insulated storage containers designed to provide fire protection for data processing records at 150°F. have been certified by the Underwriters' Laboratories, and are available from a number of different vendors.[10] Depending upon the way in which their interior space is arranged, these containers can hold only 60 to 90 items. Thus, floor load and space limitations will preclude their use for other than essential master files, related current transaction tapes, and computer programs.

Several security equipment makers claim to have developed suitable protective records vaults for disk and tape storage. However, Underwriters' Laboratories has not certified any of these units and does not certify a fire door or vault construction that will successfully maintain the contents

[9] See [U.S.] National Bureau of Standards Publication 500-101. *Care and Handling of Computer Magnetic Storage Media* by Sidney Geller. Available from: Superintendent of Documents, Government Printing Office, Washington DC 20402.

[10] Specifications for this protective storage equipment are contained in National Fire Protection Association Standard 236 *Protection of Records.* A 350°F. rated records storage container will be denied testing laboratory certification if its contents require special treatment after a fire before they can be used. However, certification will be granted for a 150°F. rated unit if after a fire its contents are capable of being "used for developing information for possible future use." Thus, tapes and disks that survive a fire in such a container possibly could not be used immediately afterward but might require extensive remedial handling before their contents could be processed reliably by a computer.

of a records vault or file room at 150°F. or less during a fire. Thus, alternate means of protecting data processing records should be used.

Necessary additional protection can be provided by copying onto duplicate tape reels to be dispersed for storage at a geographically remote company operating location or secure commercial storage facility. It is highly unlikely that files at both the company computer facility and this remote site will be subject to damage or destruction at the same time. To avoid possible employee fraud in handling these dispersed file copies, they should be placed in the custody of an internal auditor or other responsible individual at the location where they are stored.

When data files are updated periodically three generations of the file can be retained: the current version and the two previous ones. The *grandfather* (the oldest) version of the file is stored off-site until replaced by a later version. Avoid the all too common error of storing all three file versions at the same site. When data files are maintained on a disk, a *snapshot* (a copy of file content at a specific point in time) should be made periodically by copying disk contents to tape. This may not be feasible to do with any regularity when some of the newer high data density disk packs are in use. Dumping their content to tape is a time-consuming process that may be difficult to justify economically and operationally. However, where the snapshot technique can be used, the two oldest tape sets should be stored off-site until replaced in turn by later snapshots. In both instances, these stored off-site tape file copies can be used with related transaction records to reconstruct files damaged or containing extensive computer processing errors.

Where tapes are to be maintained for extended periods off-premises they should be diagnostically checked for errors and copied onto other tape. Rather than being handled haphazardly *as processing time becomes available*, this protective processing should be scheduled by computer operations in the same way that semiannual report preparation is handled.

United States Internal Revenue Service Ruling 71-20 provides for auditing of computer-maintained tax records in machine processable form. The ruling mandates retention of certain tapes and disks until after completion of tax audit and clearance. Often this will mean that these materials will be kept for anywhere from two to seven years, along with pertinent file documentation. Special steps should be taken to protect these records.

Program Library and System Files

In general, operating programs and related documentation should be protected along with the other records and files used in the computer facility. Thus, the basic recommendations in this chapter on computer facility security and records protection apply to these materials as well. Supplemental efforts should be made to restrict access to these files and the work areas in which they are used. For instance, these records may well be placed in a locked separate area *within* the computer facility. Maintain a register of individual access to particular files: a form similar to that used for the visitor's register may be suitable. Prevent overnight removal of these files and access to them on holidays or during off-hours. At least once a week these files should be inventoried and the location of all out-of-file items verified.

Summary

Improved approaches to computer room layout and design are called for. It must be made secure, yet retain its workplace environment. The most effective program for protecting the computer is one developed as an integral part of the equipment selection and installation process.

The building in which the computer is to be located should be secure against fire and flood damage. An independent power generation source should be provided.

The area in which data processing equipment and files are located must be isolated from the rest of the building and protected as a unit against fire threats. Special fire detection and extinguishing equipment should be installed. Good housekeeping practices should be rigorously enforced.

Access to the computer facility should be closely controlled and consistently monitored. Circulation of vendors and visitors within the computer facility should be sharply restricted.

Computer operating programs and related documentation should be carefully protected along with data processing tape and disk files.

Limited on-site storage should be backed up by off-premises maintenance of vital records.

Microcomputer Physical Security

Placing a microcomputer in an office setting—rather than in space specifically designed for computer use—creates a number of new security problems. These relate to location control; preventive maintenance, heating, ventilation, and air conditioning of the use site; electric power supply quality; static electricity elimination; fire protection; and magnetic media control.

- Location Control. These systems all are highly portable and easily stolen and fenced. There are three ways to reduce this loss exposure. First, apply conventional fixed asset controls to the system. Affix a serially numbered tag to each system component. The tag should also include the company name and identifying symbol, if any. Enter the data on the component and their location in the organization's asset records. Second, secure the various system components to the work surface on which they are used. (A number of standard office equipment locking devices have been modified for this use.) Third, limit casual access to the microcomputer. Either avoid placing it in an 'open office' environment, or provide hardware locks for the equipment and the office areas, with adequate supervision.

- Preventive Maintenance. Microcomputers will be located, in many instances, in areas not intended for the use of relatively sensitive electronic devices. In particular, office cleaning practices and ventilation systems operation may lead to the deposit of room dust and other debris on both diskette surfaces and within disk drives. This can cause both data read/write errors and data loss, and may cause read/write head damage as well. (A crash of one of these heads could leave the microcomputer effectively inoperable for days—or even weeks—until it is repaired or a replacement is secured.) Ban smoking and eating from the area in which the microcomputer is used. Discourage the placement of plants in that area. Require strict adherence to manufacturer-recommended drive head cleaning practices.

- Heating, ventilation, and air conditioning (HVAC). Basically, the microcomputer should be placed away from the direct flow of air in the office. (Require regular changes of air filters in the ventilation system.) And, extremes of heat and cold in this part of the building should be avoided.

- Electric power supply quality. Microcomputers are far more susceptible than conventional data terminals to ordinary fluctuations (surges and sags) in the electric power supplied to an office area. A surge suppressor may be installed between the electric power outlet and the microcomputer. Constant voltage regulators can compensate effectively for surges as well as for power level reduction associated with a sag. Small uninterruptible power supply (UPS) devices can be installed to provide even more stable electric power—effectively eliminating the impact of any surges and sags. It will also provide a short-term power supply reserve whenever the conventional power source fails completely.

- Static electricity. Friction on carpets in conditions of low humidity produces static electricity, which is capable of damaging or destroying data on magnetic media and in computer primary memory. Touch mats, sprays, and wipes are useful in bleeding off static charges.

- Fire protection. Microcomputers are located, typically, in an atmosphere that is not protected adequately against exposure to a possible fire. Most office areas, for instance, do not have smoke detectors or a water sprinkler fire extinguishing system installed. Fortunately most reported fires directly involving microcomputers have been confined to the interior of the device's cabinet and have not spread to the adjacent work area. To deal with a possible fire exposure, install a Halon 1301, CO_2, or dry chemical fire extinguisher adjacent to the microcomputer use site. Be sure that the office personnel have been taught to use the extinguisher effectively, and that the extinguisher is serviced and tested frequently.

- Magnetic media control. Diskettes are more sensitive to mishandling and far easier to compromise than are conventional tapes and disks. Among other things, diskettes should not be used as coffee cup coasters or jammed haphazardly into a shirt pocket, purse compartment, or interoffice mailing envelope. And, diskettes should not be left on top of the system monitor. (Many monitors are not shielded adequately against x-ray emission. This signal leakage may destroy part or all of the recorded content of the diskette.) Content compromise can occur because recorded diskettes too often are not secured by the microcomputer user in a locked storage container when not in actual read/write use. A stock of blank diskettes typically is available adjacent to the microcomputer. Failure to secure these blank diskettes adds to the potential for compromise. Microcomputers—like data terminals—are commonly left on throughout the workday in unattended offices, even when not in active operation. These offices, as noted earlier, rarely are locked when the occupant is away. Opportunities for uncontrolled file content copying abound in such an environment.

Physical Security Checklist

	Yes	No
Is the computer facility located away from high traffic areas?	☐	☐
Is the computer facility located away from the buildings outside walls and without windows?	☐	☐
Can the computer's power sources and air-conditioning function independently of regular utilities in an emergency?	☐	☐
Are the facility's architects and engineers familiar with computer physical and fire security requirements?	☐	☐
Is the computer facility located away from hazards such as gas stations, airports, paint storage structures, and chemical plants, and rivers or other possible causes of flooding?	☐	☐
Is the computer facility inconspicuous, without references on direction signs?	☐	☐

	Yes	No
Have telephone operators been instructed not to give unseen telephone callers directions to the computer room?	☐	☐
Are the ceilings and walls sufficiently watertight to prevent equipment damage if a pipe is ruptured?	☐	☐
Is drainage under the raised floor adequate to avoid water accumulation where flooding may occur or where water might be used to extinguish a fire?	☐	☐
Are water-level detectors installed beneath raised floors?	☐	☐
Are document destruction units placed near computer operations areas?	☐	☐
Is spoiled impact printer output destroyed before it is disposed of?	☐	☐
Is there a computer facility fire protection plan which operates independently from that for the rest of the premises?	☐	☐
Are smoking and eating prohibited within the computer facility?	☐	☐
Do the computer facility specifications indicate: flame resistant floor and wall surfaces? acoustical ceiling tiles and ductwork certified by a recognized testing laboratory? glass diffusers on lighting fixtures? fluorescent light fixtures that cannot melt or drip?	☐	☐
Are clearly marked master power control switches placed at each of the computer facility main exits?	☐	☐
Are portable fire extinguishers placed at main computer room entrances and exits?	☐	☐
Is a set of proper extinguishers within 50 feet of every point in the computer area?	☐	☐
Are water extinguishers marked: "Do not use on live electrical equipment"?	☐	☐
Is smoke and fire detection equipment approved by a recognized testing organization?	☐	☐

Yes No

Are supplemental detectors placed on underfloor space with thermostats activated by rate of heat rise? ☐ ☐

Is breathing apparatus similar to that used by fire fighters located near key extinguisher sets? ☐ ☐

Does activation of the smoke detection system result in an audible alarm in the computer area, automatic notification to the nearest fire department, switching air-conditioning to a non-recirculating mode, and startup of additional fans and blowers? ☐ ☐

Will smoke and combustion products be exhausted into the outside atmosphere? ☐ ☐

Are there flame-retardant waterproof plastic covers for major data processing equipment items? ☐ ☐

Yes No

Are the main supplies of forms and paper items located outside the computer room? ☐ ☐

Are emergency action drills held frequently? ☐ ☐

Is computer room access limited to those whose presence is necessary? ☐ ☐

Are there audible exit alarms on all doors that are not the ones used for normal access? ☐ ☐

Are access points continually observed by a receptionist or security guard? ☐ ☐

Are parcels brought in and out of the computer area routinely inspected? ☐ ☐

Are duplicate copies of data files and programs routinely kept at an off-site location? Are these duplicate files kept current? ☐ ☐

CHAPTER 12

Monitoring and Related Control Devices

By Eugene V. Redmond

Introduction

Much has been written on the need for the physical safety of the computer data center, microprocessor work stations, and the dangers of inadequate controls over data resources. This chapter analyzes and defines the remedies or options available when making a decision on a system of computer security.

Computer security is a process intended to control the people, physical plant and equipment, and the data involved in information processing so as to preserve and protect these valuable assets.

Monitoring devices are the physical means by which environmental conditions are measured in a data processing installation.

Control devices are mechanisms for preventing unwanted actions, or for initiating corrective action to remedy adverse conditions detected by monitoring devices.

Security and control monitoring measures include:

- Warning as early as possible, through sensing of a security threat
- Employing effective deterrents
- Initiating corrective action to security breaches

This chapter describes:

- The lines of defense (i.e., security systems) that can be used by the management of the computer facility
- The types of computer security devices that are available to the data center

- Advantages and constraints for various types of security devices
- Minimum data center requirements for achieving a positive security stance

Defense Planning

When considering the options open to protect computer resources, the data center manager must, as in all systems of defense, organize so that penetration in one area does not compromise the entire facility. Because of the variety and scope of responsibility in a modern data processing center, the types of protection must vary from early warning to condition red.

The first line of defense involves precautionary measures at the outer perimeter. For today's computer center, the purpose of perimeter control is to prevent unauthorized access to the premises. In turn, access control subdivides into two types:

- Security during periods of operation
- Protection when the facility is closed down

If a computer facility remains closed for a portion of the normal 24-hour day, the most effective protection is a device that prevents initial entry. Frequently the solution for this requirement is a good lock placed on all entrances. As required, the lock can be backed up by either the direct surveillance of a guard at the entrance or by indirect monitoring such as a remote TV camera.

Initial entry protection during periods of data center operation may also involve an entrance lock system with or without surveillance.

However, the problem is complicated by the need to distinguish between authorized and unauthorized access. Protection devices suitable for these applications are further defined in a subsequent section of this chapter.

The second line of defense requires protection using a form of deterrence. Although a deterrent may be used at the perimeter (for example, a low voltage charge on a door or fence), it is more frequently employed within the computer facility. Deterrents can be considered as active or passive:

- Passive devices include prominently placed cameras at key locations, sound-emitting devices that provide constant audible sounds, or power line conditioners that limit electrical aberrations.

- Active devices, typified by the alarm system, can be activated by unauthorized entry or environmental disturbances. There are many types of alarms, ranging from simple sounding of a bell or buzzer, to electronic devices that detect motion.

These devices are subsequently described in further detail in this chapter.

The final line of defense is a natural extension of the two previous categories—the system of control and response to the discovery signal. Such response typically involves a method available of investigating the indicated condition in order to take immediate action. Controlled response can include the access to and egress from the data center, control monitors continuously evaluating data from sensors, and automated response devices that are actuated without any human decisions.

Classification of Security Mechanisms

All security monitoring devices, whether serving in a perimeter, deterrent, or control capacity, fulfill at least one of the following functions:

- Surveillance. The ability to view a designated area within the abilities of human or animal sensory perception. Surveillance can be direct, as in the case of a guard at the door, or indirect, as when employing a device such

Table 12.1 Common Monitoring and Control Devices, Functions and Applications

Device/Agent	Primary Security Function			Application
	Surveillance	Detection	Control	
Guard	X	X	X	Perimeter security and alarm response
Guard dogs	X	X	X	Intrusion detection and control. Fire/smoke detection
Photographic camera	X			Perimeter/interior surveillance
Closed circuit TV camera	X			Perimeter/interior surveillance
Heat-actuated sensor		X		Room temperature detection
Flame-actuated senor		X		Flame presence detection
Smoke-actuated sensor		X		Smoke presence detection
Low frequency wave patterns		X		Space detection
Ultrasonic wave pattern		X		Space detection
Microwave device		X		Space detection
Capacitance device		X		Spot detection
Audio microphone		X		Space detection
Photoelectric beam		X		Space/spot detection
Dry contact switches		X		Spot detection
Alarm system circuitry		X	X	Indicate security incident and assure tamper-free reliable operation
Power line conditioner			X	Prevent electrical aberrations
Sprinkler system			X	Respond to fire detection
Gas discharge system			X	Respond to fire detection
Automatic dial up			X	Respond to security detection
Locks			X	Control access/egress
Coded/Imaged cards			X	Control access/egress
Hand prints			X	Control access/egress

as a camera. It may or may not include a response ability.

- Detecting. The ability to sense aberrations in a controlled environment. Sensing devices can be active or inactive.
- Control. The assurance of the security system that necessary information reaches those responsible, that appropriate response activity can be initiated, or that unwanted actions are prevented or impeded.

Surveillance, detecting, and control devices can now be examined as to equipment characteristics and their relation to the data center security system.

Table 12.1 identifies common monitoring and control devices and classifies them according to security function performed. It provides a checklist of various alternative devices to consider in planning or reviewing a data center security system.

Surveillance Devices

Visual surveillance is undoubtedly the oldest monitoring technique of security control. Modern surveillance techniques, however, are a blending of both old and new forms of technology. The oldest is based on extra ordinary development of sensory perception and logical response, while the newest is based on the technological feats of converting a viewed image into either a single snapshot print or transparency after viewing, or a multiple screening of electronic images in a live format as it occurs. There are three categories of data center security surveillance:

1. Guards
2. Dogs
3. Visual recording devices

Guards

The use of guards takes advantage of man's greatest asset over hardware—the ability to learn quickly a myriad of recognition patterns essential to data center security and to respond to the various undesirable conditions. A guard's eyesight (along with other sensory organs) permits his use in a perimeter, deterrent response, or control capacity. In a perimeter function, the most ele-

mentary and still useful applications of a guard can be to:

1. Apply recognition patterns to each access into the secure area
2. Perform a receptionist function by logging in visitors and telephoning ahead for verification of access
3. Prevent unauthorized access to unwanted individuals
4. Patrol the secured area premises

The physical presence of a guard provides a deterrent capacity. The fact that the guard is visible and able to notice unusual sounds, odors, or suspicious behavior, and is available to respond to the detected problems, is the main advantage of a guard on the premises.

Guards can also perform control functions that are a vital part of any security system. Some of these services are:

- Planning security requirements
- Maintaining order
- Crowd control
- Reporting of irregularities
- Responding to mechanical or other sources of alarms

The use of guards, however, is limited by their reliability. Despite careful preemployment screening and bonding, there is no foolproof method for overcoming this problem entirely—either in selection or training. Therefore, a security system that contains reasonable checks and balances, rather than relying on any one particular device or technique is essential. Another limitation is that the guards might not be informed, through procedural failure, which individuals are no longer authorized to be in the area.

These limitations, as well as their relative costs, should be considered in deciding whether to employ guards on permanent staff, or to use an outside agency.

Guard Dogs

Dogs were the first animal to be trained by man. Their loyalty and intelligence, coupled with a keen sense of hearing and acute sense of smell, make dogs highly useful in detecting intruders or other conditions. Dogs' ability to provide early warning of a security incident is evidenced by the fact that they can hear a sound 250 yards away that a human generally cannot detect beyond 25 yards. Also, a dog's range of hearing extends beyond 30,000 cycles, well into the ultrasonic range and beyond the ability of the human ear. In addition, a dog has a high degree of recognition ability based upon an extremely keen sense of smell.

Dogs are not limited to just the detection of unusual sounds or odors. Their ability to be trained to respond to a command and hold a potential intruder at bay until security personnel can take over make them capable of doing what an electronic detector alone cannot: perform as an automatic response mechanism.

Many breeds are suitable as guard dogs, the German shepherd leading the list. However, there are other large dogs temperamentally suited to guard duty: Dobermans, Rottweillers, Bouviers, Bull terriers, and giant Schnauzers. If dogs are trained to operate as attack dogs, they usually will first bark to chase away intruders from the areas being guarded. If an intruder penetrates the secured area, the attack dog will corner the perpetrator and hold him at bay until the police or the dog handler arrive. If the dog is trained to detect specific types of odors or sounds (such as smoke from a paper fire), he will lead the handler to the source of the disturbance.

While its obvious virtues make a dog in many ways ideal for surveillance, detection, and response to security incidents, there are disadvantages. A guard dog requires insurance coverage in the event of liability damage awards. Also, it is not safe for an authorized person to make an unscheduled appearance without the handler being present. Other disadvantages fall under the category of costs. The typical cost categories that should be budgeted when considering a guard dog are listed in Exhibit 12.1.

Exhibit 12.1
Typical Cost Categories for Maintenance and Ownership of Guard Dogs

Maintenance Costs:
    Feeding
    Veterinary license fees
    Collars and chains

Ownership Costs:
    Cost of acquisition
    Dog training
    Handler training
    Handler's salary (if additional)
    Liability insurance
    Housing

Visual Recording Devices

Since surveillance is based upon either human or animal sensory perception, surveillance devices are normally used in conjunction with guards to extend their range of perception. Typical among this group of hardware is the camera. Basically, there are two categories of visual recording devices in use—the photographic and the closed circuit TV.

Cameras   In the photographic category, there are two types in use—the motion picture camera and the single exposure sequence camera. Each camera can be activated by manual or electronic switching devices. The motion picture camera, once activated, typically runs for approximately five minutes on standard 8mm or 16mm film until all the film is exposed. Modern lenses, high-speed film, and an exposure rate of 16 to 24 frames per second are able to combine in normal room lighting to yield good pictures of a security incident. If continuing camera surveillance is desired for longer periods, time-lapse techniques can be employed with sequencing varying from one frame per second anywhere up to one frame per minute or more. Time-lapse rates enable a 100-foot roll of movie film to last from approximately 1¼ hours to 80 hours of continuous operation. Some movie cameras have an override device that enables switching from a time-lapse mode to the normal moving picture exposure rate of 16 to 24 frames per second. Typical camera timing mechanisms are built in and do not require external activation.

Single exposure sequence cameras utilize a 35mm film format, and because of the increased film size it is possible to obtain greater line resolution and improved print quality. Its exposure rate is determined by the range of the built-in timing mechanism, which typically varies from once every few seconds to one-minute intervals. A 200-foot roll of 35mm film can yield anywhere from approximately one-half hour to 25 hours of exposure. In all other respects—lenses, film, and lighting requirements—the 35mm single exposure camera is similar to the movie camera.

Photographic type cameras can only provide a viewable image if the film is processed or developed, usually off the premises. Cameras of this type are often placed in highly visible locations to serve as a form of psychological deterrent.

Closed Circuit TV (Video Recorder) The closed circuit TV camera is generally similar in function and performance to the photographic type camera, with one important difference. The TV system provides a live image of events currently taking place in the area under surveillance. This capability allows a guard in a remote location to maintain constant surveillance of key security areas. Closed circuit TV systems can be acquired with lenses that enable a guard to zoom the camera in for a close-up and to pivot or pan about the security areas. Some cameras can be mounted on an overhead conveyor rail that allows the camera to place a wider area under security surveillance. The camera carriage is propelled noiselessly by compressed air, and when combined with zoom lenses, tilting and panning controls, its ability to perform surveillance tasks is greatly enhanced. As with the photographic camera, the closed circuit TV camera can be a strong psychological deterrent.

Utilizing a video cassette recorder (VCR), closed circuit TV methodology has the advantage of economically recording an event and storing any desired events. Current advances in VCRs make this system cost-effective for visual recording.

Detecting

Strictly speaking, a detecting device is a means of sensing a change in a specific aspect of the environment. Different sensing devices have been developed to monitor various environmental aspects. These devices typically perform as follows:

Measurement Function	Detection Application
Temperature	Fire
Flame	Fire
Radioactive ionization	Fire
Wave patterns	Motion
Capacitance	Motion
Microwave patterns	Motion
Continuity	Fire/motion

Measurement Function	Detection Application
Audio amplification	Motion
Power line	Noise/spike

Definitions of the terms used to describe various detector functions are given in Exhibit 12.2.

Exhibit 12.2
Definition of Terms Used in Security Detection

Temperature detection refers to the measurement, usually in degrees Farenheit, of the room or area.

Flame detection refers to the number of cycles per second that a flame pulsates, or to the amount of infrared energy it disperses.

Radioactive ionization detection is the measurement of the gaseous residue of combustion.

Wave pattern detection is the evaluation of sound wave reflections in an enclosed area.

Capacitance detection is the measurement of an electrical field present in the monitored area.

Microwave pattern detection is the measurement of high frequency radio wave reflections in an enclosed area.

Continuity detection is the monitoring of an area to sense interruption or the breaking of a carrier beam.

Audio amplification is the detection and amplification of sound within an enclosed area.

Power line detection refers to the suppression of unwarranted interference transmitted primarily by the source of electrical power.

Usually, most sensing devices are connected to other mechanisms, either as a part of an active deterrent, such as alarms and shut-off devices, or as a passive deterrent, such as an audio microphone.

Sensing devices can also be connected to data-gathering devices that record the time of environment change at a remote location. They can also be connected to logic circuits that carry out programmed checks, dial up predetermined phone numbers, or similar activities. Typical sensing applications and their activating media are:

Sensing Application	Activating Medium
Fire	Heat
Motion detection	Reflected wave patterns and amplified sound
Intrusion detection	Continuity break

Fire Detectors

Fire detectors sense thermal combustion or its products. These devices respond to incremental changes in temperature or the products of combustion, typically as a part of an automatic fire alarm system. Fire detectors are concerned with temperature, flame, radioactive ionization, and photoelectric detection methods. Actuation can be by heat, flame, or smoke. Each of these will be treated separately.

Heat-actuated sensing devices fall into two categories:

1. Fixed-temperature detectors that function when the temperature level reaches a predetermined value.
2. Rate-of-rise detectors that operate when rate of temperature increase exceeds a predetermined value regardless of the temperature level. A typical value at which the rate-of-rise temperature detector will function is 15° to 20°F. per minute.

While a rate-of-rise temperature sensor provides a quicker alarm, particularly for highly combustible areas, it may also increase the possibility of false alarms due to its greater sensitivity. Fixed temperature devices, on the other hand, do not offer as much opportunity for false alarms, and are more reliable in detecting a slowly developing fire such as one started by a careless cigarette. Some sensors combine the two types to offer protection from both categories of fire.

Heat-actuated devices can be of the line or spot types. A line type installation is operated by a pneumatic tube or heat-sensitive cable, while the spot installation locates each sensor in zones at specified distances apart. The maximum spacing applicable for a spot installation depends upon the sensitivity of the heat detector, the ceiling materials (i.e., board or joist or concrete) used in construction, and the amount of combustibles in the area. For a flat, smooth ceiling, the maximum spacing between sensors can vary from 12½ feet to 30 feet, depending upon the type of heat-actuated device used.

Flame-actuated sensing devices can be obtained in two principal types:

1. Flame-radiation-frequency-actuated devices that sense the pulsations or flicker of the flame associated with combustion
2. Flame-energy-actuated devices that sense a portion of the infrared energy in the flame

Radiation-frequency flame-actuated devices are expensive, and therefore limited to highly specialized applications. Flame-energy-actuated devices provide ultra-high-speed detection of the infrared energy of a flame. This device has a response time of less than 5 milliseconds and can produce a voltage sufficient to release an extinguishing agent and sound an alarm. Its main application is to provide extremely fast fire detection, and, although expensive, it is recommended for the protection of valuable equipment.

Smoke-actuated devices are particularly useful as an early warning device in detecting slowly developing fires during which it is desirable to provide a quick alarm before the sprinklers are turned on. Smoke detectors are also installed in air conditioning and ventilating systems where the presence of smoke could cause serious harm. Typically, two types of smoke-actuated devices are in use—the photoelectric type and the radioactive type.

Photoelectric devices are based upon the principle of an electric current that changes when there is a variation in the light intensity reaching the photoelectric cell. There are three types currently in use today: the beam type, area-sampling type, and the spot type.

- The beam type focuses a beam of light across the protected area onto a photoelectric cell that acts as the sensor. If the beam of light is obscured by smoke, an alarm is initiated.
- The area-sampling type uses a pipe system to draw air continuously from the protected area through a light source in a detector. The presence of smoke in the air sample will cause light reflections on the photoelectric cell that in turn initiates an alarm.
- The spot type contains the light source, receiver, and photoelectric cell in one housing. When smoke enters the detector, it causes reflected light to strike the photoelectric cell

and initiate an alarm in the same manner as the area-sampling type.

Radioactive smoke detection devices contain a radioactive material in a special chamber that is part of the detector. As smoke particles or other products of combustion enter this chamber, the normal ionization current is disturbed and causes an alarm signal to be generated. Radioactive detectors are mostly of the spot type and are usually mounted on the ceiling of the protected area.

The response of a smoke detector unit during a fire can be affected by stratification of air currents surrounding the device, the nature of the products of combustion, and the color of smoke produced from such combustion. In stratification, smoke may be prevented from reaching the detector head because of circulating air currents. Some products of combustion are heavier than others and will, therefore, rise more slowly, taking a longer period of time to reach the detector. The color of the smoke can affect the response of a spot type photoelectric detector, i.e., light-colored smoke causes a quicker response than dark-colored smoke. On the other hand, radioactive detectors are able to respond to invisible products of combustion such as found in freely burning paper.

Definitive spacing standards cannot be established for the various smoke detectors because of the many variables involved. Nevertheless, it is possible to indicate some approximations that are based on current practice (Table 12.2).

Table 12.2 Sample Approximations of Smoke Detector Head Spacing

Detector	Approximate Spacing*
Radio-active ionization detector:	
• rapid response not essential	1 head per 1000 sq. ft. maximum
• medium response	500 sq. ft.
• rapid response time	250 sq. ft.
Photoelectric Detector:	
• *Spot type:* Irregular enclosed spaces	30–40 square feet
Smooth ceilings	60 ft. centers
• *Beam type*	15′–160′ centers
• *Air sampling*	6400 sq. ft. maximum

*The 1000 square feet indicated for radioactive detectors assumes flat ceilings 8–16 feet high, open spaces, and no more than 30 detectors installed on a single circuit. Similar assumptions and constraints apply to each type of detector, depending upon specific recommendations from the manufacturer or insurance agency, and the physical layout of the data center.

Smoke detectors use a minute amount of radioactive material as part of their sensing chamber to enable detection of both visible and invisible products of combustion in an adjustment-free manner over their entire life. Everyone receives a daily radiation exposure from the naturally occurring radioactive materials within the earth and from cosmic radiation from outer space. On the average, humans receive about 125 mRem (milliRems) per year from these natural sources. An mRem is a very small unit of radiation dosage. Diagnostic medical procedures, such as chest and dental x-rays, for example, result in an average additional 20 mRem per year to each person. However, a person would receive less than 0.1 mRem standing one meter away from an ionization detector 24 hours a day for a year.

Federal and state governments have strict requirements limiting additional radiation dosage from products such as television receivers, luminous wristwatches, and many types of smoke detectors to levels far below that received from natural sources. Even though some of these products do not contain radioactive materials, all produce radiation to which one may be exposed. Periodic tests should be made in offices where radiation occurs to make sure government regulations are met.

Smoke detectors are required to meet or exceed all government standards. Their manufacture and distribution are licensed by the U.S. Nuclear Regulatory Commission (formerly the Atomic Energy Commission).

Motion Detectors

Motion detectors are used to sense an unusual presence or movement within a predefined interior security area. These sensors use wave patterns, photoelectric, infrared, capacitance, and audio amplification detection methods in providing an active type deterrent. For purposes of explanation, they can be grouped into three basic categories:

1. Wave pattern sensors
2. Capacitance devices
3. Audio amplification devices

Wave pattern motion detectors can be classified according to the frequency (i.e., cycles per second) of the generated wave and include low frequency, ultrasonic, and microwave devices.

In general, low frequency, ultrasonic, and microwave detectors all operate by generating a wave pattern that is either entirely or partially reflected back within the protected area to a sensitive receiver. Undisturbed wave patterns are reflected back to the generating device at the same originating frequency and will cause no alarm to be sounded. If, however, the reflected wave pattern is modified by any motion within the protected area, the frequency of the returning wave is changed and the motion detectors are programmed to activate the alarm circuit.

The range of effective coverage for wave type detectors under ideal conditions can vary anywhere from 600 to 10,000 square feet. However, because of the many variables in room size, configurations, acoustics, and detector system characteristics, the specific number of sensors, power and control requirements will be a function of the characteristics of each data center.

Table 12.3 compares the advantages and disadvantages of the low frequency, ultrasonic, and microwave detection devices.

Capacitance detectors monitor an electrical field that is generated to surround the immediate area of the specific object requiring security measures. As such, they provide point or spot protection rather than room area or space security. Capacitance detectors require that the specific object being protected act as one part of the tuned circuit which will emit a small but measurable magnetic field when electric current is applied. The protective field is usually limited to a depth of a few inches from the secured object. However, any penetration of this field, such as by an individual, will change the capacitance sufficiently to upset the balance of the system and typically provide an output signal that causes an alarm.

Capacitance detectors are typically used to provide spot protection for one or more file cabinets, safes, or other metallic containers. In addition, it can be connected to a metal grid covering windows and doors to detect unauthorized

Table 12.3 Advantages and Disadvantages of Low Frequency, Ultrasonic and Microwave Detection Devices

Advantages	Disadvantages
Low Frequency	
• Not triggered by small objects, or sudden or slow movements.	• 700 cycle note may be disturbing to some people.
• Emits audible sound as psychological deterrent.	• Limited to areas of relatively low ambient noise.
• Responsive only to human sized objects.	• Moderate to high maintenance level.
• Permits independent control of separate zones.	
• High reliability, moderate to high resistance to defeat.	
Ultrasonic	
• Difficult to detect presence of the system.	• Limited to line of sight and enclosed areas with minimal extraneous movement such as air currents.
• Reasonably flexible for application control.	• May require reduced sensitivity to overcome disturbance factors.
• High reliability.	• May not detect very slow movements.
	• May not detect wall penetration.
	• May be irritating to some people who hear or feel the sound.
	• Only moderate resistance to defeat.
	• Moderate to high maintenance level.
Microwave	
• Radiation field difficult to detect.	• Coverage not easily confined to desired security areas.
• Not affected by air currents, noise, light or sound.	• May be accidentally tripped by other radio transmitters.
• High salvage value.	• Tube replacement (frequency generator) may be expensive.
• High reliability and resistance to defeat.	• Moderate to high maintenance level.

entry. Because of the limited depth of the protective field, the capacitance detector avoids unwanted alarms from authorized staff passing nearby.

Table 12.4 compares the advantages and disadvantages of capacitance detectors.

Table 12.4 Advantages and Disadvantages of Capacitance Detectors

Advantages

- Protective field is invisible.
- Difficult to detect a protected object.
- Authorized staff passing within a few feet will not trigger an alarm.
- Flexible applications. Can be used for any ungrounded metallic object within the maximum range of the detection system.
- Simple and compact in size.
- High reliability and resistance to defeat.

Disadvantages

- Security object must be ungrounded.
- Protective field extends only a few inches from protected object.
- Moderate to high maintenance level.

Audio detectors are different from the previous category in that they are passive and do not generate any wave patterns. Instead, they listen for sounds within the protected area. Unlike ultrasonic detectors, audio sensors can tolerate air movement or other types of motion at low levels. In addition, fans or other background noise producers can be cancelled out by placing cancellation microphones in close proximity to the noise-producing component. There are two different applications for audio detectors—one for normal room protection, and the other for vault protection.

The room protection audio detector can probably be defeated by an individual wearing tennis shoes, and for that reason it has a limited usefulness. The vault protection audio detector, on the other hand, can use more sophisticated circuitry that responds to noise or vibrations within the enclosed area.

Table 12.5 lists the advantages and disadvantages of this type of detector.

Intrusion Detectors

Intrusion detectors are used to sense a breach of perimeter security. Intrusion sensors typically employ some form of linear continuity check uti-

Table 12.5 Advantages and Disadvantages of Audio Detectors

Advantages

- Simple to install.
- Complete protection within a confined (or vault type) structure.
- Flexible for covering large or small areas.
- High salvage value because of ease in removing and reinstalling.
- High reliability.
- Moderate to high resistance to defeat.

Disadvantages

- Sensitivity to all sounds limits use to locations with low ambient sound levels.
- Needs to be combined with other type detectors for full protection.

lizing both active and passive forms of deterrence. There are two forms of intrusion detectors:

1. Photoelectric beams
2. Dry contact switches and metallic foil tape

Photoelectric sensors are used, in addition to smoke detection, to prevent penetration of walls, ceilings, or long rows of windows. Photoelectric beams require a light-emitting device and a light-sensitive receiver, the latter usually located some distance away. In normal operation, any dense object cutting off or interrupting the light from the receiver causes an alarm relay or control panel signal to be actuated. The beams emitted by the photoelectric cell are of a small cross-sectional area, and in the case of a visible (white) light beam, may be easily avoidable by stepping over, under, or around it.

Because visible light is easily detected, photoelectric beams are also designed to emit an infrared source. Although infrared beams are preferable to white light sources because of their extremely low visibility, they can be compromised by introducing a substitute source of illumination. For this reason, some infrared photoelectric beams are modulated (i.e., frequency modulation) which requires synchronizing the emitting beam with the receiver. If the corresponding pulses of the sender and receiver are not synchronized, the photoelectric detector will then sound an alarm or signal the control panel.

To overcome the limitations of the narrow cross-sectional beam area, some photoelectric detectors employ mirrors to provide a criss-cross pattern for better coverage. In this type of installation, the mirrors and associated sending

Table 12.6 Advantages and Disadvantages of Photo-Electric Beam Detectors

Advantages

- Can protect long distances with one sender-receiver combination.
- High reusability value.
- Can be used to actuate surveillance devices such as cameras.
- Can be recessed in an area where there is no room for obstructions.
- Moderate to high reliability.

Disadvantages

- Narrow cross-section linear type beams can be avoided if located.
- Substitute light sources may be used to defeat system.
- Dirt on lamps or mirrors degrade effectiveness.
- System susceptible of being knocked out of alignment.
- Careful planning needed for effective coverage.

and receiving equipment are usually concealed to prevent discovery.

Table 12.6 lists the advantages and disadvantages of photoelectric beam detectors.

Dry contact switches, with or without metallic foil tape, offer one of the most common forms of perimeter detection. Contact switches alone are typically used on a movable door or window frame, while the metallic foil tape is usually added when the protection is extended to the immovable plate glass in the door or window. Typically, these components are arranged as a continuous closed circuit loop that is connected to alarm relays in a control cabinet. Any attempt to enter the premises through a protected point when the circuit is activated will break the continuity of the electrical connections and set off an alarm or signal a control panel.

Table 12.7 lists the advantages and disadvantages of contact switches and metallic foil.

Table 12.7 Advantages and Disadvantages of Dry Contact Switches/Metallic Foil

Advantages

- Simple components easily and cheaply available.
- High reliability.
- Low maintenance level.

Disadvantages

- Unprotected walls or ceilings may be penetrated without an alarm signal.
- Low resistance to defeat.
- Low salvage value.
- Cannot detect unauthorized staff remaining after-hours until they leave premises.

Control

Control is the final classification of security mechanisms. It assures that an alarm signal generated by either a surveillance or sensing unit reaches its intended receiving device, and that appropriate measures are in force with regard to access and egress.

Control is typically a function of system design and is not only concerned with electronic signal or pulse movement within an alarm system, but can also be involved with the movement of people throughout the data center. Therefore, control involves the types of alarm systems, the security requirements necessary to assure continuous, reliable operation, the automatic response mechanisms that can be utilized in conjunction with sensing devices, and, finally, the locks and similar mechanism that constrain entry and egress of the data center premises.

Alarm Systems

Although fire, motion-sensitive, or intrusion type detectors have been described, they seldom exist except as part of an alarm system. An alarm system is defined as the process for initiating a deterrent response such as bells, sprinklers, extinguishers, guard action, and notices to police and fire services based on a signal-actuated device. Therefore, this section presents a brief description of the type of alarm systems and typical deterrents that are used with such detectors. While the alarm systems that follow are mandatory insofar as fire detectors are concerned, the system concepts apply to all types of detectors.

There are five types of alarm systems:

1. Local
2. Central station
3. Proprietary
4. Auxiliary station
5. Remote station

In a *local alarm system*, protective circuits in the secured area are connected directly to an audible alarm on the premises. The sound-producing device and the connecting cable must be protected from willful tampering and must be audible for at least 400 feet. The local alarm is a simple system and is of little value if there is no attendant to provide response.

Central-station systems are operated by private security organizations. These systems transmit signals from detectors over leased telephone lines to constantly monitored receiving and recording equipment on the premises of the security organization. Monitoring equipment may consist of TV screens for live viewing of critical areas, time-sequenced printouts of the detector status on the protected premises, signal lights to display detector circuit condition, or direct measurement equipment to indicate circuit conditions such as voltage levels. In addition to providing printed readouts and signal lights, the monitoring equipment can also produce an audible indication of any change in the security status. Most central stations are monitored 24 hours a day. Signals from a fire-monitoring detector on the protected premises are typically relayed automatically to the local fire department on an auxiliary system (see below). Response to other signals is provided by the private security organization. The central station system requirements for Underwriters Laboratory (UL) approval are that the protected premises be less than ten minutes traveling time from the central office.

Proprietary systems are similar to the central-station system, except that the receiving and monitoring functions are performed directly on the protected property, and that the alarm systems are owned or leased by the data center. Guards who operate the system are available to respond to alarms. High value protected premises may require so many different types of detectors and alarms that a specialized, dedicated computer is employed to integrate the data gathered from the many different sources into a common format. Utilizing a computer for asset protection can enable the operator to query any remote device and receive what amounts to a real-time response. It is also capable of routine interrogation and response of all stations at computer speeds. Typical components of an asset protection computer consist of an operator's console, a CPU, and a printer. These provide automatic recording of all incoming alarms and enable the operator to request special status reports and logs of equipment on-off time without manual entry or retrieval of data. Some computer equipment also provides a visual display of floor layouts and hook-ups for live TV monitoring.

Auxiliary station systems automatically cause an alarm originating in the data center to be transmitted over the local municipal fire or police alarm circuits for relaying to both the local po-

lice/fire station and the appropriate headquarters. The system is activated by either a manual (i.e., fire) alarm or an automatic sensing device that trips the master control tied to the particular municipal circuit. Both local and proprietary systems may also be connected as an auxiliary system to the municipal fire or police alarms. Permission by local authorities is required for each such connection.

Remote station systems have a direct connection between the signal initiating device at the protected property and the signal receiving device located at a remote station, such as the fire house. A remote system usually consists of a local system connected by a leased telephone circuit to the remote location. The entire remote system, including telephone lines, is supervised (see following). A remote system differs from an auxiliary system in that it does not use the municipal fire or police alarm circuits.

Line Supervision   Since alarm systems usually transmit signals for some distance over a pair of wires, the possibility of tampering or compromise exists. Line supervision, therefore, is concerned with the ability of the electrical circuit between the sensor and the central monitoring area to detect and sound an alarm if any tampering, intentionally or unintentionally, takes place. In order for a central station to be classed as Grade AA (protection of costly equipment), it must comply with the UL standard 611-1968, which states:

> *The connecting line between the central station and the protection shall be supervised so as to automatically detect a compromise attempt by methods of resistance substitution, potential substitution, or any single compromise attempt.*

Power Supplies   Because of the nature of the service provided, supervised alarm systems should receive power on a reliable electrical circuit. Power options and appropriate backup supply vary according to the type of alarm system. Separate circuitry reduces the probability of power line failure for the entire system.

- Local or auxiliary alarm systems should obtain power from a circuit separate from all other power lines (i.e., reliable power), or from storage batteries capable of operating the system for not less than 24 hours between chargings.

- Remote station alarm systems should obtain power from a reliable AC or DC source, together with storage batteries capable of operating the system for at least 60 hours without recharging.

- Proprietary and central station alarm systems require a reliable power source that is a combination of AC and battery power with the latter capable of operating for 24 hours without recharge, or a duplicate set of storage batteries used for alternating 24-hour periods. If the latter option is selected, each set of batteries in a proprietary alarm system must be capable of operating for 24 hours without recharging, and in a central station system for 60 hours without recharging.

Signal Response Mechanisms

Fire, motion, or intrusion detectors typically are connected to one or more of the three types of automatic response mechanisms: audible alarms, fire extinguishing agents, and/or automatic dial-updevices.

Audible alarms are warning bells or buzzers that sound upon transmission of a signal from the detection device. Audible alarms are simple devices that can be part of a local, central station, proprietary, or remote system.

Fire extinguishing agents consist of two main types: sprinkler systems and gas discharge systems. Both types may be found in the data center. There are four types of sprinkler systems available:

1. Wet pipe
2. Dry pipe
3. Deluge
4. Preaction

- Wet pipe sprinkler systems always contain water in the pipes connected to the nozzle devices, and therefore are considered a closed head system. Discharge is typically controlled by a 165° fixed temperature detector, although other temperature control levels are available. In the event of a heat rise to the predetermined level, the detector in the form of a fusible link melts, the two halves of a gate valve swing apart and water flows. The wet pipe sprinkler is considered to be most reliable in its action. It is also efficient in that the water flows almost instantaneously after the fixed temperature level is reached. The main disadvantage is that water may freeze in the pipes if they are exposed to the elements in a cold climate.

- Dry pipe sprinkler systems are similar in operation to a wet pipe system, except that there is no water in the pipes, since it is held back by a clapper valve. As in the wet pipe system, the fixed temperature detector will open. At the predetermined temperature level, air will then be blown out and water will flow. The main advantage of this system is that since there is no water in the pipes, there is a time delay before the water actually flows, thus providing an opportunity to shut down the systems if the fire is minor with little chance of causing damage. However, since there is a delay between the time the spray nozzle is opened and the water flows, this system is less efficient, although not necessarily less desirable in a computer installation. If deemed important, an acceleration device can be attached to speed up the delay period, and therefore make the system almost as efficient as the wet pipe.

- The deluge system is similar to the dry pipe system, except that the sprinkler head is open. It is used when it is desired to deliver a large volume of water quickly to all sprinkler heads. Water is held back at a central riser by a deluge valve, which in turn is controlled by a heat-actuated sensor. The system is not typically used at a data center because the volume of water released is excessive, and it can require extensive time to restore the computer system to its normal operating capability.

- The preaction system is a combination of a wet and dry pipe system, using a closed head. The system works in two stages: initially, the pipes are dry before a heat-actuated sensor opens an automatic water control valve that sounds an alarm and allows the pipes to fill with water. The water is not discharged until a fusible link melts as in the wet pipe system. The preaction system is used when it is desirable to prevent an accidental discharge of water by providing an advance alarm. It is recommended for computer room installations since it allows time to use a hand extinguisher before pouring water onto the computer equipment.

Gas discharge systems typically employ an inert gas under pressure in an underfloor installation. Gas discharge systems can be actuated by any type fire detector to put out an underfloor fire that can result from, for example, a breakdown in cable insulation. The advantage of a gas discharge system is that it provides a quick smothering of the fire and eliminates the necessity of mixing water and electricity. Gas discharge systems can also be used to provide total flooding within the main frame of a computer. Typical agents of a gas discharge system are carbon dioxide or Halon 1301. Since Halon 1301 has the potential for generating corrosive hydrogen fluoride, hydrogen bromide, and bromine in a deep-seated fire, it is not recommended for use in the computer room itself.

Automatic dial up enables a prerecorded message to be sent to a predetermined location such as a fire or police station. The device can be actuated by a fire, motion, or intrusion type detector, which causes the desired location to be dialed and the recorded message to be spoken. Some units have more than one channel and can be used to control more than one type detector.

The dial-up units can use existing telephone lines and have a high salvage value since they are self-contained and reusable. In general, they are relatively inexpensive devices. However, since they are not part of a supervised alarm system, the telephone lines can be compromised without causing an alarm.

Power Line Conditioners

With the proliferation of the microprocessor both at the business facility and at the home, the necessity for increased concern over the prevention of power irregularities has become an important issue. These irregularities consist of voltage surges, voltage sags, and/or line noise. The solution has been met through the availability of many devices that intercept the 120 volt power before it reaches the computer and automatically reduces or eliminates the potentially harmful irregularities.

Power line conditioners for reprocessors typically contain one or more electrical power sockets for the power lines of system components and a suitable means of connecting the conditioner to the power source.

Typical problems that power line conditioners are designed to meet are as follows:

- Voltage surge: a momentary increase in the voltage from the power source resulting in damage to the computer system. The increase can be of short duration (a spike), or long duration. Voltage spikes are probably the most common type of power irregularity.

Voltage surges or transient spikes of as much as several thousand volts can be caused by utility company line switching, lightning, or the intermittent operation of large electrical motors such as used in air conditioners, factory tools, heaters, and elevators. Smaller spikes, which are less harmful but nevertheless troublesome, can be caused by the turning on and off of household type appliances such as blenders, vacuum cleaners, and the like.

- Voltage surge protection is the primary mode of protection offered by many commercial products. Typically consisting of a solid state device known as a metal oxide varistor (MOV), it conducts excessive voltage to ground whenever the threshold voltage is exceeded.

- In selecting a voltage surge protection device, consideration should be given to a low "clamping" voltage and a low clamping time and a high current-handling ability. Clamping refers to the point at which the surge protection device takes hold. For voltage protection this would be at approximately 150+ volts, while clamping time input ranges from between one picosecond up to 50 nanoseconds. The current handling ability, i.e., energy dissipation, in watts or joules, should be as high as possible.

- Noise consists of unwanted random high frequencies present in or picked up by the power line, which interferes with the proper operation of the computer system.

Noise is the electrical interference superimposed on the power line, typically from a local source. Noise can occur when a power line acts as an antenna and picks up high frequency interference from such sources as fluorescent lighting, auto ignitions, transformers, lightning storms, and signals from local radio and television broadcasts. These frequencies are significantly higher than the basic power supply of 60 Hz and overlap the ranges at which computer operations are performed. Hence, noise can cause interference in computer processing activities resulting in unwanted loss or change of program instructions, stored data, and false output.

- Noise suppression circuitry is frequently included as part of a voltage surge protection device. Noise suppressors are more effective and more costly when designed to attenuate specific noise interference frequencies rather than averaging over a wide range. Noise suppressor effectiveness is usually designated as decibels (Db) of attenuation; the higher the Db rating, the more effective the suppression. Thus, the greater the problem of noise, the higher the Db of attenuation desired.

- Voltage sags of long duration, or brownouts, are the result of deliberate reductions in grid voltage by the power company, usually during periods of peak power consumption. Voltage sags of short duration generally occur in small areas directly affected by excessively high loads of a temporary nature.

Voltage sags or power outages are more obvious conditions that affect computer operations. While most computer equipment has an operating range of 105–120 volts, a brownout or other relatively long duration voltage fluctuations can affect the performance of the computer.

Constant voltage transformers provide voltage regulation during these periods of fluctuation. Typically, they accept an input range of 90/95 to 130/140 volts and provide a constant output of 120 volts. Constant voltage transformers may frequently be combined with surge filters and noise suppression circuits.

- Blackouts are the result of a complete interruption in electrical power, where line voltage is reduced to zero. Blackouts can be of a short duration of a few seconds, such as when a utility switches generators, or of a long duration resulting from lightning strikes or downed power lines. In either case, the computer will cease operation unless connected to an uninterruptible power supply. The key feature of the uninterruptible power supply is the inclusion of an internal battery that will automatically supply a constant source of power for a defined period of time. The transfer time from AC power to battery and the wattage available for the time period are

the key factors to be considered. The uninterruptible power supply may be combined with other power conditioning devices into a single unit.

Access Control

Next to the use of sight and sound, locks are probably one of the oldest access control techniques in use. Locks have evolved from the relatively crude devices first invented 4,000 years ago by the Egyptians to the sophisticated computer-actuated mechanisms using complex coding and sensing techniques.

For purposes of data center security, locks can be classified into two categories: preset and programmable.

Preset locks are the typical locks currently found in any door where entry requirements cannot be changed except by physically removing and substituting or modifying the locking mechanism. Basically, there are three types of preset locks: the key-in-knob, mortise, and rim.

- Key-in-knob locks have the lock cylinders in the knob used to open or close a door, and thus avoid the need to mortise a square or rectangular cavity into the door for the lockset. Although key-in-knob locks are in common use, by themselves they provide only minimal protection against forced entry unless they are a part of a security alarm system or a security-related complex.

- Mortise type locks have a separate lock cylinder and door latching devices. While these locks may possibly provide a somewhat better level of security, the improvement for preventing forced entry is minimal unless the lock is also equipped with a dead-bolt, preferably one inch long to prevent forced entry. Key-in-knob locks have a similar feature called the dead-locking latch.

- Rim locks are actually additional or auxiliary locks that are secured to the inside of a door. The action of these locks opens or closes a deadbolt through the portion of the lock attached to the door frame. A rim lock, when complemented by the primary key-in-knob or mortise lock in a metal door, will usually act as a strong deterrent against forcible entry. However, it is also important to note that any lock can be forced (or picked), given the time and lack of supplementary security measures.

Programmable locks are a more recent innovation and include both the mechanical and electronic variety. The mechanical type are typified by the combination dial commonly used to secure a vault, or, more recently, pushbuttons to open a door. A variation of the combination type has a timing mechanism which prevents opening the lock even if the combination is known, except after a predetermined time period has elapsed. The pushbutton type used more commonly in data center installations requires indexing up to five buttons in proper sequence before turning the door knob to open the deadbolt or springlatch as in a key-in-knob or mortise lock. Pushbutton locks eliminate the need for keys and their related control problems, and also simplify the process (and expense) of changing the tumblers in a conventional type lock whenever security reasons dictate this course of action. Pushbutton type locks are also suitable for installation on desks and cabinets as well as doors.

Electronic programmable locks are different from the mechanical variety in that they employ a digital keyboard input to index up to five separate, discrete digits. In a typical unit, the user can be required to enter the five-digit code within a specified time span. Correct entry allows current to flow and activates an electric lockset, door strike, or other electrically activated device. As in the mechanical pushbutton type, electronic programmable locks are an auxiliary device that supplements the key-in-knob or mortise type door control. These locks offer the same advantages of keylessness and simplified code changes as in mechanical pushbutton types. In addition, electronic programmable locks can be used as a control for many electrically activated devices such as an elevator call button, automatic doors, and parking gates, but should have a backup power supply in the event of a power failure.

Another type of access control is the *security card system*, which is used to control entrance to the data center complex, and, in large installations, to sensitive areas within the installations. Components of these systems can include card readers for accepting the coded input media, locksets which can be opened automatically or semi-automatically upon presentation of a coded

card media, and logic circuitry, which uses its capabilities to provide on-line controls. It is also possible to employ some of the previously identified sensing devices to be activated or deactivated upon presentation of the card media.

There are two basic types of security card systems: digital coded cards and photo-image cards.

Digital coded cards are typically wallet-sized identification media that are magnetically encoded by the manufacturer. The cards can be made of plastic material similar to credit cards, or heavy kraft paper. In the plastic models, they are suitable for up to three lines of fixed embossed data and the application of a picture to the identification badge without interfering with the magnetic code. Kraft paper badges are suitable when additional notations are required after issuance to the user, such as special imprinting, validation, or a signature. Or, if notations are not required, it can be laminated by the manufacturer for greater resistance to normal environmental deterioration. The magnetic codes on some cards can be scrambled in a cryptographic pattern. Card codes can only be altered by the card system manufacturer.

In operation, the coded edge of all identification cards is inserted into a seat that acts as a card reader. However, there are two types of card validation techniques. In the simpler cartridge type system, insertion of a coded card causes tumbler elements to actuate the door strike or other controls, such as a parking gate. Cartridges are located in the access door. Some models are programmable by the data center through a special program card.

The more sophisticated console systems utilize the card reader as a remote station which transmits the coded data to a memory device that compares it against a preestablished authorized list. Acceptable codes initiate an activating signal that actuates the door strike or other access control device.

The console systems, which, in effect, are small computers, make possible on-line access control through a programmable memory core that can void any previously approved card. In addition, each access event can be documented with the date, time, and access point. One type of console system can control as many as 50 access locations and 5,000 cards. Other designs, employing larger computers, can control even larger numbers. Some models of console type systems combine the card access system with the digital keyboard input for high security applications. Other models can be programmed to allow authorized access only once per 24-hour day, and thus eliminate the possibility of employees passing cards back to others for multiple use in the same day. Similar controls would apply to egress frequency. If desired, an output signal is provided to operate any of the alarm systems previously described.

Another type of digital access control uses an individual's hand geometry to make positive identification. It minimizes the main disadvantage of the digital coded card: an authorized card falling into the hands of an unauthorized person. This is achieved by measuring the precise characteristics of the human hand and magnetically encoding this data on a standard type plastic identification card. In operation, the user inserts his identity card into the machine, places his hand on the unit and presses down gently. In a cycle time of about one second, the hand is measured and compared to the coded data on the identity card. If an accept signal is generated, a door strike or other device is actuated. The system is designed for an error rate of less than one in two hundred (i.e., 199 out of 200 people would be rejected if attempting to use someone else's card). If this error rate is too high for a high security application, the tolerance can be tightened to one in 2,000. One reader unit is required at each access control point and a single card-making device is needed by the data center for the coded identity cards. Reader units can be programmed to accept only specified personnel for high security areas. In an access control system similar to hand geometry, an individual's fingerprints are compared by a reader to a master file of fingerprints. This system would have the advantage of positive identification that accompanies any fingerprint identification method, but has a high cost per access point which limits its application.

• Photo imaging on cards is utilized in two ways. Any of the foregoing cards can include a picture of the authorized card holder as a part of the normal identification routine. Or, the picture and personal data, laminated in plastic, can be used in conjunction with an access guard as an ID card. Typical ID cards are simple to prepare, usually taking about two minutes including picture taking. Photo images have the obvious advantage of definitive recognition. However, in actual practice, this recognition ability is not always fully utilized, particularly in large installations where many people require visual interrogation at one time. An interesting variation of the photo ID card system utilizes a TV camera to compare side by side the live picture of an individual requesting entrance to the data center with the picture on a preissued photo ID badge. In addition to the surveillance camera, this system requires a monitor console to display the authorized ID photo and a surveillance console for comparative viewing of the individual seeking entry.

Microcomputers

Microprocessors have unique requirements in terms of monitoring and control devices. This is so because the physical location of microprocessors is generally in the user department and not in a central location such as a data center.

Hence, all the foregoing, including perimeter control, motion detectors, smoke and heat detectors, and fire alarm systems, will apply in some degree, constrained only by cost. In addition, access control alternatives, in terms of locks and other related devices, will all be applicable to the microprocessor. Specific recommendations for controlling the proliferation of floppy disks will be found in the checklist section for this chapter.

Summary

The objectives of security monitoring are to:

• Provide early detection and warning of the security threat
• Present as high a level of deterrence to a possible security breach as is consistent with resources and available technology
• Provide a methodology of control that can assure a high level of reliability

Detection or sensing devices in the form of fire and motion detectors meet the requirement for early detection and warning of impending security threats. Typically, deterrent devices are aimed at detecting potentially dangerous changes in the data center environment.

Active and passive perimeter protection devices in the form of intrusion detectors, guards, remote TV surveillance, and some types of door locks meet the requirement for as high a level of deterrence to a potential security breach as is possible. Perimeter protection devices are primarily aimed at people, and hence are designed to prevent unauthorized entry to either the entire or a part of the data center installation.

Security control systems in the form of alarm systems, automatic response mechanisms, and automated access control systems provide methodologies for receiving data and responding to a security incident. As in an information system, a security control monitoring system involves the utilization of available resources, and therefore is concerned with both people and equipment. The system receives input, manipulates data, and provides output for initiating a response activity. Depending on the nature of the detected incident, the system response may be considered as automated. For example, in a fire, the signal generated by the heat-actuated sensing device can be designed to both turn on a sprinkler system and notify the fire department without human interference.

The selection of proper monitoring equipment is in many ways as complex as acquiring a computer. Indeed, it may also include just this possibility. Yet, the surveillance, detecting, or control requirements of the security monitoring system are different from the typical business information system hardware and software design in the key area of testing. In the event of a security system malfunction, there may not be a second chance to make corrections. The results could be catastrophic, not only in terms of heavy asset losses, but also in terms of day-to-day business operations.

Therefore, the selection and application of existing or planned security monitoring hardware require a great deal of planning and decision-making without the benefit of significant live testing. Thus, in auditing the data center's current or projected monitoring hardware requirements, important consideration should be given to the utilization of the type of monitoring equipment expertise that is available from such sources as insurance organizations. It is equally important that defining security monitoring equipment requirements for the data center organization be treated as a system design problem, with as heavy emphasis on setting objectives and determining the ramifications of input, output, and priority combinations, as in evaluating equipment specifications.

Monitoring and Related Control Devices Checklist

	Yes	No
Is list of authorized personnel readily available?	☐	☐
Are key personnel data and photos available to security personnel?	☐	☐
Are employee identification cards issued?	☐	☐
Do employee identification cards include photographs?	☐	☐
Are employee identification cards laminated or otherwise designed to prevent alteration?	☐	☐
Are employees properly instructed as to smoking and beverage restrictions in the immediate computer area?	☐	☐
Are employee identification cards collected upon termination of the employee?	☐	☐
Are employee keys or other security access devices collected upon termination?	☐	☐
Is a proper inventory and control maintained for physical access keys?	☐	☐
Is a physical access control system utilized?	☐	☐
Does access control log include in/out and person to be seen for visitors?	☐	☐
Are packages, briefcases, and similar items inspected before entering and after leaving the facility?	☐	☐
Are visitors issued badges?	☐	☐
Are visitor badges easily distinguished from those of employees?	☐	☐
Are visitors escorted to their destination?	☐	☐

	Yes	No
Are employees required to furnish advance notification for use of computer equipment during nonscheduled hours?	☐	☐
Are sign-in procedures during nonscheduled hours carried out under a guard or management supervision?	☐	☐
Are employees required to wear badges?	☐	☐
Are guards employed to control access to the computer area?	☐	☐
Are guards used at the main facility entrances?	☐	☐
Is the data center facility patrolled during nonworking hours?	☐	☐
Are guard/watchman check-in stations used during nonscheduled or nonworking hours?	☐	☐
Is closed circuit television used to monitor access to sensitive areas?	☐	☐
Are perimeter patrols beyond the building site under surveillance?	☐	☐
If keys are used to control facility access, are these keys controlled as to issuance and return?	☐	☐
Are direct line outside phones conveniently located and accessible to guards?	☐	☐
Is an emergency list of phone numbers available to guards (management, police, security service, fire department, etc.)?	☐	☐
Is an inventory maintained of all visual monitoring equipment, including television monitors, cassette recorders, and cameras?	☐	☐
Is the visual equipment checked frequently by guards or appropriate personnel?	☐	☐
Is there a procedure for reporting and following up on defective equipment?	☐	☐
Does the visual recording equipment have provision for noting the date and time?	☐	☐

	Yes	No
Is the date and time feature above regularly checked for correctness?	☐	☐
Are access control devices (i.e., locks, magnetic cards) routinely checked for tampering?	☐	☐
Are locks and/or badge coding changed frequently?	☐	☐
Are adjacent areas above, below, and next to the computer facility properly checked and controlled?	☐	☐
Is a continuity alarm system installed in the perimeter of the facility?	☐	☐
Is the continuity alarm system linked directly to the local police or security service?	☐	☐
Are motion detectors installed, checked, and maintained?	☐	☐
Are water-level detectors below false floors?	☐	☐
Are heat and/or smoke detectors suitably installed in appropriate areas?	☐	☐
Is the heat and/or smoke detector alarm linked directly to the local fire department? Is it checked periodically?	☐	☐
Is an automatic fire extinguishing system installed in equipment and data storage areas? Is it checked periodically?	☐	☐
Are portable fire extinguishers adequately disposed in and about the computer facility?	☐	☐
Are portable fire extinguishers checked periodically for recharge certificate?	☐	☐
Are the carpeting and other decorative materials manufactured from fire-resistant materials?	☐	☐
Are the electrical appliances such as clocks used in the computer area Underwriters Laboratories approved?	☐	☐
Is there an equipment inventory of microprocessors kept in user areas?	☐	☐

	Yes	No
Is filtering equipment to prevent power surges and/or noise suppression utilized for both data center and individual microprocessors?	☐	☐
Is backup power available to avoid potential damage from brownouts and blackouts? Is it checked regularly?	☐	☐
Are updated lists, including phone numbers, available for the vendors of the monitoring, alarm, and control devices used by the facility?	☐	☐

	Yes	No
Are the vendor service telephone numbers readily available to shift management?	☐	☐
Are there emergency procedures in the event of fire or unauthorized entry?	☐	☐
Are emergency procedures rehearsed at scheduled meetings with appropriate personnel?	☐	☐

PART IV
Technical Protection

CHAPTER 13

Software and Data Security

By Myles E. Walsh

Introduction

The increased use of computers, including personal computers, has given rise to a greater public awareness of the sensitive information that is resident on electronic data processing equipment. Motion pictures and newspapers have shown how easy it is to gain access to information stored on computers. In doing so, they have shattered the illusion that computers are inaccessible to all but the technical experts in charge of machines. At the same time they have created another illusion, that anyone with even a minimum amount of electronic know-how and a telephone can gain access to information stored in the most secure computer system. Both illusions are incorrect, and yet, as with other possessions, the more data that are accumulated, the more there are to protect. The purpose of this chapter is to describe the protection of data by means of software, as opposed to protection by means of equipment and external controls.

Total software security is no more attainable than is perfect security in any other area. A highly skilled programmer can almost always penetrate software safeguards written by another programmer. Of course, the same can be said for attorneys; an unprincipled lawyer can usually get around protections in a contract written by another lawyer. Yet contracts continue to be written, and, for the most part, they are effective. Computer software security routines can also be effective most of the time. A security procedure does not have to be all-encompassing; if it provides reasonable protection at an acceptable cost, it is certainly worthwhile. The basic consideration is one of degree—how important are specific elements of data and software, and how important is their security. Some data require very little security. For example, a software library containing programs that are similar to those found in many other computer installations does not require elaborate security protection against theft. On the other hand, proprietary programs and sensitive data require extensive security. A data base containing payroll information requires stringent security procedures to maintain its confidentiality.

Basic Computer Installation Security

Preceding any system of software security is the physical security of the installation. Safeguards ought to be in place to exclude unauthorized personnel and to provide environmental protection. Stationing a security guard at the main entrance of an installation is basic; keeping delivery entrances locked when not in use is another fundamental precaution. Established fire prevention procedures and strategically located extinguishers and smoke detectors are also basic and should not be overlooked. Pass keys or plastic cards can be used to restrict entry. These items, covered in detail in other chapters, represent rudimentary security provisions. Without them, the most elaborate and sophisticated software security measures can be neutralized and rendered ineffective.

Overview

Software security, in this chapter, is defined as the protection of data and programs stored in a computer system. It is in large-scale mainframe environments where the most elaborate and comprehensive software security procedures can be justified. Protection of data and programs in less complex computer environments is similar, but neither the risks nor the precautions are as extensive. A special section at the end of the chapter addresses the issue of software security in small computers.

There are three major elements to be considered: (1) protection of programs by software, (2) protection of data in on-line systems by software, and (3) protection of data in conventional "batch" processing systems by software.

Security by means of software is provided by computer programs designed to protect data and to protect themselves. Both data and software require varying degrees of protection based on sensitivity and confidentiality. Some data and software must be kept strictly confidential and be made available to selected individuals only. Other data and software must be restricted as far as modification is concerned. Substantial amounts of on-line data require periodic copying so as to facilitate restoration in the event that the original data are damaged or destroyed.

The major elements of data protection are integrity and accuracy. Data integrity involves the protection or recovery of data from damage due to equipment or software malfunction. Data accuracy involves the protection or recovery of data from errors caused by sources external to equipment or software. Data integrity is maintained by means of software and by procedures for logging, backup, backout, recovery, and restart. Data accuracy is promoted by editing, control totals, hash counts, reasonableness checks, and balancing procedures.

Security practices and methods will be discussed as they apply to protection of software systems and data.

The Layers of Software

Software Components

Considerable complexity exists within the various levels of computer software. Figure 13.1 illustrates the layers that surround data in a typical installation. It is not uncommon for a hundred program modules to be invoked from the time a single transaction is entered into a terminal device until a response is returned to the device. The dotted line represents the two-way flow of transaction and response traffic; the numbers in the schematic indicate the points at which each layer of software is invoked:

1. A "front-end" computer houses a set of software modules that are sometimes referred to as a network control program. In a computer network involving many telecommunications lines and several large-scale computers, these modules manage the traffic, routing incoming transactions to the appropriate computer and outgoing responses to the appropriate lines.

2. Security modules together with security files and tables are used to validate terminals, operators, and transactions. Unauthorized individuals or unrecognized transaction codes or undefined terminals are denied access.

3. Teleprocessing access methods contain program modules that interface with the network control program to transfer transactions and responses between the "front-end" computer and the host.

4. Data communications monitors interface between teleprocessing access methods and application programs. The teleprocessing access method notifies the data communications monitor and passes the transaction to it, the monitor then validates the transaction, invokes the appropriate application program, and then gives control to that program.

5. The application program uses the facilities of an integrated data base/data dictionary system to define and to request retrieval of information from specific files or data bases. At this juncture there is coordinated interaction among the application program, the operating system, and the physical data access method.

6. The application program, using executable file or data base definitions (frequently called control blocks) issues a CALL to the input/output modules of the physical data access method. Coordination of this interaction is handled by the operating system. The physical data access method performs the actual transfer of data between the application program's data buffers and the files or data bases.

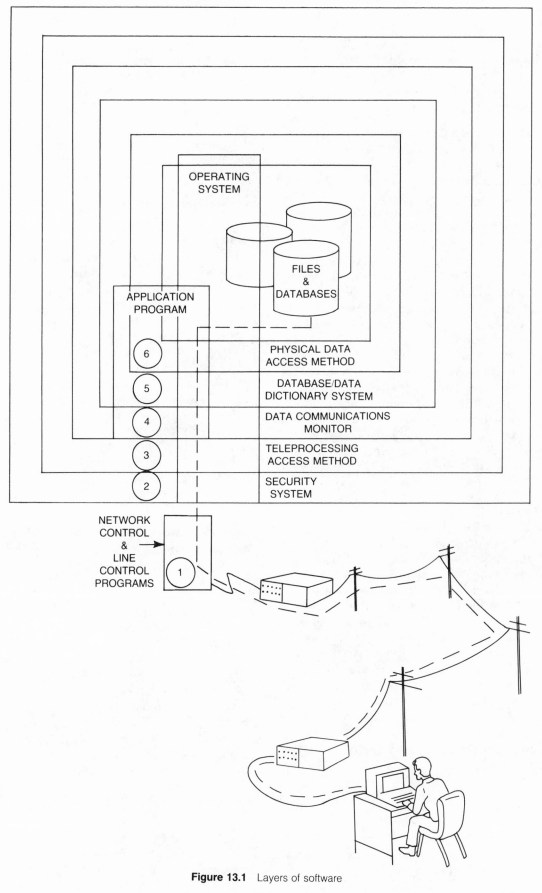

OPERATING
SYSTEM

FILES
&
DATABASES

APPLICATION
PROGRAM

6 · PHYSICAL DATA
ACCESS METHOD

5 · DATABASE/DATA
DICTIONARY SYSTEM

4 · DATA COMMUNICATIONS
MONITOR

3 · TELEPROCESSING
ACCESS METHOD

2 · SECURITY
SYSTEM

NETWORK
CONTROL
&
LINE
CONTROL
PROGRAMS

1

Figure 13.1 Layers of software

203

Once data are accessed, the same software components handle fabrication of a response, data base or file updates if necessary, and transmission of the response to a terminal device.

Concept of a Data Dictionary

The integrated data dictionary system mentioned above, if used correctly, provides some degree of security. A data dictionary is a centrally located repository containing descriptions of files or data bases used by the programs. In those situations where a data dictionary is an integral component of a data base management system, data base definitions are automatically entered into the data dictionary. Some data base management systems do not have data dictionaries as one of their features, that is, they are not integrated. In those cases procedures can be established making it mandatory that all data base definitions are entered into the data dictionary from which entries to the data base management system are generated. Under the control of a data base administration function, programs are granted access to only those files whose record definitions have been entered into the data dictionary. While it may be possible to circumvent these procedures, they do make unauthorized access more difficult.

The Tradeoff

In planning security measures, caution must be exercised so that in making data and software secure, they are not at the same time made inaccessible. Technically oriented individuals are inclined, because of their knowledge and capabilities, to develop complex security procedures that are difficult to breach. This can be counterproductive, especially in emergency situations where it may be necessary to bypass security. The establishment of security procedures involves trade-offs; they should be able to keep sensitive data reasonably secure at reasonable cost.

Elementary Protection with Software

Whether trying to provide security for software or for data, there are some rather elementary practices that can be put into effect: the use of data dictionaries, passwords, terminal and transaction restrictions, function menus, and segmentation of data records.

Data Dictionaries

A data dictionary has several ways in which it can serve as a security instrument. For example, the files or data bases of a data dictionary system can be set up as a central repository of the documentation describing an organization's data bases, files, records, data elements, and fields. Procedures can be established and enforced that can make it difficult to use descriptions that are not contained in the data dictionary.

Passwords

Individuals who require access to various data files or software modules of the computer system can be issued passwords. Passwords may be several characters in length, and specific passwords may allow certain individuals to access specific files or to invoke certain programs. Files and programs can be protected, requiring an individual attempting access to key in an appropriate password before access is permitted. In order to keep passwords confidential they can be changed periodically. Most security software products currently in use mask out passwords as they are being keyed in. This makes it difficult for one individual to "steal" another's password. A long way from being foolproof, passwords do provide at least a minimum of security for very little cost.

Terminal and Transaction Restrictions

Another way to provide some security for data is to set up within the software a table of values that correlates transactions with terminals or transactions with passwords or even terminals with passwords. These correlations might specify, for instance, that terminal ABC can only be used for transactions PDQ, XYZ, WXR, and RRD. Any attempt to enter other transactions through terminal ABC would fail. This kind of arrangement assures that no access is possible to data files from that terminal other than by those specified, and the only activity against the data bases from that terminal is that which is performed by the transactions specified. This kind of security is quite common in major on-line systems where there is a great deal of activity of a limited and repetitive nature.

Function Menus

In a number of the high-level software products currently available, provisions for security are designed right in. These products often take the form of what are called data base/data communications systems in which a list of available functions is presented as screen displays on terminal devices. These displays are commonly called menus. Users are able to select a function and the programs within the data base/data communications system that fulfill that function are invoked. Frequently, a hierarchy of menu displays makes it possible for the data base/data communications system to continually prompt the users, thereby stepping them through the process of selecting the appropriate functions to complete a job or a task. In products like this, security menus are often included. Security can be applied to terminal devices, to files, to programs to data base schemas (parts of records within files), to transactions, to applications, and to systems software. These options might constitute one menu display screen. Another menu screen might include levels of security to be given to individuals. For example, the highest level of security might be given to the security officer and a system programmer, the next level might be granted to a data base administrator, with lower levels being given out to application programmers, analysts, users, and operators.

Data Record Segmentation

Within data base management systems, there is a concept, sometimes called segmentation, that can provide another level of data security. Essentially, in segmentation, data records are subdivided into components representing different views of the information. Each of the components is in itself a retrievable entity. For example, a complete record might contain two segments. Application A might have need of one segment and application B might have need of the other. A set of specifications is made up by an individual known as a Data Base Administrator (DBA) describing each segment as a separate entity as well as describing the two segments as a complete record. Two application programs are written with each requiring a different segment. Because of the specifications made by the DBA, each of the application's programs accesses only that segment of the entire record that it needs. The other segment or view is not accessible to it. The segmentation process introduces a potential level of security that is not possible in non data base

systems where each program would have to access the entire record.

Protection of Software

Two areas of software protection are discussed here, protection of software as it is stored in a computer, in a media library, and protection of software as it is being executed by a computer.

A feature of most computer operating systems is a facility called a library. Actually, there can be several libraries in which programs can be stored. There are libraries for programs in source form (as they are coded by programmers), and for programs in executable form (machine language). There are also libraries for procedures, for operating instructions, and for other software components. Access to libraries is made through another operating system facility called a catalog. The catalog contains the names of the items (called members) that are stored in the library and their primary storage or secondary storage addresses. Primary storage, sometimes called memory, is that storage component that holds information that is immediately available to the computer processor. Secondary storage is made up of magnetic disks and magnetic tapes or other such devices, from which information must be transferred to memory before it is available to the computer processor. Catalogs and libraries lend a degree of security that is not found where software access is uncontrolled.

Libraries in large data centers are common, often with several data sets that contain only programs. One of these data sets is used to hold production status programs. These are the programs used in day-to-day operations, as opposed to copies of these same programs that are undergoing modification and testing. Test status programs become production programs eventually, but an orderly procedure for moving them from test to production status is necessary. When a program is moved from test to production status, the old production copy is generally kept for a few days just in case the new version malfunctions. Since oral communications sometimes break down, a simple form, either on paper or in the computer itself, can be used to facilitate transfers of programs from test to production status. Figure 13.2 is an example of a paper version of this concept.

CBS DATA CENTER COMPUTER SYSTEM TRANSMITTAL

STANDARDS & DOCUMENTATION	1) FROM		2) DIVISION	3) DATE
4) APPLICATION NUMBER/NAME	5) PROGRAM NUMBER/NAME		6) LOCATION	7) TELEPHONE EXT.

8) CHECK THE APPROPRIATE BOXES AND ENTER THE REQUIRED INFORMATION

A ☐ This is a new application to be installed before _____ .

B ☐ This is a change to be applied before _____ .

                    The change is: ☐ An insertion   ☐ A removal.

                    The change involves: ☐ A complete deck   ☐ Individual cards.

                    The number of cards involved is _____ .

                From   To

C ☐ Move modules   (Library) _____   (Library) _____

              (List modules to be moved under "Programmer/Analyst Remarks" below)

D ☐ Other:

9) CHECK THE APPROPRIATE BOX FOR DOCUMENTATION OF THE ABOVE NEW APPLICATION OR CHANGE.

    ☐ New documentation attached   ☐ Modified documentation attached   ☐ No documentation required.

10) Programmer/Analyst Remarks

11) AUTHORIZED BY DIVISION DIRECTOR	12) DATE CHANGE TESTED
13) PROGRAMMER/ANALYST NAME	14) HOME PHONE NUMBER *(Include Area Code)*
ACKNOWLEDGED RECEIPT ▶ 15) SIGNATURE	16) DATE APPLIED

CBS 1037 REV 6/80

SYSTEMS DIVISION COPY

Figure 13.2 CBS Data Center Computer System Transmittal

Protection of On-Line Files

Increasing numbers of computer systems contain on-line data that are accessible directly from a terminal device. In an on-line environment, when updating takes place, the data in storage prior to the change are overlaid. Unless appropriate procedures are invoked, the original data disappear without a trace. On those occasions when data are changed erroneously, inadvertently, or maliciously, steps need to be taken to recover the original data.

To guard against corruption of an on-line data base, several practices can be instituted. One of the most basic of these is copying or backing up on-line files or data bases on a periodic basis. Figure 13.3 illustrates this backup process as well as the recovery and restart discussion which follows. Backup involves nothing more than copying (dumping) the file or data base onto another device at some point in time. Files stored on magnetic disk can be copied to another magnetic disk or to magnetic tape. In its simplest form, this method could mean copying a data base at 9 AM. If damage were discovered at 11 AM, work could

be suspended, the copy made at 9 AM would be copied (restored) to another disk and represent the working data base. Then the work that had been done between the time the backup copy was made (9 AM) and the time the damage was discovered (11 AM) would have to be redone. This would result in a loss of two hours required to reenter the data.

In many installations the loss of two hours is intolerable. Where that is the case, it is possible to post each transaction to a log file. As an alternative it is possible to post to the log file an image of the record both before and after it is updated. In the event of a failure, as described above, a copy of the file made at 9 AM would be reloaded. However, rather than redoing the work, the log file would be used to apply the transactions once again, or to restore the last updated image for each record. This would normally be accomplished in minutes rather than in hours. The value of the log file increases as the time between copying and failure increases. This type of processing is sometimes known as "recovery and restart" processing.

Log files serve another important function.

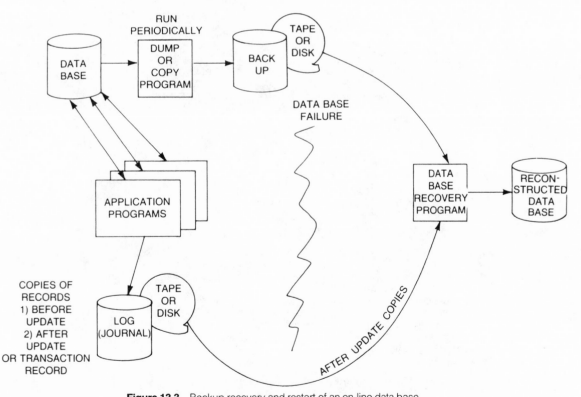

Figure 13.3 Backup recovery and restart of an on-line data base

Failures of systems that process data often take place at very awkward times. For instance, a program may malfunction right in the middle of a transaction consisting of four updates, after having completed only two. The two completed updates must be deleted (backed out) from the data base so that when the program that processes the transaction is rerun, those first two updates do not have the effect of being applied twice. A combination of programming technique and the log file makes this type of backout possible. Figure 13.4 shows the backout technique. The practices of logging, backout, recovery and restart, and backout are used to sustain data integrity. As security measures they are applied to the data bases and files to recover them after damage has been done.

There are other forms of security that attempt to prevent damage. Included are the practices examined earlier, such as password, transaction, and terminal security. Also, reasonableness checks can be made on data being used for updating purposes. An example of this might be a table of valid product codes against which an entry might be checked. If the entry contains a product code not on the table, it would be rejected as an error. This is a relatively simple kind of security measure to implement, although it does add the additional task of maintaining the product code table.

In addition to the log described above, another log can be used that constitutes an audit trail of transactions and updates made to the files or data bases. It would contain similar information to the original log, but also other information not carried on that log. Since the original log is intended for use as a backup, recovery and restart vehicle, the speed at which it can be processed is a critical factor. The amount of data contained on it is therefore kept to a minimum. The audit log, on the other hand, should contain sufficient information so that it is meaningful to the auditors. It should contain an operator identifier and a time stamp on each transaction, either update or inquiry. Again, although the system is not foolproof, awareness that an audit

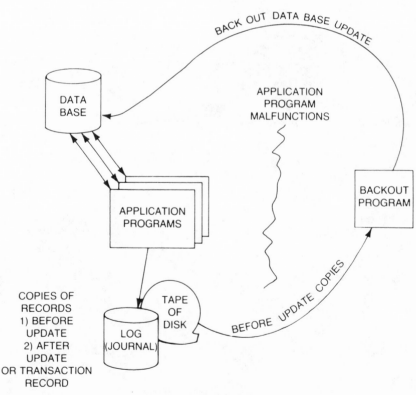

Figure 13.4 Database backout

log records such information may deter unauthorized individuals from tampering with data bases.

Protection of Data in "Batch" Systems

The practices just described are most often used with on-line or real-time systems, although some of them can also be used in batch systems. However, there are other better-known security and control practices commonly found in batch systems. In on-line systems, files or data bases have to be periodically copied or dumped onto another device because updating is done in place on the records or segments in those files and data bases. In batch processing this is not the case. In most batch systems, processing is sequential, and when updating is done, the entire file, both updated and "un-updated" records, is recopied as part of the update process (Figure 13.5). To provide

backup, a copy of the file before updating must be kept together with the activity file that updates it. In this way, if a file is damaged and cannot be reprocessed, a rerun of the job that created the file can create it again. It is generally assumed to be safe if two generations of the updated file are kept. This technique is known as the "father/grandfather" or as generation data sets.

Another type of security in batch systems is the use of batch control totals. In most batch systems, a batch of information is submitted to be processed. A common example is the input run for a batch of employee time cards submitted for processing in a payroll system. When submitted, they are accompanied with an adding machine tape containing a control total of all the hours worked for all the employee time cards in the batch. Often, there is also a count of the number of time cards in the batch. When the data are entered into a computer system, one of the first jobs to be run produces control totals. The totals

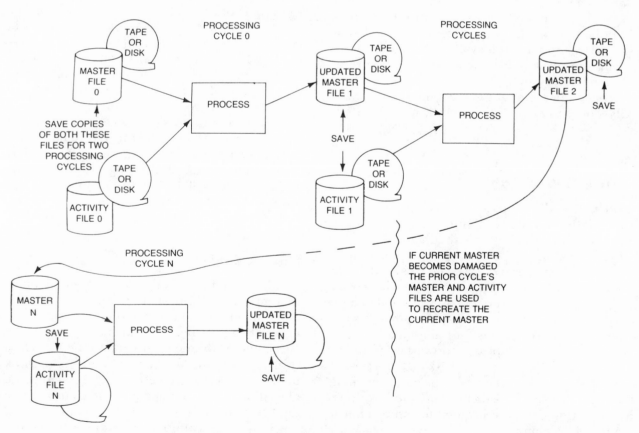

Figure 13.5 Sequential batch file backup

include the number of time cards and the total hours. The total from the computer run should be equal to the totals on the adding machine tape. If so, payroll processing continues. If not, steps are taken to determine where the error was made. Once corrected, the total balancing job is rerun to make sure that the correction was made properly. When it is shown to be correct, the payroll processing continues.

Job-to-job control totals are also kept so that if there is a malfunction as the processing progresses, it is highlighted by a discrepancy in the control totals. When this happens, processing is suspended until the problem is resolved. For instance, in a payroll system, the difference between total year-to-date earnings for the completed payroll and the year-to-date earnings before the payroll was run should be equal to the total gross payroll for the pay period being processed. If a discrepancy is discovered, payroll checks would not be produced until the discrepancy is corrected. Some systems, however, permit the continuation of a batch run in an "out-of-balance" status for later correction.

There are other types of control totals that can be used to check the successful completion of each step within a system. For example, a completed general ledger should balance to zero; in a payroll system, the dollar total in the check reconciliation file sent to the bank should equal the dollar total of all the payroll checks created.

Off-Site Storage

For files and data bases that contain data that are critical to the continuing operation of the business, and for libraries that house programs that are vital to the performance of essential business functions, copies should be stored in off-site locations. This can become somewhat costly since many files and data bases are updated on a daily basis. Libraries containing programs are not quite as volatile as files and data bases so they need not be copied and transported to off-site location as frequently. Risk analysis should be made to determine when the cost of making copies, transporting them to off-site locations, and storing them are justified to assure against a possible calamity.

Encryption

Encryption, one of the more complex methods of security, is given detailed treatment in another chapter; what follows is a brief overview. Encryption is currently being practiced on a somewhat limited scale. Basically, encryption, an outgrowth of cryptology, which had its beginnings hundreds of years ago, involves the coding of data, usually in an intricate fashion. Modern cryptology makes use of transposition and substitution methods for transforming messages into coded or cipher form. It is nothing more than an interchange of letters of the text. Substitution has the letters of the text replaced by other letters, numbers, or symbols. Cipher alphabets work essentially on a one-for-one letter replacement. Codes represent a more elaborate substitution method. Codes generally consist of thousands of words, phrases, letters, and syllables that are used as replacements for plain text elements. Code books are required, both to encode and to decode messages. One book, in sequence by plain text element, enables the user to encode messages. The other book, in sequence by code elements, enables the recipient of the messages to decode them. On the other hand, most ciphers employ keys, which specify things like the arrangement of letters within a cipher alphabet. In elaborate cipher systems, key numbers, key phrases, or key words are used.

The words encipher or encode describe the process of transforming text to a form not easily read. Decipher and decode are the words used to describe the process of restoring encoded and enciphered code to plain text. Cryptoanalysis is the process of breaking codes or ciphers.

Check Digits

Validation of individual fields of numeric information can be facilitated by the use of a check digit, an additional decimal digit appended to a decimal number field. The primary purpose of a check digit is to catch clerical oversights such as transposition and transcription errors. A check digit is arrived at by performing an arithmetic algorithm on a group of digits and using a single digit from the result as the check digit.

It is quite common for transposition and

transcription errors to take place when information is being keyed into a terminal device. For example, an operator might key in 1179 instead of 1779 or 1564 instead of 1456, the first being a transcription error and the second being a transposition error. If a calculation is performed on the number 1179 and the result produced a check digit of 8, the same calculation performed on the number 1779 would have a high probability of producing a different check digit.

Another type of validation is to compare an entry against a list of acceptable records. For example, a social security number might be verified against a list of, say, 100 social security numbers in a certain department. In this case, such a comparison would be more likely to detect an error than would a check digit; and it could, of course, be used in addition to a check digit for twofold verification.

Check digits are very useful, particularly to validate critical key fields, such as account numbers.

Security Products

Software products that have been developed for the sole purpose of protecting either data or other software are available. Some products can be used to protect certain types of data sets and program libraries from unauthorized access, and contain features that permit reports to be produced showing all authorized and unauthorized attempts to access data. Other packages have security features as part of a broader range of functions. For example, packages are available that facilitate auditing of program usage, evaluation of operational effectiveness, and allow predictions of future resource requirements.

As with the procurement of any software product, it is a commonsense practice to determine specific needs first and then to find a product that meets those needs. In order to provide a feel for what is available, two well-known products are discussed; one is called ACF2 and the other is called Guardian.

ACF2 is a product that is used to protect files and data bases in an environment where access to files is virtually wide open. An example of such would be a TSO (Time Shared Option) environment using IBM computers (see Figure 13.6). In a TSO environment, with only password and ID requirements, any individual who is able to "sign on" to the computer can gain access to any file that is not protected in some way. The ACF2 product, when initialized, makes all files inaccessible to everyone. To make files and data bases accessible to authorized individuals, specifications in the form of what are called "rules" are prepared. An individual can be assigned the responsibility of security officer, whose function is to get these rules specified and into the computer system.

When ACF2 is installed initially, it is said to be in QUIET mode. It can be kept in this mode for a period of time so that those using it can become accustomed to it. While in QUIET mode, there are essentially no perceptible changes in operating procedures. After a while ACF2 is put into LOG mode, and violations are put into a log file. Once an appropriate period of time has passed, WARNING mode is established. During that time, security violations are logged and warning messages are issued, but processing is not terminated. After a further interval of time, ACF2 is put into ABORT mode. From that point on, when violations are logged, processing is terminated. When the product is installed, some global rules have to be prepared initially so that access to some data sets, such as those in commonly used libraries, e.g., compilers, linkage editors, and sorts, is not unnecessarily inhibited.

ACF2 rules can be specified to conform to an organization's standard ID and data set naming conventions. For example, an individual's ID might be 0501063; the data set naming conventions might be generated so that the second through the eighth (the first has to be alphabetic) characters of that individual's data set would contain the ID 0501063; and a rule could be written so that the individuals would be able to access all data sets where the second through the eighth characters were 0501063. Broader rules can also be written. For example, if an individual requires access to all data sets where the first four characters were 0501, a rule could be written for that individual so that access to the multiple data sets would be possible. Rather than 0501063, the rule would contain 0501— as the data set designation. There are many other ways to develop ACF2 rules and the responsibility for knowing how to do it belongs to the security officer. How much of this

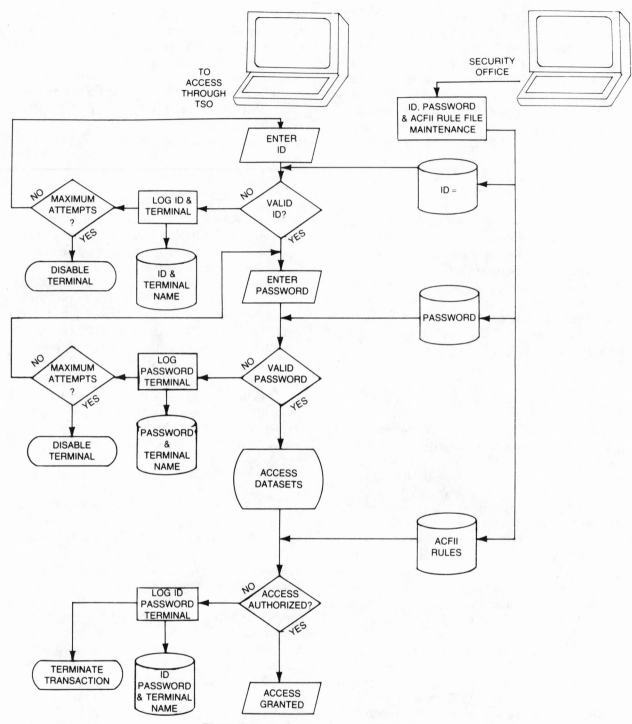

Figure 13.6 Access to files under TSO & ACFII

knowledge can be made available to others is a function of how strictly the approval process is enforced.

Guardian is a software product that is used in CICS environment. Whereas TSO is used basically as a development facility for programmers,

CICS is used basically as a vehicle for the support of a commercial data processing production environment where interactive transactions make inquiries of and update on-line data bases and files (See Figure 13.7). The initials CICS stand for Customer Information Control System. It is a

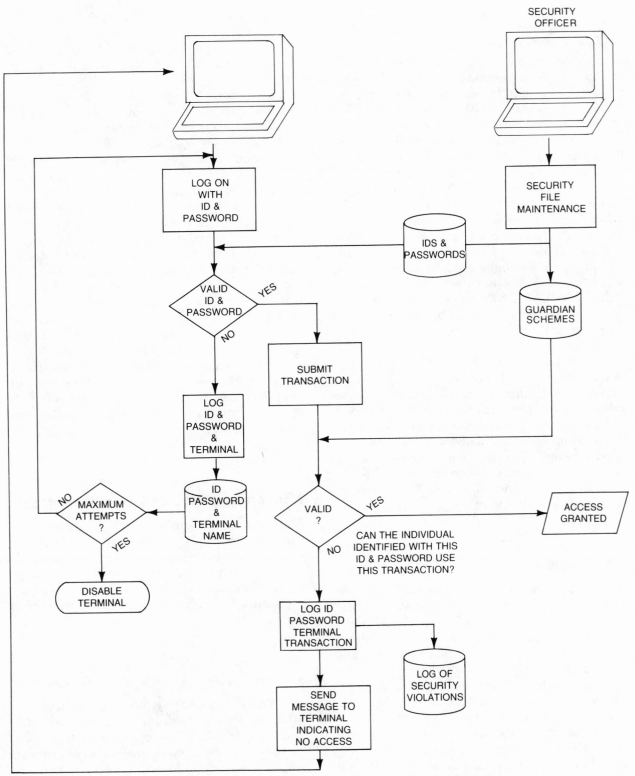

Figure 13.7 Security using GUARDIAN (also known as OMNIGUARD/CICS)

213

system software product that is used to interface transactions coming from or going to terminal devices on a communications network and the application programs that process those transactions in a host computer. The Guardian security product is used to validate the IDs and passwords of individuals who sign on a terminal and attempt to interact with on-line files and data bases using precompiled transaction programs or interactive products supported by CICS.

Guardian uses what are called schemes to identify authorized individuals. Conceptually they are quite similar to what are known as rules under ACF2. Individuals are identified by IDs and passwords. Their security profiles identify the programs, files, and even records and fields within files and data bases to which individuals can have access. Guardian also operates in QUIET, LOG, WARNING, and ABORT modes so as to give an installation an opportunity to get accustomed to the product before using all of its capabilities.

If it is found that ACF2 and Guardian or one of the other available products does not contain the security features desired, it is possible to develop a proprietary security system. Since most security products available are quite comprehensive and were developed with the objective of offering optimal protection at minimal cost, it is usually unnecessary or uneconomical to develop an in-house system, except where specific requirements demand it.

Conclusion

Difficulties arise in determining the proper security for data elements in large organizations. When responsibility for safeguarding data elements is divided among several functions within an organization, disputes generally arise. The disputes generally center around who is responsible for which data elements and how much security is required for different data elements. There are some who favor tight security and others who favor security that is somewhat loose and flexible. Those who feel that they have something to say about security include system software programmers, project leaders, end users, application programmers, security officers, data base administrators, and executives. Reaching a consensus among so many individuals can be a

trying experience. One of the major reasons for the difficulty is the lack of clear understanding of the types of security that can be applied. This chapter has attempted to enhance that understanding.

Data security is getting a great deal of coverage in data processing journals and trade papers. Stories of thievery, fraud, and accidental and malicious damage appear frequently. There is no doubt that a need exists for some level of security. And yet, it must be pointed out that the introduction of security procedures is costly in terms of money and time. It adds to the amount of time required to process a transaction, and it adds to the amount of time required to implement a system. Most software systems today, those developed by user organizations or purchased packages, are sold on the basis that they can make more information available to more people more quickly. The introduction of security systems or practices, by their very nature, mitigates against this. Security systems attempt to restrict information accessibility to selected individuals. Many levels and many types of security are possible with current software technology. It is necessary to trade off time and cash against invulnerability.

Microcomputer System Security

Software security products and procedures are available that apply specifically to small business systems. In addition, some of the same measures now taken to protect the resources of larger computer configurations are also practical. For microcomputers, software security is an issue in three basic areas:

1. Standalone microcomputer systems
2. Microcomputers in computer networks
3. Microcomputers accessible by telephone

With standalone microcomputer systems, the principle delivery medium for software products and for storage of data is the diskette. Unauthorized copying of computer software products results in significant loss of revenue to their developers. Some of those who market microcomputer software have attempted to prevent unauthorized copying and usage, but they have been only partially successful. Transferring the contents of one diskette to another ordinarily involves nothing more than the use of a commonly available utility program called a COPY or DISKCOPY. Such a program simply transfers part or all of the information from one diskette to another by executing a series of read and write instructions.

Various protection schemes have been de-

veloped to discourage copying. Before describing these attempts at securing software on diskettes, it is first necessary to explain how information is stored on diskettes. Figure 13.8 is an illustration showing a single track of a diskette. Diskettes generally consist of a number of tracks with a storage capacity of thousands of characters per track. Information is stored in sectors usually of

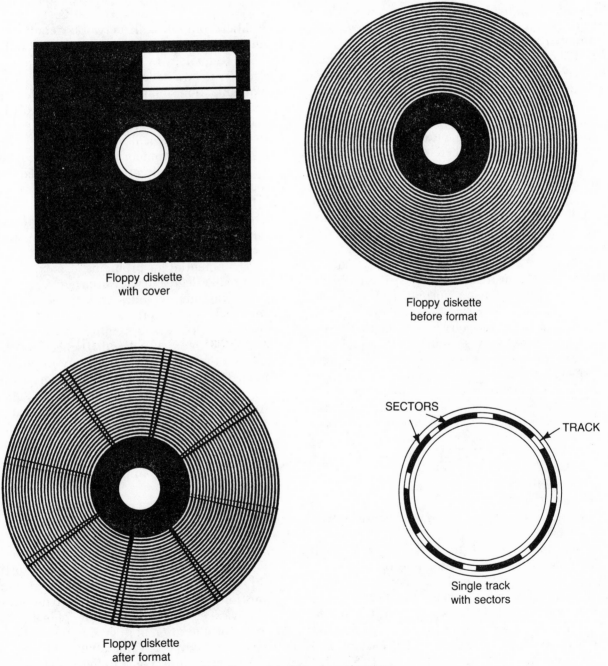

Floppy diskette
with cover

Floppy diskette
before format

Floppy diskette
after format

SECTORS

TRACK

Single track
with sectors

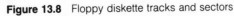

Figure 13.8   Floppy diskette tracks and sectors

128, 256, or 512 characters each. However, the number of sectors per track varies from one computer to another. Most diskettes are purchased "unsectored," and a utility program called FORMAT establishes sectors. The diskette pictured in Figure 13.8 is formatted at eight sectors per track.

Since diskettes are the most economical and practical delivery mechanism, those who developed software for small computers were obliged to use them. At the same time, software developers realized that while it was impossible to stop copying totally, it was at least possible to make it more difficult.

The first technique used was quite simple. It involved creating an unreadable bit combination in an unused sector of the diskette. Since many of the COPY utilities copied an entire diskette, they would malfunction when attempting to read the sector containing the unreadable character. The COPY would complete successfully and the material copied would appear to be of doubtful integrity.

Another technique, known as "finger printing," is more sophisticated. When a software product is put onto a diskette originally, a character is written in an area of a track outside of a sector or in an unused track. To access data in these areas requires special positioning of the read/write mechanism. Normal read/write only takes place within sectors or to and from specific tracks. However, the software product itself performs a validation with that character before it executes. If a diskette contains a copied software product, that character is not present. So when an attempt is made to execute with a copied version, it fails the validation process because the character is not there. Consequently the product does not execute. However, bootleg "bit copy" programs can be obtained that bypass the restrictions of both these techniques.

Apart from software security, diskettes are difficult to protect. Programs or data stored on diskettes can easily be put in a briefcase or even in a jacket pocket.

As they continue to get larger, the "hard disks" with capacities in the tens of millions of bytes are becoming significant as storage media for data and programs. To protect data and programs on hard disks from accidental or intentional damage, or to prevent them from being copied, requires password and ID checking and other security procedures similar to those used on larger computers.

It is also possible to copy sensitive data from hard disks to diskettes in fragments equal to the storage capacity of the diskettes. Although this is time consuming, it may be necessary in some situations where the data are sensitive. Copying data to a diskette provides a practical backup. Of course, once the data are copied to the diskettes, it then becomes necessary to keep the diskettes secure. Other backup alternatives that can be used are magnetic tape cassettes and disk cartridges.

Microcomputers in networks require more security than those that stand alone. Contemporary technology makes it possible for a microcomputer to be a node on a network that includes an organization's main computer and files, or on a network of small computers. Some of these networks include telecommunications, while others, known as local area networks (LANs), have all their equipment in the same geographical area and are directly interconnected. Both types of network invite security breaches unless, at the very least, password and ID checks as well as restrictions on read, write, and execute commands for specific files and programs are in place.

The potential for problems also exists in an even greater degree in wide area networks where a microcomputer includes a telephone and a modem. Such configurations, accessible from any telephone in the world, require access controls. In addition to password and ID checking, there are two other techniques that may improve security. The first is to limit the number of times an individual is allowed to attempt to sign on with an incorrect ID and password. With an unlimited number of attempts, the correct combination may eventually be determined. Limiting the number of attempts and automatically disconnecting when the limit is exceeded prevents this.

The second method is known as the call-back technique. When an individual calls up the computer and submits a valid ID and password, the computer hangs up and calls back to a prearranged phone number. The limitation to this technique at the present time is the built-in assumption that the individual requiring access will always call in from the same phone.

The proliferation of microcomputers has introduced new levels of vulnerability. As more and more vulnerabilities come to light new products must be developed to meet security needs.

Software Security Checklist

	Yes	No
At the very least, are passwords and IDs required to gain access to the computer system? Is access to files and programs restricted to authorized users?	☐	☐
Are files and data bases copied periodically to create backup for use in restoring data following a failure?	☐	☐
In addition to the log or journal file used in recovery and restart operations, is there an additional log or journal that can be used to provide an audit trail of activity against on-line files or data bases?	☐	☐
Do long running batch jobs have checkpoints taken periodically so as to minimize the amount of time required to rerun?	☐	☐
Do control procedures exist for matching output against input to assure the integrity and accuracy of batch reports and listings?	☐	☐
Does teleprocessing software disconnect a terminal after some period of time (usually a few minutes) if no activity has occurred?	☐	☐
Is a security profile used to restrict inquiry and update access to sensitive information?	☐	☐
Do data base management systems contain utility programs for backout,	☐	☐

	Yes	No
recovery and restart, and reorganization?		
Do data base management systems include a data administration structure that prevents indiscriminate access to data base information to individuals?	☐	☐
Is there a defined responsibility for issuing and maintaining passwords and IDs?	☐	☐
Is data encryption necessary? Can it be cost justified?	☐	☐
Can a check digit scheme be used to validate input? Will its value offset the cost of its implementation?	☐	☐
Are program modifications adequately tested before being transferred to production status?	☐	☐
Are there proper authorizations before the transfer of a program to production status?	☐	☐
Does the security software limit the number of times an individual can attempt to sign on to a computer with an incorrect ID and password?	☐	☐
Does the security software use the callback concept, where an individual attempting to sign on to a computer from a remote location has his ID and password checked; and the computer hangs up and calls back a prearranged number?	☐	☐

CHAPTER 14

Data Files

By Ralph E. Jones

Introduction

Data files are collections of information used to manage an organization and document its activities. As important information, data files warrant protection so as to meet the needs of the organization for privacy, confidentiality, and security. Data files may be described in terms of their logical contents or physical forms. They can be housed in any of the following media: magnetic tapes, magnetic disks, optical disks, input source documents, punched cards or tape, printed output, or microfilm.

This chapter describes security considerations in handling and processing data files. These files include input (local and remote, on-line and batch), and storage (on-line and off-line). The chapter also discusses how to dispose of hard copy output documents from an EDP environment when sensitive data are involved. Also included is a discussion of adequate backup for sensitive data files—remembering that backup for equipment is of no value unless backup for data files and program libraries is provided as well.

Regardless of which form of data storage is being considered, one must bear in mind a vital concept, no data processing installation can afford 100 percent security—if indeed there is such a thing. However, a manager can have reasonable security at a reasonable cost. All security measures must be viewed with one question foremost in mind: will a manager of company assets and data be considered prudent if something goes wrong and reasonable steps have not been taken to prevent it? It should be pointed out that the courts have held corporate executives personally liable to their stockholders if they have not taken appropriate actions in protecting their stock-

holders' interests (*Barr v. Chris*). The cost of data security must be weighed against the cost of restoring lost data should something go wrong. The responsibility of the prudent manager is to find the optimum level of security for his particular environment and situation.

In the business world, more and more data and information are being transferred from paper records to electronic media. Each of the electronic media must be protected from damage and unauthorized use. Precautions taken to protect data files in a centralized computer facility are often inadequate; data on microcomputer floppy disks are rarely given any consideration at all.

Data file security requirements are not limited to professional data processing facilities. With the decentralization of information, the need arises for almost every office manager to apply security procedures to protect corporate information.

Data Input

Three concerns about input are (1) preventing loss of data, (2) protecting sensitive data, and, most important, (3) preventing or reducing key entry errors.

Preventing Data Loss

A primary objective for data input is to control data documents to assure that they are not lost in transit. A common device used to prevent losing batches of input data is to establish a sequential number for each batch of work. This identifiable group of data can then have a control total or multiple control totals of dollars, shares, hours, pieces, or some other appropriate unit of measure. Each batch is then recorded in control logs by the sending, keypunch, and control functions (see Exhibit 14.1). These tight controls prevent groups of data from being lost, and assist in maintaining data integrity throughout the system. They do not, however, keep the data confidential.

Exhibit 14.1
Batch Ticket

	Date _____
Batch number _____	Last for day? Yes
Items in batch _____	No
Dollar value _____	
Created by _____	Input by _____
Control _____	

Protecting Sensitive Data

Sensitivity is a lesser issue relating to only some of the documents. In batch processing systems where data are sensitive and must not be seen by unauthorized persons, the user should mark appropriate source documents as "TOP SECRET," "SECRET," or "CONFIDENTIAL." Such marking should have very specific meanings and be defined by corporate policies. Employees must be reminded of these policies on a yearly basis. It is important that the levels be identified, explained in written corporate policy, enforced, and routinely audited for compliance. Employees must understand that any violation of security rules is grounds for disciplinary action. It should be recognized, however, that stamping documents with security classifications can be counterproductive, since a large group of people then know the documents are sensitive.

Some installations use locked bags or containers to store and transport paper containing sensitive data, with the contents itemized on a three-part receipt form. The sender retains one part of the form, the receiver signs two copies and retains one, sending the third signed copy back to the sender. Limiting the number of people who know that the contents are considered sensitive reduces the threat of unauthorized access.

Security of data keyed into terminals of an on-line system is easier if the terminals and operators are in secure locations at the originating source. Data are not then forwarded to another functional area for input into the system. The operators report directly to and are directly responsible to supervisors who control the sensitive data.

In cases where data are highly sensitive, one method to prevent its misuse is to isolate data elements from related descriptors. For instance, field names can be omitted from input forms so that entry operators are unaware of the meaning of the data they are keying. Input clerks can use plastic overlay sheets to assist in interpreting the "blank" forms while they are filling them out.

A data item is sensitive only when it is associated with descriptors, or with other identifying data. For example, this series of numbers has no apparent meaning:

$$18542 \qquad 44750 \qquad 23811$$

However, the addition of one descriptor adds some significance:

$$18542 \qquad 447.50 \text{ salary} \qquad 23811$$

A great deal more meaning is conveyed by:

18542	Senior Programmer
447.50	Salary
23811	John Johnson

Data should be tightly controlled during the input process, not only to protect sensitivity, but also to insure that all data are correctly and completely input to the system.

Inadvertent Keying Errors

The cost of inadvertent error far exceeds that of all fraud, embezzlement, and other intentional data abuse. Computer software should be designed to detect inadvertent errors in data input.

Routines to detect such errors can be very simple. For example, if dollar values input to a system should never exceed $100,000, then code could be inserted into the program to detect this and either halt processing or advise the user via a warning message. Reasonableness tests can be inserted to detect extreme conditions that should never occur. In the above example, suppose the operator keyed in $10,000,000; an appropriate test could detect the error immediately and not wait for batch controls to catch it.

It is virtually impossible to catch all entry errors in a data processing system or, in fact, in a paper processing system. Nevertheless, there must be a continuing effort to eliminate input of errors, and to correct those that slip through.

Processing Data

Processing of data within a computer consists of taking data from an input source, manipulating it, sorting, filing, performing calculations, and finally preparing output to other files, paper, or to remote terminals. During each step of the processing phase data must be kept secure, and their integrity must be maintained.

There are several techniques that can be used:

- Separate the files. It may not always be desirable for security purposes to create one large all-inclusive data bank stored at one location. Sensitive files can be physically separated to eliminate the possibility of relating one file, record, or field to another. This consideration must be weighed against the advantages of creating a central data bank.
- Encrypt the files. This will make it difficult for anyone to read their contents without possession of the proper key.
- Store files in a locked container when not in use. Depending upon the particular situation, the locked container could be anything from a simple sheet-metal cabinet designed to store tapes and disks to an underground vault. Sign-out procedures for each volume of file should be appropriately designed.

Such procedures will, in all probability, increase computer processing costs, but they can provide a high degree of data security.

Encrypting Data

Data can be encrypted by numerous methods of varying sophistication described in the chapter on that subject. It is possible to maintain sensitive data files on tape or disk in encrypted form and to encrypt files for transmission. However, data encryption will increase programming and operating costs. Encrypted files are difficult to work with, and debugging can be a painful chore.

Terminal User Security Profile

Terminal users of on-line systems create additional security problems not present in batch systems. Critical data bases must be properly protected from unauthorized use by terminal operators. One method to protect an on-line data base is to create a "security profile" for each authorized person using the system. A typical security profile record might contain the following information:

- Employee's name
- Password
- Employee number
- Department number
- Transaction or function codes authorized for use
- Terminals authorized for use
- Authorized hours

When a terminal operator indicates the transaction or function he wishes to perform, the programmed security subroutine can check to see that he is not only authorized for that function but that it is being performed at an authorized terminal, during authorized hours. Violations result in the terminal being locked, and only by action on the part of a supervisor can the terminal be unlocked. Passwords must be changed frequently for each authorized user. Authorizations and restrictions can be assigned for transaction queries, additions, changes, and deletions. Detailed security logs should be maintained indicating each unsuccessful access attempt and the nature of the violation. Reports could be produced showing activity by terminal, time, user's name, passwords, data fields addressed, and other relevant data. The log can be used by management to detect and deter attempts to subvert the security system.

Passwords

Use of passwords is a common approach to system security. Each operator is identified by a password, which is recorded within the system. Thereafter, each operator enters that password at the start of a terminal session during the logon procedures. Typical system design will allow anywhere from one to three unsuccessful attempts to gain access to the system; any additional attempts will terminate the session. The procedure can help to protect systems and data files provided that:

- Passwords cannot readily be determined by intelligent guesswork or by trial and error
- Creation of the passwords is correctly done
- Proper security and control are exercised over the password

- Management is notified each time the system denies operator access due to use of faulty passwords
- Passwords are frequently changed

While computer-generated passwords are created by programming, the user may simulate this action by striking letters, numbers, and special character keys on a typewriter. The stranger the resulting password appears, the more difficult it will be for an unauthorized user to guess. However, it will also be more difficult for the authorized user to remember, and the temptation to write the password down and keep it near the terminal must be entirely resisted. When the password is created, a copy of it must be retained in a secure place and a second copy retained by a central password control agency within the company. During the password creation process it is important to destroy all papers and computer printout containing the password, or to file them in an approved secure place. Alternatively, security systems may be designed so that password input is by video terminal, and there is no printed output. In this case, it is the responsibility of the user to remember the passwords; no central records are kept.

Password systems may be extremely simple so that any valid password provides access to all system functions. When greater security is required, the functions accessed may be restricted to certain passwords, and within those passwords may be further constrained by the use of authorization levels. As an example, the password XQ*114 with access level "3" may permit entry of time-card data into the payroll files, but only operators with access level "9" may view payroll records. In other systems, the password itself provides information about the access levels.

Regardless of the actual method used, it is important to document all password procedures, and to have them approved by the internal audit or security function. Passwords are actually electronic "keys" to an application package. As such, the "keys" should not be kept in easily accessible places, since that would lead to the system being compromised.

Electronic Data Destruction

A great threat to file security arises from the fact that instructions to delete a file do not in fact destroy the data. Only the file directory is flagged to ignore the file, but this flag can easily be reset to make the file readable again. There are several techniques that can be used to actually erase sensitive data when they are no longer required and the magnetic medium is to be reused:

- Writing a new file over the old one
- Tape degaussing, which demagnetizes an entire reel in a short time without unwinding
- Writing blanks, zeros, or some other character on the entire tape or disk

The technique of writing blanks or zeros on unused tape does not require new equipment, but it does require additional computer time, and over the years the procedure could incur considerable extra processing costs.

Indefensible Threats

One of the greatest threats, and one that has received the least attention, arises from the technical nature of the operating system, coupled with the extensive knowledge of systems programmers whose powers of manipulation are virtually without limit. Because the operating system software is responsible for the control of all input, output, processing, and storage of data, its improper functioning, whether through inadvertent error or fraudulent intent, can subvert any password system or application program safeguard. Through such technical elements as checkpoints, core dumps, and trapping procedures, the systems programmer, by his expert capabilities, is able to read, alter, or delete any data within the system. It is unrealistic to expect within any organization to find talent adequate to prevent or even detect depredations of such an individual, nor is it practicable to employ outsiders to maintain continuous surveillance. The only solution would appear to be for the entire operating system to be provided as "firmware" or read-only memory (ROM) so that it cannot be altered throughout its life.

Transmission of Data Files

Transmission of files needs to be done in ways to prevent confidential information from getting into the wrong hands, and to assure that data are moved without error.

With the increasing use of electronic data transmission, the business world is becoming more concerned with related security issues. The business world requires transportation of data files to be 100 percent safe and secure. Among the procedures that can create a fairly secure environment is data encryption. This process is more fully described in another chapter of the book.

A sensitive subject in recent years has been the procedures in use by commercial bank customers to initiate wire transfer instructions. A bank wire transfer is a mechanism used to move sums of money, usually large, from one customer's account to a beneficiary customer's account in another bank. For years the accepted practice has been for an authorized person at a corporation to send a wire or make a voice telephone call to a bank's money transfer facility, providing the necessary instructions to move funds from one bank account to another. The instructions usually consisted of the date, dollar amount, daily sequence number, and customer number. This was accompanied by a test key formed through a closely guarded algorithm or arithmetic procedure. The test key is derived from some of the data from the transaction instructions. The receiving bank also checked the daily sequence number and calculated the test key. If all was in order (and the account had sufficient funds) the transfer was completed. Some banks used the additional procedure of telephoning the authorized person at the customers' office to verify the instructions received. This is certainly safer, but it is labor intensive, slow, costly, and requires an authorized person to be available to receive the phone call prior to release of the transfer instruction.

Modern corporations now use computer terminals that are connected to bank computers either by dial-up voice or dedicated telephone lines. Authorized initiators are now identified through user identification codes and password procedures, while test keys may be automatically computed. As new technologies emerge, the movement of large amounts of money between financial institutions will likely be made with even more enhanced controls.

Additional procedures for assuring accurate transmission generate record counts, hash totals, and control totals on critical data fields, at the transmission end, and then compare these with totals generated at the receiving end. The control totals can accompany the data files in trailer records or be verified via voice communication between control personnel.

Production Standard vs. Actual Run Times

Actual program run logs and computer run times should be audited against standard schedules and run times. This enables management to detect unauthorized computer usage that could generate extra copies of critical reports.

Standard run times should be established for every scheduled production run based upon a reliable volume indicator, such as quantity of input transactions, records on a master file, or lines of printed output. The standard run times should then be compared to the actual run times and variances indicated for management's review. System performance statistics such as these can be accumulated by commercially available software packages. These packages establish a uniform method for gathering, comparing, and reporting actual hardware usage versus available hours to establish workload and hardware utilization, while simultaneously accumulating system performance statistics. A less sophisticated procedure, although highly effective, is to spotcheck daily computer console log sheets. These should be printed on prenumbered pages so that unauthorized runs cannot be hidden by disposing of unnumbered log sheets. Where this problem exists, one ply of the log could be arranged to feed automatically into a locked box behind the console typewriter.

As a further aid in reducing the rerun problem, it is useful to create a set of codes to pinpoint responsibility. This will also be of value in training personnel, as well as in detecting unauthorized usage. Unfortunately, operators cannot always be relied upon to encode a rerun properly. The ultimate responsibility rests with management, who must enforce proper procedures on supervisors and operators alike.

A suggested set of rerun reason codes may be as follows:

User Error
01 Incorrect user supplied control information
02 Incorrect or illegible source data
03 Both of above
04 Source data added after run began

DP Errors
  21 Data control
  22 Data entry
  23 Operations—wrong program
  24 Operations—wrong sequence
  25 Operations—wrong volumes
  26 Operations—wrong output
  27 Operations—wrong command
  28 Unknown

Equipment Failures
  31 Central processor
  32 Disk drive
  33 Tape drive
  34 Printer
  35 Card reader
  36 Card punch
  37 Data entry
  38 Terminal
  39 Tape reel
  40 Disk pack

Communications
  51 Lines
  52 Modems
  53 Switches
  54 Controllers

Software
  61 Application program bug
  62 Operating system bug

Power Supply
  71 Power failure
  72 Power surge

Data Output

EDP systems generate large volumes of paper, which must be disposed of properly. If data are of a sensitive nature, it is important to be concerned not only with actual hard copy output but also with the carbon paper and printer ribbons that have produced it.

For applications that are considered sensitive or confidential, strict procedures must be established to guarantee proper disposal of hard copy, either immediately or at the end of a prescribed retention period. If a records center administrator exists, that person should assist in developing appropriate procedures to identify computer outputs that must be controlled. Functional areas with potential hard copy problems include data entry, computer operations, systems and programming, end users, remote locations, microfilming, and even auditing.

Programmers, internal auditors, and end user's are frequently overlooked when it comes to disposing of hard copy documents. They may have reports, memory dumps, or listings to check out some particular problem, and then discard them in the regular office waste papter—or take them out of the office only to discard them when no longer needed.

United States mails and interoffice mails can be used to negate security precautions. Sensitive reports on paper, microfilm, floppy disks, or magnetic tape can easily be mailed, completely bypassing security guards at the doors. Proper procedures require all packages to be inspected, but microfilm, floppy disks, and small reports will usually pass unnoticed.

Appropriate controls over the generation and distribution of these media are necessary, and a conscientious program for destroying all unused data outputs must be maintained as a deterrent to unauthorized use of valuable data files.

Disposal Methods

Once it has been decided "what" to destroy, the next consideration is "how" to destroy it. For an effective procedure, costs can be of major concern and must be evaluated against the attendant risks.

In-House Procedures

Locked containers are desirable to accumulate sensitive scrap material until such time as it is destroyed. Containers should be accessible and well supervised. When containers are emptied, the waste must be guarded until the material is picked up by a disposal service or destroyed on-site.

Pick-up responsibility should rest with security personnel rather than with regular maintenance personnel. Two people should collect it as a team to prevent individual security breaches, and these employees should be alternated to discourage collusion.

Paper disposal machines are available using solvents or mechanical shredding blades. Incineration is an acceptable method providing there are no local ordinances to prevent it.

Outside Contractor Services

Special security oriented disposal services are available. They generally use closed vehicles with trained, bonded operators who are able to provide a certificate of destruction such as that in Exhibit 14.2.

Exhibit 14.2
Sample Guarantee of Destruction Affidavit

The undersigned, a member of the firm of

trading as

does hereby make the following deposition:

That the procedure hereinafter described is the method employed by this company in the removal of all papers and records from your premises, to wit;

that from the moment your records, papers, tabulating cards, or other instruments are removed from your premises, they are transported in completely enclosed vehicles directly to our plant, placed in the baling press, mangled, and transformed into solid bales under great pressure, and then shipped directly to the paper mill;

that during the entire process and proceedings above described, every step is under the personal direction of a member of this firm;

that upon arrival at the paper mill, the bales are placed in a paper beater, treated with chemicals, dissolved, pulverized, macerated, and so physically transformed in substance and in form as to lose all identity as paper, and eventually to wind up as a heavy liquid mass. All inks, writings, printings, and impressions are eradicated and washed away in this "wet-beater" process.

STATE OF NEW YORK

ss.:

COUNTY OF KINGS

Sworn to before me on this

Backup

Since EDP files can be easily altered or destroyed it is imperative that complete backup capabilities be designed into every system. This is true for a large central computer facility and equally true for a small microcomputer. Backup includes not only the appropriate hardware and software but properly trained personnel as well.

Backing up master files, secondary files, and transaction files, whether updated daily, weekly, or monthly, requires that three generations be saved. The most current copy of a file is usually retained on-site mounted for immediate use or in a secure tape library. Strict procedures must be followed to have these copies rotated on a fixed schedule in accordance with specified retention cycles. Exhibit 14.3 shows four generations of tape reels numbered 1 thru 20 with each set saved for one month. After one week of storage in the on-site library, reels 1–5 would be sent off-site on 2/11 and remain there until 3/3, the scratch date, at which time they would be erased and then returned to the on-site library for use again on 3/4. File management software can assist in these procedures.

Exhibit 14.3

Set Designation	Reel Numbers	Date Created	Send Off-Site On	Scratch Date
A	1–5	2/04	2/11	3/03
B	6–10	2/11	2/18	3/10
C	11–15	2/18	2/25	3/17
D	16–20	2/25	3/04	3/24
A	1–5	3/04	3/11	3/31
B	6–10	3/11	3/18	4/07

etc.

File storage facilities on-site with the computer itself are considered the primary storage area. Secondary sites should be located at least 500 feet away from the primary storage area and never directly above or below the computer room, so that one disaster will not destroy all files. Suitable space, facilities, and security precautions not available on a company's own premises can usually be rented at a bank vault or other physical location set up for this purpose.

Suitable facilities include:

- Vault space
- Fire protection
- Access protection
- Messenger service

For files whose value does not mandate off-site storage, if the number of tape reels is under a few hundred and disks under 25, adequate facilities can usually be provided on-site. Quantities above this will probably dictate renting of space in commercial vaults. Variable size room vaults are available at these locations for a yearly rental fee. A 6' × 10' × 15' vault may cost about $5,000 per year. Access and messenger services are also available on a per use basis.

All storage sites should have the same environmental protection as exists at the computer center. This is especially true for long-term storage of six months or more. Ordinary office space that is dependent upon office air conditioning is usually not adequate for long-term storage of tapes and disks. Punched cards are even more critical because of warping caused by humidity. Air conditioners are usually lowered or turned off after hours and on week-ends. Over a long period of time fluctuating temperature and poor humidity control can have damaging effects on tapes, disks, and cards. It is important to test the ability to read files after they have been stored for some period of time and to copy them onto new media before they deteriorate. Periodic tests should be run to ensure that the data files can be restored from the backup. This will verify that proper procedures are being followed.

Program modifications can render backup files obsolete due to changed record layouts. If this happens, either the old files must be converted to the new format or the old programs must be saved in order to process the original backup files. Similar problems can occur during equipment changeover or when implementing a new release level for an operating system. Testing the backup after each such event will minimize the possibility of discovering that backup is worthless at a time when it is most needed.

Backup files require at least as much security as do the current files. Also, on-line and batch transaction files should be backed up and retained on the same schedule, and copies of the current programs must also be stored off-site.

Because of the importance of file backup, many computer centers require that each disk file be copied to two backup tapes. As an alternative, a single tape drive can continuously record an on-line transaction file. At end of day, the log tape can be copied onto another tape. If successful, no further processing is required. If the copy is not completed owing to a bad tape, the entire updated master disk file should be backed up.

Double writing of tapes increases the tape inventory problem. If accurate retention cycles are not adhered to, an installation can easily spend an inordinate amount of money on new tapes and greatly increase its need for library storage facilities.

Microcomputers

A microcomputer is similar to a large-scale computer system when security is being considered. Data must be kept secure, whether stored and processed on a microcomputer in an open office, or on a large-scale system in a data center. The same aspects of security are involved, e.g.:

- Input source documents
- Passwords
- Processing of data
- File storage
- Data output
- Data transmission

Some users of microcomputers tend to treat their systems carelessly. The fact that the equipment is small and does not require a special room built around it tends to minimize the apparent value of data residing in a microcomputer system. Most microcomputer users are not trained as EDP people and have not been exposed to the risks of improper security procedures. Most of the recommended security measures reviewed in this chapter should be implemented in a microcomputer environment. As the use of microcomputers becomes more widespread in normal office environments, the proven principles of data security must be increasingly applied to microcomputer systems.

Word processing systems almost invariably contain valuable information that is easy to understand and easily accessible. The contents of their files can readily be displayed or printed, while the floppy disks themselves can easily be removed from office environments.

To prevent unauthorized use or loss of data, floppy disk files should never be left unattended. One copy of each floppy disk should be stored in a locked cabinet, and a second copy retained at the central data processing library or at some other closely controlled facility.

Three developments increase the risks of fraud that are of particular concern for business: (1) the spread of low-cost personal computers, (2) the increasing number of students and others who are learning how to use computers, and (3) the large number of employees who can access computers through remote terminals.

A most serious threat by knowledgeable microcomputer users is tapping into data transmission lines, either to steal proprietary information, change data, or to insert fraudulent messages into the transmission. Companies seldom monitor the authors of microcomputer programs. More than anyone else in a company, programmers are familiar with weaknesses in the systems they have designed. Because of this familiarity, they can easily commit fraud and manipulate files so as to hide the evidence.

To protect from this potential intrusion requires system designers to pay more attention to telecommunication and audit controls. The increasing presence of microcomputers results in greater vulnerability of data, which requires increased security measures and attention from EDP technicians and management.

Summary

All security precautions taken for data files must be tailored to satisfy the particular business environment at a justifiable cost. The degree of file sensitivity, the number of individual physical files, their dollar value, and their cubic volume, all tend to dictate what procedures will be used. Excessive precautions are overly expensive and could attract unnecessary attention, creating additional risks. On the other hand, inadequate procedures subject valuable corporate assets to unnecessary risks. It is the prudent manager who strikes a proper balance between the two extremes, maintaining an effective and secure function while contributing to overall cost and profit objectives.

Checklists

Data Input:

	Yes	No
Are sensitive source documents stamped with appropriate security markings?	☐	☐
Are locked bags or containers used for sensitive data?	☐	☐
Are there written procedures on the use of such markings?	☐	☐
Are control totals, hash totals, reasonableness tests, and batch totals used where appropriate?	☐	☐
Are control logs used to record input document batches?	☐	☐
Do sensitive input documents have column captions or field names removed?	☐	☐

	Yes	No
Are meaningful relationships of data removed from the files containing sensitive data?	☐	☐
Are sensitive master files broken up into separate files to remove meaningful relationships of data?	☐	☐

Processing Data:

	Yes	No
Are sensitive data files scrambled or coded?	☐	☐
Are critical files kept under lock and key?	☐	☐
Do tamperproof security logs indicate when and how sensitive data files are used?	☐	☐
Are security codes kept confidential and closely controlled on a need-to-know basis?	☐	☐
Are there written procedures for the use of security codes?	☐	☐
Are the codes changed frequently?	☐	☐
Are terminal operators sufficiently identified by the system before it allows them to enter data through the terminals, or to access data from the files?	☐	☐
Are dedicated tape reels used for sensitive applications and safeguarded appropriately?	☐	☐
Are scratch tapes from sensitive applications properly cleaned of all data before release to other applications?	☐	☐
Is sensitive data always erased after the end-of-file indicator on critical files?	☐	☐
Do external labels draw unnecessary attention to sensitive data files?	☐	☐
Can sensitive tape, disk files, or floppy disks be physically removed from company property?	☐	☐
Is the security system demonstrated to other than those with a need-to-know?	☐	☐
Are passwords kept in a secure place?	☐	☐
Are passwords changed frequently?	☐	☐

Yes No

Are there sufficient levels of password security? ☐ ☐

Do passwords adequately determine which employees are authorized to add, change, delete, or read data in each file? ☐ ☐

Are password procedures documented in writing? ☐ ☐

Are critical or sensitive data sent coded over communication lines? ☐ ☐

Are communication lines tested for the presence of wiretaps? ☐ ☐

Are proper test keys, authentications, and batch control totals used? ☐ ☐

Are critical data secure from remote terminal inquiry by unauthorized persons? ☐ ☐

Production Standard vs. Actual Run Times:

Are computer operators prevented from producing extra copies of sensitive reports? ☐ ☐

Are there tight controls over computer run times? ☐ ☐

Are actual run times equal to standards? ☐ ☐

Data Output:

Are standard run times established for each production run? ☐ ☐

Can unauthorized runs of critical data reports be made by programmers or computer operators? ☐ ☐

Are adequate disposal methods used in all areas to completely destroy waste paper, ribbons, and carbon paper that may contain sensitive data? ☐ ☐

Is it impossible to have any data security leaks via outside scavenger service? ☐ ☐

Are waste punch cards properly destroyed if they contain critical data? ☐ ☐

Yes No

Is it impossible for a sensitive report to be mailed out of the facility? ☐ ☐

Are all copies of sensitive reports tightly controlled and adequately destroyed when no longer used? ☐ ☐

Backup:

Are backup files that contain sensitive data properly protected from intrusion? ☐ ☐

Is the secondary storage site sufficiently separated from the primary storage site? ☐ ☐

Can current computer programs correctly process critical backup files? ☐ ☐

Are sufficient backup cycles retained for complete file restoration? ☐ ☐

Are there written procedures as to who can have physical access to critical backup files? ☐ ☐

Are backup tapes readable? ☐ ☐

Are critical disk files copied twice? ☐ ☐

Are critical files periodically reconstructed to test backup procedures? ☐ ☐

Do all storage sites have the same environmental protection as exists at the computer center? ☐ ☐

Microcomputers:

Are the major aspects of security—i.e., input source documents, passwords, processing of data, file storage, data output, and data transmission given proper consideration as if in a large-scale system in a data center? ☐ ☐

Are floppy disks stored in locked file cabinets? ☐ ☐

Are floppy disks safe from magnetized security badges? ☐ ☐

CHAPTER 15
Data Encryption

By Cipher A. Deavours

Terminology

Data encryption is an integral part of the science of *cryptology*, the study of concealed and secret writing. Cryptology is divided into two major areas: *cryptography* and *cryptanalysis*. Cryptography is the study of systems for putting "plaintext" into a coded cyphertext form; cryptanalysis is the study of methods for recovering the plaintext without knowledge of the specific "key" involved.

Enciphering or encryption of data uses an algorithm with a *cryptographic key* that transforms the plaintext data into its ciphered form. The term *cryptographic system* includes not only the algorithm itself but all other features of the encryption and decryption process. This comprises physical security features, selection of cryptographic personnel, generation and distribution of cryptographic keys, monitoring and testing of the cryptographic system both before and after installation, the enforcement of approved procedures, and the training of personnel who use the system. The environment in which cryptography takes place is invariably more important to the overall security achieved than the actual algorithm(s) utilized.

As an example of what cryptography does, consider the following message, which might be transformed into the form shown:

PLAINTEXT: ACCT 1234-56789 CLOSED EOT
CIPHERTEXT: 5H)-*LIKJJ3#G'8**1!2CFRGT

Clearly the scrambling succeeds admirably in making the original version unreadable on sight. To form a cryptographic network, each user must be provided with the same algorithm and keys so that messages sent by one person in the network can be deciphered by any addressee. Further examples of simple cryptographic methods are shown in Appendix 17. Cryptographic networks are depicted in Figures 15.2 to 15.5.

Cryptology is a subject about which little practical or even theoretical information is published. This problem, which makes the task of potential users even more difficult than it would ordinarily be, has arisen primarily because of the secrecy that surrounds the subject. There is little established literature to which one can turn for advice, and few persons have had more than academic experience in the design and employment of cryptographic systems.

Uses of Cryptography

The purpose of cryptography is to protect sensitive data from unauthorized disclosure. In computer systems this almost always means protecting data transmitted over insecure public carriers, or protecting data files within the system itself. In the case of data files, cryptography often operates as an adjunct to the access controls that are built into the operating system. The problem of securing static data files is the more difficult of the two situations because of their size and the fact that often much of the plaintext of the file is known to an attacker. In either application, some way must be found to protect the cryptographic keys used in scrambling the data. Often this amounts to relying on operating system access controls to safeguard key lists. In this case, the cryptographic system is no better than the operating system itself in providing security, and little, if anything, can be gained by the use of cryptography. When protection of telecommunications is the primary purpose of cryptography, the cryptographic environment is more susceptible to stringent safeguards.

Cryptographic Guidelines

Several major tenets of cryptographic practice are recognized as vital to the successful installation and functioning of a cryptographic system:

- It should be determined at the outset just what data are to be protected and what level of security is desired. This includes a general examination as to whether or not cryptography is an appropriate solution to this problem.
- The security of the cryptographic process should depend only on keeping the specific cipher keys secret and not on the secrecy of the algorithm itself.
- The system should be easy to use.
- The encryption method chosen should be the simplest one available to achieve the desired security level.
- Standards and procedures regarding the maximum length of text to be enciphered before change of key, generation and distribution of keys, and access of personnel to cryptographic data should be set before the system is put into place and should be vigorously followed thereafter.
- The cryptographic system should never be modified or "improved" in a piecemeal manner during its operational lifetime without a thorough reexamination of the consequences of the proposed adjustment.
- Usage of the system should be monitored continuously to verify that the operational guidelines for the system are being followed.

Goals

Clearly defined goals should be established before considering cryptography. Often the use of ciphering results from the knowledge that certain data should be protected. A "quick fix" is then sought with the idea that any cryptographic algorithm is better than none at all. Unfortunately,

once cryptography is employed, users tend to rely upon it for protection, possibly discarding other safeguards. This can lead to confidential data being made more easily available to an adversary than would otherwise be the case. There are seldom any clues that a cryptographic system has been attacked or penetrated and so this state of affairs may continue for a very long time before the damage is realized.

The data to be protected and the level of security desired must be clearly defined, because no one cryptographic algorithm is likely to fit all the needs of a user. If the algorithm is to be used for static file encryption, for example, this use may provide enough in the way of known plaintext so that telecommunications enciphered using the same algorithm might be deciphered even though different cryptographic keys are in use. No one algorithm is appropriate to all needs and there does not exist an algorithm strong enough to resist careless application.

The use of cryptography is a relatively expensive solution to the problem of data security. It is practical only when the data protected are worth the cost and bother involved. Since inhouse expertise is usually not available, an independent consultant, rather than a vendor of cryptographic equipment, should be engaged to assess the strengths and weaknesses of a projected cryptographic system.

Safeguarding Keys and Algorithms

That the security of a cipher must not rest on keeping the algorithm itself secret is an important point. If the system to be used is one commercially available, then it is clear that the details of the design will be known, or will become known, to a determined adversary. Similar problems exist with encryption software. The paradox here is that if few people know the construction of the machine or the software algorithm, then it probably has not received adequate scrutiny from the cryptanalytic community; if the converse is true, then the construction of the machine or algorithm can be considered to be common knowledge. In either case, the only safe course is to assume that the algorithm is known to a potential penetrator of the system and to exercise the greatest of care in protecting the keys.

Key Management

Safeguarding cryptographic keys is of paramount importance. There are several approaches that are commonly used. Setting aside the case of "public key" cryptographic systems, which will be discussed later, it is necessary for both the sender and the receiver in a cryptographic network to have some sort of secret key(s) in their common possession. One method of doing this is to install a set of "master keys" in the machine itself and to have ciphered text be preceded by "preambles" that are then used with the master keys to generate the particular key for that message. Usually the preambles are generated randomly using the system clock *and* some form of mixing or scrambling algorithm. In this type of system, the size of the key that must be kept secret is very small compared with most other approaches.

In some instances, the cipher algorithm itself is used in the key generation process, and this minimizes the amount of ROM needed for the cryptographic device. It is of advantage if the master keys need not be entered manually from a keyboard or other device where they are directly readable by personnel involved in operating the system.

It is also possible to generate large numbers of keys in advance and store them in the machine or some other device so that there is no master key at all. Each key is used only once and then destroyed. A number of commercial military systems use this approach.

For large networks that must transmit a high volume of traffic, the key management process becomes more difficult. The obvious alternative is to provide enough master keys so that every two users who will have occasion to communicate have unique master keys. Since the number of keys to be generated will increase as the square of the number of users, this can become a problem.

Alternatively, one can set up chains of users who can each communicate only with two neighboring nodes cryptographically. The chains must be formed so that there is a path leading between any two nodes of the network. In each node the text must be decrypted and reencrypted before being passed to the next link in the communication chain. The disadvantage here is that the plaintext of the message travels, providing multiple opportunities for breaching security. Fur-

thermore, the fact that the same message appears reciphered in many different keys provides a cryptanalyst with more information of the type that makes codebreaking easier. Finally, one inoperative or compromised node can destroy the security of the entire network.

The generation of suitable keys for a cryptographic algorithm can itself be a problem. There are cipher devices on the public market for which "bad" keys can produce easy to solve ciphertexts.

As far as possible, the key generation process should be random and under automatic control; the amount of human intervention allowed should be as little as is practical. There is the example of a certain organization that used the Federal Data Encryption Standard (DES), an algorithm devised by IBM and several United States government agencies. Because it was necessary for someone to construct cipher keys for the company's files, the job was given to a junior administrator who knew little about cryptology. Each DES key was to consist of 14 hexadecimal characters. After three days, the administrator returned to complain to his superior that the task was not going well because he was having trouble thinking up enough meaningful words and expressions that could be formed from the 6 hexadecimal values A, B, C, D, E, F! (This has been called the "BAD FAD" case.) When questioned, the administrator claimed that he was only following good security procedures, since, if a key were not easy to remember it would necessarily have to be written down and might then be stolen. The administrator was obviously unaware of the ease with which such a limited set of passwords could be broken.

In another case involving DES, an employee with some cryptologic training managed to solve the cipher because, although he did not have access to the weekly DES key, he did have the ability to submit plaintext to the encryption system for encipherment. The DES algorithm enciphers data in 64 bit blocks (8 bytes) in its simplest form. An examination of the (funds transfer) data being enciphered showed him that there were a few thousand eight-character blocks that occurred with high frequency in the texts being sent. From his desktop PC he could thus submit a list of high frequency plaintext blocks for encipherment and read quite a high percentage of the coded text by later comparisons between the transfer data and his enciphered list of blocks. It was further found that the value of many other blocks could be determined from inference once a portion of the text had been recovered. In this particular case, the bank's repetition of data and the employee's easy access to account numbers allowed cryptanalysis to proceed with less data than might otherwise be necessary, but the same general approach can be used in more difficult situations.

This is a case where the cipher algorithm was not at fault, but only its method of use. Although the cipher keys for this particular example were selected with caution, the fact that sample texts could be deciphered without knowledge of the key shows what surprising and unexpected weaknesses can invalidate all attempts at security.

Ease of Use

It goes without saying that ease of use is as important in cryptography as in hardware and software engineering. If long random keys need to be entered from a terminal or long delays are experienced as data are enciphered by the system, users will be increasingly dissatisfied with the results. This, in turn, will lead to misuse or outright avoidance of the system. There is a fine line between the much sought after user friendliness and the complexities of a secure system. Only experience can draw the line properly.

It is seldom found necessary to provide cryptographic protection for data over very long periods of time. While there are exceptions, most data become quickly stale and relatively useless to adversaries. Since cryptography really provides no "absolute" protection, it is better to think in terms of *delaying* intrusion beyond the point where the information will be of value, and to change the keys within this time interval, rather than attempting to prevent intrusion forever. This usually allows the use of simpler (and less expensive) cryptographic methods.

Operational Factors

Cryptologic history demonstrates the importance of considering the encryption environment when selecting and determining the security provided by a given algorithm. Once an optimal system has been determined and its usage set out, changes in the operating procedures associated

with the system should not be made or taken lightly.

A well-designed cryptographic system may be rendered less secure through some later modification that seemed harmless at the time. In one case, a new message key was generated every 30 seconds. In the interest of impressing superiors, a systems programmer for the user's company modified the program so that one contiguous text had only one key. The running time of the program was thereby decreased about 10 percent. Unfortunately the "timewasting" reinitialization was done to prevent a certain method of cryptanalysis from being applied. In fact it had been decided during the design of the algorithm that the reinitialization had actually greatly decreased the encryption time because it avoided the need for a much more complex ciphering process. The apparent improvement was, in reality, a serious degradation of the security of the cipher.

Constant monitoring of an operational cryptographic system is a necessity. There is no guarantee that a well-designed and implemented system will remain so. In fact, quite the reverse is likely to occur as old personnel leave and are replaced by new ones who may not be as thoroughly trained in the procedures to be used in operating the system. Electronic devices also can fail to function properly. In one case the mechanism for generating random preamble sequences began to drift toward nonrandomness in one cipher unit (for a reason that was never fully understood). If allowed to continue, a number of identically keyed messages could have been sent that, for that particular system, was tantamount to solution of the ciphertext. Advances in technology sometimes make yesterday's secure cipher much less secure today. This could result from increasing CPU speeds, added parallelism in computations, and large-scale, inexpensive memory chips and processors.

The need for operational safeguards should not be looked on as a reason to avoid the use of cryptology, but only as a consideration that should receive attention *if* cryptology is to be effective.

Authentication

A technique related to cryptographic protection is the use of authenticators. While cryptography is primarily a provider of *privacy*, authentication does not attempt to hide data, only to verify their integrity. There are two cases where authentication is a must. First, when the data are not to be encrypted and are susceptible to interception and subsequent alteration or forgery; second, when the common exclusive-or (XOR) encryption method of adding plaintext bits to a random-looking keystream of bits, modulo two, is used.

The American Bankers Association recommends the use of DES-based authentication for funds transfers. The actual data may be sent encrypted or unencrypted, but in either case a 32-bit quantity derived using the DES algorithm is to be attached to the end of each text. This four-byte quantity depends in a complex manner on all of the bits of the message. If any bit in the plaintext is altered, after the authentication is determined, or if a message is sent by someone unaware of the authentication key, then when the receiver deciphers and recalculates the authenticator, it will be obvious that a transmission error had occurred, or that an intruder was at work.

Encryption can be used without authentication, but how well this works depends on the nature of the cipher used. Many cipher algorithms are of the "key stream generator" type. An algorithm of this type is primarily a producer of a pseudorandom stream of keying bits, which are then XORed to the plaintext to produce the ciphertext. (DES can also be used this way in the output feedback mode.) No matter how complex the process that generates the key stream, the ciphertext is trivial to alter if one knows some plaintext. For example, suppose one believed the following cipher and plaintext equivalences hold:

Plain	Cipher
S	4D
1	61
.	A2
1	8C
0	77
0	AC
0	E3
•	53
0	04
0	71

The amount here can be altered without detection. To change the leading "1" to a "9" it is necessary to calculate what the key stream byte must have been and make the required replacement. Since the ASCII value of "1" is 31 then the key byte required must have been 31 XOR 61 which is 50. Thus, if we replace the cipher text byte 61 with 39 XOR 50, or 69, then this byte deciphers to the decimal value of "9." (See Exhibit 15.1.)

Exhibit 15.1
ASCII Cyphertext Replacement Example

Original

0011	0001 = 31
0110	0001 = 61
0101	0000 = 50

Altered

0011	1001 = 39
0101	0000 = 50
0110	1001 = 69

The use of a well-designed authenticator can prevent this type of attack, because the thief would not know how to change the authenticator to compensate for the change in the ciphertext.

The idea of text authentication is not new, even for the commercial world. The authentication systems of the past were primarily of the pencil and paper type, and these systems are still used. Shortly after World War I, the American cipher machine inventor Edward Hebern was promoting one of the first electromechanical cipher machines as a check authentication device. The famous cryptologist William Friedman designed an authentication system for Morgan Guaranty Trust of New York during the 1930s. Friedman's device, for which he was to be paid $25,000, was based on a system then in use for government communications. The system turned out to be a failure when one of the bank's employees solved the system in short order. (See Figure 15.1.)

Starting during the 1950s an increasing number of patents were filed in the United States and Europe for devices to perform authentication tasks that ranged from banking to controlling building access. Most of these systems were transparently simple to overcome, but, as more and more electronics came into play, methods of greater complexity evolved. By the mid-1960s most authentication methods being patented relied heavily upon traditional cryptographic practices.

DAY OF WEEK
TENS OF MILLIONS
MILLIONS
TENS OF THOUSANDS
THOUSANDS
HUNDREDS
UNITS
MONTH
FROM
TO

It is also possible that the need for authentication can be obviated by the use of certain types of ciphers. Algorithms that have an autokey feature actually offer a form of self-authentication. In an autokey cipher, the ciphertext or plaintext itself enters into the process of generating the message key, and so a change in either of these usually garbles at least some of the deciphered message. Such ciphers are of value when the communications line does not have a high error rate or when the transmitted ciphertext is further enclosed in error detecting and error correcting coding such as is commonly done in packet switching networks.

The DES Cipher

The major problem facing anyone interested in using cryptography is choosing from amongst many commercially available products. In 1985 there were roughly 60 firms in the world seriously involved in the sale and production of cryptographic devices and software. Of these, only a handful were in the United States, where emphasis was mainly on the Data Encryption Standard, or DES.

The decision of the U.S. government to promote the design of a public cryptographic algorithm in the 1970s has been a mixed blessing toward advancing the use of cryptography where it is increasingly needed in the private sector. At the direction of the government, the U.S. Bureau of Standards advertised in the *Federal Record* for a data encryption algorithm to be used for the protection of unclassified information. At the time there were increasing fears that much vital national information was being lost to foreign powers because of open and easily tapped U.S. communications media.

There was considerable interest on the part of academic and entrepreneurial persons in the subject of cryptology. Eventually, it was IBM who designed the resulting algorithm that is known as the Federal Data Encryption Standard (DES).

The DES algorithm has been the subject of controversy since its unveiling. First it was discovered that the National Security Agency (NSA) of the U.S. Defense Department had aided in the supposed "public" design of the cipher although this was denied at first. This realization gave rise to fears that the algorithm was being pushed on both government and public organizations because NSA wanted an algorithm in use that was reasonably strong but one that they themselves could break if need be. The relatively small key size of 56 bits reinforced this viewpoint.

Manufacturers were encouraged to produce and to promote the use of DES, especially in the growing electronic funds transfer field. The Bureau of Standards agreed to certify DES products, but only those produced in a hardware configuration.

Public Key Cryptosystems

The last decade has also seen the development of a novel type of cipher system, the public key cryptosystem. In a conventional cipher system the deciphering key for an algorithm is easily calculated given the enciphering key. In theory, it is possible to develop ciphers for which, even with the enciphering key known, the deciphering key is not readily determinable. These "asymmetric" cryptographic systems can be of great practical importance because they make the key management problem much simpler. Cryptographic networks can be set up in which the correspondents need not exchange cipher keys in advance. One such system, known for Rivest, Shamir, and Adleman, its authors, as the RSA public key system, is based on several elementary theorems of number theory. It is the subject of intense study, and may emerge as a widely used network protocol.

It is not yet clear what the role of public key cryptography will finally be because the algorithms that have been proposed all have disadvantages: encryption rates are exceedingly slow, the "public" keys are very large, and the protocols of using a system such as the RSA have not yet been worked out satisfactorily. It is possible to use public key systems to exchange cipher keys only, with the actual ciphering being done by conventional algorithms. There are currently several commercial products that use this approach.

Proponents of the public key approach usually argue that their cryptographic systems are safe because they are based on problems that are known to be difficult mathematically. The RSA algorithm depends on the difficulty of factoring large numbers, but the very example given in the initial description of the algorithm was solvable by a method not envisioned by the authors, that of "cycling."

Public key advocates as well as workers in the general field of cryptology may attempt to increase the security of a cryptographic system by repeated encryption. This means that the ciphertext is enciphered again as if it were plaintext. Both DES and public key systems have been advocated with this technique, but the idea that doing something twice improves security when one is not really sure of the security level in the first place, is not entirely convincing.

It does appear true at this time that the complexity of public key methods can limit their use, both in terms of analytical understanding and of encryption speed and key size. Nevertheless, public key concepts are too important to be discarded and it seems certain that public key cryptosystems will play an important role in future designs. Currently, however, caution dictates the use of conventional systems until the strengths and weaknesses of the newer systems are better understood.

NSA and the Public Sector

In October 1985, the National Security Agency announced plans to phase out its advocacy of DES in favor of a new and unique approach to public cryptography. The agency has launched a drive to "embed" cryptography into electronic communications within the United States. This will include allowing "trusted" companies to produce cryptographic chips for sale to qualified buyers. In order to make the whole matter practical, NSA says they will work with private industry to define I/O standards for the cryptographic chips so that they may be designed into new equipment and employed without expensive modifications and adjustments. As a first step, NSA has selected a number of private companies to develop a secure telephone system that can be used to encrypt both voice and data communications. The finished product is expected to cost about $2,000 a unit. One model of the telephone will be cellular in design. This system is ultimately to be used by some government agencies, private contractors who do government business, and by other "qualified" organizations who need the additional security.

In order to prevent the diffusion of cryptographic secrets, the cryptographic chips will be "reverse engineering proof." This means that someone having a chip will not be able to determine the algorithm used by that chip. The ciphers used on the chips are to have weak keys in the sense that certain choices of key will produce ciphertext that is easy to solve. Since the algorithms will be unknown to the user, the method of avoiding such bad key choices will not be known either. This will prevent nonqualified users who may obtain the chips from using them with any certainty of success. NSA will provide strong keys for those entitled to them, and some methods of generating such keys may be disclosed to selected users. Nothing about the exact nature of the cryptographic algorithms has been discussed by agency officials who consider this tantamount to giving away national security secrets. It appears that the RSA public key system may be used in some instances to exchange cryptographic keys between users.

Authority to expand its activities to such an extent was granted to NSA when President Reagan signed National Security Decision Directive Number 145 in September 1984. This directive was the result of growing concern about the threat to United States interests posed by the interception of American public communications by foreign powers.

What the outcome of NSA's new policy will be is difficult to determine. The overall level of cryptographic security achieved by this one-dimensional approach may fall short of what the agency wants. The algorithms cannot be expected to remain secret from those who have the time and money to pursue them. Private algorithm developers are to have no part in the new process.

While the new approach puts the government directly in competition with private algorithm designers, it does not obviate the need for private algorithms because NSA has publicly admitted that it possesses the ability to solve the ciphers created by these devices. Very probably, others will learn to do so as well.

Two major considerations may prevent the National Security Agency from enforcing this new approach as a replacement for the Data Encryption Standard. One is the immensity of the task required to maintain centralized control over such a system. The other is the possibility of overwhelming public disapproval of any cryptographic system designed and controlled by the Federal government, with all keys in its possession.

Toward Security

The process of setting up and using a cryptographic system calls for considerable study and forethought. Whether a proprietary system is to be designed or a commercial product installed, its strengths and weaknesses should be fully analyzed. In-house experts should be utilized if available, and if necessary private consultants should be employed to crosscheck and verify claims made by the vendor of the cryptographic system. An acceptable level of security can be achieved only if the decision process is carefully thought out and implemented.

There is no substitute for a thorough analysis of the need for cryptography and the uses to which it will be put. This should not merely be a matter of discussion but should be put into writing for comment and amendment by company personnel. Future uses as well as present needs should be given consideration, since planning during this phase of design will produce better, less expensive systems.

System selection should be based on the needs of the company, cost of implementation, and appropriateness of the solution. The methods for generating, distributing, and using cryptographic keys should be studied before a system is selected. Since the security of the keys is the most important cryptographic issue, a system of controls should be decided upon and risk assessment done of these controls. This process should be done in a realistic manner, and not by merely assuming a secure area with restricted access. The needs of specific company personnel for sensitive data must be determined with exactness. Otherwise, constant exceptions will be made, and the entire security structure endangered.

To use risk assessment properly, potential exposures must be identified along with the extent of the damage that could take place. The most likely threats to cryptographic security do not come from cryptanalysts but from the personnel using the system. Only after weak points in the system have been identified can one take corrective action. In most instances, the greatest risks arise from mismanagement of cryptographic keys. To a lesser extent, the risks involved depend on the sensitivity of the algorithm itself.

Penetration may be effected when a cryptographic unit is placed near a window allowing someone in an opposing building to view the keyboard entries being made, or to read the cipher keys directly. Electronic bugs can detect cryptographic information; the shrinking size and costs of such units make their use all the more probable. These methods and others have been used in the past and will continue to be used in the future to penetrate and circumvent security systems.

The monitoring of a cryptographic system can be partially automated. Generally speaking, attention has to be paid to prevent the use of keys that are nonrandom and easy to guess, or keys that are used repeatedly. The system itself, or an external computer program, can perform this function. The amount of data that are to be encrypted with one key can also be checked and controlled automatically by the operating system. A periodic report concerning system usage and keying data should be studied by responsible company personnel to verify that guidelines are being met and to detect trends that may require action. Auditing is an important part of system security. A log of failed access attempts should be examined daily to stop users who may be "playing" with the system, or attempting to find weak places in the encryption implementation.

Clearly defined lines of responsibility should be drawn in the operation and monitoring of a cryptographic system. This tends to make employees more conscious of system security and more dedicated to carrying out their own missions.

Finally, it would be advantageous if employees handling cryptographic assignments could be given formal education about the subject. This might include a general discussion of the history of the subject with the accent on mistakes made in the past, recent case histories of fraud or attempted crime involving security systems, and a general review of sound cryptographic practices. This type of experience can be very helpful in getting personnel started toward thinking about the need to maintain cryptographic security and the pitfalls to be avoided while doing so.

In summary, the process of introducing cryptography into a computer or communications system should consist of the following steps:

- *Define the problem.* Specify what is to be encrypted, encipherment rates needed, degree of security desired, volume of traffic to be enciphered, and, in the case of telecommunications, the transmission characteristics of the network that will be used.
- *Market survey.* Gather descriptions of commercially available products and proposals for proprietary algorithms. Reject those not meeting requirements previously established. Do not attempt to forcefit a system to the application.
- *Select the system.* A tentative choice as to the equipment or algorithms to be used can now be made. Select the simplest and most cost-effective device or algorithm that performs the required job.
- *Test the system.* This includes not only inquiring of the vendor or developer what algorithm testing has been done to insure the security of the cryptographic system but having company personnel use the proposed system if possible. It is not a good idea to accept statements about the security of any device or algorithm without seeing how these facts are backed up by testing. There are no standard tests that can determine the strength of a cryptographic algorithm, and only experienced personnel can be expected to have much feeling about where potential vulnerabilities may exist. In no case should any system be considered for purchase if the vendor refuses to disclose the details of the system. On the other hand, it is reasonable that a vendor ask for nondisclosure agreements and other legal protection before revealing any system details.
- *Configure the system.* Personnel selection and training, traffic management policies, site preparation, and key generation and distribution methods are to be worked out and implemented. Care must be taken that nothing in the handling of data or keys could compromise the cryptographic system used.
- *Install the system and institute monitoring.* During the early life of a cryptographic system, unforeseen problems will arise that require some adjustment in the established operating guidelines. Monitoring of traffic loads, keying procedures, and operational analysis should be conducted on an ongoing basis. The security of the system should be reviewed at periodic intervals to make certain that the level of security provided remains adequate.

Microcomputers

Cryptography can be of value for both stored data and for data in transit, involving computers of any size or power. The proliferation of the microprocessor has brought forth both the need and some of the means for cryptographic security on small systems.

There are a number of hardware and software devices and programs available whose security ranges from very good to negligible. Price has been found to be no guide in this regard. If a concern has, in fact, designed a reasonable product, then the methods used to test and verify the security of the product should be available to the potential purchaser. In many cases, little testing has been done, and the security offered by a product may not be worth the time and effort to install it. The algorithm itself should certainly be examined by knowledgeable experts before proceeding with any purchase agreements.

Well-designed products can offer security in telecommunications. Software encryption rates in the 20,000–40,000 bits/second range are achieved with current technology, while hardware rates are an order of magnitude faster, or even more.

With microcomputers as with mainframes, any encryption method will foil casual browsers, but not necessarily the knowledgeable, determined intruder. With or without encryption, the greatest threat to security lies not in faulty technology, but rather in the carelessness or venality of human beings. Questions may be raised about the "breakability" of the DES standard, or any other algorithm, but there can be no question about the ease with which a valid key can provide access to a secured system—whether that key is thoughtlessly left exposed or sold for personal gain.

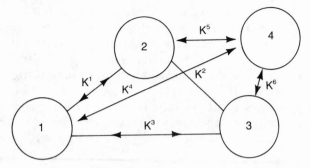

Figure 15.2 A fully connected, end-to-end network

The greatest efforts toward security should be directed at the human elements, rather than to technological measures.

Figure 15.2 shows a fully connected, end-to-end network. In this setup each pair of stations in the network has a unique master key for cryptographic communication. The number of keys required is $N(N-1)/2$ where N is the number of stations linked by the network.

A link encrypted network is shown in Figure 15.3. Each ciphered transmission is deciphered and reenciphered as it transverses a node. The minimum number of keys required is $N-1$, but this type of system is inherently weak since the solution of a single key will compromise all communications through the corresponding station.

Figure 15.4 shows a hybrid network. In this system there is communication between a large number of secondary stations and a single main station all using separate master keys. Similarly, a few main stations intercommunicate among themselves.

The central key distribution facility in Figure 15.5 is most useful when it is undesirable to entrust individual stations with control of cryptographic keys. Two stations wishing to communicate request a session key from the central station. The key generated by the central station is sent to each of the two stations, encrypted in each station's master key. The master key list is known only to the central station. Once the session keys are received the two stations can commence communications on their own.

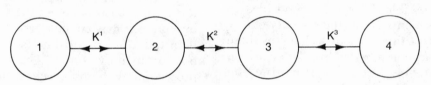

Figure 15.3 A link encrypted network

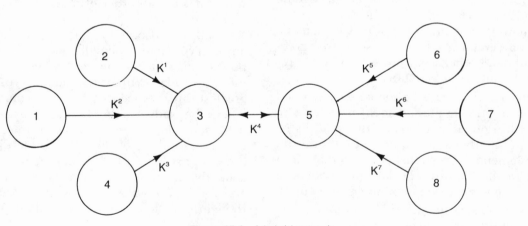

Figure 15.4 A hybrid network

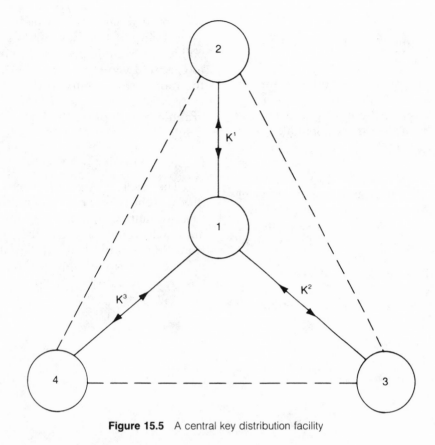

Figure 15.5 A central key distribution facility

Checklist

The decision of whether or not cryptography is desirable in a given situation is often most perplexing. The following list of questions should be carefully considered before embarking on this pursuit.

	Yes	No
Has a list been made and approved of the data to be protected and its characteristics?	☐	☐

For system-resident data this includes the number and size of files to be protected, the length of time protection will be needed, the level of security desired, and the frequency and method of access for file use. For telecommunications data, the same questions should be answered relative to use of the communications line.

	Yes	No
Have estimates been made of the financial value of each data item to be protected, and of the costs of protection?	☐	☐

Answers obtained in the procedure bring to light the cost-effectiveness of the entire process of cryptographic protection.

	Yes	No
Have the access groups who will be using cryptography been defined along with their relationship to one another?	☐	☐

In situations requiring a hierarchal system of access rights to certain files, multilevel cryptographic protection may be needed. Without knowledge of access groups, cryptographic systems cannot be examined realistically in view of company needs.

	Yes	No
Have physical security levels been evaluated?	☐	☐

If secure areas must be set up, can this be done? Is there any established access control mechanism for personnel entering and leaving such areas? Is physical security adequate?

	Yes	No
Is it possible to safeguard cryptographic keys?	☐	☐

Are there secure provisions for *distributing* and for *safeguarding* cryptographic master keys? Who will have ultimate access to the key lists and how will keys be provided for users of the system? How many keys will be required based on previous considerations about the level and amount of data to be protected? How will the required keys be generated and by whom? How often will keys be changed?

	Yes	No
Can the system be monitored?	☐	☐

Are there personnel available who will do the monitoring of the system? Is the expense and bother of assigning personnel to monitoring tasks too great? Even more importantly, to whom are the monitoring agents to report their findings? How can the presence of an inadequate cryptographic system prevent a false sense of security?

	Yes	No
Is there a simpler solution?	☐	☐

The essence of good business practice is to find the cheapest and most reasonable solution to a problem. Cryptography is often not the best approach to data security in a particular situation. Comparable time and effort expended in more conventional approaches may produce a faster, better, and less expensive degree of security.

Bibliography

For general reading about cryptology, the masterwork on the subject is David Kahn, *The Codebreakers*, New York: Macmillan & Co., 1967. This book is available in several different editions and languages.

A technical discussion of automated cryptography during the post–World War I era up to the early 1960s is Deavours and Kruh, *Cryptography and Modern Cryptanalysis*, Boston: Artech House Inc., 1985.

For a mathematical treatment of the subject of cryptology including a discussion of public key systems and recent work in the field of computer security, a good source is Dorothy Denning, *Cryptography and Data Security*, Reading, MA: Addison-Wesley, 1982.

Also see *NSA to Provide Secret Codes*, *Science* 4:230 (October 1985): 45–46.

CHAPTER 16

Data Communications Networks

By Lindsay L. Baird, Jr.

There has been significant growth in data communications recently, and there is every indication that this rapid growth will accelerate in coming years. Data communications networks—private and public—are employed in a multitude of applications, from accessing private and public data bases, transmitting data to and from hosts and remote terminals, electronic funds transfer, automatic teller machines, electronic banking, point-of-sales terminals, and a host of other applications. Just how safe and secure are these communications paths over which perhaps a trillion dollars or more pass every business day? Not too safe or secure in all too many instances.

There does not exist a complete solution to the numerous communications-related vulnerabilities that exist today, and certainly not to the vulnerabilities that can reasonably be expected to increase with tomorrow's technology. The purpose of this chapter is to acquaint the reader with some of the common exposures that both the private and public sectors fail to address adequately, and to describe a few examples of how computing systems have been manipulated remotely. Also briefly discussed are some of the difficulties experienced in identifying those individuals who have successfully gained unauthorized access to computing systems via communications networks. A number of approaches are described that can reduce these exposures.

Open System Interconnection (OSI) and Other Conventions

Telecommunications provide the electronic means for interconnecting systems users to exchange information with each other. The familiar telephone call is such an example. Today, there is a great need for interconnecting computers for the exchange of information among appropriate parties. If the user's equipment and interconnecting systems are all of the same manufacture and design, such communications should easily be realized.

In today's competitive world, however, there is a need for interconnection of systems with a wide range of design technology. When such systems can only communicate internally, they are *closed systems*, but when they wish to communicate externally, they must become *open systems*. The system user may require any sort of task from a simple file transfer to a very complex series of operations. In performing these tasks, application programs may need to communicate with other application programs to share information or to accomplish a larger task. In order to be able to communicate outside the local environment of the system performing the application program, a convention is needed to provide an environment that will facilitate communication among heterogeneous end-user systems. One such environment that is gaining support as a standard is the *open system interconnection*. Within the OSI environment, a standard architecture with associated interfaces and protocols is employed to provide the widest range of applications with the flexibility required for communicating in an effective and economical manner.

The International Standards Organization (ISO), the International Telegraph Telephone Consultative Committee (CCITT), and the International Telecommunications Union (ITU) are organizations that are either part of the United Nations (UN) or are supportive. They have developed a basic reference model defining standard architecture of an *open system interconnection* (OSI). The model provides:

- A universally applicable structure
- Standard specifications
- Compatible interconnections for communication programs
- Evolution of advanced technology into the future

It appears probable that the open system interconnection being formulated by the International Standards Organization and other organizations working on the problem will evolve as the worldwide standard. This assumption is based upon the fact that business and commerce today are international to a very large measure, and all those engaged in such activities must be able to transmit data among themselves. A common approach must be found, and that being developed under the direction of ISO has been accepted by most of our nation's trading partners.

There are other conventions in place that apply to transmission media, such as:

- Dedicated circuits
  - Point-to-point
  - Multipoint
- Switched networks
- Circuit-switched networks
- Packet-switched networks
- Virtual circuit service

Because a single international convention is necessary for efficient international data exchanges, these alternative conventions will be utilized only by those who do not have a need to move data across international borders, or they will be entirely replaced by the OSI standards.

No matter how or when standardization becomes universal, it is in the best interest of all users and data communication services to concern themselves with the vulnerabilities associated with audit, control, integrity, and security of data and systems. Some of these exposures are addressed in the pages that follow.

Microwave Communications

The air waves are not secure at all. A good portion of the nation's communications network consists of microwave transmitters and receivers scat-

tered on the high ground throughout the country. Each microwave link, usually no longer than 15 to 30 miles in length, consists of antennas, transmitters, receivers, repeaters, and associated equipment, employing highly directional, narrow beams of microwave radio energy. These microwave beams, traveling between the called and calling parties, can each carry data or voice communications.

Microwave carrier circuits operate at superhigh frequencies—normally in the order of four, six, or eleven gigaHertz (billions of cycles per second). On the other hand, ordinary AM broadcasting is transmitted in the 1000 kiloHertz range, while FM broadcasting, which was once considered very high frequency transmission, is down in the region of 100 megaHertz (one hundred million cycles per second).

Microwave data and voice channels share a band of frequencies by employing technology known as multiplexing. Every time a call is placed, a pair of multiplexed channels is utilized, one circuit in each direction. Communications cannot be initiated before a series of address codes are exchanged. This set of a dozen or so signals contains the high frequency beeping sounds heard while dialing a long distance call. The tones identify the called number and cause the switching equipment to establish a circuit with the called party. The technique of sending multifrequency address codes or tones over the same channel which will subsequently be utilized for data or voice communications is known as "in-band" signaling. This technology is the most widely used, but it is easily exploited by sophisticated interlopers.

Those engaged in industrial and international espionage find microwave communications easy to penetrate, as would any interested person. Electronic snooping into microwave circuits may be achieved at any point within the beam path. In addition, interception may be accomplished outside the beam path by a capture facility that is located near a microwave tower and in a position to pick up the spillover energy in the side lobes of the antenna. It is known that the Soviet Union is actively engaged in intercepting microwave data and voice communications at its Washington, D.C., embassy. This fact was reported in a *New York Times* article captioned "Soviet Monitoring Many Calls," dated July 10, 1977, and subsequently confirmed by the U.S. State Department.

A microwave communications capture facility can be established using available microelectronic technology, which is completely automatic, unmanned, and no larger than a typical high-fidelity receiver. The signal-capturing antennas do not have to be larger than an ordinary dinner plate, one facing in each direction, to capture both sides of the communication being intercepted. The capture equipment is configured to separate the respective communication circuits by a process of demodulation and demultiplexing. Each of the communications channels can be continuously scanned by the capture equipment, using a microcomputer to determine the presence of those multifrequency tone sequences that correspond to a targeted telephone number of particular interest.

The costs involved in capturing microwave signals are relatively low. The antennas required cost less than $500, and the complete microcomputer can be obtained for $5,000 or less. Because the technology is available to intercept microwave communications, both data and voice, at relatively low cost and with little risk of detection, it is realistic to assume that both international and domestic espionage benefit widely from these techniques.

Satellite Communications

The use of satellites for communications began in 1960 with the United States' launching of a passive repeater, Echo I. This satellite, which remained in orbit until 1968, relayed voice and television signals across the Atlantic Ocean between Andover in Maine, Goonhilly in England, and Bodou in France.[1]

Commercial satellite operation is considered by most to have begun with the passage of the Communications Satellite Act of 1962. This was followed by the establishment of the Communications Satellite Corporation (COMSAT), in 1963, the formation of the International Telecommunications Satellite Consortium (INTELSAT), in 1964, and the launching, in 1965, of the first satellite to provide commercial service. There are now a number of satellites orbiting the world that provide data, voice, and video communications.[2]

Satellite data communications, like standard microwave transmissions, are subject to capture by interlopers. The only difference is that the interloper requires more advanced equipment to sort out and capture the target signals. However, this can be accomplished with the aid of a microcomputer and a receiver dish. The cost would be about $2,000 for a 1½ meter dish antenna, plus, the cost of a microcomputer. The interloper must also have a parametric amplifier, microwave FM receiver, and a selective level meter. The time and cost involved in purchasing hardware and developing software for such an enterprise are certainly not prohibitive, considering the market value of transmitted data. A common example of capturing satellite signals involves the unauthorized reception of television programs by individuals at a total cost of $2,000 to $3,000. As sales and manufacturing volume increases, the costs for capture equipment can be expected to drop significantly. The ease with which satellite communications can be subverted was demonstrated, in 1986, when a hacker completely overrode cable television transmissions and substituted his own message, which was beamed to all subscribers.

Satellite communications are already widespread, and as time passes, even greater use will be made of satellite communications for data, voice, and video. It is known that many governments monitor international communications, and it is highly probable that commercial and industrial competitors are doing so as well.

Successful Penetrations

Potential exposures involve communications linkages, most configurations, user identification, systems access protocols, operating system vulnerabilities, and application program shortfalls. Communications linkage exists between traditional regulated suppliers such as the Bell systems, American Telephone & Telegraph, International Telephone & Telegraph, and services provided by overseas government-controlled systems such as Post, Telephone & Telegraph in

[1]The MITRE Corporation, Metrek Division, MITRE Technical Report, MTR-7439, Vol. II, "Study of Vulnerability of Electronic Communication Systems to Electronic Interception," 1977, pp. 43–94.

[2]Ibid.

Europe and Nippon Telegraph & Telephone in the Far East. In addition, there are a number of independent value-added data communications suppliers such as Telenet, Tymnet, Datapac, Europac, and Nippon Information Management Service.

For any linkage, it should be possible to grant unrestricted access or to establish a secure environment through a system of passwords and user identification. Where access is unrestricted, it is generally for the convenience of a group of users, such as students and faculty of a university who require generous amounts of computer time. In this case it is only necessary to check for exorbitant usages that might indicate business applications for private gain. Where access is not adequately restricted, entry is possible from any computer or computer terminal, anywhere in the world.

User identification and password protocols are the main approach employed for restricting system access. Unfortunately, many users who cannot commit their passwords to memory, write or tape them to their terminals where they can be appropriated by anyone. To avoid the necessity for doing this, some users select passwords that are very easily memorized. Individual initials, names of a spouse or child, and office telephone or extension numbers are frequently used. It is not at all difficult for hackers or those engaged in espionage (foreign or industrial) to breach systems employing such access protocols.

User IDs or application names, tend to be composed of organization initials (ABC Company) plus a suffix such as AP (accounts payable), AR (accounts receivable), INV (inventory), RD (research & development), etc. A hypothetical user ID might be constructed as ABCAP, ABCAR, ABCINV, and ABCRD.

Privileged Access

There are a number of individuals within any data processing installation who have privileged access authority. This authority permits those users to gain virtually unrestricted systems access. For example, the privileged access protocol for some computers consists of a three- to five-character user ID plus a password of one to six characters. The first character of the user ID indicates access authority. For example, "O" is re-

served for manufacturers or third party maintenance functions that require total access authority, and "1" (or any other single digit) is normally set aside for those with access to all systems facilities except maintenance functions. The second character in these access protocols is always a "," (comma), which in turn is followed by one or more numeric characters. Very often passwords are not employed, but a suffix is appended to the numeric, comma, numeric string that takes the place of password protocol. For example: The maintenance access protocol may be "0,1 MAINT" while the systems operator might employ "1,1 SYSOPN" or "1,1 OPNS". It only takes a little trial and error before one has taken complete control of the operating system and thus the entire computing system.

Some manufacturers have improved their operating system software to make unauthorized access more difficult. Unfortunately, not all users have upgraded their operating systems to the more secure later versions. The procedure with earlier systems is quite simple. With one system, for example, once a circuit has been established, the computer advises the terminal user what operating system is in use and then displays an "@" prompt. The user need only enter the following two lines following the "@" prompt:

- "LOGIN SYSTEM-ON"
- "MFD XXXXXX O"

This procedure places the user into the 0 platter of the disk resident operating system, which, in turn, provides direct access to all Master File Directories (MFD), associated User File Directories (UFD), and the individual passwords associated with each. Other computer hardware manufacturers' systems can also be accessed remotely, by using a factory-installed universal access protocol or by attacking the privileged access account structure.

Many organizations restrict user access to specific data bases; others take a more open approach concerning access authority. A computer system is a tool that is designed and set in place to facilitate employee productivity and to make timely and accurate information available to managers at all levels. However, in many instances the "need for access" principle is not followed, which results in people without a need to know having access to sensitive information. All organizations should go through the process of determining just who requires systems access, what portions of the data base they need to interface with, and the systems facilities (read, write, change, or delete) each user should be authorized to employ.

Telephone Access

Determining the origin of an attempted or actual break-in is almost impossible when the call is made by a dial-up unit using either standard telephone lines or a value-added network (VAN) gateway node. A VAN gateway node is actually a computer located near a group of users to provide access to a particular VAN. For these calls there is no record maintained by the telephone company, and the originator cannot readily be traced.

A dial-up terminal can consist of a microcomputer, minicomputer, mainframe, or even a pushbutton telephone. The one common element each must have is a modem (modulator–demodulator) —an electronic device that translates a computer or terminal digital output into an analog format that can be transmitted over standard telecommunications facilities in one direction, and then reformats the signal back into digital representation at the receiving end. Both the calling and receiving equipment must have this type of signal conversion equipment in place.

Dial-up communications, unlike leased or dedicated lines, establish a link simply by dialing a telephone number that is connected to a computer access port. Hackers and others involved in unauthorized access generally use dial-up facilities rather than attempting to tap into dedicated lines. Dial-up linkages present two major problems. First, the called host has no idea where the calling computer or terminal is located unless the call is made collect. There is little chance of this occurring if a hacker or espionage agent is involved. Second, there is a very low probability that an unauthorized user can be tracked down via call-tracing equipment. This is a very complex and expensive task to accomplish, and communication providers will not undertake a call-tracing project unless theft of services is obvious and the victim is committed to bringing charges against the interloper.

Dial-up vulnerability can be countered in several ways. Many portable terminals have imbedded in their read-only memory (ROM) a unique terminal identifier—normally a unit serial number and other data elements. This unique terminal identifier can be recorded in the host normally accessed. If the terminal involved has a "HERE IS" key, the host or communications front end will request that the "HERE IS" key be depressed, thus transmitting the unique terminal identifier for validation against the recorded authorizations. Some organizations employ a call-back protocol in which a calling terminal transmits its identifier to a host. The connection is then automatically disconnected, and the receiving host dials a preestablished telephone number at which the identified and authorized user is located. This technique cannot be used by traveling salespeople or executives who cannot call from predetermined locations. The "HERE IS" key, built into a portable terminal, and a password are best employed for these situations.

Access via value-added network (VAN) facilities poses similar identification problems when such services are entered via a local node. VAN services have installed many hundreds, perhaps thousands, of local gateway nodes for dial-up users. Most are accessed via non-toll charge telephone numbers—the call to a node in most instances is "free" and the local telephone company has no record of the time and place of origin. Once a user has access to a gateway node, it is a relatively simple matter to communicate with any host, even one that accepts collect calls, without leaving a trace.

The identity of a remote systems user is just as difficult to determine when a communications service such as Sprint or MCI is employed. Dial-up access is gained normally via the local telephone company which provides the linkage from a personal computer to some other carrier's gateway node. Once in this node, the user simply addresses the desired remote host and the circuit is established. In this situation the communications network can identify the gateway node through which the circuit was initiated, but they can identify only the area code, not the actual phone number employed to access the gateway node. It is possible to further mask the identity and location of unauthorized users by employing two or more individual networks in establishing a simple circuit. In an actual incident involving this approach, a computing system of a large Canadian corporation was accessed by an unauthorized user and the data bases were maliciously damaged or destroyed one-by-one. In all, approximately 70 percent of the on-line files were affected. Fortunately, many of the files and data bases were in a backup storage facility, but not all. An unsuccessful attempt was made to backtrack through the communications networks employed to determine where the calls were initiated. It was learned that the perpetrator utilized three networks (Telenet, Tymnet, and finally Datapac) and a gateway node somewhere within the United States to establish this circuit. Records available at the value-added networks were of little value, and the perpetrators were never identified or apprehended.

A recent study provides an excellent example of how those engaged in industrial espionage, as well as "hackers," develop clever methodologies for gaining free communications and unauthorized access to unsuspecting target hosts. The methodology described in the following paragraphs was employed by many unauthorized users, perhaps thousands, over a period of five or more years without detection.

The U.S. Department of Agriculture (USDA) leased a TP4000 terminal concentrator from Telenet, which was installed in Las Vegas, Nevada. There were four IN WATS "800" telephones that could access this gateway node. The facility was intended to be utilized by USDA field personnel, such as the Forest Service and others, to input data and access data bases maintained on hosts in Kansas City, Missouri. That set of hosts, as well as USDA hosts in Fort Collins, Colorado, Beltsville, Maryland, and several contractor facilities, would accept collect calls from dial-up as well as host-to-host users. The assigned Telenet identification address of the Las Vegas terminal concentrator was "702 28". The "702" represents the telephone area code for Las Vegas as well as the rest of the state, while "28" was the unique computer identifier. Dial-up terminals as well as hosts gained access via the "800" numbers and then went on to place collect calls to other unsuspecting victims. VAN circuit connection protocols are different from those employed by local and international telephone service providers, they are not like the standard telephone number protocol which consists of ten numbers (area code—3 digits; exchange—3 digits; and individual number—4 digits).

Hackers and other unauthorized users, specifically those engaged in industrial espionage, became aware of the USDA "800" IN WATS telephone numbers. Possibly these telephone numbers were first obtained by hackers employing "War Games Dialers" (programs that automatically dial all 10,000 phone numbers in a particular telephone exchange, 800 or otherwise, recording those numbers that provide a computer carrier tone) who then posted their findings on computer bulletin boards. The USDA did not change their "800" numbers even once during the years that they had been in place. No doubt many other users of similar IN WATS service have not changed their "800" numbers over the years. Considering normal turnover of data processing, communications and other professionals in any organization, it is certain that many former employees and others have knowledge of specific communication linkages that can provide unauthorized access to a substantial number of hosts throughout the country, and even internationally.

In the case of the USDA, it was determined that unauthorized access to the Las Vegas switch was being made from some 35 to 40 area codes within the United States. It took a great deal of time and effort on the part of all concerned (the victim, USDA, AT&T Long Lines, many regional Bell Telephone Companies, and other communications network services) to gather this limited amount of information. It would have taken an inordinate amount of manpower, time, and equipment to track these unauthorized users through to telephone branch exchanges (the first three digits in the local telephone number) and then down to the specific line (the last four digits of a telephone number).

The perpetrator's approach for obtaining free communications and computer usage was quite simple. One of the USDA IN WATS "800" numbers was used to gain access to the Telenet TP4000 in Las Vegas—the U.S. government paid for that circuit linkage. Next, a collect call was placed to a host in New Jersey. Once the perpetrators were in the New Jersey host, they immediately executed a prepaid NETLINK using the intermediate host as a switch, in order to move on to another host. The New Jersey facility was paying for both the communications linkage from Las Vegas to New Jersey and from New Jersey to the target host.

In the aforementioned case, the perpetrators, when their activities were completed, did not logoff the system—they simply executed a "hang-up" that broke the circuit. The net result was that a login/logout history record was not created. The only internal records that would show that the New Jersey host had been used as an intermediate switch were the console log and the monthly Telenet billing tape. The former is not normally subjected to detailed review unless a systems problem is encountered, while the latter was difficult to interpret in the form provided by the carrier.

Figure 16.1 provides a visual presentation of the communication linkages that were exploited by unauthorized users in attacking unsuspecting and inadequately safeguarded hosts throughout the country. Some 247 banks including the Federal Reserve, Bank of America, Wells Fargo, and Citibank, as well as Edunet, Arparnet, numerous manufacturing and engineering concerns, hospitals, transportation companies, various government agencies (including the Pentagon), and many other computer systems were illegally accessed on a regular basis. It is possible that many of these organizations are still being exploited, although the USDA has dismantled their Las Vegas TP4000 switch.

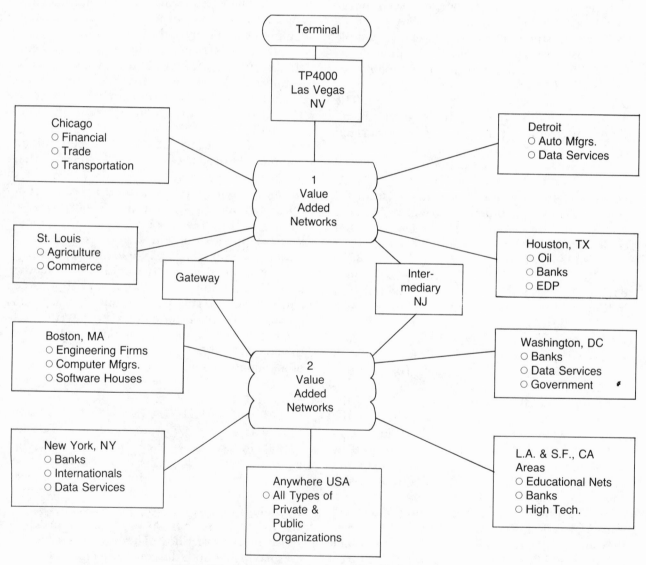

Figure 16.1 Value Added Networks Call Tracking Vulnerabilities

In another case, a computer manufacturer had its research and development, marketing, maintenance, and business systems penetrated by competitors and others. These unlawful systems accesses had been going on undetected for a number of years, with ultimate costs to the company in the millions of dollars. This particular victim, once made aware of the problem, corrected existing deficiencies and took one perpetrator to court charging theft of R&D data concerning a new piece of hardware then being marketed. This firm is now one of the most security-conscious companies in the United States, and a by-product of their unfortunate experiences has been the incorporation of their concerns into the design of their computer product line.

Breaking into Systems

Gaining unauthorized systems access via telecommunications circuits is easy when proper network controls are not in place. Apart from communications, there are many ways that the security of the computing system itself may be threatened. Computers, when shipped from manufacturers, have embedded within them one or more standard initialization and maintenance access protocols. Not many end users question the existence of such protocols—in fact, many do not know that they exist. Most mainframe and minicomputer suppliers offer clients maintenance contracts, or the client can obtain similar service from a third-party maintenance company. Many maintenance diagnostic functions, as well as operating systems upgrades, are accomplished remotely. The suppliers of these services generally employ the protocols embedded in the systems when they were manufactured. Maintenance personnel need complete unrestricted access to a system if they are to perform their job properly. This includes the ability to get into the operating system and all utilities. They need to be able to bypass all systems audit, control, integrity, and security features, in order to troubleshoot or perform maintenance.

In addition to maintenance access protocols, manufacturers normally ship systems with one or more general access protocols embedded that permit direct systems access, bypassing whatever user logon and password protection features may have been installed. Several common commands encountered include:

- LIST
- SYS
- SYSTEM
- SYSTEMS
- TEST

All manufacturers provide software packages that enable the hardware to function as intended. There are fairly frequent changes made to the operating system (OS) and to restricted and non-restricted utility programs. However, it is the so-called restricted utilities that are of primary concern. They are the standard tools utilized by systems programmers and other personnel in the performance of their technical systems-related tasks. Examples of restricted utilities include:

- IBM
  —Data Interfile Transfer, Testing & Operations (DITTO)
  —Superzap
  —Patch
  —Data File Utility (DFU)
  —Alter/Display
- BURROUGHS
  —Amend
  —Modify
  —Data Control System (DCS)
- DEC
  —Patch
  —SOS Editor
  —Primer
- HONEYWELL
  —Edit/Testedit
- PRIME
  —File Utility (FUTIL)
  —Direct Disk Editor
  —Edit
- HEWLETT PACKARD
  —Stand Alone Diagnostic Utility (SANDU-TIL)
  —Patch

There are many other utilities associated with these and other hardware manufacturers that present avenues of attack.

Communications Billing Records

Both public telephone and value-added networks forward monthly billing tapes or a printed bill listing all calls placed or accepted during a particular billing cycle. Unfortunately, billing records are often too voluminous for easy study and, in any event, often lack information about specific identification of the calling party.

Perpetrators often use IN WATS (800 toll-free numbers). Many organizations install such service for applications such as on-the-road salespersons to enter their daily orders directly into a central computer system. Telephone company billings normally only give hours of usage and in some cases they will provide usage data concerning a geographical area. There is no simple way that an organization can determine who is accessing their systems and from what particular telephone number.

Hackers seek to obtain a carrier tone as they browse through the various IN WATS (800) exchanges throughout the country. "War Games" is a term they use when referring to the use of a simple program (normally written in BASIC) that automatically dials all 10,000 possible numbers associated with any particular exchange. The program is so structured that whenever a carrier tone is obtained a notation is made that contains the full telephone number of the host concerned. A complete scan of 10,000 numbers can be automatically accomplished in between 15–20 hours employing a 300 baud modem, or approximately one-third the time when a 1200 baud modem is used. War Gaming is very common, and the successful results of any one hacker's efforts are flashed through the country via a comprehensive network of hackers' bulletin boards.

Common Vulnerabilities

General
Data communications facilities and interface protocols were developed and implemented before concerns about computing systems audit, control, integrity, and security were raised. Data communication networks were designed to make their use as easy as possible—just as some computing systems, utilities, and application programs are made "user-friendly." Unfortunately, ease of access applies to both authorized and unauthorized personal systems access. Where controls are inadequate, access may even be obtained through accidental misdialing.

Communications providers such as AT&T, IT&T, local telephone operating companies, MCI, GTE Sprint, Western Union, Satellite Business Systems, Telenet, Tymnet, Datapack, and Europack are only concerned with providing the communications linkage from one point to another. They are not responsible for the privacy or security of the information being transmitted between points—that remains the exclusive domain of network users.

Former Employees
It is quite common in both the private and public sectors for employers not to revoke systems access rights when an employee is terminated. The main cause for this omission is the lack of coordinated control policies. It would be prudent to have a notation included in every employee's personnel record that details what systems access authority may have been granted and by whom. One method that has been quite effective is to require as a routine part of any employee outprocessing, transfer, or promotion, to contact the employee's current department head and insure that systems access authority has been voided. Those organizations that have in place systems security administrators or security departments should be required to record and control access authority, at initial employment and upon employee transfer or termination.

It is not uncommon for organizations to establish universal access protocols. One victim of massive loss of very sensitive and valuable information had established common systems access protocols for its R&D network. Once communications was established between the called and calling parties, the perpetrator only needed to enter "GUEST" or "MOXIE" at the appropriate prompt to gain access to all systems facilities. This victim learned a lesson the hard way and only after it had sustained losses of many millions of dollars. Many of this firm's employees had changed jobs during the course of years, most going with competitors, and yet no one gave any thought to the vulnerabilities that are associated with standard and unchanged universal access protocols.

Many organizations utilize direct digital dial (DDD) facilities for employees to communicate with computing systems. It is common for firms to have their sales staff call in at the end of a business day and directly communicate orders into a central system. Another practice employed by many organizations is to permit data processing technical personnel, managers, and other employees systems access from their homes after normal business hours. This practice, while of benefit in some ways, may be costing the organization a great deal in unauthorized and fraudulent activities. Most organizations do not know what actually constitutes their specific network configuration, or exactly who is authorized systems access.

Network Shortfalls

Value-added networks have a number of built-in vulnerabilities. Perhaps the most serious is their inability to identify the precise telephone number utilized to access one of their gateway nodes. Local access numbers permit someone to connect with the local access node without being recorded by the local telephone company. This lack of record is a major cause of concern. A person can access these networks and the only information victims will be able to discern from their monthly billings is that someone accessed their systems via a public access node from some geographical area and that their organization paid for the communication linkage.

Corporate and Individual Responsibility

Most victims of computer-related crime are not willing to prosecute. The victims are often concerned that stockholders will find out that the organization has not been able to protect their assets. Since officers and directors of public companies are obliged to exercise due diligence and prudence in safeguarding corporate assets placed in their custody, they may be individually liable for suit and payment of damages up to three times the actual loss. For this reason, it is rare that a notation appears in reports to stockholders that a reduction in earnings was the direct result of computer abuse or criminal activity. Such losses are usually hidden and included as either administrative, sales, or operating expenses.

Systems Programmers

Trained technical employees are in great demand at hardware manufacturers, software development firms, and user installations. The frequent turnover of systems programmers and other highly skilled employees produces serious exposure whereby significant amounts of proprietary information may move within a firm as well as from one firm to another.

To minimize the likelihood of technical employees revealing proprietary information to competitors, using such information for their own purposes, or possibly even causing damage intentionally, the following actions are recommended:

- Use care and thorough checks to secure honest and reliable employees.
- Obtain signed commitments from employees not to disclose sensitive data to unauthorized persons, during and subsequent to employment. What is sensitive should be clearly defined.
- Delete access codes of departing employees as soon as they leave.

Hardware Maintenance Personnel

Maintenance service for computer equipment is provided by hardware manufacturers, by third party maintenance companies, and by in-house personnel. With any of these, there is a substantial risk to be guarded against. Maintenance technicians have the power, inadvertently or through intent, to destroy or alter records, files, or an entire data base. A basic preventive measure is to change the computer manufacturer's universal maintenance protocol. Maintenance personnel should, as all others, be allowed to gain systems access only with the specific authority of the operations manager and systems security officer.

A great deal of systems troubleshooting is being done remotely at central diagnostic facilities utilizing telephone lines for communications linkage and the "super user" systems access protocol. Personnel providing these remote services do not always advise operations managers when they will access a system, nor are the users immediately aware of changes that have been made. Here, too, the potential for inadvertent or intentional misuse is great. Audit, control, security, and integrity of existing systems have often been of lesser concern than developing new applications.

Hackers

There are actually three general groups that engage in hacking—*hackers*, *crashers*, and *phone phreaks*. For the most part, they are young, bright, and technically oriented. Some are thrill seeking, some simply curious, and others enjoy the challenge of "beating" access controls on computers and data communications network systems. All three groups pose serious threats to both the private and public sectors.

Hackers for the most part are not intentionally destructive. The vast majority of them are teenagers and young college students. Their main objectives are to gain unauthorized systems access, utilize systems facilities such as storage and computational power, and find out what the data bases contain. They are also looking for systems that accept collect calls. Many systems have games resident in them—Star Wars is an excellent example. The hackers will spend hours playing these games at no personal expense. Although most hackers try not to cause damage, there have been cases where they have inadvertently crashed systems as they move through data bases—a costly accident as far as the victim is concerned.

Crashers tend to be older than hackers and a step above them in technical skills. Their basic intention is to gain unauthorized systems access and to deliberately crash the system, accomplishing as much damage as possible.

In one instance, a crasher wove his way through three different value-added networks before striking the target host in Canada. He or she destroyed approximately 70 percent of the on-line systems data base, in addition to modifying the operating systems. The perpetrator created a great deal of havoc and adversely affected company operations. Fortunately, the company had a large portion of its data bases backed up, although not all; they had to expend a substantial amount to recreate those destroyed data bases.

Phone-phreaks in general engage in the same activities as the other two groups. Most are electronic whiz kids who are experts in both computer and telecommunication technology. Their primary ambition is to obtain "free" data and voice communications from local Bell companies, AT&T, IT&T, and VANs. Phreaking first became an organized activity in 1971, when West Coast students decided to beat the phone companies out of what they considered to be outrageous charges for service. They were quite successful in that goal with the development of the blue, black, yellow, red, gray, and other electronic boxes that simulate the electronic tones made as a call is routed. One telephone company alone estimated that it lost about $130 million in revenue during 1984 owing to such theft of services.

Electronic Bulletin Boards, known as BBSs, started springing up in the mid to late 1970s with the introduction of personal computers and modems at affordable prices. Many BBSs were set up by user groups to legally pass electronic information about specific microcomputers, their operating systems, software, application programs, and games. However, many others were set up to pass along information pertaining to hacking, crashing, and phreaking. It is these latter groups that are of concern from a security point of view.

Hackers received a great deal of notoriety durng late 1984 and afterward. The 414 group, a number of bright, young high school students operating out of area code 414 (Milwaukee, Wisconsin), were virtually lionized by the media and, to a lesser extent, by the U.S. Senate, overlooking the fact that these young people are actually felons. They deliberately accessed and modified data bases at government contractor facilities in Los Alamos, New Mexico, as well as the Sloan-Kettering Medical Center in New York City. Just how many other hosts they improperly accessed is not known, but the number may be substantial. A few excerpts from a 125-foot long listing dumped from a New York BBS provided some insight as to what was being freely passed around. In the following listing, real numbers have been replaced with others randomly selected:

Item: About TELENET Numbers
From: (Name deleted)
To: ALL CALLS
Here are a few TELENET numbers to try for some fun and games. You will have to figure out password codes for yourself in most cases. Just dial your local TELENET switch, then try one of the following:
—C 46322 American Express Company (Type Command "Information")
—C 86743 Newsnet 75
—C 732140 "DPVM"
  I don't know what this means
—C 46721 SLVAX 1 "Ditto"
—C 46743 Credit Information Time Sharing
—C 68921 American Hospital Supply
—C 41342/66 TRAVENOL Systems A/B
—C 38492 (Here's a good one for you!!)
—C 86791 Alternate Network
  **Acct: 4200-8888 Password "AID" to read

the help files. This is an international system a lot like TELENET serving England, Australia, etc. and the code shown here is the interchange between them and TELENET. Of course, the number and password is a "DEMO" for new clients on their systems. In addition these have local access numbers in local communities: see the section on 'local access' above.

—C 86720 Stanford University WYLBUR System. Answer with HX.GST, account number, and no password is required.

In future messages, I shall discuss more TELENET numbers if anyone is interested, plus, similar items from DATANET, the Canadian 'cousin' to TELENET.

Item: Interesting Phone Numbers
From: (Name deleted)
To: All Calls
Here are some interesting phone numbers for you to try out—
—Chicago (312) 482-7600
    University of Illinois
    (Circle) Computer Room
—Chicago (312) 444-7000
    Quaker Oats Company
—Chicago (312) 872-8787
    Argonne National Labs
    You come in on a BBS "front."
    Log in as follows to break the BBS and access the 420-
    (F) CHARLEY
    (L) Hornaday DEPARTMENT AI
    Then on BBS you can break out if you check the menu and use your instincts.
—Colorado (303) 877-6482
    A good phreak board in the Rockies!!.
—Manhattan (212) 412-6220
    Account # 320,200
    Password "DALTON", it will ask you to attach to an open job. Use number shown.

These are only two messages out of a total of 218 messages contained on this one bulletin board, and there are many similar BBSs throughout the country.

Hacker BBSs have more security built into their individual and collective systems than most corporations. An individual BBS may serve hackers, crashers, and phone phreaks, with a specific access security level assigned for each category of user. Within each category there may be as many as ten sublevels of security. Access is most restrictive in the better BBSs, especially those that have available what is considered to be sensitive information.

The authorization required to obtain the messages quoted earlier was level 4 of 8 access levels. Before access rights are given to users on BBSs containing sensitive information, it is common practice for the SYS OPS to require two references (other hackers known to the BBS), a voice line (telephone) number, a real name, a network "handle," home address, and a few other personal facts. The SYS OPS on the more notorious BBSs will not grant anything but the lowest level 1 access authority, granting only the ability to read and post general interest items, until known and trusted hackers have been queried and responded with favorable reports. Hacker bulletin boards are often more secure than the operating systems of either the private or public sectors.

The Federal Bureau of Investigation, U.S. Secret Service, local telephone companies, value-added networks, and some corporations often try to gain access to BBSs in order to monitor their activities, with some success. During the spring of 1985 six of the more notorious BBSs were put out of action, including Sherwood Forest, Crypton, and Crypton 2. Much more work has to be accomplished before these threats are eliminated, or even substantially reduced.

When apprehended for running a BBS that receives, stores, and transmits sensitive information, young hackers receive little if any punishment. Sometimes their computing systems are confiscated, and they are placed on some form of probation. Older hackers also have little to fear when apprehended. Most states do not have criminal statutes that adequately address this type of activity, and those that do tend to treat such offenses as either minor crimes or low level felonies. A case in point is that pertaining to the former hacker, known as Captain ZAP, who now is employed as a computing systems security consultant.

Captain ZAP was arrested along with five or six other young men, all in their early twenties, in 1982. They had gained unlawful access to the business systems computer of a public data base service provider. Once in that system they read more than 1,800 valid Visa account numbers, holders' names, credit limits, and their associated expiration dates. Using this purloined information, they ordered and received some $351,000 worth of microcomputer hardware, which they charged to these stolen account numbers before they were caught. Only Captain ZAP was charged, as he was considered the central figure by state and federal authorities. His punishment consisted of a $1,000 fine, three years probation, ten hours of community service per week during the probation period, and the confiscation of his personal computer system. Fortunately, all but a few thousand dollars worth of the unlawfully gained hardware was recovered. How many unreformed hackers are still at work is not known, but the number is assuredly large and growing.

Although there are many vulnerabilities and exposures that can adversely affect the integrity and security of data processing and associated telecommunication systems, relatively simple steps can be taken to provide a high degree of security at modest cost. There are also a number of relatively complex and costly approaches to problem resolution that can be explored. The important points to keep in mind when considering systems protective measures are the value of the data, as measured by the criticality of the continued and unadulterated availability to the organization. The best approach to determining an organization's network security needs is one in which management applies the rules of reasonableness and prudence. Risk analysis, as described in another chapter, may provide a practical means for evaluating exposures and developing countermeasures in most data processing environments. There are always exceptions as data processing systems configuration, telecommunications, and associated networks are not identical in most instances. As a minimum, each organization should closely monitor and control its network and systems users, its network configurations, the physical locations of hardware, user access authorization, user IDs, and passwords.

Vulnerabilities associated with easily interrupted microwave and satellite transmission systems are a matter of special concern. For all data communications, the best approach available is data encryption. There are a number of hardware manufacturers that have incorporated the U.S. Bureau of Standards recommended Data Encryption Standard (DES) in terminal, host, and interface equipment.

There is a major administrative problem associated with any data encryption system. While the encryption algorithm may be in the public domain, as is the DES, it is the security of key changes (daily, weekly, monthly, or quarterly) that needs to be addressed. Encryption keys need to be changed with some regularity, and their values must be maintained under strict security at all times.

A communications front end controller is a practical and cost-effective approach to reduce unauthorized systems access. This hardware device and associated software stands between the host and the communication circuits. Resident in the unit are the identity of all authorized systems users, VAN address numbers, telephone numbers for dial-up terminal users, and related data. This facility can be greatly enhanced by incorporating circuit-break and call-back features. In this instance, an incoming call goes through normal access protocol. The front end controller does a table lookup on the user ID, breaks the communication circuit, then automatically redials the registered official telephone or network address number and reestablishes the circuit. Although this creates an added expense for communications, it is a fairly foolproof method of insuring that all callers are authorized system users.

Traveling salespeople and others who are required to access systems while moving from place to place can be identified by user ID and password, while the portable terminals they are using can be identified by a specially transmitted electronic signature. A number of portable terminal manufacturers install unique electronic signatures in ROM (read only memory) of each terminal. This electronic signature normally consists of the unit's serial number, which is transmitted automatically by pressing the "HERE IS" key. The signature for each portable terminal is registered at the front-end controller or host. At the time of LOGIN, the terminal transmits its electronic signature to the front-end controller or host, where it is compared with that on file. This validation, plus proper user ID and password, provides proof that the terminal is authorized systems access.

Frequent changes of user IDs and passwords help provide greater systems security. Passwords should consist of at least six alpha-numeric characters. The use of names, birth dates, and similar easy to remember items should be avoided. Passwords, as well as user IDs, need to be changed not less than quarterly and upon the transfer, promotion, or termination of any employee who had systems access. It is not uncommon for employees to share or otherwise acquire knowledge of each other's access protocol. This should be forcefully discouraged.

Microcomputers

In recent years many high schools and some elementary schools have added computer literacy to their curricula, while a number of colleges have even required that entering freshmen be equipped with a personal computer and modem. Technological education in data processing is certainly desirable, but it is equally important to instill a social conscience that reflects the impact improper use of computers and communications can have upon society. There are hundreds of Captain ZAPs in the country, and indeed throughout the world, all playing with corporate or governmental computing systems. In addition to a large number of microcomputers in school networks, it has been estimated that at the end of 1984 between two and three million personal computers were equipped with modems that permit them to communicate with other computers of all types. In time, microcomputers with communications capabilities may be as common in America as the radio, telephone, and television. The increased installation of cable television service throughout the country provides a natural medium for transmission of data among homes, banks, retail businesses, credit card services, stockbrokers, and a host of other organizations.

The ability of computers to communicate with one another has had a very positive impact on both the private and public sectors. Increased speed and efficiency will continue to be incorporated into data communications equipment in the future, as costs continue to decline. However, communications capabilities in the hands of some personal computer owners have been put to unlawful use. The losses from their unlawful activities have been staggering. A home owner in northern New Jersey received a monthly telephone bill in the amount of $197,587.54. His AT&T credit card number had been flashed around the country via the BBS (bulletin boards) networks in a matter of hours. During the next 20 days the hackers completed long-distance telephone calls all over the world. It is estimated that telephone service providers during 1984 lost some $300 million in revenue as a result of unlawful telephone use.

The illicit uses to which microcomputers can be put is limited only by the imagination and the ethics of their owners.

Protective Measures

Although there are many vulnerabilities that can adversely affect data processing systems' integrity, communications, and security, relatively simple steps can provide a high degree of security at modest cost. There are also a number of relatively complex and costly approaches to problem resolution that can be explored if warranted. The important points when considering protective measures are the value of the data, and the criticality of their continued and unadulterated availability to the organization. The best approach to determining network security needs is one in which management applies the rules of reasonableness and prudence.

Many organizations do not truly know the scope of their network configuration. That is, who are authorized network and system users, what is their equipment configuration, physical location of both the hardware and users, user access authorizations, user IDs and passwords? This information must be recorded and maintained in a current state, as a first step in developing network and systems security requirements.

Those organizations utilizing 800 (IN WATS) service that provide direct access to their computing systems need to give thought to changing their 800 number from time to time. True, hackers can war games an exchange in less than a day using a dialer program—at no communications expense to them. Yet, it would be prudent for organizations, based upon the sensitivity of information resident in or on systems, to eliminate their 800 numbers or at least have them changed from time to time. This, of course, creates extra expense; however, the extra expense may well be justified based upon information sensitivity and the impact compromise, damage, alteration, or loss of data may have upon an organization.

Summary

The cost of data processing systems and associated communications facilities has come down in price significantly in the past 10 years; there is every indication that this trend will continue. At the same time computational power has been increased significantly. Many new communication (data and voice) providers have entered the marketplace. The favorable price performance ratio has encouraged organizations to put in place computer systems with both internal and external communication systems. The introduction of the microcomputer has not only made it possible for organizations to provide employees access to host resident data bases, it also provided a large segment of the general population with that same ability, enabling access by the hacker communities as well as those engaged in espionage.

Many organizations in both the private and public sectors have not recognized the vulnerabilities communication systems present concerning their data processing environments. It has been the intent of this chapter to describe these exposures and approaches for eliminating or at least reducing unauthorized systems access via communication linkages.

Data Communications Checklist

	Yes	No
Are sensitive data encrypted or otherwise protected when transmitted between separated facilities via land lines, value-added networks, microwave, or satellite communications?	☐	☐
Are network configurations specifically defined with the identity and location of authorized system specified, and information pertaining to them maintained current?	☐	☐
Are monthly data communications billings compared against the network configuration authorized users?	☐	☐
Are systems console logs reviewed in detail daily for any suspect activity—both external and internal?	☐	☐

	Yes	No
Do user IDs and passwords consist of both alpha and numeric characters?	☐	☐
Are all user IDs and passwords changed at least quarterly?	☐	☐
Are all user IDs and passwords within a functional organizational element changed whenever an employee is transferred to another department or terminated?	☐	☐
Are dial-up port telephone numbers changed on some scheduled basis?	☐	☐
Is it required that all portable terminals be configured with factory-installed ROM (read only memory) unique electronic identifiers?	☐	☐
If the above is not required, then does the system automatically break a dial-up connection after user identification and call the user back at a predetermined telephone or value-added network address number?	☐	☐
Is it required that privileged systems access authority protocols be changed at least quarterly and whenever an employee with such access is terminated or transferred to another department?	☐	☐
Are computer manufacturer-installed access protocols changed, such as those used by maintenance personnel, remote diagnostic facilities, and others?	☐	☐
Are one-time systems access protocols issued each time manufacturer or third party hardware maintenance is required?	☐	☐
Is all systems access authority based upon the principle of "need for access"?	☐	☐
Are confidential personal, proprietary, or otherwise sensitive data, records, files, and data bases defined and identified?	☐	☐

	Yes	No

Is user data base, file, and record access based upon the "need to know" principle—not the "nice to have" principle? ☐ ☐

Have the systems facilities each user requires to perform his duties (read, write, change, and delete) been determined, and are appropriate system controls in place? ☐ ☐

Are prepaid value-added network calls accepted only, and systems access permitted only after the calling host has been properly identified? ☐ ☐

Is access to restricted utilities limited to only those data processing and maintenance personnel who must have access? ☐ ☐

Are appropriate audit, control, data integrity, and security procedures in place to determine in a timely manner when any abnormal activity concerning data, application programs, or logical grouping of programs or systems has taken or is taking place? ☐ ☐

Do internal audit departments have staff members who are comfortable in the data processing and telecommunication environments? ☐ ☐

Are internal auditors involved in the systems development life cycle, network configuration, and resultant data communications methodologies? ☐ ☐

Is serious consideration given to providing security managers and investigative personnel some training in data processing and both data and voice communications? ☐ ☐

Has the organization established a central data systems and communications security function, which is not part of the data processing department? Has that organization developed security policies in order to assign, monitor, grant, and revoke systems access? ☐ ☐

Are procedures in place to monitor both communications and systems usage and perform other related functions? ☐ ☐

Have all actual or suspected unauthorized systems access involving external communications been reported to the service provider? ☐ ☐

PART V
Special Protection Issues

CHAPTER 17

Forms and Related Supplies

By Robert A. Daley

Introduction

Computer operations usually produce printed reports as their most important function. In the area of forms security, careful planning is necessary to provide for day-to-day operations and for operations under emergency conditions.

The objective of this chapter is to point up the need for forms security and to describe methods for accomplishing it. The principal need is to provide for continuous operation of the computer facility under all conditions, by having the correct forms and related supplies on hand in sufficient quantities to meet printing schedules.

Planning for continuous operations requires establishing and implementing procedures for normal and emergency conditions. Such procedures should address shipping, receiving, storage, accountability, backup, control, rotation, and disposal. Establishing and implementing procedures for emergency conditions should cover adapting stock forms, alternate methods of report preparation, alternate methods of preparing input data, off-site storage, logistics, handling, and control procedures.

Forms are often taken for granted, but they are essential, and should be given the same consideration as all other areas of computer security. In forms security planning as in other planning, Murphy's Law applies, "If it is at all possible for anything to go wrong, it will."

Subjects to be discussed in this chapter include:

Forms Handling—outlines procedures necessary for labeling, shipping, receiving, storage, accountability, backup control, rotation, and obsolescence of vital, necessary, convenient, and useful forms.

Check Handling—because of its importance this subject is discussed in a separate section.

Emergency Planning—defines objectives, tasks, responsibilities, and results to be accomplished.

Emergency Backup—describes alternative methods for preparing input data and for producing reports under emergency conditions.

In security planning, forms problems will vary depending on the size and nature of the operation. A large organization may be able to assemble a task force from different departments to tackle the problem. A small organization may have one person wearing several hats. In either case, the problems are the same, varying only in degree.

Regardless of the size of the organization the following should be provided for:

Planning for an adequate supply of forms for assurance of continued operations in event of emergency.

Control of vital forms on a day-to-day basis and under emergency conditions.

Establishing procedures for control, handling, auditing, accountability, supply, backup supplies, and rotation of forms and related supplies.

Forms Handling and Control

The proper control and handling of forms is an essential element of computer security. Requirements vary according to the classification of forms as described in Exhibit 17.1. In brief, vital forms represent potential cash value, necessary forms are essential to the operations of systems, and convenient forms include all others.

Exhibit 17.1
Classification of EDP Forms

1. VITAL FORMS

   Vital forms usually represent legal evidence of financial transactions, and are customarily preprinted. Examples are checks, purchase orders, bills of lading, invoices, security trading forms, and stock certificates.

2. NECESSARY FORMS

   Necessary forms do not represent legal evidence of financial transactions but are required for systems operations. They include preprinted forms such as: statements, confirmations, and sales orders. In addition, stock paper should be available in at least one standard width, together with certain supplies such as punch paper tapes, printer ribbons, printer carriage control tapes, and unit record (punch) cards.

3. CONVENIENT FORMS

   Convenient forms are time saving when available, but not essential because blank stock can easily be substituted in their place. Manual records such as incident reports, tape or disk scratch logs, and batch control logs are typical of this type of form.

Controls for vital, necessary, and convenient forms are described below in one general sequence of events from their creation to their ultimate disposition.

Vital Forms
Ordering of Forms
- The supplier must imprint forms with control numbers, in sequence, as shown on the purchase order. There should be no missing sequence numbers, and the packing slip should so state. If this is not possible, the cartons and the printer's packing slip must indicate all breaks in sequence.
- Form names should not be printed on the outside of cartons. Form designations such as checks, purchase orders, or bills of lading should not appear on external shipping labels. Forms should be identified by code numbers only.
- List beginning and ending sequence numbers on the packing slip, invoice, and each carton.

Shipping
- Shipments should be by bonded carriers, insured and signed for at each point during transit.
- For intracompany shipments, record each movement to each location, showing se-

quence numbers and responsible handlers. Shipping should be by bonded carriers.

Receiving
- Delivery should be to a separate secure receiving area, if possible.
- Receiving should check each carton against the order to ascertain that no forms are missing.
- Forms should be delivered to the officer who maintains control (auditor, treasurer, controller, etc.) and who will provide a receipt. After receipting for delivery, forms should be logged in and placed in secure, protected storage.

Backup
- The backup supply of vital forms should be stored off-site, preferably in a vault or bonded storage.
- Determination of backup quantity will depend on usage, storage available, distance, and other factors. The quantity stored as backup should be about 20 percent greater than the quantity normally used during the period of time required for delivery of a new order.

Accountability
- Vital forms should be controlled by an auditor or treasurer with appropriate control procedures, accounting for all unused and spoiled forms and logging forms in and out.
- Periodic or surprise audits should be made of all forms in on-site, off-site, and vendor storage.
- All serialized forms issued to data processing should be logged in and out by data processing control.
- Physical inventory counts must be made periodically as a further control measure.
- Minimum stock reorder points must be established, periodically reevaluated, and regularly observed.
- Usage reports should include reruns, spoilage, and changes in demand in order to ensure continued availability of vital forms.

Necessary Forms
- These forms and related supplies may be kept in a common storeroom or warehouse but should be protected from extremes of heat, cold, and humidity.

- Inventory control personnel should be responsible for maintaining control of numbered forms and their issuance in correct numerical sequence.
- Once issued, forms are the responsibility of the user departments.
- Backup forms and related supplies should be stored separately from the working supply in a secure location, preferably off-site.

Control of Unnumbered Forms
- In some installations, continuous forms for advices, statements, etc., are not prenumbered; consecutive numbers are printed by the program. For control purposes, an additional set of consecutive numbers should be preprinted in some unobtrusive location on the form, such as in the pin feed margin, or at the bottom of the form.

Convenient Forms

These forms may be stored in a common stockroom. Rigid control is unnecessary, the only requirement being that an adequate level of supply be maintained to meet operational necessities.

Other Considerations for All Types of Forms
Rotation
- When a new order of forms is received, the older forms should be brought from backup storage to working storage.
- Care should be exercised to use the oldest forms first. Other supplies such as punched cards, paper tape, magnetic tape, cassettes, and diskettes must also be rotated regularly; otherwise the backup may consist of obsolete and deteriorated forms and supplies, with unwanted color changes, dried out glue, and brittleness.

Obsolete Forms
- When a form is redesigned or becomes obsolete, all copies should be removed from backup storage and replaced by the new form.
- Obsolete vital forms should be destroyed by shredding, chemical dilution, or burning under control procedures.
- Obsolete necessary forms may be disposed of as common trash or sold to a reliable waste paper dealer.

Forms Printer's Services
- The forms printer can offer a variety of services that are extremely useful. The availability of such services is often a factor in choosing a supplier. Among the services that may be offered are environmentally controlled backup storage, inventory control, forms control, and reorder notification.

Check Handling and Control

The control and handling of checks is a major concern of most companies. Even after check control and handling procedures have been established, it is extremely risky to assume that all risks have been eliminated. Procedures and policies should be constantly reviewed and tested, and security must be enforced. The size of the operation may require a staff whose principal function is control and handling of checks.

In order to minimize the possibility of blank checks falling into the wrong hands, check control and handling procedures should be instituted to include:

1. Security at the check printer's plant and warehouse
2. Carrier's security procedures
3. Physical facilities and access restrictions at the receiving location
4. Design and ordering of checks

Check printers usually observe stringent security measures at their plants and warehouses, and bonded carriers have had extensive experience in the shipping and delivery of checks. Despite all of this, breaches of security do occur, and only stringent internal controls will detect such breaches early enough to prevent serious loss.

A survey of the user's physical facility should be undertaken with special attention to critical areas such as receiving points, storage facilities, and the data processing area. Procedures followed at these locations, and the work habits of the employees should be reviewed.

Some basic precautions should be observed in the design and ordering of checks:

- The paper should be special check paper.
- MICR characters must be positioned in exactly prescribed locations, vertically and horizontally, using the special magnetized

ink and type style prescribed by the American Bankers Association.

- If required, provision may be made for multiple check copies, but more than one copy of the actual check is inefficient. Internal control is better served by providing copies of the check register for distribution to affected departments.

Precautions to be observed in check handling and control are as follows:

At the Printers Prior to Delivery
- The order must have beginning and ending check numbers.
- Samples of the checks must **not** be affixed to the outside of the cartons.
- Labels should **not** bear the word "CHECKS." Contents are to be identified by code numbers. Beginning and ending consecutive numbers of checks enclosed should be shown on the labels, along with the affirmation "No Missing Numbers" or a listing of any missed numbers.

Shipping
- Ship by bonded carrier.
- Insure during shipping.
- Shipment should be checked and a receipt obtained at each point of handling during shipment.

Receiving
- If possible, use a separate secure receiving area. Each carton must be checked against the order to assure that no checks are missing in the shipment.

Internal Storage
- Checks are to be delivered to storage under guard, and receipts obtained as evidence that the checks were placed in storage.
- All checks received should be logged in.

- All personnel entering the storage area are to be logged in and out.
- A log should be maintained for the issue and return of checks, showing to whom checks were released, the disposition of the used checks (including spoilage), and an accounting for the return of unused checks. See Exhibits 17.2 and 17.3.

Shipments to Branches
- Ship under guard by bonded carrier.
- Record the consecutive check numbers shipped to each location.
- Obtain receipt from the person(s) handling shipments.

Internal Controls
- The check printing program should provide the total number of checks printed.
- Verification of the number of checks used should be done by a control section or other independent department.
- Provide sufficient copies of the check register to meet the needs of general accounting, auditing, the user department, and data processing.
- Check signing equipment. Maintain a check signer control log (Exhibit 17.4) showing:
    - Date of check issuance
    - Application or purpose
    - Meter readings of signer counter
    - Number of checks signed
    - Notes listing irregularities or adjustments
- When the check signing is completed, the signature die should be removed, boxed, and placed in secure storage (vault); logged in and out; and the log should be sent to the control section for comparison with the check register.

Exhibit 17.2
Cancelled/Spoiled Checks

| | | Check Numbers | | Number of Checks | |
Date	Check	From	To	Spoiled	Remarks
6/17/86	Accts Payable	246579	246581	3	
6/20/86	Payroll	579006	579037	32	Printer Alignment Error

Exhibit 17.3
Check Control

Check: Accounts Payable
Numbers: From 100,000 to 200,000 inc.

Date	Opening Balance Recipient	Numbers Issued From	To	Numbers Returned From	To	Quantity Used	Balance
10/15/85	100000						100000
10/30/85	K. Night	100000	200000	105000	200000	5000	95000
11/7/85	C. Miau	105000	200000	111000	200000	6000	89000
11/15/85	J. Doe	111000	200000	120000	200000	9000	80000

Obsolete Checks

Checks may become obsolete due to redesign, or because a retention period has expired for a check printed for a special application, or because of preprinted dates. (e.g., Dividend No. 105 dated October 1, 1985).

- Destruction procedures should specify method of destruction, i.e., shredding, chemical dilution, incineration.
- Checks scheduled for destruction should be logged out of storage and a receipt obtained from the person(s) accepting custody.
- Obtain receipt from the person(s) handling shipment to the destruction site.
- Destruction should be witnessed and a certificate of destruction obtained.
- All documents relating to the disposal and destruction of obsolete checks should be given to the official responsible for the handling and control of checks.

Mailing
- When inserting and mailing is performed by an outside organization, an agreement with the mailing organization concerning control and handling procedures would provide assurance of security. If the mailing organization has its own control procedures, they should be reviewed for adequacy.

In any computer installation where checks are printed the greatest possibility exists for inadvertent error or fraudulent actions with immediately damaging consequences. With a form this vital, none of the above details in handling and control should be overlooked.

Emergency Planning

The objective of emergency planning is to provide for continued operations in the event that on-site storage is destroyed, or the premises are rendered unusable and operations must be transferred to a backup facility.

Requirements
In addition to functional needs, there may be statutory requirements that hold directors or

Exhibit 17.4
Check Signer Control

Date	Application	Signer Counter Meter Readings From	To	Number of Checks Signed	Notes
1/10/86	Expense	105010	105490	480	
1/14/86	Dividends	105490	116990	11500	
1/15/86	Payroll	116990	119205	2215	
1/16/86	Accounts payable	119205	121021	1816	

managers responsible for continuing operations and financially liable for losses due to their interruption.

Considerations

It is necessary to conduct a study to determine forms volumes and timing requirements so that backup quantities, emergency storage, program changes, and transportation will be able to cope with any emergency. The planning should provide for operations under emergency conditions for periods of time ranging up to at least six months. In emergency planning, consideration should be given to:

* Maintaining an adequate backup supply of forms
* Alternate methods of report preparation
    - As a substitute for preprinted forms use stock forms with computer generated headings.
    - Arrange for off-line printing from magnetic media at a service bureau or a backup site.
    - Eliminate printing of low priority reports.

- If laser printer or xerographic printing process is available, use forms overlays to substitute for preprinted forms.
    - Use exception reporting to reduce print load; however, such procedures must be thoroughly tested in advance.
* Use of microfilm forms flashers
    - This involves magnetic tape output projected on a cathode ray tube and photographed through a glass plate negative (forms flasher), printing on the microfilm an image of the form itself as well as the fill-in data. Report copies can then be made from the microfilm. This could be an expensive service bureau operation, but may be worthwhile if the volume is great enough. See Fig. 17.1 for a diagram showing the steps in such an operation.
* Alternate method of preparing input data
    - Use a service bureau or data entry specialists.
    - Rent key entry equipment and facilities on a temporary basis.
    - Institute reciprocal agreements with other organizations.

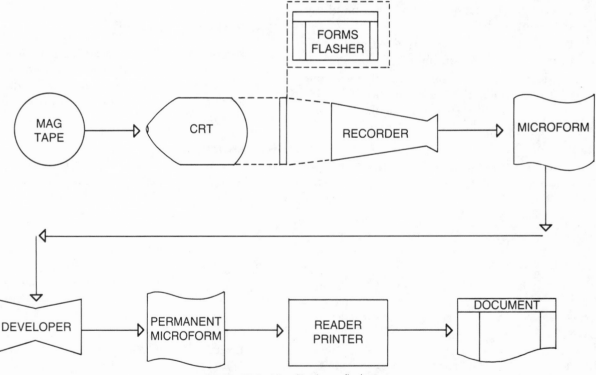

Figure 17.1 Microfilm forms flasher

- Off-site storage for backup forms and related supplies
    - Use area with controlled temperature and humidity.
    - Provide fire protection and controlled access.
- Logistical methods of assuring a continuous supply
    - Control of form movements.
    - Periodic inventory of backup supply.
    - Periodic rotation and replacement of backup forms.
- Forms and document distribution procedures
    - Arrange for alternate quarters and equipment to burst, decollate, and mail or deliver forms and documents.
- Alternative sources of forms supplies
    - Establish and maintain relationships with more than one forms supplier.
    - Periodically place orders with alternate vendors.

Responsibility

To assemble a forms security program requires coordination of responsibility. The areas of the organization to be involved include: forms control, systems and programming, computer operations, purchasing, inventory control, administrative management, personnel, the backup facility, and the forms supplier. The functions and responsibilities are:

- Forms Control

    Devise alternate methods of creating forms by the use of stock forms, overlays, copiers, forms flashers, and microfilm. Provide an estimate of the storage areas available for the stocking of forms and supplies at the backup facility, and review procedures for control of vital forms stored on these premises.

- Systems

    Prepare manual procedures, alternate methods of preparing input data and alternate methods of report preparation, such as adapting stock forms for emergencies.

- Programming

    Have available necessary program changes to cope with emergency conditions. For example, a routine could be available to print form headings on stock paper. Provide

items such as printer carriage control tapes with documentation and run books, which can be made available at the backup facility when needed.

- Computer Operations

    Provide estimates, according to operations schedules, of quantity and type of report forms needed for a given period of time.

- Inventory Control

    Determine from the records the necessary quantities of input forms drawn to meet operational requirements.

- Purchasing

    Arrange for shipments of forms and supplies to emergency storage and backup facilities. Ship enough to cover operational needs, without taxing the backup facility's storage area.

- Administrative Management

    Provide for protected emergency storage for forms and related supplies, as near to the backup facility as feasible or at the closest branch office. A bank vault or other fireproof and temperature-controlled storage would be suitable. Establish procedures for delivery of forms and related supplies to the backup facility from either the company storeroom, emergency storage, or vendor's storage. Establish procedures and alternate quarters for the mailing of checks, reports, advices, statements, etc., should it be impractical to use the company mailroom. Establish schedules for the delivery of forms, input data, and supplies to the backup facility and for the return of reports and other data to the company's premises.

- Personnel

    Hire necessary temporary employees, such as messengers, data entry operators, control clerks, etc. Provide time sheets, payroll forms, and other necessary forms for personnel expenses if backup is at a remote location. Rent temporary quarters to house employees if it is inconvenient for them to commute from home daily. Arrange for emergency transportation for employees.

The functions outlined above may in some instances overlap. Each company's own organization structure will determine responsibilities for the tasks to be accomplished. It is recommended that a project coordinator be named who will assign specific responsibilities and be responsible for implementation of this program.

Microcomputers

Forms safeguards for microcomputer operations should follow the same general rules as for forms used with larger computers. Most microcomputer operations do not use complex or vital forms because microcomputers, being suitable for smaller volume procedures, are more apt to have their output on plain paper or standard off-the-shelf labels. However, when a microcomputer is used with important or vital forms, such as with payroll or accounts payable systems, it is necessary to apply the security measures described for all such forms, for example, keeping a reserve supply off-site, and maintaining accurate logs and controls of the checks.

Summary

This chapter has been prepared to emphasize the importance of forms in business operations and the need for protection of forms in the data processing environment. Good forms security requires careful attention to detail in day-to-day operations and under emergency conditions in order to ensure that operations are continuous, or if disrupted that they can be restored with a minimum of time lost. Special protection must be provided for vital forms, and adequate backup of forms and related supplies must be maintained.

Having a backup facility does not guarantee that emergencies are provided for, unless there are also periodic tests and checks of procedures, logistics, and forms supplies.

Security of forms on a day-to-day basis can be maintained by frequent monitoring of forms handling procedures and controls. Nothing should be taken for granted, especially in regard to checks and other vital forms.

In planning for an emergency, be sure that stock forms and special forms are made available. Consideration should be given to alternate methods of reports preparation, and alternate methods of preparing input data.

Although the recommendations outlined in this chapter are applicable to all installations, varying in size from microcomputers to mainframes, there are differences in how these recommendations are applied. Microcomputers present special security problems that need to be addressed in a practical way. A security program generally must be tailored for each installation and organization.

A checklist is provided in questionnaire form, designed to elicit yes or no answers. An answer in the negative indicates an area requiring attention.

Forms and Related Supplies Checklist

VITAL FORMS

Forms Printer:

	Yes	No
Do orders have beginning and ending consecutive numbers?	☐	☐
Are copies of forms omitted from outside of cartons?	☐	☐
Are form names omitted from labels and are forms identified by code numbers?	☐	☐
Are beginning and ending consecutive numbers shown on label?	☐	☐
Does label state "no missing numbers" or are missing numbers listed.	☐	☐

Shipping:

Are shipments by bonded carriers?	☐	☐
Are shipments insured?	☐	☐
Are shipments checked and receipted for at each point handled during shipment?	☐	☐

Receiving:

Are deliveries made to a secure receiving area?	☐	☐
Does receiving check each carton against order for assurance that no forms are missing?	☐	☐
Are forms delivered to a responsible person who will give receipt?	☐	☐

Yes No

Storage:

Are forms logged in and receipt given for delivery? ☐ ☐

Is a log maintained for all persons entering and leaving storage area? ☐ ☐

As forms are issued, is receipt obtained and are they logged out? ☐ ☐

Is receipt given for spoiled and unused forms returned and are they logged in? ☐ ☐

Shipping to Branches:

Are shipments logged out? ☐ ☐

Is each shipment recorded with consecutive numbers to each location? ☐ ☐

Is receipt obtained from person(s) handling shipments? ☐ ☐

Are shipments insured? ☐ ☐

Is shipping by bonded carrier? ☐ ☐

Accountability:

Do you have control procedures? ☐ ☐

Are all spoiled and unused forms accounted for? ☐ ☐

Are forms logged in and out? ☐ ☐

Are periodic and/or surprise audits taken of forms in on-site, off-site, and vendor storage? ☐ ☐

Backup:

Do you have off-site secure storage for backup forms? ☐ ☐

Have you determined necessary quantities of backup forms? ☐ ☐

NECESSARY, CONVENIENT, AND USEFUL FORMS:

Does storage protect against extremes of heat, cold, and humidity? ☐ ☐

Is there control of numbered forms and are they issued in correct numerical sequence? ☐ ☐

Does anyone assume responsibility for control after issue? ☐ ☐

Yes No

Is backup supply stored separate from main supply? ☐ ☐

Are console typewriter sheets consecutively numbered? ☐ ☐

Rotation:

Are forms rotated regularly, maintaining proper numerical sequence, from printer to backup to main supply? ☐ ☐

Are unnumbered forms, supplies, tab cards, magnetic tapes, etc., also regularly rotated from vendor to backup to main supply? ☐ ☐

Are regular audits taken of on-site, off-site, and vendor storage? ☐ ☐

Obsolete Forms:

Are obsolete forms removed from backup storage and replaced by new forms? ☐ ☐

Do you have control procedures for destruction of obsolete vital forms? ☐ ☐

Do you have provision for removal and disposal of other obsolete forms? ☐ ☐

CHECK HANDLING

At the printer prior to delivery:

Does the order have beginning and ending consecutive numbers? ☐ ☐

No copies of checks attached to outside of cartons? ☐ ☐

Is the word "checks" omitted from labels? ☐ ☐

Are contents identified by code numbers on label? ☐ ☐

Are beginning and ending consecutive numbers shown on labels for each carton and the words "no missing numbers" or a list of missing numbers also shown on label? ☐ ☐

Shipping:

Are shipments by bonded carrier? ☐ ☐

Are shipments insured? ☐ ☐

	Yes	No		Yes	No

Are shipments checked and receipted for at each point handled during shipment? ☐ ☐

Obsolete Checks:
Are procedures in effect governing destruction of obsolete checks? ☐ ☐

Are obsolete checks logged out of storage and receipt obtained? ☐ ☐

Receiving:
Are deliveries made to a secure receiving area? ☐ ☐

Is receipt obtained from person(s) handling shipment to destruction site? ☐ ☐

Is each carton checked against order for assurance that delivery is complete? ☐ ☐

Do destruction procedures provide for witnessing destruction and certification of destruction? ☐ ☐

Are checks delivered to a responsible person who will give receipt? ☐ ☐

Mailing by Outside Organizations:
Do you have an agreement with mailers for control of checks on their premises: ☐ ☐

Storage:
Are checks stored in a secure area (vault)? ☐ ☐

Have you reviewed control procedures of mailers? ☐ ☐

Are they delivered under guard and is receipt obtained for delivery? ☐ ☐

Are checks logged in? ☐ ☐

Are all personnel entering storage logged in and out? ☐ ☐

EMERGENCY PLANNING
Do you have emergency or off-site storage? ☐ ☐

Do you maintain logs for issue and return of checks accounting for spoiled and unused checks? ☐ ☐

Have you determined necessary back-up quantities of forms and related supplies? ☐ ☐

Does the backup facility have space for your forms? ☐ ☐

Shipments to Branches:
Are shipments made under guard and by bonded carrier? ☐ ☐

Have you made provision for control of vital forms at the backup facility? ☐ ☐

Are shipments recorded with consecutive numbers for each location? ☐ ☐

Do you have a schedule prepared for deliveries to backup facility? ☐ ☐

Is receipt obtained from person(s) handling shipment? ☐ ☐

Do you have a schedule prepared for messenger delivery of input data and pick up of completed reports? ☐ ☐

Internal Accounting:
Are check control logs used? ☐ ☐

Have you provided for vehicle hire or rescheduling of company's automotive equipment in event of emergency? ☐ ☐

Does check printing program print total of checks issued and cancelled? ☐ ☐

Are sufficient copies of check register provided for control purposes? ☐ ☐

Have you provided for hiring necessary temporary employees for the emergency? ☐ ☐

Is a check signer control log used? ☐ ☐

Is check signing die protected when not in use? ☐ ☐

Have you provided for temporary office space and living quarters for employees? ☐ ☐

	Yes	No
Have you provided for necessary forms of personnel expenses if backup is at a remote location?	☐	☐

ALTERNATE METHODS OF REPORTS PREPARATION

	Yes	No
Have you considered an optional print routine for printing form headings on stock forms?	☐	☐
Have you considered the use of COM with transparent overlays as an alternative method?	☐	☐

ALTERNATE METHODS OF PREPARING INPUT DATA

	Yes	No
Have you made arrangements for equipment rental, a backup facility, or a service bureau?	☐	☐
Have you prepared manual procedures and coding forms as source documents for alternate input preparation?	☐	☐
Have you arranged for other methods of input preparation if yours cannot be duplicated?	☐	☐

CHAPTER 18
Outside Contract Services

By Theodore W. Christiansen

Introduction

Outside contract services have been used by nearly every company that has data processing equipment to perform data processing related operations. Outside service companies can provide skilled personnel not otherwise obtainable for relatively short periods of time to meet peak and irregular requirements.

A primary reason for deciding to use a service company is its capacity to provide a technical competence or service more economically and quickly than could be done internally. Other benefits may arise from the service organization's greater depth of experience and its objective viewpoint.

The use of outside services often creates opportunities to establish superior policies and procedures to properly control these activities and to ensure security. Non-data processing services such as outside auditors, guards, and truckers, as well as data processing services require special security measures. Security requirements increase the cost of outside services, as they do for normal internal operations.

Basic Considerations

Outside contracting services related to data processing involve security considerations similar to those for the same functions performed internally. For example, security in systems analysis and development whether performed by staff programmers or outside consultants requires in-depth planning in each area of risk. A risk assessment performed on a system to be developed, with system specifications covering security measures, should give management a good picture of costs and benefits.

One of the more important areas of security is file management. It is desirable to keep sensitive files encrypted and to limit access with passwords. Access to company confidential data should be restricted to employees with a business need to know, and edit procedures should be set up to test the validity of new data.

Computer systems and their programs are investments that can provide a company with a competitive edge. It is equally necessary to prevent contractors and company personnel from willfully destroying files and from selling their contents to others.

Providing timely data can make a substantial difference in decisions made by management. For this reason, many companies permit inquiry via terminals into company files, rather than requiring personnel to wait for printed reports. Information availability and integrity can affect a company to a far greater extent than with most other company assets, so that special precautions are necessary to prevent abuses.

Security considerations require separation and control of production and testing. A programmers' library should be set up, restricting programmer access only to test data. Production data should not be available to contract programmers doing development work, and their programs should not be put into production libraries except by qualified company personnel. Conversely, production personnel should not have access to the "source code," so as to prevent their changing programs that run in a production mode.

A company should permit outside personnel

access only to those procedures and data that are required to do their assigned jobs. It is a good practice to review regularly a consultant's work, to ensure that what is being done conforms to company standards, and to ensure the ability to maintain the system in the future.

Project activity reports can be useful in monitoring system development work an outside services and by internal personnel; see Exhibits 18.1 and 18.2 as examples.

Identification of a Reputable Service Company

In searching for a reputable service organization, it is helpful to ask business contacts for suggestions as to potential firms. Inquiries can be made of associates in professional societies, in CPA and legal firms, and among the service company's vendors and customers.

It is desirable to investigate at least two or three potential sources for a large contract in order to select the most appropriate technical personnel as well as to insure good working relationships with staff personnel. Before selecting a service company, client references should be verified. The personnel who would do the work should be interviewed and their competence evaluated by the client company's management or technical personnel.

In addition to adequate technical experience and knowledge, the service firm's reliability from a security standpoint should be checked, and in some instances, bonding of their personnel may be desirable. Many of the non-data processing services, such as guard and trucking services, usually will have their personnel bonded, and, except in the most sensitive applications, such personnel may automatically be approved without additional investigation.

The willingness of service companies to provide references can be an indication of their professional integrity as well as of their past successful performances.

Publicly owned software houses provide annual reports from which judgments can be made as to their stability and the likelihood of their being in business for the contract period. In certain states, banking institutions have a legal obligation to obtain financial data from vendors.

Where the value of a contract service is substantial, it is also desirable to secure verification of the service organization's financial stability from a credit reporting service. Where such credit reports are not available, the potential service company can be asked for a financial statement certified by its public accounting firm.

Exhibit 18.1
Project Activity Report

Project Task: _____

Task Status: _____

Problems Found: _____

Time used this week: _____ Hrs.   Time task to date: _____ Hrs.
Latest estimate total time required this task: _____ Hrs.
Define the requirement if more manpower or different skills are needed: _____

Reporting to: _____   Reported by: _____
Title: _____   Date: _____

Notes: Project Task: What was planned to be done.

Task Status: What has been done. Where we stand at the end of the week.

Problems Found: Is the task taking longer than planned? Have unforeseen obstacles occurred?

Project manager should break down projects to definable tasks and may develop a PERT chart to define steps and completion dates.

Exhibit 18.2
Weekly Activity Report

By: Date: _____ / _____ / _____

Tasks Worked on This Week

Project: Inventory System

ID#	Description	Completion/Schedule
503	Issue Screen	
504	Issue Edit Program	
505	Purchase Order File	
506	Purchase Order Screen	

Problems with current tasks which may delay or prevent completion on schedule: _____
_____
_____
_____

Time spent during the week: _____ Hours

ID#	Systems	Programming	Training	Documentation	Test	Totals
503						
504						
505						
506						
Total						

Software and Programming Services

Types of Services

Purchased software has become the dominant expenditure for outside services by many companies, large and small. The types of software purchased can vary in many ways, from large systems such as the operation of major credit cards, to small ones such as personal computer spreadsheet programs, and from completely customized programs, to programs bought and installed without a change. In some cases the seller installs the software, or the purchaser may perform that function.

Vulnerabilities

When software is procured from an outside vendor or service, instead of being created and designed by the using organization's employees, there are these special security vulnerabilities that must be recognized and dealt with:

- If the programs are created by an outside consultant or service, the outsiders may have access to confidential or sensitive information about the client's operations.

- When purchased programs are identical or similar to programs used by competitors, the opportunity for unauthorized persons, especially competitors, to access data is greatly increased.

- Proprietary software may be disclosed to a competitor.

- Some software designers are not as reliable or competent as the application warrants.

- If the source code is not provided along with the object code, it will be impossible for the purchaser to modify the program without the seller's assistance.

- Software providers may go out of business, which can make for difficulties, or even disasters, if the customer has not protected himself against that possibility.

- Personal computer program applications are usually not formally documented, therefore, it may be difficult or impossible to continue their use if an operating problem occurs in the absence of the program's creator.

Protective Measures

It is important to investigate carefully the competence and reliability of the outside service, if that service is to design, adapt, or install a computer system or computer program. If it is a standard program, research should be undertaken to determine the program's effectiveness, and the degree and nature of problems that other users may have experienced.

If software is to be developed, or if an existing package is to be modified, then particular caution must be exercised to determine the reliability of the vendor and to assure that there is a history of past successes. Personal contact with a representative sample of past customers is possibly the best approach. Vendors who cannot supply recent satisfied client references should usually be avoided.

Source programs should be obtained along with object code wherever possible. If, as is often the case, the vendor is unwilling to provide the source programs, agree to have them held in escrow. In the event that the vendor is unable or unwilling to make desired modifications, or if he goes out of business, the source code would then be released to the contractor.

It is necessary, especially when dealing with small vendors, to arrange for access to the source code in the event of the vendor's business termination or his inability or unwillingness to maintain the program. Software contracts can be written so as to require the vendor to place the source code in escrow, using an independent third party, with provision for allowing the buyer conditional access to the source code. To rely upon this type of protection, one must verify the reliability of the third party escrow holder and obtain legal and technical guidance in the drafting the escrow agreement.

When systems and programs are purchased that are similar to those used by competitors, it is particularly important to apply access controls such as passwords, terminal access identifications, call-back requirements, and related features to prevent unauthorized persons from obtaining or modifying the system's data.

In all cases with purchased software, it is desirable to obtain clear and complete documentation so that the system is fully understood by the purchaser's personnel and can be modified, if possible, without reliance on the vendor.

Since many personal computer programs are developed informally, without documentation, it is important that at least one person besides the program's creator become familiar enough with it so that he can resolve operating problems. Obviously full documentation of every system should be required, but few organizations have recognized the importance of this action, and fewer still have the personnel to accomplish it.

Service Bureaus

Types of Services

Jobs can be sent to a service bureau to be processed, or the service bureau's equipment and operators can be rented or leased by the hour, shift, or day. It is also possible to rent a block of time and use the service's equipment with one's own operators on a regular basis.

Until recently, service bureaus have not been promoting the use of microcomputers to interface with their computers. They were more interested in selling mainframe time, and they believed that to download files and programs for off-line editing, calculating, and reporting was not in their own best interests. More recently, faced with a declining market share, service bureaus have increasingly turned to microcomputers. Service bureaus now often offer standalone minicomputer systems and microcomputers as on-line terminals to their mainframe.

Many service bureaus offer a combination of on-line and batch services. Typically this means that the customer is supplied with a terminal that is used for entry of data during the month. All transactions are stored on the service bureau's computer. It is then possible to inquire as to the status of various records, current on hand inventory, current orders, price of product, employee's pay rate, etc. At stipulated time periods the printed reports for payroll, accounts receivable, accounts payable, general ledger, or other activities are run from the data in the files. Payroll applications have been successful in this mode because a small amount of data are entered, and many calculations and reports are generated. The entry of basic data for new employees, hours worked by employee for the week, and changes to basic file data (infrequent) results in pay checks, bank transfer drafts, check registers, W-2 forms, 941 reports, and data for budgets or cost accounting analyses. The on-line batch combination has also been widely used for inventory, accounts receivable, and sales order processing.

Vulnerabilities

When service bureaus are used, a variety of potential dangers to security are created or increased. The following are principal weaknesses to security that might arise from the contracted use of service bureaus. Appropriate protective measures are described in the succeeding section.

- The service bureau may not be capable of performing the required work on schedule or with the necessary quality and absence of errors.

- The service bureau may not remain in business or might not be available during the hours desired by its customer.

- The service bureau's employees might allow access to sensitive information by unauthorized persons.

- The service bureau might not adequately prevent the loss of files, which could result in high costs and delays in reconstructing the records, as well as the possibility of disastrous damage to the business.

- An in-house facility or a service bureau that allows its programmer to execute jobs circumvents the safeguards provided by divisions of responsibilities. Such programmers can make unauthorized changes without others being aware of them.

- Loss of records and facilities in a fire or other disaster might create a crisis for the customer unless the facilities and data are properly backed up.

- Delays may result when a service bureau uses equipment from several manufacturers who may disagree as to the cause of the equipment problems.

Protective Measures

Various protective measures should be undertaken when service bureaus are engaged, to make sure that they are sufficiently reliable, durable, and equipped with security safeguards to minimize risks and dangers cited in the section above.

Service bureaus should provide the names of other customers as references. These references should be contacted to discuss their experiences with the particular service bureau. Trade organizations, professional societies, and user groups may provide useful contacts for this type of information.

A danger of service bureaus to some companies is the improper use of a principal company programmer doubling as a computer operator to execute jobs off-site during periods with peak workloads or equipment problems. This should be avoided because it puts division of responsibilities established for normal operations, control of file data, program changes, and report data, all in the hands of one individual who has the knowledge and ability to make unauthorized changes.

Whenever a service bureau is employed for the processing and retention of company files, backup and security procedures must be carefully scrutinized. It is important to determine how the service bureau will recover files in the event of an equipment failure and how long recovery will take. With the backup techniques available today no records should be lost except the ones being entered when the equipment goes down. The nominal cost to recover may be borne by the service bureau, but, if the time to recover is excessive, the cost in terms of lost business can be disastrous.

Agreement should be reached on the storage of supplies for analysts and programmers when using a service bureau for system development. The ready availability of supplies, miscellaneous equipment, and programming manuals at the service bureau's office may avert unnecessary delays at a critical time. Space requirements when operating at a service bureau and security procedures to safeguard materials should be reviewed. If the customer is to rent block time at an off-site location, the storage there of required paper, tapes, programs, disk packs, and instruction manuals is necessary. Instructions on how to run the equipment and run the jobs should be available.

Data security rules for service bureau employees should be spelled out in the agreement. It is essential to establish backup procedures to be followed in the event of equipment or program failures and to establish who will have responsibility for duplicating and storing such records. It is also desirable to be able to inspect facilities and to have an agreement providing for random visits by auditors to check data security and the use of proper procedures.

Physical security and fire protection at a service bureau should be reviewed in the same manner as for internal operations. Often, safety for critical files may be better at a service bureau than would be practical for a small company. One service bureau that does a large volume of payroll work maintains all on-site tapes in fireproof safes. Most small companies are not willing to pay for such protection. Procedures should be established to insure the storage of vital programs and files, no matter how extensive the on-site security.

Consideration must be given to who will perform the work at the service company. Most service bureaus will certify that their employees are bonded. Service bureaus may use trainees to do contract work because much of it is repetitive, and that type of work is useful for training new employees. It is useful to have contractual protection to guarantee performance.

Limiting unauthorized on-line access can often be accomplished by locking the terminal with a key or with a password restricting usage. Access can be further limited in software by means of menus that permit only the specified users to access particular jobs or functions. Another techniques is to restrict use of "objects" on the computer, objects being defined as files, programs, and procedures. Systems can also be designed to restrict a user to the content of only specified libraries.

Service companies providing on-line service usually offer file recovery and backup; but it is desirable to have a written understanding of how the records will be safeguarded, and how long recovery would take under worst-case conditions.

Facilities Management

Some service companies, termed facility managers, run a data processing operation on a customer's site for the customer's use only. The usual reason for using a facility management firm is to avoid personnel and management problems in handling data processing professionals. The facilities management firm provides skilled people to run such an operation so that the customer avoids the need for special recruitment efforts, or having data processing personnel's pay conflict with internal pay standards. Also eliminated are turnover problems, training costs, and detailed scheduling required to make use of expensive equipment.

One of the dangers of facilities management

is the necessity for observation of company records by outside personnel. Another possible danger is the loss of key people by the facilities management firm, a circumstance over which the user has less control than he would have over in-house staff. Agreement should be made in advance about ownership of software that is developed on behalf of the company. Management must still be involved in periodic reviews of security, from computer room access, to where and how backup is performed.

Major costs often result when management terminates a facilities management contract. Only rarely will it be possible to retain key members of the contractor's on-site team. Hiring and training replacements usually involve considerable costs in time and money. Other problems may result from inadequate documentation of original systems and procedures, as well as of changes that were developed during the period of the contract. Requiring that all documentation meet a defined standard would prevent this problem. Without good documentation a firm may be locked into its facilities management contract despite rising costs and declining service levels. Good documentation is the key to freedom of action, permitting a change in facilities managers, or recruiting an in-house staff to do the work.

It is useful to provide incentives to the facilities management company to suggest and develop improvements in company operations. Contractual commitments can provide financial incentives to the facilities management company to develop savings for operations eliminated or for reductions in the cost of operations. All such changes require documented revisions of programs, data files, procedures, and schedules to insure that operational savings will continue after such changes.

Controls, recovery procedures, and documentation considerations are the same for facilities management operations as for internally managed operations. It should be required that employees be bonded by the facilities manager and that company audit teams and outside auditors be able to review operations at the facilities management site at any time. The contract with the facilities management firm should specify that all programs and procedures developed or changed be considered the client's property and not that of the facilities management company.

Documentation Service

Documentation is the backbone of security in data processing. In order to maintain a program properly it is necessary to know the current file structures, program logic, and formats of input and output. Otherwise, program bugs or system changes may become irreparable.

Documentation requirements are often developed by the systems and programming personnel of an outside company as a part of its software design and programming service. Alternatively a service company may be retained to document the systems that have been developed by the client company itself. In either event it is necessary that the documentation be done thoroughly and properly. Exhibit 18.3 lists the documentation required for each program, and Exhibit 18.4 lists the total systems documentation. Good practice dictates that these be immediately available at the processing site. In addition, as shown in Exhibit 18.5, copies of all documentation and necessary supplies should also be retained as off-site backup.

Exhibit 18.3
Program Documentation

- Description of the program and system name
- Copy of program source
- Logic charts
- Codes and tables
- Layout of screens
- List of files and records accessed or updated
- Operator instructions
- Halt and error messages
- Restart, rerun, and recovery procedures
- Data entry instructions
- List of operations procedures
- Controls and control procedure
- Estimates of run times and file sizes

Maintenance and Repairs

Maintenance of computer equipment was once provided only by the equipment manufacturers. They alone had trained customer engineers capable of repairing the computer and its peripheral devices.

Exhibit 18.4
System Documentation

- System description requirements
- Block diagram of system
- Description of system work flow
- Contents of master files with fields defined
- Copies of input documents and forms
- Copies of output documents and reports
- Proposed scheduling
- System control requirements
- Test and audit considerations
- Procedures for user departments

Full-service contracts are now available from independent third party companies, who can guarantee to provide as timely a service as any manufacturer. Further assurances may be offered that if repairs are not made within a specified time the maintenance service company will replace the equipment until the original unit is repaired. It is also desirable for the contract to guarantee that at its termination the equipment will be acceptable for servicing by the original manufacturer.

There are major differences in the terms and prices of available service contracts, principally, a fixed price per year or a charge based on time and materials for each individual service call. A service company with a fixed price contract is apt to replace a marginal part so as to avoid a subsequent trip if the part should fail. The per call service, on the other hand, may avoid replacing the doubtful part since a later trip to replace it would give it more revenue. In actual

Exhibit 18.5
Backup Documentation

- All system documentation
- All programming documentation
- Supply of critical preprinted forms
  -Computer output
  -Customer input
- Printer carriage tapes
- Copies of current master files in hard copy and magnetic media
- Current transaction files in hard copy and magnetic media

practice, a reliable service company will provide conscientious service under either arrangement. However, it is usual to give first priority to those customers who are under a fixed-priced contract rather than those on a time and materials basis.

The security vulnerabilities to consider in selecting and working with maintenance and service companies are twofold: (1) undue delays in repairs that might prevent continuous or timely operation of the computer, and (2) the danger of sensitive data being made available to unauthorized personnel.

The danger of delays in operations should be avoided by verifying the reliability of the service organization selected, and making sure, if it is other than the equipment manufacturer, that it has the skills and availability of parts to be able to effect repairs in a timely manner.

Sensitive data on equipment being serviced must be protected from unauthorized access. One way is to remove all sensitive files from the equipment, replacing them with meaningless test data or with obsolete data which are no longer sensitive. Another precaution is to have a reliable employee stay with the repairman to make sure he does not observe confidential information unnecessarily or remove such data from the area. These protective measures are particularly important because the manufacturer or service company's customer engineers usually have "super-users" passwords that permit them to circumvent the user's security systems.

Backup Facilities

A major disaster such as a fire or flood may make the computer inoperable for an extended period. The possibility of such a disaster makes it important to plan for the use of an alternate facility during the time it takes to repair or replace the original.

A number of commercial recovery services are available for such a need. They include:

- Commercial service bureaus
- Fully equipped recovery centers
- Empty shell facilities
- Time brokers
- Hardware vendor facilities

Computer service bureaus have data processing facilities that are operated for the conven-

ience of their customers. They generally offer both batch and on-line, or time-sharing services. For a fee some service bureaus will obligate themselves to hold sufficient reserved capacity to handle a customer's workload in the event of a disaster. If a service bureau is to be used as a contingency resource, a number of preparatory steps need to be taken:

- Access information and passwords should be obtained and tested for on-line use.
- JCL statements should be prepared and tested for batch systems.
- Training should be conducted for employees who would be involved in the backup operations.
- Provisions should be made for storage of all required source code, object code, and data on disks and tapes in advance of an actual emergency.
- Disaster events should be simulated periodically, so that all of the elements necessary for recovery are fully tested.

Although this approach may be quite costly, it is effective for critical applications such as payroll processing, which must be performed at specific times.

Fully equipped recovery centers provide standby data processing facilities for organizations that have experienced a total computer disaster and need to reconstitute their processing capabilities quickly.

A completely operating EDP facility is immediately available, including communications capabilities and office space for customer's employees. Some recovery centers operate as service bureaus, but that function is instantly superseded by a customer's need for all or part of the center for disaster recovery. Other centers are used only to rehearse contingency plans and to assure the operation of critical functions during an emergency.

Shell facilities do not include computers, but do provide those items that typically require long lead-times for installation, such as raised flooring, air conditioning, utilities, and communication lines.

Shells are cheaper than equipped rooms but are slower to start up, because computers must be installed after the disaster. The time delay is too long for most critical applications, although this alternative can be used effectively as a longer term solution. Arrangements can also be made to limit the number of organizations that might need the shell simultaneously, but the inability to test backup in an empty shell is a major drawback.

Time brokers specialize in locating processing time for one organization on a compatible system owned by another. The broker will, for a fee, "guarantee" the availability of specialized computer facilities at scheduled times.

The major drawback of this service is the possibility of conflicting requests for the same facilities at the same time. This possibility must be discussed and resolved before commitments are made.

Hardware vendor facilities are run by computer manufacturers, generally for demonstration purposes, but also as a marketing aid by providing customer backup.

A problem with this service is that the vendor normally has only a small system set up for demonstration purposes and is constantly changing its configuration or adding special features. Another concern may be loose access security, although vendors who have committed to provide this service are prepared to turn their showrooms into secure facilities to aid customers in emergencies.

Housekeeping, Guard Service, and Deliveries

Housekeeping
Housekeeping, or the cleaning of the data processing facilities, is usually done at night. The use of contract cleaning personnel has resulted in the theoretical danger that outside personnel have access to important or sensitive data. Although it may be thought that cleaning personnel would not have the passwords, the knowledge of what to look for, or the ability to access or change data, a determined and knowledgeable person could quite easily gain access in this way. In a small shop the computer should be shut down and locked after work hours. In a larger installation television camera observation by the guards or night operators should provide continuous monitoring.

Most cleaning companies bond their employees and specify two or more to be together when cleaning certain areas. Collusion is then required to breach security. A standard procedure of locking up all files, tapes, disks, and other records when not in use reduces security risks as well as permits faster housecleaning. Data that are not accessible cannot be stolen or compromised.

Guard Service
Guards who provide security to computer operations may be employees or may be obtained from an outside guard service on a contract basis. Their primary functions are to see that only authorized persons are permitted in the computer areas and to check packages removed from the premises for proper authorization.

The use of guards provided by an outside service could be considered to increase security vulnerability. Contracted guard services place outsiders in positions of control, and possibly afford them access to sensitive information. As a practical matter, the procedures by which contracted services interview, investigate, hire, and supervise the guards they employ should be no less stringent than those the customer itself would use. In addition, all guards should be individually bonded.

Delivery
Outside delivery service is often required to pick up input documents and to deliver reports and other outputs on a regular basis. Service bureaus usually provide regular delivery service to and from their customers and include that function in their service fees.

The risks associated with outside trucking services are loss of record materials, misplaced materials, damaged records, delayed deliveries, and sensitive information getting into the wrong hands. Loss of an only payroll master file would be a disaster. Loss of any materials would, at the very least, cost time and money for replacement.

To minimize these risks:

- Keep backup copies of all records that are being transported, in electronic or paper form.
- Schedule shipments with a time "cushion" to absorb expected delays, and monitor to detect nondelivery.
- Verify the reliability of the transportation service, whether service bureau, an independent trucker, or a courier.

- Assure that the delivery employees are bonded.
- Obtain insurance to cover losses that may occur in the process of moving computer materials.

Legal Considerations

When arranging for outside services, either with a contract company or an individual, and when purchasing computer equipment and software, written agreements are necessary to ensure a mutual understanding of what is to be done and by whom. Employee agreements on patents or copyrights is another area that requires attention as a result of data processing operations.

The writing or review of a contract's specifications may require a lawyer, depending on the type of arrangement and the type of service involved. Usually the agency providing the service takes the initiative in proposing at least the initial draft of the contract. Contracts should define the service to be performed or the products to be provided, and specify what constitutes performance agreeable to both parties.

Equipment Contracts

Equipment contracts are normally executed for the lease, purchase, or maintenance of significant items of computer hardware.

The legal department or an outside attorney should examine important equipment contracts to ensure that important oral representations are actually in the written agreement, and that the contract covers in unambiguous language all the terms that are important to the customer. Oral promises by a salesman are not binding. A knowledgeable data processing person should collaborate with the legal professional in this review. The types of provisions that the contract should include are:

- Scope
- Technical specifications
- Delivery and acceptance
- Installation
- Training
- Performance guarantees
- Modification
- Maintainability

- Warranties
- Termination of contract

Service Bureau Contracts

Service bureaus usually present standard contracts to potential customers, but it is almost always possible to negotiate changes.

It is prudent to plan and include terms for the time when the contract expires. The contract should allow for a warning period should either party wish to terminate or alter the agreement. The service bureau should not be allowed to unilaterally change its price for its services.

Security procedures at the service bureau should be described in detail. Physical access controls, employee bonding and supervision, handling and storage of records, files, and programs, and backup and recovery procedures are elements to be considered. Ownership of files, program media, and documentation should be clearly delineated.

Employee Agreements

Employee agreements should specify that all software and systems developed or purchased for the company are the property of the company. They should include a provision that there may be no "sharing" of such knowledge with other companies or individuals including the employee's friends in other companies. The employee contract should also specify that neither documentation, reports, files, or programs in any media are to be removed from company premises without written approval. Computer software purchase agreements usually provide that the software may not be duplicated except for internal backup or archival use. Employees should be forced to adhere to software terms by a provision in their employment agreement and by the publication of an appropriate policy.

Programming and Software Agreements

When contracting for original programs or complete systems, the quoted price will depend to a degree on whether exclusive ownership passes to the purchaser or the developer, or is shared for mutual benefit. For purposes of security, it is most advisable that the programs not be available for sale to others. Contracts should, therefore, specify exclusive ownership by the purchaser, with strong nondisclosure stipulations agreed to by the developer.

It is desirable for original systems specifications to include performance standards and to provide for the desired levels of documentation. Systems controls and file security provisions are of equally great or even greater importance, and they must be spelled out. Acceptance testing must not be considered complete until all of the security measures have been tested and approved.

Microcomputers

Contracts that involve small business computers should address the same security provisions as for large mainframes. Unfortunately, the relative low costs of microcomputer products often precludes costly security measures that are mandatory on mainframes.

Most microcomputer programs, such as spreadsheets, word processors, and data base managers, are purchased as standard packages, with few, if any, security provisions. Some users write their own programs, others contract for custom programs. Another type of vendor, the "turnkey" supplier, sells the hardware along with their own proprietary software and is responsible for the entire system's installation and for training the purchaser's personnel in its operations.

The security requirements for microcomputer programs or systems to be designed by outsiders are threefold: (1) making sure the vendor is reliable and competent, (2) being assured the vendor will continue to be available to help with problems or need modifications, and (3) verifying that the vendor incorporates security features in the system.

Even large software firms with a known reputation may assign trainees to a specific project. It is necessary, therefore, to verify that the individuals who will provide the actual services are properly qualified. Small firms and individual programmers need to be checked more carefully, generally by contacting people they have served on systems similar to the one being considered. With many systems, it is important that the program supplier be avilable for making revisions to and maintaining the system over its entire useful life, which may span many years. In general, larger and longer established firms provide better assurance as to their viability.

The purchaser of microcomputer services should verify that the vendor will incorporate those security requirements, described in detail elsewhere in this handbook, that are deemed necessary. These security features include backup of data and programs in case the originals are lost or destroyed, access control such as passwords and IDs, a disaster recovery plan, and measures to prevent theft of sensitive data.

Summary

Despite some of the additional security safeguards necessary when employing outside contract services, the economic advantages of time and skills obtained are so great that the practice will continue to thrive. General experience has proven that most service companies expect great efforts to assure that their customers' data are not compromised. Most consulting firms have approached their operations with the same ethical and professional standards as the public accounting field, and do not discuss, nor permit their employees to discuss, systems or reports developed for client companies.

It is necessary to define the level of security appropriate for various data processing operations and to be aware of what can happen to prevent those security objectives from being accomplished. Outside service people frequently have the ability and the opportunity to tamper with software, data files, and transactions. It is desirable to establish in advance what they will work on, where, when, with whom, and why, and to provide supervision where necessary so as to minimize the company's risk exposure.

Security priorities should be set and efforts made to attain a high degree of protection at a reasonable cost, consistent with company objectives.

Checklist Outside Contract Services

SOFTWARE AND PROGRAMMING SERVICES

	Yes	No
Has each system task been defined and documented?	☐	☐
Are firm specifications part of the contract?	☐	☐

Yes No

Has a definite time schedule been established? ☐ ☐

Were references checked? ☐ ☐

Was the consultant personally interviewed by a knowledgeable person? ☐ ☐

Is there an agreement with management on the cost and scope of each project? ☐ ☐

Has a review procedure been established and responsibility for review assigned? ☐ ☐

Has a decision been made on actions to be taken if time or cost exceeds estimates? ☐ ☐

Are the programs compatible with equipment and languages? ☐ ☐

Is each program package fully tested before acceptance? ☐ ☐

Is documentation adequate to permit correction and audit of the system? ☐ ☐

Was the system reviewed for conformance to security requirements? ☐ ☐

Is the system compatible with the company backup and security standards and procedures. ☐ ☐

SERVICE BUREAUS

Are controls maintained to at least the same degree they would be if the work was done in-house? ☐ ☐

Are security procedures described in detail? Have they been verified? ☐ ☐

Are the files or duplicated records safely backed up off-site? ☐ ☐

Is storage space available for company records to reduce transportation requirements? ☐ ☐

Does the agreement specify ownership of programs, files, media, and documentation? ☐ ☐

Does the agreement specify that all customer's property need be returned immediately in the event of termination? ☐ ☐

Yes No

FACILITIES MANAGEMENT

Do the documentation and operating procedures for the companies work? ☐ ☐

Are records protected and backed up? ☐ ☐

Does the operation have adequate controls? ☐ ☐

Is there physical security for the center? ☐ ☐

Has a backup plan been developed and tested? ☐ ☐

What assurances are there of employee reliability? ☐ ☐

DOCUMENTATION SERVICES

Would outside services do the job at less cost than in-house personnel? ☐ ☐

Is the extent of desired documentation known? ☐ ☐

Once established how is it to be maintained? ☐ ☐

Are documentation standards established for new projects? ☐ ☐

Is backup documentation retained? ☐ ☐

BACKUP FACILITIES

When would the facility be available for use? ☐ ☐

What time schedule would be required to stay in business? ☐ ☐

Is agreement between other companies possible to trade use in an emergency? If so, are systems designed to permit transportation to another similar equipment? ☐ ☐

Has a live test to recover from backup records been made? ☐ ☐

HOUSEKEEPING

What is the reputation of the service company? ☐ ☐

Does the service company bond its employees? . ☐ ☐

Yes No

Is the cleaning done in the presence of the organization's employees? ☐ ☐

Are your records secure prior to access by the service company employees? ☐ ☐

GUARD SERVICES

Is there planned guard use and schedule to maximize protection? ☐ ☐

Are there procedures for authorized access to facility for guards to enforce? ☐ ☐

Can they completely observe all exits? ☐ ☐

Are there procedures limiting removal of materials and requiring authorization? ☐ ☐

Are there defined guard responsibilities? ☐ ☐

Are the guards individually bonded? ☐ ☐

Yes No

TRUCKING

Is material insured when in the hands of truckers? ☐ ☐

Have definite schedules been established for delivery? ☐ ☐

Are materials transported listed and checked off? ☐ ☐

LEGAL CONSIDERATIONS

Has a regular procedure been established of what should be reviewed with a lawyer? ☐ ☐

Have cost and performance requirements been established for outside services? ☐ ☐

Have attempts been made to alter contracts from service companies that have undesirable clauses? ☐ ☐

CHAPTER 19

Security for Minicomputers and Microcomputers

By Carol W. Brown

Seldom has any industry seen such explosive change as has occurred in the computer field in the last 30 years. Because of this rapid change, users find themselves increasingly in need of more stringent security measures.

The first step toward achieving security is a complete understanding of the environment and the functions to be secured. This chapter gives an overview of how minicomputers and microcomputers are used, by whom, and for what purposes. It lists the objectives to be achieved and the risks that should be minimized in the security process. Finally, it offers specific suggestions that can aid the user in creating a more secure environment for minicomputers and microcomputers.

Thirty years ago, mainframe computers were operated in a central location, and processed in a batch fashion, performing one job at a time. Data came into the machine just to perform the specific task at hand, and then left the machine, to be retained in the form of punched cards, magnetic tape, or printed reports.

Minicomputers appeared in the early 1970s, offering as much computing power as earlier mainframes. This new breed of computer was decidedly cheaper, and far easier to operate, and thus brought computers down to a whole new class of users, including smaller companies and separate departments of larger companies.

In the mid-1970s microcomputers became available, and began a new wave of technology, creativity, and even lower costs. A mix of 1,700 typical data processing applications requiring millions of computer instructions cost $14.54 and required 375 seconds in 1955. In 1983 the same task cost seven cents and took one second to complete.

What Are Minicomputers and Microcomputers?

Meaningful definitions of these terms are elusive. As mainframe manufacturers have expanded their product lines, their computers have become both larger and smaller. The smaller mainframes are similar to larger minicomputers, or "superminis." The minicomputer manufacturers are also expanding their product lines in both directions, so that their low-end products are similar to the high-end of the microcomputer product lines in many ways. As one definition, mainframes can be classified as needing a raised floor and air conditioning. Minicomputers, in general, do not have the extensive cabling that requires a raised floor, but they do generate enough heat to require air conditioning. Microcomputers need neither a raised floor nor air conditioning.

While the progression from mainframe to mini to micro may seem like evolution, it is interesting to notice the revolutionary ways in which computing has become available for everyday use. All of today's users wish to control their own computers, to operate, program, repair, and dispose of them at relatively modest cost. Until the advent of small computers, this was neither economically nor technologically feasible.

Similarities Between Minicomputers and Microcomputers

Both a minicomputer and a microcomputer have a CPU, or central processing unit, where instructions are performed. Both have input devices, such as a keyboard or CRT (cathode ray tube). Both create output, in the form of a printed page or terminal display. Both have devices with which to perform storage functions, usually magnetic disk or magnetic tape. Both need software, which is the term for collections of logical machine instructions designed to perform specific tasks. Both have an *operating system*, which is the name for a group of specialized software programs that control the various components of a computer, while *application programs* actually do the tasks required by the user.

Differences Between Minicomputers and Microcomputers

Recognizing that the distinctions do not apply universally, a number of differences can be noted.

Most minicomputers are designed for operation by more than one user at a time. These users are generally provided with terminals, which are controlled by the CPU. There are generally provisions made in the operating system to handle the inevitable problems that occur in a multi-user environment, such as several users wanting to control the same device or piece of data.

Most minicomputers do not use the smaller capacity and slower storage components used by the microcomputers. Cassettes and diskettes are devices almost solely used by microcomputers. On the other hand, microcomputers are steadily infringing on the territories of the minicomputer through increasing use of multimillion character hard disks and magnetic tape drives.

Earlier microcomputers did not include the so-called higher level languages, such as COBOL or FORTRAN. These languages, which require compilation before execution, required more memory than was present in the CPUs of most early microcomputers. With the price of memory elements steadily dropping, high-level compiler languages are becoming available on a growing number of microcomputers.

Minicomputers have not replaced mainframes, as many claimed would be the case. Instead, they have augmented and extended their usefulness, by providing a way to "off-load" tasks that were not cost-effective on mainframes to a less costly mode of processing. In the same way, microcomputers are not likely to replace minicomputers, although they can also "off-load" tasks that microcomputers can perform at lower cost. But, overwhelmingly, microcomputers now make it possible to perform tasks that were never done economically on any computer, and this is the reason for their widespread popularity.

The Interactive Environment

In the early days of computing, all handling of data was done at a centralized place, the computer room or center. This area was off-limits to all but authorized personnel. Data could be checked, "hash-totalled," and otherwise verified. Rarely were the end-users of the data present for verification or correction of errors. Work was processed in batches, usually one batch at a time. The information needed to run each batch (such as the lists of valid customers) stayed in the computer only long enough for the work to be performed, and was then replaced by the data for the next batch of work.

In the present world of computers, users themselves are part of an interactive process. For example, an airline reservation system with terminals in hundreds of cities around the country would be impossible to operate with "batches" of work, because each request for information must be handled immediately as it is received. In order for the exchange to be useful, it must include the ability to trap and prevent errors. The term "interactive" means that the user and the system have a continuing and immediate dialogue in the form of data. In simple terms, such a dialogue might go like this:

Computer: Who are you?

Operator: I am operator 6006 with password (xxx) [password doesn't display].

Computer: What shall I do for you?

Operator: Show me flights from LaGuardia to Cleveland on January 13.

Computer: Flight 950 at 10 AM, flight 973 at 2 PM local time.

Operator: I want 2 coach seats on flight 974.

Computer: Flight 974 does not go from LaGuardia to Cleveland.

Operator: Make that flight 973, the names are C. Brown, M. Williams.

Computer: That space is confirmed. Your ticket is now printing on the printer.

The term *real-time* is used to describe this same function, since in addition to immediate dialogue, the transaction is actually processed at the same time. In this example, the file containing reservations for flight 973 is updated, and the ticket printed immediately as a result of this interactive dialogue.

The Interactive Environment Changes the Nature of Security

Even in this simple example, a number of security objectives can be identified:

- The operator is verified to be a valid user of the system.
- A person accompanying the operator cannot see the password.
- The operator is prevented from making a clerical error on the flight number.
- Another operator is prevented from booking the same two seats.
- More seats cannot be sold than are available, unless by intent.
- Duplicate tickets cannot be printed.

How Are Minicomputers and Microcomputers Used?

Personal Computers in the Home

Practical applications were not obvious when personal computers first appeared on the market. The applications available then consisted largely of such things as recipe files, Christmas card lists, and checkbook balancing. While there is nothing wrong with doing these things on a personal computer, they hardly justified the expense and effort involved. The general public has not yet realized the potential value in the home, not even in the areas of education and entertainment. This situation is unlikely to change until a truly valuable application with widespread appeal is available.

Through the addition of a device called a *modem*, a computer may be linked to an ordinary telephone line, instantly broadening the number of possibilities available. Certainly the long-range uses of the home computer will include acting as a communications terminal able to effect transactions in banking and shopping, for example. A consumer could pay his bills, seek investment advice, and inquire about and purchase tickets for concerts, sports events, and airline travel. Consumers could identify various sources for the desired purchase, and make effective cost comparisons in the process. In one application, monitoring the security of a home, various appliances could be turned on and off by computer control, while the status of doors and windows would be continuously monitored by appropriate sensors. In the event of fire, flood, or intrusion, the computer would dial the proper agency, report on the event, and request that help be dispatched. Despite all of the opportunities, it will probably be some time before the public becomes convinced that computers are as necessary as telephones.

Personal Computers in Corporations

It was the corporate small computer user who really launched the microcomputer on its way. A single kind of new program, the "spreadsheet," was itself responsible for the sale of hundreds of thousands of microcomputers.

Freed from the enormous drudgery of manually recalculating all of a worksheet when one of its figures changed, a spreadsheet user could vary the data and their interrelationships easily.

This sort of application has reached a mature state; where at first only the technically knowledgeable manager might be able to utilize these tools, many nontechnical managers now feel equally at home with them. Corporate users are an important segment of the marketplace, as it is their needs which most suppliers address.

Communications Computers

The communications area continues to involve a number of technical decisions with a multiplicity of conflicting standards.

Several kinds of computer communications arrangements exist, such as wide area networks and local area networks, bulletin boards, remote computing, banking transactions, and data base access. With the exception of some local area networks, they require the use of a modem. The term stands for the phrase "modulator demodulator," which describes how the device converts digital computer characters to and from analog telephone frequencies. With a modem attached, one computer may call another computer that possesses a compatible modem, over ordinary telephone lines, at either short or long distances. Most modems are able to originate or receive calls, though not both at the same time.

Computers for Data Base Access

One popular use of computer communications is to access computerized data bases such as airline schedules, news, legal decisions, and stock quotations. There are literally hundreds of data bases available. Some on-line data bases merely offer references to selected texts, while others offer complete texts (of articles, for example) with capabilities for searching via key words, names, and phrases. Microcomputers are providing large numbers of people with the means to access large bodies of information at attractive levels of convenience and cost.

Bulletin Boards

Electronic, computerized bulletin boards are actually data bases that may be accessed freely for posting or reading items of interest. Bulletin board services are often free to the caller, except for telephone charges. Bulletin boards serve as a means of communication between members of a group with common interests, for example, the users of a particular brand of computer. More free-form than the commercial data bases, these bulletin boards are frequently operated from an individual's home.

Some bulletin board services have received bad publicity and have been charged with promoting criminal and unethical activities. It is known that these so-called pirate bulletin boards have displayed numbers and names of stolen retail and telephone credit cards, along with telephone numbers and passwords to the mainframe computer systems of unsuspecting corporations, libraries, hospitals, and the like. As a result of some recent arrests, the courts will have to decide whether the operator of a bulletin board displaying such information is committing a crime. The courts' decision is certain to have its effect on the bulletin boards of the future.

Who Uses Microcomputers, and for What?

A recent article describes a microcomputer system used by Eskimos to record their disappearing tribal languages and culture. Another article describes the growing trend in computer usage among senior citizens. Computer camps for campers of all ages are popular. Sales and donations of computers to third world countries are on the rise. A whole new way of finding a job or hiring an employee seems to be emerging through various special purpose data bases. Another article describes programs that provide simulations of medical cases, which enable doctors to sharpen their diagnostic skills. Still another new program

enables students who wish to be farmers to access a national network of information, news, and training modules concerning agriculture. If there is one sure thing to say about who uses microcomputers and for what, it is "anyone, for anything."

Future Trends

The ideal system of the future would be able to do the following things:

- Perform the most widely used applications competently in a standalone environment. These applications include spreadsheets, word processing, business accounting, business graphics, and data base manipulation.
- Be able to exchange information between these applications conveniently.
- Be able to communicate with mainframes, minicomputers, and other microcomputer systems, emulating whatever terminal is required and being able to "upload" and "download" data as necessary.
- Do these processes automatically, conveniently, and perhaps unattended.
- Provide appropriate security features.
- Provide benefits that justify the costs involved.

The system builders who come the closest to offering such a system in one integrated package will meet the minimum demands of the future. Most of the pieces exist now, but no one system has them all.

The role of the data processing manager has changed enormously and will continue to do so. Initially, professional data processing managers greeted the "upstart" micros with contempt or indifference. As the use of small computers spread from the initial knowledgeable users to others less experienced, corporate data processing departments became deluged with calls for advice and assistance. Worse yet, these staffs were asked to explain errors and differences in figures not produced by their systems. Increasingly, managers of large data processing installations are becoming active in purchasing and standardizing microcomputer systems with the long-range goal of strengthening their operations. Microcomputers will continue to comprise an increasing share of corporate data processing budgets. Corporate data processing managers are hoping for a commensurate decrease in the applications backlog for specialized systems, and in lower expense for special-purpose terminals and for outside time-sharing services.

Users will continue to pressure data processing managers with their need to integrate personal computers into mainframes and communications networks. They will increasingly seek to use their personal computers in word processing, electronic mail, and general office systems.

The future is certain to bring greatly accelerated use of computer telecommunications for a host of applications. Users of on-line data base services will increase their usage of electronic mail as more users join the network. Already company letterheads are beginning to show their "Compuserve" or "Source" identification codes just as they list their telephone numbers. One of the few obstacles to unlimited growth of small computer usage is their apparent inability to resolve issues of security and privacy.

The Objectives of Security for Microcomputers and Minicomputers

Threats to the Buyer

Whether the buyer is an individual, purchasing a single unit in a computer store or through mail order or a corporation making a bulk purchase, rarely is an opportunity given in advance to operate and test all elements of the product. The purchaser of computer products therefore needs protection against the following hazards.

- Consumer fraud. Counterfeiters of consumer hardware and vendors of pirated software continue to function despite efforts at prosecution. Mail order fraud has also been perpetrated by vendors who have failed to fill paid orders that they advertised at tempting discounts.

- Defective merchandise. The consumer with a defective product has the double burden of determining which of several components is not functioning correctly, and then getting it repaired or replaced.

- Lack of warranty or merchantability. The consumer may have no guarantee that the product he is purchasing will serve the de-

sired function. This problem is compounded when the function he desires must be produced by an integrated system, and he must purchase the system from separate sources one component at a time.

- Obsolete or incompatible components. The velocity of change in this industry is extremely high. Even if the user buys only the most widely sold components, there is tremendous danger that some parts of his system will not be expandable or compatible with other parts in the future.

- Poor instructions and documentation. It may prove very difficult to operate or modify a system because of inadequate written guidance. This shortcoming is rampant in the products of this young and fast-changing industry.

Clearly, there is a need for caution on the part of the buyer before finalizing an acquisition. Improved consumer education for computer buyers is of prime importance.

Threats to the Seller

No industry will flourish unless buyers and sellers alike have the opportunity to operate profitably. The entire microcomputer software industry is being threatened by the practice of software piracy, the term currently given when computer programs are copied, sold, or given to others without the owner's consent. In the process, the owner or author of the software is denied a potential sale. It is not a simple issue.

There are many reasons why users might want to make copies of programs. Here are just a few:

- Make a backup copy in case the original becomes unreadable.

- Make a copy for a second computer owned by the same user.

- Make a copy for all the students in the classroom.

- Make a copy for the person in the next office.

- Make a copy for other departments.

- Make a copy for demonstration or testing.

- Make a copy available to all users on a communications network.

- Make a copy for the challenge of figuring out how.

- Make a copy because it's not supposed to be done.
- Make a copy to sell it for profit.

While some of these reasons are obviously unethical, some are legitimate and others are debatable. The ethics of copying software are not clearly defined. Some consider it nothing more than simple "sharing." Others rationalize that they are entitled to make copies of software because it is not bug free, or well enough documented, or reasonably enough priced.

Current copyright law is interpreted by some as prohibiting any duplication at all, regardless of whether or not the copying was done for the purpose of resale. Most current licensing agreements specify that the software may be executed only upon one computer, even if the buyer owns several machines for his own personal use.

Laws are being strengthened on both the federal and the state levels. The concept that the buyer agrees to abide by the terms printed on the outside of a package that he has opened is being extended to forbid explicitly the unauthorized duplication of software, regardless of existing copyright laws.

Manufacturers continue to strive to produce new kinds of devices to prevent copying. These developments often take the direction of encoding storage media with electronic fingerprints or signatures that cannot be erased. Some software vendors are calling for the cooperation of hardware vendors in tying a system's unique serial number to the software that it may execute. One vendor of a security product has advertised a contest in which a prize of $10,000 was to be awarded to anyone who could successfully copy the competition diskette within the allotted 30-day period. While these products are successful at deterring the casual copier, they also serve as a challenge for the serious ones. At the same time, several companies offer software that can be used to permit copying of almost any program disk, regardless of its copy protection scheme. Ostensibly these are to be used only for backup or archival purposes.

A software protection fund has been established by one group of vendors, and a major advertising campaign was launched to promote antipiracy sentiments. Several users have had lawsuits filed against them for having permitted copies of programs to be distributed within their companies. These lawsuits will be inconvenient and nonproductive trouble to defend at best.

The combination of ethical appeals, technological innovation, and legal strictures may reduce the incidence of unauthorized program use of copying, but it is unlikely to eliminate it. Perhaps the trend toward extremely low priced software will render the entire issue moot. When programs and documentation are available for little more than the cost of copying, the incentive for piracy disappears.

Threats to the Public

Now that 1984 has come and gone, it is ironic to realize that the Big Brother whose constant surveillance had been so dreaded may easily have become the teenager down the block. An increasing amount of data about an increasing number of people is stored on computers. Information containing bank account data, credit card purchases, names and addresses of family members, and employment history exists for literally millions of people. Tied together by the commonality of the social security number, data stored in consumer credit agencies, law firms' files, governmental files, hospital records and more will become increasingly vulnerable to invasion, inspection, misuse and destruction. Consider the fact that a single hard disk unit small enough to sit on top of a desk could contain the name and address of every person living in a large city. Existing legislation regarding individuals' rights to privacy may prove inadequate in the face of advances in recording, transmission, and access techniques.

It would be ostrichlike to pretend that these threats do not exist. Most large businesses and institutions would not, in fact could not, operate without large data bases. They are searched and shared rapidly in the normal course of business, and are integrated into the accounting, marketing, and billing procedures at the hearts of those businesses.

Current legislation has as its theme that computerized information should not be used in ways other than that for which it was collected, and that the subject of the data should have access to it for the purpose of correcting errors. Unfortunately, the sheer volume of data bases makes this almost unworkable.

As George Orwell envisioned 1984, there would be a single enormous data base, owned and operated by the State. He did not imagine that there would be hundreds of public, private, commercial, and nonprofit collections of data. Courts have generally ruled that data belong to their "keepers," but certainly the keepers must recognize that they are not going to build strong businesses in the long run by taking irresponsible steps with their customers' data. A commercial bank making depositor information available intentionally or inadvertently could not earn the level of customer confidence necessary to sustain its business operations.

Hackers

A widely publicized case in 1983 involved the "414"s, a group of young people in Milwaukee (area code 414) with personal computers, who were able to penetrate a few poorly secured systems. It is important to note that the actual dollar damage caused by the 414s was small. They were caught in the process of accessing a bank with a very good security system. Although there was much publicity given to this case, the really significant issue is the inadequacy of the security systems that they did enter. One can imagine the allure of "beating the system" to a group of adolescents, and the thrill of posting the victory anonymously on the appropriate bulletin board.

There is some evidence that the hacker problem is very serious indeed. Some feel that it has reached epidemic proportions, and that much of it has gone underground since the publicity given to the 414s. The offenses being committed are said to range from simple tricks and malicious mischief to serious criminal behavior. The offenses tend to fall into four main categories. The first category, theft of long distance services, is the activity that enables the rest of the offenses to occur. This activity has been called "phone-phreaking." Through the creation of so-called black boxes, which permit the user to place long distance calls anywhere without detection, and "blue boxes," which allow the user to receive calls in the same way, networks of shared intelligence can prosper. To some technically oriented youths these activities may have become a rite of passage into adulthood.

The second kind of offense, sharing pirated copies of software programs and stolen credit card information, can easily be done once the structure exists in which unlimited communications are freely available.

The third class of offense, breaking into large mainframe systems, is perhaps the most threatening, for here the issues of privacy and security intersect, and the potential losses are of inestimable value.

The fourth type of offense is theft of tangible property. Microcomputers, monitors, printers, and circuit boards all are small enough to be carried easily and unobtrusively.

A group of teens in Atlanta stole a quarter of a million dollars worth of computer equipment from office complexes. Often they would steal an entire system just to get one particular circuit board. They swapped parts as casually as boys swapped baseball cards 30 years ago. They used stacks of diskettes containing valuable corporate data to copy games on. The value of the components that were useful to them in some way was only a tiny fraction of the dollar value of the damage they caused.

Law enforcement agencies have been accused of not considering crimes to be serious where people were invading systems that were poorly protected. Their campaign against hackers has not been easy to wage. There has been no one single federal law that prohibits computer crime. In addition, juvenile offenders could not be prosecuted to the full extent of whatever state laws did apply. Juveniles could not even be interviewed unless their parents were present.

The role of the FBI is such that they cannot deter or detect crimes, but must respond when called in to assist with a crime that has already occurred, usually when amounts of $20,000 or more are involved. The FBI has made efforts to improve its ability to operate in the computer environment. It is admittedly difficult for them to make their agents computer-literate. There is frequently not enough staff in any one location to do the long-term "stake outs" and "stings" necessary to catch the offenders.

Banking is an industry that is most vulnerable to large losses. Billions of dollars around the world are transferred each day through computerized electronic fund transfer systems. The educated insider is an insidious threat to these systems, as was the case when a consultant in California nearly succeeded in diverting more than $10 million to his Swiss bank account. He might not have been detected had he simply made off with the proceeds of his theft.

Banks and other organizations are understandably reticent to publicize losses they may have suffered through weaknesses in their security systems. Rather than risk losing the confidence of their customers, they often prefer to absorb their losses silently. Security officers should monitor the hackers' bulletin boards and newsletters, and for sensitive telecommunications private leased-lines should replace public networks in order to shield transactions from "phone-phreaking" and dial-up intrusions.

The Dangers To Protect Against

Loss of Data

Trade secrets and sensitive data need to be protected against industrial espionage and malicious mischief. For example, a list of potential customers assembled with consirable effort or expense could be of great value to a competitor.

Just as real a problem is the deliberate or mischievous destruction of data. Unfortunately, the people most likely to commit such acts are employees or others entrusted with protection of the data who believe that they have cause for vengeful actions.

However, more data have been lost through careless or accidental destruction than through intentional damage or theft. The problem is exacerbated by the fact that there are no industry standards for the normal processes that all users need to employ. With one system, choices may be made from a menu. With others, striking different combinations of keys may issue the same command, while in some applications, several techniques may be used within the same program. As a consequence, some users accidentally erase important files and cause errors while trying to perform ordinary activities.

Misuse or Misinterpretation of Data

As increasing numbers of executives obtain data from their corporate data bases, and then analyze them with their own spreadsheet and data base programs, provision must be made to assure that the data remain up to date and accurate. Other issues need to be addressed, such as: (1) Does it really represent the facts he thinks it does? (2) What is the time period for which the data will remain meaningful? (3) In situations where the executive is permitted to "upload" data back into the data base, what protections exist that this in-jection of data will not destroy the integrity of the corporate data base? (4) In applications where users share data, is one user permitted to access data that another user might be in the process of modifying?

Loss of an Asset

The financial investment in a computer system must be protected. The user should avoid investing in obsolescent systems with elements or components that will become incompatible. Some purchasers restrict themselves only to the major vendors of hardware and software, feeling that they are safer being part of a large number of users. The motto "If the current is swift, stay in the middle" provides a generally useful guideline.

Protecting the financial investment includes protecting the physical equipment as well, and the traditional means of guarding, securing, and insuring physical assets should be applied. The scale of costs must relate to the value of the equipment itself and the information maintained within in.

Loss of the Ability to Process

Protection of the ability to process is often critical. Building a successful computer system almost always brings with it some dependence on that system. Alternate equipment, backup sites, and emergency plans must be available to justify that dependence.

Theft of Services

Theft of computer services produces lost revenues to service bureaus, telecommunications networks, and other vendors. In the corporate setting, the budgeting and cost allocation processes can become unmanageable unless accurate accounting is made of the system's usage.

Principles of Security for the Small Computer

Despite the fast-changing nature of this environment, there are several straightforward and constant factors that must be acknowledged.

1.   Involving more people requires more security. Security is intrinsically a problem of people. Their habits, attitudes, motivations, capa-

bilities, and concerns are the central elements in all security environments. Smaller computers involve more people and therefore complicate security. Having total control over individuals' use of small computers would be equivalent to trying to control how each employee handled the papers on his desk.

2. Integrated applications give their users access to more applications. Essentially, "the front door opens to a bigger house."

3. Trends toward portability and miniaturization widen the circle of security issues even further. For example, the advent of the lap-sized computer now means that a company must worry that its marketing budgets or other valuable information might be scrutinized by passengers in adjacent seats on airplanes and trains.

4. Smaller computers are usually operated with less supervision and assistance from data processing professionals. Computer professionals will be less accountable for information products than they have been in the past.

5. "User-friendly" systems are equally "misuser-friendly." On the other hand, the totally secure system is one that no one can penetrate— or even operate.

6. True security may not in fact exist on small computers. They are by definition excellent copying devices. They are not good homes for confidential data, without extensive precautions.

7. One hundred percent security cannot be achieved. The most effective systems apply security protection techniques in layers. Each layer of protection diminishes the chances of someone breaking through the barriers.

8. The most important single element in achieving a secure system is the use of common sense. A careful analysis of the risks to be avoided must first be done. Then techniques must be developed to reduce or eliminate those risks in a cost-effective manner.

9. Because computers are increasingly small and portable, concern for their environment must now be applied over a broader range of situations. Small computers are increasingly likely to be found in areas where there has been no preplanning for computer use. If it is undesirable to slow down the introduction of computers, then it is absolutely necessary that a thorough audit of their security and integrity be performed at the earliest possible moment.

Security Techniques

There are important aspects of a computer's environment that must be considered.

Clean Power

Power problems fall into three general categories. First there is power line "noise," or unexpected signals caused by the use of other equipment on the same line. Then there are fluctuations in voltage, which can damage equipment and cause a loss of data. Finally there are power outages, which for sensitive applications need to be anticipated and handled.

Small computers often are forced to coexist with numerous other electrical devices in the home and office. Elevators, coffee makers, copiers, and adding machines are notorious for causing spikes and surges on electrical lines. Small computers have not been designed to handle great surges or drops in power levels and may have their data damaged or destroyed where these phenomena occur.

A wide range of products is present for handling all three kinds of power problems. Professional help may have to be consulted in order to identify the specific kinds of problems that occur, and to select the appropriate device to prevent problems.

Uninterrupted Power

It is not only airline reservations systems or other critical mainframe systems that can justify the expense of an uninterruptible power supply (UPS), a device that supplies electricity in the event of a power failure. While it is often true that large systems deserve expensive devices to provide an alternate source of electricity, very small UPS systems also exist, and are reasonably priced. These devices contain enough power to enable a small computer to operate for minutes to hours after a complete power failure occurs. During this time the computer can be shut down in the prescribed manner, with no loss of data.

Static Electricity

Static electricity is often responsible for operational problems, especially during the winter when humidity is low. People build up a static charge while walking on carpets, for example. The discharge of this static to a computer can have the effect of a miniature lightning bolt.

Specially treated floor mats, humidifiers, and antistatic spray can help.

The Traveling Computer

Portable computer users must be increasingly concerned with the quality of electrical power in remote locations. Adapters, batteries, and specially pronged plugs should be carried along. In addition to checking out the kind of power that will be present at a foreign location, the international traveler who wishes to take his computer along should check ahead on several important matters. First, some airlines will not permit use of a computer on board, as they fear interference with navigating equipment. Second, travelers to foreign countries must register their computers with customs officials before departing so as to avoid difficulty in reentering the country of origination. Third, the United States government has restrictions on export of certain types of hardware and software, to prevent foreign powers from obtaining advanced computer technologies with military applications.

The General Environment

Smaller computers are generally engineered to be able to function in the same environments as their human operators. While some systems are specially encased in shielding to deter espionage, and others are built to withstand shock, vibration, and water, most systems can function only within normal ranges of temperature, humidity, contamination, and handling. In simple terms, most personal computers require more kind treatment than the average television set but less than a baby. Computers do better when their environments stay at relatively constant levels, especially with respect to temperature and humidity.

Good Housekeeping

Storage media should be treated with respect, as their information contents can be quite valuable. Because the data are invariably far most costly than the medium itself, it is penny-wise and pound-foolish to buy cheap diskettes and tapes. Even with high-quality media, attention should be given to disk and tape age and wear, as there is a finite limit to the read and write processing that any magnetic tape or disk can provide. Appreciably before this level is reached, data should

be copied to a new tape or disk and the old one discarded.

A critical aspect of good housekeeping is the regular creation of backup copies of a system's disk contents. Operators in large system environments are accustomed to backing up their systems on a regular basis. Users of smaller systems who are less experienced in data processing must learn to follow almost identical procedures. Backup copies of data are needed if there has been a hardware or software malfunction or a storage medium or its data has become damaged. They are also called upon when accidental erasures, improper entries of data, or an error in processing have occurred.

Some common sense practices for protecting microcomputer data on diskettes include:

Keep diskettes away from magnetic fields, including paperclip holders, magnetic clips, and even the telephone, which produces a magnetic field when it rings.

Use external storage labels consistently and carefully, writing on them only with a soft tip pen.

Avoid contact with food, beverages, and smoking materials. Any particles of solid matter, any liquids, and even smoke can do substantial damage to data and media.

Avoid contaminants such as dust, hair, fingerprints, and chemicals.

Keep all devices covered with static-resistant covers when not in use.

Be especially careful to avoid any contact with the exposed portions of tape or disk media.

Planning Ahead

Emergency plans should be made so that the ability to process is not jeopardized. Some users make reciprocal arrangements with others having similar hardware. Each will let the other process in case of need.

Some fail-safe, or fault-tolerant systems contain duplicate sets of devices. Through positive redundancy, these systems continue to operate even after failure of critical elements. Systems performing breathing assistance, spacecraft positioning, or air traffic control functions obviously must take these sorts of precautions. Commercial systems such as banking also use redundant mainframes and minicomputers, but for microcomputers it is feasible to retain one or more complete units as spares, to replace any malfunctioning unit.

Maintenance contracts that guarantee timely hardware repairs are prudent precautions against inevitable breakdowns. A maintenance log should be kept, which lists all equipment with manufacturer's serial number and details all maintenance procedures performed on the equipment.

When operating any electrical equipment, it is sensible to have a carbon dioxide or Halon fire extinguisher nearby. While most manufacturers suggest only that the power plug be pulled on a smoking microcomputer, if there is flame or evidence of fire, the carbon dioxide or Halon can be sprayed inside the vents on the cover. Carbon dioxide should not be sprayed directly on the CRT lest the sudden change of temperature cause an implosion and shatter the glass.

Plan ahead too for the availability of software assistance on a guaranteed basis. Software developers and independent companies offer a service where users can call a "hot-line" manned by technicians experienced in one or more of the major microcomputer software packages and their usage. For a fee, the user can guarantee that this sort of help will be available when needed.

Insurance plays an important role in planning ahead. Small computer users would be well advised to check that they have coverage for at least these risks:

- Damage from the user's own negligence
- Losses incurred on or off the premises
- Damage caused by power surges or lightning
- Damage caused by fire or water
- Costs of replacing purchased and internally developed data and programs
- Business interruption expense
- Loss or damage to equipment rented, borrowed, or leased

Ordinary business insurance and homeowners' policies often require riders or separate policies in order to cover these items, while specially designed insurance policies for small computer users may be more desirable.

Protecting Physical Equipment

Computer equipment needs to be protected from theft, loss, and vandalism, but the trends toward miniaturization and portability as well as widespread distribution make protection increasingly difficult. Locks, alarms, and surveillance cameras should be selected to fit the needs of the particular situation.

Personally owned computers can have the owner's name and identifiers etched or engraved upon the cover. Company-owned equipment should be permanently marked in a similar way.

Some specialized products have been introduced in order to meet the special needs of the small-computer user. One device literally sticks the computer to its work surface so tightly that the entire desk would have to be removed to carry it away. Several kinds of cases and cabinets place locks around the power supply and disk drives of the computer, or they disable some part of the system so that it cannot be successfully operated, much as the front tire of an expensive bicycle can be removed.

Protecting Communications Pathways

Except for service bureaus and other public facilities, it is important that a computer's incoming telephone number be kept confidential. Often telephone numbers of various systems are written in plain sight near the terminals of authorized users. While it is true that criminals seeking computer entry may use programs that successively dial thousands of numbers in a matter of hours, such tactics are not necessary when telephone numbers are not guarded with adequate security measures.

One protective technique is to obtain a nonlocal exchange telephone number. This reduces the possibility that a system will be called with repetitive-dialing equipment in the same area code.

Another technique is to verify that the caller is a bona fide one. As sentries have asked "Who goes there?" for thousands of years, the system must also ask for a user's identification. The usual method is to request the entry of a password.

People responsible for selecting their own passwords often choose very predictable, easily remembered ones. By doing simple research it is possible to obtain names of wives, children, friends, and dogs, which quite often are used as passwords. It is also possible to learn passwords by watching an authorized user key them. To prevent this, passwords should never be displayed or printed as they are used, and care should be taken to shield the keyboard from observation.

Passwords can sometimes be obtained by successively keying all the possibilities. A one- or two-letter password can be identified in minutes manually or by a program that tries all of the combinations and permutations in turn. By using longer passwords the time required to do this is extended geometrically. Even more effective is the use of special characters, and especially control characters. These are made by the combination of ordinary keys and a key usually marked "control" on the keyboard. Control characters resemble ordinary characters visually but are not the same internally. The use of longer passwords and control characters makes passwords much more difficult to determine automatically.

Devices exist that identify users based on biomedically unique characteristics, such as hand-span or retinal patterns, but the password is generally the most cost-effective means of authenticating a user. The National Bureau of Standards publication *Password Usage Standard* covers in considerable detail the factors relating to the design, implementation, and use of password systems.

The modem itself, or an associated device, can also play a role in rejecting intruders. Modems are available with enough intelligence to detect repeated calls and invalid password entries. These devices can be programmed to shut down the port after a predetermined number of invalid attempts. Logs can also be kept that record each attempt. These logs should be analyzed on a regular basis to determine whether changes in the security arrangements need to be made.

An important technique involves the ability to consult files containing the identities and telephone numbers of all valid system users. Once an incoming call signals that a user wishes to log onto the system, the device verifies that the user is a bona fide one. It then terminates the incoming call and calls the user back at his stored telephone number. This technique may prevent hackers from accessing a system, but it is not appropriate for travelers or other users who do not call from a predetermined telephone number.

Limiting Access to Data

In the corporate environment, policies must be set up and enforced so that only appropriate people have access to data and computers. The problem is intensified with wide-area and local-area networks that are able to link computers and their data bases. Questions of who shares which data become increasingly critical as these networks grow in popularity, and passwords become increasingly necessary.

Passwords are as valuable as the data they protect. They should be changed frequently, reflecting the various privilege levels of their users. They should not be stored in a microcomputer as a convenience in performing automatic logon to a mainframe computer, nor should they be posted in public view.

Record locking must be used so data are not subject to simultaneous update by different users. Confidential memos and data that were once hand carried between offices can now be read by everyone on an electronic mail network unless adequate security controls are installed.

Encryption should be used to protect highly sensitive data. It is effective in foiling browsers, but the keys, like passwords, must be protected with great care, and changed frequently.

Menu techniques are useful in limiting an unsophisticated user's access. Once a person has identified himself as a valid user, a menu only appropriate to his privilege level can be placed before him. In this way, a member of the accounting department, for example, could not access personnel applications and vice versa. Similarly, sensitive files can be hidden by preventing them from appearing in on-screen directory listings.

Logging techniques are effective when they record the activities of users as they occur. A logging system should record each time a user enters or leaves the system, and it should record any access to sensitive or restricted data. It should also deny a user access after a specified number of invalid password attempts or other transgressions has occurred.

Thinking Securely

Users must be trained to be security conscious. Each organization should prepare, circulate, and enforce a written security policy. This document should present the firm's rationale for initiating its security procedures, and detail how these procedures would affect employees' jobs. The policy should be presented to all groups of users, particularly addressing any reservations on their part. A security coordinator should be appointed within each major group of users, with responsibility for data resources of the group.

The penalties for security infractions should be clearly stated and imposed when necessary. Continuing audit and reinforcement of proper procedures will help to ensure that everyone is security conscious and conforms to company policy.

Conclusion

This chapter has discussed minicomputers and microcomputers, the role they are currently playing in the computer industry, and the security issues facing their users. These issues are essentially the same as those facing mainframe computer users, but with important variations. Small size, portability, low cost, and use by ever larger numbers of people bring additional levels of challenge to computer security problems.

For another summary of related minicomputer security issues, see Appendix 18, a copy of Personal Computer Security Considerations published by the National Computer Security Center.

Microcomputer Checklist

	Yes	No
Are data copied to new diskettes and tapes before age and wear cause loss of or damage to the data they contain?	☐	☐
Are backup copies of each system's disk contents made promptly and regularly?	☐	☐
Are diskettes kept away from magnetic fields?	☐	☐
Are external storage labels written on with a soft tip pen?	☐	☐
Are food, beverages, and smoking materials kept out of microcomputer areas?	☐	☐
Are contaminants avoided, such as dust, hair, fingerprints, and chemicals?	☐	☐

	Yes	No
Are all devices covered with static-resistant covers when not in use?	☐	☐
Is contact with exposed portions of tape or disk media avoided?	☐	☐
Do maintenance contracts guarantee timely repairs?	☐	☐
Is a carbon dioxide or Halon fire extinguisher kept near each microcomputer?	☐	☐
Does insurance cover damage from users' negligence; losses on or off the premises; damage caused by power surges, fire, or water; cost of replacing data and programs; business interruption expense; and loss of or damage to equipment rented, borrowed, or leased?	☐	☐
Is owner's identification etched on equipment covers?	☐	☐
Is the equipment housed in a locked cabinet, or locked or firmly attached to fixed adjacent furniture?	☐	☐
Is the microcomputer's incoming telephone number kept confidential?	☐	☐
Is a password required for initiating use of the microcomputer if it contains sensitive data?	☐	☐
Are passwords never displayed or printed as they are used?	☐	☐
Are logs maintained which record each attempt to use the microcomputer?	☐	☐
Must a user via telephone be called back at his stored telephone number before access is granted?	☐	☐
Are passwords changed frequently?	☐	☐
Is encryption used to protect highly sensitive data?	☐	☐
Are menus designed to prevent use by someone unfamiliar with the system?	☐	☐
Are sensitive files kept from appearing in on-screen listings?	☐	☐
Are users trained to be security conscious?	☐	☐

	Yes	No
Is a written security policy circulated and enforced?	☐	☐
Has a security coordinator been appointed with responsibility for data resources?	☐	☐

	Yes	No
Are penalties for security infractions clearly stated and imposed when necessary?	☐	☐
Are proper procedures and security rules audited regularly?	☐	☐

Suppliers of Computer Based Risk Analysis Software

IST/RAMP (Risk Analysis and Management Program)
International Security Technology, Inc.
11250 Roger Bacon Drive, Suite 11
Reston, VA 22090

RISKPAC (Qualitative Analysis)
RISKCALC (Quantitative Analysis)
Profile Analysis Corp.
P.O. Box 875
454 Main Street
Ridgefield, CT 06877

RA/SYS (Risk Analysis SYStem)
Nander Brown
2315 Freetown Court, Unit 1B
Reston, VA 22091

RISKA
Chesapeake Computer Group
440 Sycamore Valley Road West
Danville, CA 94526

CAPARS (Computer Assets Protection and Risk Reduction System)
The Concorde Group, Inc.
2000 Bering Drive–Suite 850
Houston, TX 77057

BDSS (Bayesian Decision Support System)
Ozier-Perry Associates
870 Marset Street, Suite 1001
San Francisco, CA 94102

APPENDIX 2

Security Standards Manual
Table of Contents
(Sample)

1.1 General Security Standards

    1.1.1 Introduction
    1.1.2 Organizational Responsibilities
    1.1.3 Security Evaluation and Updating
    1.1.4 Reporting Security Violations
    1.1.5 Security Auditing

1.2 Physical Facility Security

    1.2.1 Site Selection
    1.2.2 Facility Design and Construction
    1.2.3 Fire and Accident Prevention
    1.2.4 Access Control
    1.2.5 Computer Room Emergency Procedures
    1.2.6 Contingency Plan

1.3 Data Security

    1.3.1 Data Protection
    1.3.2 File Backup/Recovery
    1.3.3 Off-Site Storage Procedures
    1.3.4 Release of Production Programs
    1.3.5 File/Data Integrity
    1.3.6 Telecommunications Security

1.4 Personnel Security

    1.4.1 Pre-Employment Screening
    1.4.2 Hiring Practices
    1.4.3 Security Orientation and Training
    1.4.4 Termination/Transfer Procedures
    1.4.5 Personnel Security Assessment
    1.4.6 Contract Personnel

Confidentiality Agreement (Sample)

This AGREEMENT is entered into as of _____, by _____(Employee Name)_____ (hereinafter "Employee"), an employee of _____(Company Name)_____, with offices at _____(Company Address)_____ (hereinafter "Employer").

FOR AND IN CONSIDERATION OF employment by Employer, the Employee agrees, during the term of his employment and forever thereafter to keep confidential all information and material provided to him by Employer, excepting only such information as is already known to the public, and including any such information and material relating to any customer, vendor or other party transacting business with the Employer, and not to release, use or disclose the same except with the prior written permission of Employer. The within understandings shall survive the termination or cancellation of this Agreement or of the Employee's employment, even if occasioned by the Employer's breach or wrongful termination. Employee recognizes that the disclosure of information by the Employee may give rise to irreparable injury to the Employer or to the owner of such information, inadequately compensible in damages and that, accordingly, the Employer or such other party may seek and obtain injunctive relief against the breach or threatened breach of the within undertakings, in addition to any other legal remedies which may be available.

By _____   _____
                                        Date
Title _____

Admissibility of Computer Records

Part VIA
Computer Evidence

59a. Interpretation. In this Part, unless the contrary intention appears—

"computer" means a device that is by electronic, electromechanical, mechanical or other means capable of recording and processing data according to mathematical and logical rules and of reproducing that data or mathematical or logical consequences thereof:

"computer output" or "output" means a statement or representation (whether in written, pictorial, graphical or other form) purporting to be a statement or representation of fact—

(a) produced by a computer;

or

(b) accurately translated from a statement or representation so produced:

"data" means a statement or representation of fact that has been trancribed by methods, the accuracy of which is verifiable, into the form appropriate to the computer into which it is, or is to be, introduced.

59b. Admissibility of computer output. (1) Subject to this section, computer output shall be admissible as evidence in any civil proceedings.

(2) The court must be satisfied—

(a) that the computer is correctly programmed and regularly used to produce output of the same kind as that tendered in evidence pursuant to this section;

(b) that the data from which the output is produced by the computer is systematically prepared upon the basis of information that would normally be acceptable in a court of law as evidence of the statements or representations contained in or constituted by the output;

(c) that, in the case of the output tendered in evidence, there is, upon the evidence before the court, no reasonable cause to suspect any departure from the system, or any error in the preparation of the data;

(d) that the computer has not, during a period extending from the time of the introduction of the data to that of the production of the output, been subject to a malfunction that might reasonably be expected to affect the accuracy of the output;

(e) that during that period there have been no alterations to the mechanism or processes of the computer that might reasonably be expected adversely to affect the accuracy of the output;

(f) that records have been kept by a responsible person in charge of the computer of alterations to the mechanism and processes of the computer during that period;

and

(g) that there is no reasonable cause to believe that the accuracy or validity of the output has been adversely affected by the use of any improper process or procedure or by inadequate safeguards in the use of the computer.

(3) Where two or more computers have been involved, in combination or succession, in the recording of data and the production of output derived therefrom and tendered in evidence under this section, the court must be satisfied that the requirements of subsection (2) of this section have been satisfied in relation to each computer so far as those requirements are relevant in relation to that computer to the accuracy or validity of the output, and that the use of more than one computer has not introduced any factor that might reasonably be expected adversely to affect the accuracy or validity of the output.

(4) A certificate under the hand of a person having prescribed qualifications in computer system analysis and operation or a person responsible for the management or operation of the computer system as to all or any of the matters referred to in subsection (2) or (3) of this section shall, subject to subsection (6) of this section, be accepted in any legal proceedings, in the

absence of contrary evidence, as proof of the matters certified.

(5) An apparently genuine document purporting to be a record kept in accordance with subsection (2) of this section, or purporting to be a certificate under subsection (4) of this section shall, in any legal proceedings, be accepted as such in the absence of contrary evidence.

(6) The court may, if it thinks fit, require that oral evidence be given of any matters comprised in a certificate under this section, or that a person by whom such a certificate has been given attend for examination or cross-examination upon any of the matters comprised in the certificate.

59c. Regulations. The Governor may make such regulations as he deems necessary or expedient for the purposes of this Part, and without limiting the generality of the foregoing those regulations may—

(a) make any provision for the purposes of this Part with respect to the preparation, auditing or verification of data, or the methods by which it is prepared;

and

(b) prescribe the qualifications of a person by whom a certificate may be given, or a translation made, under this Part.

Revenue Procedure 86–19: IRS Guidelines for ADP Records

Section 1. Purpose.

.01 The purpose of this revenue procedure is to update Rev. Proc. 64–12, 1964-1 (Part 1) C.B. 672, and Rev. Proc. 80–42, 1980-2 C.B. 776, and to specify the basic requirements that the Internal Revenue Service considers to be essential in cases where a taxpayer's records are maintained within an Automatic Data Processing (ADP) system. Rev. Proc. 64–12 provides guidelines for record requirements to be followed in cases where part or all of the accounting records are maintained within an ADP system, and Rev. Proc. 80–42 extended the ADP requirements to the windfall profit tax under section 4997 to the Internal Revenue Code. References here to ADP systems include all accounting and/or financial systems that process all or part of a taxpayer's transactions, records, or data by other than manual methods.

.02 The technology of automatic data processing has evolved rapidly, and new methods and techniques are constantly being devised and adopted. The requirements set forth in Section 5 of this revenue procedure are intended to ensure that all machine-sensible records generated by a taxpayer's automatic data processing system are retained so long as they may become material in the administration of any internal revenue law. These requirements will be modified and amended as the need indicates to keep pace with developments in automatic data processing systems.

.03 This revenue procedure pertains to taxpayers with assets of $10 million or more. For the purpose of this revenue procedure, a controlled group of corporations will be considered to be one corporation and the assets of all members of the group will be aggregated.

.04 The District director has the authority to enter into an agreement with the taxpayer to modify or waive any or all of the specific requirements of this revenue procedure. The taxpayer remains subject to all requirements of this procedure that are not specifically modified or waived by the agreement.

Section 2. Background.

.01 Section 6001 of the Code provides that every person liable for any tax imposed by the Code, or for the collection thereof, shall keep such records as the Secretary may from time to time prescribe.

.02 Rev. Rul. 71–20, 1971-1 C.B. 392, establishes that all machine-sensible data media used for recording, consolidating, and summarizing accounting transactions and records within a taxpayer's automatic data processing system are records within the meaning of section 6001 of the Code and section 1.6001-1 of the Income Tax Regulations and are required to be retained so long as the contents may be material in the administration of any internal revenue law. Accordingly, a taxpayer is required to retain all machine-sensible files generated by its automatic data processing system unless a retention agreement is reached with the District Director to limit the retention to certain specified records.

Section 3. Scope and Objectives.

.01 Modern data processing accounting systems are capable of recording business transactions much more rapidly and accurately than manual systems, and they are capable of retaining and producing vast amounts of data. The ability to produce in legible form data necessary to determine at a later date whether or not the correct tax liability has been reported must be carefully considered in designing and programming an ADP system. This factor may add to the complexity of the system and require additional cost, but this cost may be negligible in comparison to the expense that may be incurred at a later date if the system cannot practically and readily provide the information needed to support and substantiate the accuracy of the previously reported tax liability. This revenue procedure encompasses all types of data processing systems, including those using a Data Base Management System.

.02 The requirements of this revenue procedure pertain to income, windfall profit, excise, employment, and estate and gift taxes.

.03 The requirements of this revenue procedure are applicable to the machine-sensible records generated by a Controlled Foreign Corporation (CFC), since the definition of "records" in section 964(c) and 982(d) of the Code and the regulations thereunder has the same meaning as "records" as used in section 6001 and section 1.6001-1(a) of the regulations.

.04 Machine-sensible records used by an insurance company to determine its loss deduction under section 832(b)(5) of the Code must be retained in accordance with the requirements of this revenue procedure and Rev. Proc. 75–56, 1975-2 C.B. 596. The machine-sensible file(s) for a particular taxable year include(s) that year and the seven preceding years, all of which must be retained so long as they are material to the examination of the return. Normally that materiality continues until the expiration of the statute of limitations (including extensions) for the tax year under examination.

Section 4. Machine-Sensible Records Evaluation.

.01 A record evaluation may be conducted by the District Director to determine of a taxpayer may limit its retention of machine-sensible records. This evaluation of the data processing and accounting systems may be initiated by the District Director or requested by the taxpayer and is not an "examination," "investigation," or "inspection" within the meaning of section 7605(b) of the Code, since such an evaluation is not directly related to the determination of tax liability for a particular taxable period.

.02 The District Director may periodically initiate tests to establish the readability and completeness of the machine-sensible records retained under a retention agreement. Such test are not an examination of the books and records within the meaning of section 7605(b) of the Code, since they are not directly related to the determination of tax liability for a particular taxable period.

Section 5. Requirements.

.01 All machine-sensible records must be retained by the taxpayer. The retained records must be in a retrievable format that provides the information necessary to determine the correct tax liability. The utilization of a service bureau or time-sharing service does not relieve the taxpayer of its responsibilities as described in this revenue procedure.

.02 Documentation that provides a complete description of the ADP portion of the accounting system and those files that feed into the accounting system must be retained. The statements and illustrations as to the scope of operations should be sufficiently detailed to indicate: (a) the application being performed, (b) the procedures employed in each application, and (c) the controls used to insure accurate and reliable processing. The following specific documentation for all files must also be retained:

1. record formats (including the meaning of all "codes" used to represent information);

2. flowcharts (system and program);

3. label descriptions;

4. source program listings of programs that created the files retained; and

5. detailed charts of accounts (for specific periods).

Major changes to the ADP system, together with their effective dates, should be noted in order to preserve an accurate chronological record. This record should include any changes to software or systems and any changes to the formats of files. Audit trails should be designed to insure that details underlying the summary accounting data, such as invoices and vouchers, may be easily identified and made available to the Service upon request.

.03 The records are required to be retained so long as their contents may become material in the administration of any internal revenue law. At a minimum, this materiality is possible until the expiration of the statute of limitations (including extensions) for each tax year. In certain situations, files should be retained for a longer period (for example, fixed assets and insurance loss reserve).

.04 The provisions of this revenue procedure do not relieve taxpayers of their responsibility for retaining hardcopy records. The hardcopy records may be retained in microfiche or microfilm format in accordance with the requirements outlined in Rev. Proc. 81–46, 1981-2 C.B. 621. These records are *not* a substitute for the machine-sensible records required to be retained as described in section 5.01 above.

.05 All retained records must be clearly labeled and stored in a secure environment. For example, supplemental labels with the statement, "Retain for IRS until _____" or "Retain for IRS, Consult Tax Manager Before Releasing" should be used and affixed to each tape reel, disk pack, or diskette being retained, with a retention date on the internal label. Back up machine-sensible files being retained for the Service should be stored at an off-site location.

.06 The taxpayer must have the capability to access the retained records at the time of a Service examination. When the data processing system that created the records is being replaced by a system in which the records would not be compatible, the taxpayer must convert them to a compatible system. Any changes in the accessibility of the retained records must be reported to the Service. The District Director has the authority to enter into an agreement with the taxpayer to modify or waive any or all of the requirements for conversion or to approve substitute procedures. The taxpayer remains subject to all requirements that the agreement does not specifically modify, waive, or replace.

.07 The limitation pursuant to a retention agreement on machine-sensible records to be retained does not apply to subsidiary companies acquired, or accounting and tax systems added, subsequent to the completion of the record evaluation or re-evaluation. All machine-sensible records produced by these companies or systems must be retained until such time as a reevaluation is conducted by the District Director. On disposition of a subsidiary the files being retained for the Service by, or for, the disposed subsidiary should be retained until a new evaluation can be made by the District Director. A reevaluation can be requested by the taxpayer.

.08 The taxpayer should make periodic checks on all files being retained for use by the Service. If any machine-sensible records required to be retained are subsequently lost, destroyed, damaged, or found to be incomplete or materially inaccurate, the taxpayer must report this to the District Director and re-create the files within a reasonable period of time.

.09 The use of Data Base Management Systems (DBMS) necessitates the implementation by the taxpayer of appropriate procedures to ensure that required records and other needed documentation are retained to comply with this revenue procedure. A taxpayer is in compliance if it creates, for Service use, a sequential file(s) that contains all detail transactions necessary to create an audit trail to trace back to the underlying source documents. All necessary fields must be identified and the file documentation must follow the rules in section 5.02 above. This process should be reviewed by the Service prior to creation. These sequential files must be processible by conventional means. As a minimum, the following documentation must be made available:

1. Data Base Description (DBD);
2. Record layout of each segment with respect to the fields in the segments;
3. Systems Control Language;
4. Program Specification Block (PSB);
5. Program Communication Block (PCB).

Any taxpayer that has questions or is uncertain as to its responsibilities with respect to the retention of data when utilizing a DBMS should contact the District Director.

Section 6. Penalties.

Failure to comply with the provisions of this revenue procedure may result in the assertion of the addition to tax under section 6653(a) of the Code, a civil penalty. The criminal penalty under section 7203 may also be applicable. *See* Rev. Rul. 81–205, 1981-2 C.B. 225. In addition, the District Director may issue a Notice of Inadequate Records if machine-sensible records were not properly retained as required by this revenue procedure. . . .

IRS Revenue Ruling 71-20: What Are Records

26 CFR 1.6001–1: Records. (Code Sec 6001)

Rev. Rul. 71–20[1] Advice has been requested whether punched cards, magnetic tapes, disks, and other machine-sensible data media used in the automatic data processing of accounting transactions constitute records withing the meaning of section 6001 of the Internal Revenue Code of 1954 and section 1.6001–1 of the Income Tax Regulations.

In the typical situation the taxpayer maintains records within his automatic data processing (ADP) system. Daily transactions are recorded on punched cards and processed by the taxpayer's computer which prints daily listings and accumulates the individual transaction records for a month's business on magnetic tapes. At the month's end the tapes are used to print out monthly journals, registers, and subsidiary ledgers and to prepare account summary totals entered on punched cards. The summary data from these cards is posted to the general ledger and a monthly printout is generated to reflect opening balances, summary total postings, and closing balances. At the year's end several closing ledger runs are made to record adjusting entries. In other situations taxpayers use punched cards, disks, or other machine-sensible data media to store accounting information.

Section 6001 of the Code provides that every person liable for any tax imposed by the Code, or for the collection thereof, shall keep such records as the Secretary of the Treasury or his delegate may from time to time prescribe.

Section 1.6001-1(a) of the Income Tax Regulations provides that any person subject to income tax shall keep such permanent books of account of records, including inventories, as are sufficient to establish the amount of gross income, deductions, credits, or other matters required to be shown by such person in any return of such tax.

Section 1.6001-1(e) of the regulations provides that the books and records required by this section shall be retained so long as the contents thereof may become material in the administration of any internal revenue law.

It is held that punched cards, magnetic tapes, disks, and other machine-sensible data media used for recording, consolidating, and summarizing accounting transactions and records within a taxpayer's automatic data processing system are records within the meaning of section 6001 of the Code and section 1.6001-1 of the regulations and are required to be retained so long as the contents may become material in the administration of any internal revenue law.

However, where punched cards are used merely as a means of input to the system and the information is duplicated on magnetic tapes, disks, or other machine-sensible records, such punched cards need not be retained.

It is the desire of the Internal Revenue Service to provide fair and equitable treatment to all taxpayers using ADP accounting systems and to minimize undue hardships of ADP recordkeeping. It is recognized that ADP accounting systems will vary from taxpayer to taxpayer and, usually, will be designed to fit the specific needs of the taxpayer. Accordingly, taxpayers who are in doubt as to which records are to be retained or who desire further information should contact their District Director for assistance.

---

[1] Also released as Technical Information Release 1062, dated December 31, 1970.

Confidential and Proprietary Information Agreement (Sample)

To:_____   Date:_____

You have this day agreed to be employed by Able Computing Services Corporation (the "Company"). As you have been advised, the business of the Company involves valuable, confidential and/or proprietary data and information of various kinds. Such data and information concern, among other things:

a. the names of the Company's customers and the nature of the Company's relationships with such customers;

b. the Company's computer systems;

c. developments, improvements and inventions that are or may be produced in the course of the Company's operations; and

d. the business of the Company's customers and potential customers, which submit private material to the Company for handling and processing.

It will hurt the Company if any such data or information become known to the Company's competitors or to people not employed by the Company; or if any such developments, improvements or inventions are not disclosed and transferred to the Company. It is therefore required, as a condition of your employment and of your continuing employment by the Company, and in consideration of the Company's accepting and continuing to accept you as an employee, that you agree with the Company as hereinafter set forth. THIS AGREEMENT WILL CREATE OBLIGATIONS WHICH ARE BINDING ON YOU. IT IS IMPORTANT. PLEASE READ IT IN FULL BEFORE YOU SIGN.

1. **Disclosure of Information.** You recognize and acknowledge that the following are valuable, special and unique assets of the Company's business:

a. the lists of the Company's customers; and

b. the Company's various computer systems, as such systems may exist from time to time, including, without limitation, computer hardware, computer programs, computer languages, and other computer software, and methods, techniques or algorithms of organizing or applying the same (collectively referred to herein as the "Company's Computer Systems").

You will not, during or after the term of your employment, use for your own benefit, or, without the prior consent of the Company, disclose to any person (other than in the ordinary conduct of the Company's business):

a. the lists of the Company's customers, or any part thereof;

b. any of the Company's Computer Systems, or any part thereof; or

c. any other information, not generally known, concerning the Company or its operations, products, personnel or business, acquired, disclosed, or made known to you while in the employ of the Company, which, if used or disclosed, could, with reasonable possibility, materially and adversely affect the business of the Company, or accord to a competitor of the Company a material competitive advantage.

In addition, you will not, during or after the term of your employment, use for your own benefit or, without the prior consent of the Company, disclose to any person (other than in the ordinary conduct of the Company's business) any private material submitted to the Company by any customer, potential customers, supplier or co-venturer.

2. **Surrender of Written Material on Termination.** Upon termination of your employment, in any manner or for any reason, you will promptly surrender to the Company all copies of any of the following in your possession, custody or control:

a. lists of the Company's customers, or any part thereof;

b. any of the Company's Computer Systems, or any part thereof; or

c. any memoranda, manuals, brochures, external or internal specifications, listings, papers, or other documents or documentation, and other materials and equipment belonging to the Company or relating to the Company's Computer Systems, or the operations, products, personnel or business of the Company, or the business of any of its customers or prospective customers.

3. Disclosure and Assignment of Proprietary Information, Inventions, Etc. You will forthwith fully and completely disclose to the Company:

a. any and all Computer Systems, including, without limitation, computer hardware, computer programs, computer languages and other computer software, and methods, techniques or algorithms of organizing or applying the same, and improvements and developments thereof; and

b. any and all innovations, inventions, developments and improvements (whether or not patentable) and all writings (whether or not copyrightable) pertaining to any aspect of the manufacture, use or application of computers, or computer hardware or software, or pertaining to the compilation of data or information or the methods or standards of selecting or arranging data or information, or pertaining to any business in which the Company is now or may hereafter be engaged during your employment;

made, developed and/or conceived by you, alone or jointly with others, at any time heretofore, or any time hereafter, during your employment or within six months after termination thereof.

You will, and hereby do, assign to the Company or its nominee or designee (without any separate remuneration or compensation to you, other than the compensation paid to you from time to time in the course of your employment hereunder), all of your right, title and interest in and to such Computer Systems, hardware, programs, languages, software, methods, techniques and algorithms, and improvements and developments pertaining thereto, and such innovations, inventions, developments, improvements and writings. You will furnish to the Company, upon its request and at its expense, all such assignments, transfers, affidavits, certificates, certifications and other documents and assurances as the Company may reasonably request in order to confirm the fact of the Company's ownership thereof.

You further agree that the provisions of this paragraph 3 shall be binding upon you, irrespective of the duration of your employment by the Company, the reason for the cessation of your employment by the Company, or the amount of your compensation.

4. Enforcement. You agree that, in the event of a breach or threatened breach by you of the provisions of paragraphs 1, 2, or 3 of this Agreement, the Company's remedies at law would be inadequate, and the Company shall be entitled to an injunction to enforce such provisions (without any bond or other security being required), but nothing herein shall be construed to preclude the Company from pursuing any action or further remedy, at law or in equity, for any breach or threatened breach of such provisions or any other provisions of this Agreement, including, but not limited to, the recovery of damages.

5. Miscellaneous. The rights and obligations of the Company under this Agreement shall inure to the benefit of and shall be binding upon the successor and assigns of the Company. The laws of the State of New Hampshire shall govern all questions relative to the interpretation and constructions of this Agreement, and to the performance hereof. No waiver by the Company of any default by you hereunder shall in any way prejudice the Company with respect to any subsequent default by you hereunder (whether or not similar). This Agreement contains the entire understanding of the parties respecting the subject matter hereof. It may not be changed orally, but only by an agreement in writing signed by both parties against whom enforcement of any waiver, change, modification, extension or discharge is sought.

If you agree to the foregoing, kindly sign both copies of this Agreement at the indicated place below and return one copy to the Company, WHEREUPON THIS AGREEMENT SHALL BE BINDING. Please retain the other copy for your personal use.

ABLE COMPUTING SERVICES CORPORATION

By:_____
Title:_____

I have read and agree to the foregoing and acknowledge receipt of a signed copy of this Agreement. I accept employment on the terms stated above.

_____
(Employee's Signature)
Witness:_____

Extract from IBM License Agreement on Limitations on Use of Programs

"IBM will ... grant the Customer a nontransferable and nonexclusive license in the United States and Puerto Rico to use the licensed program materials. ..."

Definitions

The term "licensed program" in this Agreement shall mean a licensed data processing program consisting of a series of instructions or statements in machine readable form, and/or any licensed data base consisting of a systematized collection of data in machine readable form, and any related licensed materials such as, but not limited to, flow charts, logic diagrams, and listings provided for use in connection with the licensed data processing program.

. . .

The term "use" in this Agreement shall mean copying any portion of the licensed program materials into a machine and/or transmitting them to a machine for processing of the machine instructions, statements or data contained in such materials.

. . .

IBM may discontinue any license or terminate this Agreement upon written notice effective immediately if the Customer fails to comply with any of the terms and conditions of this Agreement.

. . .

License

Each license granted under this Agreement authorizes the Customer to

a. use the licensed program materials in machine readable form on the machine or machines (hereinafter referred to as "machine") designated in an applicable Supplement for such licensed program materials and in conjunction therewith to store the licensed program materials in, transmit them through, or display them on, units associated with such designated machine.

. . .

c. copy or translate the licensed program materials in machine readable form into any machine read-

able or printed form to provide sufficient copies to support the Customer's use of the licensed program as authorized under this Agreement. Licensed program materials provided by IBM in printed form, microfiche or other non-machine readable form may not be copied. Additional copies may be obtained under license from IBM at the charges then in effect.

. . .

For any licensed program that is a data base, the license granted in this section is further limited to permit access to such data base exclusively by the Customer. Except as provided in the section entitled "Protection and Security of Licensed Program Materials," the Customer shall not make or permit any manner of access to any form of such data base, or part thereof, for the purpose of making available to any other person any data contained in such data base.

The Customer shall not use, print, copy, translate or display the licensed program materials, in whole or in part, unless expressly authorized in this Agreement.

The Customer shall not reverse assemble or reverse compile the licensed programs in whole or in part.

. . .

Change in Designated Machine

The Customer may notify IBM of the Customer's intention to change the designation of the machine on which licensed program materials are to be used. The change of designation will be effective upon the date set forth in the form entitled "Confirmation of Change in Designated Machine" furnished to the Customer by IBM.

Risk of Loss

If licensed program materials are lost or damaged during shipment from IBM, IBM will replace such licensed program materials and program storage media at no additional charge to the Customer.

If licensed program materials are lost or damaged while in the possession of the Customer, IBM will replace such licensed program materials at the applicable charges, if any, for processing, distribution, and/or program storage media.

. . .

Protection and Security of Licensed Program Materials

The Customer will take appropriate action, by instruction, agreement or otherwise, with any persons permitted access to licensed program materials so as to enable the Customer to satisfy the Customer's obligation under this Agreement.

All copies of licensed program materials provided by IBM or made by the Customer including translations or compilations or partial copies within modifications, derivative works, and updated works are the property of IBM and may not be distributed by the Customer to any other persons, including other licensees of the licensed program, without IBM's prior written consent. The Customer will reproduce and include the copyright notice on any such copies made by the Customer in accordance with the copyright instructions provided by IBM.

The Customer will maintain records of the number and location of all copies of licensed program materials and will notify IBM in writing if the original or any copy of the licensed program materials will be kept at an installation (or location, when IBM has specified "Location License Applies") other than that of the machine designated in the applicable Supplement.

The Customer will insure, prior to disposing of any media, that any licensed program materials contained thereon have been erased or otherwise destroyed.

The Customer will not provide or otherwise make available any licensed program materials in any form without IBM's prior written consent except to Customer employees or IBM employees, or to other persons during the period such other persons are on the Customer's premises for purposes specifically related to the Customer's authorized use of the licensed program.

. . .

Return or Destruction of Licensed Program Materials

Within one month after the date of discontinuance of any license granted hereunder, unless the requirement is waived by IBM, the Customer will furnish to IBM a completed form entitled "IBM Licensed Program Certificate of Return or Destruction" certifying that through the Customer's best effort, and to the best of the customer's knowledge, the original and all copies of the licensed program materials received from IBM or made in connection with such license have been returned to IBM or destroyed. This requirement will apply to all copies in any form including translations or compilations or partial copies within modifications, derivative works, and updated works, whether partial or complete, and whether or not modified or merged into other program materials as authorized herein. However, upon prior written authorization from IBM, the Customer may retain a copy for archival purposes only.

The requirement to return or destroy will apply to a licensed data base; it will not apply to individual pieces of data obtained by the Customer from such data base and which constitute a minor portion of such data base.

. . .

General

This Agreement is not assignable; none of the licenses granted hereunder nor any of the licensed program materials or copies thereof may be sublicensed, assigned or transferred by the Customer without the prior written consent of IBM. Any attempt to sublicense, assign or transfer any of the rights, duties or obligations under this Agreement is void.

. . .

Licensed program materials furnished under this Agreement are to be used only on machines located in the United States and Puerto Rico.

Employee Nondisclosure Agreement (Sample)

I, _____, an employee of _____ (Employer), acknowledge that my Employer has been granted certain rights to use the Licensed Software. I further acknowledge that the Licensed Software has tangible value, contains valuable trade secrets, copyrights and confidential information of Able Computing Services Corp. ("Able"), and is the sole property of Able.

I shall not print or copy, in whole or in part, any Licensed Software except in accordance with the terms of my Employer's license that are attached hereto, which I have read and understand. Furthermore, I shall not disclose, provide or otherwise make available, in whole or in part, such Licensed Software other than to my Employer's employees and/or consultants who have executed confidentiality agreements. Such disclosure shall be in confidence for purposes specifically related to my Employer's use of the Licensed Software during the time such employees and/or consultants are on my Employer's premises with my Employer's permission and are subject to my Employer's security and control.

I shall take all appropriate action, whether by instruction, agreement or otherwise, to ensure the protection, confidentiality and security of the Licensed Software and to satisfy my obligations under this Nondisclosure Agreement. I agree that my obligations with respect to the confidentiality and security of all information disclosed to me shall survive the termination of any agreement or relationship between Able, its distributor, my Employer and/or me. This Agreement shall be interpreted in accordance with the laws of the State of New Hampshire.

ACKNOWLEDGED AND ACCEPTED:

_____   _____
      (Employee)   (Employer)

Address: By:_____

_____   Title:_____
_____   Date:_____

Date:_____

APPENDIX 10

State Privacy Statutes (Selected Citations)

Arkansas Statutes, Section 16-804
California Civil Code, Section 1798
Connecticut Public Acts 76-421
Indiana Code 4-1, Chapter 6
Massachusetts General Laws, Chapter 66A
Minnesota Stat. 1974, Chapter 401

New Hampshire Revised Statutes, Chapter 7A
New York Stat. 1983, Chapter 652
Ohio Sections 1347.01, et seq.
Utah Section 63-30-10
Virginia Title 2.1, Chapter 26

APPENDIX 11

Crime and High Technology: A Case in Point

Robert Bigelow*

Just as technology does not stand still, so crime does not stand still. The invention and development of the computer since World War II, and its incredible penetration of commerce, has, in turn, led to the development of computer crime (so-called), in which the computer is manipulated by persons inside or outside the enterprise for their own benefit. Most of the cases reported to date involve the theft or embezzlement of corporate assets, although such assets may be in forms not previously known. However, the development of this new technology has also led to crimes of a new, indeed unique, nature, such as the widely reported use of 'hacking'. However, the majority of computer crimes appear to be old crimes in a new guise—perhaps new wine in old bottles.

While the theft of money (usually by insiders) appears to be the most prevalent, there have also been cases involving the theft of computer time, computer programs, and of information stored upon computers. The use of computerized files to store information has led in several cases to the illegal deletion of information. There have been assaults upon computer systems, both by terrorists and others and by insiders for personal reasons. Perhaps the most interesting development in the computer crime area is the discovery by individuals—often juveniles—that the system can be accessed from a remote location for their own amusement; this is the so-called Computer Hacking and by some (often the popular press) is considered nothing more than a juvenile prank or 'good clean fun'. However, companies and organizations that have suffered the deprivations do not concur with this assessment.

Specific Information

An interesting question facing prosecutors has been whether the criminal statutes already in place are sufficient to cover the particular crimes involved. The American experience has been mixed, although it appears that in most cases offenders have been convicted under laws enacted without reference to the computer. However, because of computer crime's wide publicity, a number of American states have enacted specific legislation aimed at computer crime. The United States Congress has also enacted such legislation.

A discussion of all the cases in the United States, much less those elsewhere, is beyond the scope of this paper. However, a few specific instances may assist in showing how the law can be applied to prosecute offenders successfully under ordinary criminal statutes.

- One of the more interesting cases involved the invention by an accounts payable supervisor of a Toronto company of a false vendor code, specifically in the name of his sister in Baltimore, Maryland, USA. After certain invoices from the Whirlpool Corporation, an American company, had been verified, the supervisor changed the accounts payable slip to the new vendor code. The document was then forwarded to the keypunch area. The keypunch operator routinely ordered the computer to process the altered information, and in due course a check was automatically printed payable to 'A.L.E. Jones', although the company had intended to pay Whirlpool. Mrs. Jones was prosecuted in the United States under the National Stolen Property Act;[2] the indictment was dismissed at the trial level[3] but was reinstated upon appeal.[4] It is reported also that the account supervisor in Toronto pleaded guilty to deceit and fraud, and was sentenced to serve two years (less one day).[5]

* Reprinted from *Computer Law & Practice* (Canada), January/February 1985, © Robert P. Bigelow 1985, 1987.

- In another case, a bank president arranged to have his account computer coded so that the checks he drew would be removed and held, rather than being routinely posted through the computer. Periodically, the defendant collected the actual checks and recorded them as cash items so that his account would not be debited.[6]

- In *U.S. v. Sampson*,[7] it was held that an indictment alleging theft of computer time as theft of 'a thing of value' was sufficient for an indictment under 18 U.S.C. Section 641 (embezzlement or theft of United States property). A similar result was reached in *State v. McGraw*.[8]

- Defendant's motion to dismiss the information (a kind of indictment) was denied under the California trade secret statute[9] in *Ward v. Superior Court of California*,[10] where the defendant was alleged to have obtained a computer program from a competitor through a terminal at the defendant's office. An interesting point in this case was that physical movement was necessary for conviction; this was found to exist because the defendant took the printout of the program from the terminal to his desk. Theft of a program was also held to violate the federal wire fraud statute,[11] where the defendant in the Commonwealth of Virginia, using a terminal located in his house, abstracted a program from the computer located in the State of Maryland, thus crossing state borders and becoming interstate commerce.[12]

- The theft of information from a computerised data base has also been held to be a 'thing of value' under federal antitheft statutes.[13] However, in a case involving non-computerized information, a Colorado court held that hospital record information was not a thing of value;[14] this decision is in part responsible for the enactment of the Colorado computer crime law.[15]

- In *United States v. Alston*,[16] the defendant paid to have an accomplice delete adverse information from, and insert favorable fictitious information into, a computerized credit file of individuals who had difficulty obtaining credit; he was convicted of wire fraud.[17] This kind of deletion and insertion of information in computerized records, as well as the making of false entries, appears to have been responsible for a number of business failures, including Saxon Industries, a photocopier company;[18] it was certainly a factor in the famed Equity Funding case,[19] as well as in major write-offs, for example, the closing of the syndication unit of the J. Walter Thompson Advertising Agency after the recording of over $30 million in fictitious revenues.[20]

- Among the most widely publicised incidents of computer crime are those in which computer systems are accessed by individuals who have no relationship to the organisation using telecommunications. Such incidents include a group of schoolboys in New York,[21] the Milwaukee 414 operation,[22] other access to the public packet switched networks,[23] and destruction of the computerized files of a leasing company.[24] And a popular motion picture, 'War Games', is based on unauthorized third party access to computerised national security information (although such an event appears to be impossible). The same penal statutes may be available for prosecution in these cases. For example, in *United States v. Muni*,[25] the defendant, a storekeeper, was convicted of wire fraud in using counterfeit credit cards to charge non-existent purchases. He telephoned the bank's authorization clerk in the same state for approval of the transaction; however, this clerk in turn queried computer files located in another state. It was held that this inquiry across state lines was sufficient to satisfy the requirements of the federal wire fraud statute.

Despite successes in conviction in the United States under present statutes, there have, as noted above, been some occasions on which the accused was released because his crime did not exactly fit the law that was available. A number of states have now enacted specific computer related crime laws, as noted in the footnote.[26] However, such statutes may suffer from imprecision or overbroadness. For example, the definition of a computer in the Florida computer crime law[27] is '*an internally-programmed, automatic device that performs data processing*'. This definition will cover a computer; unfortunately, it also covers a calculator, a digital watch, and even a microwave oven. Should the 'computer' be destroyed or injured without authority, or stolen, and have a value greater than $200, the offender is guilty of a felony.[28]

Some states have enacted statutes relating to specific aspects of computer crime, particularly with respect to electronic funds transfer systems.[29] Similarly, Massachusetts has amended its trade secrets larceny statute to provide that the secret no longer need be in tangible form. A trade secret now '*means and includes anything tangible or electronically kept or stored*'.[30,31]

It is a hacking case that gave rise to what the author believes is the only computer crime case considered by the highest court of appeal in a nation. In *Queen v. McLaughlin*,[32] the Supreme Court of Canada held that where a computer hacker made use of a terminal at the University of Alberta to access the University's central processing unit, the entire computer system was a unit and was not a 'telecommunication facility' as that term is used in Section 287 of the Canadian Criminal Code, but rather was a data processing facility. The defendants, therefore, were acquitted. To the same effect is *Queen v. Marine Resource Analysts, Ltd.*,[33] where programs were removed by individuals who were terminating their affiliation with the owner of the system. However, in this case, they were convicted of an attempt to defraud the government, because the government was charged for the cost of the computing, an amount of $27.30. A computer crime law is now pending in the Canadian Parliament.[34]

Other Nations

The foregoing discussion of American and Canadian cases is not meant to indicate that computer crime does not exist in other nations. For example, it has been reported that in Japan a bank clerk, at her lover's request, opened savings accounts under assumed names and channeled funds into the accounts by false entries in the bank computer system; in Australia, an operator changed the time clock in the state-run horse betting agency to make it late by three minutes, thereby successfully betting on the winner; and in West Germany, a programmer added fictitious people to the company's payroll system.[35] Several cases in Sweden have occurred, some of which involve violations of the Swedish Data Act.[36] At least 67 computer frauds were reported in the United Kingdom by 1983,[37] while it has been stated that there were 288 bank computer fraud cases in Japan in 1981.[38]

A special kind of computer crime against business is related to violations of data protection acts. For example, the Austrian law[39] defines persons affected as including *'legal persons or associations of persons under commercial law, about whom data are collected, processed or disclosed.'*[40] The law applies to computerised systems, limits disclosure of processed data to certain specific situations, and provides criminal sanctions in certain situations. The Act also provides a penalty for unlawful erasure, falsification or other alteration of computerized data.[41] (In the United States, at least one state provides civil penalties for unauthorised disclosure by a computer service bureau of information about its customers.)[42]

Notes

1. 18 U.S.C. § 1030, as amended by PL99-474(1986); see also Electronic Communications Privacy Act of 1986, PL99-508.

2. 18 U.S.C. Sections 2314 and 2315.

3. *U.S. v. Jones*, 414 F. Supp. 964 (D.Md. 1976).

4. *U.S. v. Jones*, 553 F.2d 351 (4th Cir. 1977).

5. Bigelow, 'Computer Operator Acted as an Innocent Agent in Fraud', Computer Data, November 1976, p. 9.

6. *U.S. v. Duncan*, 598 F.2d 839, 846 (4th Cir.), cert. den. 444 U.S. 871 (1979); the conviction was for misappropriation under 18 U.S.C. Section 656.

7. 6 CLSR 879 (N.D.Cal. 1978).

8. 459 N.E.2d 61 (Indiana App. 1984); contra, *Lund v. Commonwealth*, 232 S.E.2d 745 (Va. 1977); *People v. Weg*, 113 Misc.2d 1017 (N.Y. 1982).

9. California Penal Code, Section 499c.

10. 3 CLSR 206 (Cal. Super. 1972).

11. 18 U.S.C. Section 1343.

12. *U.S. v. Seidlitz*, 589 F.2d 152 (4th Cir. 1978).

13. *U.S. v. Girard*, 601 F.2d 69 (2d Cir. 1968), construing 18 U.S.C. Section 641 making it an offense to sell, without authority, a 'record . . . or thing of value' of the United States.

14. *People v. Home Insurance Co.*, 591 P.2d 1036 (1979).

15. See, infra, Footnote 28.

16. 609 F.2d 531 (D.C. Cir. 1979).

17. 18 U.S.C. Section 1343.

18. Edpacs, January 1984, p. 10; Computerworld, October 25, 1982.

19. See Seidler, Andrews and Epstein, **The Equity Funding Papers**, Wiley-Hamilton (1977). See also Becker, 'Trial of a Computer Crime in the United States', New Law Journal, August 27, 1981, 2 Computer/Law Journal 441 (1980).

20. Edpacs, December 1982, p.14; Forbes, February, 27, 1984, p. 121. Even the courts have not been exempt. The alteration of traffic citations and arrest warrants in the Dallas, Texas Municipal Court's computer system has been reported (Computerworld, November 8, 1982, p. 9).

21. 'The New York School Gang' in Parker, **Fighting Computer Crime**, Scribners, 1983, Chapter 20. The computer systems involved were in the United States and Canada.

22. Software News, April 1984, p. 4; Computerworld, May 14, 1984, p. 18; Computer Security Digest, May 1984, p. 2.

23. Edpacs, March 1984, p. 12; Computerworld, May 21, 1984, p. 16.

24. Computerworld, June 28, 1982, p. 7.

25. 668 F.2d 87 (2d Cir. 1981).

26. Alabama Sections 13A-8-10 et seq.; Alaska 11.46.200(a), 11.46.985, 11.46.999; Arizona Section 13-2316; California Penal Code Section 502; Colorado Criminal Code Article 18-5.5; Connecticut § 53a-250-61; Delaware Title II, §§ 931–939; Florida Chapter 78–92; Georgia Title 16, Chapter 9, Article 6; Hawaii §§ 708-890 to 896; Idaho §§ 18-2201, 2202; Illinois Chapter 38, Section 16–9; Iowa Sections 716A.1–716A.16; Kansas § 21-3755; Kentucky §§ 434.840–860; Louisiana §§ 73.1–73.5; Maine Art. 27, § 357; Maryland Section 146, Section 45A; Massachu-

setts, c 167B § 21, c 266 § 30; Michigan Public Acts 1979, Chapter 53; Minnesota Sections 609.87 et seq.; Mississippi §§ 97-45-1 to 13; Missouri § 569.093–.099; Montana Statutes 1981, Chapter 485; Nebraska §§ 28-1343 to 1348; Nevada §§ 205.473-.477; New Hampshire §§ 638.16-.19; New Jersey Ch. 20c, Title 2c, §§ 1–31, Title A, §§ 38A-1-38A-3; New Mexico Statutes 1979, Chapter 176; New York SB 5743-B (1985); North Carolina Statutes 1979, Chapter 831; North Dakota §§ 12.1-1.06.1-01(3) and 1.06-08; Ohio § 2901.01 (J), 2913.01; Oklahoma Code, Title 21, Section 1952; Oregon §§ 164.125, 164.345–365; Pennsylvania Statutes 1983, Chapter 67; Rhode Island Title 11, Chapter 52; South Carolina § 16-16-10 to 40; South Dakota § 43-43B-1 to 8; Tennessee 39-3-1401 to 1406; Texas Title 7, §§ 33.01 to .05; Utah Statutes 1979, HB103; Virginia Title 18.2, Article 7.1; Washington Statutes 1984, Chapter 273; Wisconsin Statutes, Section 943.70; Wyoming §§ 6-3-501 to 505. [The assistance of Susan H. Nycum of the Palo Alto California bar in compiling this list is appreciated.]

27. Section 815.03(s).
28. Section 185.05(2).
29. See Tennessee Section 39-3-1401 and Massachusetts General Laws Chapter 167B, Section 21.
30. Massachusetts General Laws Chapter 266, Section 30, as amended by Stat. 1983, Chapter 147.
31. For a further discussion of computer crime, see 2 Computer/Law Journal 275–803 (1980);
32. 2 Can. S. Ct. 331, 7 CLSR 1420 (1980).
33. 7 CLSR 1411 (Nova Scotia District Appeal 1980).
34. Proposed Criminal Code, Section 301.2; see Bigelow, 'Canada Proposes Computer Crime Law', Computer Law and Tax Report, May 1984, p. 6.
35. Computerworld, December 26, 1983, p. 59.
36. 7 CLSR 1457 et seq.
37. Edpacs, May 1983, p. 14; May 1984, p. 1.
38. Computing, November 25, 1982, p. 9.
39. Federal Act of 18th October 1978.
40. Section 3, paragraph 2.
41. Section 49.
42. North Dakota, Stat. 1981, SB 2051, Computer Law and Tax Report, July 1980, p. 1.

APPENDIX 12

Computer Abuse: Ward v. Superior Court of the State of California, County of Alameda

Superior Court of the State of California, March 22, 1972
3 CLSR 206

[2-2] Theft of program by remote access
[4-4] Source program as trade secret
[6-3] Theft of trade secret information

In action against computer service company employee charging him with theft by remote access of computer program from another computer company, defendant's motion to dismiss information was denied where probable cause existed to believe that program was trade secret within meaning of statute prohibiting theft of trade secrets or within meaning of grand theft statute prohibiting theft of property.

Facts

SPARROW, Judge. Defendant Ward, an employee of UCC, a computer service company in Palo Alto, is charged in a two-count Information with the theft on January 19, 1971, of a trade secret belonging to ISD, a computer company in Oakland, in violation of Penal Code Section 499c and 487 (Grand Theft). Both UCC and ISD compete in providing computer services to Shell Development in Emeryville and Aerojet General in Sacramento, among others.

The alleged trade secret is a computer program, Plot/Trans, developed by ISD and valued at $5,000. The program makes it possible to provide a remote plotting service from the ISD Univac 1108 computer, through a CTMC switching attachment, over telephone wires to customers distant from ISD's Oakland office who have a Calcomp plotter and transceiver unit. As of January 19, 1971, only Aerojet had such a transceiver unit and only ISD had the CTMC computer attachment which made it possible automatically to switch telephone calls to and from the remote transceiver unit directly into ISD's Univac computer and its Fastrans memory bank attachment. The Plot/Trans Program eliminates the need for ISD to buy or lease an expensive Calcomp 611 sending unit, and, in conjunction with the CTMC, eliminates the need for a manual magnetic tape exchange of the executive program to be remotely plotted from the computer to the sending unit.

Since competitors of ISD had neither a CTMC nor a program such as Plot/Trans, they could not provide a telephonic remote plotting service without the added expense of securing a Calcomp 611 sending unit and the added time to effectuate a manual tape exchange, both of which the Plot/Trans Program avoided. The evidence clearly indicates that ISD did not sell the details of the Plot/Trans *program* itself but rather sold only the remote plotting *service*, which it made possible. Because of the saving in time and equipment, ISD could provide such a *service* at a lesser cost than its competitors, including UCC.

As of January 19, 1971, the details of the Plot/Trans Program itself were stored in the Fastrans memory bank attached to ISD's Univac computer in two forms: (1) in source code, i.e. man readable symbolics, and (2) in object code, i.e. machine readable symbolics. Access to the details of the Plot/Trans Program in source or object code could be secured at that time by one using a special data phone dial-up who knew three sets of numbers: (1) the unlisted telephone number of the ISD computer, (2) the two-character site code number of any ISD customer, and (3) an account or billing number of that customer. The form in which the details of any computer program comes off the drum of a Univac computer is by way of either a print-out or a deck of cards punched out (i.e. computer software).

The evidence indicates that on January 19, 1971, someone using a PT&T data phone dialed the ISD computer, furnished the Shell Development's site and billing numbers[1] and secured a printout of the source code form of ISD's Plot/Trans Program. (Contemporaneously, the ISD computer in Oakland punched out

---

[1] At Shell's insistence, it had the same site and billing number at both UCC and ISD, a fact presumably known to Ward.

cards of what had been accessed, together with the time of access.) When the punched out cards were delived to Shell, and the latter billed for the service, it was learned that Shell had not in fact, accessed the program. A check with the telephone company indicated that the call to the ISD computer at the time in question was from UCC, not Shell. A search warrant was secured and ISD's Plot/Trans Program printout was discovered in defendant Ward's UCC office in Palo Alto.

Penal Code Section 499c

Insofar as pertinent to this case, Section 499c(b) of the Penal Code provides "Every person is guilty of theft who, with intent to deprive or withhold from the owner thereof the control of a trade secret . . . does any of the following:

1. Steals, takes, or carries away any article representing a trade secret.

. . .

3. Having unlawfully obtained access to the article, without authority makes or causes to be made a copy of any article representing a trade secret."

Since the defendant Ward was neither an employee of, nor was he in a fiduciary relationship with ISD, subdivisions 2 and 4 are here inapplicable.

Implicit in the definition of "article" contained in Section 499c (a) is that it must be something *tangible*, even though the trade secret which the article represents may itself be *intangible*. Based upon the record here, the defendant Ward did not carry any tangible thing representing ISD's Plot/Trans Program from the ISD computer to the UCC computer unless the impulses which defendant allegedly caused to be transmitted over the telephone wire could be said to be tangible. *It is the opinion of the Court that such impulses are not tangible and hence do not constitute an "article"* within the definition contained in Section 499c(a)(1) as inclusive of "object, material, device or substance or copy thereof, including any writing, record, recording, drawing, sample, specimen, prototype, model, photograph, microorganism, blueprint or map." All of the foregoing things are tangible, and under the principle of ejusdem generis telephonic impulses would not constitute an article representing a trade secret.

However, the preliminary transcript does establish probable cause to believe that the defendant Ward, after unlawfully obtaining access to the Plot/Trans Program, did, without the authority of ISD, make a copy thereof through use of the UCC computer and thereafter carried that copy from the UCC computer to his office at UCC, thus providing the asportation required under subdivision (1) of Section 499c(b).

In any event, a violation of Section 499c(b)(3) is established by probable cause to believe that defendant

made a copy, consisting of 2 printouts, of the Plot/Trans Program, irrespective of its asportation.

To adopt and expand the library analogy suggested by defense counsel at the preliminary hearing (Tr Vol IV p 9): ISD had in its computer and Fastrans memory bank a library of computer recorded information, including the Plot/Trans Program which is the subject of the alleged theft. Other than being physically present at the ISD office itself, no one could gain access to this recorded information except by telephone. Telephonic access could lawfully be secured either (1) by a direct leased line from a customer into the ISD computer, or (2) by an ordinary dial line by a customer using a data phone into the ISD computer provided the customer knew three sets of numbers: (1) The unlisted telephone number of the computer; (2) a two-character site number; and (3) an account number identifying the customer for billing purposes. In other words, the ISD "library" was a private, not a public, library and access thereto was restricted to customers authorized by ISD to use a "library card" consisting of the unlisted telephone number, the site number, and the billing number. Anyone else using this library card to gain access to the library would be doing so unlawfully and without authorization of ISD. And the fact, if it be a fact, that ISD was negligent in leaving the source code to the Plot/Trans Program in the Fastrans memory bank, as it did on January 19, 1971, so that the program could be accessed and copied by one using the library card without authorization does not make noncriminal that which otherwise would constitute a crime. To adopt defendants' argument would mean that because from the standpoint of maximum security an owner might place his jewelry in a safe, it could never be the subject of a theft if he places it in a less secure location.

The evidence adduced at the preliminary thus established probable cause to believe that:

1. The Plot/Trans Program is secret in that ISD took measures to prevent it from becoming available to persons other than those selected by ISD to have access thereto for the limited purpose of utilizing the *service* it provided. (No one, not even a customer, was authorized by ISD to access and copy the *program* itself.)

2. The Plot/Trans Program was not generally available to the public;

3. Use by ISD of the Plot/Trans Program gave the latter an advantage over competitors including UCC, the employer of defendant, who did not know of or use the program. (Indeed, the evidence establishes that no competitor of ISD at the time of the alleged theft on January 19, 1971, even had the capability of providing a remote plotting service because none had CTMC.)

4. Defendant Ward on January 19, 1971, used the

unlisted telephone number of the ISD computer, together with the Shell Development Company site and billing numbers to access the ISD computer in Oakland from the UCC office in Palo Alto and make a computer printout copy of the Plot/Trans Program through the UCC computer.

5.   The Defendant carried the printout copy of the trade secret from the UCC computer to his office, thus providing the asportation required by subdivision (1), or Section 499c(b) (although, as above noted, asportation is not a requirement of subdivision (3); cf. People v. Dolbeer (1963) 214 CA 2nd 619).

Demurrer and Motion to Dismiss

The Legislature specifically states that the purpose of Section 499c of the Penal Code is to "clarify and restate existing law with respect to crimes involving trade secrets and to make it clear that articles representing trade secrets, including the trade secrets representing thereby, constitute goods, chattels, materials and property. . . ."

Mr. Witkin in 1 California Crimes, 1969 Supplement, page 155, Section 518 F, notes that the enactment of Section 499c, "brings the wrongful appropriation of any trade secret *within the scope of the crimes of theft and bibery.*" (Emphasis added.) A trade secret or an article representing it therefore is now, if it was not previously, "money, goods, chattels, things in action, and evidence of debt." (See Annot, Computer Programs as Property Subject To Theft, 18 ALR3rd 1121.)

It follows that a wrongful appropriation of any trade secret, or article representing it, can properly be charged either as (1) a theft of property under Section 487 of the Penal Code, provided the requisite value and intent elements are established, or (2) as a violation of Section 499c of the Penal Code, which neither requires proof of value nor of an intent permanently to deprive. Accordingly, since the elements of the crime set forth under Penal Code Section 487 and 499c are not identical, it is proper to charge both violations in a single Information, notwithstanding each arises out of the same transaction. (Penal Code Sec 954.)

The count charging a violation of Penal Code Section 499c states an offense under that section. The record establishes that ISD took "measures to prevent it from becoming available to other than those selected by the owner to have access thereto for limited purposes" within the meaning of Section 499c(a)(3). These measures, as above indicated, consisted of an unlisted telephone number, a two-character site code number, and a billing number, all of which had to be known and used to make the Plot/Trans Program in the ISD computer available to those seeking it. The program is, therefore, presumed to be secret under the definition of "Trade Secret" contained in Section 499c(a)(3). Anyone using these numbers for the purpose of securing access to the Plot/Trans Program without the authority of the owner would be acting unlawfully within the meaning of Section 499c(b)(3). The fact that the owner might have taken additional measures to make the program more secure such as by scrambling or adopting one of the number of other methods testified to by Dr. Chapin is immaterial. Finally, the record establishes that the Plot/Trans Program was not generally available to the public and that its use gave ISD an advantage over competitors such as UCC who, although knowing of the Plot/Trans *service*, did not know or use the *program* itself.

There is probable cause to believe that offenses under Sections 499c and 487 of the Penal Code were committed and the defendant committed them. Accordingly, the motion to dismiss the Information under Section 995 of the Penal Code is denied and the demurrer thereto overruled.

Federal Information Processing Standards: Abstracts

Abstract-FIPS PUB 31

This publication provides guidelines to be used by Federal organizations in structuring physical security programs for their ADP facilities. It treats security analysis, natural disasters, supporting utilities, system reliability, procedural measures and controls, off-site facilities, contingency plans, security awareness and security audit. It contains statistics and information relevant to physical security of computer data and facilities and references many applicable publications for a more exhaustive treatment of specific subjects.

Abstract-FIPS PUB 39

This glossary provides an alphabetic listing of approximately 170 terms and definitions pertaining to privacy, and security related to data, information systems hardware and software. Multiple word terms are listed in natural order, synonyms are referenced, and glossary terms appearing within a definition are indicated.

Abstract-FIPS PUB 41

This publication provides guidelines for use by Federal ADP organizations in implementing the computer security safeguards necessary for compliance with Public Law 93-579, the Privacy Act of 1974. A wide variety of technical and related procedural safeguards are described. These fall into three broad categories: Physical security, information management practices, and computer system/network security controls. As each organization processing personal data has unique characteristics, specific organizations should draw upon the material provided in order to select a well-balanced combination of safeguards which meets their particular requirements.

Abstract-FIPS PUB 46

The selective application of technological and related procedural safeguards is an important responsibility of every Federal organization in providing adequate security to its ADP systems. This publication provides a standard to be used by Federal organizations when these organizations specify that cryptographic protection is to be used for sensitive or valuable computer data. Protection of computer data during transmission between electronic components or while in storage may be necessary to maintain the confidentiality and integrity of the information represented by that data. The standard specifies an encryption algorithm which is to be implemented in an electronic device for use in Federal ADP systems and networks. The algorithm uniquely defines the mathematical steps required to transform computer data into a cryptographic cipher. It also specifies the steps required to transform the cipher back to its original form. A device performing this algorithm may be used in many applications areas where cryptographic data protection is needed. Within the context of a total security program comprising physical security procedures, good information management practices and computer system/network access controls, the Data Encryption Standard is being made available for use by Federal agencies.

Abstract-FIPS PUB 48

This publication provides a guideline to be used by Federal organizations in the selection and evaluation of techniques for automatically verifying the identity of individuals seeking access to computer systems and networks via terminals, where controlled accessibility is required for security purposes. The guideline describes various techniques for verifying identity and provides a set of criteria for the evaluation of automated identification systems embodying these techniques.

Abstract-FIPS PUB 65

This document presents a technique for conducting a risk analysis of an ADP facility and related assets. Risk analysis produces annual loss exposure values based on estimated costs and potential losses. The annual loss exposure values are fundamental to the cost effective selection of safeguards for the security of the facility. An ADP facility of a hypothetical government agency is used for an example. The characteristics and attributes of a computer system which must be known in order to perform a risk analysis are described and an example is given of the process of analyzing some of the assets, showing how the risk analysis can be handled.

Abstract-FIPS PUB 73

Security decisions should be an integral part of the entire planning, development, and operation of a computer application. This guideline describes the technical and managerial decisions that should be made in order to assure that adequate controls are included in new and existing computer applications to protect them from natural and human-made hazards and to assure that critical functions are performed correctly and with no harmful side effects. The multifaceted nature of computer security is described, and differences in security objectives, sensitivity levels, and vulnerabilities that must be considered are identified. Fundamental security controls such as data validation, user identity verification, authorization, journalling, variance detection, and encryption are discussed as well as security-related decisions that should be made at each stage in the life cycle of a computer application. These include questions about security feasibility and risk assessment that should be asked during initial planning, decisions that should be made during the design, programming and testing phases, controls that should be enforced during the development process, and security provisions that should be enforced during the day-to-day operation of the system.

Abstract-FIPS PUB 74

The Data Encryption Standard (DES) was published as Federal Information Processing Standards Publication (FIPS PUB) 46 on January 15, 1977 [2]. The DES specifies a cryptographic algorithm for protecting computer data. FIPS PUB 81[3] defines four modes of operation for the DES which may be employed in a wide variety of applications. These guidelines are to be applied in conjunction with FIPS PUB 46 and FIPS PUB 81 when implementing and using the Data Encryption Standard. They provide information on what encryption is, general guidance on how encryption protects against certain vulnerabilities of computer networks, and specific guidance on the DES modes of operation in data communication applications. When used with the proper administrative procedures and when implemented in accordance with these guidelines, electronic devices performing the encryption and decryption operations of the standard can provide a high level of cryptographic protection to data in computer systems and networks.

Abstract-FIPS PUB 81

The Federal Data Encryption Standard (DES) (FIPS 46) specifies a cryptographic algorithm to be used for the cryptographic protection of sensitive, but unclassified, computer data. This FIPS defines four modes of operation for the DES which may be used in a wide variety of applications. The modes specify how data will be encrypted (cryptographically protected) and decrypted (returned to original form). The modes included in this standard are the Electronic Codebook (ECB) mode, the Cipher Block Chaining (CBC) mode, the Cipher Feedback (CFB) mode, and the Output Feedback (OFB) mode.

Abstract-FIPS PUB 83

This Guideline provides information and guidance to Federal agencies on techniques and practices which can be used to control access to computer resources via remote terminals and networks. A variety of methods are described for verifying the identity of persons using remote terminals, as a safeguard against unauthorized usage. This Guideline discusses the three basic ways which may serve as a basis for verifying a person's identity: something the person KNOWS, such as a password; something the person HAS, such as a key or access card; or something ABOUT the person, such as fingerprints, signature, voice, or other personal attribute. The ability to automatically verify a person's identity via a unique personal attribute offers the prospect of greater security, and equipment for accomplishing this is beginning to emerge. There are several promising laboratory developments, although such equipment has not yet been interfaced to computer terminals to any great extent. In view of the present dependence on authentication techniques other than personal attributes, this Guideline provides advice on the effective use of passwords. This Guideline also discusses a variety of cards and badges with various forms of machine-readable coding that may be used for access control. In order to protect information used for identity verification, encryption is recommended.

Abstract-FIPS PUB 87

This document provides guidelines to be used in the preparation of ADP contingency plans. The objective is to ensure that ADP personnel, and others who may be involved in the planning process, are aware of the types of information which should be included in such plans; to provide a recommended structure and a suggested format; and generally to make those responsible aware of the criticality of the contingency planning process.

Abstract-FIPS PUB 102

This Guideline is intended for use by ADP managers and technical staff in establishing and carrying out a program and a technical process for computer security certification and accreditation of sensitive computer applications. It identifies and describes the steps involved in performing computer security certification and accreditation; it identifies and discusses important issues in managing a computer security certification and accreditation program; it identifies and describes the principal functional roles needed within an organization to carry out such a program; and it contains sample outlines of an Application Certification Plan and a Security Evaluation Report as well as a sample Accreditation Statement and sensitivity classification scheme. A discussion of recertification and reaccreditation and its relation to change control is also included. The Guideline also relates certification and accreditation to risk analysis, EDP audit, validation, verification and testing (VV&T), and the system life cycle. A comprehensive list of references is included.

Comments on Copyright Infringement of Software*

A. Introduction

Copying software is not too much different from copying a book or a newsletter; both are illegal. However, the problem is much more serious with software for at least the following reasons.

1. *The copying mechanisms are simple*. Anyone with the equipment to run the software will almost automatically have everything needed to make a copy.

2. With a book, the copy will be fairly costly in relation to the cost of another book and is likely to be of a lesser quality. With software, the copy will be just as good as the original, and the cost will be only a fraction of the cost of another license.

3. Some users are not as familiar with the copyright laws for software as they are for books. With a book or a newsletter, the copyright notice appears in a conspicuous place. With a software program, the copyright for the program is less conspicuous, and some people simply are not aware that the program is copyrighted. Other users do not seem to see anything wrong with copying programs.

B. The Problem and the Question

Copying software is clearly illegal. At least one suit has already been filed. It was filed by Lotus against a company allegedly making about a dozen unauthorized copies for its other divisions. Lotus asked for $10,000,000 in damages. The case has been highly publicized. (*Business Week,* April 30, 1984, and numerous other business publications.) We understand it has been settled out of court for a substantial payment.[1]

Should we assume that our people know better, or should we try to do something to prevent the problem? If so, what should we do?

C. Options and Suggestions

We offer you the following list of options and our conclusions as to what may be a reasonable approach at this time.

1. Do nothing.

This problem is not likely to be one of the more serious concerns facing corporate America. Doing nothing is not so much evidence of a disregard for the rights of those from whom we license software as it is a reflection that, to date at least, the evidence of copyright infringement problems has been limited. To our knowledge, we have only the one lawsuit.[2]

On the other hand, *we cannot recommend this approach.* Given the publicity this problem has attained over the past months, we think a "do nothing" approach is unwise.

2. Take steps to make sure people do not infringe software copyrights.

a. Keep track of which of your computers is authorized to run certain software, and keep a complete log of all your programs. Auditors can then check to see that no one is using unauthorized programs on an unauthorized computer. We understand from *Business Week* (April 30, 1984), that Travelers Corporation takes this approach.

b. Refuse to sign any request for purchase of a computer unless it also includes a request to license the software which it is supposed to be running. We understand from the same *Business Week* article that Chemical Bank does this.

c. Require each manager to certify that the computers under his responsibility all have licensed software, as opposed to software which has been copied from another department.

d. Require each person using a computer or a program to certify that he will not make copies, and that the copy he is using is a licensed one.

e. Ask your internal auditors, when they visit other departments or facilities, to make inquiries as to the origin of the software.

* Reprinted from the June 15, 1984 issue of *The Lawyer's Brief*, copyright 1984 by Business Laws, Inc., P.O. Box 24162, Cleveland, Ohio 44124.

1. Since this was written, there have been many copyright infringement suits involving software, and the plaintiff has usually been successful. [EDS.]

2. No longer true. [EDS.]

f. ***Establish a policy and publicize it.*** We assume that most companies already have a general policy of legal and ethical conduct. When one of these new problems comes up, the obvious question is why establish a new policy or send out another memo which says "obey the law" in simply another context. That is the argument against the policy/memo approach.

The argument for the policy/memo approach is that it appears to be a reasonable compromise between the "do nothing" and the "send in the auditors" approaches. Further, if the memo is worded properly, it should accomplish its desired objective without accusing anyone of copyright infringement.

D. The Memorandum

We recommend serious consideration of the following sort of memo for any company with many computers—especially the small decentralized microcomputers which are the ones at the base of this problem. Of course, the memo should be tailored to your company's communication style.

1. Who Should Get the Memo?

In this day and age, it is practically impossible to go through any corporate department without finding some small computers. The law department, virtually all of the financial departments, and even the personnel and purchasing departments use them. Any department with clerical people is likely to have at least some word-processing equipment. It is, therefore, difficult to think of a department which would not be a possible recipient of the memo/policy. If you have a list of "managers," it may be an appropriate starting point.

2. Should the Recipient Do Anything with the Memo?

We think not. We do not suggest asking the recipient to acknowledge his receipt (unless this is a normal practice with these types of memos), nor would we ask for any specific action such as asking the recipient to verify that he has distributed the memo to the appropriate people, or that he is not aware of any "infringing" programs. We feel that these options are just too severe for this problem at this time.

3. What Should the Memo Say?

Here is a start—which is included to clarify what we have in mind rather than to suggest any specific wording. We know that these types of communications are rather sensitive points within the company, and each company has its own style. It is the thought that counts.

To: All Managers
From: (President, chief executive officer, or whoever typically sends out memos to managers. The chief legal officer of the company could sign it, but we would consider that a second-best approach. This is not really a legal issue as much as it is a "moral" one.)
Re: Company licensed software programs.

The news media has recently pointed out that there may be quite a bit of illegal or improper copying of software. In fact, there has already been one lawsuit. We would like to clarify the following points.

— Most software is protected by a copyright. This means that it is illegal for us to make copies (except for backup or security purposes). Any user of software should assume that the programs he uses are protected by a copyright, or a provision in the license agreement, which prohibits all copying (except for backup or security purposes), unless he has specific advice from the company's lawyers to the contrary.

— Making unauthorized copies of software is against the law. Such conduct could subject both the company and the person making the copies to serious consequences.

— Our company's policy is to have a license for each and every program we use. Employees are not to make copies of any licensed program for other employees. This includes copies for employees in the same department, in another department, or in another part of the company.

[Optional]

Some companies have master agreements with software vendors. You may want to describe those at this point. Tell the recipients of the memo how they can order programs through the company's master discount program. If you do not have such a master or "volume discount" arrangement, and you license quite a few programs, it might be something to consider. The savings can be substantial.

A few companies have negotiated a "site license" by which, for a stated sum, you can make up to a certain number of copies. The software vendors do not like this approach, and many of them will not do it. However, it should be considered as a possibility.

FDIC Examination Questionnaire

	Number	Date of Examination
SERVICED BANK QUESTIONNAIRE	Total Assets	

Name and Location of Bank

SUMMARY COMMENTS

No. of Hours	Name of Examiner	Signature

FDIC 6601/106 (10-81) PAGE ONE

GENERAL INFORMATION

Name and Address of Servicer(s)	Applications Processed (By Servicer)

Indicate any affiliated relationship between the serviced institution and the servicer(s).

Discuss future EDP related plans. Detail any new applications scheduled for conversion. Indicate projected completion dates.

If available, obtain the following materials for review:

1. The latest EDP Report of Examination of the servicer and any subsequent correspondence.

2. The servicer's latest audit or third party review.

3. Internal and external audit reports that pertain to outside servicing.

4. Current service contracts.

5. Insurance policies relating to EDP services (*including the blanket bond*).

6. The servicer's most recent financial statement (*if not a financial institution*).

7. Current user manuals for each application.

QUESTIONNAIRE

	YES	NO	COMMENTS
Servicer Selection			
1. Before entering into any service arrangement, did management consider:			
a. Alternative services?			
b. Financial stability of the servicer?			
c. Control environment at the data center?			
d. Emergency backup provisions?			
e. The ability of the servicer to handle future processing requirements?			
f. Requirements for termination of service?			
g. Quality of reports?			
h. Insurance requirements?			
2. Is there an annual re-evaluation of the servicer's performance that includes:			
a. Financial condition?			
b. Costs?			
c. Ability to meet future needs?			
d. Quality of service?			
Contracts			
3. Is each automated application covered by a written contract?			
4. Were contracts reviewed by legal counsel?			
5. Does each service contract cover the following areas:			
a. Ownership and confidentiality of files and programs?			
b. Liability limits for errors and omissions?			
c. Frequency, content, and format of input and output?			
d. Fee structure, including:			
1. Current fees?			
2. Provisions for changing fees?			
3. Fees for special requests?			
e. Provisions for backup and record protection? *(Detail)*			
f. Notice required *(both parties)* for termination of service and the return of customer records in machine readable form? *(Detail)*			
g. Time schedules for receipt and delivery of work, including processing priorities?			
h. Insurance carried by the servicer?			
i. Liability for documents in transit?			
j. Audit responsibility?			
k. Provision to supply the serviced institution with yearly financial statements *(preferrably audited with both consolidated and unconsolidated figures when applicable)*?			

QUESTIONNAIRE

	YES	NO	COMMENTS

Insurance

6. Does the serviced institution's insurance coverage include the following provisions:
   a. Extended blanket bond fidelity coverage to employees of the servicer?
   b. Insurance on documents in transit including the cash letter?
   c. If the serviced institution is relying on the servicer and/or an independent courier for insurance covered in a and b respectively, is adequate evidence of that coverage on file?

Operational Controls

7. Are duties adequately separated for the following functions:
   a. Input preparation?
   b. Operation of data-entry equipment?
   c. Preparation of rejects and non-reads for re-entry?
   d. Reconcilement of output to input?
   e. Output distribution?
   f. Reconcilement of output to general ledger?
   g. Posting general ledger?
   h. Statement preparation?

8. Are employee duties periodically rotated for control and training purposes?

9. Do supervisors and/or officers:
   a. Adequately review exception reports?
   b. Approve adjusting entries?

10. Are servicer personnel prohibited from initiating transactions or correcting data?

11. Can any individual initiate or authorize a transaction and then execute it?

12. Are employees at the serviced institution required to be absent from their duties *(by vacation or job rotation)* for two consecutive weeks?

13. Are master file changes:
    a. Requested in writing?
    b. Approved by a supervisor?
    c. Verified correct after processing?

14. Are exception reports prepared for:
    a. Unposted and rejected items?
    b. Supervisory override transactions?

QUESTIONNAIRE

	YES	NO	COMMENTS
Operational Controls (cont'd)			
c. Master file changes *(before and after)?*			
d. Dormant account activity?			
15. Does each user department:			
a. Establish dollar and non-dollar controls before they are sent for processing?			
b. Receive all scheduled output reports even when report contains no activity?			
c. Effectively review all output and exception reports?			
16. Are current user manuals available for each application and are they used by the employees?			
17. Does each user manual cover:			
a. Preparation and control of source documents?			
b. Control, format and usage of output?			
c. Settlement and reconcilement procedures?			
18. Are users satisfied with the servicer's performance and output reports? *(If not, explain)*			
19. Are computer generated entries subsequently reviewed and approved by appropriate officials?			
20. Does the serviced institution microfilm or microfiche all source documents, including cash letters, before they leave the premises? If so:			
a. Is the microfilm/microfiche stored in a secure location with limited access?			
b. Is an inventory and usage log maintained?			
Communication Controls			
21. Is user access to the data communication network controlled by:			
a. User number?			
b. Physical keys?			
c. Passwords?			
d. Other? *(Explain)*			
22. Are periodic changes made to numbers/keys/ passwords and are they adequately controlled?			
23. Are identification numbers/passwords suppressed on all printed output and video displays?			
24. Are terminals controlled as to:			
a. What files they can access?			

QUESTIONNAIRE

	YES	NO	COMMENTS

Communication Controls (cont'd)

b. What transactions they can initiate?

c. Specific hours of operation?

25. Do controls over restricted transactions and overrides include:

   a. Supervisory approval?

   b. Periodic management review?

26. Are there exception reports which indicate:

   a. All transactions made at a terminal?

   b. All transactions made by an operator?

   c. Restricted transactions?

   d. Correcting and reversing entries?

   e. Dates and times of transactions?

   f. Unsuccessful attempts to gain access to the system and/or to restricted information?

   g. Unusual activity?

27. Overall, are there adequate procedures in effect that prevent unauthorized use of the data communication systems?

28. To backup on-line systems:

   a. Are off-line modes available? (*Explain*)

   b. Are the off-line capabilities periodically tested?

Audit

29. Is there an internal auditor or member of management not directly involved in EDP activities who has been assigned responsibility for the audit function?

30. Does that individual have any specialized audit/or EDP training?

31. Are there written internal audit standards and procedures that require:

   a. Review of all automated applications?

   b. Reports to the Board of Directors?

   c. Audit workpapers?

32. Does the person responsible for the audit function perform the following procedures:

   a. Test balancing procedures of all automated applications including the disposition of rejected and unposted items?

   b. Periodically sample masterfile information to verify it against source documents?

QUESTIONNAIRE

	YES	NO	COMMENTS
Audit (cont'd)			
c. Spot check computer calculations such as interest on deposits, loans, securities, loan rebates, service charges and past due loans?			
d. Verify output report totals?			
e. Check accuracy of exception reports?			
f. Review masterfile changes for accuracy and authorization?			
g. Trace transactions to final disposition to determine adequacy of audit trails?			
h. Review controls over program change requests?			
i. Perform customer confirmations?			
j. Other? *(Explain)*			
33. Does the serviced institution obtain and review the servicer's internal or external audits and/or third party reviews? *(If yes, detail exceptions and corrective action)*			
34. Has the serviced institution used an independent auditor to evaluate EDP servicing? *(If yes, detail exceptions and corrective action)*			
35. Is the overall audit program for serviced applications considered adequate?			

FDIC 6601/106 (10-81) PAGE THREE

Appendix 16

Work Program for Electronic Data Processing Examinations

Federal Financial Institutions Examination Council
Form No. 008

WORK PROGRAM FOR ELECTRONIC DATA PROCESSING EXAMINATIONS

Name of Financial Institution or Servicer	City	State	Region/District	Number

Examination Commenced_____M., on _____
                                                                                     Day   Date

Examination Closed_____M., on _____
                                                                                     Day   Date

The information contained in this work program presents a fair evaluation of the EDP activities of this financial institution/servicer in accordance with the instructions outlined below.

I have reviewed the information included in this work program and concur with the examination findings except where noted.

_____   _____   _____   _____
       (EDP Examiner in Charge)   (Date)   (EDP Review Examiner)   (Date)

GENERAL INSTRUCTIONS

This program presents examination procedures for an electronic data processing system. It assists the examiner in determining the extent and quality of the financial institution's EDP-related internal control procedures. The program should be used in conjunction with the EDP Examination Handbook. Upon completion of the work program, the examiner should be able to assess the adequacy of the institution's EDP controls. The report of examination will be prepared on the basis of the information in the work program. All significant exceptions should be discussed with the financial institution or servicer management together with any promised corrective action noted in both the work program and report of examination. Where applicable, significant deficiencies should also be discussed with the examiner-in-charge of other examination areas.

The applicable work program sections should be completed in pencil for each data center examined. A data center may include multiple computers located in the same general areas and subject to common administration. If the data center provides services for other financial institutions, the examiner should also complete the customer services section of this work program. The work program should include conditions during multiple shifts and overtime hours, as well as during normal work hours. The EDP examination should be conducted concurrently with the commercial examination, when possible, especially if internal controls are suspected of being weak. Prior to an EDP examination, the EDP examiner should review the most recent commercial, holding company, trust, and consumer reports (as applicable).

The examiner should obtain all materials necessary to complete the questionnaire for each section of the program. In most instances, this material should be retained until the specific examination area is completed. If a work step in the program is marked with an asterisk (*), the material obtained from the data center or developed by the examiner should be included in the work papers, together with any other information needed to fully describe the existent internal controls. Exhibits should be bound on the upper portion of the work program folder. Exhibits having continuing significance should be carried forward from worksheets of previous examinations. The completed work program should be bound on the bottom portion of the work program folder.

Each examination should include a review of exceptions in prior work programs, examination reports, and follow-up correspondence. Any unresolved exceptions should be included in the "Summary of Exceptions." In addition, any significant changes that would affect future examinations should be documented in the work program and administrative section of the report of examination.

Work program questions and phrases printed in upper case type are critical to a sound EDP operation. All questions have been designed so that a "yes" (affirmative) answer indicates the presence of strong internal controls. However, a "no" (negative) answer may not necessarily indicate a deficiency if compensating controls exist. This must be evaluated by the examiner. ALL NEGATIVE ANSWERS MUST BE EXPLAINED. IN INSTANCES WHERE THERE ARE ADEQUATE COMPENSATING CONTROLS, COMMENTS NEED NOT APPEAR IN THE EXAMINATION REPORT OR IN THE "SUMMARY OF EXCEPTIONS." HOWEVER, THE COMPENSATING CONTROLS MUST BE DESCRIBED IN THE WORK PROGRAM UNDER "COMMENTS." Many questions may require elaboration beyond "yes" or "not applicable" (N/A) answer. Such elaboration should be made in the comments section of the work program or in exhibits or attachments. Additionally, answers to the less critical questions may evidence improvement or weakness in the overall condition of EDP operations and should be evaluated by the examiner.

When weaknesses in internal controls appear grossly deficient and/or little progress toward correction is promised by management, the examiner may elect to perform supplemental examination procedures. Such procedures should be clearly documented in the work program.

The completed work program and questionnaire will be retained as part of the examination work papers and used for guidance in the next examination. Accordingly, the programs and questionnaires should be completed in an organized and legible manner.

SUMMARY OF EXCEPTIONS

This section should summarize deficiencies and management's response and projected date for correction.

SECTION	EXCEPTIONS	RESPONSE AND CORRECTIVE ACTION PROMISED
1. EDP Audit		
2. Management		
3. Systems and Programming		
4. Data Integrity		
5. Computer Operations		
6. Teleprocessing		
7. Customer Service		

SECTION 1

EDP Audit

EXAMINER'S
INITIALS   COMMENTS

The purpose of this section is to determine whether the internal and/or external auditors are conducting an effective on-going EDP audit program. This evaluation will reveal the adequacy of EDP audit coverage and to what extent, if any, the examiner may rely upon the procedures performed by the auditors in determining the scope of the EDP examination.

WORK STEPS

*1.1   OBTAIN AND REVIEW THE AUDIT DEPARTMENT'S WRITTEN CHARTER/DECLARATION FROM THE BOARD OF DIRECTORS. (1.15)

*1.2   REVIEW AND SUMMARIZE THE MINUTES OF THE BOARD OF DIRECTORS, AUDIT COMMITTEE AND OTHER EDP RELATED COMMITTEES IN WHICH THE AUDIT DEPARTMENT IS REPRESENTED. (1.16 to 1.21)

*1.3   DETERMINE THE ORGANIZATIONAL STRUCTURE OF THE INTERNAL AUDIT FUNCTION. (1.22 to 1.29)

*1.4   OBTAIN A BRIEF RESUME OR COMPLETE A "BIOGRAPHICAL DATA WORKSHEET" ON ALL KEY PERSONNEL IN THE AUDIT DEPARTMENT. INCLUDE BANKING AND AUDIT RELATED EDUCATION AND EXPERIENCE. (1.30 to 1.36)

1.5   REVIEW THE EDP AUDIT STANDARDS MANUALS AND/OR EDP RELATED SECTIONS OF THE GENERAL AUDIT MANUAL. DOCUMENT ANY DEFICIENCIES. (1.37 to 1.48)

*1.6   REVIEW A SAMPLE OF EDP AUDIT PROCEDURES FOR DATA PROCESSING. DOCUMENT PROCEDURES REVIEWED AND ANY LACK OF SCOPE OR COMPREHENSIVENESS. (1.49 to 1.58)

*1.7   OBTAIN OR PREPARE A LIST OF AUDIT SOFTWARE PROGRAMS. INDICATE APPLICATION, PROGRAM NAME, FUNCTION PERFORMED, BY WHOM DEVELOPED AND DATE OF LAST USE.

*1.8   SELECT A SAMPLE OF AUDIT SOFTWARE PROGRAMS. REVIEW THE DOCUMENTATION AND COMPLETE THE "DOCUMENTATION WORKSHEET" FOR THESE PROGRAMS. (1.59)

Section 1 — EDP Audit (continued)

EXAMINER'S
INITIALS   COMMENTS

*1.9   REVIEW THE MOST RECENT EXTERNAL EDP AUDIT REPORTS AND/OR MANAGEMENT LETTERS. DOCUMENT THE REVIEW AND ANY DEFICIENCIES. (1.60 and 1.61)

*1.10   REVIEW A SAMPLE OF INTERNAL EDP AUDIT REPORTS AND RELATED WORK PAPERS PREPARED SINCE THE LAST EXAMINATION. DOCUMENT THE REVIEW AND ANY DEFICIENCIES (1.62, 1.66 to 1.68)

*1.11   EXAMINE AUDIT DEPARTMENT FOLLOW-UP ON EXCEPTION ITEMS NOTED IN THE AUDIT REPORTS REVIEWED IN 1.9 AND 1.10. DOCUMENT ANY SIGNIFICANT UNRESOLVED EXCEPTIONS AND/OR ANY LACK OF FOLLOW-UP. (1.63 to 1.65)

1.12   REVIEW THE PHYSICAL SECURITY AND CONTROLS EXERCISED OVER SENSITIVE AUDIT MATERIAL, SUCH AS WORK PAPERS, REPORTS, CORRESPONDENCE, SOFTWARE AND SOFTWARE DOCUMENTATION. (1.69)

*1.13   SUMMARIZE STRENGTHS AND WEAKNESSES OF EDP AUDIT AND COMPLETE THE "SUMMARY OF EXCEPTIONS" FOR THIS SECTION.

*1.14   IF ANY PROCEDURES ARE TO BE LIMITED OR OMITTED BECAUSE OF RELIANCE UPON THE WORK OF THE INTERNAL OR EXTERNAL AUDITORS, DESCRIBE THE AREAS OF RELIANCE AND NOTE THE AUDITORS' CONCLUSIONS. FOLLOW UP ON ALL THE SIGNIFICANT AUDITOR CRITICISMS AND CARRY FORWARD EXISTING DEFICIENCIES IN THE EDP REPORT OF EXAMINATION.

QUESTIONNAIRE

YES   NO

1.15   Does the corporate charter/by-laws contain a resolution from the board of directors that:

a. Provides for adequate and effective audit coverage?
b. Includes a requirement that the auditor provide assurances for adequate audit trails and internal control mechanisms in each system?

1.16   Has a budget been established for EDP audit?

1.17   Does the board of directors or audit committee:

   a. REVIEW AND APPROVE THE EDP AUDIT SCHEDULES AND OBJECTIVES AT
       LEAST ANNUALLY?   ____ ____
   b. INCLUDE IN THEIR AUDIT REVIEW COMPARISONS OF ACHIEVEMENTS TO
       OBJECTIVES AND SCHEDULES PREVIOUSLY APPROVED BY THE BOARD OR
       THE AUDIT COMMITTEE?   ____ ____
   c. ADEQUATELY REVIEW ALL EDP RELATED AUDIT REPORTS?   ____ ____

1.18   IF NEITHER THE BOARD OF DIRECTORS NOR THE AUDIT COMMITTEE REVIEWS
       ALL EDP RELATED AUDIT REPORTS, IS THE SELECTION CRITERIA
       SATISFACTORY?   ____ ____

1.19   Do the minutes of the board of directors and the audit committee indicate:

   a. Attendance?   ____ ____
   b. Subjects discussed?   ____ ____
   c. Decisions made?   ____ ____

1.20   Is audit committee membership limited to outside directors? ____ ____

1.21   Do non-members attend meetings only at the specific request of the audit committee? ____ ____

1.22   Does the EDP auditor:

   a. Attend meetings of committees that consider the acquisition of new
       hardware/software?   ____ ____
   b. Routinely report audit matters to the board of directors or the audit committee? ____ ____
   c. Report audit matters to a senior officer to assure adequate response to audit
       exceptions?   ____ ____

1.23   DOES THE EDP AUDITOR PARTICIPATE IN THE DESIGN OR SELECTION OF
       NEW SOFTWARE SYSTEMS TO ENSURE THAT PROPER AUDIT CONTROLS ARE
       INCLUDED?   ____ ____

1.24   IS IT POLICY TO INFORM THE EDP AUDITOR OF EDP PROBLEMS IDENTIFIED BY
       MANAGEMENT?   ____ ____

1.25   Is there a written policy describing actions to be taken in case of a dispute over the
       adequacy of management response to an audit?   ____ ____

1.26   Does this policy include arbitration by the board of directors or audit committee? ____ ____

1.27   Does written policy prohibit auditors from engaging in activities which may be subject
       to audit?   ____ ____

1.28   IS INTERNAL AUDIT BOTH FUNCTIONALLY AND ADMINISTRATIVELY UNDER
       THE OVERALL DIRECTION OF THE BOARD OF DIRECTORS OR AUDIT
       COMMITTEE?   ____ ____

1.29   ARE THE INTERNAL AUDITORS FREE FROM PERFORMING ANY ACTIVITIES
       WHICH THEY MAY AUDIT?   ____ ____

EDP Audit Staff

1.30   Has management established minimum qualifications for EDP auditors? ____ ____

1.31   Based upon the review of personnel files or resumes for EDP auditors, have these
       employees met management's minimum qualifications, if established, for:

   a. Education?   ____ ____
   b. Experience?   ____ ____

1.32   Is there an adequate education program to provide training for the audit staff in:

   a. AUDIT TECHNIQUES AND PHILOSOPHY?   ____ ____
   b. PROGRAMMING, SYSTEMS DESIGN AND PROJECT MANAGEMENT?   ____ ____
   c. COMPUTER OPERATIONS AND TELEPROCESSING?   ____ ____
   d. OTHER RELEVANT TECHNICAL SUBJECTS?   ____ ____

1.33   DOES THE EDUCATION PROGRAM PROVIDE SUPERVISORY OR MANAGERIAL
       COURSES FOR APPROPRIATE PERSONNEL?   ____ ____

1.34   When planning the EDP audit schedule, does the EDP auditor/audit manager consider
       all EDP related activities?   ____ ____

1.35   HAS THE EDP AUDITOR/AUDIT MANAGER CONSISTENTLY ACHIEVED THE
       OBJECTIVES PREVIOUSLY APPROVED BY THE BOARD OF DIRECTORS?   ____ ____

Section 1 — EDP Audit (continued)   YES   NO   COMMENTS

1.36   Does authorized staffing appear adequate in the following respects:

    a. ARE ALL AUTHORIZED STAFF POSITIONS FILLED?   ____ ____
    b. IS THE TURNOVER RATE OF EDP AUDIT EMPLOYEES CONSIDERED
      REASONABLE?   ____ ____
    c. IS EDP AUDIT MANAGEMENT SUCCESSION ADEQUATE?   ____ ____

EDP Audit Standards

1.37   Do standards for EDP audit include selection criteria (risk analysis) to determine audit
    frequency for specific areas and functions?   ____ ____

1.38   IF SELECTION CRITERIA EXISTS, HAS IT BEEN APPROVED BY THE BOARD OF
    DIRECTORS OR THE AUDIT COMMITTEE?   ____ ____

1.39   DOES THE SELECTION CRITERIA PROVIDE ASSURANCE THAT ALL
    SIGNIFICANT EDP FUNCTIONS AND SYSTEMS WILL BE AUDITED WITH
    ADEQUATE FREQUENCY?   ____ ____

1.40   HAS A WRITTEN EDP AUDIT SCHEDULE BEEN DEVELOPED WHICH
    CONFORMS TO THE SELECTION CRITERIA?   ____ ____

1.41   Do standards exist for EDP audit reports including:

    a. Sample formats?   ____ ____
    b. Description of audit scope?   ____ ____
    c. Recommendations for improvements in criticized areas?   ____ ____
    d. Deficiency descriptions which contain background information and reasons why
      the deficiency should be corrected?   ____ ____

1.42   Do standards for the follow-up of EDP audit reports include:

    a. Timeliness of management response?   ____ ____
    b. Criteria for scheduling follow-up audits and a policy for determining the adequacy
      of management's response?   ____ ____

Section 1 — EDP Audit (continued)   YES   NO   COMMENTS

1.43   Do standards for EDP audit work papers include:

    a. Documentation of all audit work performed, with a uniform filing system for easy
      reference?   ____ ____
    b. A statement of the audit objectives?   ____ ____
    c. A description of the area to be audited, including its operating standards and control
      points?   ____ ____
    d. A description of audit scope?   ____ ____
    e. A documented review of previous exceptions?   ____ ____
    f. A determination of compliance with established policies and procedures?   ____ ____

1.44   Do EDP audit standards establish procedures for:

    a. AUDITING EDP OPERATIONS?   ____ ____
    b. AUDITING AUTOMATED APPLICATIONS?   ____ ____
    c. THE REVIEW OF NEW APPLICATION SYSTEMS?   ____ ____

1.45   DO STANDARDS REQUIRE POST-IMPLEMENTATION REVIEWS OF RECENTLY
    INSTALLED APPLICATIONS?   ____ ____

1.46   Do standards for EDP audit include the use of audit software and require that:

    a. PROGRAM DOCUMENTATION IS ADEQUATE?   ____ ____
    b. ALL SIGNIFICANT APPLICATIONS ARE COVERED?   ____ ____
    c. CONFIRMATIONS ARE PREPARED, WHERE APPROPRIATE?   ____ ____
    d FILES ARE FOOTED?   ____ ____
    e. CALCULATIONS AND ACCRUALS ARE VERIFIED?   ____ ____

1.47   Do software standards include criteria for developing or purchasing audit software?   ____ ____

1.48   Do EDP audit standards require adequate security measures to protect:

    a. Work papers?   ____ ____
    b. Reports?   ____ ____
    c. Responses?   ____ ____
    d. Software?   ____ ____
    e. Software documentation?   ____ ____

YES   NO   COMMENTS

EDP Audit Scope

1.49 Are periodic audits performed which cover:

a. RECONCILEMENTS?   ____ ____
b. DATA PREPARATION?   ____ ____
c. PROOF AND TRANSIT?   ____ ____
d. COMPUTER OPERATIONS?   ____ ____
e. SYSTEMS AND PROGRAMMING?   ____ ____
f. TELEPROCESSING?   ____ ____
g. SIGNIFICANT APPLICATION SOFTWARE?   ____ ____
h. SOFTWARE DOCUMENTATION?   ____ ____
i. USER DEPARTMENT DATA PROCESSING CONTROLS?   ____ ____

1.50 Do audit procedures reveal whether proper segregation of duties exists for input
preparation, reject/re-entry handling and output balancing/review?   ____ ____

1.51 Do procedures for data preparation audits consider whether:

a. Monetary and non-monetary control totals are provided?   ____ ____
b. Processed data is verified?   ____ ____
c. Adjusting entries are prepared in accordance with established procedures?   ____ ____
d. Reference manuals are available and current?   ____ ____

1.52 Do procedures for output distribution audits consider whether:

a. Process control totals are reconciled prior to output distribution?   ____ ____
b. CURRENT INSTRUCTIONS ARE AVAILABLE FOR THE DISTRIBUTION OF ALL
OUTPUT REPORTS?   ____ ____
c. ADEQUATE PROCEDURES HAVE BEEN ESTABLISHED TO CONTROL
SENSITIVE INFORMATION?   ____ ____

YES   NO   COMMENTS

1.53 Do procedures for computer operations audits adequately consider:

a. COMPUTER OPERATIONS STANDARDS AND PROCEDURES AND
COMPLIANCE WITH THEM?   ____ ____
b. REPORTING MECHANISMS USED BY MANAGEMENT TO MONITOR EDP
OPERATIONS?   ____ ____
c. EQUIPMENT MAINTENANCE, SERVICE AGREEMENTS AND RECORDS OF
EQUIPMENT PROBLEMS?   ____ ____
d. PHYSICAL SECURITY AND CONTROLS OVER DATA PROCESSING
EQUIPMENT?   ____ ____
e. PHYSICAL SECURITY AND CONTROLS OVER DATA FILES AND
PRODUCTION PROGRAM LIBRARIES?   ____ ____
f. EMERGENCY PROCEDURES?   ____ ____
g. DISASTER/RECOVERY PROCEDURES AND EQUIPMENT BACKUP?   ____ ____
h. EDP RELATED INSURANCE COVERAGE?   ____ ____
i. COMPUTER OPERATIONS' ORGANIZATION AND SEPARATION OF DUTIES?   ____ ____
j. WHETHER OPERATOR RUN MANUALS ARE CURRENT AND COMPLETE?   ____ ____

1.54 Do procedures for application system audits adequately consider:

a. AUDIT TRAILS AND CONTROL MECHANISMS?   ____ ____
b. DOCUMENTATION?   ____ ____
c. COMPLIANCE WITH PROGRAMMING STANDARDS?   ____ ____

and for new application system audits, do they consider:

d. CONFORMANCE TO DESIGN OBJECTIVES?   ____ ____
e. AUTHORIZATIONS BY MANAGEMENT AT SPECIFIED MILESTONES IN
THE DEVELOPMENT PROCESS?   ____ ____
f. ADEQUACY OF TEST PLANS AND RESULTS?   ____ ____

Section 1 — EDP Audit (continued)   YES   NO   COMMENTS

1.55   Do procedures for system and programming audits adequately consider:

    a. PROGRAM STANDARDS AND PROCEDURES AND COMPLIANCE WITH
       THEM?   ____ ____

    b. CONTROLS OVER UTILITY PROGRAMS THAT HAVE DATA FILE OR
       PROGRAM ALTERING CAPABILITIES?   ____ ____

    c. PHYSICAL SECURITY AND CONTROL OVER OPERATING SYSTEM AND
       APPLICATION SYSTEM DOCUMENTATION?   ____ ____

    d. DOCUMENTATION FOR THE OPERATING SYSTEM AND APPLICATION
       SYSTEMS?   ____ ____

    e. CONTROLS OVER CHANGES TO THE OPERATING SYSTEM AND
       APPLICATION PROGRAMS?   ____ ____

    f. SYSTEMS AND PROGRAMMING ORGANIZATION AND SEPARATION OF
       DUTIES?   ____ ____

1.56   If teleprocessing systems are in use, do auditors determine whether:

    a. ACCESS TO THE SYSTEM IS LIMITED BY USER IDENTIFICATION CODES
       AND/OR PASSWORDS?   ____ ____

    b. PASSWORDS AND USER IDENTIFICATION CODES ARE PROPERLY
       PROTECTED?   ____ ____

    c. AN ADEQUATE TRANSACTION FILE IS MAINTAINED FOR ALL MESSAGES
       RECEIVED FROM THE TERMINALS?   ____ ____

    d. UNAUTHORIZED ATTEMPTS TO GAIN ACCESS TO THE SYSTEM ARE
       MONITORED?   ____ ____

    e. USER MANUALS ADEQUATELY DESCRIBE CURRENT PROCESSING
       REQUIREMENTS?   ____ ____

    f. ALTERNATE PROCESSING PROCEDURES ARE ADEQUATE?   ____ ____

1.57   Do auditors:

    a. REVIEW MAJOR PROGRAM CHANGES PRIOR TO THEIR
       IMPLEMENTATION?   ____ ____

    b. INDEPENDENTLY PROVE EVERY AUTOMATED APPLICATION TO THE
       GENERAL LEDGER CONTROLS AT LEAST ANNUALLY?   ____ ____

    c. RECOMMEND CONTROL CHANGES TO EXISTING AUTOMATED
       APPLICATIONS, WHERE NECESSARY?   ____ ____

Section 1 — EDP Audit (continued)   YES   NO   COMMENTS

1.58   Do procedures for the review of EDP customer/user services adequately consider:

    a. CONTRACTS FOR EDP SERVICING?   ____ ____

    b. BILLING AND INCOME COLLECTION?   ____ ____

1.59   If audit software is used by internal auditors in performing audits, is:

    a. AUDIT SOFTWARE, WHICH WAS NOT DEVELOPED BY THE EDP AUDIT
       STAFF, REVIEWED BY QUALIFIED AUDIT PERSONNEL?   ____ ____

    b. VENDOR SUPPORT OF THE SOFTWARE PACKAGE ADEQUATE?   ____ ____

    c. CONTROL OVER AUDIT SOFTWARE PROGRAM CHANGES ADEQUATE? ____ ____

    d. THE SOFTWARE APPROPRIATE FOR THE SIZE AND COMPLEXITY OF THE
       APPLICATIONS PROCESSED AND EFFECTIVE IN PROVIDING
       INFORMATION TO AUDITORS?   ____ ____

    e. AVAILABLE DOCUMENTATION ADEQUATE TO SUPPORT THE CONTINUED
       USEFULNESS OF AUDIT SOFTWARE?   ____ ____

    f. The systems and programming department's documentation standards followed by
       the audit department?   ____ ____

    g. AUDIT SOFTWARE AND SUPPORTING DOCUMENTATION BACKED-UP
       OFF-SITE IN A CONTROLLED ENVIRONMENT?   ____ ____

1.60   If an external EDP audit was performed, did the report/management letter
      adequately:

    a. DESCRIBE SCOPE AND OBJECTIVES?   ____ ____

    b. DESCRIBE DEFICIENCIES?   ____ ____

    c. SUGGEST CORRECTIVE ACTION?   ____ ____

1.61   Did the scope of the external audit include:

    a. Organization and planning?   ____ ____

    b. Systems and programming controls?   ____ ____

    c. Computer operations?   ____ ____

    d. Physical security?   ____ ____

    e. Input, processing and output controls?   ____ ____

    f. Data communications?   ____ ____

    g. Customer servicing?   ____ ____

    h. Internal audit coverage?   ____ ____

Section 1 — EDP Audit (continued)

EDP AUDIT REPORT AND WORK PAPER REVIEW WORKSHEET

NAME OF EDP AUDIT REPORT: _____

_____

AUDITOR NAME: _____

REPORT DATE: _____ DATE OF MANAGEMENT RESPONSE: _____

DATE OF AUDIT: _____ DATE OF AUDITOR FOLLOW-UP: _____

DATE OF LAST AUDIT: _____

		YES	NO	COMMENTS
1.62	Is the audit report:			
	a. IN COMPLIANCE TO THE STANDARD FORMAT?	___	___	
	b. LOGICAL, EFFECTIVE, AND UNDERSTANDABLE?	___	___	
	c. ADEQUATE IN DESCRIBING AUDIT OBJECTIVES AND SCOPE?	___	___	
	d. ADEQUATE IN SUGGESTING CORRECTIVE MEASURES FOR DEFICIENCIES?	___	___	
	e. ADEQUATE IN COMMUNICATING SIGNIFICANT INFORMATION?	___	___	
1.63	Did management respond:			
	a. TO NOTED EXCEPTIONS?	___	___	
	b. IN A TIMELY MANNER?	___	___	
	c. SPECIFICALLY TO THE ISSUES?	___	___	
1.64	Did the EDP auditor:			
	a. REVIEW THE RESPONSES FOR COMPLETENESS AND APPROPRIATENESS?	___	___	
	b. PERFORM A FOLLOW-UP AUDIT TO VERIFY CORRECTIVE ACTIONS?	___	___	
1.65	Have major deficiencies noted in audit reports been resolved to the satisfaction of the auditor or referred to the board of directors for final resolution?	___	___	
1.66	Are the objectives of the audit reasonable and sufficient?	___	___	

Section 1 — EDP Audit (continued)

		YES	NO	COMMENTS
1.67	Do work papers for system development and/or application system audits document if:			
	a. DESIGN OBJECTIVES HAVE BEEN MET?	___	___	
	b. PROGRAMS ARE IN COMPLIANCE TO STANDARDS?	___	___	
	c. AUDIT TRAILS AND CONTROL MECHANISMS ARE SATISFACTORY?	___	___	
	d. TEST PLANS ARE ADEQUATE?	___	___	
	e. TEST RESULTS ARE SATISFACTORY?	___	___	
	f. DOCUMENTATION IS ADEQUATE?	___	___	
	g. PROGRAM CHANGES ARE ADEQUATELY REVIEWED?	___	___	
1.68	Are work papers filed in uniform manner for easy reference?	___	___	
1.69	Were the reviewed audit reports, work papers, and follow-up documents:			
	a. IN CONFORMANCE WITH EDP AUDIT STANDARDS?	___	___	
	b. ADEQUATELY SAFEGUARDED?	___	___	

SECTION 2

Management

A detailed knowledge of the computer center's organization is essential to the examiner's review of the data processing function. Proper organization and management supervision of that function should be evaluated in terms of clearly defined lines of authority and an appropriate separation of duties.

WORK STEPS

*2.1 OBTAIN OR PREPARE AN ORGANIZATION CHART FOR THE OVERALL CORPORATE STRUCTURE, INDICATING THE RELATIONSHIP OF DATA CENTER MANAGEMENT TO SENIOR MANAGEMENT. INCLUDE NAMES AND TITLES OF PERSONS HOLDING KEY POSITIONS. ALSO OBTAIN OR PREPARE DETAILED ORGANIZATION CHARTS FOR THE DATA PROCESSING FUNCTION, INCLUDING SYSTEMS AND PROGRAMMING, COMPUTER OPERATIONS, INPUT/OUTPUT AND DATA CONTROL AREAS. (2.12 to 2.14)

*2.2 OBTAIN A "BIOGRAPHICAL DATA WORKSHEET" OR RESUME FOR THE EDP DEPARTMENT, SYSTEMS AND PROGRAMMING, AND OPERATIONS MANAGEMENT. INCLUDE A LIST OF ANNUAL SALARIES FOR KEY PERSONNEL IN EACH AREA. (2.15 to 2.17)

*2.3 OBTAIN OR PREPARE A LIST OF ALL EDP RELATED COMMITTEES. INCLUDE NAMES AND TITLES OF MEMBERS AND A BRIEF DESCRIPTION OF COMMITTEE FUNCTIONS. ANY COMMITTEE LISTED IN SECTION 1 MAY BE INCORPORATED BY REFERENCE.

*2.4 OBTAIN OR PREPARE A LIST OF MEMBERS OF THE BOARD OF DIRECTORS. INDICATE NAME, OCCUPATION AND PRINCIPAL BUSINESS AFFILIATION. IF THE CENTER IS NOT A FINANCIAL INSTITUTION, INCLUDE PRINCIPAL OWNERS (10 PERCENT OR MORE).

*2.5 SELECTIVELY REVIEW THE MINUTES OF THE BOARD OF DIRECTORS AND OF ANY COMMITTEES LISTED IN WORK STEP 2.3. SUMMARIZE ANY EDP RELATED MATTERS. REFER TO WORK STEP 1.2, IF APPLICABLE. (2.18 to 2.23, 2.37 to 2.40)

*2.6 REVIEW ADMINISTRATIVE MANUALS CONTAINING WRITTEN JOB DESCRIPTIONS AND GENERAL PERSONNEL POLICY. REVIEW KEY JOB DESCRIPTIONS BASED ON WORK STEP 2.1 AND CONSIDER SAMPLING OTHERS. (2.24 to 2.32)

Section 2 — Management (continued)

*2.7 SUMMARIZE ANY MANAGEMENT PLANS FOR CHANGING SOFTWARE, HARDWARE, ORGANIZATION OR CONTROL PROCEDURES. (2.33 and 2.34)

*2.8 REVIEW SIGNIFICANT EXCEPTIONS NOTED IN PRIOR EDP EXAMINATION AND AUDIT REPORTS. DOCUMENT MANAGEMENT ACTION TAKEN TO CORRECT THOSE EXCEPTIONS. (2.35 and 2.36)

*2.9 CONSIDERING WORK STEPS 1.11 AND 2.8, DETERMINE WHETHER MANAGEMENT HAS TAKEN REASONABLE ACTION TO CORRECT SIGNIFICANT DEFICIENCIES. SUMMARIZE YOUR CONCLUSIONS.

2.10 REVIEW MANAGEMENT REPORTS WHICH ARE USED TO MONITOR EDP ACTIVITIES. (2.41)

*2.11 SUMMARIZE STRENGTHS AND WEAKNESSES OF MANAGEMENT AND COMPLETE THE "SUMMARY OF EXCEPTIONS" FOR THIS SECTION.

QUESTIONNAIRE

YES   NO

2.12 Does the center's organization chart properly reflect the current reporting structure?

2.13 DOES THE MANAGER OF THE EDP DEPARTMENT REPORT DIRECTLY TO A SENIOR OFFICIAL?

2.14 DOES THE ORGANIZATION CHART REFLECT ADEQUATE SEGREGATION OF DUTIES?

2.15 Have minimum personnel qualifications been established for key EDP positions and have these qualifications been met?

2.16 Is there a continuing education program for EDP personnel which includes:

    a. Technical training?
    b. Management participation?

2.17 Are there persons within the organization who have the experience and training necessary to provide for succession of management?

Section 2 — Management (continued)   YES   NO   COMMENTS

2.18   Are EDP matters considered when senior management establishes overall policy?   ____ ____

2.19   Does senior management or a committee thereof, such as an EDP steering committee,
        review and approve:
        a. EDP POLICIES?   ____ ____
        b. Resource allocations by project?   ____ ____
        c. PROCEDURES FOR SECURITY AND CONTROL MEASURES?   ____ ____
        d. Research and development studies?   ____ ____
        e. EDP BUDGETS?   ____ ____
        f. EDP PRIORITIES?   ____ ____
        g. MAJOR SYSTEM, ORGANIZATION AND EQUIPMENT CHANGES?   ____ ____
        h. THE STATUS OF MAJOR PROJECTS AND THE ACHIEVEMENT OF
           OBJECTIVES?   ____ ____
        i. EDP LONG RANGE PLANNING?   ____ ____

2.20   During the most recent budget period, were actual costs for the EDP function within
        budgeted amounts?   ____ ____

2.21   IS AUDIT DEPARTMENT ADVICE SOUGHT ON INTERNAL CONTROLS AND
        AUDIT MATTERS?   ____ ____

2.22   DO USER DEPARTMENTS PARTICIPATE IN DETERMINING THE USE OF EDP
        RESOURCES?   ____ ____

2.23   ARE MANAGEMENT POLICY DECISIONS ADEQUATELY DOCUMENTED IN
        COMMITTEE MINUTES OR MEMORANDA?   ____ ____

2.24   HAS MANAGEMENT DEVELOPED A WRITTEN PERSONNEL POLICY?   ____ ____

2.25   DOES THE POLICY INCLUDE A DESCRIPTION OF JOB POSITIONS AND
        RESPONSIBILITIES IN THE EDP DEPARTMENT?   ____ ____

2.26   DO THE DUTIES PERFORMED BY EDP PERSONNEL CONFORM TO THEIR JOB
        DESCRIPTIONS?   ____ ____

2.27   Have new employees received adequate clearance before being given access to secure
        areas, confidential information or financial data?   ____ ____

2.28   ARE ALL AUTHORIZED STAFF POSITIONS FILLED?   ____ ____

Section 2 — Management (continued)   YES   NO   COMMENTS

2.29   Has employee or supervisory turnover been within reasonable limits?   ____ ____

2.30   IS THE QUANTITY AND QUALITY OF THE STAFF ADEQUATE?   ____ ____

2.31   ARE EDP EMPLOYEES PROHIBITED FROM HAVING AUTHORITY,
        RESPONSIBILITY OR SIGNIFICANT DUTIES IN ANY OTHER DEPARTMENTS? ____ ____

2.32   If EDP employees have duties in other departments: ____ ____

        a. IS MANAGEMENT AWARE OF ANY POTENTIAL CONFLICTS THAT SUCH
           DUTIES MAY CAUSE?   ____ ____
        b. DOES MANAGEMENT REVIEW CONFLICTING FUNCTIONS?   ____ ____

2.33   HAS MANAGEMENT DEVELOPED LONG AND SHORT RANGE PLANS AND
        HAVE THESE BEEN DOCUMENTED IN BOARD MINUTES OR OTHER WRITTEN
        FORM?   ____ ____

2.34   Are long range plans periodically updated to reflect current management philosophy?   ____ ____

2.35   HAS MANAGEMENT TAKEN POSITIVE ACTION TOWARD CORRECTING
        EXCEPTIONS REPORTED IN PRIOR EDP EXAMINATION REPORTS?   ____ ____

2.36   DOES MANAGEMENT GIVE ADEQUATE CONSIDERATION TO CORRECTION
        OF DEFICIENCIES NOTED IN AUDIT REPORTS?   ____ ____

2.37   Is risk analysis or some other management technique used to determine the types and
        amounts of EDP related insurance purchased by the institution? ____ ____

2.38   DOES EDP MANAGEMENT REVIEW EDP INSURANCE COVERAGE AT LEAST
        ANNUALLY AND IS IT SUBSEQUENTLY APPROVED BY THE BOARD OF
        DIRECTORS?   ____ ____

2.39   HAS AN EDP SECURITY PROGRAM BEEN DEVELOPED AND IS IT REVIEWED
        AND APPROVED AT LEAST ANNUALLY BY THE BOARD AND EDP
        MANAGEMENT?   ____ ____

2.40   Has a person been assigned the overall responsibility for EDP department security?   ____ ____

2.41   IS AN EFFECTIVE MANAGEMENT REPORTING SYSTEM USED BY SENIOR
        MANAGEMENT TO MONITOR THE EDP FUNCTION?   ____ ____

SECTION 3

Systems and Programming

Systems and programming standards should guide the development, maintenance and modification of computer applications. By reviewing those standards, the examiner should understand the general system techniques and controls in effect at the installation. Compliance with systems standards should be documented and safeguarded adequately so that the center does not become overly dependent upon the originators of the system.

Documentation communicates to the user the essential elements of the data processing system and the logic of the various computer programs. The examiner reviews documentation to determine the existence of programmed and other controls. In addition, the examiner ascertains whether such controls can provide the bank with the continuing ability to produce reliable financial data.

WORK STEPS

3.1 REVIEW THE STANDARDS MANUAL FOR SYSTEMS AND PROGRAMMING. DOCUMENT ANY NONCOMPLIANCE WITH THE GUIDELINES PROVIDED IN SECTION 3 OF THE EDP EXAMINATION HANDBOOK. (3.12 to 3.20)

3.2 SELECTIVELY REVIEW WRITTEN REPORTS THAT COMMUNICATE PROJECT STATUS TO SENIOR MANAGEMENT. (3.21 and 3.22)

3.3 REVIEW WRITTEN DOCUMENTS THAT PRESENT EDP OBJECTIVES/ PROJECTS, BUDGETS FOR THE CURRENT PLANNING CYCLE AND COST/BENEFIT ANALYSES FOR SELECT PROJECTS. (3.23 to 3.27)

3.4 REVIEW THE DOCUMENTATION FOR THE CURRENT OPERATING SYSTEM GENERATION. (3.28 to 3.31)

*3.5 OBTAIN OR PREPARE A LIST OF UTILITY PROGRAMS THAT HAVE DATA FILE OR PROGRAM ALTERING CAPABILITY.

*3.6 OBTAIN OR PREPARE A LIST OF ALL AUTOMATED APPLICATIONS. INCLUDE PROGRAMMERS ASSIGNED TO THE APPLICATION AND THE PROGRAMMING LANGUAGE. IF SOFTWARE IS PURCHASED, INCLUDE NAME OF VENDOR AND PURCHASE PRICE, ORIGINAL AND CURRENT BOOK VALUE, AND AMORTIZATION. (3.32 and 3.33)

3.7 REVIEW THE CONTROLS AND PHYSICAL SECURITY FOR SYSTEMS AND PROGRAMMING. (3.34 to 3.40)

Section 3— Systems and Programming (continued)

*3.8 DOCUMENT THE PROCEDURES REQUIRED TO EFFECT A PROGRAM CHANGE. (3.41 to 3.50)

*3.9 SELECT APPLICATIONS FOR REVIEW AND COMPLETE THE "DOCUMENTATION WORKSHEET." (3.51 to 3.59)

3.10 DETERMINE WHETHER THE INSTITUTION MARKETS ANY SOFTWARE. IF SO, FOR EACH SOFTWARE PACKAGE, LIST THE CUSTOMER FINANCIAL INSTITUTIONS AND INDICATE IF SOFTWARE SUPPORT IS PROVIDED.

3.11 SUMMARIZE STRENGTHS AND WEAKNESSES IN SYSTEMS AND PROGRAMMING AND COMPLETE THE "SUMMARY OF EXCEPTIONS" FOR THIS SECTION.

QUESTIONNAIRE

YES   NO

Standards and Procedures

3.12 Have written standards been developed for:

   a. SYSTEM DESIGN/DEVELOPMENT?
   b. PACKAGE SELECTION?
   c. PROGRAMMING PROCEDURES?
   d. TESTING?
   e. IMPLEMENTATION?
   f. PROGRAM APPROVAL AND CATALOG PROCEDURES?
   g. PROGRAM CHANGE PROCEDURES?
   h. ACTIVITIES PERFORMED BY OPERATING SYSTEMS PROGRAMMERS?

3.13 Are standards properly maintained in a current status?

3.14 Do application system design/development standards require:

   a. A project-feasibility study?
   b. A project cost/benefit analysis?
   c. Performance of specific development tasks in a specified sequence?
   d. Periodic review and approval of system design through the development cycle?
   e. Written user approval of design prior to coding?
   f. Acceptance testing of systems by users and computer operations?
   g. Written user system acceptance?
   h. A post-implementation review of systems?

Section 3— Systems and Programming (continued)　　　　　　　　　　YES　　NO　　　　　　　COMMENTS

3.15　Do software package selection standards require:

　　　a. Thorough analysis of software products of alternative vendors?　　　___　___
　　　b. A cost/benefit analysis of alternative vendor packages?　　　___　___

3.16　Do programming standards require:

　　　a. Use of control totals, batch totals and item counts, wherever possible?　　　___　___
　　　b. Programmed edit and validation checks of input before any processing is done?　　　___　___
　　　c. Use of file labels to authenticate file input?　　　___　___
　　　d. That checkpoint restart capability be programmed, wherever possible?　　　___　___
　　　e. Capture of transactions for audit trails?　　　___　___
　　　f. Use of standardized routines, wherever possible?　　　___　___
　　　g. Use of exception reports of uncommon transactions?　　　___　___

3.17　Do testing standards require:

　　　a. Parallel testing of all new systems, when feasible?　　　___　___
　　　b. Independent verification of test results?　　　___　___
　　　c. That no tests be run against live files?　　　___　___
　　　d. Testing of all conceivable error conditions?　　　___　___
　　　e. Review and approval of final test results by all affected parties?　　　___　___
　　　f. Testing of all program changes prior to implementation?　　　___　___

3.18　Do implementation standards require:

　　　a. Formal system acceptance by users and the computer operations function?　　　___　___
　　　b. Distribution of final versions of user manuals and operator run manuals?　　　___　___
　　　c. Completion of user training?　　　___　___
　　　d. Completion of all documentation?　　　___　___

3.19　ARE WRITTEN STANDARDS CONSIDERED ADEQUATE?　　　___　___

3.20　DOES THE APPLICATION SYSTEM DEVELOPMENT DOCUMENTATION
　　　ADHERE TO THE STANDARDS PRESCRIBED IN THE STANDARDS MANUAL?　　　___　___

Section 3— Systems and Programming (continued)　　　　　　　　　　YES　　NO　　　　　　　COMMENTS

3.21　If projects have been designated for development during the current budget cycle:

　　　a. HAS A MEANINGFUL COST/BENEFIT ANALYSIS BEEN USED TO SELECT
　　　　 PROJECTS WITH THE GREATEST POTENTIAL ADVANTAGES?　　　___　___
　　　b. Are budget targets established for selected projects and incorporated into the overall
　　　　 budget for the organization?　　　___　___
　　　c. HAVE SPECIFIC TARGET DATES BEEN SET FOR ALL PROJECTS?　　　___　___

3.22　Is a formal project control system employed?　　　___　___

3.23　If yes, does the control system require:

　　　a. Designation of a project target completion date?　　　___　___
　　　b. Designation of interim target dates for project tasks?　　　___　___
　　　c. Periodic project status reports that identify tasks completed and remaining?　　　___　___
　　　d. Clear identification of target date revisions?　　　___　___

3.24　Are post-implementation reviews conducted?　　　___　___

3.25　Do post-implementation reviews include:

　　　a. Analysis of planned and actual development costs?　　　___　___
　　　b. Comparison of planned and actual timeframes for development?　　　___　___
　　　c. Comparison of planned and actual operational savings?　　　___　___
　　　d. Identification of system operational problems and required enhancements?　　　___　___
　　　e. Comparison of planned and attained system benefits?　　　___　___

3.26　DOES PROGRESS INFORMATION APPEAR ACCURATE AND USEABLE IN
　　　COMMUNICATING CURRENT STATUS AND LOCATING PROBLEMS?　　　___　___

3.27　Were prior period objectives and time and cost targets for projects generally attained?
　　　(If not, document reasons.)　　　___　___

Software Controls

3.28　ARE THE OPERATING SYSTEM VENDOR OPTIONS PROPERLY DOCUMENTED?　　　___　___

3.29　ARE USER MODIFICATIONS PROPERLY DOCUMENTED?　　　___　___

Section 3 — Systems and Programming (continued)   YES   NO   COMMENTS

3.30 Does the most recent operating system generation include the following features or
      their equivalent:

    a. Storage or boundary protections?   —— ——
    b. Fetch protection?   —— ——

3.31 IS THERE A FUNCTIONAL DIVISION OF DUTIES BETWEEN SYSTEMS
      PROGRAMMING AND APPLICATION PROGRAMMING?   —— ——

3.32 Is maintenance expertise available and specifically assigned for each major application?   —— ——

3.33 Are there persons with sufficient training and experience to provide backup for the
      major systems and programming function?   —— ——

3.34 If any applications are written in low level languages, are programmers prohibited from
      executing instructions normally restricted to the operating system?   —— ——

3.35 IS ACCESS TO STORAGE DUMPS RESTRICTED TO THOSE PERSONS WHO MUST
      USE THEM FOR DIAGNOSTIC PURPOSES?   —— ——

3.36 ARE SYSTEMS PROGRAMMERS DENIED ACCESS TO APPLICATION PROGRAM
      LIABRARIES AND DOCUMENTATION?   —— ——

3.37 ARE PROGRAMMERS DENIED ACCESS TO LIVE DATA FILES?   —— ——

3.38 Are application programmers denied access to:

    a. DOCUMENTATION AND SOURCE LISTINGS FOR THE OPERATING SYSTEM?   —— ——
    b. PRODUCTION PROGRAM LIBRARIES?   —— ——

3.39 Are program listings used by programmers properly secured and destroyed when no
      longer needed?   —— ——

3.40 Are source listings for purchased programs either on-premises or readily accessible?   —— ——

Section 3 — Systems and Programming (continued)   YES   NO   COMMENTS

Program Change Controls

3.41 IS THERE A WRITTEN AUTHORIZATION PROCEDURE FOR MAKING PROGRAM
      CHANGES?   —— ——

3.42 Does the program change procedure include:

    a. PRE-NUMBERED OR CONTROLLED SEQUENCE NUMBER CHANGE FORMS?   —— ——
    b. A NARRATIVE DESCRIPTION OF THE PROBLEM OR REASON FOR CHANGE?   —— ——
    c. APPROVAL OF THE CHANGE REQUEST BY THE AFFECTED PARTIES?   —— ——
    d. THE NAME OF PROGRAMMER MAKING THE CHANGE?   —— ——
    e. THE SIGNATURE OF ANOTHER PROGRAMMER OR SUPERVISOR WHO
       REVIEWED AND APPROVED THE ACTUAL PROGRAM CHANGE?   —— ——
    f. SENDING A COPY OF THE APPROVAL TO THE AUDIT DEPARTMENT?   —— ——

3.43 ARE PROGRAM CHANGE REQUEST FORMS REVIEWED FOR PROPRIETY
      BEFORE ACCEPTANCE BY THE PROGRAMMING DEPARTMENT?   —— ——

3.44 Are program change requests reviewed to determine:

    a. Alternate methods to accomplish the change?   —— ——
    b. The cost of making the change?   —— ——
    c. The time requirements necessary to make the change?   —— ——

3.45 ARE PROGRAM MODIFICATIONS REVIEWED AND APPROVED PRIOR TO
      IMPLEMENTATION?   —— ——

3.46 ARE CHANGES TO THE OPERATING SYSTEM SUBJECT TO THE SAME CONTROL
      PROCEDURES AS APPLICATION PROGRAMS?   —— ——

3.47 ARE RECORDS OF PATCHES OR TEMPORARY PROGRAM CHANGES
      MAINTAINED, INCLUDING THE APPROPRIATE APPROVALS, RECORDS OF THE
      INSTRUCTIONS ALTERED, THE NAME OF THE PERSONS MAKING THE
      CHANGES AND THE REASON FOR THE CHANGES?   —— ——

3.48 ARE PROGRAM PATCHES OR TEMPORARY PROGRAM CHANGES REPLACED
      BY PROPERLY AUTHORIZED AND PROCESSED SOURCE LEVEL PROGRAM
      CHANGES AS SOON AS PRACTICABLE?   —— ——

Section 3 — Systems and Programming (continued)

YES   NO   COMMENTS

3.49   IS PROGRAM DOCUMENTATION UPDATED TO REFLECT PROGRAM CHANGES AS SOON AS PRACTICABLE AFTER THE CHANGE HAS BEEN MADE?

3.50   ARE PROGRAM CHANGES RECORDED IN A MANNER THAT PROVIDES AN ACCURATE CHRONOLOGICAL RECORD OF THE SYSTEM?

Documentation Controls

3.51   Do documentation standards require:

   a. SYSTEMS NARRATIVES?
   b. SYSTEMS FLOWCHARTS?
   c. PROGRAM NARRATIVES?
   d. RECORD LAYOUT SCHEMATICS AND OUTPUT FORMATS?
   e. DESCRIPTION OF EDIT CHECKING AND PROGRAMMED CONTROLS?
   f. CURRENT SOURCE LISTINGS?
   g. OPERATOR INSTRUCTIONS?
   h. USER MANUALS?
   i. HISTORY OF PROGRAM CHANGES?

3.52   BASED ON A REVIEW OF APPLICATION DOCUMENTATION (WORK STEP 3.9), DOES THE DOCUMENTATION ADHERE TO STANDARDS PRESCRIBED IN THE DOCUMENTATION STANDARDS MANUAL AND IS IT ADEQUATE?

3.53   IS THE DOCUMENTATION WELL ORGANIZED AND PROPERLY MAINTAINED?

3.54   ARE PERIODIC DOCUMENTATION REVIEWS CONDUCTED BY EDP MANAGEMENT OR ITS REPRESENTATIVE?

3.55   IF NOT, ARE ALTERNATIVE METHODS USED TO DETERMINE COMPLIANCE WITH DOCUMENTATION STANDARDS?

3.56   Do program source listings indicate:

   a. The date last compiled?
   b. The program version number, if applicable?
   c. Source code changes, if applicable?

Section 3 — Systems and Programming (continued)

YES   NO   COMMENTS

3.57   HAVE USER MANUALS BEEN DISTRIBUTED TO ALL APPROPRIATE USER DEPARTMENTS?

3.58   Does the installation employ a documentation librarian who has no conflicting duties?

3.59   ARE THE FOLLOWING DOCUMENTATION LIBRARIAN FUNCTIONS PERFORMED:

   a. Reviewing documentation at system development time to ensure adherence to standards and appropriate authorization of exceptions?
   b. CONTROLLING AND PROTECTING DOCUMENTATION?
   c. HANDLING OF DOCUMENTATION REVISIONS?
   d. NOTIFYING AND DISTRIBUTING DOCUMENTATION TO AUTHORIZED PARTIES?
   e. MAINTAINING ALL DOCUMENTATION AND STANDARDS TO ENSURE CURRENT VERSIONS?

SECTION 4

Data Integrity

To ensure the integrity of data, control procedures should be established for transaction processing. The examiner evaluates these procedures to determine that access and use of data is properly controlled.

WORK STEPS

*4.1 FOR THE APPLICATION(S) SELECTED FOR REVIEW IN WORK PROGRAM STEP 3.9, OBTAIN OR PREPARE A DESCRIPTION OF THE WORKFLOW FROM THE POINT OF INPUT TO THE DATA CENTER, THROUGH PROCESSING AND FINAL OUTPUT DISTRIBUTION. IDENTIFY ALL PROCESSING STEPS AND CONTROLS. A FLOWCHART MAY BE HELPFUL.

4.2 REVIEW THE CONTROLS IN EFFECT FOR NEGOTIABLE INSTRUMENTS, INPUT PREPARATION AND OUTPUT DISTRIBUTION. (4.8 to 4.29)

4.3 REVIEW THE RECONCILEMENT PROCEDURES FOR EACH CATEGORY OF DATA ENCOUNTERED IN THE PRIOR WORK STEP (INCLUDING ANY INCLEARINGS, AUTOMATICALLY GENERATED ACTIVITY, WORK GENERATED BY USER AREAS AND REJECTS). (4.30 to 4.34)

4.4 REVIEW THE DATA BASE ADMINISTRATOR'S FUNCTIONS AND RESPONSIBILITIES. NOTE ANY CONCENTRATION OF DUTIES THAT MAY EXIST (IF APPLICABLE). (4.35 to 4.37)

4.5 REVIEW THE DATA DICTIONARY AND PROCEDURES IN EFFECT TO MAINTAIN IT (IF APPLICABLE). (4.38 to 4.40)

4.6 REVIEW THE DATA BASE TRANSACTION LOGS AND PROCEDURES IN PLACE FOR THE SECURITY AND RECOVERY OF THE DATA BASE (IF APPLICABLE). (4.41 to 4.43)

*4.7 SUMMARIZE THE STRENGTHS AND WEAKNESSES OF DATA INTEGRITY AND COMPLETE THE "SUMMARY OF EXCEPTIONS" FOR THIS SECTION.

QUESTIONNAIRE

Input/Output Controls

YES   NO

4.8 IS ALL WORK RECEIVED BY THE INPUT/OUTPUT SECTION ACCOMPANIED BY TRANSMITTAL FORMS AND CONTROL TOTALS?

4.9 Is a log maintained of the work received for each user branch and application?

Section 4 — Data Integrity (continued)

YES   NO   COMMENTS

4.10 Are proof tapes that are received with the input data retained in an orderly and logical manner for final balancing of the day's processing?

4.11 Are non-dollar transactions subject to similar controls as dollar transactions?

4.12 Is it a requirement that master file change requests:

    a. BE IN WRITING?
    b. IDENTIFY THE ORIGINATING PERSONNEL?
    c. BEAR SUPERVISORY APPROVAL?

4.13 When clearings are received at the data center from Federal Reserve banks or correspondent banks, have procedures been established for timely reporting of the cash letter totals to the user's accounting office?

4.14 IF THE DATA CENTER IS REMOTE FROM USERS, ARE SOURCE DOCUMENTS MICROFILMED OR OTHERWISE RECORDED BEFORE BEING SENT TO THE CENTER?

4.15 ARE REFERENCE MANUALS THAT INCLUDE ILLUSTRATIONS OF ALL INPUT FORMS AVAILABLE TO DATA ENTRY PERSONNEL?

4.16 Is key input verified by a second data entry operator to ensure accuracy of critical control fields?

4.17 Are monetary totals and item counts developed for control purposes on key-to-disk and key-to-tape systems?

4.18 For input reconstruction, are key-to-disk and key-to-tape data duplicated or otherwise retained for a minimum of 24 hours?

4.19 Is MICR encoded data retained in batch or block sequence for a sufficient period to facilitate the location of rejected items?

4.20 ARE DATA ENTRY PERSONNEL PROHIBITED FROM ORIGINATING ENTRIES FOR PROCESSING?

4.21 Are control totals on related reports cross-compared?

Section 4 — Data Integrity (continued)   YES   NO   COMMENTS

4.22   Are reports reviewed for quality of output (paper aligned properly, no strings of meaningless characters, etc.) prior to distribution?   ____   ____

4.23   Are control procedures in effect to ensure that ¬ll reports are produced and delivered as scheduled?   ____   ____

4.24   Has a systematic and orderly plan for pick-up, processing and delivery of data been established?   ____   ____

4.25   ARE DISTRIBUTION PROCEDURES SUFFICIENT TO PROVIDE FOR DELIVERY OF REPORTS TO THE PROPER USER?   ____   ____

4.26   Do the procedures include control over the disposal of all output containing individual customer information?   ____   ____

4.27   Are negotiable items which are computer processed (i.e., blank checks, stock certificates, and plastics) and facsimile signature plates:

    a. ISSUED ONLY AS REQUIRED?   ____   ____
    b. KEPT LOCKED IN A SECURE LOCATION?   ____   ____
    c. CONTROLLED BY ACCESS LOGS?   ____   ____
    d. PERIODICALLY INVENTORIED?   ____   ____

4.28   WHEN MICROFILM OR MICROFICHE OUTPUT IS PRODUCED, ARE CONTROLS IN EFFECT WHICH ARE SIMILAR TO THOSE FOR HARD COPY OUTPUT?   ____   ____

4.29   Is microfilm/microfiche (input and output) stored in a secure location with:

    a. ACCESS LIMITED?   ____   ____
    b. A LOG TO RECORD USAGE?   ____   ____
    c. A RECORD OF INVENTORY?   ____   ____
    d. PHYSICAL INVENTORIES CONDUCTED PERIODICALLY?   ____   ____

4.30   ARE LISTINGS OF UNPOSTED ENTRIES USED TO CONTROL RESUBMISSIONS?   ____   ____

4.31   ARE REJECTED ITEMS, TOGETHER WITH THE LISTINGS OF CAPTURED ITEMS, DELIVERED TO THE RECONCILEMENT CLERKS FOR BALANCING?   ____   ____

4.32   ARE ALL CONTROL TOTALS DEVELOPED BY THE USER AND THE DATA CENTER CROSS-COMPARED?   ____   ____

Section 4 — Data Integrity (continued)   YES   NO   COMMENTS

4.33   Are rejected and unposted items (with listings) charged back to the appropriate user area?   ____   ____

4.34   Is official approval obtained for adjusting entries arising from:

    a. Entries received by, but not charged to, the data center?   ____   ____
    b. Entries charged to, but not received by, the data center?   ____   ____

Control of Data Base Management Systems (DBMS) (if applicable)

4.35   HAS A DATA BASE ADMINISTRATOR BEEN ASSIGNED THE RESPONSIBILITY OF COORDINATING AND CONTROLLING THE USE OF THE DATA BASE?   ____   ____

4.36   HAS THE DATA BASE ADMINISTRATOR ESTABLISHED STANDARDS FOR DATA RECORDS AND FILES USED BY PROGRAMMERS?   ____   ____

4.37   IS THE DATA BASE ADMINISTRATOR'S ACCESS TO LIVE DATA, APPLICATION SOURCE LISTINGS AND OTHER APPLICATION PROGRAM DOCUMENTATION ADEQUATELY RESTRICTED?   ____   ____

4.38   Are detailed definitions of data items contained in a data dictionary or central catalog?   ____   ____

4.39   MUST CHANGES TO THE DICTIONARY BE AUTHORIZED THROUGH THE DATA BASE ADMINISTRATOR?   ____   ____

4.40   Are there procedures in place to assure that the data dictionary remains current and accurate?   ____   ____

4.41   IS THERE A FACILITY FOR DATA BASE RECOVERY IN THE EVENT OF HARDWARE OR SOFTWARE FAILURES?   ____   ____

4.42   IS THERE A TRANSACTION LOG WHICH PROVIDES AN AUDIT TRAIL OF ENTRIES?   ____   ____

4.43   DOES THE LOG INDICATE PROCEDURAL VIOLATIONS OR ATTEMPTS TO VIOLATE DBMS SECURITY?   ____   ____

SECTION 5

Computer Operations

Adequate operating procedures/controls contribute to the reliability of information produced by the computer system. Inadequate procedures/controls may result in the processing of erroneous data or may allow data to be destroyed or compromised. Additionally, adequate procedures may mean the difference between a computer center surviving a physical disaster or being unable to process for long periods of time.

WORK STEPS

*5.1   OBTAIN OR PREPARE A SCHEDULE OF MAJOR EDP EQUIPMENT. IF EQUIPMENT IS LEASED, INDICATE NAME OF LESSOR AND TERMS OF LEASE.

*5.2   REVIEW THE STANDARDS MANUAL FOR COMPUTER OPERATIONS, INCLUDING SECURITY PROCEDURES, HOUSEKEEPING, EQUIPMENT MAINTENANCE, SCHEDULING, EQUIPMENT OPERATION, AND THE DATA AND PROGRAM FILE LIBRARY. INDICATE ANY AREAS THAT ARE NOT INCLUDED.

*5.3   DETERMINE THE COMPUTER CENTER'S OPERATING SCHEDULE, INCLUDING HOURS PER SHIFT, SHIFTS PER DAY AND DAYS PER WEEK THAT THE CENTER OPERATES. (5.15 to 5.24)

*5.4   REVIEW THE REPORTS PRODUCED TO ASSIST MANAGEMENT IN EVALUATING OPERATIONAL EFFICIENCY. SUMMARIZE PERTINENT CONCLUSIONS FOR THE MANAGEMENT SECTION. (5.25 to 5.31)

5.5   OBTAIN A LIST OF PERSONNEL AUTHORIZED TO OPERATE COMPUTER EQUIPMENT. COMPARE THIS LIST TO THE ORGANIZATION CHART AND TO ANY LISTING OF INDIVIDUALS GRANTED UNRESTRICTED ACCESS TO THE COMPUTER ROOM. (5.32 to 5.36)

5.6   REVIEW OVERALL PROCEDURES FOR EQUIPMENT SERVICE, INCLUDING MAINTENANCE AGREEMENTS, PREVENTATIVE MAINTENANCE SCHEDULES, AND PROBLEM/REPAIR LOGS. (5.37 to 5.45)

5.7   REVIEW THE PHYSICAL SECURITY AND CONTROLS FOR THE USE OF DATA FILES, UTILITY PROGRAMS AND PROGRAM LIBRARIES. (5.46 to 5.66, 5.70 to 5.81)

Section 5 — Computer Operations (continued)

5.8   DETERMINE THE PROGRAM NAMING CONVENTIONS IN EFFECT FOR SOURCE AND OBJECT PRODUCTION SOFTWARE.

*5.9   For the application(s) selected for review in work step 3.8:

   a. OBTAIN A COMPUTER LISTING DIRECTORY OF THE SOURCE AND OBJECT PROGRAMS CATALOGED IN THE PRODUCTION LIBRARIES.
   b. COMPARE THE PROGRAMS LISTED ON THE SOURCE LIBRARY TO THOSE LISTED ON THE OBJECT LIBRARY. DOCUMENT AND INVESTIGATE ANY DIFFERENCES. (5.67 to 5.69)

*5.10 For the application(s) selected for review in work step 3.8:

   a. OBTAIN A LIST OF ALL RELATED TAPES, DISKS, DOCUMENTATION, ETC., AT THE OFF-PREMISE STORAGE SITE.
   b. VERIFY THE LIST BY VISITING THE OFF-PREMISE STORAGE SITE. (5.82 to 5.85)

5.11   REVIEW THE PHYSICAL SECURITY AND OTHER CONTROLS IN EFFECT FOR THE MACHINE ROOM AND INPUT/OUTPUT AREAS. (5.86 to 5.100)

5.12   Review:

   a. THE DATA CENTER'S PROCEDURES FOR THE PROTECTION OF PERSONNEL, EQUIPMENT AND RECORDS IN THE EVENT OF EMERGENCIES.
   b. THE DATA CENTER'S CONTINGENCY (DISASTER/RECOVERY) PLANS FOR CONTINUANCE OF OPERATIONS IF ON-SITE PROCESSING CAPABILITIES ARE LOST. (5.101 to 5.115)

*5.13 REVIEW EDP RELATED INSURANCE POLICIES AND LIST THE TYPE AND AMOUNT OF INSURANCE. (5.116 and 5.117)

*5.14 SUMMARIZE STRENGTHS AND WEAKNESSES OF COMPUTER OPERATIONS AND COMPLETE THE "SUMMARY OF EXCEPTIONS" FOR THIS SECTION.

YES   NO   COMMENTS

QUESTIONNAIRE

Operational Controls

5.15   Is separation of duties adequate for:

    a. PREPARING INPUT?
    b. OPERATING THE DATA ENTRY EQUIPMENT?
    c. OPERATING THE COMPUTER AND SORTING EQUIPMENT?
    d. PREPARING REJECTS AND NON-READS FOR REENTRY?
    e. RECONCILING OUTPUT?
    f. DISTRIBUTING OUTPUT?

5.16   Does the computer operations manual include formalized procedures for operations scheduling?

5.17   Does the procedure require the use of a written or automated schedule?

5.18   ARE RUN FREQUENCIES ADEQUATE RELATIVE TO SIGNIFICANCE OF APPLICATIONS?

5.19   IS THE CENTER'S OVERALL OPERATING SCHEDULE ADEQUATE FOR THE CURRENT VOLUME OF WORK?

5.20   Are all jobs assigned a processing priority?

5.21   ARE ALL NON-SCHEDULED COMPUTER RUNS SUPPORTED BY A WORK REQUEST OR OTHER WRITTEN AUTHORIZATION?

5.22   ARE OPERATORS PROHIBITED FROM DEVIATING FROM THE ESTABLISHED WORK SCHEDULE WITHOUT SUPERVISORY APPROVAL?

5.23   ARE SIGNIFICANT DEVIATIONS FROM THE SCHEDULE INVESTIGATED?

5.24   Is a procedure in effect to cover late arrival of all or part of the input?

5.25   ARE MACHINE LOGS KEPT WHICH DETAIL PROGRAM IDENTIFICATION, JOB STARTING AND ENDING TIMES, RERUNS, DOWNTIME AND OPERATOR IDENTIFICATION?

YES   NO   COMMENTS

5.26   Are machine logs initialed or otherwise documented in support of a review for unusual activity?

5.27   ARE THERE MANAGEMENT REPORTS OF MACHINE UTILIZATION AND PERFORMANCE OF SCHEDULED OPERATIONS (SYSTEM ACTIVITY, JOB ACCOUNTING, ETC.)?

5.28   ARE THESE REPORTS PRODUCED AT SUFFICIENT INTERVALS TO ALLOW PROPER CONTROL AND MANAGEMENT REVIEW?

5.29   Are the console printer pages pre-numbered or otherwise controlled?

5.30   Are console logs or automated summaries of such logs reviewed for unusual activity?

5.31   DOES THE DATA CENTER ACCOUNT FOR ALL COMPUTER TIME?

5.32   IS THE OPERATION OF EQUIPMENT RESTRICTED TO AUTHORIZED PERSONNEL?

5.33   Are two or more operators required to be in the computer room whenever the system is in operation?

5.34   ARE OPERATORS CROSS-TRAINED TO PROVIDE BACKUP AND REDUCE DEPENDENCE ON KEY PERSONNEL?

5.35   ARE OPERATORS PERIODICALLY ROTATED EITHER BETWEEN SHIFTS OR BETWEEN TASKS WITHIN SHIFTS?

5.36   IF OPERATORS ARE NOT ROTATED, ARE THERE OTHER COMPENSATING CONTROLS IN EFFECT?

5.37   IS THERE A WRITTEN MAINTENANCE CONTRACT FOR ALL EQUIPMENT?

5.38   Does the service and maintenance agreement:

    a. Provide for repair service?
    b. Define what preventive maintenance will be performed?
    c. Address the schedule for performance of maintenance?
    d. Provide for maintenance boundaries where hardware from more than one manufacturer is used?

Section 5— Computer Operations (continued)   YES   NO   COMMENTS

5.39   ARE WRITTEN LOGS MAINTAINED OF ALL HARDWARE PROBLEMS?   ____ ____

5.40   Does an operator remain in the computer room with all data files dismounted or
       otherwise controlled when hardware or system maintenance is being performed?   ____ ____

5.41   Are data center personnel prohibited from performing equipment repairs?   ____ ____

5.42   IS PREVENTIVE MAINTENANCE PERFORMED (BOTH INTERNAL AND VENDOR
       SUPPLIED) ACCORDING TO A PREDETERMINED SCHEDULE RATHER THAN ON
       A RANDOM BASIS?   ____ ____

5.43   Does this preventive maintenance schedule provide (where applicable) for the cleaning
       of:
       a. Printers?   ____ ____
       b. Card devices?   ____ ____
       c. Tape units?   ____ ____
       d. MICR reader/sorters?   ____ ____
       e. Under floor areas?   ____ ____

5.44   IS THE SCHEDULE FOR PREVENTIVE MAINTENANCE SUFFICIENT BASED ON
       THE SIZE OF THE INSTALLATION, THE VOLUME OF WORK PROCESSED, AND
       MANUFACTURER RECOMMENDATIONS?   ____ ____

5.45   IS PREVENTIVE MAINTENANCE DOCUMENTED AND MONITORED TO ENSURE
       THAT IT IS BEING PERFORMED AS SCHEDULED?   ____ ____

Software and Data Protection

5.46   ARE OPERATORS DENIED ACCESS TO SOURCE PROGRAMS, PROGRAM
       LISTINGS AND OTHER DOCUMENTATION THAT IS UNNECESSARY TO THE
       PROCESSING OF APPLICATIONS?   ____ ____

5.47   ARE OPERATORS PROHIBITED FROM COPYING SOURCE OR OBJECT
       PROGRAMS WITHOUT PRIOR APPROVAL?   ____ ____

5.48   Are data files and program libraries protected by passwords or other means?   ____ ____

5.49   IF PASSWORDS ARE USED, ARE THEY CHANGED PERIODICALLY?   ____ ____

Section 5— Computer Operations (continued)   YES   NO   COMMENTS

5.50   ARE INTERNAL LABELS USED FOR ALL DATA AND PROGRAM FILES?   ____ ____

5.51   ARE OPERATORS PROHIBITED FROM OVERRIDING INTERNAL LABELS OR
       OTHER SYSTEM CHECKS WITHOUT SUPERVISORY APPROVAL?   ____ ____

5.52   IS THE USE OF UTILITY PROGRAMS WITH DATA FILE OR PROGRAM ALTERING
       CAPABILITIES ADEQUATELY CONTROLLED?   ____ ____

5.53   Are operators prohibited from:
       a. ORIGINATING ENTRIES FOR PROCESSING?   ____ ____
       b. CORRECTING DATA EXCEPTIONS, UNPOSTED OR REJECTED ITEMS?   ____ ____
       c. PREPARING ANY GENERAL LEDGER OR SUBSIDARY LEDGER ENTRIES?   ____ ____
       d. PERFORMING ANY BALANCING FUNCTIONS OTHER THAN RUN-TO-RUN
          CONTROL?   ____ ____
       e. RUNNING TEST PROGRAMS AGAINST LIVE OR BACKUP FILES?   ____ ____
       f. EXECUTING PROGRAMS FROM THE TEST LIBRARY DURING PRODUCTION
          RUNS?   ____ ____

5.54   DO WRITTEN PROCEDURES COVER THE ACCEPTANCE AND CATALOGING OF
       PRODUCTION PROGRAMS?   ____ ____

5.55   ARE OPERATORS PROHIBITED FROM RUNNING UNCATALOGED OBJECT
       PROGRAMS WITHOUT WRITTEN SUPERVISORY APPROVAL?   ____ ____

5.56   ARE OPERATORS PROHIBITED FROM RUNNING UNCATALOGED OBJECT
       PROGRAMS WITHOUT PRIOR AUTHORIZATION?   ____ ____

5.57   ARE ALL PROGRAM CHANGES TO THE PRODUCTION LIBRARIES, INCLUDING
       DELETIONS, APPROVED AND ACCOUNTED FOR?   ____ ____

5.58   DOES DATA CENTER MANAGEMENT PERIODICALLY REVIEW AND UPDATE
       CONTROLS AND SECURITY RELATING TO DATA FILES AND PROGRAM
       LIBRARIES?   ____ ____

5.59   IS A DATA FILE LIBRARY MANUAL MAINTAINED?   ____ ____

Section 5 — Computer Operations (continued)   YES   NO   COMMENTS

5.60   Does the data file library manual contain descriptions of:

      a. LIBRARY CONTROLS AND PROCEDURES?
      b. THE AUTOMATED TAPE LIBRARY SYSTEM OR MANUAL SYSTEM BEING USED?   ____ ____
      c. DATA FILE RETENTION SCHEDULES?   ____ ____
      d. LABELING AND STORAGE CONVENTIONS?   ____ ____
      e. PROCEDURES FOR NEW TAPES AND DISKS AND FOR THOSE TAPES AND
          DISKS RETIRED FROM USE?   ____ ____
      f. PROCEDURES FOR PERIODIC INVENTORIES OF BOTH ON AND
          OFF-PREMISE TAPES AND DISKS?   ____ ____

5.61   ARE MAGNETIC TAPES AND DISK PACKS STORED IN A CLOSED, DUST FREE,
      FIRE RESISTANT AND LIMITED ACCESS LIBRARY?   ____ ____

5.62   Does the library have:

      a. A sprinkler or other suitable fire extinguisher system?   ____ ____
      b. An adequate air conditioning system?   ____ ____
      c. An adequate fire alarm system?   ____ ____

5.63   Do tape library operations cover all shifts?   ____ ____

5.64   IS THE LIBRARIAN FUNCTION ASSIGNED TO A PERSON WHO HAS NO
      CONFLICTING DUTIES?   ____ ____

5.65   Has specific responsibility been assigned for the maintenance of production libraries?   ____ ____

5.66   IS AT LEAST ONE CURRENT COPY OF THE SUPERVISOR AND APPLICATION
      PROGRAM LIBRARIES MAINTAINED IN THE DATA FILE LIBRARY AS
      IMMEDIATE BACKUP?   ____ ____

5.67   BASED ON THE APPLICATIONS SELECTED FOR REVIEW IN WORK PROGRAM
      SECTION 3, IS A MACHINE-READABLE SOURCE PROGRAM MAINTAINED FOR
      EACH APPLICATION PROGRAM LISTED IN THE PRODUCTION OBJECT
      LIBRARY?   ____ ____

Section 5 — Computer Operations (continued)   YES   NO   COMMENTS

5.68   ARE ALL CURRENT OBJECT LANGUAGE VERSIONS OF PRODUCTION
      PROGRAMS GENERATED FROM CURRENT SOURCE LANGUAGE VERSIONS?   ____ ____

5.69   Are obsolete and/or unused programs deleted from the production libraries?   ____ ____

5.70   ARE EXTERNAL LABELS ADEQUATE TO IDENTIFY THE FILE USE AND
      CONTENTS?   ____ ____

5.71   DO INVENTORY LISTINGS OF TAPES AND DISK PACKS EXIST?   ____ ____

5.72   If so, do they include:

      a. STORAGE LOCATION?   ____ ____
      b. VOLUME SERIAL NUMBER?   ____ ____
      c. CREATION AND EXPIRATION DATE?   ____ ____

5.73   Are live data tapes and scratch tapes physically separated and clearly identified in the
      library?   ____ ____

5.74   IS DATA FILE ACCESS LIMITED TO AUTHORIZED PERSONNEL?   ____ ____

5.75   ARE DATA FILES ISSUED ONLY ON THE BASIS OF ESTABLISHED RUN
      SCHEDULES OR OTHER EVIDENCE OF PROPER APPROVAL?   ____ ____

5.76   Are operator run instructions current/adequate?   ____ ____

5.77   IF BACKUP COPIES OF THE SUPERVISOR PROGRAM, APPLICATION
      PROGRAM LIBRARIES, TRANSACTION FILES OR MASTER FILES MUST BE
      USED, ARE THEY DUPLICATED BEFORE BEING PUT INTO PRODUCTION?   ____ ____

5.78   ARE THE BACKUP SUPERVISOR PROGRAMS AND APPLICATION
      PROGRAM LIBRARIES PERIODICALLY TESTED?   ____ ____

5.79   ARE ON-SITE BACKUP SUPERVISOR PROGRAMS, APPLICATION
      PROGRAM LIBRARIES AND DATA FILES CURRENT?   ____ ____

Section 5 — Computer Operations (continued)   YES   NO   COMMENTS

5.80   IF A DATA BASE MANAGEMENT SYSTEM IS USED, ARE CRITICAL RECORDS
        PERIODICALLY DUMPED AND STORED FOR BACKUP PURPOSES?   ____ ____

5.81   Are data files duplicated before being released to outside auditors, consultants, or
        vendors?   ____ ____

5.82   Is there adequate/current off-premise storage of:

        a. SOURCE AND OBJECT PRODUCTION PROGRAMS?   ____ ____
        b. DATA FILES?   ____ ____
        c. SYSTEM AND PROGRAM DOCUMENTATION?   ____ ____
        d. OPERATING SYSTEMS AND UTILITY PROGRAMS?   ____ ____

5.83   ARE OFF-PREMISE PROGRAMS AND FILES MAINTAINED IN
        MACHINE-READABLE FORM?   ____ ____

5.84   IS ACCESS TO THE ITEMS STORED AT THE REMOTE STORAGE FACILITY
        ADEQUATELY CONTROLLED?   ____ ____

5.85   Is a record of entry to the remote storage site maintained?   ____ ____

Hardware Protection

5.86   Is the accumulation and disposal of trash in or near the computer facility handled in a
        manner which minimizes exposure to fire and maximizes control over sensitive
        information?   ____ ____

5.87   Is smoking, eating and drinking prohibited in the computer room?   ____ ____

5.88   Is the supply of paper, magnetic media and other combustibles in the computer room
        limited to that necessary to complete the daily work?   ____ ____

5.89   Are all nonessential paper supplies stored in an area away from the computer room and
        protected by fire suppression equipment?   ____ ____

5.90   Are all flammable fluids, as well as cleaning supplies and equipment, stored away from
        the computer room and paper storage areas?   ____ ____

Section 5 — Computer Operations (continued)   YES   NO   COMMENTS

5.91   Is the computer room maintained in a neat and orderly manner?   ____ ____

5.92   Is entry to the data center controlled by properly instructed guards or other employees?   ____ ____

5.93   Do personnel attempt to identify all visitors within the data center?   ____ ____

5.94   Are janitorial and maintenance personnel appropriately identified prior to admittance
        to the computer room?   ____ ____

5.95   ARE ADEQUATE SAFEGUARDS IN EFFECT TO ENSURE THAT ONLY
        AUTHORIZED PERSONS ARE PERMITTED IN THE COMPUTER OR MACHINE
        AREAS?   ____ ____

5.96   ARE SERVICE ENTRANCES, STORM DRAINS, EXHAUST DUCTS, EXTERIOR
        DOORS AND WINDOWS AND EMERGENCY EXITS ADEQUATELY SECURED
        TO PREVENT UNAUTHORIZED ENTRY TO THE DATA CENTER FROM
        ADJACENT UNSECURED AREAS?   ____ ____

5.97   Is the data facility adequately protected with:

        a. HEAT OR SMOKE DETECTORS?   ____ ____
        b. HAND EXTINGUISHERS?   ____ ____
        c. A suitable fire control system?   ____ ____
        d. TEMPERATURE/HUMIDITY CONTROL EQUIPMENT?   ____ ____
        e. Intrusion detection devices?   ____ ____
        f. Alternate power supply?   ____ ____

5.98   Do detective devices:

        a. PROVIDE 24-HOUR COVERAGE?   ____ ____
        b. TRIGGER AN INTERNAL ALARM SYSTEM?   ____ ____
        c. Trigger an alarm at police/fire stations?   ____ ____

5.99   Have precautions been taken to protect the computer equipment from water damage?   ____ ____

5.100   Are floor tile pullers visible and available to operations personnel?   ____ ____

Section 5 — Computer Operations (continued)   YES   NO   COMMENTS

5.101   HAS HARDWARE BACKUP BEEN ADEQUATELY CONSIDERED AND HAVE
MANAGEMENT'S DECISIONS BEEN DOCUMENTED?   ____   ____

5.102   If in-house backup is used, is each system in a separate physical location?   ____   ____

5.103   If in-house backup systems are in separate physical locations:

    a. Are they on different power/water grids?   ____   ____
    b. Is the equipment at each location capable of independently processing critical
       applications?   ____   ____
    c. Are the systems fully compatible?   ____   ____

5.104   If the institution has more than one processing site in a single location:

    a. Is alternative electric power and water available?   ____   ____
    b. Are peripherals switchable between systems?   ____   ____
    c. If one unit fails, can the other unit(s) process the critical applications?   ____   ____

5.105   Is the institution relying on a recovery operations center or another outside facility for a
recovery site?   ____   ____

5.106   IF THE INSTALLATION IS RELYING ON OUTSIDE FACILITIES FOR BACKUP, IS A
WRITTEN AGREEMENT IN EFFECT?   ____   ____

5.107   HAVE BACKUP ARRANGEMENTS ACTUALLY BEEN USED OR TESTED IN THE
PAST YEAR?   ____   ____

5.108   IS THE CENTER ADVISED OF HARDWARE AND SYSTEM SOFTWARE CHANGES
MADE AT THE BACKUP LOCATION?   ____   ____

5.109   Is management satisfied that the backup facility has available computer time?   ____   ____

5.110   Are there comprehensive written plans that adequately:

    a. PROVIDE FOR PHYSICAL SECURITY OF THE COMPUTER INSTALLATION?   ____   ____
    b. IDENTIFY ACTION TO BE TAKEN IN SPECIFIC EMERGENCY SITUATIONS?   ____   ____
    c. DESCRIBE CONTINGENCY PROCEDURES IN THE EVENT RECOVERY FROM A
       DISASTER IS NECESSARY?   ____   ____

Section 5 — Computer Operations (continued)   YES   NO   COMMENTS

5.111   ARE ASPECTS OF THESE PLANS PERIODICALLY TESTED?   ____   ____

5.112   Do physical security aspects of the plan:

    a. PROVIDE REASONABLE PROTECTION TO PERSONNEL, EQUIPMENT AND
       DATA?   ____   ____
    b. PREVENT UNAUTHORIZED ACCESS TO THE DATA FACILITY, COMPUTER
       ROOM, FILES AND DOCUMENTATION?   ____   ____
    c. SPECIFY VARIOUS PROTECTIVE SYSTEMS OR DEVICES TO BE UTILIZED?   ____   ____
    d. INCLUDE INSURANCE CONSIDERATIONS?   ____   ____
    e. PROVIDE FOR EMPLOYEE INSTRUCTION IN THE USE OF EMERGENCY
       EQUIPMENT?   ____   ____

5.113   Does the emergency plan provide for:

    a. RESPONSE TO THREATS IN A MANNER THAT LIMITS DAMAGE AND
       ENSURES CONTINUED OPERATIONS?   ____   ____
    b. PERSONNEL EVACUATION?   ____   ____
    c. INSTRUCTIONS FOR EMPLOYEES TO COVER FIRE, FLOOD, INTRUDERS,
       BOMBS, OR OTHER THREATS?   ____   ____
    d. SAFE STORAGE OF DATA FILES AND DOCUMENTS?   ____   ____
    e. POWER-OFF PROCEDURES?   ____   ____
    f. RESTART AND RECOVERY PROCEDURES FOR EQUIPMENT FAILURE?   ____   ____

5.114   Does the data center contingency (disaster/recovery) plan include:

    a. ASSIGNMENT OF DUTIES FOR RECONSTRUCTION AND OFF-SITE
       PROCESSING?   ____   ____
    b. UNDER WHAT CONDITIONS THE BACKUP SITE WOULD BE USED?   ____   ____
    c. DECISION RESPONSIBILITY TO USE THE BACKUP SITE?   ____   ____
    d. SEQUENCE IN WHICH EMPLOYEES WILL BE NOTIFIED OF THE DECISION?   ____   ____
    e. PROCEDURES FOR NOTIFYING THE BACKUP SITE?   ____   ____
    f. WHAT FILES, DATA, PROGRAMS AND DOCUMENTATION ARE TO BE
       TAKEN TO THE BACKUP SITE AND HOW THEY ARE TO BE TRANSPORTED?   ____   ____
    g. PROCESSING PRIORITIES TO BE FOLLOWED?   ____   ____
    h. PROVISIONS FOR RESERVE SUPPLIES?   ____   ____
    i. BACKUP OF PROCESSING FACILITIES AND VITAL DATA?   ____   ____

5.115   ARE APPROPRIATE PARTS OF THE OVERALL CONTINGENCY PLANS
DISPLAYED AND COMMUNICATED TO EMPLOYEES?   ____   ____

Section 5 — Computer Operations (continued)   YES   NO   COMMENTS

INSURANCE

5.116   Does insurance coverage provide adequate protection (if applicable) for:

    a. EMPLOYEE FIDELITY?
    b. EDP EQUIPMENT AND FACILITIES?
    c. MEDIA RECONSTRUCTION?
    d. EFTS ACTIVITIES?
    e. LOSS RESULTING FROM BUSINESS INTERRUPTIONS?
    f. ERRORS AND OMISSIONS?
    g. EXTRA EXPENSES, INCLUDING BACKUP SITE EXPENSES?
    h. ITEMS IN TRANSIT?
    i. OTHER PROBABLE RISKS?

5.117   IF THE LESSEE MAINTAINS INSURANCE COVERAGE FOR LEASED
    EQUIPMENT, IS THE AMOUNT SUFFICIENT TO COVER OBLIGATIONS FOR THE
    EQUIPMENT?

SECTION 6

Teleprocessing

The controls and safeguards built into a teleprocessing system are often more subtle than in a batch system because they tend to be integrated into the software and hardware. The integration of controls and additional sources of risk inherent in on-line data processing require an expanded review of security, integrity and continuity of on-line data processing systems.

In a batch processing mode, arrangement for alternate processing capabilities in the event of a disruption of service is considered imperative. However, in a teleprocessing system, these arrangements are further complicated by the availability of communication lines and equipment. A thorough review should be made of the center's backup procedures and the relative importance of the applications in terms of risk to the financial institution.

WORK STEPS

*6.1 IF THE ON-LINE SYSTEM HAS BEEN MODIFIED SINCE THE LAST EXAMINATION, OBTAIN OR PREPARE A BRIEF DESCRIPTION OF ANY CHANGES IN EQUIPMENT USED, LOCATIONS SERVED AND APPLICATIONS OFFERED BY THE INSTALLATION. (NOTE: IF IT IS THE FIRST EXAMINATION OF THE ON-LINE SYSTEM, THE ABOVE INFORMATION SHOULD BE OBTAINED FOR THE ENTIRE SYSTEM. ALSO INCLUDE DATA FOR THE INSTITUTION'S DOLLAR INVESTMENT IN THE ON-LINE SYSTEM).

*6.2 REVIEW AND BRIEF DOCUMENTATION RELATIVE TO SECURITY CONTROLS ESTABLISHED FOR THE DATA COMMUNICATIONS NETWORK. (6.5 to 6.43)

6.3 REVIEW THE CENTER'S ALTERNATE PROCESSING PROCEDURES AS THEY RELATE TO THE ON-LINE NETWORK AND APPLICATIONS. (6.44 to 6.50)

*6.4 SUMMARIZE STRENGTHS AND WEAKNESSES OF TELEPROCESSING AND COMPLETE THE "SUMMARY OF EXCEPTIONS" FOR THIS SECTION.

QUESTIONNAIRE

YES   NO

Communications Security

6.5 Is access to the system terminals appropriately limited by means of:

a. TERMINAL LOCKS?
b. TERMINAL IDENTIFICATION CHECKS?
c. A PHYSICALLY SECURE LOCATION?
d. USER IDENTIFICATION?

Section 6 — Teleprocessing (continued)

YES   NO   COMMENTS

6.6 Are all terminals controlled as to:

a. What files they can access?
b. What transactions they can initiate?

6.7 DOES THE SYSTEM ASSURE THAT ALL TRANSMISSIONS ARE RECEIVED FROM ONLY AUTHORIZED TERMINALS AND USERS (i.e., polling list, user ID/password, call-back)?

6.8 ARE ADEQUATE SAFEGUARDS IN EFFECT TO ENSURE THAT ONLY AUTHORIZED PERSONS MAY ACCESS TELEPHONE EQUIPMENT ROOMS AND OTHER DATA COMMUNICATIONS EQUIPMENT AREAS?

6.9 Are teleprocessing communications lines in the equipment rooms free from identifying labels?

6.10 Are messages encrypted or similarly protected during transmission?

6.11 IF ENCRYPTION IS USED, DOES ADEQUATE CONTROL EXIST OVER ENCRYPTION KEYS?

6.12 Have network trouble shooting procedures been formulated and maintenance responsibility established?

User Identification

6.13 IS THE USE OF EACH USER IDENTIFICATION CODE LIMITED TO ONE INDIVIDUAL?

6.14 WHEN USER IDENTIFICATION PASSWORDS AND SECURITY CODES ARE ISSUED AND/OR CHANGED, ARE THEY RECORDED AND DISTRIBUTED IN SUCH A WAY AS TO MAINTAIN THEIR USEFULNESS AS A CONTROL MECHANISM?

6.15 ARE IDENTIFICATION NUMBERS AND PASSWORDS SUPPRESSED ON ALL PRINTED, VIDEO AND AUDIO OUTPUT?

6.16 ARE USER IDENTIFICATION CODES, SECURITY CODES AND DIAL-UP PHONE NUMBERS PERIODICALLY CHANGED?

Section 6 — Teleprocessing (continued)   YES   NO   COMMENTS

6.17   ARE PASSWORDS, SECURITY KEYS AND AUTHORIZATION TABLES LOCATED
       IN MEMORY AND/OR PERIPHERAL STORAGE ENCRYPTED OR OTHERWISE
       PROTECTED?   ____   ____

6.18   Are dial-up lines controlled by either an automatic callback procedure or physical
       connection (manual intercept) by operations personnel at the data center?   ____   ____

6.19   Are all users restricted as to:

       a. WHAT FILES THEY CAN ACCESS?   ____   ____
       b. WHAT TRANSACTIONS THEY CAN IMITATE?   ____   ____

6.20   ARE THESE USER LEVELS OF ACCESS AND AUTHORITY APPROVED AND
       PERIODICALLY REVIEWED BY MANAGEMENT?   ____   ____

6.21   Are department employees restricted to using terminals only in that department?   ____   ____

6.22   Are automatic time-out controls used, whenever practicable?   ____   ____

6.23   Are time of day controls used, whenever practicable?   ____   ____

6.24   IS SUPERVISORY APPROVAL REQUIRED FOR TERMINAL ACCESS MADE AT
       OTHER THAN AUTHORIZED TIMES?   ____   ____

6.25   ARE TRAINING MATERIALS, INCLUDING USER MANUALS OR
       PRE-PROGRAMMED USER INSTRUCTIONS, AVAILABLE TO ALL TERMINAL
       OPERATORS?   ____   ____

6.26   IS TERMINAL OPERATOR TRAINING CONDUCTED IN A MANNER THAT WILL
       NOT JEOPARDIZE THE INTEGRITY OF LIVE DATA OR MEMO FILES?   ____   ____

6.27   IS TERMINAL INPUT SUBJECT TO AUTOMATIC EDITING TO REDUCE INPUT
       ERRORS?   ____   ____

6.28   Does the system check message contain or use a coding scheme to establish the validity
       of each transmission?   ____   ____

6.29   Are accumulators for both item counts and dollar totals used at the terminals and the
       central computer?   ____   ____

Section 6 — Teleprocessing (continued)   YES   NO   COMMENTS

6.30   IS THERE DAILY INPUT BALANCING TO EACH TERMINAL OR USER IN THE
       SYSTEM?   ____   ____

6.31   ARE ALL CORRECTING AND REVERSING ENTRIES IDENTIFIED AND REPORTED
       AS SUCH?   ____   ____

6.32   DO CORRECTING AND REVERSING ENTRIES AS WELL AS OVERRIDES REQUIRE
       SUPERVISORY APPROVAL?   ____   ____

6.33   Are exception reports generated which record:

       a. UNUSUAL APPLICATION RELATED ACTIVITY?   ____   ____
       b. UNSUCCESSFUL ATTEMPTS TO GAIN ACCESS TO THE TELEPROCESSING
           SYSTEM OR APPLICATIONS?   ____   ____
       c. TELEPROCESSING NETWORK PROBLEMS/STATISTICS?   ____   ____

6.34   DO EXCEPTION REPORTS APPEAR TO MEET THE NEEDS OF MANAGEMENT,
       USERS AND THE AUDIT DEPARTMENT?   ____   ____

6.35   ARE EXCEPTION REPORTS REVIEWED REGULARLY BY MANAGEMENT
       PERSONNEL RESPONSIBLE FOR INSTITUTING FOLLOW-UP ACTION? ____   ____

6.36   ARE POLICIES ESTABLISHED BY THE USER DEPARTMENT FOR SOURCE
       DOCUMENT RETENTION ADEQUATE FOR TERMINAL INITIATED
       TRANSACTIONS?   ____   ____

Data Integrity

6.37   IS A TRANSACTION FILE MAINTAINED FOR ALL MESSAGES RECEIVED FROM
       ALL TERMINALS?   ____   ____

6.38   Does this transaction file record the:

       a. IDENTITY OF THE USER?   ____   ____
       b. TERMINAL?   ____   ____
       c. TRANSACTION CODE?   ____   ____
       d. DETAIL TO IDENTIFY THE TRANSACTION?   ____   ____
       e. DATE AND TIME OF TRANSACTION?   ____   ____

6.39   Are periodic checks made on the network during normal operation to verify proper functioning and to detect line errors?   _____ _____

On-Line Programming

6.40   DOES ON-LINE INTERACTIVE PROGRAMMING IN LOW LEVEL LANGUAGES REQUIRE MANAGEMENT APPROVAL?   _____ _____

6.41   ARE ON-LINE PROGRAMMING TERMINALS PROPERLY CONTROLLED TO PROHIBIT PROGRAMMERS FROM TESTING AGAINST LIVE FILES?   _____ _____

6.42   IF MODIFICATIONS (CHANGES) TO PROGRAM LIBRARIES ARE ALLOWED FROM ON-LINE TERMINALS, ARE THEY PROPERLY CONTROLLED?   _____ _____

6.43   IS AN ADEQUATE DETAILED RECORD AUTOMATICALLY GENERATED BY THE SYSTEM TO DOCUMENT ALL ON-LINE ACCESS AND MODIFICATIONS TO PROGRAM LIBRARIES?   _____ _____

On-Line Backup

6.44   Are the following provisions for backup of teleprocessing facilities available:

   a. Backup transmission lines?   _____ _____
   b. Automatic switching of backup lines?   _____ _____
   c. Backup terminals at critical locations?   _____ _____
   d. Backup communications control units?   _____ _____
   e. A backup computer system?   _____ _____
   f. Redundant data/transaction files?   _____ _____

6.45   ARE DATA COMMUNICATIONS FACILITIES ADEQUATELY BACKED UP (see question above), REPLACEABLE BY BATCH PROCESSING OR NOT CRITICAL TO DAILY OPERATIONS?   _____ _____

6.46   If replaceable by batch processing, is this backup capability:
   a. SUPPORTED BY APPROPRIATE WRITTEN PROCEDURES, INPUT FORMS, PROOF FORMS, ETC.?
   b. FEASIBLE IN LIGHT OF PROCESSING VOLUMES?   _____ _____

Section 6 — Teleprocessing (continued)

6.47   Are terminals capable of operating off-line or off-host in the event of computer failure?   _____ _____

6.48   Does the system provide for graceful degradation of terminals in the event of system failure?   _____ _____

6.49   HAVE PROCEDURES BEEN ESTABLISHED TO PREVENT LOSS OR DOUBLE POSTING OF TRANSACTIONS WHEN THE SYSTEM RECOVERS FROM A FAILURE?   _____ _____

6.50   ARE BACKUP PROVISIONS PERIODICALLY TESTED?   _____ _____

SECTION 7

Customer Service

Services provided by the computer center to financial institutions must be reviewed during the EDP examination. To assess the customer service performed, the examiner should be familiar with the contracts/agreements between the servicer and the customers.

WORK STEPS

*7.1   OBTAIN OR PREPARE A LIST OF ALL FINANCIAL INSTITUTIONS BEING SERVICED. INCLUDE SERVICES PROVIDED AND APPLICATIONS PROCESSED.   _____

*7.2   OBTAIN OR PREPARE A LIST OF ALL SERVICES PROVIDED AND APPLICATIONS PROCESSED FOR CUSTOMERS OTHER THAN FINANCIAL INSTITUTIONS. INDICATE THE NUMBER OF CUSTOMERS FOR EACH APPLICATION.   _____

*7.3   INDICATE ANY SUBSIDIARIES OR AFFILIATES OF THE DATA CENTER FOR WHICH SERVICES ARE PROVIDED.   _____

*7.4   OBTAIN AND REVIEW A COPY OF EACH TYPE OF SERVICE CONTRACT USED.   _____

7.5   REVIEW THE WRITTEN SERVICE CONTRACT ON FILE. (7.12 to 7.14)   _____

7.6   REVIEW CUSTOMER COMPLAINT PROCEDURES. (7.15 to 7.17)   _____

7.7   REVIEW CUSTOMER BILLING AND COLLECTION PROCEDURES. (7.18 to 7.20)   _____

7.8   REVIEW A SAMPLE OF USER MANUALS WHICH HAVE BEEN DISTRIBUTED TO VARIOUS CUSTOMERS. (7.21 to 7.24)   _____

7.9   REVIEW INPUT PROCEDURES USED TO CONTROL RECEIPT OF SOURCE DOCUMENTS AT THE DATA CENTER AND OUTPUT DISTRIBUTION PROCEDURES USED TO CONTROL DELIVERY OF SOURCE DOCUMENTS AND REPORTS. (7.25 and 7.26)   _____

*7.10   REVIEW THE FINANCIAL CONDITION OF THE DATA CENTER. (7.27)   _____

Section 7 — Customer Service (continued)

*7.11   SUMMARIZE STRENGTHS AND WEAKNESSES OF CUSTOMER SERVICES AND COMPLETE THE "SUMMARY OF EXCEPTIONS" FOR THIS SECTION.   _____

QUESTIONNAIRE   YES   NO

7.12   ARE WRITTEN CONTRACTS IN EFFECT FOR ALL CUSTOMERS?   ____ ____

7.13   Do contract provisions specify:

     a. Specific work to be performed by the servicer and the frequency and general contents of the related reports?   ____ ____

     b. The basis of costs, including development, conversion and processing, and additional charges for special requests?   ____ ____

     c. The established time schedules for receipt and delivery of work?   ____ ____

     d. Audit responsibility, including the right of user representatives to perform audit procedures?   ____ ____

     e. Backup and record protection provisions (equipment, programs, data files) to ensure timely processing by the service center in emergencies?   ____ ____

     f. Liability for source documents while in transit to and from the service center? (If the service center is responsible, the servicer should have adequate insurance coverage for such liabilities.)   ____ ____

     g. Maintenance of adequate insurance in the case of data losses from error and omissions?   ____ ____

     h. Confidential treatment of records?   ____ ____

     i. Ownership of computer programs and related documentation?   ____ ____

     j. Ownership of master and transaction data files and their return in machine-readable format upon the termination of the contract or agreement?   ____ ____

     k. Price changes, cost and method of cancellation of the contract or withdrawal from the servicing arrangement by either party, including adequate time allowance?   ____ ____

     l. Processing priorities?   ____ ____

     m. Notification from the service center to the users of all changes that would affect procedures, reports, etc.?   ____ ____

     n. That financial information is to be periodically (preferably annually) provided by the servicer to serviced institutions?   ____ ____

7.14   DO THE TERMS OF THE CONTRACTS PROVIDE ADEQUATE PROTECTION AND ESTABLISH LIMITS OF LIABILITY FOR BOTH THE SERVICER AND THE USER?   ____ ____

Section 7 — Customer Service (continued)   YES   NO   COMMENTS

7.15   Are services performed according to the contract terms?   _____   _____

7.16   Does the data center maintain a customer complaint file?   _____   _____

7.17   Does the data center investigate and attempt to resolve all complaints received?   _____   _____

7.18   Has data center management established a method to determine operating costs and
       user fees?   _____   _____

7.19   ARE THE FEES CHARGED TO AFFILIATES AND SUBSIDIARIES APPROPRIATE?   _____   _____

7.20   ARE CONTROLS OVER CUSTOMER BILLING AND RECEIPT ADEQUATE?   _____   _____

7.21   ARE CUSTOMERS PROVIDED WITH CURRENT USER MANUALS?   _____   _____

7.22   Does each user manual cover:

       a. The preparation and control of source documents?   _____   _____
       b. Control, format and use of output?   _____   _____
       c. Settlement and reconcilement procedures?   _____   _____

7.23   DO EXCEPTION REPORTS MEET THE NEEDS OF THE USERS?   _____   _____

7.24   Are users provided training to understand the output reports produced for each
       automated application?   _____   _____

7.25   Are customers required to receipt the delivery of their output reports and source
       documents?   _____   _____

7.26   Are all scheduled output reports produced each day, even if there is no information to
       report?   _____   _____

7.27   IS THE FINANCIAL CONDITION OF THE DATA CENTER SUFFICIENT TO
       REASONABLY ENSURE CONTINUANCE OF OPERATIONS?   _____   _____

SECTION 8

Electronic Funds Transfer Systems

This Section may be used separately or in conjunction with sections 1 through 7 of the EDP Examination Work Program. Examiners should assess the adequacy of the organization's EFT function by reviewing the wire transfer area and other selected EFT applications. To ensure that the control procedures employed offer maximum protection against loss to both the financial institution and its customers, the examiner should visit related remote EFT locations such as point-of-sale terminals and automated teller machines during the examination.

WORK STEPS

The following work steps may be incorporated by reference if they have been briefed in other sections of the EDP Work Program.

*8.1   OBTAIN OR PREPARE AN ORGANIZATION CHART FOR ALL EFT FUNCTIONS.

*8.2   REVIEW MINUTES OF THE BOARD AND ANY EFT COMMITTEES AND BRIEF ANY RELATED MATTERS.

*8.3   OBTAIN OR PREPARE A BRIEF DESCRIPTION OF ANY CHANGES IN EFT EQUIP-MENT USED, LOCATIONS SERVED OR SERVICES OFFERED. (NOTE: IF IT IS THE FIRST EFT EXAM, OBTAIN INFORMATION FOR THE ENTIRE SYSTEM. INCLUDE DATA REGARDING THE FINANCIAL INSTITUTION'S DOLLAR INVESTMENT.)

*8.4   REVIEW AND BRIEF THE BONDING AND OTHER INSURANCE COVERAGE APPLICABLE TO THE EFT SYSTEM. (8.10 TO 8.16)

*8.5   REVIEW THE CONTROLS AND PROCEDURES FOR THE WIRE TRANSFER DEPARTMENT. (8.17 TO 8.80)

*8.6   IF THE INSTITUTION PARTICIPATES IN ONE OR MORE OF THE LARGE DOLLAR TRANSFER SYSTEMS (E.G., FEDWIRE, CHIPS, CASHWIRE AND CHESS) EVALU-ATE THE CONTROLS RELATED TO OVERDRAFTS, ADVANCES AGAINST UN-COLLECTED OR ANTICIPATED DEPOSITS AND SETTLEMENT RISK. (8.81 TO 8.104)

*8.7   REVIEW THE CONTROL PROCEDURES FOR ISSUANCE, DISTRIBUTION AND CHANGE OF PINS AND PLASTIC CARDS. (8.105 TO 8.129)

Section 8 – Electronic Funds Transfer Systems (continued)

*8.8   Select an EFT application(s), visit a related remote processing site(s) and review the following procedures and controls (8.130 to 8.161):

     a. TERMINAL SHARING/NETWORK SWITCHING SYSTEMS.

     b. AUTHORIZATIONS.

     c. CONTRACT PROVISIONS.

     d. DOCUMENTATION RELATIVE TO SECURITY CONTROLS ESTABLISHED FOR THE DATA COMMUNICATIONS NETWORK.

     e. CLERICAL PROCEDURE MANUALS.

     f. SECURITY AND CONTROL PROCEDURES.

     g. ALTERNATE PROCESSING PROCEDURES.

     h. AUDIT PROCEDURES.

*8.9   SUMMARIZE THE STRENGTHS AND WEAKNESSES OF ELECTRONIC FUNDS TRANSFER SYSTEM(S) AND COMPLETE THE "SUMMARY OF EXCEPTIONS" FOR THIS SECTION.

---

*Note – Material obtained from the data center or developed by the examiner should be included in the work papers together with any other information needed to fully describe existent internal controls.

Section 8 – Electronic Funds Transfer Systems (continued)

	YES	NO	COMMENTS

QUESTIONNAIRE

INSURANCE COVERAGE

8.10   HAS INSURANCE COVERAGE BEEN CONSIDERED FOR ALL ASPECTS OF EFT BEING OFFERED TO FINANCIAL INSTITUTION CUSTOMERS?   ____ ____

8.11   HAS THE EFT INSURANCE BEEN APPROVED BY THE BOARD OF THE FINANCIAL INSTITUTION?   ____ ____

8.12   IF THE FINANCIAL INSTITUTION'S BLANKET BOND DELETES COVERAGE FOR ANY FORM OF EFT, HAS MANAGEMENT CONSIDERED SPECIALIZED EFT INSURANCE?   ____ ____

8.13   DOES THE FINANCIAL INSTITUTION HAVE INSURANCE RIDERS FOR ATM/ACH SERVICES IN THEIR BLANKET BOND WHICH GIVE ADEQUATE PROTECTION?   ____ ____

8.14   IF MANAGEMENT HAS ELECTED TO BE SELF-INSURING, HAS THE BOARD OF THE FINANCIAL INSTITUTION ADOPTED A RESOLUTION STATING SUCH?   ____ ____

8.15   IF OTHER PARTIES ARE INVOLVED IN THE EFT SYSTEM IS THERE ADEQUATE FIDELITY COVERAGE FOR THE FIRM AND EMPLOYEES INVOLVED?   ____ ____

8.16   IF MERCHANT PERSONNEL ARE UNBONDED OR EXCLUDED FROM FIDELITY COVERAGE, DOES THE FINANCIAL INSTITUTION CONSIDER ALTERNATIVE MEANS TO ENSURE THAT REPAYMENT OF MISAPPROPRIATED FUNDS IS POSSIBLE?   ____ ____

Section 8 – Electronic Funds Transfer Systems (continued)

	YES	NO	COMMENTS

Wire Transfer (Fed Wire, SWIFT, CHIPS and/or Bank Wire II)

PERSONNEL

8.17   HAS THE INSTITUTION TAKEN STEPS TO ENSURE THAT SCREENING PROCEDURES ARE APPLIED TO PERSONNEL HIRED FOR SENSITIVE POSITIONS IN THE WIRE TRANSFER DEPARTMENT?   ____ ____

8.18   Is special attention paid by supervisory staff to new employees assigned to work in the wire transfer function?   ____ ____

8.19   Are temporary employees excluded from working in sensitive areas?   ____ ____
       If not, is the number of such employees limited?   ____ ____

8.20   Are statements of indebtedness required of employees in sensitive positions of the wire transfer function?   ____ ____

8.21   ARE EMPLOYEES SUBJECT TO UNANNOUNCED ROTATION OF RESPONSIBILITIES REGARDLESS OF THE SIZE OF THE INSTITUTION?   ____ ____

8.22   Are relatives of employees in the wire transfer function precluded from working in the same institution's bookkeeping or data processing departments?   ____ ____

8.23   DOES THE INSTITUTION REQUIRE THAT ALL EMPLOYEES TAKE A MINIMUM NUMBER OF CONSECUTIVE DAYS AS PART OF THEIR ANNUAL VACATION?   ____ ____

       List any exceptions.

8.24   DOES MANAGEMENT IMMEDIATELY REASSIGN EMPLOYEES WHO HAVE GIVEN NOTICE OF RESIGNATION OR BEEN GIVEN TERMINATION NOTICES FROM SENSITIVE AREAS OF THE WIRE TRANSFER FUNCTION?   ____ ____

8.25   Is a training program utilized to alert personnel to the current trends in wire transfer activities and to the necessity of adequate internal control?   ____ ____

Section 8 – Electronic Funds Transfer Systems (continued)　　　　YES　NO　　　　　　　COMMENTS

OPERATING PROCEDURES

8.26　DO WRITTEN OPERATING PROCEDURES EXIST FOR EMPLOYEES IN THE IN-
COMING, PREPARATION, DATA ENTRY, BALANCE VERIFICATION, TRANSMIS-
SION, ACCOUNTING, RECONCILING AND SECURITY AREAS OF THE WIRE
TRANSFER FUNCTION?　　　　　　　　　　　　　　　———　———

8.27　Do the procedures cover:

　　　a. Access to the wire transfer area and user files?　　　———　———

　　　b. Terminal security and password control?　　　　　———　———

　　　c. Origination of wire transfer transactions and the modification and deletion of pay-
　　　　ment orders or messages?　　　　　　　　　　　———　———

　　　d. Verification of sequence numbers?　　　　　　　———　———

　　　e. End of day accounting for all transfers request and message traffic?　———　———

　　　f. Control over messages or payment orders received too late to process the same
　　　　day?　　　　　　　　　　　　　　　　　　　———　———

　　　g. Control over payment orders with future value dates?　———　———

　　　h. Supervisory review of all adjustments, reversals, reasons for reversals and open
　　　　items?　　　　　　　　　　　　　　　　　　———　———

　　　i. Contingency planning?　　　　　　　　　　　———　———

8.28　ARE THESE PROCEDURES PERIODICALLY REVIEWED AND UPDATED?　———　———

Section 8 – Electronic Funds Transfer Systems (continued)　　　　YES　NO　　　　　　　COMMENTS

AGREEMENTS

8.29　ARE AGREEMENTS CONCERNING WIRE TRANSFER OPERATIONS BETWEEN
THE FINANCIAL INSTITUTION AND ITS HARDWARE AND SOFTWARE VENDORS,
MAINTENANCE COMPANIES, CUSTOMERS, CORRESPONDENT BANKS, AND
THE FEDERAL RESERVE BANK IN EFFECT AND CURRENT?　　———　———

8.30　DO THE AGREEMENTS FIX RESPONSIBILITIES AND ACCOUNTABILITY
BETWEEN THE PARTIES?　　　　　　　　　　　　　———　———

8.31　Do both the hardware and software vendors guarantee continuity of service in the
event of a failure?　　　　　　　　　　　　　　　———　———
If so, does the guarantee specify recovery time?　　　　———　———

8.32　Are there agreements between the financial institution and vendor setting forth the
vendor's liability for actions performed by their employees?　———　———

8.33　HAVE WRITTEN CONTINGENCY PLANS BEEN DEVELOPED FOR PARTIAL OR
COMPLETE FAILURE OF THE SYSTEMS AND/OR COMMUNICATION LINES
BETWEEN THE FINANCIAL INSTITUTION, FEDERAL RESERVE BANK, DATA CEN-
TERS AND/OR SERVICE COMPANIES?　　　　　　　　———　———

8.34　ARE THESE CONTINGENCY PLANS REVIEWED REGULARLY AND TESTED
PERIODICALLY?　　　　　　　　　　　　　　　　———　———

8.35　HAS MANAGEMENT DISTRIBUTED THESE PLANS TO ALL WIRE TRANSFER
PERSONNEL?　　　　　　　　　　　　　　　　　———　———

8.36　Are sensitive information and equipment adequately secured before evacuation in an
emergency and is further access to the affected areas denied by security personnel?　———　———

Section 8 – Electronic Funds Transfer Systems (continued)   YES   NO   COMMENTS

OPERATING CONTROLS

8.37   DOES MANAGEMENT MAINTAIN A CURRENT LIST OF INSTITUTION PERSONNEL AUTHORIZED TO INITIATE A TRANSFER REQUEST?   ____ ____

8.38   ARE AUTHORIZED EMPLOYEE SIGNATURE CARDS KEPT UNDER DUAL CONTROL?   ____ ____

8.39   DOES THE INSTITUTION MAINTAIN A CURRENT LIST OR CARD FILE OF AUTHORIZED SIGNERS FOR CUSTOMERS WHO USE THE FUNDS TRANSFER SERVICES?   ____ ____

8.40   ARE CUSTOMER SIGNATURE CARDS MAINTAINED UNDER DUAL CONTROL OR OTHERWISE PROTECTED?   ____ ____

8.41   Do customer signature cards specify the amount of funds that an individual is authorized to transfer?   ____ ____

8.42   Has the institution established guidelines for what information should be obtained from a person making funds transfer request by telephone?   ____ ____

8.43   Does the institution:

     a. Advise its customer callers that telephone transfer requests are being recorded?   ____ ____

     b. USE A CALL-BACK PROCEDURE THAT INCLUDES A TEST CODE OR PASSWORD AUTHENTICATION TO VERIFY TELEPHONE TRANSFER REQUESTS?   ____ ____

     c. Limit call-back to transactions over a certain dollar amount?   ____ ____

8.44   Are transfer requests recorded in a log at the time received?   ____ ____

Section 8 – Electronic Funds Transfer Systems (continued)   YES   NO   COMMENTS

8.45   Do the records of transfer requests contain:

     a. A SEQUENCE NUMBER?   ____ ____

     b. AN AMOUNT?   ____ ____

     c. THE PERSON, FIRM OR INSTITUTION MAKING REQUEST (ALSO, SPECIFIC TRANSFEROR)?   ____ ____

     d. THE DATE?   ____ ____

     e. The test code authentication?   ____ ____

     f. PAYING INSTRUCTIONS?   ____ ____

     g. Authorizing signatures for certain types and dollar amount transfers?   ____ ____

8.46   IS SOMEONE RESPONSIBLE FOR REVIEWING ALL TRANSFER REQUESTS TO DETERMINE THAT THEY HAVE BEEN PROPERLY RECEIVED AND PROCESSED?   ____ ____

8.47   Are payment orders and message requests reviewed by someone other than the receipt clerk for:

     a. PROPRIETY OF THE TRANSACTIONS?   ____ ____

     b. FUTURE DATES, ESPECIALLY FOR MULTIPLE TRANSACTION REQUESTS?   ____ ____

8.48   Is an unbroken copy of all messages kept throughout the business day and does it receive adequate review?   ____ ____

8.49   Are the receipt, data entry, authentication and balancing functions in the wire transfer area adequately segregated?   ____ ____

8.50   Are all transactions checked by a supervisor prior to release of the payments?   ____ ____

Section 8 – Electronic Funds Transfer Systems (continued)   YES   NO   COMMENTS

RECONCILEMENT PROCEDURES

8.51   DOES THE WIRE TRANSFER DEPARTMENT OF THE INSTITUTION PREPARE A DAILY RECONCILEMENT OF FUNDS TRANSFER ACTIVITY BY DOLLAR AMOUNT AND NUMBER OF MESSAGES?   ____ ____

8.52   IS THE DAILY RECONCILEMENT OF FUNDS TRANSFER ACTIVITY REVIEWED BY SUPERVISORY PERSONNEL?   ____ ____

8.53   Are customer transfer and message requests which have been rejected by an in-house terminal carefully controlled and assigned a sequence number for accountability purposes?   ____ ____

8.54   Are all pre-numbered forms, including cancellations, accounted for in the end-of-day proof?   ____ ____

8.55   Does the wire transfer department verify that work sent to other institution departments agrees with its totals?   ____ ____

8.56   IS EACH NETWORK STATEMENT (FED WIRE, BANK WIRE, ETC.) REVIEWED DAILY TO DETERMINE IF THERE ARE "OPEN" FUNDS TRANSFER ITEMS AND THE REASONS FOR THE OUTSTANDING ITEMS?   ____ ____

8.57   DOES THE WIRE TRANSFER DEPARTMENT OR ANOTHER AREA OF THE INSTITUTION HAVE PROCEDURES IN EFFECT TO PROHIBIT TRANSFERS OF FUNDS AGAINST ACCOUNTS THAT DO NOT HAVE PRE-AUTHORIZED CREDIT AVAILABILITY AND HAVE UNCOLLECTED BALANCES?   ____ ____

8.58   IF THE INSTITUTION ACCEPTS TRANSFER REQUESTS AFTER THE CLOSE OF A BUSINESS DAY, ARE PROCEDURES IN EFFECT TO ENSURE THAT REQUESTS ARE RECORDED AND PROMPTLY PROCESSED ON THE FOLLOWING DAY?   ____ ____

8.59   Does the institution maintain adequate records as required by the Currency and Foreign Transactions Reporting Act of 1970 (also known as the Bank Secrecy Act)?   ____ ____

Section 8 – Electronic Funds Transfer Systems (continued)   YES   NO   COMMENTS

TESTING

8.60   ARE THE FUNCTIONS OF RECEIPT, TESTING AND TRANSMISSION OF FUNDS TRANSFER REQUESTS PERFORMED BY DIFFERENT EMPLOYEES?   ____ ____

8.61   ARE TEST CODES USED FOR TELEPHONIC REQUESTS FOR WIRE TRANSFER TRANSACTIONS?   ____ ____

8.62   ARE TEST CODES USED FOR TRANSACTIONS VERIFIED BY SOMEONE OTHER THAN THE PERSON WHO RECEIVES THE REQUEST?   ____ ____

8.63   ARE THESE CODES RESTRICTED TO AUTHORIZED PERSONNEL?   ____ ____

8.64   IS THE RESPONSIBILITY FOR ISSUING AND CANCELLING TEST KEYS ASSIGNED TO SOMEONE WHO IS NOT RESPONSIBLE FOR TESTING THE AUTHENTICITY OF TRANSFER REQUESTS?   ____ ____

8.65   ARE THE FILES CONTAINING THE KEY FORMULAS MAINTAINED UNDER DUAL CONTROL OR OTHERWISE PROTECTED?   ____ ____

8.66   Is the testing area physically separated from the remainder of the operation?   ____ ____

PHYSICAL SECURITY

8.67   IS ACCESS TO THE WIRE TRANSFER AREA RESTRICTED TO AUTHORIZED PERSONNEL?   ____ ____

8.68   Are visitors to the wire transfer area required to:

   a. BE IDENTIFIED?   ____ ____

   b. SIGN IN?   ____ ____

   c. CONTINUOUSLY DISPLAY IDENTIFICATION?   ____ ____

   d. BE ACCOMPANIED AT ALL TIMES?   ____ ____

Section 8 – Electronic Funds Transfer Systems (continued)

	YES	NO	COMMENTS

8.69   Are personnel who are permitted entry to the operating area properly identified and required to continuously display identification?

8.70   IS WRITTEN AUTHORIZATION GIVEN BY A SUPERVISOR TO THOSE EMPLOYEES WHO REMAIN IN THE WIRE TRANSFER AREA AFTER NORMAL WORKING HOURS?

8.71   DO PROCEDURES PREVENT DATA PROCESSING PERSONNEL FROM GAINING ACCESS TO WIRE TRANSFER EQUIPMENT AND TEST KEY INFORMATION WITHOUT PRIOR SUPERVISORY APPROVAL?

8.72   Are terminals in the wire transfer area regulated by:

     a. AUTOMATIC TIME-OUT CONTROLS?

     b. TIME-OF-DAY CONTROLS?

8.73   ARE TERMINALS AND OTHER HARDWARE IN THE WIRE TRANSFER AREA SHUT DOWN AFTER NORMAL WORKING HOURS?

8.74   IS TERMINAL OPERATOR TRAINING CONDUCTED IN A MANNER THAT WILL NOT JEOPARDIZE THE INTEGRITY OF LIVE DATE OR MEMO FILES?

8.75   ARE PASSWORDS SUPPRESSED WHEN ENTERED IN TERMINALS?

8.76   ARE TERMINAL OPERATOR PASSWORDS FREQUENTLY CHANGED? IF SO, HOW OFTEN

8.77   Is supervisory approval required for terminal access made at other than authorized times?

Section 8 – Electronic Funds Transfer Systems (continued)

	YES	NO	COMMENTS

8.78   ARE PASSWORDS RESTRICTED TO DIFFERENT LEVELS OF ACCESS SUCH AS DATA FILES AND TRANSACTIONS THAT CAN BE INITIATED?

8.79   ARE EMPLOYEES PROHIBITED FROM TAKING KEYS FOR SENSITIVE EQUIPMENT OUT OF THE WIRE TRANSFER AREA?

8.80   Has the institution established procedures and time limits for the retention of accounting records in the wire transfer department?

SUPERVISORY AND ACCOUNTING CONTROLS

Supervision by Directors and Senior Management

8.81   ARE THE DIRECTORS AND SENIOR MANAGEMENT KEPT INFORMED REGARDING THE NATURE AND MAGNITUDE OF THE RISKS IN THE FUNDS TRANSFER ACTIVITY?

8.82   HAS THE BOARD OF DIRECTORS AND/OR SENIOR MANAGEMENT REVIEWED AND APPROVED ANY LIMITS RELATING TO THE RISKS IN THE FUNDS TRANSFER ACTIVITIES?

     IF SO, WHEN WERE THE LIMITS LAST REVIEWED?

8.83   IS SENIOR MANAGEMENT AND/OR THE BOARD OF DIRECTORS ADVISED OF CUSTOMERS WITH LARGE INTRADAY AND OVERNIGHT OVERDRAFTS? IF SO, ARE OTHER EXTENSIONS OF CREDIT TO THE SAME CUSTOMERS COMBINED TO SHOW THE TOTAL CREDIT EXPOSURES?

8.84   IS SENIOR MANAGEMENT AND/OR THE BOARD OF DIRECTORS ADVISED OF CUSTOMERS WITH LARGE DRAWINGS AGAINST UNCOLLECTED FUNDS?

Section 8 – Electronic Funds Transfer Systems (continued)   YES   NO   COMMENTS

8.85   Is senior management and/or the board of directors, under established policies and
        procedures, required to review at predetermined frequencies:

        a. THE VOLUME OF TRANSACTIONS, THE CREDITWORTHINESS OF CUSTOM-
           ERS, AND THE RISK INVOLVED IN THE FUNDS TRANSFER ACTIVITY?   ____ ____

        b. CREDIT AND OTHER EXPOSURES RELATED TO SAFE AND SOUND BANKING
           PRACTICES?   ____ ____

        c. The capabilities of the staff and the adequacy of the equipment relative to current
           and expected volume?   ____ ____

        Credit Evaluation and Approval

8.86   What is the basis for accepting customers for the CHIPS clearing activity?

        a. If the examined institution is a settling CHIPS participant, what are the criteria for
           accepting a nonsettling participant as a respondent?

        b. At what level of management is this decision made, and how frequently is it
           reviewed?

8.87   ARE PERIODIC CREDIT REVIEW OF FUNDS TRANSFER CUSTOMERS
        PERFORMED?   ____ ____

        If so, how frequently?

        a. Are the reviews adequately documented?   ____ ____

        b. ARE THE REVIEWS CONDUCTED BY COMPETENT CREDIT PERSONNEL IN-
           DEPENDENT OF ACCOUNT AND OPERATIONS OFFICERS?   ____ ____

Section 8 – Electronic Funds Transfer Systems (continued)   YES   NO   COMMENTS

8.88   Does the institution make payments in anticipation of the receipt of covering funds?   ____ ____

        IF SO, ARE SUCH PAYMENTS APPROVED BY OFFICERS WITH APPROPRIATE
        CREDIT AUTHORITY?   ____ ____

8.89   ARE INTRADAY EXPOSURES LIMITED TO AMOUNTS EXPECTED TO BE RE-
        CEIVED THE SAME DAY?   ____ ____

8.90   HAVE CUSTOMER LIMITS BEEN ESTABLISHED FOR INTRADAY AND OVER-
        NIGHT OVERDRAFTS?   ____ ____

        a. ARE GROUPS OF AFFILIATED CUSTOMERS INCLUDED IN SUCH LIMITS?   ____ ____

        b. DO THE LIMITS APPEAR REASONABLE IN VIEW OF THE INSTITUTIONS CAPI-
           TAL POSITION AND THE CREDITWORTHINESS OF THE RESPECTIVE
           CUSTOMERS?   ____ ____

        c. How often are the limits reviewed and updated?

8.91   ARE PAYMENTS IN EXCESS OF ESTABLISHED LIMITS APPROVED ON THE
        BASIS OF INFORMATION INDICATING THAT COVERING FUNDS ARE IN TRANSIT
        TO THE FINANCIAL INSTITUTION?   ____ ____

        IF SO, WHO IS AUTHORIZED TO MAKE SUCH APPROVALS?

8.92   ARE PAYMENTS AGAINST UNCOLLECTED FUNDS AND INTRADAY OVER-
        DRAFTS IN EXCESS OF ESTABLISHED LIMITS REFERRED TO A PERSON WITH
        APPROPRIATE CREDIT AUTHORITY FOR APPROVAL BEFORE RELEASING
        PAYMENTS?   ____ ____

        IF SO, IS A RECORD OF APPROVALS OF SUCH RELEASES MAINTAINED?   ____ ____

Section 8 – Electronic Funds Transfer Systems (continued)

YES   NO   COMMENTS

8.93   Review the funds transfer activities report for the number of items received and the number of items paid over CHIPS, Bank Wire and Fedwire.

a. Are there any unresolved open payment items?   —— ——

b. If payments exceed the established limits, are steps taken in a timely manner to obtain covering funds?   —— ——

c. If the institution is a settling participant in CHIPS, list the nonsettling participants and total amount settled for each as of the examination date.   —— ——

8.94   Is the volume of transactions on each of the funds transfer systems considered large relative to the size of the institution?   —— ——

8.95   Determine where suspense items are posted.

a. Age the items.

b. Determine who reviews suspense items for resolution.

c. Review management reports on suspense items.

d. Are they adequately controlled and resolved in a timely manner?   —— ——

8.96   DOES THE INSTITUTION RECEIVE CABLE OR OTHER ADVICES FROM ITS CUSTOMERS INDICATING AMOUNTS TO BE PAID AND RECEIVED AND THE SOURCE OF COVERING FUNDS?   —— ——

a. IF THE DETAIL OF RECEIPTS IS NOT RECEIVED, IS THE INSTITUTION ADVISED BY ITS CUSTOMER OF THE TOTAL AMOUNT TO BE RECEIVED FOR THE DAY?   —— ——

b. IS THIS INFORMATION MAINTAINED AND FOLLOWED-UP FOR EXCEPTIONS?   —— ——

Section 8 – Electronic Funds Transfer Systems (continued)

YES   NO   COMMENTS

8.97   IS AN INTRADAY POSTING RECORD KEPT FOR EACH CUSTOMER SHOWING OPENING COLLECTED AND UNCOLLECTED BALANCES, TRANSFERS IN, TRANSFERS OUT, AND THE COLLECTED BALANCE AT THE TIME PAYMENTS ARE RELEASED?   —— ——

8.98   ARE SIGNIFICANT WIRE TRANSFER PAYMENTS AND RECEIPTS BY OTHER DEPARTMENTS OF THE INSTITUTION ON BEHALF OF A CUSTOMER COMMUNICATED TO A MONITORING UNIT IN A TIMELY FASHION DURING THE DAY TO PROVIDE ADEQUATE INFORMATION ON EACH CUSTOMER'S OVERALL EXPOSURE?   —— ——

8.99   DOES THE DEMAND DEPOSIT ACCOUNTING SYSTEM GIVE AN ACCURATE COLLECTED FUNDS POSITION?   —— ——

8.100   WHEN AN OVERNIGHT OVERDRAFT OCCURS, IS A DETERMINATION MADE AS TO WHETHER A FAIL CAUSED THE OVERDRAFT?   —— ——

a. IF SO, IS THIS PROPERLY DOCUMENTED?   —— ——

b. IS ADEQUATE FOLLOW-UP MADE TO OBTAIN THE COVERING FUNDS IN A TIMELY MANNER?   —— ——

8.101   DOES THE INSTITUTION HAVE A RECORD OF PAYMENTS IT FAILED TO MAKE IN A TIMELY FASHION?   —— ——

a. If so, is the record reviewed to evaluate the efficiency of the department?   —— ——

b. Indicate the level of management making such reviews.

c. IS CORRECTIVE ACTION INITIATED WHEN APPROPRIATE?   —— ——

d. Show the total expenses the institution has incurred during the last calendar year and year-to-date for failing to make payments as instructed by its customers.

e. ARE INVESTIGATIONS AND FOLLOW-UPS FOR FAILED PAYMENTS CONDUCTED BY PERSONNEL INDEPENDENT OF THE OPERATING UNIT?   —— ——

Section 8 – Electronic Funds Transfer Systems (continued)   YES   NO   COMMENTS

8.102   Do credit advices sent to customers clearly indicate that credits to their accounts received through wire transfer are conditional until the next day when they are considered final.   ____ ____

8.103   FOR SETTLING INSTITUTIONS ON CHIPS, ARE THE NET DEBT POSITIONS OF THE NON-SETTLING PARTICIPANTS RELAYED TO APPROPRIATE PERSONNEL AS SOON AS THEY BECOME KNOWN?   ____ ____

   a. Who is responsible for verifying that respondents' net debt positions are covered the same day?   ____ ____

   b. ARE THE FOLLOW-UP PROCEDURES ADEQUATE TO FACILITATE THE RECEIPT OF FUNDS?   ____ ____

   c. Is senior management required to make the decision to refuse to cover a net debt settlement position of a respondent?   ____ ____

8.104   Has the institution devised and maintained an adequate system of internal accounting controls as required by the Foreign Corrupt Practices Act of 1977?   ____ ____

PIN (Personal Identification Number)

8.105   DOES EACH CUSTOMER HAVE A UNIQUE PIN FOR EACH TYPE OF EFT SYSTEM?   ____ ____

8.106   If customers are allowed to select PINS, are they discouraged from using common number sequences or words?   ____ ____

8.107   In the event a customer's PIN is lost or forgotten:

   a. HAVE ADEQUATE CONTROL PROCEDURES BEEN ESTABLISHED FOR OLD PIN LOOK-UP AND NEW PIN ISSUANCE?   ____ ____

   b. IS THERE ACCOUNTABILITY TO THE PERSON INITIATING SUCH TRANSACTIONS?   ____ ____

8.108   Is it a standard that no PIN information be released over the telephone?   ____ ____

Section 8 – Electronic Funds Transfer Systems (continued)   YES   NO   COMMENTS

8.109   If PINS and corresponding account numbers appear in format where they could be matched, are adequate controls maintained to prevent compromising situations?   ____ ____

8.110   Is the PIN encrypted or otherwise disguised when:

   a. TRANSMITTED OVER TELEPHONE LINES?   ____ ____

   b. STORED ON THE COMPUTER FILES, EITHER MASTER OR DATA BASE?   ____ ____

8.111   Has all documentation relating to encryption, decryption and the PIN generation process been properly secured?   ____ ____

8.112   IF MANAGEMENT INSISTS THAT THEY MUST HAVE ACCESS TO CUSTOMER PINS AND ACCOUNT NUMBERS, HAVE ADEQUATE COMPENSATING CONTROLS BEEN IMPLEMENTED?   ____ ____

PLASTIC CARDS

8.113   ARE BLANK CARDS KEPT UNDER EFFECTIVE DUAL CONTROL AND ACCOUNTED FOR IN EACH OF THE VARIOUS STEPS IN ENCODING, EMBOSSING, STUFFING AND MAILING?   ____ ____

8.114   Is the working supply of plastics securely stored?   ____ ____

8.115   IS ACCESS TO THE PHYSICAL AREA IN WHICH ENCODING IS PERFORMED RESTRICTED TO AUTHORIZED PERSONNEL?   ____ ____

8.116   Are there adequate controls over use of encoding equipment?   ____ ____

8.117   ARE SPOILED CARDS DESTROYED UNDER DUAL CONTROL AND IS THE DESTRUCTION PROPERLY DOCUMENTED?   ____ ____

8.118   Are test or demonstration cards adequately controlled?   ____ ____

8.119   Are adequate controls maintained over any duplicate cards which were not issued to the customer?   ____ ____

Section 8 – Electronic Funds Transfer Systems (continued)

	YES	NO	COMMENTS

8.120 If cards are issued at more than one location, e.g., branches, have card maintenance control procedures been established for these locations?

8.121 IF CARDS ARE PRODUCED BY CARD VENDORS, HAVE THE CONTRACTS FOR SUCH SERVICES BEEN REVIEWED BY LEGAL COUNSEL?

8.122 IS THE SHIPMENT OF CARDS FROM THE VENDOR TO THE INSTITUTION DONE IN A SECURE MANNER?

8.123 ARE CARDS MAILED TO CUSTOMERS IN ENVELOPES WITH A RETURN AD-DRESS WHICH DOES NOT IDENTIFY THE FINANCIAL INSTITUTION'S NAME OR USUAL PLACE OF BUSINESS?

8.124 ARE RETURNED CARDS CONTROLLED AND ACCOUNTED FOR BY INDIVIDUALS OTHER THAN THOSE WITH CARD ISSUER OR SYSTEMS/OPERATIONS RESPONSIBILITIES?

8.125 IS IT AGAINST POLICY FOR THE FINANCIAL INSTITUTION TO MAIL UN-SOLICITED CARDS?

8.126 ARE CARDS WHICH WERE LEFT INADVERTENTLY OR CAPTURED AT EFT LO-CATIONS PROPERLY CONTROLLED?

8.127 ARE PLASTIC CARDS AND PINS ALWAYS MAILED SEPARATELY AND WITH A SUFFICIENT PERIOD OF TIME BETWEEN MAILINGS?

8.128 After the card is issued, is there a follow-up mailing to ascertain whether both card and PIN were received/utilized by the proper customer?

8.129 ARE PROCEDURES SUCH AS "HOT" CARD LISTS AND EXPIRATION DATES USED TO LIMIT THE PERIOD OF EXPOSURE IF A CARD IS LOST, STOLEN OR PURPOSELY MISUSED?

Section 8 – Electronic Funds Transfer Systems (continued)

	YES	NO	COMMENTS

APPLICATION REVIEW

Review the following control procedures for each type of EFT application examined (ATM, POS, ACH, Telephone Bill Paying, Transfers and/or Debit Cards). Omit any questions that do not apply to the application(s) being reviewed.

INTERCHANGE OR TERMINAL SHARING

8.130 IF THE FINANCIAL INSTITUTION SHARES TERMINALS, DOES THE WRITTEN AGREEMENT BETWEEN/AMONG INSTITUTIONS CLEARLY SET FORTH THE RIGHTS AND RESPONSIBILITIES OF ALL PARTIES, INCLUDING REQUIREMENTS FOR INSTALLING AND SERVICING AS WELL AS TRAINING CUSTOMERS?

8.131 Are responsibilities of each financial institution known in the event of equipment failure?

8.132 IF ONE PART OF THE SWITCH EQUIPMENT IS INOPERATIVE, HAVE ADEQUATE STORE AND FORWARD PROCEDURES BEEN ESTABLISHED TO UPDATE THE SYSTEM AT A LATER TIME?

8.133 Does the maintenance contract establish the responsibilities of the supplier or vendor?

8.134 Is there adequate control over terminal access?

8.135 CAN THE FINANCIAL INSTITUTION IDENTIFY EACH TERMINAL OR COMMUNICA-TIONS DEVICE IN THE NETWORK?

8.136 IS THERE A DAILY SETTLEMENT PROCEDURE FOR EACH SHARED DEVICE?

Section 8 – Electronic Funds Transfer Systems (continued)   YES   NO   COMMENTS

AUTHORIZATIONS

8.137   ARE TERMINAL AND OPERATOR IDENTIFICATION/AUTHORIZATION CODES
USED TO EFFECT ALL TYPES OF EFT TRANSACTIONS?   —— ——

8.138   Are customers required to pre-authorize:

a. PAY-BY-PHONE PAYMENTS TO SPECIFIC MERCHANTS?   —— ——

b. TELEPHONE TRANSFERS BETWEEN ACCOUNTS?   —— ——

8.139   If pre-authorizations are accepted over the telephone are confirmations promptly sent
to customers and merchants?   —— ——

OPERATIONAL CONTROLS

8.140   Does the financial institution have:

a. WRITTEN AGREEMENTS ON FILE THAT ADEQUATELY SET FORTH RE-
SPONSIBILITIES OF THE FINANCIAL INSTITUTION AND CUSTOMERS, MER-
CHANTS, EFT SERVICERS AND/OR OTHER PARTICIPATING INSTITUTIONS?   —— ——

b. WRITTEN POLICIES THAT COVER CREDIT AND CHECK AUTHORIZATION,
FLOOR LIMITS, OVERRIDE PROCEDURES, ETC. FOR THE EFT FUNCTIONS?   —— ——

c. MAINTENANCE AGREEMENTS ON THE EFT EQUIPMENT (TERMINALS AND
COMMUNICATIONS)?   —— ——

8.141   IS THE EFT SYSTEM RECONCILED DAILY?   —— ——

8.142   Are all transactions promptly posted to customer accounts?   —— ——

8.143   ARE "HOT" CARD OR CUSTOMER SUSPECT LISTS REGULARLY UPDATED AND
DISTRIBUTED TO REMOTE USER LOCATIONS?   —— ——

Section 8 – Electronic Funds Transfer Systems (continued)   YES   NO   COMMENTS

8.144   Does the financial institution take adequate measures to:

a. PREVENT CUSTOMER CHARGES FROM EXCEEDING THE AVAILABLE BAL-
ANCE IN THE ACCOUNT AND/OR THE APPROVED OVERDRAFT LINE?   —— ——

b. ENSURE CHECKS ARE RETURNED TO MERCHANT ACCOUNTS BEFORE
FUNDS BECOME AVAILABLE FOR CUSTOMER USE?   —— ——

8.145   ARE ACCESS AND USE OF TERMINALS USED TO CHANGE CUSTOMER CREDIT
LINES AND ACCOUNT INFORMATION ADEQUATELY CONTROLLED?   —— ——

8.146   ARE MERCHANT EMPLOYEES PROHIBITED FROM ACCESSING CUSTOMER
ACCOUNTS OR ACCOUNT iNFORMATION THAT ARE MAINTAINED BY THE FI-
NANCIAL INSTITUTION?   —— ——

8.147   Is the EFT equipment keyboard and/or display properly shielded to avoid disclosure of
a customer's PIN?   —— ——

8.148   Do customers receive a receipt showing the date, time and location for each EFT transaction they make?   —— ——

8.149   IS EACH EFT TRANSACTION ASSIGNED A SEQUENCE NUMBER TO PROVIDE
AN AUDIT TRAIL?   —— ——

8.150   ARE ACH TAPES VERIFIED BEFORE THEY ARE PROCESSED?   —— ——

8.151   Are reports provided for the EFT system that indicate:

a. increased customer usage?   —— ——

b. completed and attempted transactions?   —— ——

c. large currency transactions?   —— ——

Section 8 – Electronic Funds Transfer Systems (continued)   YES   NO   COMMENTS

8.152   Do exception reports:

    a. MEET THE NEEDS OF MANAGEMENT, USER DEPARTMENTS AND AUDIT
    DEPARTMENTS?   ____   ____

    b. RECEIVE SUPERVISORY REVIEW IN USER DEPARTMENTS DAILY?   ____   ____

8.153   Is the name and address procedure sufficiently controlled to preclude unauthorized
changes which may circumvent normal controls?   ____   ____

8.154   Are the clerical procedure manuals adequate?   ____   ____

8.155   Does the data processing center control EFT system tests and is each test logged and
verified?   ____   ____

8.156   ARE SECURITY DEVICES AND PROCEDURES FOR EACH EFT FACILITY
ADEQUATE?   ____   ____

8.157   Does the financial institution control and monitor maintenance engineers' access to the
EFT equipment?   ____   ____

BACKUP

8.158   DOES THE FINANCIAL INSTITUTION HAVE ADEQUATE ALTERNATE PROCESS-
ING PROCEDURES FOR THE EFT SYSTEM(S)?   ____   ____

8.159   IS THE EFT CONTINGENCY PLAN PERIODICALLY TESTED?   ____   ____

AUDIT COVERAGE

8.160   IS THERE ADEQUATE AUDIT COVERAGE FOR THE EFT APPLICATION(S)?   ____   ____

8.161   IS THE AUDIT DEPARTMENT NOTIFIED OF ALL HARDWARE, SOFTWARE AND
PROCEDURAL CHANGES MADE TO THE EFT SYSTEM OR APPLICATION(S)?   ____   ____

BIOGRAPHICAL DATA WORKSHEET

Exhibit No.: _____
Date _____
Prepared by _____

PERSONAL

(Name) _____ (Birth Date) _____

(Title) _____

(Responsibilities) _____

_____

_____

(Years with Bank/Center) _____ (Years in Present Position) _____

(Previous Position) _____

(Responsibilities) _____

If employed by bank/center less than two years, provide the following:

(Previous Employer) _____ (Years with that Employer) _____

(Highest Position Attained) _____

(Responsibilities) _____

PROFESSIONAL

(Education): High School _____ College _____ Bus. College _____ Major Field _____
(Indicate no. years attended or Degree)

(Continuing Education):

Seminar/Course Title	Presented By	Dates Attended
1.		
2.		
3.		
4.		
5.		
6.		
7.		
8.		
9.		
10.		

(Membership in Business/Professional Organizations) _____

EDP EXAMINATION DOCUMENTATION WORKSHEET

Section No. _____
Exhibit No. _____
Date _____
Prepared by _____

Application Name	SYSTEM					SYSTEM					SYSTEM					SYSTEM				
Date/performed by																				
Individual Program ID																				
System Level Feasibility Study System Narrative System Flowchart																				
Program Level Source Listing Program Narrative Record Layout																				

*List additional items required by documentation standards.
**Individual items may be filed with systems documentation, but are applicable to individual programs.

Codes: Y = Yes   I = Incomplete
       N = No   NA = Not Applicable

Appendix 17

Examples of Simple Cryptographic Systems

Ciphers of great complexity can be produced by using combinations of three basic cryptographic operations:

- Transposition
- Substitution
- Fractionization

Transposition

A transposition system merely rearranges the plaintext characters without changing their identities. The system shown in Figure A17–a uses a geometrical figure. In this case, the plaintext, NOVUS ORDO SECLORUM, is written into the triangle shown in rows and copied out in columns according to the numeric columnar keys as shown. The resultant ciphertext is then divided into five character groups as is customary.

Substitution

The simplest form of substitution cipher merely replaces each plaintext character with a substitute ciphertext character. Figure A17–b shows a simple substitution using a 5 × 5 or "Polybius" square where each plaintext letter is represented by a two-digit ciphertext character comprising its row and column coordinates. The letters in the square were arranged by choosing a "keyword," PARIS, and filling in the remaining letters of the alphabet while leaving out the letters of the keyword. (The letter "J" is omitted entirely, and "Y" may be used in its place.)

More complex substitutions are often constructed by adding (modulo 10) a long, random-looking key to the previous ciphertext as shown in Figure A17–c.

The "random" key is formed in this example by picking a five digit "seed," 61702, and then adding modulo 10 to the first two digits to get the next digit in the key, adding the second digit in the key to the third in order to get the succeeding digit, and continuing this process for as much key as is desired. Thus, $6+1=7$, $1+7=8$, $7+0=7$, etc. Similarly, the ciphertext is derived by adding, modulo 10, each character of the plaintext to the corresponding character of the key.

Fractionization

A fractionating system is one that literally tears apart the individual components of a plaintext by character and scatters them in the ciphertext. Perhaps the best known such system is the "bifid" cipher in Figure A17–d. Using the previous Polybius square, the plaintext letters are represented by their row and column coordinates as before, but these coordinates are then recombined using the same square in the manner demonstrated.

The alphabet square of Figure A17–e, termed the Vigenere Table by cryptologists can be used to perform the modulo (26) addition of the letters of the alphabet. The key letter is found in the leftmost column and the letter to be enciphered is found in the topmost row. The intersection of the row and column thus determined yields the ciphertext letter. For example, C + F = H, W + B = X, etc. In modulo (26), all numerals to be enciphered must be spelled out. For example, 26 must be transliterated to "twenty six" or "two six" before it can be enciphered.

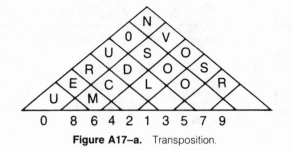

Figure A17–a. Transposition.

	1	2	3	4	5
1	P	A	R	I	S
2	B	C	D	E	F
3	G	H	K	L	M
4	N	O	Q	T	U
5	V	W	X	Y	Z

PLAINTEXT: NOVUS ORDO SECLORUM
CIPHERTEXT: 41 42 51 45 15   42 13 23 42 15   24 22 34 42 13   45 35 12 41 54

Figure A17–b. Substitution.

PLAINTEXT: 41 42 51 45 15 42 13 23 42 15 24 22 34 42 13 45 35
KEY: 61 70 27 87 29 55 91 40 40 54 44 59 88 94 76 73 13
CIPHERTEXT: 02 12 78 22 34 97 04 63 82 69 68 71 12 36 89 18 48

Figure A17–c. Substitution with "random" key.

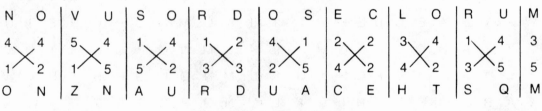

Figure A17–d. Fractionization.

	A	B	C	D	E	F	G	H	I	J	K	L	M	N	O	P	Q	R	S	T	U	V	W	X	Y	Z
A	A	B	C	D	E	F	G	H	I	J	K	L	M	N	O	P	Q	R	S	T	U	V	W	X	Y	Z
B	B	C	D	E	F	G	H	I	J	K	L	M	N	O	P	Q	R	S	T	U	V	W	X	Y	Z	A
C	C	D	E	F	G	H	I	J	K	L	M	N	O	P	Q	R	S	T	U	V	W	X	Y	Z	A	B
D	D	E	F	G	H	I	J	K	L	M	N	O	P	Q	R	S	T	U	V	W	X	Y	Z	A	B	C
E	E	F	G	H	I	J	K	L	M	N	O	P	Q	R	S	T	U	V	W	X	Y	Z	A	B	C	D
F	F	G	H	I	J	K	L	M	N	O	P	Q	R	S	T	U	V	W	X	Y	Z	A	B	C	D	E
G	G	H	I	J	K	L	M	N	O	P	Q	R	S	T	U	V	W	X	Y	Z	A	B	C	D	E	F
H	H	I	J	K	L	M	N	O	P	Q	R	S	T	U	V	W	X	Y	Z	A	B	C	D	E	F	G
I	I	J	K	L	M	N	O	P	Q	R	S	T	U	V	W	X	Y	Z	A	B	C	D	E	F	G	H
J	J	K	L	M	N	O	P	Q	R	S	T	U	V	W	X	Y	Z	A	B	C	D	E	F	G	H	I
K	K	L	M	N	O	P	Q	R	S	T	U	V	W	X	Y	Z	A	B	C	D	E	F	G	H	I	J
L	L	M	N	O	P	Q	R	S	T	U	V	W	X	Y	Z	A	B	C	D	E	F	G	H	I	J	K
M	M	N	O	P	Q	R	S	T	U	V	W	X	Y	Z	A	B	C	D	E	F	G	H	I	J	K	L
N	N	O	P	Q	R	S	T	U	V	W	X	Y	Z	A	B	C	D	E	F	G	H	I	J	K	L	M
O	O	P	Q	R	S	T	U	V	W	X	Y	Z	A	B	C	D	E	F	G	H	I	J	K	L	M	N
P	P	Q	R	S	T	U	V	W	X	Y	Z	A	B	C	D	E	F	G	H	I	J	K	L	M	N	O
Q	Q	R	S	T	U	V	W	X	Y	Z	A	B	C	D	E	F	G	H	I	J	K	L	M	N	O	P
R	R	S	T	U	V	W	X	Y	Z	A	B	C	D	E	F	G	H	I	J	K	L	M	N	O	P	Q
S	S	T	U	V	W	X	Y	Z	A	B	C	D	E	F	G	H	I	J	K	L	M	N	O	P	Q	R
T	T	U	V	W	X	Y	Z	A	B	C	D	E	F	G	H	I	J	K	L	M	N	O	P	Q	R	S
U	U	V	W	X	Y	Z	A	B	C	D	E	F	G	H	I	J	K	L	M	N	O	P	Q	R	S	T
V	V	W	X	Y	Z	A	B	C	D	E	F	G	H	I	J	K	L	M	N	O	P	Q	R	S	T	U
W	W	X	Y	Z	A	B	C	D	E	F	G	H	I	J	K	L	M	N	O	P	Q	R	S	T	U	V
X	X	Y	Z	A	B	C	D	E	F	G	H	I	J	K	L	M	N	O	P	Q	R	S	T	U	V	W
Y	Y	Z	A	B	C	D	E	F	G	H	I	J	K	L	M	N	O	P	Q	R	S	T	U	V	W	X
Z	Z	A	B	C	D	E	F	G	H	I	J	K	L	M	N	O	P	Q	R	S	T	U	V	W	X	Y

Figure A17–e. Vigenere table.

Personal Computer Security Considerations

Preface

This publication provides a general discussion of a number of issues that are pertinent to microcomputer security in the home and business environment. This is not a formal National Computer Security Center policy document, but rather an information memorandum intended to raise the computer security awareness of the reader.

Table of Contents

NOTE: This material was provided by the National Computer Service Center as document NCSC-WA-002-85, originally published December 1985.

1. Introduction

Computer security is one of the biggest problems in the computer industry. A recent computer security survey conducted by the American Bar Association indicated that 40 percent of the respondents had detected and verified "incidents of computer crime" within their organizations during the year immediately preceding the survey. The survey pegged those single-year losses at between $145 million and $730 million. These figures only hint at the true cost of security-related losses since many either are unaware of the occurrence(s) of security breach or are aware but refuse to do anything that might create negative publicity about their ability to protect their assets. Some experts have estimated that the true cost of computer crime may exceed $15 billion. [1]

Personal computer (PC) security is a relatively new, but rapidly growing computer security issue. Although elaborate security measures can be employed on mainframe computers, PCs afford almost unlimited opportunity for intrusion into the PC itself, and through it into any mainframe system or network to which it may connect. The current trend to integrate

PCs into networks and mainframe computers now makes vulnerable data once considered to be secure.

This document briefly discusses some of the security considerations associated with the use of personal computer systems. The key consideration in protecting computer systems or, more importantly, the sensitive data they process is for users and managers to develop a security mind-set.

2. Basic Information Security Concerns

The basic principle of information security is the control of access to information. Only properly authorized individuals should have the ability to review, create, delete, or modify information. [2]

2.1 Security Objectives

Information security as applied to computer systems requires that the following security objectives be met:

- *Confidentiality* of personal, proprietary, or otherwise sensitive data handled by the system.
- *Integrity* and accuracy of data and the processes that handle the data.
- *Availability* of systems and the data or services they support. [5, 7]

2.2 Threats

The accomplishment of these objectives can be adversely affected by a wide range of events or conditions. These include:

- Lack of awareness or concern for the implications of computer security issues
- Carelessness, errors, or omissions
- Equipment and media failure hazards
- Intentional attacks by disgruntled or dishonest personnel, hackers, or hostile agents

The various manifestations of each type of threat are limited only by the specific characteristics of the system, data, and operational environment. [5]

3. PC Security Concerns

Although considerable effort has been expended in securing centralized, mainframe computer systems, relatively little attention has been given to the protection of personal computer systems. In general, PCs have been designed and developed without much consideration for security issues. PCs have traditionally been treated as single-user rather than shared systems; therefore, security was not perceived as a problem. As a result, weaknesses exist which can threaten the confidentiality, integrity, or availability of information resources.

3.1 Hardware Concerns

Before reviewing sophisticated data security issues, it is necessary to consider the basic physical protection of the equipment itself.

3.1.1 Access   Access to PCs should be physically limited to authorized users. Untrained or malicious individuals could damage or make inappropriate use of the equipment or the accessible data.

3.1.2 Theft   Personal computers and their component parts are high-value items. Secure the rooms where the hardware is located, or install lockdown systems securing the equipment to a table or desk.

3.1.3 Environmental Damage

a. PCs are sensitive to the quality of electrical power. Use surge protectors. Also, PCs should be powered from a source isolated from heavy appliances or office equipment.

b. Smoking, drinking, and eating should be prohibited in the vicinity of personal computers. Smoke can damage disks. Food and ashes that are dropped on the keyboard can work down into the mechanism and cause malfunctions.

c. Static electricity can badly damage a PC. This danger can be minimized through the use of anti-static sprays, carpets, or pads.

3.1.4 Magnetic Media Protection   Particular attention should be given to the protection of magnetic media, as it is the primary means of data storage.

a. Floppy disks should always be handled with care:

- Always store in the protective jacket
- Protect from bending or similar handling
- Maintain an acceptable temperature range (50-125°F)
- Avoid contact with magnetic fields (e.g., avoid contact with telephone handsets)
- Do not write on diskette, either directly or through the jacket or sleeve [5]

b. Rough handling of fixed disk devices may damage the disk or the drive read/write heads. Take care never to jostle the unit unnecessarily; never power off the system without performing the recommended shutdown procedures.

3.1.5 Media Declassification or Destruction   Magnetic media, such as disks, diskettes, and tapes that contain sensitive or classified information should not be put in regular waste containers. They should be cleared by degaussing and reused, or rendered useless by shredding or burning.

Defective or damaged magnetic storage media that have been used in a sensitive environment should not be returned to the vendor unless they have been degaussed. This is required since many PC "erase" commands do not actually erase the file. For example, the IBM MS/DOS/ERASE procedure performs only a logical erase by blanking out the filename and zeroing sector pointers in the File Allocation Table. The actual data remains unchanged until that portion of the disk is reused. "Erased" files can consequently be recovered using utility programs like the Norton Utilities. The Department of Defense-approved erasure method requires three overwrites of the file; first overwrite with "1"s, then "0"s, and then random bits. Each overwrite should be verified by visually inspecting the file contents, using some low level DEBUG-like facility.

3.1.6 Lack of Built-in Security Mechanisms A major security weakness shared by most PCs is the lack of built-in hardware mechanisms needed to isolate PC users from sensitive, security-related system functions. The typical personal computer is a single-state machine and therefore does not support the following security mechanisms common to larger systems:

- Multiple processor states—enabling separate "domains" for users and system processes;
- Privileged instructions—limiting access to certain functions (e.g., reading and writing to disk) to trusted system processes; and
- Memory protection features—preventing unauthorized access to sensitive parts of the system.

Without such hardware features it is virtually impossible to prevent user programs from accessing or modifying parts of the operating system and thereby circumventing any intended security mechanisms. Without protecting the hardware, it is impossible to guarantee that any hardware-based security mechanisms have not been modified or removed. [5]

3.1.7 Electromagnetic Emanations All electronic equipments emanate electromagnetic signals. Emanations produced by computers, terminals, and communication lines can be detected and translated into readable form by monitoring devices. Security measures intended to combat these radio frequency emissions are known as "Tempest" controls. Tempest-certified equipment is available, and used regularly by government organizations and contractors processing classified data.

3.1.8 Hardware Modifications Hardware modifications should be strictly controlled. Uncontrolled or poorly considered hardware modifications can adversely affect the operation of the PC. For example,

any modifications to Tempest-approved devices may invalidate their emanation-shielding ability. The configuration of any hardware system used for sensitive processing should be very carefully monitored. Such devices should be sealed to prevent tampering, and modifications made only by trusted, qualified personnel.

3.1.9 Hardware Attacks Advanced microelectronic techniques make PCs vulnerable to "bugging." A transmitter chip could be installed by a hostile technician under the guise of system repair or upgrade. Therefore, the user should be certain that the technician performing maintenance is both authorized and qualified. Also, circuit boards or components removed in the course of any maintenance at a classified facility should not leave without qualified technical review.

3.2 Data Concerns

3.2.1 Nature of the Data The information processed and stored on personal computer systems is more easily accessed (potentially by unauthorized interlopers) than that found on larger, multi-user systems. This is due primarily to the fact that the information on PCs is often in the form of memoranda, reports, or simple lists which are readily accessible using software tools familiar to all personal computer users. Also, the data will tend to be in relatively "final" form. This makes the interloper's job of searching for specific information much easier than on a large system.

3.2.2 Labeling Sensitive or classified information resources must be clearly labeled. These "resources" include both the hardware and the storage media.

a. PCs should have external classification labels indicating the highest sensitivity of data processed on the device. Avoid using hard disk systems for sensitive processing as the data stored on a hard disk cannot be reliably removed except by degaussing the entire disk drive. Also, it is very difficult to ascertain that sensitive data has not been stored on the disk. Consequently, hard disk systems must be labeled to indicate the highest level of data sensitivity to which they have ever been exposed.

b. Label all floppy disks to indicate the type and sensitivity of data on the disk. A floppy must be considered to assume the sensitivity level of the device in which it is inserted. For example, a fixed disk system, that has some sensitive data, must always be considered to be a sensitive device; and any floppy disks inserted into it must assume that level of sensitivity. Conversely, if the floppy were more sensitive than the fixed disk device, the device must now assume the higher sensitivity of the floppy.

c. Files stored on a fixed disk system containing any sensitive files must be handled as carefully as the most sensitive data stored on the system. On such a system, even files that are assumed to be not sensitive cannot be readily confirmed as such. Visual inspection of a file's printed image does not really confirm what is physically stored in the filespace. Sensitive files, if they must be stored on hard disk systems, should be handled very carefully. One means of emphasizing which files are sensitive is to store them in a separate disk partition. However, such methods, no matter how carefully controlled, do not ensure data integrity.

d. Data encryption provides a partial solution to the problem of labeling as well as providing access control. Encryption is a technique for rendering information unintelligible to those who don't have access to the tools necessary to see it. Encryption is performed based on an algorithm (usually a mathematical formula), and a key (usually a string of bits or characters). The longer the key, the more difficult it may be to break the encryption. The algorithm should be designed in such a way that even if an intruder knows the algorithm, it does him absolutely no good unless he also knows the specific key used. The algorithm used in most commercial applications is the Data Encryption Standard (DES), adopted in 1977 by the National Bureau of Standards as a Federal standard. DES is not approved for classified applications. Encryption is described in detail in the Federal Information Processing Systems publication on the DES, FIPS PUB Number 46.

The DES and other algorithms have been implemented in both hardware and software. Hardware implementations can provide a higher degree of security since software-based implementations are susceptible to penetration by interlopers. However, take steps to assure the integrity of the device. Sensitive equipment should be sealed and the internal configuration audited.

3.2.3 Securing Data Media

a. Lock floppy diskettes in a secure container. Be sure that the keys are unique (i.e., not interchangeable with the keys to other locks).

b. When feasible, use removable hard disk systems instead of fixed disk storage. At minimum, keep hard disk systems in a secure area. Also, consider installing power-on locks that restrict access to the machine to individuals with lock keys. Again, the keys should be unique.

c. Make back-up copies of all important software and data files.

d. Clear the PC's memory between users. For some equipment, such as an unmodified IBM PC model 5150, this appears to be achievable by turning the machine off, and leaving it off for at least 5 seconds.

This procedure may also be effective for other equipment.

3.2.4 Data Corruption Because of the lack of hardware security features, PCs cannot be trusted to prevent the corruption of the data they handle. For example, when editing an unsensitive file on a PC that has been used to process sensitive data, a SAVE command may actually append residual sensitive data from the computer memory after the end of the document file on disk. As a result, the supposedly unsensitive disk now actually contains sensitive data. Therefore:

a. Media exposed to a sensitive environment should always be considered to assume that level of sensitivity. For example, if the Wordstar text editor is used to edit sensitive data, the Wordstar disk employed should be considered to be as sensitive as the data processed. Write protection of floppy disks using write-protect tabs will, in many instances, provide adequate protection from this type of corruption. For example, the IBM PC family write-protect sensor disables the diskette drive's electronic circuits whenever a write-protect tab is applied to the diskette. However, if the sensor is damaged, floppies may be overwritten despite the presence of a write-protect tab.

b. PCs should go through a power-off, power-on sequence, as described in 3.2.3 (b), when changing processing sensitivity levels. After processing sensitive data, all diskettes should be removed, and the machine powered off, before the device is used to process unsensitive data. However, this procedure, which is intended to clear memory, is only valid for some devices—check manufacturers' specifications. Any expansion boards inserted into the device may also affect the validity of this procedure. Note also that this process is valid only for floppy disk systems—hard disk systems must always be considered to be operating at their highest sensitivity level.

3.2.5 Data Transmission Personal computers can enable users to transfer data to or from a mainframe computer. Transferring sensitive data should be carefully controlled and monitored. The PC user is responsible for ensuring that sensitive or classified data is transferred only to other computers designated for sensitive data. The PC user is also responsible for the data transferred from the mainframe to the PC. Note that such transmissions may include data which the user may not have perceived as being transferred.

3.3 Software Concerns

3.3.1 Software Vulnerabilities The lack of PC hardware security engenders software insecurity. Because modifications cannot be prevented, critical software, including operating system routines, can be modified or destroyed. For example, encryption schemes implemented in software can be forced to reveal their decryption key.

3.3.2 Operating System Weaknesses

Unlike many mainframe computer operating systems, PC operating systems generally have not been developed with any great consideration for security. Also, most PCs (including all those based on the Zilog Z80 series, the Intel 8086, 8088, or earlier version CPU chips) do not have the architectural capacity to assure any protection mechanisms. Consequently, they cannot be trusted. For example, DOS provides the means to set file status to "read-only," "system," or "hidden." This feature is intended to supply a small measure of discretionary access control. However, the switches that control these states are not protected and can be easily manipulated. Thus, access to files cannot be restricted—a file residing on the system is available to anyone with physical access to the PC. Xenix and PC/IX, two Unix derivatives, provide the standard Unix discretionary access control mechanism, which allows the user to set read, execute, and write access to his files. This is an improvement over DOS, and provides some measure of security, but can be subverted by a knowledgeable individual through circumventing, or modifying, or completely overwriting the operating system.

PC operating systems cannot be trusted since certain commands do not function as reasonably expected. For example, as mentioned previously, the DOS ERASE command does not actually erase files—it merely releases the file space, leaving its data intact.

3.3.3 User Identification and Authentication

User identification is the process by which an individual identifies himself to the system as a valid user. Authentication is the procedure by which the user establishes that he is indeed that user, and has a right to use the system. This process is generally employed on mainframe computer systems, but normally implemented only on PCs that are used by more than one person. A simple authentication system can effectively prevent office prowlers from poring through your hard disk files. For example, hardware-based access control systems exist that require the user to enter a password before the PC will boot up.

In order for discretionary access control mechanisms (as discussed in the previous section) to be enforced, it is necessary that users be identified to the system. This can be accomplished by some type of "login" process in which the user provides an identifier (e.g., name or account number) and a password to authenticate that identification. Another means of authentication is to attach an ID card reader, which will electronically transmit identification information. This solution usually requires an add-on board inside the computer, a card-reading device external to the computer, and the issuance of control ID cards.

Authentication (and, for multiple-user PCs, identification) should occur whenever the system is powered up or rebooted. Unix derivative PC operating systems, for example, provide for both identification and authentication; however, the authentication process is implemented in software and thus subject to unauthorized modification because the PC hardware does not provide sufficient protection.

3.3.4 Software Attacks—Trapdoors/Trojan Horses/Viruses

Despite a growing interest in securing computer systems—especially against mischievous "hackers"—most (if not all) computer systems (both PCs and mainframe computers) are susceptible to software attacks.

One attack, known as a trapdoor attack, involves the insertion of a mechanism that provides the attacker the means to later gain unauthorized access to the system. Such a mechanism inserted in a mainframe computer could, for example, grant the attacker access to a privileged system account after he presents a control sequence or password.

Another attack, called the Trojan horse attack, involves the insertion of unauthorized algorithms into the system. Many times, a trapdoor is used to activate a Trojan horse. A Trojan horse is a body of code that is designed to subvert the person or process that uses it. A sample Trojan horse might be a text editor that copies every file it creates into the attacker's directory. Beware of programs on bulletin boards and in the public domain. These programs purport to be useful utilities, but, in reality, may be designed to sack your system. One example is EGABTR, a program that claims to maximize features of the IBM Enhanced Graphics Adapter, but actually erases the file allocation tables (FAT)s on your hard disk, and clobbers any floppy disks that are present. After it has erased the FATs, it displays, "Got you! Arf! Arf!." An even more insidious attack is known as a "Virus." [1]

A "virus" is a software attack that infects computer systems much the same way as a biological virus infects humans. A computer virus is a small program that searches the computer for a program that is uninfected, or "germ-free." When it finds one, it makes a copy of itself and inserts the "germ" in the beginning of the healthy program. This insertion could take place in a fraction of a second—a delay that is impossible to detect. The infected program will subsequently execute the virus code prior to beginning its normal processing. A sample PC virus might copy itself onto any diskette inserted into the disk drive, and after a certain number of operations on that disk, erase it. According to the 23 March 1985 issue of the *Minneapolis Star and Tribune*, a number of viruses of this nature have been injected into the Apple PC community of Minneapolis.

The knowledge needed to create a Trojan horse or virus is basic, and no foolproof system exists to detect one. PCs are especially susceptible to these attacks because of the volume of software exchanged between users. Consequently, don't use any public-domain program that is not a known quantity. At a minimum, examine it with DEBUG, looking at all the ASCII strings and data. If there is anything even slightly suspicious about it, do a cursory disassembly. Be wary of disk calls (interrupt 13H), especially if the program has no business writing to the disks. As noted in the 23 July 1985 issue of *PC*: "Speaking of Greeks bearing gifts, Aristotle said that the unexamined life is not worth living. The unexamined program is not worth running."

3.3.5 Communications Attacks Personal computers are in increasing use as terminal devices to larger host systems or to connect two or more personal computers in networks. The security concerns raised in these situations include all those issues that have always existed in multi-user host systems and data communication networks, as well as certain concerns unique to PCs.

Information transmitted over unprotected communications lines can be intercepted by someone masquerading as you, actively receiving your information, or through passive eavesdropping. Therefore, sensitive information should be protected during transmission. Masquerading can be thwarted through the use of dial-back. Dial-back is an interactive security measure that works like this: The answering modem requests the identification of the caller, then disconnects. If the caller's ID matches an authorized ID in the answering system's user directory, the answering system will call back the originating system at a prearranged number. [4] The effectiveness of dial-back as a security measure is questionable due to the widespread use of digital PBXs (private branch exchange telephone systems) and convenience features like call forwarding. Also, various methods of call back protection have been broken by hackers. Encryption is one sure method of transmission protection.

Encryption can be adapted as a means of remote user authentication. A user key, entered at the keyboard, authenticates the user. A second encryption key can be stored in encrypted form in the calling system firmware that authenticates the calling system as an approved communication endpoint. When dial-back is used in conjunction with two-key encryption, data access can be restricted to authorized users (with the user key) with authorized systems (those whose modems have the correct second key), located at authorized locations (those with phone numbers listed in the answering system's phone directory).

Remote connections to other systems make PCs susceptible to remote attacks. A PC connected to a network, for example, may be subjected to attack by other network users. The attacker could transmit control characters that affect the interrupt logic of the PC in such a way as to permit him to obtain full access to the PC and its peripherals, even if he is incapable of passing the system's login challenge. The attacker could use other techniques to examine the user's communication package for dial-up phone numbers, access codes, passwords, etc.

4. Management

It is management's responsibility to provide direction in assuring security for personal computer systems. Management should focus on protecting information, not computers.

4.1 User Responsibility

Traditionally, the operational and security-related tasks associated with the use of computer systems were performed by small, well-trained groups of systems and support personnel. This responsibility now rests with each individual PC user. Thus the need for PC security training throughout an entire organization is a major issue.

4.2 Strategies

PC information security management requires the implementation of three basic strategies:

- *Prevent* threats from striking;
- *Detect* that threats have struck; and
- *Recover* from damaging effects.

Any given security measures will fall into one of these categories. The objective of security management is to select cost-effective measures that address all of the above strategies. [5]

4.3 A Plan of Action

Successful information security management requires the development of a plan of action. Elements key to such a plan are described below.

a. Security Policy—A formal information security policy is a prerequisite for a workable security program. This requires identifying the types of information needing protection, and outlining control measures.

b. Risk Assessment—Evaluate the value of the assets being protected, the vulnerabilities of these assets, the nature and likelihood of threats, and the cost-effectiveness of potential safeguards.

c. Select Control Measures—If the risks are determined to be unacceptable, additional control measures must be implemented. In general, such controls will fall into one of the following categories:

Physical Protection—Limit access to, and into, the devices.

Administrative Procedures—Detailed, understandable instructions that explain the threats, and measures for countering them.

Self-Developed Software—In many cases, simple in-house developed programs or automated procedures can be used to provide a relatively controlled environment for users.

Commercial Security Products—A growing number of security-enhancing products are available commercially. However, because of the fundamental weaknesses of easy physical accessibility and lack of internal security mechanisms, users should be wary of claims for products (particularly software) which claim to provide "absolute" security.

d. Security Monitoring and Enforcement—After implementing the appropriate security measures, management should ensure that periodic audits are conducted. [5]

5. Where to Find Assistance

Personal computer security is an issue of special dimensions, but is still an extension of the overall problem of computer security. As such, PC security concerns often can be addressed by existing resources, including professional organizations, consultants, trade publications, and literature.

The National Computer Security Center was established in 1981 as the Department of Defense Computer Security Center, and subsequently expanded to encompass national scope in 1985. The Center actively participates in fostering an increasing awareness of computer security problems and solutions. Letter requests for information should be address to:

National Computer Security Center
ATTN: C42
9800 Savage Rd.
Ft. Meade, Md. 20755-6000

List of References

1. "PC Data Is Vulnerable to Attack," *PC*, Vol 4 Number 15, July 23, 1985, pp 33–36.

2. CSC-STD-001-83—Department of Defense Trusted Computer Systems Evaluation Criteria, August 1983.

3. FEMA Manual 1540.2—Automated Information Systems (AIS) Security, September 1984.

4. "Data Security: Can Your Computer Keep a Secret?," *Computing for Business*, Vol 10, Issue 4 1985, pp 33–36.

5. NBS Special Publication 500-120—Security of Personal Computer Systems: A Management Guide, January 1985.

6. DOE/MA-0181—Security Guidelines for Microcomputers and Word Processors, March 1985.

7. Department of Defense Trusted Network Evaluation Criteria, 29 July 1985, Draft.

Glossary

Access Method Technique and/or program code for moving data between main storage and input/output devices.

Access Mode A technique used to obtain a specific record from, or to place a specific record into, a specific file. See also Random Access and Serial Access.

Access Time The amount of time required for a computer to locate and transfer a character of data from its storage position and make it available for processing or to return a character from the processing unit to the storage location.

Acoustical Coupler A data communications device that converts electrical data signals to/from tones for transmission over a telephone line using a conventional telephone headset.

Acronym A word formed from the initial letter or letters of each word in a name or phrase; for example, COBOL from COmmon Business Oriented Language.

Active Security Consists of alarm systems activated by an unauthorized entry or environmental disturbance.

Address The specific location where data are stored in a computer system. A symbolic (numerical or alphabetical) designation of the storage location of data or machine unit to be used.

Algorithm A specific set of defined rules of processes for the solution of a problem in a finite series of steps. Contrast with Heuristics.

Alphameric Same as alphanumeric, that is, containing both letters and numbers.

Analyst Person who analyzes and defines problems and develops algorithms and procedures for their solution.

Application A program or series of programs which covers the processing of related records in one area of work, such as Accounts Payable.

Application Program A computer program designed to perform specific tasks to meet the needs of the end user.

Application Programmer One who designs, develops, debugs, maintains, and documents computer application programs.

ASCII (American Standard Code for Information Interchange). An 8-bit code representing up to 256 characters or symbols. Widely used in communications.

Assembler A computer program that assembles programs written in symbolic coding to produce machine language programs.

Audit Function Periodic or continuous verification of an organization's assets, liabilities, income, and expenses.

Audit Trail A means of identifying the actions taken in processing input data or in preparing an output such that data on a source document can be traced forward to an output (a report, for example) and an output can be traced back to the source items from which it is derived.

Autokey Cipher A cipher system in which the plain or ciphertext itself enters into the generation of the ciphering key.

Backup Pertaining to equipment or procedures that are available for use in the event of failure or overloading of normally used equipment or procedures. The provision of adequate backup facilities is important to the design of all data processing systems, especially real time systems, where a system failure may bring the total operations of the business to a virtual standstill.

Batch Processing A type of computer processing where data are stored, manipulated, retrieved, and displayed in groups. Processing is always serial and usually sequential. The classical example of batch processing is payroll; time cards are batched, balanced, input, sorted, run against the payroll master file, with checks, registers, and other reports produced at the end of the process.

Binary Pertaining to the number system with the radix of two, or to a characteristic or property involving a choice or condition in which there are two possibilities. Used by computers for data representation.

Bit A binary digit. A digit (0 or 1) in the representation of a number in binary notation.

Blackout A complete interruption of electrical power reducing the line voltage to zero.

Blanket Bond, Blanket Crime Policy Specific types of crime insurance contracts designed for commercial (as opposed to financial institution) businesses. The contracts protect primarily against employee dishonesty and robbery, burglary, mysterious and unexplainable disappearance, and forgery.

Bonding To place (an employee or merchandise, for example) under bond or guarantee.

Bug A mistake in the design of a program or computer system, or an equipment fault.

Byte A group of adjacent bits operated on as a unit and usually shorter than a word. Note: in a number of current computer systems, this term stands specifically for a group of eight adjacent bits that can represent one alphanumeric character or two decimal character digits.

CICS An acronym for Customer Information Control System. Pronounced "C-I-C-S" by United States users and "kicks" by Canadians and Europeans, CICS is a monitor program that interfaces between transactions and application programs in an on-line environment.

CPU Central Processing Unit, the computer component that contains the electronics controlling the interpretation and execution of instruction.

CRT Acronym for Cathode Ray Tube. A name widely used for terminal devices with screens and keyboards, although new versions do not actually contain the cathode ray tube component. See also VDT.

Central Station Alarm System A means of transmitting signals from detectors over leased telephone lines for purposes of monitoring the receiving and recording equipment maintained on the premises of the monitoring security organization.

Character One of a set of elementary signals which may include decimal digits 0 through 9, the letters A through Z, punctuation marks, and any other symbols acceptable to a computer for reading, writing, or storing.

Checkpoint A point in a routine at which sufficient information can be stored to permit restarting the computation from that point.

Clause At law a term used often to describe a sentence, paragraph, or section with legal significance.

Collusion A secret agreement between two or more persons for a deceitful or fraudulent purpose; a conspiracy.

Common Carrier In telecommunications, a company in the business of transferring messages.

Compile To prepare a machine-language program from a program written in another programming language. The compilation usually involves examining and making use of the overall structure of the program, and/or generating more than one object program instruction for each source program statement. Same as assemble.

Compiler A special program that converts programming language statements into machine language.

Computer Security A process intended to control the people, physical plant and equipment, and the data involved in information processing so as to preserve and protect these valuable assets.

Confidentiality Agreement A contract signed by an employee, consultant, or other person agreeing not to disclose the company's confidential information.

Configuration A specific set of equipment units interconnected and programmed to operate as a system.

Control Block A control block contains the compiled file or data base definitions that are used by a computer program as it executes, to retrieve information from files and data bases.

Control Devices Mechanisms for preventing unwanted actions, or for initiating corrective action to remedy adverse conditions detected by monitoring devices.

Control Point A control point is a point of activity, a subject, an object, or a function at which the probability of a threat occurring is very high. A control point is a subdivision of the control zone.

Control Zone A control zone or exposure zone is a logical subdivision of the application system which is selected for risk analysis, exposure quantification, and controls building.

Control, Safeguard or Countermeasure This refers to a provision, standard, procedure, device, individual, or function which is designed to offset the level of exposure.

Copyright The right of an author to prevent others from copying, translating, abridging, or otherwise using the words and pictures developed by the author.

Copyright Notice A notice in the form specified by the Copyright Office to protect the copyright owner when a copyrighted work is published.

Crime An act committed in violation of a law.

Cryptanalysis Recovery of the plaintext of a ciphered message without knowledge of a cryptographic key.

Cryptography The science of concealed and secret writing. The study of algorithms used to encipher and encrypt data.

DBA Acronym for Data Base Administration or Data Base Administrator. The tasks of defining the physical structures that hold the data elements that comprise a data base, monitoring the performance, and preparing and entering specifications into a data dictionary belong in a data base administration and are performed by data base administrators.

DBMS (Data Base Management System). Establishes and employs rules about file organization and processing (e.g., personnel record file) and establishes relationships between files and records in each file. This provides for integration or sharing of common data items that can be processed by one or more application programs.

DES The Federal Data Encryption Standard, an encryption algorithm developed jointly by IBM and the National Security Agency for encryption of unclassified government data files.

DOS Acronym for Disk Operating System. Used to refer to the operating system used on IBM personal computers as well as that used on medium and large-scale IBM machines, even though they are not the same operating system.

Data Base Data items that must be stored in order to meet the information processing and retrieval needs of an organization. Note: The term implies an integrated file used by many processing applications as opposed to an individual file for a particular application.

Data Communications The process of transmitting data using common carrier communications facilities. Data communications may or may not involve the use of computers. See also Teleprocessing, Telecommunications.

Data Diddling Unauthorized alteration of information in a data base.

Data Element A piece of information carried in a program or data file.

Data File A collection of related data records organized in a specific manner for a particular application.

Data Set A collection of related data elements; it may be a file of conventional records, a program library, or a table of values.

Debug To trace and eliminate mistakes in a program or faults in equipment. Same as troubleshoot.

Degaussing, tape A procedure in which a reel of magnetic tape is inserted into a small cabinet device where a magnetic field demagnetizes an entire reel without unwinding it.

Detail File A file containing relatively transient information; for example, records of individual transactions that occurred during a particular period of time. Synonymous with transaction file. Contrast with Master File.

Detecting The ability to sense aberrations in a controlled environment. Sensing devices may be active or inactive.

Detection Device A means of sensing a change in a specific aspect of the environment, such as temperature, flame, ionization, motion, and noise.

Direct Access Pertaining to a storage device where data or blocks of data can be read in any particular order. See Random Access.

Disk Drive The hardware component that houses magnetic disk storage.

Disk or Disc A rotating data storage device for the electronic storing of data files and programs.

Diskette A magnetic disk generally between three and eight inches in diameter. Also known as a floppy disk due to the flexible nature of the recording medium.

Display A visual presentation of information on a CRT screen.

Double Tape Writing The procedure of redundantly writing computer files out to two identical tape files. Used for critical system restart tapes to preclude the possibility that a file might not be readable once it is written. When it is determined that the tape is readable the second tape is unnecessary.

Downtime The elapsed time when a computer system is not operating correctly because of the failure of one or more components.

Dry Pipe Sprinkler A system of pipes similar to the wet pipe sprinkler system, except that the water is held back at a central point by a clapper valve which is programmed to open at a fixed temperature.

EBCDIC (Extended Binary Coded Decimal Interchange Code). An 8-bit code that represents up to 256 distinct characters and is used in many current computers. See also ASCII.

EDP Acronym for Electronic Data Processing, referring to the equipment, software, and people who are involved in the processing of information with computer equipment.

Exposure Exposure refers to the loss resulting from the occurrence of threat at a given frequency of occurrence. Exposure can be tangible and measurable in monetary terms and intangible or not directly measurable. Tangible exposure is computed by multiplying risk (frequency of occurrence) times loss per occurrence.

FIPS PUB Standards in the data processing area adopted by the National Bureau of Standards.

Federal Privacy Act A statute enacted in 1974 limiting the use by federal agencies of personal information.

Field A subdivision of a record.

File A collection of information manifesting a common relationship; a group of records.

File Processing The periodic updating of master files to reflect the effects of current data, often transaction data contained in detail files, for example, a weekly payroll run updating the payroll master file.

File Protection Ring A removable plastic or metal ring, the presence or absence of which (depending upon the computer manufacturer) prevents writing on a magnetic tape and thereby prevents the accidental destruction of its contents. Note: The most common method involves insertion of the ring to allow writing and its removal to prevent writing.

Firmware Computer instructions that normally can only be read. Firmware cannot be altered throughout the life of the computer except through use of special procedures. Frequently referred to as read-only-memory (ROM).

Floppy Disk A magnetic storage device made out of a flexible material and contained in a sealed plastic envelope. Generally between three and eight inches in diameter, it is inserted into a disk drive. See also Diskette.

Foreign Corrupt Practices Act A federal law requiring certain companies to maintain reasonably accurate financial records.

Fraud The intentional misrepresentation of a material fact which when relied upon causes an individual either to part with property or value or to surrender a legal right.

Grandfather Cycle The period/series of three generations (or versions) during which, for instance, magnetic tape records are retained before reusing so that records can be reconstructed in the event of loss of information stored on magnetic tape.

Hacker A term used to designate an individual who, without authorization, attempts to gain access to a computer system.

Hard Copy Medium of data, either input or output, in paper form including punched cards, printouts, checks, etc.

Hardware The physical equipment and devices of a computer system.

Hashing The process of using an algorithm to convert key values into storage addresses for the purpose of direct access storage and retrieval of information.

Heuristics Exploratory methods of problem solving in which solutions are arrived at by an interactive, self-learning method. Contrast with Algorithm.

Host A computer which is the primary or controlling computer in a computer network, generally involving data communications or a local area network.

Housekeeping Operations in a program or computer system that do not contribute directly to the EDP solution of a user's problems but are necessary to maintain control of the processing.

Injunction A court order telling someone to do or not to do, a specific action.

Input Data that are going into a particular process or program.

Input/Output (I/O) A term referring to the transfer of information between peripheral devices and the primary storage of a computer.

Input/Output Device A device that can both take and receive information.

Interrupt A signal, condition, or event that causes an interruption; for example, the completion of an input or output operation, the detection of incorrect parity, or the attempt to execute an illegal instruction or to write in a protected location.

JCL Acronym for Job Control Language. A means of instructing a computer to run various steps of a task or job sequenced one after another.

Job A task or defined unit of work for a computer, often requiring a number of programs, files, and commands to be linked together when performed.

Judgment (in court cases) The order of the court and the end of a lawsuit; also often the amount of money that one party is to pay to the other.

K An abbreviation for 2 raised to the 10th power, or 1024. Considered roughly a thousand, it is commonly used to describe the storage capacity of a computer or disk in bytes, for example, a computer with 64K of memory.

Key One or more characters associated with a particular item or record and used to identify that item or record, especially in sorting or collating operations.

Libel The defamation of an individual in writing.

Library A facility of an operating system that is used to store data sets. Libraries are used for the storage of source programs, object programs, load modules, file definitions, and JCL job streams, for example.

License An agreement under which the possessor of a program, manual, copyright, trade secret, or patent authorizes another to use, copy, distribute, or otherwise deal with the protected item.

Line Supervision A means of automatically detecting data being input into a computer system.

Local Input Data Punch card data or local terminal data being input into a computer system.

Log File A file containing copies of transactions which have updated on-line files. May also contain copies of records affected before and after the logged transaction. Log files are used to recover damaged on-line files.

Logic Bomb A program insertion designed to cause damage at a later time.

MB An abbreviation used for approximately one million bytes, which is actually 2^{20} or 1,048,576 characters. See K.

Machine Readable Describes media containing data in a form which is processible by a mechanical device.

Machine-sensible Data Media Internal Revenue Service term for all data storage media that can be read by machine.

Mainframe A large-scale computer processor.

Master File   A main reference file of information used in a computer system. It provides information to be used by the program and can be updated and maintained to reflect the results of the processing operation.

Microcomputer   A very small computer, designed for use in small business or personal computer applications. See also PC.

Microprocessor   A tiny processor on a single semiconductor chip. Used in watches, calculators, microcomputers, and as components in large-scale computers.

Modem   (MOdulator-DEModulator.) A physical device that converts impulses from the terminal into waves that can be sent via telephone lines. The process is reversed for waves from phone lines into impulses for the terminal.

Monitoring Devices   The physical means by which environmental conditions are measured in a data processing installation.

Multiple Interfaces   A series of common links between automatic data processing systems or between parts of a simple system.

Negligence   Failure to perform a duty, resulting in a tort.

Noise   The electrical interference superimposed on a power line causing unwanted losses of or damage to program instructions and/or stored data.

Nondisclosure Agreement   An agreement not to disclose information belonging to another.

Object Language   A language that is the output from a translation process. Contrast with Source Language.

Object Program   A program that is expressed in an object language; for example, a machine-language program that can be directly executed by a computer.

Off-Line   (Or Offline) Pertaining to equipment or devices that are not in direct communications with the central processor of a computer system. Note: Off-line devices cannot be controlled by a computer except through human intervention. Contrast with On-Line.

On-Line   Descriptive of a data processing system where peripheral devices are under the control of a central processing unit and information reflecting current activity is introduced into the system as soon as it occurs.

Operating System   An organized collection of routines and procedures for operating a computer. Functions performed include (1) scheduling, loading, initiating, and supervising the execution of programs; (2) allocating storage and other facilities; (3) initiating and controlling input/output operations; (4) handling errors; etc.

Order of Magnitude   A factor of ten.

Organization Structure   The systematic arrangement of functions to operate in an orderly manner.

Output   Information displayed by a computer on a display screen or in printed form. Information stored on secondary storage devices can also be referred to as output.

PC   Acronym for Personal Computer. Generally, a computer utilizing a microprocessor.

Packing   A method of storing numeric information compactly. Using a common technique two numeric characters can be stored in one byte.

Padding   Filling out a field or a block with a filler character such as a zero or a blank.

Passive Security   Consists of prominently placed video devices, sound-emitting devices, or power line conditioners to limit electrical aberrations.

Password   A unique word or string of characters that a program, computer operator, or user must supply to meet security requirements, before gaining access to data or to data processing facilities.

Patching   Correcting or modifying a program in a rough or expedient way by adding new sections of coding. Patches should be used only as temporary modifications of object language, as opposed to a more permanent change in the source program.

Plaintext   The unenciphered data, also called cleartext.

Policy   A course of action or guiding principle formally established by an organization, designed to influence and determine corporate decisions or actions.

Power Line Conditioner   A means of reducing or suppressing electrical voltage surges, sags, and line noise.

Pre-Action Sprinkler System   A combination of wet and dry sprinkler systems that releases the water in stages in order to prevent accidental discharge of water.

Primary Storage Area   On-site storage facilities for computer tapes, punch cards, paper forms, etc. It is often a room adjacent to a computer room. Primary storage areas should never be located above a computer room.

Privacy   An individual's right to be left alone.

Proc   A term meaning procedure; frequently referring to a series of JCL statements stored in a library. See JCL.

Procedure   A set of established methods or steps in the conduct of business affairs.

Programming Language   A language developed for people to give instructions to computers more easily. A programmer must follow the rules of grammar and syntax of the programming language.

Proprietary Alarm Systems   A means of transmitting signals from detectors to a monitoring function.

Proximate Cause   The act or action that is an immediate cause of an injury.

Publication (of copyrighted material) The offering of the material for sale or its disclosure to a big audience.

Query A request for information from an operator or user.

Query Language A language designed for nontechnical personnel to make queries with English-like request statements.

Queue A waiting line. Queues are used to hold jobs waiting to be run, transactions waiting to be executed, messages waiting to be sent, and reports waiting to be printed. Queues are often stored on primary or secondary storage devices. See Spooling.

RAM Acronym for Random Access Memory. Refers to the primary storage component of a computer system.

Random Access 1. Direct access, generally through the use of a hashing algorithm which calculates the storage location from the key of the item to be accessed; 2. pertaining to a storage device whose access time is not significantly affected by the location of the data to be accessed. See Direct Access. Contrast with Serial Access.

ROM (Read-only-memory) Computer instructions in a certain part of memory that cannot be altered, except by special procedures. Read-only-memory is rarely altered through the life of the computer. Used for computer operating systems.

Record A physically interrelated group of logically related fields that contain attributes and characteristics of a person, place, or thing. Examples include a payroll record for an individual or a part record for a subassembly.

Record (in privacy sense) Information about an individual.

Record System (in privacy sense) A series of records maintained by an agency.

Regulation A rule of general applicability adopted by a government agency.

Remote Access The ability to input or receive output from a device not at the immediate site of the central processing unit.

Remote Input Data Data being input from distant terminals to a computer system. Could also refer to Remote Job Entry Input Data.

Remote Job Entry (RJE) Input of a batch job from a remote site and receipt of the output via a line printer or card punch at a remote site. The technique allows various systems to share the resources of a batch oriented computer by giving the user access to centrally located data files and the power necessary to process those files.

Response Time The amount of time it takes for a computer system to respond to an entry mode through a terminal. Usually measured as the time elasped between the depressing of the Enter key and the appearance of information on the user's terminal.

Restart/Recovery Procedures designed to recover and restart applications after an equipment failure in which on-line files or data bases have been damaged. These procedures usually involve obtaining backup files and applying transactions logged since the creation of the backup files. See Backup, Log File.

Risk The likelihood or probability of occurrence of a threat.

Risk Analysis The process by which one identifies threats, quantifies the risk, and calculates the exposure leading to the selection of cost-effective controls.

Rule An authoritative direction for the conduct of the business of the organization.

Secondary Storage Storage that supplements a computer's primary internal storage. Note: In general, auxiliary storage has a much larger capacity but a longer access time than primary storage. Same as mass storage, auxiliary storage.

Secondary Storage Area Storage facilities located at least 500 feet away from a primary storage area. Samples are bank vaults, other storage vaults, rented storage space, etc. Should contain suitable space, facilities, and security precautions.

Sector A section of a track on a diskette or disk pack. Where sectors are used, data are often transferred a sector at a time.

Security Control The assurance of the security system that necessary information reaches those responsible, that appropriate response activity can be initiated, or that unwanted actions are prevented or impeded.

Serial Access Pertaining to a storage device in which there is a sequential relationship between the access times to successive location, as in the case of magnetic tape. Contrast with random access.

Software A collection of programs (stored sets of instructions) which govern the operation of a computer system and make the hardware run. Contrast with Hardware.

Source Document The document from which data entry is initiated.

Source Language A language that is an input to a translation process. Contrast with Object Language.

Source Program A computer program written in source language (for example, a program written in COBOL) or symbolic language which will be converted into an absolute language object program using a compiler or assembler.

Spooling The procedure of reading and writing input and output streams on auxiliary storage devices, concurrently with job execution, in a format convenient for later processing or output operations. By staging the output destined for slow devices into a queue on mass storage devices to await transmission, more efficient use of the system is allowed since programs using low-speed devices can run to completion quickly and make room for others.

Standards The formal set of policies, practices, and procedures defining work methods and performance. Also a commonly agreed set of specifications for representation of information, or equipment functions, or equipment interface, etc.

Statute A law enacted by an authorized legislative body such as Congress or a state legislature.

Storage Protection Protection against unauthorized writing in or reading from all or part of a storage device. Effective storage protection is vital in multi-programming and timesharing systems for preventing concurrently operating programs from interfering with one another.

Substitution Cipher A cipher in which each unit of plaintext is replaced by a ciphertext unit.

Surveillance The ability to view a designated area within the abilities of sensory preception. Surveillance can be direct, as in the case of a guard at the door, or indirect, as when employing a device such as a camera. It may or may not include a response ability.

System A set or arrangement of entities that form an organized whole. Since the term is general and applies to both hardware and software entities, it is meaningful only when carefully qualified; for example: computer system, management information system, operating system.

System Program A computer program designed to coordinate the processing of the software with the hardware.

System Software The programs and procedures that instruct the system how to operate its own devices.

TSO Acronym for Time Sharing Option, a feature of some IBM operating systems, making it possible for users to interact with their computer, using a terminal device.

Tape Generally an electronically polarized flexible linear medium for storing information. Other types of tape, such as paper or plastic tape which move past sensory or recording heads, can be encoded to capture or transmit information.

Tariff The rates filed by a public utility for its services, often including limitations on the company's liabilities—essentially the contract between the utility and its customer.

Telecommunications The activity of transmitting data, using computer equipment and software.

Terminal A device connected to a computer, either locally or by means of a communications facility, that is used to enter or retrieve data from the computer. The most commonly used is the keyboard/display screen variety. Printers with keyboards are also used. See also CRT and VDT.

Test Key A number used to authenticate data and instructions in a voice telephone call. The key is computed using a closely guarded algorithm.

Theft Unlawful or felonious taking away of another's property without his consent and with the intention of depriving him of it.

Threat A threat is an adverse event or occurrence that takes place at particular control points to give rise to a business's exposure to loss or damage.

Throughput A measure of the amount of batch processing work performed in a finite time period. See also Response Time.

Time-Sharing A method of operation in which the resources of a computer facility are shared by users via terminals for different purposes at the same time. Although the computer actually services each user in sequence, the high speed of the computer makes it appear that all users are handled simultaneously.

Tort A civil wrong—analogous to a crime except that the lawsuit is brought by the individual who is hurt, and the relief is (usually) money, while in a criminal case the perpetrator may be sent to jail.

Track A physical subdivision of the surface of a magnetic disk or diskette, usually one of a number of concentric circles.

Trade Secret Company information of business value that is kept confidential by appropriate security measures.

Transaction A unit of data which triggers processing. The processing may be a response to a query, or an update of various files.

Transposition Cipher A method of encryption in which the characters of plaintext are rearranged without change in their form.

Utilities A general class of programs and programming aids used to facilitate tasks which are frequently performed such as copying data, listing directories, etc.

VDT Acronym for Video Display Tube. See also CRT.

VSAM Acronym for Virtual Storage Access Method, an IBM access method which permits the processing of serial, indexed, and relative data sets.

VTAM Acronym for Virtual Telecommunications Access Method, an IBM access method which handles transactions and messages being transferred between computers and terminal devices on communications networks.

Virtual Storage A combination of hardware and software which gives the user the ability to process as though he had unlimited primary storage. Using techniques of "paging" data to and from secondary storage on an as-needed basis, virtual storage is accomplished dynamically and is transparent to the user.

Visual Recording Device A photographic or magnetic device capable of recording an image automatically or under direct control.

Voltage Sag A temporary reduction in the line voltage sufficient to affect the performance of a computer.

Voltage Surge A momentary increase in the line voltage from the power source that could damage a computer system.

Wet Pipe Sprinkler A system of pipes containing water programmed to discharge when a fixed temperature is reached, usually 165°F.

Index